ROUTLEDGE LIBRARY EDITIONS:
BUSINESS AND ECONOMICS IN ASIA

Volume 27

P.R.C. LAWS FOR CHINA TRADERS AND INVESTORS

P.R.C. LAWS FOR CHINA TRADERS AND INVESTORS

THOMAS C.W. CHIU

Routledge
Taylor & Francis Group

LONDON AND NEW YORK

First published in 1988 by Taylor & Francis Inc.

This edition first published in 2019
by Routledge
2 Park Square, Milton Park, Abingdon, Oxon OX14 4RN

and by Routledge
52 Vanderbilt Avenue, New York, NY 10017

Routledge is an imprint of the Taylor & Francis Group, an informa business

© 1988 Taylor & Francis Inc.

British Library Cataloguing in Publication Data
A catalogue record for this book is available from the British Library

ISBN: 978-1-138-48274-6 (Set)
ISBN: 978-0-429-42825-8 (Set) (ebk)
ISBN: 978-1-138-36892-7 (Volume 27) (hbk)
ISBN: 978-1-138-36893-4 (Volume 27) (pbk)
ISBN: 978-0-429-42895-1 (Volume 27) (ebk)

Publisher's Note
The publisher has gone to great lengths to ensure the quality of this reprint but points out that some imperfections in the original copies may be apparent.

Disclaimer
The publisher has made every effort to trace copyright holders and would welcome correspondence from those they have been unable to trace.

P.R.C. LAWS
FOR
CHINA TRADERS
AND INVESTORS
Second Edition, Revised

Thomas C.W. Chiu

Taylor & Francis
Philadelphia • New York • London

USA	Publishing Office:	Taylor & Francis • New York
		3 East 44th St., New York, NY 10017
	Sales Office:	Taylor & Francis • Philadelphia
		242 Cherry St., Philadelphia, PA 19106-1906
UK		Taylor & Francis Ltd.
		4 John St., London WC1N 2ET

PRC Laws for China Traders and Investors Second edition, revised

First Edition published 1983. Second Edition 1988
Typeset by Four Way Phototypesetting Co., Hong Kong
Printed in the United States of America

Library of Congress Cataloging in Publication Data

PRC laws for China traders and investors.

   1. Law—China. 2. Foreign trade regulation—China.
3. Investments, Foreign—Law and legislation—China.
I. Chiu, C. W. (Chor-wing) II. PRC laws for China
traders & investors.

| LAW | 346.51'07 | 87-33570 |
| ISBN 0-8002-8002-4 | 345.1067 | |

To S.K.

Contents

x *Contents*

Chapter Three: Oil and Other Energy Resources

Chapter Four : Trademark

Preface

Everyone will agree China is, so far, the largest unexplored market in the world. It was in mid 1979 that China opened its market to foreigners, results of which were evidenced by the achievements of China's Sixth Five-Year Plan for Economic and Social Developments 1981-1985.

Now, China's Seventh Five-Year Plan has been enforced for a year. It is confident that targets stipulated in the Plan will be achieved by 1990. In order to provide a background knowledge of China's present foreign trade policy, excerpts of the Plan are covered in Chapters 33-40.

In the five-year period, the total volume of imports and exports is expected to grow at an average annual rate of 7 per cent, reaching $83 billion by 1990. Exports to grow at a rate of 8.1 per cent and import at a rate of 6.1 per cent.

We shall continue to increase exports of such goods as petroleum, coal, non-ferrous metals, grain and cotton. In addition, we shall gradually increase the proportion of manufactured goods in the total export volume.

As far as imports are concerned, priority will be given to computer software, advanced technologies and key equipment, as well as to certain essential means of production that are in short supply in the domestic market.

To promote foreign trade we shall continue to reform the system by which it is managed. For some time to come, our most important task will be to strengthen macroeconomic control and the management system, and to regulate imports and exports by increased use of such economic levers as exchange rates, customs duties, taxation and export credits, to be supplemented with administrative means when necessary. We shall delegate more decision-making power to government departments and local authorities and, in particular, to enterprises engaging in export, in order to encourage them to expand foreign trade.

In using foreign funds, we shall give first priority to construction projects in such areas as energy, transport, communications, and raw and semi-finished materials, and especially to projects for power generation, port facilities and the petroleum industry, and also to the technological transformation of the machine-building and electronics industries.

In introducing foreign technology, we shall give priority to the transformation of existing enterprises. First we shall import technology and equipment that will help increase our capacity to export and to produce substitutes for imports.

We shall enhance our co-operation with foreign engineers and technicians and invite foreign experts to China to advise and consult with us.

In the Special Economic Zones of Shenzhen, Zhuhai, Shantou and Xiamen, we shall make greater efforts to improve the existing infrastructure and develop supporting industries for projects that use foreign capital. We shall concentrate on completing construction in those areas where development has already begun, thus gradually building an export-oriented economy that is based on industry and advanced technology and earns foreign exchange through export.

The 14 open coastal cities and Hainan Island should, in the light of their own conditions and characteristics, exploit their advantages to introduce investment from abroad and establish lateral ties at home. In this way they will systematically expand economic and trade relations with other countries and increase technological exchanges with them.

In the open areas such as the Yangtze River and Zhujiang River deltas, and the triangular area in southern Fujian Province, we shall gradually build an economic structure in which agriculture serves processing industry and processing industry serves trade.

We expect to receive 5 million tourists from abroad in 1990. Under unified State planning, we shall mobilize to develop places of interest for tourists, we shall speed up the training of people engaged in the tourist industry and expand the production and sale of tourist commodities.

We must try to increase foreign exchange earnings and economize on their use, maintaining a basic balance and keeping necessary reserves. We shall tighten centralized control over foreign exchange and foreign loans, rationally readjust the spending of foreign exchange and rigorously enforce discipline in this regard.

Of the total investment in fixed assets for State enterprises and institutions, funds spent for equipment renewal and technological transformation will increase from 27.9 per cent in period of the Sixth Five-Year Plan to 30.8 per cent. Of total investment in capital construction for State enterprises and institutions, funds spent on renovation and expansion will grow from 56 to 57 per cent.

Of total investment in capital construction for State enterprises and institutions, funds spent on energy, transport and communications will increase to 37.4 per cent as against 34.4 per cent during the period of the Sixth Five-Year Plan.

With the exception of necessary tourist facilities, we shall cut back on non-productive construction projects, such as office buildings, exhibition halls and centres of all kinds. As far as geographical distribution of investment is concerned, priority will be given in the eastern region to technological transformation, renovation and expansion of existing enterprises, in the central region to the construction projects for the energy and raw and semifinished materials industries, and in the western region to active preparation for development.

The total investment in capital construction for State enterprises and institutions will be 500 billion yuan. Funds to be allocated by central departments will come to 375 billion yuan, and funds allocated by local authorities will total 112.5 billion yuan.

Investment in the four special economic zones in Guangdong and Fujian provinces and in a nuclear power station in Guangdong will amount to 12.5 billion yuan.

Nine hundred and twenty-five large and medium-sized capital contruction projects will be undertaken during the Seventh Five-Year Plan period. Of these, 350 will be projects started from scratch and projects for the renovation or expansion of existing facilities. Four hundred and fifty will be completed and put into operation. (China Daily APRIL 22, 1986)

Apart from mapping out priorities for foreign trade as above, China also has ideas of developing more areas as economic zones.

In Chapter 20, Section 2. Networks of Economic Zones, The Chinese Government said:

(1)   We shall accelerate the formation and expansion of a National Network of Economic Zones. These will include the Shanghai Economic Zone, the Northeastern Economic Zone, the energy production bases centering around Shanxi province, the Beijing-Tianjin-Tangshan Zone, the Southwestern Zone (Yunnan, Guizhou and Sichuan provinces, Guangxi Zhuang autonomous region and the municipality of Chongging.)

(2)   We shall establish a Second-echelon Network of Economic Zones linking provincial capitals, designated ports, and cities located along vital communication lines.

(3)   We shall establish a Third-echelon Network of Economic Zones, with the cities directly under the jurisdiction of provincial governments as centres.

Section 3.   Readjustment and Technological Transformation of Enterprises in the "Third-line Regions":

(1)   Those enterprises which are rationally distributed geographically, turn out marketable products and have good economic returns should continue to raise their technological level and improve their operations and management.

(2)   Those enterprises which are basically successful but are operating under capacity due to shortages of energy, transport, information services etc. should nevertheless make efforts to upgrade their technology and increase their production capacity.

(3)   Those few enterprises which are badly located, poorly market-orientated and unable to carry on should undergo readjustment. They should move to other places, convert to the manufacture of other products, amalgamate with other enterprises, suspend operations, or shut down."

(Xinhua News Bulletin APRIL 15, 1986)

In order to achieve the above as well as other targets stipulated in the Seventh Five-Year Plan, China's foreign trade policy will definitely be more flexible and tailor-made to meet the demands of China traders.

In this second edition, I have amended all the out dated materials and added new references. The aim of this edition is to provide a concise reference of the laws and practice relating to China Trade. I hope readers will find this book a useful tool for doing business with China.

The author wishes to acknowledge the advice he has received in the preparation of this book from Professor Luo Xiujin, former First Secretary of Education, Embassy of the People's Republic of China, Professor Yu Yuwen of the Materia Medicia, Beijing China, Professor Li Ling and Professor Zhang Ding of Academy of Social Sciences, China, and Professor Sheung Jiemin of School of Laws, Ning Po University, China.

The author is grateful to Anthony R Selvey, Managing Director of the Taylor & Francis Group, Kate McKay, President of Taylor & Francis, Inc. and Colin Walsh and Tony Littlechild of Book Product Consultants, Cambridge, England for arranging the publication of this book.

My thanks to Jung Ra, Book Publishing Manager of Taylor & Francis Inc., for his proofreading the manuscripts. My thanks to Benedict Chiu, for his research and assistance. My special thanks to Peter Caraye OBE formarly Director, British Council Hong Kong, for his encouragement and advice.

The author also grateful to Joyce Chan for typing up manuscripts of this book and Grace Ho and Frankie Ho of Four Way Photo-type setting Co. for typesetting the manuscripts.

The author has endeavoured to ensure that all opinions and facts, expressed or contained in this book are fair and accurate. However, any errors and omissions which may remain are their own. The laws contained in the book are the laws of the People's Republic of China in force on September 1, 1987.

T.C.W.C.

CHAPTER ONE

CUSTOMS & DUTIES

Brief Introduction

In the past few years, laws and regulations regarding customs and duties have been changed drastically. Certain important legislations have been repealed, namely:

1. The Provisional Law of the PRC on Customs now repealed and superseded by the Customs Law of the People's Republic of China, with effect from July 1, 1987. The latter was promulgated by the State Council on January 22, 1987, surprisingly, the General Customs Bureau of PRC was so efficient to have the Implementation Details on the Administration Penalties of the Customs Law approved by the State Council on June 30, 1987 and announced it with immediate effect on July 1, 1987, the same day when the Customs Law comes into force. The Implementation Details were drafted by reference to Article 60 of the Customs Law, readers may refer to the text of the Customs Law for details.

2. The Import & Export Tariff of Customs of the PRC, now repealed and substituted by a new set of tariff with the same title effective from August 13, 1985. To compare with the previous set of tariff, there is an average of 20% reduction of import tariff rates. However, readers should consult the Commercial Department of the Chinese Embassy in their countries for updated tariff rates as the Chinese authority will adjust individual import tariff rates from time to time.

Apart from the above changes, readers should also pay attention to some of the laws of regulations of customs concerning foreign investors and traders; namely:

1. Provisions for Bonded factories Processing Imported Materials (announced on January 1, 1984)

2. Regulations concerning Import & Export of Articles by Resident Offices of Foreign Enterprises and Presses and Their Staff Stationed in China (announced on April 20, 1984)

3. Implementing Details of the Customs of the PRC on confiscation of Import & Export Obscene Materials (announced on June 5, 1985)
4. Regulations of the General Customs Bureau of the PRC on Administration over the Goods, Vehicles, Luggage & Postal Delivered Goods Entering or Leaving the Special Economics Zone.

Readers will appreciate it that it is not necesssary to list all the customs laws and regulations here as some of the them are either less important or less concern to the majority China traders and investors. For this reason, this Chapter is devoted on the major issues. I believe, they are suffice to assist you in your China trade venture or your understanding about the customs and duties of China.

The Customs General Administration of China have prepared a pamphlet for foreign visitor' reference, I list hereunder the contents of this pamphlet as conclusion of this article.

DECLARATION

As a visitor to China, you are required to fill out a Baggage declaration upon your arrival. Members of a family travelling together may prepare a joint delcaration, with children under the age of 16. You are not supposed to carry any articles on behalf of others.

Your should declare in writing the descriptions and quantities ect, of the articles itemized in the declaration form if your baggage contains such items. Articles released with a registration must be taken out of China when you depart.

Unaccompanied baggage, if any, must be declared with regard to the number of pieces and the entry port, and be imported within 6 months from the date of your entry.

Failure to declare or inaccurate declaration may cause inconvenience and delay.

EXEMPTIONS

If you come to China on a short stay, you may bring in, without incruing duty, a reasonable amount of articles for private consumption duriang your trip and sojourn.

In addition, you have a duty-free allowance of 400 cigarettes and 2 litres of alcoholic beverages if you are 16 or older.

Those who have obtained the permission to have a long term residence in China are entitled to some special concessions. For detailed information, please contact one of the customs offices listed at the back of this pamphlet.

FOREIGN CURRENCY

There is no restrictions on the amount of the foreign currency, RMB traveller's checques, traveller's letters of credit and other RMB payment instruments convertible into foreign currency that you carry into China, yet declaration is required on your arrival. In case you want to take them out of the country, you should produce the original declaration form completed at the time of entry. Foreign currency and RMB payment instruments convertible into foreign currency acquired otherwise, if to be taken out of China, shall be released against certification by the Bank of China.

GOLD, SILVER AND SUCH WARES

Gold, silver and objects made of them are to declared and the released with a registration. When you take them out, the amount and weight must not exceed those previously delcared in the delcaration form at the time of entry. Gold and silver ornaments (including newly-designed handicraft such as inlaid ornaments and wares) you have bought with foreign currency within China are permitted to be carried or shipped out of China against a Special Invoice provided by the silver and gold shops.

ANTIQUES
To carry antiques out of China, you are advised to submit them to the cultural relics administration for appraisal in advance and truthfully declare them on your departure. They will be checked and released on the evidence of the wax seals affixed by cultural relics administration, together with the invoice, or on the strength of the cultural relics export certificate issued by the cultural relics administration. Failure to declare any antiques, whether they are hidden or not, will constitute an act of smuggling.

TRADITIONAL CHINESE MEDICINE
When you end your trip in China, you may take out Chinese medicinal materials and traditional Chinese medicine at a total value of 200 (RMB) Yuan, However, that value will be reduced to 100 Yuan if you leave for the Hong Kong and Macao regions.

PROHIBITED ARTICLES FOR IMPORTATION
Arms, ammunition and explosives of all kinds;
Radio transmitter-receivers and principal parts;
Renminbi (With the exception of those in compliance with an aggreement or protocol on the exchange of nationsl currency notes);
Manuscripts, printed matter, films photographs, gramophone records, cinematographic films, loaded recording tapes and video-tapes, etc. detrimental to Chinese political, economic, cultural and moral interests;
Poisonour drugs, habit-forming drugs, opium, morphia, heroin, etc.;
Animals, plants, and products thereof infected with or carrying disease germs and insect pests;
Unsanitary foodstuffs and germ-carrying foodstuffs from infected area,
Other articles the importation of which is prohibited by state regulations.

PROHIBITED ARTICLES FOR EXPORTATION
Arms, ammunition and explosives of all kinds;
Radio transmitter-receivers and principal parts;
Renminbi and securities, etc, in Renminbi;
Foreign currencies, bill and securities in foreign currencies (with the exception of those allowed to be taken out);
Manuscripts, printed matter, films, photographs, gramophone records, cinematographic films, loaded recording tapes and video-tapes, etc. which contain state secrets or other-wise prohibited export;
Valuable cultural relics and rare books relating to Chinese revolution, history, culture and art;
Rare animals, rare plants and their seeds;
Precious metals and articles made thereof, jewelry, diamonds and ornaments made thereof (with the exception of those within the quantity allowed to be taken out by out-going passengers);
Other articles the exportation of which is prohibited by state regulations.

Customs General Aministration:

Tai Ping Qiao Street, Beijing China	Tel. 668981
Beijing Customs	595568
Shanghai Customs	230770
Guangzhou Customs	85926
Jiulong Customs	22314

I CUSTOMS LAW

SECTION A: Overall policy

Customs Law of the People's Republic of China

*(Adopted on January 22, 1987 at the 19th Session of the
Standing Committee of the National People's Congress)*

Chapter I: **General Provisions**

Article 1: This Law has been formulated with a view of safeguarding national sovereignty and interests, strengthening Customs control, promoting exchanges in the areas of economy, trade, science, technology and culture with foreign countries and protecting the construction of socialist modernization.

Article 2: The Customs of the People's Republic of China is a state organ responsible for the control over inbound and outbound activities through the Customs territory. The Customs shall, in accordance with this Law and other related laws and regulations, exercise control over the inbound and outbound means of transport, goods, traveller's luggage, and postal items and other articles (hereinafter referred to as inbound and outbound means of transport, goods and articles); collect Customs duties and other taxes and fees; prevent smuggling; compile Customs statistics and deal with other Customs affairs.

Article 3: The State Council establishes the Customs General Administration to govern uniformly all Customs in the country.

The State establishes the Customs at the ports open to foreign countries and other localities where Customs affairs are concentrated. Administratively Customs offices are not subordinate to the government administration of various levels.

The local Customs shall perform its functions and exercise its powers independently and be accountable only to the Customs General Administration.

Article 4: The Customs is invested with the following powers:

(1) To check the inbound and outbound menas of transport, examine inbound and outbound goods and articles; to detain those in violation of this Law or other related laws and regulations;

(2) To verify the papers and identifications of inbound and outbound personnel; to interrogate those suspected of violating this Law or other related laws and regulations, and to investigate their illegal activities;

(3) To examine or make copy of contracts, invoices, accounts, bills, records, documents, business letters, tape recordings, video recordings and other data which are related to the inbound and outbound means of transport, goods and articles; to detain those connected with the means of transport, goods and articles which are involved in violations of this Law or other laws and regulations;

(4) To search the means of transport suspected of smuggling and storage places suspected of concealment of smuggled goods and to search those persons suspected of smuggling within the Customs surveillance zone and specified border and coastal areas near a Customs office. Upon the approval of the director of the Customs house, to detain the suspected smuggler and hand him over to the judicial organ. The duration of detention shall not exceed 24 hours under normal circumstances, but it may be extended to 48 hours in special cases.

The range of the specified border and coastal areas shall be defined by the Customs General Administration in conjunction with the Ministry of Public Security and provincial governments concerned.

(5) To pursue and seize those inbound and outbound means of transport, or persons defying and escaping from Customs control, the pursuit of which may be continued beyond the Customs surveillance zone or the specified nearby border and coastal areas so that the transport means or persons in question may be booked and dealt with according to the proper procedures.

(6) The Customs may be provided with fire arms for performing its duty. The rules governing the bearing and using of fire arms by the Customs officer shall be drawn up by the Customs General Administration in conjunction with the Ministry of Public Security and approved by the State Council.

Article 5: All inbound and outbound means of transport, goods, articles shall enter or leave the country at places (points) where a Customs office is located. Where temporary inbound or outbound passage at a place without a Customs office is requested in a special case, permission shall have to be obtained from the State Council or a department empowered by the State Council and the Customs formalities shall be followed in accordance with relevent provisions of this Law.

Article 6: Unless otherwise provided for, all import and export goods shall be declared and their duties paid by declaration units which have been registered with the Customs or by enterprises authorized to engage in import or export business. The declarants of the above-mentioned units and enterprises shall be tested and approved by the Customs.

The Customs formalities concerning declaration and duty payment of inbound and outbound articles may be fulfilled by the owner or other person entrusted by the owner as his agent.

The agent entrusted for Customs declaration purposes shall abide by all provisions of this Law applicable to the owner.

Article 7: All Customs officers shall abide by the laws and regulations, enforce the law justly, be loyal to their duties and perform them in a manner as befits a public service.

No units or individuals shall obstruct the Customs in performing its duties.

Where such obstruction occurs while the Customs officer performs his duty, the public security organs and the troop of the People's Armed Police responsible for such matters shall provide assistance.

Chapter II: Inbound and Outbound Means of Transport

Article 8: When inbound and outbound means of transport call at or intend to leave a place where a Customs office is located, the carrier shall make an accurate delcaration, lodge or present papers and documents to the Customs and be subject to Customs control.

All inbound and outbound means of transport that stop or berth at a place where a Customs office is located shall not depart without prior approval by the Customs.

Before any inbound or outbound means of transport intends to move from one Customs point to another, requirements for Customs control shall be met, Customs formalities shall be followed and any deviation to foreign territory before it is cleared by the Customs is prohibited.

Article 9: Inbound means of transport pending declaration to the Customs after entering the territory and outbound menas of transport pending to leave the territory after being cleared by the Customs shall both move along the route specified by the competent communications organs or the Customs in case the communications organs have no such specification.

Article 10: The time of arrival or departure, the place of stay, any moving during their stay and the time for loading or discharging the cargoes or articles of all inbound and outbound vessels, trains and aircraft shall be notified in advance to the Customs by the carrier or related communications and transport units.

Article 11: The loading and discharging of inbound and outbound cargoes and articles, the embarking and disembarking of inbound and outbound passengers from or to the means of transport shall be carried out under Customs control.

Upon the completion of loading or discharging of such goods and articles, the carrier shall submit to the Customs the delivery receipt and records containing the actual situation.

Articles carried by the person embarking or disembarking the inbound and outbound means of transport shall be declared to the Customs accurately and subject to Customs examination.

Article 12: While the inbound or outbound means of transport is being searched by the Customs, the officer in charge of the carrier shall be present and the hatches of holds and the doors of cabins, rooms and vehicles shall remain open as required by the Customs. In case that smuggling is suspected, the compartment where smuggled goods may be stored shall be dismantled and the goods or materials shall be removed.

When deemed necessary, the Customs may dispatch officers to perform duties on board the means of transport and the officer in charge of the carrier shall render the necessary assistance or facilities.

Article 13:   Inbound means of transport of foreign registry and outbound means of transport of domestic registry shall not have their ownership transferred or used for other purpose before having gone through the Customs formalities and their Customs duties paid.

Article 14:   Where inbound and outbound vessels and aircraft are also engaged in transport of goods or passengers within the territory of China, Customs approval shall be obtained and requirements for Customs control shall be satisfield.

Inbound or outbound means of transport that change over to transport isnide the territory of China shall go through the Customs formalities before hand as required.

Article 15:   Coastal vessels, fishing boats and special ships engaged in operation on sea shall not carry, exchange, purchase, or transfer the ownership of inbound or outbound goods and articles without prior Customs approval.

Article 16:   Where an inbound or outbound vessel or aircraft is forced to call or land at places without a Customs office, or jettison or discharge goods at such places owing to force majeure, the officer of the carrier in charge shall report the matter to the nearby Customs without delay.

Chapter III: Inbound and Outbound Goods

Article 17:   All the following goods shall be subject to Customs control: import goods from the time of entering the territory of China till the completion of the Customs formalities, export goods from the time the Customs declaration is made right up the time of leaving the territory, and goods in transit, transshipment and through-shipment from the time they enter the territory up to the time they leave the territory.

Article 18:   The consignee for import goods and consignor for export goods shall make an accurate declaration, submit the import or export license and the relevant papers and documents to the Customs. Without an import or an export license, goods subject to import or export control by the State shall not be released. Details shall be specified by the State Council.

Declaration with the Customs shall be made by the consignee for import goods within 14 days after the inbound means of transport declares its arrival and, unless specially approved by the Customs, 24 hours before loading for export goods by the consignor.

Where the consignee of import goods fails to declare with the Customs within the time limit mentioned above, a fee for delayed declaration shall be charged by the Customs.

Article 19:   All import and export goods shall be subject to Customs examination. While goods are being examined by the Customs, the consignee for import goods or consignor for export goods shall be present and respon-sible for moving the goods, opening and restoring the package. Where deemed necessary, the Customs may examine, re-examine the goods or take samples in the absence of the consignee or the consignor.

Upon the application of the consignee or consignor and being approved by the Customs General Administration, import or export goods may be exempted from examination.

Article 20: Unless specially approved by the Customs, import and export goods shall be released only upon endorsement by the Customs after duties have been paid or a proper guarantee has been submitted.

Article 21: Where the consignee falls to declare with the Customs within 3 months from the date of declaration of the means of transport concerned, the goods shall be taken over and sold off by the Customs. The balance of the proceeds of the sale after deduction of expenses for transport, loading and discharging, storage, duties and taxes, may be returned to the consignee within one year upon application. If a claim is not made within the time limit, the money shall be turned over to the State Treasury.

For inbound goods, which are proven to have been misdischarged or over-discharged, after being verified by the Customs, the necessary procedures for their reshipment back to the original destination or for their import shall be undertaken by the office of the carrier in charge of the means of transport which carried them or the consignee or the consignor of the goods within 3 months from the date of discharging from the means of transport. The duration, when necessary, may be extended another 3 months upon Customs approval. If the formalities are not accomplished within the time limit, the goods shall be disposed of by the Customs in accordance with the preceding provision.

In case that the above-mentioned goods are not suitable for storage over a long period of time, they shall be disposed of before the time limit by the Customs accordingto the actual situation.

Import goods abandoned by the consignee or the owner with a statement to that effect shall be taken over and sold off by the Customs, and the proceeds of such sale, after deducting the expense for transport, discharge, and storage, shall be turned over to the State Treasury.

Article 22: Goods that are imported or exported on a temporary basis and approved by the Customs shall be takenout of or into the territory within 6 months. In special cases, this time limit may be extended upon Customs approval.

Article 23: The operation of the storage, processing, assembling and consignment sales of the bonded goods shall be approved by and registered with the Customs.

Article 24: Customs formalities for import goods shall be completed by the consignee at the place where the goods entering the territory and for export goods, by the consignor, at the place where the goods leave the territory.

Upon the application of consignee or consignor, and being approved by the Customs, formalities for import goods may be completed at the place of destination, and for export goods, at the place of departure, provided that these places have a Customs office. The transport of such goods from one Customs to another shall comply with the Customs control requirements. When deemed necessary, such conveyance shall be done under the escort of a Customs officer.

Where goods entering or leaving the territory by electric cable, pipeline or other specific modes of transport, the business units concerned shall make the declaration with the designated Customs and complete the Customs formalities at regular intervals.

Article 25: All transit, transshipment and through-shipment goods shall be declared with the Customs at the place where they enter the territory or are shipped out of the territory within the specified time limit.

Where deemed necessary, the Customs may examine such goods.

Article 26: Without Customs approval, goods under Customs control shall not be opened, picked up, delivered, conveyed, replaced, repacked, mortgaged or transferred, and their identifications or marks shall not be changed by any unit or person.

Seals affixed by the Customs shall not be opened or broken by any person without Customs authorization.

The manager ofwarehouses and places which store the goods under Customs control shall fulfill the formalities of keeping an account for the receipt and delivery in accordance with the Customs provides.

The storage of goods under Customs control at a place outside the Customs surveillance zone shall be approved by the Customs and subject to Customs control.

Article 27: Rules governing the inbound and outbound containers, rules governing the salvage of inbound and outbound goods and sunken ships, rules governing import and export goods under small-scale border trade and rules governing other inbound and outbound goods not specified in this Law shall be drawn up by the Customs General Administration independently or in conjunction with the relevant department under the State Council.

Chapter IV: Inbound and Outbound Articles

Article 28: Inbound and outbound luggage carried by individuals and inbound and outbound articles sent by post shall be for personal use, in reasonable quantities and subject to Customs control.

Article 29: All inbound and outbound articles shall be accurately declared with the Customs by the owner, and be subject to Customs examination.

Seals affixed by the Customs shall not be opened or broken by any person without authorization.

Article 30: The loading, unloading, conveyance and transit of inbound and outbound mail bags shall be subject to Customs control, and a covering way bill shall be lodged with the Customs by the Units engaged in postal service.

The units engaged in postal service shall inform the Customs in advance of the time for the opening and sealing of international mail bags; the Customs shall dispatch officers to the spot to exercise control over the bags in time.

Article 31: Inbound and outbound articles sent by post shall be delivered or handed over only after they have been examined and released by the Customs.

Article 32: Inbound or outbound articles registered with the Customs and temporarily exempted from Customs duty upon approval shall be brought out or into the territory again by the person on his own.

Persons passing through the territory shall not leave behind the articles they carry in the territory without Customs approval.

Article 33: Inbound and outbound articles that are abandoned by the owner with a statement, unclaimed for which Customs formalities are not completed within the specified time limit, or postal articles which can neither be delivered nor sent back, shall be disposed of by the Customs in accordance with Article 21 of this Law.

Article 34: Inbound and outbound articles intended for official or personal use by foreign missions or personnel enjoying diplomatic privileges and immunity shall be dealt with in accordance with the Regulations on Diplomatic Privileges and Immunity of the People's Republic of China.

Chapter V : Customs Duties

Article 35: Unless otherwise provided for in this Law, Customs duties shall be collected in accordance with the Import and Export Tariff (schedules) on goods permitted to be imported or exported and articles permitted to enter or leave the territory. The Tariff shall be made public.

Article 36: The consignee of import goods, the consignor of export goods and the owner of inbound and outbound articles are obligatory Customs duty payer.

Article 37: The obligatory duty payer of import or export goods shall pay the amount levied within 7 days following the date of issuance of the duty memorandum. At the expiration of this time-limit, a fee for delayed payment shall be collected by the Customs. Where the delay exceeds 3 months, the Customs may either instruct the guarantor to pay the duty or sell off the goods for compensation. When deemed necessary, the Customs may request the bank to deduct the amount of duties from the deposits of the guarantor or the obligatory duty payer.

The payment of duty on inbound or outbound articles shall be made by the obligatory duty payer prior to their release.

Article 38: The price for duty assessement of import goods shall be the normal CIF price, which shall be recognized by the Customs; the price for duty assessment of export goods shall be the FOB price, which shall be recognized by the Customs, minus the export duty. Wthere CIF or FOB price can not be ascertained, the price for duty assessment shall be estimated and fixed by the Customs.

Article 39: Duty reduction or exemption shall be granted for the import and export goods and inbound and outbound articles listed below:
  (1) Advertising matters and trade samples of no commercial value;
  (2) Materials by foreign governments or international organizations;
  (3) Goods suffering damage or loss prior to Customs release;
  (4) Articles of a quantity or value below the fixed limit;
  (5) Other goods and articles enjoying duty reductiuon or exemption in accordance with the laws and regulations;
  (6) Goods and articles enjoying duty reduction or exemption in accordance with the international treaties to which the People's Republic of China is either a contracting or an acceding party.

Article 40: Duty reduction or exemption shall be granted to goods imported or exported by the Special Economic Zones and other specified areas, and by Sino-foreign joint ventures, contractual joint ventures and wholly foreign-owned enterprises, and to goods imported or exported for specific purposes, and to materials donated for public welfare. The State Council will specify the exact items and enact rules on such reduction and exemption.

The State Council or the department empowered by the State Council shall also specify the duty reduction or exemption items of small-scale border trade and draw up detailed rules on such reduction or exemption.

Article 41 : All import goods and articles to which duty reduction or exemption is granted in accordance with the preceding article shall be used only in specified areas and enterprises and for specific purposes. They shall not be utilized otherwise unless Customs approval is obtained and duties duly paid.

Article 42 : Duty reduction or exemption of an odd nature and beyound the ambit of Articles 39 and 40 of this Law shall be examined and approved by the Customs General Administration independently or jointly with the financial department under the State Council in accordance with the regulations of the State Council.

Article 43 : Temporary duty exemption shall be granted to goods temporarily imported or exported and to bonded import goods upon Customs approval after a guarantee or a deposit equal to the duty has been lodged with the Customs by the consignee or the consignor of the goods.

Article 44 : Upon discovery of a short-or non-payment of Customs duty on import or export goods, or inbound or outbound articles after their release, the Customs shall collect the money payable from the obligatory duty payer within 1 year of the previous duty payment or the release of the goods or the articles. If the short-or non-payment of the duty is due to a breach of the Customs regulations by the obligatory duty payer, the Customs is entitled to recover the unpaid duty within 3 years.

Article 45 : Where an over-levy of duty is discovered, the Customs, shall refund the money without delay; the duty payer is entitled to ask the Customs for the refunding withint 1 year of the date of duty payment.

Article 46 : Where the obligatory duty payer is involved in a dispute over duty payment with the Customs, he shall first make the payment of the duty, and then apply to the Customs in writing for a reconsideration of the case within 30 days of the issuance of the duty memorandum. The Customs shall reach a decision within 15 days after receipt of the application. In case the obligatory duty payer still has objection against the decision, he is entitled to apply to the Customs General Administration for a reconsideration of the case within 15 days after receipt of the decision. If the decision of the Customs General Administration is still considered unacceptable, the obligatory duty payer may take legal action at the People's Court within 15 days after receipt of the decision.

Chapter VI : Legal Responsibilities

Article 47 : Any one of the following acts to evade Customs control constitutes a crime of smuggling:

    (1)   To transport, carry or send by post into or out of the territory drugs, weapons and counterfeit currencies which are prohibited by the State from importation or exportation; to transport, carry or send by post obscene objects into or out of the territory aiming at commercial gain or dissemination, or to transport, carry or send by post out of the territory precious cultural relics which are prohibited by the State from exportation;

    (2)   For the purpose of commercial gain, to transport, carry or send by post into or out of the territory the goods or articles which are not listed above but also prohibited by the State from importation or exportation, and goods and articles in relatively large quantities or

of relatively high value which are restricted by the State from importation or exportation or subject to Customs duties in accordance with laws and regulations;

(3) To sell without Customs approval and payment of duties, the bonded goods imported upon special permission or goods enjoying specified duty reduction or exemption in relatively large quantities or of relatively high value.

Any armed smuggling of goods and articles or resistence by violence to Customs examination over smuggled goods and articles constitutes a crime of smuggling, regardless of the quantity of value of the goods and articles involved.

Criminal sanctions imposed by the People's Court on persons guilty of smuggling shall include a fine and confiscation of the smuggled goods and articles, the means of transport carrying them and the illegal incomes obtained therefrom.

Where an enterprise, and undertaking, a government department or a social organization commits a crime of smuggling, criminal sanctiuons shall be imposed on the person in charge and the person directly responsible for the offence by the judicial organ, a fine and confiscation of the smuggled goods and articles, the means of transport carrying them and the illegal incomes obtained therefrom may also be imposed on such unit.

Article 48: If the smuggled goods and articles involved in one of the acts listed under 2 and 3 of Article 47 of this Law are not large in quantity, nor high in value or where the carrying or sending by post of obscene objects into or out of the territory does not yet constitute a crime of smuggling, the Customs, while confiscating the goods, articles or illegal incomes obtained therefrom, may at the same time impose a fine on the person concerned.

Article 49: Any of the following acts shall be dealt with as a crime of smuggling and punishable in accordance with the provisions of Article 47 of this Law:

(1) To purchase directly and illegally from the smuggler articles which are prohibited by the State from importation, or to purchase directly and illegally from the smuggler other smuggled goods and articles in relatively large quantities or of relatively high value.

(2) To transport, purchase or sell on coastal or territorial waters articles which are prohibited by the State from importation and exportation, or transport, purchase or sell without legal certification goods and articles which are restricted by the State from importation or exportation in relatively large quantities or of relatively high value. Where an act listed above does not yet constitute a crime of smuggling, the provisions concerning punishments under Article 48 shall be applied.

Article 50: Any individual who carries or sends by post articles for personal use into or out of the territory in a quantity exceeding the reasonable limit and fails to declare them to the Customs shall be made to pay the duties and a fine.

Article 51: Apenalty may be imposed for any of the following acts which violate the regulations on Customs control:

(1) For a means of transport, to enter or leave the territory at a place without Customs office;

(2) Failure to inform the Customs of the arrival and the departure time

of the means of transport and the place of its intended stay or any change of the place during its stay;

(3) Failure to declare to the Customs accurately the import and export goods and the transit, transshipment and through goods;

(4) Failure to submit to the checking and examination by the Customs of the means of transport, goods and articles in accordance with relevant regulations;

(5) For an inbound or outbound means of transport, to load or unload inbound or outbound goods and articles, or to embark and disemark passengers without Customs approval;

(6) For an inbound or outbound means of transport staying at a place where a Customs office is located, to leave without Customs approval;

(7) For inbound or outbound means of transport intended from one place having a Customs office to another place having a Customs office, to move out of the territory or to a point in the territory where there is no Customs office before completing the clearance formalities and obtaining the Customs approval;

(8) For an inbound and outbound means of transport, to engage concurrently in, or change to, water transport within the territory without Customs approval;

(9) For an inbound or outbound vessel or aircraft which by force majeure stops or lands at a place without a Customs office, or jettisons or discharges cargo in the territory, to fail to report to the Customs nearby without a valid reason;

(10) To open, pick up, deliver, forward, replace, repack, mortgage or transfer goods that are under Customs control without Customs approval;

(11) To open or damage seals affixed by the Customs;

(12) Violations of other Customs control regulations contained in this Law that result in failure or suspension of Customs control over inbound and outbound means of transport, goods and articles.

Article 52: All smuggled goods and articles, the smuggling means of transport employed in the smuggling and the illegal incomes therefrom which are confiscated by the order of the People's Court or by the decision of the Customs together with the fines paid shall be turned over to the State Treasury. It shall be the Customs to deal with and turn over to the State treasury in accordance with the regulations of the State Council, all smuggled goods and articles and the means of transport confiscated by the order of the People's Court and the decision of the Customs.

Article 53: Where the person concerned objects to the Customs decision of punishment, he may apply for reconsideration of the case either to the Customs making the decision or to one at a higher level, within 30 days after receipt of the notification of punishment or 30 days after the punishment is made public in case it is impossible to send such notification. If the person concerned finds the decision reached after the reconsideration still unacceptable, he may take his case to the People's Court within 30 days after receipt of the decision. The person concerned may also take his case directly to People's Court within 30 days after receipt of the notification of punishment or 30 days after the punishment is made public. If the person concerned refuses to carry out the Customs decision and fails to apply for a reconsideration of the case or take the case to the People's Court within the time-limit , the Customs making the decisiion may confiscate the deposit of the person concerned, sell off his goods, articles and means of transport detained, or apply to the People's Court for an injunction to enforce the execution of the decision.

Article 54: Any damage to any inbound and outbound goods or articles caused by Customs examination, the actual loss shall made up by the Customs.

Article 55: Any criminal responsibility shall be prosecuted in accordance with Article 155 of the Criminal Law of the People's Republic of China in case the Customs personnel divide up the confiscated smuggled goods and articles among themselves.

No Customs personnel shall purchase confiscated smuggled goods and articles. Those who have done so shall be made to return the goods and articles, and may be subject to disciplinary actions.

Article 56: Disciplinary actions shall be imposed on those Customs personnel who abuse their power and intentionally create difficulties or procrastinate the control and examination; disciplinary or legal actions shall be taken on those who practise graft, neglect their duties or indulge in smuggling, depending on the seriousness of the case.

Chapter VII: Supplementary Provisions

Article 57: Terms used in this Law are defined as follows :

The term "inbound and outbound means of transport" means various vessels, vehicles, aircraft and animals which enter or leave the territory for carrying passengers, goods and articles.

The term "transit, transshipment and through goods" means goods which come from a place outside the territory and pass through the territory en route to a place outside the territory. Among them, "transit goods" are those passing through the territory by land,"transshipment goods" are those only changing the means of transport at a place having a Customs office and without passing through the territory by land, and "through goods" are those carried into and out of the territory by the same vessel or aircraft.

The term "goods under Customs control" means import and export goods enumerated in Article 17 of this Law, transit goods, transshipment goods, through goods, temporary import and export goods, bonded goods and other inbound and outbound goods for which Customs formalities have not been completed.

The term "bonded goods" means goods which have entered the territory with formalities of duty payment being exempted upon Customs approval and will be reshipped out of the territory after being stored, processed or assembled in the territory.

The term "Customs surveillance zone" means exports, railway and highway station, airports, border passes and international postal matter exchanges for which a Customs office is provided, other places where Customs control is conducted and places without a Customs office but have been approved by the State Council as a point of entry or exit.

Article 58: The Customs shall reward individuals or units providing information or assistance which is helpful for the exposing of offences against this Law; the identities of such individuals or units shall be kept strictly confidential by the Customs.

Article 59: Rules governing the control over the means of transport, goods and articles of other parts of the territory entering or leaving the Special Economic Zones and other specially designated areas shall be enacted by the State Council.

Article 60: Detailed rules and regulations for the implementation of this Law shall be drawn up by the Customs General Administration and be put into force after being approved by the State Council.

Article 61: This Law shall enter into force on July 1, 1987, on which date the Provisional Customs Law of the People's Republic of China promulgated on April 18, 1951 shall be abrogated.

Implementation Details on the Administration and Penalties of the Customs Law of the People's Republic of China

(Approved by the State Council on June 30, 1987.
Promulgated by General Administration of Customs
on July 1, 1987)

Chapter I: General Principles

Article 1:   These detail are legislated by reference to Article 60 of the Customs Law of the People's Republic of China (hereinafter called Customs Law), to implement the principles concerning the legal obligations as prescribed in said law.

Article 2:   These details shall be applicable to smuggling behavior which does not constitute a criminal offense as such, which constitutes a criminal offense but against which prosecution has been dropped or the penalty on which has been exempted in accordance with the principles of the law, as well as to actions against any activity which has violated the authority and control of the Customs.

Chapter II: Smuggling and Penalties

Article 3:   Any of the following activities constitutes an act of smuggling:

(1)   Without prior State Council's permission or permission from the authorities entrusted by the State Council, to transport, carry or send by mail articles at places where no Customs office has been set up that are prohibited by the State from entering or leaving the country, goods and articles that are restricted from entering or leaving the country and goods that are subject to paying Customs duties by reference to the law.

(2)   Purposedly trying to evade Customs supervision or control when

transporting, carrying or sending by mail article that are prohibited by the State from entering or leaving the country, good and articles that are restricted from entering or leaving the country and goods that are subject to paying Customs duties as required by the law by means of concealing, falsifing, deceiving, forging or other means at places where Customs offices have been set up.

(3)   With out Customs permission and not having paid the Customs duties that should have been paid originally when engaging in unauthorized sales of bonded warehouse goods, goods that have been put under Customs supervision and means of transportation which have been driven, flown, or sailed into the country.

(4)   Without Customs permission and not having paid the Customs duties that should have been paid originally when engaging in unauthorized sales of duty-free imported goods which are to be used by a particular enterprise for a particular purpose; or to transport without authorization such goods to be used by that particular enterprise in that particular area to other parts of the country.

Article 4:   Any of the following activities also constitutes an act of smuggling:

(1)   Illicit purchase of smuggled goods and articles directly from a smuggler.

(2)   Transporting, buying or selling articles that are prohibited from entering or leaving the country on China's inland sea or territorial water; or transporting, buying or selling goods and articles that are restricted from entering or leaving the country without the required legal documents.

Article 5:   Penalties shall be given according to the following clauses if any of the actions mentioned in Articles 3 and 4 is found to have been committed:

(1)   Confiscate the prohibited imports or exports and the illegal gains as a result of such activities plus a fine of up to RMB 50,000;

(2)   For smuggling of goods and articles that are restricted by the State on entering or leaving the country or goods and articles that are subject to paying Customs duties according to the law the penalty shall be confiscation of the smuggled goods and articles and the illegal gains as a result of the smuggling plus a fine of not more than the equivalent value of the smuggled goods and articles or up to three times the Customs duties payable.

(3)   Goods and articles that are specially used to conceal the smuggled goods and articles shall be confiscated and those specially designed instruments for concealing the smuggled goods and articles shall be ordered to be confiscated or destroyed.

In case the smuggled goods and articles are beyond the possibility of confiscation, a sum of money equal to the value of the smuggled goods and articles shall be charged.

Article 6:   Smuggling involving two persons or more than two shall be subject to prosecution under which each person shall be treated individually according to the seriousness of each case and the degree of involvement.

Individuals who knew about the smuggling but did not report it to the authorities and facilitated the smugglers shall be punished by confiscating their illegal gains as a result of the smuggling plus a fine of not more than two times the amount of their illegal gains. In case no illegal gains is involved, a fine up to RMB 5,000 shall be imposed.

Article 7: By virtue of those penalties in Article 5 of the present rules, less severe terms shall be given to persons who prepared tools and created conditions for the smuggling.

Article 8: Any of the following activities shall be given punishments that are less severe in terms or exemption:

(1) Minor smuggling

(2) The party concerned has confessed on its own initiative and information so provided has led to cracking of the crime by the authorities, or

(3) Smuggling only discovered three years afterwards.

The duration provided in Clause (3) of Article 8 shall be calculated as from the day the smuggling is committed. In case the smuggling is conducted continuously over a certain period of time, the duration shall calculated as from the last day the smuggling is committed.

Chapter III: Acts in Violation of the Provision on Customs Supervision and Control and Their Penalties

Article 9: Any acts in violation of the Customs Law but do not yet constitute a crime of smuggling are misconducts in breach of the provisions of the Customs Law regarding Customs supervision and control.

Article 10: Goods imported or exported without the required license or in violation of the rules in relation to the import and export administration shall be confiscated or ordered to be transported back or to refuse shipment. In the event the required license is only obtained after the shipments have arrived, a fine equal to the value of the shipments shall be imposed.

Article 11: In case of any of the following actions, a fine of not more than the equivalent value of the goods and articles concerned or up to two times of the Customs duties payable shall be imposed;

(1) To evade Customs supervision and control and to transport, carry or send by mail goods and articles into or out of the country - although such goods and articles do not belong to the kinds of goods that are prohibited or restricted from entering or leaving the country or are not subject to paying Customs duties by reference to the law.

(2) To open, pick up, deliver, forward, replace, re-assemble or transfer goods and articles that have been put under Customs supervision and control or goods and articles that have not been released by Customs.

(3) Failure to provide the authentic records or appropriate reasons for the loss in quantity of the bonded warehouse goods when engaged in the business of handling the transport, storage, processing, assembling or sales-on-consignment of bonded warehouse goods.

(4) To use, without prior approval from Customs, the duty-reduced or duty-exempted imported goods and articles for purposes other than what was declared earlier.

(5) To purposely misdeclare the goods when entering or leaving the country.

(6) To keep goods inside the country that are allowed to be imported

only on a temporary basis and that should be re-exported under the re-exportation requirement of provisions concerned, for to keep goods outside the country that are allowed to be exported only on a temporary basis and that should be re-imported into the country under the re-importation requirement of the provisions concerned.

(7)   Failure to transport the transit goods, trans-shipment goods or through, shipment goods out of the country within the required time period but instead keeping such goods inside the country without authorization.

(8)   Without Customs approval and not paying Customs duties required, when engaged in unauthorized sales of materials and articles of means of transportation after entering or leaving the country.

Article 12:   Any of the following actions shall be subject to a fine of up to RMB 50,000:

(1)   Without State Council's approval or approval by authorities entrusted by the State Council, when means of transportation enter or leave the country at places where no Customs office has been set up.

(2)   Inbound or outbound means of transportation leaving the Customs Surveillance Zone without prior Customs permission.

(3)   Before completing Customs procedure or without Customs approval, inbound or outbound means of transportation when going from one Customs point to another Customs point change course without authorization for places out of the country or for places where no Customs office is there.

Article 13:   Any of the following actions shall be subject to a fine up to RMB 30,000:

(1)   When inbound or outbound means of transportation enter or leave a place where a Customs office has been set up but fail to provide the relevant documents to the Customs for examination by reference to the provisions concerned or the documents provided are not authentic.

(2)   Inbound or outbound means of transportation or goods and articles upon entering or leaving the country fail to submit to checking or inspection by the Customs by reference to the the provisions concerned.

(3)   Inbound or outbound means of transportation load or unload cargoes or passengers without Customs approval.

(4)   Without Customs approval, inbound or outbound means of transportation that are to be used for the transportation of cargoes or passengers into or out of the country engage in unauthorized transportation business inside the country or are used for other unauthorized activities.

(5)   Without going through the Customs procedures according to the provisions concerned, inbound or outbound means of transportation engage in unauthorized transportation business.

(6)   When engaged in the storage, assembling, processing tf sales-on-consignment of bonded warehouse goods, failure to go through the required procedures on receiving, delivering, bookkeeping and selling procedures by reference to the provisions concerned. Or failure to go through the required Customs procedures on termination, extension, or transfer of the relevant contracts according to the provisions concerned.

(7)   Without Customs permission or refusing to accept Customs super-

vision or control to keep outside the Customs Surveillance Zone goods that have been put under Customs supervision or control.

(8) To destroy or damage Customs seals on means of transportation, warehouse or goods.

Article 14: Any of the following actions shall be subject to a fine up to RMB 20,000:

(1) Inbound means of transportation that enter the country but have not completed their Customs procedures fail to go along the route designated by the competent transportation organ or the Customs, or outbound means of transportation that have completed their Customs procedures but have not left the country fail to go along the routes designated by the competent transportation organ or the Customs.

(2) Ships or vehicles carrying goods into or out of the country which have been put under the supervision or control of the Customs fail to go along the routes designated by the Customs.

(3) Failure to report to the nearest Customs with a valid reason when ships or aircraft are found to have stopped, landed or unloaded goods and articles due to force majeure at places where no Customs office is there.

Article 15: Payment of over-due Customs duties, return of the articles concerned and a fine not exceeding the value of the articles concerned shall be imposed simultaneously for any of the following actions:

(1) In a small quantity and for personal use, carried by persons or sent by mail into or out of the country articles the amount of which has exceeded the amount allowed by the Customs without declaring to the Customs.

(2) False declaration of or refusal to accept Customs inspection on articles carried by persons or sent by mail into or out of the country.

(3) When, in contravention of the relevant provisions, articles that originally have been allowed to leave/enter after they have been registered with the Customs and granted temporary exemption on their Customs duties are taken into or out of the country again without authorization.

(4) Transit passengers leave their belongings inside the country without Customs permission.

Article 16: Any of the following actions shall be subject to a fine of up to RMB 1,000:

(1) Without a special reason, failure to notify Customs in advance the time and place of arrival, or the new time and place after the original ones have been changed, of ships, trains or aircraft that are entering or leaving the country.

(2) Destruction of or damage to without authorization Customs seals made on articles.

(3) Violations of Customs provisions which prevent or disrupt Customs supervision or control over incoming or outgoing means of transportation, goods and articles.

Article 17: Confiscation, order to return or withholding of shipments and/or fine depending on the seriousness of the case may be imposed on the party concerned who reports to the Customs before Customs inspection about the carrying or mailing of articles into or out of the country that are prohibited by the State.

Article 18:   Minor penalties or exemption may be accorded in case of slight breaches of the Customs provisions or on those who volunteer to confess.
Activities in breach of Customs provisions but were only discovered three years after the activities were committed shall be exempted from prosecution.

Chapter IV: Disposition on Smuggling and Actions Violating the Provisions on Customs Supervision and Control of the Customs Law

Article 19:   Actions that constitute an act of smuggling or actions that are in violation of the provisions on Customs supervisiion and control of the Customs Law shall be dealt with in accordance with the relevant decisions made by the Customs director.

Article 20:   When detaining goods, articles or means of transportation Customs shall issue the necessary documentation to that effect to the parties concerned.
Such documentation forms shall be prepared by the General Administration of Customs in a unified way.

Article 21:   Customs may charge the party concerned an amount of money which is the equivalent value of the goods, articles or means of transportation that shall be detained in the form of deposit or pledge in kind if such goods, articles or means of transportation cannot be detained or are unsuitable to detain.

Article 22:   Goods, articles or menas of transportation under Customs detention according to the law cannot be disposed of before a court order is issued or before the Customs decision goes into effect. But for those fresh, live or perishable goods or articles, or goods or articles that easily lose their started effectiveness Customs may sell them, safekeep the proceeds therefrom and notify the owner/owners accordingly.

Article 23:   Customs may notify the banks or post offices in writing to temporarily suspend withdrawal or payment on deposits or remittance if the money has been proved to have derived from smuggling activities. Customs shall simultaneously notify the person/persons in title of the deposits or remittance of the suspension. A suspension cannot be longer than three months. After a court order is made. Customs shall have the authority to dispose of the money which they have suspended withdrawal or payment according to the provisions of the Customs Law and the present rules.

Article 24:   In case of violation of the Customs Law by enterprises, institutions, government departments or public organization, Customs may impose a fine up to RMB1,000 on the person/persons in charge of the said units in addition to penalities to be imposed on the said units.

Article 25:   In case of violation of the Customs Law by enterprises, institutions, government departments or public organizations, Customs may in light of the seriousness of the case suspend the preferential treatment on Customs duties that the said units are enjoying, declare null and void their eligibility on Customs clearance or revoke the Customs clearance certificate held by the person(s) in charge of the said units.

Article 26:   A disposition notice shall be sent by the Customs to the party concerned in respect of the penalities imposed for violations of Customs supervision and control or smuggling activities.

If the party concerned objects to the Customs decisions, the said party may apply for reconsideration in writing within 30 days after receipt of the disposition notice to the Customs making the decision or to one at a higher level. The Customs which receives the reconsideration application shall make a decision within 90 days after receipt of the application, notify the party concerned to that effect, and to whom the reconsideration decision in writing should be sent.

If the party concerned objects to the reconsideration decision, the said party may take the case to the People's Court within 30 days after receipt of the reconsideration decision in writing.

Instead of applying to the Customs for reconsideration, the party concerned may consider taking the case directly to the People's Court for a decision within 30 days after receipt of the disposition notice. Under such circumstances, the party concerned cannot apply to Customs for reconsideration.

Both the disposition notice and reconsideration decision in writing shall be prepared by the General Administration of Customs in a unified way.

Article 27: Customs may choose to send the disposition notice and reconsideration decision in writing by special delivery or by mail. Signature of the party concerned shall be required if the delivery is made by person. If the delivery is made through the mail, the date of receipt of the registered mail shall be the data of delivery. In case of unsuccessful delivery Customs may make a public announcement to that effect, in which case the public announcement shall be accepted as proof of delivery.

Article 28: If the party concerned fails to apply for reconsideration or take the case before the People's Court before the said time limit, the disposition shall be enforced accordingly.

Fine, illegal gains and sums of money equivalent to the value of the smuggled goods, articles or means of transportation that should have been paid according to law shall be paid or handed over within the time limit stipulated by Customs.

Article 29: If the party concerned who is found guilty according to the Customs' ruling does not have permanant residency in the country, the said party shall pay or hand over the fine, illegal gains and the sums of money equivalent to the value of the smuggled goods, articles or means of transportation before leaving the country. If the party concerned is going to leave the country but objects to the Customs decision or the same party is going to leave the country but fails to pay the required fine, the said party may make deposits or pledge in kind which is the equivalent value of the required fine or any other forms of guarantees that are acceptable to the Customs.

Customs shall return the deposits or pledge in kind of the party concerned and the guarantee so made shall become null and void after the party concerned has performed the obligations of the disposition decisions of the Customs within the required time limit.

Article 30: In case of non-performance of Customs decision on the disposition or in the absence of a reconsideration application or lawsuit, the Customs which made the disposition decision may confiscate the deposits or the pledge in kind and sell those goods, articles or means of transportation that have been put under detention. The Customs may also apply to the People's Court for an injunction to enforce the execution of the disposition.

Article 31 : The party concerned shall not be exempted from paying the Customs duties and completing the Customs procedures on goods, articles or means of transportation that have not been confiscated even though the said party has paid the fine(s) imposed according to these implementation details.

Chapter V : Supplementary Provisions

Article 32 : Disciplinary actions shall be taken against those Customs personnel who abuse their power and intentionally create difficulties or procrastinate while on Customs control and examination duties. The State Council provisions on the reward and penalities on government personnel shall be the term of reference for such disciplinary action. The State Council provision on the reward and penalties on government personnel shall, according to the seriousness of the case, be referred to in disciplinary or legal actions against those who practise graft, neglect their duties or indulge in smuggling.

Article 33 : Terms used in these implementation details are defined as follows:
The term ''articles'' includes money, gold and silver and negotiable securities.
The term ''the equivalent value of '' means the prevailing market price in local State-run markets; Customs shall have the authority to determine the price of the commodity if the market price cannot be determined.
The term ''up to'' or ''not more than'' are inclusive of the amount they designated.

Article 34 : A list of goods that are restricted by the State from entering or leaving the country shall be announced by the departments in charge under the State Council.
A list of those articles that are prohibited by the State from entering or leaving the country shall be prepared by the General Administration of Customs together with other departments in charge under the State Council by referring to the Customs Law and any other relevant laws and regulations and shall be announced by the General Administration of Customs.
A list of articles that are restricted by the State from entering or leaving the country shall be announced by the General Administration of Customs.

Article 35 : The General Administration of Customs shall be responsible for the interpretation of the present rules.

Article 36 : The present rules shall be effective from July 1, 1987.

Regulations of the People's Republic of China on Import and Export Duties

(March 10, 1985)

Chapter I: General Provisions

Article 1:   With a view to implementing the policy of opening to the outside world, bringing the tariff economic lever into full play and promoting the development of economic external relation, foreign trade and national economy, the present regulations are hereby formulated.

Article 2:   All goods permitted to be imported into or exported out of the People's Republic of China are subject to import or export duty to be collected by the Customs according to "The Customs Import and Export Tariff of the People's Republic of China" (hereinafter referred to as "Customs Import and Export Tariff"), unless otherwise provided for.

"Customs Import and Export Tariff" is an integral part of the present regulations.

Article 3:   The Tariff Commission shall be responsible for the amendment of the "Customs Import and Export Tariff" and the establishment of temporary tariff rates and submit them to the State Council for approval and promulgation.

The Tariff Commission is composed of the representatives of the Customs General Administration, the Ministry of Foreign Economic Relations and Trade, the Ministry of Finance, the National Planning Commission, the National Economic Commission and other relevant departments.

Article 4:   The consignee (or shipper) or his agent shall be held responsible for the payment of import (or export) duty.

Article 5:   Rules governing the levy of import duty on articles of passengers' baggage and personal postal parcel shall be formulated separately.

Chapter II:　The Application of Tariff Rates

Article 6:　The tariff rates for imports fall into two categories: general tariff rates and minimum tariff rates. The general tariff rates apply to the imports originating in the countries with which the People's Republic of China has not concluded trade treaties or agreements with reciprocal favourable tariff clauses therein; the minimum tariff rates apply to imports originating in the countries with which the People's Republic of China has concluded trade treaties or agreements with reciprocal favorable tariff clauses therein.

Article 7:　No export duty shall be levied on the export items against which the export duty rates are not specified in the "Customs Import and Export Tariff".

Article 8:　Imports or exports shall be levied customs duty at the tariff rates in force on the date of application by the consignee (or shipper) or his agent.

　　　　　Imports which have been granted permission by the Customs to be applied for before their arrival, shall be charged import duties at the tariff rates in force on the date of entry of the means of conveyance in connection therewith.

Chapter III:　Assessment of the Duty Paying Value

Article 9:　The duty-paying value for imports shall be calculated on the basis of CIF value of the goods, which means the normal wholesale price prevailing at the place of purchase plus all charges incurred before discharge at the place of importation in China, such as packing charges, freight, insurance premiums, commissions, etc., all of which are to be scrutinized and determined by the Customs.

Article 10:　When the normal wholesale price of the imports prevailing at the place of purchase cannot be ascertained by the Customs, the duty-paying value shall be assessed on the basis of the normal domestic wholesale price of the similar goods at the place of importation prevailing at the time of application minus the import duty and product tax (or value added tax) paid at importation and normal freight storage fee and other business expenses incurred after importation.

　　　　　When the normal domestic wholesale price of the similar goods cannot be ascertained, or the business transaction is of a special nature, the duty-paying value shall be assessed by the Customs.

Article 11:　The duty-paying value for the machinery and appliance, means of conveyance and other goods, which have been sent abroad for repairs and re-imported, shall be assessed on the basis of the normal charges for repairs, materials or parts used, all of which shall be scrutinized and determined by the Customs, provided that such machinery and appliance, etc, were declared to the Customs at the time of exportation and re-imported within the prescribed time limit.

Article 12:　The duty-paying value for the goods sent abroad for processing shall be assessed on the basis of the difference between the CIF value of the processed goods and the CIF value of the original exports at the time of re-importation, provided that the goods sent for processing were declared to the Customs at the time of exportation and re-imported within the prescribed time limit.

Article 13 : The duty-paying value for the goods imported on lease (whether contractual or financial) shall be assessed by the Customs on the basis of the normal rent of the goods concerned.

Article 14 : The duty-paying value for exports shall be calculated on the basis of FOB value of the goods sold abroad less export duty, which shall be scrutinized and determined by the Customs.

Article 15 : The consignee (or shipper) or his agent shall, at the time of handing in import (or export) application, produce simultaneously a bona fide invoice enumerated with such items as price, freight, insurance premiums and other expenses incurred for the goods (with manufacturer's invoice attached, if any), packing lists and other relevant papers.

The above mentioned invoices and papers shall be certified true and correct by the consignee (or shipper) or his agent.

Article 16 : In scrutinizing the duty-paying value of imports and exports, the Customs has the authority to accept or refuse the invoices, contracts and other papers produced by the consignee (or shipper) or his agent, and if necessary, to examine the relevant documents, contracts, accounts and bills of both the buyers and sellers or make further investigations. The Customs may also check the accounts, bills of the goods concerned even after the release of the goods on payment of customs duty.

Article 17 : Where the consignee (or shipper) or his agent fails to produce the relevant papers laid down in Article 15 at the time of handing in the application, the imports (or exports) shall be levied customs duty on the basis of duty-paying value assessed by the Customs. After the duty has been collected, the duty amount shall not be adjusted even though the relevant papers have been subsequently produced to Customs.

Article 18 : Where the CIF value and FOB value or rents for imports or exports are in terms of foreign currency, the amount shall be converted into RMB at the average rate between the buying and selling rates, quoted by the administrative organ in charge of exchange control in the "Schedule of Exchange Rate of RMB against Foreign Currencies" available to the Customs on the date of issue of duty memorandum. In case the official exchange rate is not available, the Customs may use the exchange rate set by the above mentioned administrative organ.

Chapter IV : Payment, Refund or Recovery of Customs Duty

Article 19 : The consignee (or shipper) or his agent shall pay customs duty at the designated bank within 7 days (excluding Sundays and official holidays, the same below) from the date following the issue of the duty memorandum by the Customs, beyond which the Customs may, in addition to urge the consignee (or shipper) or his agent to pay the duty in time, charge an overdue fine at 0.1% of the total duty amount a day from the 8th day to date of payment of duty.

Article 20 : The Customs shall levy customs duty and overdue fine in RMB unless otherwise provided for.

Article 21 : The Customs shall issue receipts in the forms set forth by the Customs General Administration for levying customs duty and overdue fine.

Article 22 : Under any of the following circumstances, the consignee (or shipper) or his agent may, within a year from the date of payment of customs duty, apply for a refund by handing in to the Customs a written statement with details of the case and relevant duty memorandom attached, failing which his application for refund shall not be entertained:

(a) Duty overpaid on imports or exports as a result of wrong assessment by the Customs;

(b) Full amount of duty having been paid on cargo passed without Customs examination and subsequently found to have been short-landed and verified correct by the Customs;

(c) Duty paid and released exports having not been shipped, owing to special reasons, and duly reported to the Customs at shut-out cargo and verified correct by the Customs.

Article 23: Upon discovery of any duty being short-paid on imports or exports, the Customs may, within one year from the date of duty payment, recover the amount of duty short-paid from the consignee (or shipper) or his agent; if the duty was short-paid by fraudulent means, the amount short-paid may be recovered within 3 years.

Chapter V: Duty Reduction or Exemption and the Procedure Therefore

Article 24: The following goods may be exempted from customs duty upon verification by the Customs:

(a) The duty amount to be paid for a consignment of goods comes below RMB 10;

(b) Advertising matters and trade samples of no commercial value;

(c) Goods sent from abroad free of charge by international organizations or governments;

(d) Native exports returned from abroad for any justifiable reasons, if applied for re-importation by the original shipper or his agent with supporting documentary evidence covering original export and vertified true by the Customs. But the exports duty already paid shall not be refunded;

(e) Fuels, stores, beverages and provisions loaded on the means of conveyance entering or leaving the country for use en route.

Article 25: Under any of the following circumstances, the Customs may grant duty reduction or exemption on imports as the case may be:

(a) Goods suffering damage or loss en route or at the time of discharge;

(b) Goods suffering damage or loss by force majeure after discharge but prior to Customs clearance;

(c) Goods found leaky, damaged or rotten at the time of Customs examination, such damage, etc. being through no fault in custody on the part of the warehouse-keeper or other persons concerned.

Article 26: Trade samples, exhibits, engineering equipment and vehicles for construction, instruments and tools for installation, cinemato-graphic and television apparatus, containers, theatrical costumes and paraphernalia, which are permitted by the Customs to be temporarily imported (or temporarily exported) and guaranteed to be re-imported) within 6 months, shall be exempted from the payment of import (or export) duty.

The time limit prescribed above may be extended at the discretion of the Customs.

Article 27: Raw materials, subsidiary materials, parts, accessaries, components and packing materials, supplied by foreign enterprise for inward processing or assembling or brought from abroad to make goods for foreign market, shall be exempted from import duty on the basis of the quantity of the material, parts etc., actually used in the processing or assembling and re-exported.

Article 28: Rules governing duty collection or exemption for free replacement goods shall be formulated by the Customs General Administration separately.

Article 29: Duty reduction or exemption shall be accorded, in accordance with relevant laws and regulations, to goods imported into or exported from the special economic zones, to goods imported or exported by joint ventures, contractual joint ventures or enterprises using exclusive foreign investment and to goods entitled to enjoy preferential treatment by relevant rules

Article 30: In case, the consignee (or shipper) or his agent, due to special reasons, has to apply for duty reduction or exemption, he shall, prior to the importation or exportation of the goods concerned, hand in to the local Customs a written application with reasons clearly stated and documentary evidence attached. After verification, the local Customs shall transmit the case to the Customs General Administration for consideration. Applications with false reasons or without adequate documentary evidence shall not be entertained.

Chapter VI: Procedures for Appeal

Article 31: Should the consignee (or shipper) or his agent dissatisfied with the Customs decision, he shall pay the duty first and lodge with the Customs an appeal in writing within 14 days (excluding Sundays and official holidays) from the data following the issue of the duty memorandum. Any appeal not lodged within the prescribed time limit shall not be entertained.

Article 32: On receipt of the above-mentioned appeal, the Customs concerned shall, within 7 days, reconsider the case in question and may modify the original decision. If however, the original decision is sustained, the Customs concerned shall transmit the appeal together with their comments to the Customs General Administration for consideration.
Should the consignee (or shipper) or his agent be still dissatisfied with the modified decision, he may lodge a second appeal within 7 days from the date of receipt of the notification of the modified decision. The Customs will transmit the second appeal within 7 days from the data of receipt of the appeal together with their comments to the Customs General Administration for consideration.

Article 33: On receipt fo the appeal or the second appeal, the Customs General Administration shall, except in special circumstance, scrutinize the case, reach a decision and issue a written notification of the decision within 14 days which shall be communicated to the appellant through the Customs concerned. If the notification cannot be delivered, a public notice shall be posted at the Customs concerned.

Chapter VII: Penalty

Article 34:   Any act violating the present regulations shall be dealt with in accordance with the Customs Law and other relevant regulations.

Chapter VIII: Supplementary Provisions

Article 35:   All individuals have the right to expose or report any activities of duty-evasion. The Customs shall issue rewards to the persons concerned and undertake to keep secret after the case has been verified true and dealt with accordingly.

Article 36:   The Customs General Administration is authorized to interpret the present regulations.

Article 37:   The present regulations shall come into force on March 10, 1985.

II CUSTOMS DUTIES

SECTION A: Goods & Products

The Import & Export Tariff of Customs of the People's Republic of China

(Enforced on March 10, 1985)

Remarks:

The Import and Export Tariff of China are presented hereunder in table form. Since export tariff is not levied on most of the items, I have deleted this colume in the table and specified the export tariff (E.T.) whenever it is applicable.

Readers should consult the Commercial Department of the Chinese Embassy in their country for the latest tariff rates as China may amend certain tariff rates from time to time.

Keys: Min(%)   means Minimum Percentage
       Ord(%)   menas Ordinary Percentage
       E.T.   means Export Tariff

Import Tariff			
No.	**Discriptions**	**Min. (%)**	**Ord. (%)**

I. Live Animals; Animal Products

No.	Discriptions	Min. (%)	Ord. (%)
1.	Live Animals		
01.01	Live horses, asses, mules and hinnies:		
	(A) Horses and asses:		
	(1) For improvement of breeds	NIL	NIL
	(2) Other	20	30
	(B) Mules and hinnies		
01.02	Live animals of the bovine species:		
	(A) For improvement of breeds	NIL	NIL
	(B) Other	20	20
01.03	Live swine:		
	(A) For improvement of breed	NIL	NIL
	(B) Other	40	50
01.04	Live sheep and goats:		
	(A) For improvement of breeds	NIL	NIL
	(B) Other	40	50
01.05	Live poultry, that is to say, fowls, ducks, geese, turkeys and guinea fowls:		
	(A) For improvement of breeds	NIL	NIL
	(B) Other	40	50

Import Tariffs

No.	Descriptions	Min.(%)	Ord.(%)
01.06	Other live animals:		
	(A) For improvement of breeds	NIL	NIL
	(B) Other	40	50
2.	**Meat and Edible Meat Offals**		
02.01	Meat and edible offals of the animals falling within Nos 01.01, 01.02, 01.03, 01.04, fresh, chilled or frozen	50	70
02.02	Dead poultry (that is to say, fowls, ducks, geese, turkeys and guinea fowls) and edible offals thereof (except liver), fresh, chilled or frozen	50	50
02.03	Poultry liver, fresh, chilled, frozen, salted or in brine:		
	(A) Fresh, chilled or frozen	50	70
	(B) Other	60	80
02.04	Other meat and edible meat offals, fresh, chilled or frozen	50	70
02.05	Pig fat free of lean meat and poultry fat (not rendered or solvent-extracted), fresh chilled, frozen, salted, in brine, dried or smoked	40	50
02.06	Meat and edible meat offals (except poultry liver), salted, in brine, dried or smoked:		
	(A) Beche-de-mer	60	80
	(B) Jelly fish (E.T. 20%)	50	70
	(C) Other	60	80
3.	**Fish, Crustaceans and Molluscs**		
03.01	Fish, fresh (live or dead), chilled or frozen:		
	(A) Fish fry:		
	(1) Eel (E.T. 60%)	NIL	NIL
	(2) Other	NIL	NIL
	(B) Fish and roes, fresh or chilled:		
	(1) Fresh water fish (E.T. 20%)	30	40
	(2) Other fish	30	40
	(3) Herring roes (E.T. 40%)	50	70
	(4) Other roes	50	70
	(C) Fish and roes, frozen:		
	(1) Fresh water fish (E.T. 20%)	30	40
	(2) Other fish	30	40
	(3) Herring roes (E.T. 40%)	50	70
	(4) Other roes	50	70
	(D) Fillets	50	70
	(E) Edible fish lips, fish maws and sharks' fins	60	80

Import Tariffs

No.	Descriptions	Min. (%)	Ord. (%)
03.02	Fish, dried, salted or in brine: smoked fish, whether or not cooked before or during the smoking process:		
	(1) Edible fish lips, fish maws and sharks' fins	60	80
	(2) Herring roes (E.T. 40%)	60	80
	(3) Other	60	80
03.03	Crustaceans and molluscs, whether in shell or not, fresh (live or dead). Chilled, frozen, salted, in brine or dried: Crustaceans, in shell, simply boiled in water:		
	(A) Young crustaceans and molluscs for cultivation purpose	NIL	NIL
	(B) Shrimps, prawns and lobsters:		
	(1) Prawns, fresh, chilled or frozen (E.T. 30%)	50	70
	(2) Other	50	70
	(C) Crabs	50	70
	(D) Cuttle-fish and calamaries	50	70
	(E) Awabi and compoy	60	80
	(F) Other molluscs	50	70
	(G) Other	50	70
4.	Dairy Produce; Birds' Eggs; Natural Honey; Edible Products of Animal Origin not Specified or Included		
04.01	Milk and cream, fresh, not concentrated or sweetened	60	80
04.02	Milk and cream, preserved, concentrated or sweetened:		
	(A) Whey	20	30
	(B) Milk and cream in powder	30	40
	(C) Condensed milk	70	90
	(D) Other	70	90
04.03	Butter	70	90
04.04	Cheese and curd	70	90
04.05	Birds' eggs and egg yolks, fresh, dried or otherwise preserved, sweetened or not:		
	(A) Eggs for hatching	NIL	NIL
	(B) Other eggs in shell, fresh	60	80
	(C) Eggs in shell, preserved	70	90
	(D) Other	70	90
04.06	Natural honey	60	80
04.07	Edible products of animal origin, not specified or included:		
	(A) Birds' nests	60	80
	(B) Other	50	70

Import Tariffs

No.	Descriptions	Min. (%)	Ord. (%)
5.	Products of Animal Origin, not Specified or Included		
05.01	Human hair, unworked, whether or not washed or scoured: waste of human hair	70	90
05.02	Pigs', hogs' and boars' bristles or hair: badger hair and other brush making hair: waste of such bristles and hair:		
	(A) Bristles	70	90
	(B) Other	70	90
05.03	Horsehair and horsehair waste, whether or not put up on a layer or between two layers of other material	70	90
05.04	Guts, bladders and stomachs of animals (other than fish), whole and pieces thereof:		
	(A) Casings	70	90
	(B) Other	60	80
05.05	Fish waste	25	35
05.06/ 05.07	Skins and other parts of birds, with their feathers or down, feathers and parts of feathers (whether or not with trimmed edges) and down, not further worked than cleaned, disinfected or treated for preservation; powder and waste of feathers or parts of feathers:		
	(A) Feathers and down	80	100
	(B) Powder and waste of feathers	25	35
	(C) Other	70	90
05.08	Bones and horn-cores, unworked, defatted, simply prepared (but not cut to shape) treated with acid or degelatinised; powder and waste of these products:		
	(A) Powder and waste of bones	25	35
	(B) Other	40	50
05.09	Ivory, tortoise-shell, horns, antlers, hooves, nails, claws and beaks, unworked or simply prepared but not cut to shape, and waste and power of these products; whalebone and the like, unworked or simply prepared but not cut to shape, and hair and waste of these products:		
	(A) Ivory:		
	(1) Elephants' tusks	20	30
	(2) Rhinoceros horns	9	14
	(3) Other	40	50
	(B) Tortoise-shell	40	50
	(C) Horns and antlers:		
	(1) Pilose antler	20	30
	(2) Antelope horns	9	14
	(3) Other	40	50

Import Tariffs

No.	Descriptions	Min.(%)	Ord.(%)
	(D) Hooves, nails claws and beaks:whale bone and the like	40	50
	(E) Powder and waste:		
	(1) Of elephants' tusks	20	30
	(2) Of thinoceros horns	9	14
	(3) Powder of pilose antler	20	30
	(4) Of antelope horns	9	14
	(5) Other	40	50
05.10/ 05.12	Coral and similar substances, unworked or simply prepared but not otherwise worked; shells, unworked or simply prepared but not cut to shape; powder and waste of shells:		
	(A) Coral and the like	40	50
	(B) Shells	40	50
	(C) Powder and waste of shells	25	35
05.13	Natural sponges	50	70
05.14	Ambergris, castoreum, civer and musk; cantharides; bile, whether or not dried; animal products, fresh, chilled or frozen, or otherwide provisionally preserved, of a kind used in the preparation of pharmaceutical products:		
	(A) Ambergris, castoreum and civet	40	50
	(B) Musk	15	20
	(C) Cantharides	40	50
	(D) Bile	15	20
	(E) Bezoar	9	14
	(F) Pipefish and sea horses	15	20
	(G) Other	15	20
05.15	Animal products not elsewhere specified or included; dead animals of Section 1 or Section 3, unfit for human consumption:		
	(A) Animal semen	NIL	NIL
	(B) Silkworm eggs	25	35
	(C) Other	25	35

II. Vegetable Products

No.	Descriptions	Min.(%)	Ord.(%)
6.	Live Trees & Other Plants; Bulbs Roots & the Like; Cut Flowers & Ornamental Foliage		
06.01	Bulbs, tubers, tuberous roots, corms, crowns and rhizomes, dormant, in growth or in flower:		
	(A) For improvement of species	NIL	NIL
	(B) Other	60	80

Import Tariffs

No.	Descriptions	Min. (%)	Ord. (%)
06.02	Other live plants, including trees, shrubs, bushes, roots, cuttings and slips:		
	(A) Seedlings	NIL	NIL
	(B) Other	60	80
06.03	Cut flowers and flower buds of a kind suitable for bouquets or for ornamental purposes, fresh, dried, dyed, bleached, impregnated or otherwise prepared	80	100
06.04	Foliage, branches and other parts (other than flowers or buds) of trees, shrubs, bushes and other plants, and mosses, lichens and grasses, being goods of a kind suitable for bouquets or ornamental purposes, fresh, dried, dyed, bleached, impregnated or otherwise prepared	80	100
7.	Edible Vegetables & Certain Roots & Tubers		
07.01	Vegetables, fresh or chilled:		
	(A) Edible fungi	70	90
	(B) Other	50	70
07.02	Vegetables (whether or not cooked), preserved by freezing	50	70
07.03	Vegetables provisionally preserved in brine, in sulphur water or in other preservative solutions, but not specially prepared for immediate consumption:		
	(A) Edible fungi	80	100
	(B) Bamboo shoots	50	70
	(C) Other	50	70
07.04	Dried, dehydrated or evaporated vegetables, whole, cut, sliced, broken or in powder, but not further prepared:		
	(A) Edible fungi:		
	(1) Mushrooms and truffles	70	90
	(2) Black fungus	60	80
	(3) White fungus	80	100
	(4) Other	80	100
	(B) Lily flowers	60	80
	(C) Wei-cai (osmunda japonica)	60	80
	(D) Bamboo shoots, sliced or shredded	60	80
	(E) Other	60	80
07.05	Dried leguminous vegetables, shelled, whether or not skinned or split:		
	(A) Mung beans	6	11
	(B) Red beans	9	14
	(C) Broad beans	15	20
	(D) Kidney beans	15	20
	(E) Other	15	20

Import Tariffs

No.	Descriptions	Min. (%)	Ord. (%)
07.06	Manioc, arrowroot, salep, Jerusalem artichokes, sweet potatoes and other similar roots and tubers with high starch or inulin content, fresh or dried, whole or sliced:		
	sago pith	40	50
8.	Edible Fruit & Nuts; Peel of Melons or Fruit		
08.01	Dates, bananas, coconuts, Brazil nuts, cashew nuts, pineapples, avocados, mangoes, guavas and mangosteens, fresh or dried, shelled or not:		
	(A) Dates	30	40
	(B) Bananas	30	40
	(C) Cashew nuts	12	17
	(D) Other	30	40
08.02	Citrus fruit, fresh or dried	50	70
08.03	Figs, fresh or dried	50	70
08.04	Grapes, fresh or dried	50	70
08.05	Nuts other than those falling within No. 08.01. fresh or dried, shelled or not:		
	(A) Chestnuts (E.T. 10%)	50	70
	(B) Other	50	70
08.06	Apples, pears and quinces, fresh	50	70
08.07	Stone fruit, fresh	50	70
08.08	Berries, fresh	50	70
08.09	Other fruit, fresh	50	70
08.10	Fruit (whether or not cooked), preserved by freezing, not containing added sugar	50	70
08.11	Fruit provisionally preserved (for example by sulphur dioxide gas, in brine, in sulphur water or in other preservative solutions), but unsuitable in that state for immediate consumption	50	70
08.12	Fruit, dried, other than falling within No. 08.01, 08.02, 08.03, 08.04 or 08.05	50	70
08.13	Peel of melons and citrus fruit, fresh, frozen, dried, or provisionally preserved in brine, in sulphur, water or in other preservative solutions		
	(A) Peels, orange and pomelo	40	50
	(B) Other	50	70
9.	Coffee, Tea, Mate & Spices		
09.01	Coffee, whether roasted or not or free of caffeine; coffee husks and skins; coffee substitutes containing coffee in any proportion:		

Import Tariffs

No.	Descriptions	Min.(%)	Ord.(%)
	(A) Coffee	20	30
	(B) Coffee husks and skins	20	30
	(C) Coffee substitutes	60	80
09.02	Tea	80	100
09.03	Mate	80	100
09.04	Pepper of the genus ''Piper''; pimento of the genus ''Capsicum'' or the genus ''Pimenta''	50	70
09.05	Vanilla	40	50
09.06	Cinnamon and cinnamon-tree flowers:		
	(A) Cinnamon, cassis, lignea (E.T. 50%)	40	50
	(B) Other	40	50
09.07	Cloves (whole fruit, cloves and stems)	9	14
09.08	Nutmeg, mace and cardamoms:		
	(A) Nutmeg and mace	20	30
	(B) Cardamoms, inferior or superior	9	14
09.09	Seeds of anise, badian, fennel, coriander, cumin, caraway and juniper:		
	(A) Star anise	70	90
	(B) Coriander seeds	40	50
	(C) Other	40	50
09.10	Thyme, saffron and bay leaves, other spices:		
	(A) Saffron	9	14
	(B) Ginger	40	50
	(C) Other	40	50
10.	Cereals		
10.01	Wheat and mesin (mixed wheat and rye)	NIL	NIL
10.02	Rye	3	8
10.03	Barley	3	8
10.04	Oats	3	8
10.05	Maize	NIL	NIL
10.06	Rice	NIL	NIL
10.07	Buckwheat, millet, canary seed and grain sorghum; other cereals	3	8
11.	Products of the Milling Industry: Malt & Starches; Gluten; Inulin		
11.01	Cereal flours:		
	(A) Wheat flour	6	11
	(B) Flour of glutinous rice	9	14
	(C) Other	9	14
11.02	Cereal, groats and cereal; meal; other worked cereal; grains (e.g. rolled, flaked, polished, pearled or kibbled but not further prepared), except rice falling within No. 10.16; germs of cereals, whole, rolled, flaked or ground:		

Import Tariffs

No.	Descriptions		Min. (%)	Ord. (%)
	(A)	Cereal groats and meal	9	14
	(B)	Rolled oats	40	50
	(C)	Other	40	50
11.03/	Flour of the dried leguminous vegetables			
11.04	falling within No. 07.05 or of the fruits falling within any heading in Section 8; flour and meal of sago and of roots and tubers falling within No. 07.06:			
	(A)	Flour of legumes	20	30
	(B)	Flour of fruits	60	80
	(C)	Other	40	50
11.05	Flour, meal and flakes of potato		40	50
11.06/07	Malt, roasted or not		40	50
11.08	Starches; inulin:			
	(A)	Starches:		
		(1) For industrial use	40	50
		(2) Other	60	80
	(B)	Inulin	40	50
11.09	Wheat gluten, whether or not dried		60	80
12.	Oil Seeds & Oleaginous Fruit; Miscellaneous Grains, Seeds & Fruit; Industrial & Medical Plants; Straw & Fodder			
12.01	Oil seeds and oleaginous fruit, whole or broken:			
	(A)	Ground-nuts	50	70
	(B)	Soya beans:		
		(1) Yellow beans	3	8
		(2) Other	6	11
	(C)	Sunflower seeds	50	70
	(D)	Sesame seeds	50	70
	(E)	Rape seeds	50	70
	(F)	Copra	20	30
	(G)	Castor seeds	50	70
	(H)	Other	50	70
12.02	Flours or meals of oil seeds or oleaginour fruit, non-defatted, (excluding mustard flour):			
	(A)	Of soya beans	9	14
	(B)	Other	60	80
12.03	Seeds, fruit and spores, of a kind used for sowing		NIL	NIL
12.04	Sugar beer, whole or sliced, fresh, dried or powdered: sugar cane		50	70
12.05/06	Hop cones and lupulin		40	50

Import Tariffs

No.	Descriptions	Min. (%)	Ord. (%)
12.07	Plants and parts (including seeds and fruit) of trees, bushes, shrubs or other plants, being goods of a kind used primarily in perfumery, in pharmacy, or for insecticidal, fungicidal or similar purposes, fresh or dried, whole, cut, crushed, ground or powdered:		
	(A) Dang Gui (cryptotaenia canadensis (E.T. 50%)	20	30
	(B) Boxthorn fruit (E.T. 40%)	20	30
	(C) Hoantchy (astragalus membranaceus bge.) (E.T. 60%)	20	30
	(D) Ginseng:		
	(1) Wild ginseng (other than American ginseng)	70	90
	(2) American ginseng	50	70
	(3) Other	40	50
	(E) Betelnuts and betelnut husks	20	30
	(F) Liquorice	20	30
	(G) Other vegetable medicinal substances	15	20
	(H) Vegetable spices	40	50
	(I) Vegetable insecticidal or fungicidal substances:		
	(1) Derris roots and pyrethrum	6	11
	(2) Other	20	30
12.08	Chicory roots, fresh or dried, whole or cut, unroasted; locust beans, fresh or dried, whether or not kibbled or ground, but not further prepared; fruit kernels and other vegetable products		
	(A) Edible fruit kernels:		
	(1) Of apricot (E.T. 10%)	60	80
	(2) Other	60	80
	(B) Other	50	70
12.09	Cereal straw and husks, unprepared, or chopped but not otherwise prepared	25	35
12.10	Mangolds, swedes, fodder roots: hay, lucerne, clover, sainfoin, forage kale, lupines, vetches and similar forage products	25	35
13.	Lacs; Gums, Resins & Other Vegetables Saps & Extracts		

Import Tariffs

No.	Descriptions	Min. (%)	Ord. (%)
13.01/02	Shellac, seed lac, stick lac and other lacs; natural gums, resins, gum-resins and balsams:		
	(A) Shellac, seed lac, stick lac and other lacs	30	40
	(B) Gums, resins, gum-resins and balsams:		
	(1) Gum Arabic and gum tragacanth	30	40
	(2) Gum olibanum, gum myrth, gum dragon's-blood and asafoetida	12	17
	(3) Other	35	45
13.03	Vegetable saps and extracts: pectic substances, pectinates and pectates: agar-agar and other mucilages and thickeners, derived from vegetable products:		
	(A) Agar-agar	60	80
	(B) Crude lacquer (E.T. 30%)	70	90
	(C) Other:		
	(1) For medicinal or pesticidal use	15	20
	(2) Other	60	80
14.	Vegetable Plaiting Materials; Vegetable Products Not Specified Or Included		
14.01	Vegetable materials of a kind used primarily for plaiting (e.g. cereal straw, cleaned, bleached or dyed, osier, reeds rushes, rattans, bamboos, raffia and lime bark):		
	(A) Straw (other than wheat straw)	25	35
	(B) Wheat straw	50	70
	(C) Rattans	25	35
	(D) Bamboos	50	70
	(E) Other	50	70
14.02	Vegetable materials, whether or not put up on a layer or between two layers of other material, of a kind used primarily as stuffing or as padding (e.g. kapok, vegetable hair and eel-grass)	50	70
14.03	Vegetable materials of a kind used primarily in brushes or in brooms (e.g. sorgho, piassava, couch-grass and istle), whether or not in bundles or hanks	50	70
14.04/ 14.05	Vegetable products not elsewhere specified included:		
	(A) Algae (including seaweeds)	50	70
	(B) Hard seeds, pips, hulls and nuts of a kind used for carving	50	70
	(C) Vegetable products used primarily in dyeing or tanning	35	45

Import Tariffs

No.	Descriptions	Min. (%)	Ord. (%)
III.	**Animal & Vegetable Fats & Oils & their Cleavage Products; Prepared Edible Fats; Animal & Vegetable Waxes**		
15.	Animal & Vegetable Fats & Oils & Their Cleavage Products; Prepared Edible Fats; Animal & Vegetables Waxes		
15.01	Lard, other pig fat and poultry fat, rendered or solvent-extracted	25	35
15.02	Fats of bovine cattle, sheep or goats, unrendered; rendered or solvent-extracted fats (including "premier jus") obtained from those unrendered fats:		
	(A) Fats of bovine cattle, sheep or goats, unrendered	50	70
	(B) Other	20	30
15.03	Lard stearin, oleostearin and tallow stearin: lard oil, oleo-oil, and tallow oil, not emulsified or mixed or prepared in any way	20	30
15.04	Fats and oil, of fish and marine mammals, whether or not refined:		
	(A) Fish-liver oil	20	30
	(B) Other	40	50
15.05	Wool grease and fatty substances derived therefrom (including lanolin)	50	70
15.06	Other animal oils and fats (including neat's-foot oil and fats from bones or waste)	50	70
15.07	Fixed vegetable oils, fluid or solidd, crude, refined or purified:		
	(A) Soya bean oil	6	11
	(B) Groundnut oil	6	11
	(C) Sesame oil, rapeseed oil	9	14
	(D) Wood oil (Tung oil)	50	70
	(E) Linseed oil	50	70
	(F) Palm oil, palm kernel oil and coconut oil	20	30
	(G) Olive oil	20	30
	(H) Castor oil	50	70
	(I) Other	50	70
15.08	Animal and vegetable oils, boiled, oxidised, dehydrated, sulphurised, blown or polymerised by heat in vacuum or in inert gas, or otherwise modified	60	80
15.09/	Fatty acids; acid oils from refining; fatty		

Import Tariffs

No.	Descriptions	Min. (%)	Ord. (%)
15.10	alcohols:		
	(A) Fatty acids and acid oils from refining:		
	(1) Crude stearic acid	40	50
	(2) Other	40	50
	(B) Fatty alcohols	40	50
15.11	Glycerol and glycerol lyes	40	50
15.12	Animal or vegetable oils and fats, wholly or partly hydrogenated, or solidified or hardened by any other process, whether or not refined, but not further prepared:		
	(A) Hardened fat of whale oil	40	50
	(B) Other	50	70
15.13	Margarine, imitation lard and other prepared edible fats	60	80
15.14/ 15.15	Spermaceti, crude, pressed or refined, whether or not coloured: beeswax and other insect waxes, whether or not coloured	60	80
15.16	Vegetable waxes, whether or not coloured	60	80
15.17	Degras: residues resulting from the treatment of fatty substances or animal or vegetable waxes	40	50

IV. Prepared Foodstaffs; Beverages, Spirits & Vinegar; Tobacco

No.	Descriptions	Min. (%)	Ord. (%)
16.	Preparations of Meat, of Fish, of Crusta Ceans or Molluscs		
16.01	Sausages and the like, of meat; meat offal or animal blood	70	90
16.02	Other prepared or preserved meat or meat offal	70	90
16.03	Meat extracts and meat luices; fish extracts	70	90
16.04	Prepared or preserved fish, including caviar and caviar substitutes	70	90
16.05	Crustaceans and molluscs, prepared or preserved	70	90

This Section does not cover meat, meat offal, fish, crustaceans or molluscs, prepared or preserved by the processes specified in Section 2 and 3.

No.	Descriptions	Min. (%)	Ord. (%)
17.	Sugars & Sugar Confectionery		
17.01	Beet sugar and cane sugar, in solid form:		
	(A) Raw sugar, soft sugar, granulated sugar and brown slab sugar (E.T. 20%)	30	40
	(B) Other	60	80

Import Tariffs

No.	Descriptions	Min. (%)	Ord. (%)
17.02	Other sugars in solid form; sugar syrups, not containing added flavouring or colouring matter; artificial honey, whether or not mixed with natural honey; caramel:		
	(A) Glucose	60	80
	(B) Artificial honey	60	80
	(C) Other	70	80
17.03	Molasses	40	50
17.04/05	Sugar confectionery, not containing cocoa	70	90

18.   Cocoa & Cocoa Preparations

No.	Descriptions	Min. (%)	Ord. (%)
18.01	Cocoa beans, whole or broken, raw or roasted	20	30
18.02	Cocoa shels, husks, skins and waste	20	30
18.03	Cocoa paste (in bulk or in block), whether or not defatted	20	30
18.04	Cocoa butter (fat or oil)	50	70
18.05	Cocoa powder, unsweetened	30	40
18.06	Chocolate and other food preparations containing cocoa	70	90

19.   Preparations Of Cereals, Flour Or Starch; Pastrycooks' Products

No.	Descriptions	Min. (%)	Ord. (%)
19.01/ 19.02	Malt extract: preparations of flour, meal, starch or malt extract, of a kind used as infant food or for dietetic or culinary purposes, containing less than 50% by weight of cocoa:		
	(A) Milk powder substitutes	30	40
	(B) Extract of malt and milk (Lacovo)	60	80
	(C) Other	60	80
19.03	Macaroni, spaghetti and similar products	60	80
19.04	Tapioca and sago; tapioca and sago substitutes obtained from potato or other starches	60	80
19.05	Prepared foods obtained by the swelling or roasting of cereals or cereal products (puffed rice, corn flakes and similar products)	60	80
19.06/ 19.07	Bread, ships' biscuits and other ordinary bakers' wares, not containing added sugar, honey, eggs, fats, cheese or fruit; communion wafers, cachets of a kind suitable for pharmaceutical use, sealing wafers, rice paper and similar products:		
	(A) Cachets for pharmaceutical use	30	40
	(B) Other	60	80

No.	Descriptions	Min. (%)	Ord. (%)
	Import Tariffs		
19.08	Pastry, biscuits, cakes and other fine bakers' wares, whether or not containing cocoa in any proportion	60	80
20.	Preparations Of Vegetables, Fruit Or Other Parts Of Plants		
20.01	Vegetables and fruit, prepared or preserved by vinegar or acetic acid, with or without sugar, whether or not containing salt, spices or mustard:		
	(A) Canned	60	80
	(B) Other	50	70
20.02	Vegetables prepared or preserved otherwise than by vinegar or acetic acie:		
	(A) Canned:		
	(1) Mushrooms	70	90
	(2) Other edible fungi	70	90
	(3) Other	60	80
	(B) Other:		
	(1) Edible fungi	70	90
	(2) Other	50	70
20.03	Fruit preserved by freezing, containing added sugar	60	80
20.04	Fruit, fruit-peel and parts of plants, preserved by sugar (drained, glacé or crystallised)	70	90
20.05	Jams, fruit jellies, marmalades, fruit purée and fruit pastes, being cooked preparations, whether or not containing added sugar:		
	(A) Canned	70	80
	(B) Other	60	80
20.06	Fruit otherwise prepared or preserved, whether or not containing added sugar or spirit:		
	(A) Canned	70	90
	(B) Other	60	80
20.07	Fruit juices (including grape must) and vegetable juices, whether or not containing added sugar, but unfermented and not containing spirit:		
	(A) Canned:		
	(1) Fruit juices	70	90
	(2) Other	60	80
	(B) Other:		
	(1) Fruit juices	70	90
	(2) Other	60	80
21.	Miscellaneous Edible Preparations		

Import Tariffs

No.	Descriptions	Min. (%)	Ord. (%)
21.01/02	Extracts, essences or concentrates, of coffee, tea or mate and preparations with a basis of those extracts, essences or concentrates: roasted chicory and other roasted coffee substitutes and extracts, essences and concentrates thereof:		
	(A) Extracts, essences or concentrates of coffee and preparations with a basis of those extracts, essences or concentrates	60	80
	(B) Extracts, essences or concentrates of tea or mate and preparations with a basis of those extracts, essences or concentrates	100	130
	(C) Other	60	80
21.03	Mustard flour and prepared mustard	50	70
21.04	Sauces; mixed condiments and mixed seasonings:		
	(A) Gourmet powder	70	90
	(B) Other	50	70
21.05	Soups and broths, in liquid, solid or powder form; homogenised composite food preparations	70	90
21.06	Natural yeasts (active or inactive); prepared baking powders:		
	(A) Natural yeasts	60	80
	(B) Prepared baking powder	50	70
21.07	Food preparations not specified or included	70	90
22.	Beverages, Spirit & Vinegar		
22.01	Waters including spa waters and aerated waters; ice and snow:		
	(A) Natural water	20	30
	(B) Spa waters and aerated waters	70	90
	(C) Other	20	30
22.02	Lemonade, flavoured spa waters and flavoured aerated waters, and other non-alcoholic beverages, not including fruit and vegetable juices falling within No. 20.07	70	90
22.03	Beer made from malt	120	150
22.04	Crape must, in fermentation or with fermentation arrested otherwise than by the addition of alcohol	70	90
22.05	Wine of fresh grapes: grape must with fermentation arrested by the addition of alcohol	150	180

Import Tariffs

No.	Descriptions	Min. (%)	Ord. (%)
22.06	Vermouths, and other wines of fresh grapes flavoured with aromatic extracts	150	180
22.07	Other fermented beverages (e.g. cider, perry and mead)	150	180
22.08	Ethyl alcohol or neutral spirits, undernatured, of a strength of 80° or higher: denatured spirts (including ethyl alcohol and neutral spirits) of any strength:		
	(A) Undenatured	80	100
	(B) Denatured	60	80
22.09	spirits (other than those of No. 22.08); liqueurs and other spirituous beverages; compound alcoholic preparations (known as "concentrated extracts") for the manufacture of beverages	150	180
22.10	Vinegar and substitutes for vinegar	50	70
23.	Residues & Waste from the Food industries; Prepared Animal Fodder		
23.01	Flours and meals, of meat, offals, fish, crustaceans or molluscs, unfit for human consumption; greaves:		
	(A) Flours and meals of meat and offals; greaves:		
	(1) Greaves	40	50
	(2) Other	20	30
	(B) Other:		
	(1) Of fish, for animal feeding	6	11
	(2) Other	20	30
23.02	Bran, sharps and other residues derived from the sifting, milling or working of cereals or of leguminous vegetable	20	30
23.03	Beet-pulp, bagasse and other waste of sugar manufacture; brewing and distilling dregs and waste; residues of starch manufacture and similar residues	20	30
23.04	Oil-cake and other residues (except dregs) resulting from the extraction of vegetable oils	20	30
23.05	Wine lees; argol	20	30
23.06	Products of vegetable origin of a kind used for animal food, not elsewhere specified or included	25	35
23.07	Sweetened forage: Other preparations of a kind used in animal feeding	9	14

Import Tariffs

No.	Descriptions	Min.(%)	Ord.(%)
24.	Tobacco		
24.01	Unmanufactured tobacco; tocacco refuse	50	70
24.02	Manufactured tobacco; tobacco extracts and essences	150	180

V.   Mineral Products

No.	Descriptions	Min.(%)	Ord.(%)
25.01	Common salt (including rock salt, sea salt and table salt); pure sodium chloride; salt liquors; sea water:		
	(A) Common salt	NIL	NIL
	(B) Pure sodium chloride	25	35
	(C) Salt liquors and sea water	NIL	NIL
25.02	Unroasted iron pyrites	15	20
25.03	Sulphur of all kinds, other than sublimed sulphur, precipitated sulphur and colloidal sulphur	25	35
25.04	Natural graphit	20	30
25.05	Natural sands of all kinds, whether or not coloured, other than metal-bearing sands falling within No. 26.01	30	40
25.06	Quartz (other than natural sands); quartzite, including quartzite not further worked than roughly split, roughly squared or squared by sawing	30	40
25.07	Clay (e.g. kaolin and bentonite), andalusite, kyanite and sillimanite, whether or not calcined, but not including expanded clays falling within No. 68.07; mullite; chamotte and dinas earths:		
	(A) Clay	40	50
	(B) Fireclay	15	20
	(C) Other	30	40
25.08	Chalk	35	45
25.09/ 25.10	Natural calcium phosphates, natural aluminium calcium phosphates, apatite and phosphatic chalk:		
	(A) Apatite	6	11
	(B) Other	15	20
25.11	Natural barium sulphate (barytes); natural barium carbonate (witherite), whether or not calcined, other than barium oxide	35	45
25.12	Siliceous fossil meals and similar siliceous earth (e.g. kieselguhr, tripolite or diatomite), whether or not calcined, of an apparent specific gravity of 1 or less	30	40

Import Tariffs

No.	Descriptions	Min.(%)	Ord.(%)
25.13	Pumice stone; emery; natural corundum, natural garnet and other natural abrasives, whether or not heat-treated:		
	(A) Pumice stone	25	35
	(B) Other	12	17
25.14	Slate, including slate not further worked than roughly split, roughly squared or squared by sawing	40	50
25.15	Marble, travertine, ecaussine and other calcareous monumental and building stone of an apparent specific gravity of 2.5 or more and alabaster, including such stone not further worked then roughly split, roughly squared or squared by sawing:		
	(A) Marble	60	80
	(B) Other	40	50
25.16	Granite, porphyry, basalt, sandstone and other monumental and building stone, including such stone not further worked than roughly split, roughly squared or squared by sawing	40	50
25.17	Pebbles and crushed or broken stone (whether or not heat-treated), gravel, macadam and tarred macadam, of a kind commonly used for concrete aggregates, for road metalling or for railway or other ballast; flint and shingle, whether or not heat-treated; granules and chippings (whether or not heat-treated) and powder of stones falling within No. 25.15 or 25.16:		
	(A) Flint and shingle	60	80
	(B) Other	40	50
25.18	Dolomite, whether or not calcined, including dolomite not further worked than roughly split, roughly squared or squared by sawing; agglomerated dolomite (including tarred dolomite)	30	40
25.19	Natural magnesium carbonate (magnesite); fused magnesia; dead-burned (sintered) magnesia, whether or not containing small quantities of other oxides added before sintering; other magnesium oxide, whether or not chemically pure:		
	(A) Magnesium oxide, chemically pure	25	35
	(B) Other	30	40

Import Tariffs

No.	Descriptions	Min.(%)	Ord.(%)
25.20	Gypsum; anhydrite; calcined gypsum, and plasters with a basis of calcium sulphate, whether or not coloured, but not including plasters specially prepared for use in dentistry	60	80
25.21	Limestone flux and calcareous stone, commonly used for the manufacture of the or cement	40	50
25.22	Quicklime, slaked lime and hydraulic lime, other than calcium oxide and hydroxide	60	80
25.23	Portland cement, cement fondu, slag cement, supersulphate cement and similar hydraulic cements, whether or not coloured or in the form of clinker	20	30
25.24	Asbestos	25	35
25.25/26	Mica, including splittings; mica waste	20	30
25.27	Natural steatite, including natural steatite not further worked than roughly split, roughly squared or squared by sawing; talc	40	50
25.28	Natural cryolite and natural chiolite	40	50
25.29/ 25.30	Crude natural borates and concentrates thereof (calcined or not), but not including borates separated from natural brine; crude natural boric acid containing not more than 85% of H_3BO_3 calculated on the dry weight	20	30
25.31	Felspar, leucite, nepheline and nepheline syenite; fluorspar	40	50
25.32	Mineral substances not elsewhere specified or included:		
	(A) Amber, meerschaum and jet	40	50
	(B) Mineral medicinal substance	20	30
	(C) Other	40	50
26.	Metallic Ores, Slag & Ash		
26.01	Metallic ores and concentrates and roasted iron pyrites:		
	(A) Iron ores and concentrates	NIL	NIL
	(B) Copper ores and concentrates	NIL	NIL
	(C) Chromium ores and concentrates	NIL	NIL
	(D) Tungsten ores and concentrates (E.T. 20%)	NIL	NIL
	(E) Cinnabar	9	14
	(F) Ores and concentrates of precious metals	NIL	NIL
	(G) Ores and concentrates of molybdenum, niobium, tantalum, titanium, vanadium or zirconium	NIL	NIL

No.	Descriptions	Min.(%)	Ord.(%)
	(H) Antimony ores and concentrates:		
	(1) Crude antimony (E.T. 20%)	NIL	NIL
	(2) Other	NIL	NIL
	(G) Other	NIL	NIL
26.02	Slag, dross, scalings and similar waste from the manufacture of irn or steel	25	35
26.03	Ash and residues (other than from the manufacture of iron or steel), containing metals or metallic compounds	25	35
26.04	Other slag and ash including kelp	25	35
27.	Minerals Fuels Mineral Oils & Products Of Their Distillation; Bituminous Substances; Mineral Waxes		
27.01	Coal; briquettes, ovoids and similar solid fuels manufactured from coal:		
	(A) Coal (E.T. 40%)	15	20
	(B) Other	40	50
27.02	Lignite, whether or not agglomerated (E.T. 40%)	15	20
27.03	Peat (including peat litter), whether or not agglomerated (E.T. 40%)	15	20
27.04	Coke and semi-coke of coal, of lignite or of peat, whether or not agglomerated; retort carbon	6	11
27.05	Coal gas, water gas, producer gas and similar gases	15	20
27.06	Tar distilled from coal, from lignite or from peat, and other mineral tars, including partially distilled tars and blends of pitch with creosote oils or with other coal tar distillation products	20	30
27.07	Oils and other products of the distillation of high temperature coal tar; similar products as defined in Note 2 to this Section	20	30
27.08	Pitch and pitch coke, obtained from coal tar or from other mineral tars:		
	(A) Pitch	25	35
	(B) Pitch coke	6	11
27.09	Petroleum oils and oils obtained from bituminous minerals, crude	3	8
27.10	Petroleum oils and obtained from bituminous minerals, other than crude; preparations not elsewhere specified or included, containing not less than 70% by weight of petroleum oils or of oils obtained from bituminous minerals, these oils being the basic constituents of the preparations:		

Import Tariffs

No.	Descriptions	Min. (%)	Ord. (%)
	(A) Gasoline	9	14
	(B) White spirit	20	30
	(C) Other light oils and preparation	15	20
	(D) Kerosene	9	14
	(E) Diesel oil	6	11
	(F) Other medium oils and preparations	15	20
	(G) Fuel oils	15	20
	(H) Lubricating oils, grease	12	17
	(I) Other	15	20
27.11	Petroleum gases and other gaseous hydrocarbons	15	20
27.12	Petroleum jelly	35	45
27.13	Paraffin wax, micro-crystalline wax, slack wax, ozokerite, lignite wax, peat wax and other mineral waxes, whether or not coloured	35	45
27.14	Petroleum bitumen, petroleum coke and other residues of petroleum oils or of oils obtained from bituminour minerals:		
	(A) Petroleum coke	6	11
	(B) Other	25	35
27.15	Bitumen and asphalt, natural; bituminous shale, asphaltic rock and tar sands:		
	(A) Bitumen and asphalt, natural	25	35
	(B) Other	15	20
27.16	Bituminour mixtures based on natural asphalt, on natural bitumen, on petroleum bitumen, on mineral tar or on mineral tar pitch (for example, bituminous mastics, cut-backs)	25	35

VI. Productions of the Chemical & Allied Industries

No.	Descriptions	Min. (%)	Ord. (%)
28.	Inorganic Chemicals; Organic & Inorganic Compounds Of Precious Metals, Of Rare Earth Metals, Of Radio-Active Elements & Of Isotopes		
28.01	Halogens (fluorine, chlorine, bromine and iodine):		
	(A) Chlorine	60	80
	(B) Fluorine, bromine and iodine	20	30
28.02	Sulphur, sublimed or precipitated; colloidal sulphur	12	17
28.03	Carbon (including carbon black)	25	35
28.04	Hydrogen, rare gases and other non-metals:		
	(A) Oxygen	60	80
	(B) Nitrogen, hydrogen and rare gases	20	30
	(C) Phosphorus	20	30

No.	Descriptions	Min. (%)	Ord. (%)
	(D) Crystals doped for use in electronics, in the form of cylinders or rods:		
	(1) Monocrystalline silicon, 7.5cm, or more in diameter	6	11
	(2) Other	12	17
	(E) Other	20	30
28.05	Alkali and alkaline-earth metals; rare earth metals, yttrium and scandium and intermixtures or interalloys thereof; mercury:		
	(A) Alkali and alkaline-earth metals	20	30
	(B) Mercury	12	17
	(C) Other	20	30
28.06	Hydrochloric acid and chlorosulphuric acid:		
	(A) Hydrochloric acid	60	80
	(B) Chlorosulphuric acid	30	40
28.07/08	Sulphuric acid; oleum	25	35
28.09	Nitric acid; sulphonitric acids	30	40
28.10	Phosphorus pentoxide and phosphoric acids (meta-, ortho- and pyro-)	3	8
28.11/12	Boric oxide and boric acid	20	30
28.13	Other inorganic acids and oxygen compounds of non-metals (excluding water):		
	(A) Inorganic acids	25	35
	(B) Oxygen compounds of non-metals	20	30
28.14	Halides, oxyhalids and other halogen compounds of non-metals	20	30
28.15	Sulphides of non-metals; phosphorus trisulphide	20	30
28.16	Ammonia, anhydrous or in aqueous solution	25	35
28.17	Sodium hydroxide (caustic soda); potassium hydroxide (caustic potash); peroxides of sodium or potassium:		
	(A) Sodium phdroxide (caustic soda)	25	35
	(B) Other	20	30
28.18	Hydroxide and peroxide of magnesium; oxides, hydroxides and peroxides, of strontium or barium	20	30
28.19	Zinc oxide and zinc peroxide:		
	(A) Zinc oxide	30	40
	(B) Zinc peroxide	20	30
28.20	Aluminium oxide and hydroxide; artificial corundum:		
	(A) Aluminium oxide and aluminium	20	30
	(B) Artificial corundum	15	20

Import Tariffs			
No.	**Descriptions**	**Min. (%)**	**Ord. (%)**
28.21	Chromium oxides and hydroxides:		
	(A) Chromic oxide	20	30
	(B) Chromium trioxide (chromic acid)	15	20
	(C) Other	20	30
28.22	Manganese oxides:		
	(A) Managanese dioxide	30	40
	(B) Other	20	30
28.23	Iron oxides and hydroxides; earth colours containing 70% or more by weight of combined iron evaluated as Fe_2O_3:		
	(A) Earth colours	35	45
	(B) Other	20	30
28.24	Cobalt oxides and hydroxides; commercial cobalt oxides:		
	(A) Cobalt monoxide and commercial cobalt oxides	20	30
	(B) Other	20	30
28.25	Titanium oxides:		
	(A) Titanium dioxide	20	30
	(B) Other	20	30
28.26/	Lead oxides; red lead and orange lead:		
28.27	(A) Lead oxides	20	30
	(B) Red lead or orange lead	35	45
28.28	Hydraxine and hydroxylamine and their inorganic salts; other inorganic bases and metallic oxides, hydroxides and peroxides	20	30
28.29	Fluorides; fluorosilicates, fluoroborates and other complex fluorine salts	20	30
28.30	Chlorides, oxchlorides and hydroxychlorides; bromides and oxyromides; iodides and oxylodides:		
	(A) Ammonium chloride:		
	(1) As a fertilizer	6	11
	(2) Other	20	30
	(B) Calcium chloride and zinc chloride	40	50
	(C) Other chlorides, oxychlorides and hydroxychlorides	20	30
	(D) Bromides and oxybromides	20	30
	(E) Iodides and oxylodides	20	30
28.31	Hypochlorites: commercial calcium hypochlorite; chlorites; hypobromites:		
	(A) Calcium hypochlorite (including commercial calcium hypochlorite):		

No.	Descriptions	Min.(%)	Ord.(%)
	(1) Bleaching powder (i.e. chlorinated lime)	70	90
	(2) Bleaching powder, concertrated	60	80
	(3) Other	60	80
	(B) Hypochlorites and chlorites;	20	30
	(C) Hypobromites	20	30
28.32	Chlorates and perchlorates; bromates and perbromates; Iodates and periodates:		
	(A) Potassium chlorate	15	20
	(B) Other	20	30
28.33/	Sulphides; polysulphides:		
28.35	(A) Mercury sulphide (vermillion	35	45
	(B) Sodium sulphide	30	40
	(C) Molybdenum trisulphide	20	30
	(D) Antimony trisulphide	35	45
	(E) Other	20	30
28.36	Dithionites, including those stabilised with organic substances; sulphoxylates:		
	(A) Sodium hydrosulphite	20	30
	(B) Other	20	30
28.37	Sulphites and thiosulphates:		
	(A) Sodium bisulphite	20	30
	(B) Sodium hyposulphite	20	30
	(C) Other	20	30
28.38	Sulphates (including alums) and persulphates:		
	(A) Barium sulphate	20	30
	(B) Sodium sulphate	30	40
	(C) Sodium hydrogen sulphate and sodium pyrosulphate	20	30
	(D) Chrome alum	20	30
	(E) Copper sulphate	35	45
	(F) Ferrous sulphate	35	45
	(G) Alum, shite	35	45
	(H) Other	20	30
28.39	Nitrites and nitrates:		
	(A) Potassium nitrate:		
	(1) As a fertilezer	6	11
	(2) Other	20	30
	(B) Other	20	30
28.40	Phosphites, hypophosphites and phosphates:		
	(A) Sodium metaphosphate	15	20
	(B) Other	15	20
28.41/	Carbonates and percarbonates; commercial		

Import Tariffs

No.	Descriptions	Min. (%)	Ord. (%)
28.42	ammonium carbonate containing ammonium carbamate:		
	(A) Sodium carbonate (soda ash)	25	35
	(B) Sodium bicarbonate	35	45
	(C) Barium carbonate	30	40
	(D) Magnesium carbonate, calcium carbonate and basic lead carbonate (white lead)	35	45
	(E) Other	20	30
28.43	Cyanides and complex cyanides:		
	(A) Sodium cyanide	15	20
	(B) Potassium cyanide	15	20
	(C) Potassium ferrocyanide	20	30
	(D) Other	20	30
28.44	Fulminates, cyanates and thiocyanates	20	30
28.45	Silicates; commercial sodium and potassium silicates:		
	(A) Sodium silicate	30	40
	(B) Other	20	30
28.46	Borates and perborates:		
	(A) Sodium tetraborate (borax)	15	20
	(B) Other	20	30
28.47	Salts of metallic acids (for example, chromates, permanganates, stannates):		
	(A) Sodium bichromate	15	20
	(B) Potassium bichromate	15	20
	(C) Potassium permanganate	20	30
	(D) Lead chromate, basic lead chromate and zinc chromate	30	40
	(E) Ammonium molybdate	20	30
	(F) Stannates	20	30
	(G) Other	20	30
28.48	Other salts and peroxysalts of inorganic acids, but not including azides	20	30
28.49	Colloidal precious metals; amalgams of precious metals; salts and other compounds, inorganic or organic, of precious metals, including albuminates, proteinates, tannates and similar compounds, whether or not chemically defined	20	30
28.50	Fissile chemical elements and isotopes; other radio-active chemical elements and radio-active isotopes; compounds, inorganic or organic, of such elements or isotopes, whether or not chemically defined; alloys, dispersions and cermets, containing any of these elements, isotopes or compounds:		

Import Tariffs

No.	Descriptions	Min.(%)	Ord.(%)
	(A) Radium and its salts	9	14
	(B) Other	20	30
28.51	Isotopes and their compounds, inorganic or organic, whether or not chemically defined, other than isotopes and compounds falling with No. 28.05	20	30
28.52	Compounds, inorganic or organic, of thorium, of uranium depleted in U 235, of rare earth metals, of yttrium or of scandium, whether or not mixed together	20	30
28.53/54	Hydrogen peroxide (including solid hydrogen peroxide)	20	30
28.55	Phosophides, whether or not chemically defined	15	20
28.56	Carbides, whether or not chemically defined:		
	(A) Calcium carbide	35	45
	(B) Other	20	30
28.57	Hydrides, nitrides, azides, silicides and borides, whether or not chemically defined	20	30
28.58	Other inorganic compounds (including distilled and conductivity water and water of similar purity); liquid air (whether or not rare gases have been removed); compressed air; amalgams, other than amalgams of precious metals	20	30
29.	Organic Chemicals		
29.01	Hydrocarbons:		
	(A) Acyclic Hydrocarbons:		
	(1) Ethylene	20	30
	(2) Propylene	20	30
	(3) Butylenes, butadienes and methylbutadienes	20	30
	(4) Acetylene	35	45
	(5) Other	20	30
	(B) Cyclic hydrocarbons:		
	(1) Benzene	15	20
	(2) Toluene	20	30
	(3) Xylenes	15	20
	(4) Styrene	20	30
	(5) Ethylbenzene	20	30
	(6) Naphthalene	25	35
	(7) Dodecylbezene	20	30
	(8) Other	20	30
29.02	Halogenated derivatives of hydrocarbons	20	30

Import Tariffs

No.	Descriptions	Min. (%)	Ord. (%)
29.03	Sulphonated, nitrated or nitrosated derivatives of hydrocarbons:		
	(A) Dinitrochlorobenzene, dinitrotoluene and nitrobenzene	15	20
	(B) Trinitrotoluene (TNT)	30	40
	(C) Other	20	30
29.04	Acyclic alcohols and their halogenated, sulphonated, nitrated or nitrosated derivatives:		
	(A) Methyl alcohol	20	30
	(B) Propyl or isopropyl alcohols	20	30
	(C) Butyl alcohols	20	30
	(D) Octyl alcohols	20	30
	(E) Ethylene glycol	20	30
	(F) Other	20	30
29.05	Cyclic alcohols and their halogenated, sulphonated, nitrated or nitrosated derivatives:		
	(A) Menthol crystals	50	70
	(B) Borneol (borneo camphor)	20	30
	(C) Inositol (cyclohexanhexol)	20	30
	(D) Other	20	30
29.06	Phenols and phenol-alcohols:		
	(A) Phenol (carbolic acid)	20	30
	(B) Other	20	30
29.07	Halogenated, sulphonated, nitrated or nitrosated derivatives of phenols or phenol-alcohols	20	30
29.08	Ethers, ether-alcohols, ether-phenols, ether-alcohol-phenols, alcohol peroxides and ether peroxides, and their halogenated, sulphonated, nitrated or nitrosated derivatives	20	30
29.09	Epoxides, epoxyalcohols, epoxyphenols and epoxyethers, with a three or four member ring, and their halogenated, sulphonated, nitrated or nitrosated derivatives	20	30
29.10	Acetals and hemiacetals and single or complex oxygen-function acetals and hemiacetals, and their haiogenated, sulphonated, nitrated or nitrosated derivatives	20	30
29.11	Aldehydes, aldehyde-alcohols, aldehyde-ethers, aldehyde-phenols and other single or complex oxygen-function aldehydes, cyclic polymers of aldehydes; paraformaldehyde:		
	(A) Formaldehyde	20	30
	(B) Other	20	30
29.12	Halogenated, sulphonated, nitrated or nitrosated derivatives of products falling within No. 29.11	20	30

Import Tariffs

No.	Descriptions	Min. (%)	Ord. (%)
29.13	Ketones, ketone-alcohols, ketone-phenols, ketone-aldehydes, quinones, quinone-alcohols, quinone-phenols, quinone-aldehydes and other single or complex oxygen-function ketones and quinones, and their halogenated sulphonated, nitrated or nitrosated derivatives:		
	(A) Acetone	15	20
	(B) Ethyl methyl ketone	20	30
	(C) Camphor	30	40
	(D) Other	20	30
29.14	Monocarboxylic acids and their Gnhydrides, halides, peroxides and peracids, and their halogenated, sulphonated nitrated or nitrosated derivatives:		
	(A) Formic acid	30	40
	(B) Acetic acid and its salts:		
	(1) Acetic acid	40	50
	(2) Acetic acid, glacial	20	30
	(3) Salts of acetic acid	40	50
	(C) Acetic anhydride	40	50
	(D) Esters of acetic acid	20	30
	(E) Methacrylic acid and its salts and esters	20	30
	(F) Stearic acid	40	50
	(G) Sodium benzoate	20	30
	(H) Other	20	30
29.15	Polycarboxylic acids and their anhydrides, halides, peroxides and peracids, and their halogenated, sulphonated, nitrated or nitrosated derivatives:.		
	(A) Oxalic acid	30	40
	(B) Phthalic anhydried	20	30
	(C) Dioctyl orthophthalates	20	30
	(D) Esters of terephthalic acid	20	30
	(E) Maleic anhydride	20	30
	(F) Other	20	30
29.16	Carboxylic acids with alcohol, phenol, aldehyde or ketone function and other single or complex oxygen-function carboxylic acids and their anhydrides, halides, peroxides and peracids, and their halogenated, sulphonated, nitrated or nitrosated derivatives:		
	(A) salicylic acid and sodium salicylate	15	20
	(B) Acetylsalicylic acid (aspirin)	15	20
	(C) Citric acid	25	35
	(D) Tartaric acid	25	35
	(E) Other	20	30

Import Tariffs

No.	Descriptions	Min. (%)	Ord. (%)
29.17/ 29.19	Phosphoric esters and their salts, including lactophosphates, and their halogenated, sulphonated, nitrated or nitrosated derivatives	20	30
29.20/ 29.21	Other esters of mineral acids (excluding halides) and their salts, and their halogenated, sulphonated, nitrated or nitrosated derivatives	20	30
29.22	Amine-function compounds:		
	(A) Phenylamine	15	20
	(B) Other	20	30
29.23	Single or complex oxygen-function amino-compounds:		
	(A) H acid and J acid	20	30
	(B) Amino acid	15	20
	(C) Procaine	15	20
	(D) Other	20	30
29.24	Quaternary ammonium salts and hydroxides; lecithins and other phospho-aminolipins	20	30
29.25	Carboxyamide-function compounds; amide-function compounds of carbonic acid:		
	(A) Phenacetin	15	20
	(B) Paracetanol (acetaminophen)	20	30
	(C) Other	20	30
29.26	Carboxyimide-function compounds (including ortho-benzoicsulphimide and its salts) and imine-function compounds (including hexamethylenetetramine and trimethylenetrinitramine):		
	(A) O-benzoic sulphimide (saccharin)	70	90
	(B) Other	20	30
29.27	Nitrile-function compounds:		
	(A) Acrylonitrile	20	30
	(B) Other	20	30
28.28	Diazo-, azo- and azoxy-compounds	20	30
29.29	Organic derivatives of hydraxine or of hydroxylamine	15	20
29.30	Compounds with other nitrogen-function	20	30
29.31	Organo-sulphur compounds	20	30
29.32/33	Organo-mercury compounds	20	30
29.34	Other organo-inorganic compounds	20	30
29.35	Heterocyclic compounds; nucleic acids:		
	(A) Lactam:		
	(1) Caprolactam	25	35
	(2) Other	15	20
	(B) Other heterocyclic compounds	15	20
	(C) Nucleic acids	25	35

Import Tariffs

No.	Descriptions	Min. (%)	Ord. (%)
29.36	Sulphonamides	25	35
29.37	sultones and sultams	20	30
29.38	Provitamins and vitamins, natural or reproduced by synthesis (including natural concentrates), derivatives thereof used primarily as vitamins, and intermixtures of the foregoing, whether or not in any solvent	15	20
29.39	Hormones, natural or reproduced by synthesis; derivatives thereof, used primarily as hormones; other steriods used primarily as hormones:		
	(A) Insuline	12	17
	(B) Pituitary (anterior) and similar hormones	15	20
	(C) Adremal cortical hormones	15	20
	(D) Other	20	30
29.40/ 29.41	Glycosides, natural or reproduced by synthesis, and their salts, ethers, esters and other derivatives	15	20
29.42	Vegetable alkaloids, natural or reproduced by synthesis, and their salts, ethers, esters and other derivatives:		
	(A) Morphine and its derivatives	40	50
	(B) Cocaine	12	17
	(C) Papaverin and its derivatives	40	50
	(D) Quinine and its salts	20	30
	(E) Ephedrine and its salts	15	20
	(F) Cafferne and its salts	15	20
	(G) Strychnine and its salts	12	17
	(H) Other	15	20
29.43	Sugars, chemically pure, other than sucrose, glucose and lactose; sugar ethers and sugar esters, and their salts, other than products of Nos. 29.39, 29.41 and 29.42	20	30
29.44	Antibiotics	15	20
29.45	Other organic compounds	20	30
30.	Pharmaceutical Products		
30.01	Organo-therapeutic glands or other organs, dried, whether or not powdered; organo-therapeutic extracts of glands or other organs or of their secretions; other animal substances prepared for therapeutic or prophylactic uses, not elsewhere specified or included	20	30
30.02	Antisera: microbial vaccines, toxins, microbial cultures (including ferments but excluding yeasts) and similar products	15	20

Import Tariffs

No.	Descriptions	Min. (%)	Ord. (%)
30.03	Medicaments (including veterinary medicaments):		
	(A) Preparations of antibiotics	20	30
	(B) Preparations of hormones	20	30
	(C) Preparation of vegetable alkaloids:		
	(1) Compounds and preparations of quinine or its salts	25	35
	(2) Other	20	30
	(D) Sulfa drugs	30	40
	(E) Preparations of vitamins	30	40
	(F) Contraceptives	NIL	NIL
	(G) Other	20	30
30.04	Wadding, gauze, bandages and similar articles (e.g. dressings, adhesive plasters, poultices), impregnated or coated with pharmaceutical substances or put up in retail packings for medical or surgical purposes, other than goods specified in Note 3 to this Section:		
	(A) Absorbent cotton, gauze, bandages and adhesive plasters	50	70
	(B) Other	25	35
30.05	Other pharmaceutical goods:		
	(A) Dental cements and fillings	20	30
	(B) Opacifying preparations for X-ray examinations and diagnostic reagents	20	30
	(C) Blood-grouping reagents	15	20
	(D) Sterile surgical catgut	20	30
	(E) Other	20	30
31. Fertilisers			
31.01	Cuano and other natural animal or vegetable fertilisers, whether or not mixed together, but not chemically treated:		
	(A) Guano	6	11
	(B) Other	20	30
31.02	Mineral or chemical fertilisers, nitrogenous:		
	(A) Ammonium sulphate	6	11
	(B) Ammonium chloride, not chemically pure	6	11
	(C) Ammonium nitrate	6	11
	(D) Urea	6	11
	(E)Other	6	11
31.03	Mineral or chemical fertilisers, phosphatic:		
	(A) Calcium superphosphate	6	11
	(B) Other	6	11

Import Tariffs

No.	Descriptions	Min. (%)	Ord. (%)
31.04	Mineral or chemical fertilisers, potassic:		
	(A) Potassium chloride	6	11
	(B) Potassium sulphate	6	11
	(C) Other	6	11
31.05	Other fertilisers; goods of the present Chapter in tablets, lozenges and similar prepared forms or inn packings of a gross weight not exceeding 10kg:		
	(A) Fertilisers, containing the three fertilising substances nitrogen, phosphorus and potassium	6	11
	(B) Fertilisers, containing the two fertilising substances nitrogen and phosphorus		
	(1) Ammonium monohydric phosphate	6	11
	(2) Other	6	11
	(C) Fertilisers, containing the two fertilising substances nitrogen and potassium	6	11
	(D) Other	6	11
32.	Tanning & Dyeing Extracts; Tannins & Their Derivatives; Dyes, Colors, Paints & Varnishes; Putty, Fillers & Stoppings; Inks		
32.01	Tanning extracts of vegetable origin; tannins (tannic acids), including water-extracted gall-nut tannin, and their salts, ethers, esters and other derivatives:		
	(A) Tanning extracts:		
	(1) Quebracho extract	25	35
	(2) Wattle (mimosa) extract	25	35
	(3) Other	30	40
	(B) Tannins	25	35
	(C) Other	25	35
32.02/ 32.03	Synthetic organic tanning substances, and inorganic tanning substances; tanning preparations, whether or not containing natural tanning materials; enzymatic preparations for pre-tanning (e.g. of enzymatic, pancreatic, or bacterial origin)	25	35
32.04	Colouring matter of vegetable origin (including dyewood extract and other vegetable dyeing extracts, but excluding indigo) or of animal origin:		

Import Tariffs

No.	Descriptions	Min. (%)	Ord. (%)
	(A) Colouring matter of vegetable origin:		
	(1) Cunao (false gambier)	35	45
	(2) Cutch	30	40
	(3) Logwood extract	40	50
	(4) Other	35	45
	(B) Colouring matter of animal origin	40	50
32.05	Synthetic organic dyestuffs (including pigment dyestuffs); synthetic organic products of a kind used as luminophores; products of the kind known as optical bleaching agents, substantive to the fibre; natural indigo.		
	(A) Synthetic organic dyestuffs:		
	(1) Disperse dyes	25	35
	(2) Vat dyes	25	35
	(3) Reactive dyes	25	35
	(4) Other	25	35
	(B) Natural indigo	60	80
	(C) Biological stains and dye indicators	15	20
	(D) Other	30	40
32.06	Colour lakes	25	35
32.07	Other colouring matter; inorganic products of a kind used as luminophores:		
	(A) Lithophone	20	30
	(B) Titanium whites	20	30
	(C) Other	25	35
32.08	Prepared pigments, prepared opacifiers and prepared colours, vitrifiable enamels and glazes, liquid lustres and similar products, of the kind used in the ceramic, enamelling and glass industries; engobes (slips); glass frit and other glass, in the form of powder, granules or flakes	40	50
32.09	Varnishes and lacquers; distempers; prepared water pigments of the kind used for finishing leather; paints and enamels; pigments dispersed in linseed oil, white spirit, spirits of turpentine or other media of a kind used in the manufacture of paints or enamels; stamping foils; dyes or other colouring matter in forms or packings of a kind sold by retail; solutions as defined by Note 4 to this Section	40	50
32.10	Artists', students' and signboard painters' colour, modifying tints, amusement colours and the like, in tablets, tubes, jars, bottles, pans or in similar forms or packings, including such colours in sets or outfits, with or without brushes, palettes or other accessories	50	70

Import Tariffs

No.	Descriptions	Min. (%)	Ord. (%)
32.11	Prepared driers	40	50
32.12	Glaziers' putty; grafting putty; painters' fillings; non-refractory surfacing preparations; stoppings, sealing and similar mastics, including resin mastics and cements	50	70
32.13	Writing and drawing inks:		
	(A) Writing and drawing inks:		
	(1) Chinese ink, solid or liquid	60	80
	(2) Other	50	70
	(B) Printing inks	35	45
	(C) Other inks:		
	(1) Inks for duplicating machines	35	45
	(2) Other	50	70
33.	Essential Oils & Resinoids; Perfumery, Cosmetic or Toilet Preparations		
33.01	Essential oils (terpeneless or not), concretes and absolutes; resinoids; concentrates of essential oils in fats, in fixed oils, or in waxes or the like, obtained by cold absorption or by maceration; terpenic by products of the deterpenation of essential oils:		
	(A) Camphor oil	70	90
	(B) Peppermint oil	70	90
	(C) Citronella oil	50	70
	(D) Other	60	80
33.02-04	Mixtures of two or more odoriferous substances (natural or artificial) and mixtures (including alcoholic solutions) with a basis of one or more of these substances, of a kind used as raw materials in the perfumery, food, drink or other industries	60	80
33.05/ 33.06	Perfumery, cosmetic or toilet preparations; aqueous distillates and aqueous solutions of essential oils, including such products suitable for medicinal uses:		
	(A) Perfumery, cosmetic or toilet preparations	100	130
	(B) Aqueous distillates and aqueous solutions of essential oils	60	80
34.	Soap, Organic Surface-active Agents, Washing Preparations, Lubricating Preparations, Artificial Waxes, Prepared Waxes, Polishing & Scouring Preparations, Candles & Similar Articles, Modelling Pastes & Pental Waxes		

No.	Descriptions	Min. (%)	Ord. (%)
	Import Tariffs		
34.01	Soap: organic surface-active products and preparations for use as soap, in the form of bars, cakes or moulded pieces or shapes, whether or not combined with soap	60	80
34.02	Organic surface-active agent: surface-active preparations and washing preparations, whether or not containing soap:		
	(A) Organic surface-active	20	30
	(B) Washing powder	60	80
	(C) Other	60	80
34.03	Lubricating preparations, and preparations of a kind used for oil or grease treatment of textiles, leather or other materials, but not including preparations containing 70% or more by weight of petroleum oils or of oils obtained from bituminous minerals	40	50
34.04	Artificial waxes (including water-soluble waxes): prepared waxes, not emulsified or containing solvents	50	70
34.05	Polishes and creams, for footwear, furniture or floors, metal polished, scouring powders and similar preparations, but excluding prepared waxes falling within No. 34.04	60	80
34.06	Candles, tapers, night-lights and the like	100	130
34.07	Modelling pastes (including those put up for childres's amusement and assorted modelling pastes); preparations of a kind known as ''dental wax'' or as ''detal impression compounds'', in plates, horseshoe shapes, sticks and similar forms:		
	(A) Preparations of a kind known as ''dental wax'' or as ''dental impression compounds''	20	30
	(B) Other	80	100
35. Albuminoidal Substances; Glues; Enzymes			
35.01	Casein, caseinates and other casein derivatives; casein glues	25	35
35.02	Albumins, albuminates and other albumin derivatives:		
	(A) Albumen	60	80
	(B) Other	25	35

Import Tariffs

No.	Descriptions	Min.(%)	Ord.(%)
35.03	Gelatin (including gelatin in rectangles, whether or not coloured or surface-worked) and gelatin derivatives; glues derived from bones, hides, nerves, tendons or from similar products, and fish glues; isinglass:		
	(A) Gelatin and its derivatives:		
	(1) Gelatin	25	35
	(2) Gelatin derivative	25	35
	(B) Other:		
	(1) Glues derived from bones	40	50
	(2) Other	40	50
35.04	Peptones and other protein substances (excluding enzymes of No. 35.07) and their derivatives; hide powder, whether or not chromed:		
	(A) Peptone	6	11
	(B) Other	25	35
35.05	Dextrins and dextrin glues; soluble or roasted starches; starch glues	40	50
35.06	Prepared glues not elsewhere specified or included; products suitable for use as glues put up for sale by retail as glues in packages not exceeding a net weight of 1 kg	70	90
35.07	Enzymes; prepared enzymes not elsewhere specified or included	20	30
36.	Explosives; Pyrotechnic Products; Matches; Pyrophoric Alloys; Certain Combustible Preparations		
36.01	Propellent powders	40	50
36.02	Prepared explosives, other than propellent powders	40	50
36.03/ 36.04	Safety fuses; detonating fuses; percussion and detonating caps; igniters; detonators	40	50
36.05	Pyrotechnic articles (e.g. railway fog signals, amorces, rain rockets		
	(A) Firecrackers and fireworks	100	130
	(B) Other	80	100
36.06	Matches (excluding Bengal matches)	80	100
36.07/ 36.08	Ferro-cerium and other pyrophoric alloys in all forms; articles of combustible materials:		
	(A) Ferro-cerium and other pyrophoric alloys:		
	(1) Cut to shape, for immediate use	60	80
	(2) Other	40	50
	(B) Articles of combustible materials	60	80

No.	Descriptions	Min. (%)	Ord. (%)
	Import Tariffs		

37. Photographic & Cinematographic Goods

No.	Descriptions	Min. (%)	Ord. (%)
37.01	Photographic plates and film in the flat, sensitised, unexposed, of any material other than paper, paperboard or cloth:		
	(A) For X-ray use	6	11
	(B) For photomechanical use	30	40
	(C) For scientific use only	9	14
	(D) Other	50	70
37.02	Film in rolls, sensitised, unexposed, perforated or not:		
	(A) Cinematograph film	20	30
	(B) For scientific use only	9	14
	(C) Other	50	70
37.03	Sensitised paper, paperboard and cloth, unexposed or exposed but not developed	50	70
37.04	Sensitised plates and film exposed but not developed, negative or positive:		
	(A) Cinematograph film	20	30
	(B) Other	50	70
37.05	Plates, unperforated film and perforated film (other than cinematograph film), exposed and developed, negative or positive:		
	(A) Magic lantern slides, for educational use only	NIL	NIL
	(B) Plates and film of books and data	NIL	NIL
	(C) Other	50	70
37.06/07	Cinematograph film, exposed and developed, whether or not incorporating sound track or consisting only of sound track, negative or positive:		
	(A) For educational use only	NIL	NIL
	(B) Other	9	14
37.08	Chemical products and flash light materials, of a kind and in a form suitable for use in photography	25	35
38. Miscellaneous Chemical Products			
38.01	artificial graphite; colloidal graphite, other than suspensions in oil	20	30
38.02/ 38.03	Activated carbon; activated natural mineral products; animal black, including spent animal black:		
	(A) Activated carbon	15	20
	(B) Activated natural mineral products	35	45
	(C) Animal black	40	50

Import Tariffs

No.	Descriptions	Min. (%)	Ord. (%)
38.04/05	Tall oil	25	35
38.06	Concentrated sulphite lye	25	35
38.07	Spirits of turpentine (gum, wood and sulphate) and other terpenic solvents produced by the distillation or other treatment of coniferous woods; crude dipentene; sulphite turpentine; pine oil (excluding ''pine oils'' not rich in terpineol):		
	(A) Spirits of turpentine	40	50
	(B) Other	40	50
38.08	Rosin and resin acids, and derivatives thereof other than ester gums included in No. 39.05;rosin spirit and rosin oils:		
	(A) Rosin	50	70
	(B) Other	30	40
38.09	Wood tar: wood tar oils (other than the composite solvents and thinners falling within No. 38.18); wood creosote; wood naphtha; acetone oil; vegetable pitch of all kinds; brewers' pitch and similar compounds based on rosin or on vegetable pitch; foundry core binders based on natural resinous products	25	35
38.10 38.11	Disinfectants, insecitcides, fungicides, rat prisons, herbicides, anti-sprouting products, plant-growth regulators and similar products, put up in forms or packings for sale by retail or as preparations or articles (for example, sulphur-treated bands, wicks and candles, fly-papers):		
	(A) Disinfectants	25	35
	(B) Insecticides:		
	(1) Put up in packings for sale by retail	9	14
	(2) Other	6	11
	(C) Fungicides:		
	(1) Put up in packings for sale by retail	9	14
	(2) Other	6	11
	(D) Herbicides	6	11
	(E) Mosquito smudges	60	80
	(F) Fly-papers	60	80
	(G) Other:		
	(1) Put up in packings for sale by retail	15	20
	(2) Other	9	14

Import Tariffs

No.	Descriptions	Min. (%)	Ord. (%)
38.12	Prepared glazings, prepared dressings and prepared mordants, of a kind used in the textile, paper, leather or like industries	25	35
38.13	Pickling preparations for metal surfaces; fluxes and other auxiliary preparations for soldering, brazing or welding; soldering, brazing or welding powders and pastes consisting of metal and other materials; preparations of a kind used as cores or coatings for welding rods and electrodes:		
	(A) Soldering, brazing or welding powder and pastes	25	35
	(B) Other	25	35
38.14	Anti-knock preparations, oxidation inhibitors, gum inhibitors, viscosity improvers, anti-corrosive preparations and similar prepared additives for mineral oils	25	35
38.15	Prepared rubber accelerators	15	20
38.16	Prepared culture media for development of micro-organisms	6	11
38.17	Preparations and charges for fire-extinguishers; charged fire-extinguishing grenades:		
	(A) Preparations and charges for fire-extinguishers	25	35
	(B) Charged fire-extinguishing grenades	50	70
38.18	Composite solvents and thinners for varnishes and similar products	40	50
38.19	Chemical products and preparations of the chemical or allied industries (including those consisting of mixtures of natural products), not elsewhere specified or included; residual products of the chemical or allied industries not elsewhere specified or included:		
	(A) Composite laboratory reagents	15	20
	(B) Rubber antioxidants	15	20
	(C) Fusel oil	30	40
	(D) Ink-removers and stencil correctors and the like	60	80
	(E) Plasters and preparations with a basis of plaster specially prepared for dentistry	30	40
	(F) Crystals doped for used in electronics:		
	(1) Monocrystalline silicon, in the form of discs, wafer or similar forms, 7.5cm, or more in diameter	6	11
	(2) Other	12	17
	(G) Other	25	35

Import Tariffs

No.	Descriptions	Min. (%)	Ord. (%)
VII.	**Artificial Resins and Plastic Materials, Cellulose Esters and Ethers, and Articles Thereof; Rubber, Synthetic Rubber, Factice, and Related Articles**		
39.	Artificial Resins & Plastic Materials, Cellulose Esters & Ethers		
39.01	Condensation, polycondensation and polyaddition products, whether or not modified or polymerised, and whether or not linear (for example, phenoplasts, aminoplasts, alkyds, polyallyl esters and other unsaturated polyesters, silicones):		
	(A) Ion exchangers	35	45
	(B) Liquids and pastes; blocks, lumps, powder, granules, flakes and similar forms	35	45
	(C) Plates, sheets, strip, film and foil	35	45
	(D) In other forms, including waste and scrap	40	50
39.02	Polymerisation and copolymerisation products (for example, polyethylene, polytetrahaloethylenes, polyisolbutylene, polystyrene, polyvinyl chloride, polyvinyl acetate, polyvinyl chloroacetate and other polyvinyl derivatives, polyacrylic and polymethacrylic derivatives, coumaroneindene resina):		
	(A) Ion exchangers	35	45
	(B) Liquids and pastes; blocks, lumps, powder, granules, flakes and similar forms	35	45
	(C) Monofil, seamless tubes, rods, sticks and similar forms	35	45
	(D) Plates, sheets, strip, film and foil	35	45
	(E) In other forms, including waste and scrap	40	50
39.03	Regenerated cellulose: cellulose nitrate, cellulose acetate and other cellulose esters, cellulose ethers and other chemical derivatives of cellulose, plasticised or not (for example, collodions, celluloid); vulcanised fibre:		
	(A) Regenerated cellulose	35	45
	(B) Cellulose nitrates	35	45
	(C) Cellulose acetates	35	45
	(D) Vulcanised fibre	25	35
	(E) Other	35	45

Import Tariffs

No.	Descriptions	Min. (%)	Ord. (%)
39.04	Hardened proteins (e.g. hardened casein and hardened gelatin)	40	50
39.05	Natural resins modified by fusion (run gums): artificial resins obtained by esterification of natural resins or of resinic acids (ester gums): chemical derivatives of natural rubber (e.g. chlorinated rubber, rubber hydrochloride, oxidised rubber, cyclised rubber)	40	50
39.06	Other high polymers, artificial resins and artificial plastic materials, including alginic acid, its salts and esters; linoxyn:		
	(A) Alginic acid, its salts and esters	35	45
	(B) Linoxyn	50	70
	(C) Other	35	45
39.07	Articles of materials of the kinds described in Nos. 39.01 to 39.06:		
	(A) Ornamental articles and objects of personal adornment and for household furnishing	80	100
	(B) Parts for machines and instruments	25	35
	(C) Other	60	80
40. Rubber, Synthetic Rubber, Factice			
40.01	Natural rubber latex, whether or not with added synthetic rubber latex; pre-vulcanised natural rubber lates; natural rubber, balata, gutta-percha and similar natural gums	20	30
40.02	Synthetic rubber latex; pre-vulcanised synthetic rubber latex; synthetic rubber; factice derived from oils	9	14
40.03	Reclaimed rubber	20	30
40.04	Waste and parings of unhardened rubber; scrap of unhardened rubber, fit only for the recovery of rubber; powder obtained from waste or scrap of unhardened rubber	20	30
40.05	Plates, sheets and strip, of unvulcanised natural or synthetic rubber, other than smoked sheets and crepe sheets of No. 40.01 or 40.02; granules of unvulcanised natural or synthetic rubber compounded ready for vulcanisation; unvulcanised natural or synthetic rubber, compounded before or after coagulation either with carbon black (with or without the addition of mineral oil) or with silica (with or without the addition of mineral oil), in any form, of a kind known as masterbatch	25	35

Import Tariffs

No.	Descriptions	Min. (%)	Ord. (%)
40.06	Unvulcanised natural or synthetic rubber, including rubber latex, in other forms or states (e.g. rods, tubes and profile shapes, solutions and dispersions); articles of unvulcanised natural or synthetic rubber (e.g. coated or impregnated textile thread; rings and discs):		
	(A) Materials	25	35
	(B) Articles	60	80
40.07	Vulcanised rubber thread and cord, whether or not textile covered, and textile thread covered or impregnated with vulcanised rubber	60	80
40.08	Plates, sheets, strip, rods and profile shapes, of unhardened vulcanised rubber:	25	35
40.09	Piping and tubing, of unhardened vulcanised rubber:		
	(A) Flexible hose	30	40
	(B) Other	25	35
40.10	Transmission, conveyor or elevator bells or belting, of vulcanised rubber	25	35
40.11	Rubber tyres, tyre cases, interchangeable tyre treads, inner tubes and tyre flaps, for wheels of all kinds:		
	(A) For motor cars and trucks	40	50
	(B) For motor cycles or bicycles	60	80
	(C) For aircrafts	6	11
	(D) Other	60	80
40.12	Hygienic and pharmaceutical articles (including teats), of unhardened vulcanised rubber, with or without fittings of hardened rubber:		
	(A) Pharmaceutical articles	20	30
	(B) Other	60	80
40.13	Articles of apparel and clothing accessories (including gloves), for all purposes, of unhardened vulcanised rubber:		
	(A) Appeal for medical purpose	20	30
	(B) Gloves:		
	(1) For medical purpose	20	30
	(2) Other	60	80
	(C) Other	70	90
40.14	Other articles of unhardened vulcanised rubber:		
	(A) Offset blankets	25	35
	(B) Parts for machines and instruments	20	30
	(C) Other	60	80

Import Tariffs

No.	Descriptions	Min. (%)	Ord. (%)
VII.	**Raw Hides and Skins, Leather, Furskins and Articles Thereof; Saddlery and Harness; Travel Goods, Handbags and Similar Containers; Articles of Gut (other than silk-worm gut)**		
41.	Raw Hides & Skins (other than furskins) & Leather		
41.01	Raw hides and skins (fresh, salted, dried, pickled or limed), whether or not split, including speepskins in the wool:		
	(A) Bovine hides	12	17
	(B) Equine hides	20	30
	(C) Goat skins and kid skins:		
	(1) Goat skins (E.T. 20%)	25	35
	(2) Other	20	30
	(D) Sheep or lamb skins	20	30
	(E) Other	20	30
41.02	Bovine cattle leather (including buffalo leather) and equine leather, except leather falling within No. 41.06 or 41.08:		
	(A) Leather for machinery belting	15	20
	(B) Other	25	35
41.03	Sheep and lamb skin leather, except leather falling within No. 41.06 or 41.08	40	50
41.04	Goat and kid sking leather, except leather falling within No. 41.06 or 41.08	40	50
41.05	Other kinds of leather, except leather falling within No. 41.06 or 41.08	40	50
41.06	Chamois-dressed leather	40	50
41.07/ 41.08	Patent leather and imitation patent leather; metallised leather	40	50
41.09	Parings and other waste, of leather or of composition or parchment-dressed leather, not suitable for the manufacture of articles of leather; leather dust, powder and flour	40	50
41.10	Composition leather with a basis of leather or leather fibre, in slabs, in sheets or in rolls	40	50
42.	Articles of Leather; Saddlery & Harness; Travel Goods, Handbags & Similar Containers; Articles of Animal Gut (other than silk-worm gut)		
42.01	Saddlery and harness, of any material (e.g. saddles, harness, collars, traces, knee-pads and boots) for any kind of animal	80	100

Import Tariffs

No.	Descriptions	Min.(%)	Ord.(%)
42.02	Travel goods (e.g. trunks, suit-cases, hat-boxes, travelling-bags, rucksacks), shopping-bags, handbags, satchels, brief-cases, wallets, purses, toilet-cases, tool-cases, tobacco-pouches, sheaths, cases, boxes (e.g. for arms, muscial instruments, binoculars, jewellery, bottles, collars, footwear, brushes) and similar containers, of leather or of composition leather, of vulcanised fibre, of artificial plastic sheeting, of paperboard or of textile fabric	80	100
42.03	Articles of apparel and clothing accessories, of leather or of composition leather	80	100
42.04	Articles of leather or of ocmposition leather of a kind used in machinery or mechanical appliances or for other industrial purposes	25	35
42.05	Other articles of leather or of composition leather	80	100
42.06	Articles made from gut (other than silk-worm gut), from goldbeater's skin, from bladders or from tendons	70	90

43. Furskins & Artificial Fur

No.	Descriptions	Min.(%)	Ord.(%)
43.01	Raw furskins:		
	(A) Of grey squirrel, ermine, sable, marten, fox, otter, marmot and lynx	80	100
	(B) Weasel tails	40	50
	(C) Other	70	90
43.02	Furskins, tanned or dressed, including furskins assembled in plates, crosses and similar forms; pieces or cuttings, of furskin, tanned or dressed, including heads, paws, tails and the like (not being fabricated):		
	(A) Of grey squirrel, ermine, sable, marten, fox, otter, marmot and lynx	100	130
	(B) Other	80	100
43.03	Articles of furskin	120	150
43.04	Artificial fur and articles made thereof:		
	(A) Artificial fur	100	130
	(B) Articles	120	150

Import Tariffs

No.	Descriptions	Min.(%)	Ord.(%)
IX.	**Wood and Articles of Wood; Wood Charcoal; Cork and Articles of Cork; Manufactures of Straw, of Esparto and of Other Plaiting Materials; Basket-ware and Wickerwork**		
44.	Wood & Articles of Wood; Wood Charcoal		
44.01	Fuel wood, in logs, in billets, in twigs or in faggots; wood waste, including sawdust:		
	(A)Fuel wood	50	70
	(B)Wood waste	3	8
44.02	Wood charcoal (including shell and nut charcoal), agglomerated or not	50	70
44.03	Wood in the rough, whether or not stripped of its bark or merely roughed down:		
	(A) Pulpwood	3	8
	(B) Wood of coniferous species	3	8
	(C) Wood of non-coniferous species:		
	(1) Teak	25	35
	(2) Camphor-wood, sandal-wood, garoo-wood, Tie-mu (lignum vitae) Nan-mu (phoebe Nan-mu)	25	35
	(3) Rose-wood	25	35
	(4) Red-wood, fragrant-wood, sugar-wood, (myoporum platy-carpum), camagon-wood, puru-wood, ebony-wood and kranjee-wood	25	35
	(5) Chinese parasol wood	3	8
	(6) Lauan-wood	3	8
	(7) Other	3	8
44.04	Wood, roughly squared or half-squared, but not further manufactured:		
	(A) Wood of coniferous species	3	8
	(B) Wood of non-coniferous species:		
	(1) Teak, camphor-wood, sandal-wood, garoo-wood, Tie-mu (lignum vitae) and Nan-mu (phoebe Nan-mu)	25	35
	(2) Red-wood, rose-wood, fragrant-wood, sugar-wood (myoporum platycarpum), camagon-wood, puru-wood, ebony-wood and kranjee-wood	25	35
	(3) Other	3	8

Import Tariffs

No.	Descriptions	Min. (%)	Ord. (%)
44.05	Wood sawn lengthwide, sliced or peeled, but not further prepared, of a thickness exceeding 5mm:		
	(A)　Wood of coniferous species	9	14
	(B)　Wood of non-coniferous species:		
	(1)　Teak, camphor-wood, sandal-wood, garoo-wood, Tie-mu (lignum vitae) and Nan-mu (phoebe Nam-mu)	30	40
	(2)　Red-wood, rose-wood, fragrant-wood, sugar-wood, (myoporum platycarpum), camagon-wood, puru-wood, ebony-wood and kranjee-wood	30	40
	(3)　Other	9	14
44.06/07	Railway or tramway sleepers of wood		
44.08/ 44.09	Hoopwood; split poles; piles, pickets and stakes of wood, pointed but not sawn lengthwise; chipwood; drawn wood; pulpwood in chips or particles; wood shavings of a kind suitable for use in the manufacture of vinegar or for the clarification of liquids; wooden sticks, roughly trimmed but not turned, bent or other-wide worked, suitable for the manufacture of walking-sticks, umbrella handles, tool handles or the like:		
	(A)　Pulpwood in chips or particles	3	8
	(B)　Other	40	50
44.10/ 44.11	Fibre building board of wood or other vegetable material, whether or not bonded with natural or artificial resins or with other organic binders	30	40
44.12	Wood wool and wood flour	30	40
44.13	Wood (including blocks, strips and friezes for parquit or wood block flooring, not assembled), planed, tongued, grooved, rebated, chamfered, V-jointed, centre V-jointed, beaded, centre-beaded or the like, but not further manu-factured	40	50
44.14	Wood sawn lengthwise, sliced or peeled but not further prepared, of a thickness not exceeding 5mm; veneer sheets and sheets for plywood, of a thickness not exceeding 5mm:		
	(A)　Veneer sheets	30	40
	(B)　Other	20	30

Import Tariffs

No.	Descriptions	Min. (%)	Ord. (%)
44.15	Plywood, blockboard, laminboard, battenboard and similar laminated wood products (including veneered panels and sheets); inlaid wood and wood marquetry:		
	(A) Plywood and similar laminated wood	12	17
	(B) Inlaid wood and wood marquetry	35	45
44.16	Cellular wood panels, whether or not faced will base metal	30	40
44.17	"Improved" wood, in sheets, blocks or the like	15	20
44.18	Reconstituted wood, being wood shavings, wood chips, sawdust, wood flour or other ligneous waste agglomerated with natural or artificial resins or other organic binding substances, in sheets, blocks or the like	30	40
44.19	Wooden beadings and mouldings, including moulded skirting and other moulded boards	60	80
44.20	Wooden picture frames, photograph frames, mirror frames and the like	80	100
44.21	Complete wooden packing cases, boxes, crates, drums and similar packings	60	80
44.22	Casks, barrels, vats, tubs, buckets and other coopers' products and parts thereof, of wood, including staves	60	80
44.23	Builders' carpentry and joinery (including prefabricated and sectional buildings and assembled parquet flooring panels)	50	70
44.24	Household utensils of wood	80	100
44.25	Wooden tools, tool bodies, tool handles, broom and brush bodies and handles; boot and shoe lasts and trees, of wood	60	80
44.26	Spools, cops, bobbins, sewing thread reels and the like, of turned wood	60	80
44.27	Standard lamps, table lamps and other lighting fittings, of wood; articles of furniture, of wood, not falling within Section 94; caskets, cigarette boxes, trays, fruit bowls, ornaments and other fancy articles, of wood; cases for cutlery, for drawing instruments or for violins, and similar receptacles, of wood; article of wood for personal use or adornment, of a kind normally carried in the pocket, in the handbag or on the person; parts of the foregoing articles, of wood	80	100
44.28	Other articles of wood:		
	(A) Wood splints for the manufacture of matches	15	20
	(B) Other	70	90

Import Tariffs

No.	Descriptions	Min. (%)	Ord. (%)
45.	Cork & Articles of Cork		
45.01	Natural cork, unworked, crushed, granulated or ground; waste cork	12	17
45.02	Natural cork in blocks, plates, sheets or strips (including cubes or square slabs, cut to size for corks or stoppers)	20	30
45.03	Article of natural cork:		
	(A) Cork discs for making crown corks	30	40
	(B) Other	50	70
45.04	Agglomerated cork (being cork agglomerated with or without a binding substance) and articles of agglomerated cork:		
	(A) Agglomerated cork	20	30
	(B) Articles:		
	(1) Cork discs for making crown corks	30	40
	(2) Other	50	70
46.	Manufactures of Straw, of Esparto & of Other Plaiting Materials; Basketware & Wickerwork		
46.01/ 46.02	Plaits and similar products of plaiting materials, for all uses, whether or not assembled into strips; plaiting materials bound together in parallel strands or woven, in sheet form, including matting, mats and screens; straw envelopes for bottles:		
	(A) Of rattan	80	100
	(B) Other	70	90
46.03	Basketwork, wickerwork and other articles of plaiting materials, made directly to shape; articles made up from goods falling within No. 46.02; article of loofah	80	100

X. Paper-making Material; Paper and Paperboard and Articles Thereof

No.	Descriptions	Min. (%)	Ord. (%)
47.	Paper-making Materials		
47.01	Pulp derived by mechanical or chemical means from any fibrous vegetable material	3	8
47.02	Waste paper and paperboard; scrap articles of paper or of paperboard, fit only for use in paper-making	3	8
48.	Paper & Paperboard; Articles of Paper Pulp, of Paper or of Paperboard		

Import Tariffs

No.	Descriptions	Min. (%)	Ord. (%)
48.01	Paper and paperboard (including cellulose wadding), in rolls or sheets:		
	(A) Hand-made paper	50	70
	(B) Newsprint	20	30
	(C) Bank-note paper	20	30
	(D) Other printing and writing paper	20	30
	(E) Kraft paper	20	30
	(F) Other packing and wrapping paper	20	30
	(G) Cigarette paper	80	100
	(H) Other paper:		
	(1) Filter paper	20	30
	(2) White duplex board	20	30
	(3) Other	30	40
	(I) Paperboard:		
	(1) White duplex board	20	30
	(2) Jacquard or silk board (chip-board) and matrix board (dry flong)	20	30
	(3) Kraft board	20	30
	(4) Other	30	40
48.02/ 48.03	Parchment or greaseproof paper and paperboard, and imitations thereof, and glazed transparent paper, in rolls or sheets:		
	(A) Tracing paper	20	30
	(B) Glazed transparent paper(cellophane paper)	30	40
	(C) Other	30	40
48.04	Composite paper or paperboard (made by sticking flat layers together with an adhesive), not surface-coated or impregnated, whether or not internally reinforced, in rolls or sheets	30	40
48.05	Paper and paperboard, corrugated (with or without flat surface sheets), creped, crinkled, embossed or perforated, in rolls or sheets:		
	(A) Corrugated paper and board	20	30
	(B) Other	30	40
48.06/ 48.07	Paper and paperboard, impregnated, coated, surface-coloured, surface-decorated or printed (not constituting printed matter with Section 49), in rolls or sheets:		
	(A) Printing or writing paper, impregnated, coated, surface-coloured, surface-decoratedor printed:		
	(1) Coated art printing paper	30	40
	(2) Ruled, lined or squared paper	30	40
	(3) Other	30	40

No.	Descriptions	Min. (%)	Ord. (%)
(B)	Paper and paperboard (other than printing or writing paper), coated impregnated with artificial or synthetic resins:		
	(1) Electrical insulating paper and board	20	30
	(2) Other	30	40
(C)	Tarred, bituminised or asphalted paper and paperboard	30	40
(D)	Other:		
	(1) Paper for chemical tests	20	30
	(2) Electrical insulating paper and board	20	30
	(3) Other	30	40
48.08/09	Filter blocks, slabs and plates, of paper pulp	20	30
48.10	Cigarette paper, cut to size, whether or not in the form of booklets or tubes	80	100
48.11	Wallpaper and lincrusta; window transparencies of paper:		
(A)	Wallpaper and lincrusta	40	50
(B)	Window transparencies of paper	50	70
48.12	Floor coverings prepared on a base of paper or of paperboard, whether or not cut to size, with or without a coating of linoleum compound	70	90
48.13	Carbon and other copying papers (including duplicator stencils) and transfer papers, cut to size, whether or not put up in boxes:		
(A)	Carbon and other copying papers (including duplicator stencils)	50	70
(B)	Transfer papers	30	40
48.14	Writing blocks, envelopes, letter cards, plain postcards, correspondence cards; boxes, pouches, wallets and writing compendiums, of paper or paperboard, containing only an assortment of paper stationery	60	80
48.15	Other paper and paperboard, cut to size or shape:		
(A)	Paper for use of machines and instruments	20	30
(B)	Filter paper	20	30
(C)	Paper for chemical tests	20	30
(D)	Electrical insulating paper and board	20	30
(E)	Gummed or adhesive paper	40	50
(F)	Other	60	80

Import Tariffs

No.	Descriptions	Min. (%)	Ord. (%)
48.16	Boxes, bags and other packing containers, of paper or paperboard; box files, letter trays and similar articles, of paper or paperboard, of a kind commonly used in offices, shops and the like:		
	(A) Paper bags for packing cement	25	35
	(B) Other	60	80
48.17/ 48.18	Registers, exercise books, note books, memorandum blocks, order books, receipt books, diaries, blotting-pads, binders(loose-leaf or other), file covers and other stationery of paper or paperboard; sample and other albums and book covers, of paper or paperboard	60	80
48.19	Paper or paperboard labels, whether or not printed or gummed	40	50
48.20	Bobbins, spools, cops and similar supports of paper pulp, paper or paperboard (whether or not perforated or hardened)	50	70
48.21	Other articles of paper pulp, paper, paperboard or cellulose wadding:		
	(A) Joss paper and the like	150	180
	(B) For use of machines and instruments	20	30
	(C) Other	70	90
49.	Printed Books, Newspapers, Pictures & Other Products of the Printing Industry; Manuscripts typescripts & Plans		
49.01	Printed books, brochures, leaflets and similar printed matter, whether or not in single sheets	NIL	NIL
49.02	Newspapers, journals and periodicals, whether or not illustrated	NIL	NIL
49.03	Children's picture books and painting books	NIL	NIL
49.04	Music, printed or in manuscript, whether or not bound or illustrated	NIL	NIL
49.05	Maps and hydrographic and similar charts of all kinds, including atlases, wall maps and topographical plans, printed; printed globes (terrestrial or celestial)	NIL	NIL
49.06	Plans and drawings, for industrial architectural, engineering, commercial or similar purposes, whether original or reproductions on sensitised paper; manuscripts and typescripts	NIL	NIL
49.07	Unused postage, revenue and similar stamps of current or new issue in the country to which they are destined; stamp-impressed paper; banknotes, stock, share and bond certificates and similar documents of title; cheque books	40	50

Import Tariffs

No.	Descriptions	Min. (%)	Ord. (%)
49.08	Transfers (Decalcomanias)	40	50
49.09	Picture postcards, Christmas and other picture greeting cards, printed by any process, with or without trimmings	40	50
49.10	Calendars of any kind, of paper or paperboard, including calendar blocks	40	50
49.11	Other printed matter, including printed pictures and photographs:		
	(A) Printed matter exclusively for revolutionary propaganda or for imparting educational ideas for revolutionary reconstruction	NIL	NIL
	(B) Trade advertising material, commercial catalogues and the like:		
	(1) No commercial value	NIL	NIL
	(2) Other	40	50
	(C) Other	40	50

XI. Textiles & Textile Article

50. Silk & Waste Silk (Continuous)

No.	Descriptions	Min. (%)	Ord. (%)
50.01	Silk-worm cocoons suitable for reeling	50	70
50.02	Raw silk (not thrown)	60	80
50.03	Silk waste (including cocoons unsuitable for reeling, silk noils and pulled or garnetted rags)	50	70
50.04	Silk yarn, other than yarn of noil or other waste silk, not put up for retail sale	70	90
50.05	Yarn spun from noil or other waste silk, not put up for retail sale	70	90
50.06/ 50.07	Silk yarn and yarn spun from noil or other waste silk, put up for retail sale; silk-worm gut; imitation catgut of silk	80	100
50.08-10	Woven fabrics of silk, of noil or other waste silk	100	130

51. Man-made Fibres

No.	Descriptions	Min. (%)	Ord. (%)
51.01	Yarn of man-made fibres (continuous), not put up for retail sale:		
	(A) Yarn of synthetic fibres:		
	(1) Polyester textured filament (yuan)	70	90
	(2) Nylon textured filament (yarn)	60	80
	(3) Other	50	70
	(B) Yarn of regenerated fibres	25	35
51.02	Monofil, strip (artificial straw and the like) and imitation catgut, of man-made fibre materials	60	80

Import Tariffs

No.	Descriptions	Min. (%)	Ord. (%)
51.03	Yarn of man-made fibres (continuous), put up for retail sale	70	90
51.04	Woven fabrics of man-made fibres (continuous), including woven fabrics of monofil or strip of 51.01 or 51.02:		
	(A) Tyre cord fabrics and the like, of synthetic textile materials	30	40
	(B) Other fabrics of synthetic textile materials	100	130
	(C) Tyre core fabrics and the like, of regenerated textile materials	30	40
	(D) Other fabrics of regenerated textile materials	100	130
52.	Metallised Textiles		
52.01	Metallised yarn, being textile yarn spun with metal or covered with metal by any process:		
	(A) Of cotton	40	50
	(B) Of man-made fibres	60	80
	(C) Other	50	70
52.02	Woven fabrics of metal thread or of metallised yarn, of a kind used in articles of apparel, as furnishing fabrics or the like:		
	(A) Of cotton yarn	70	90
	(B) Of man-made fibre yarn	100	130
	(C) Other	80	100
53.	Wool & Other Animal Hair		
53.01	Sheep's or lambs' wool, not carded or combed	15	20
53.02	Other animal hair (fine or coarse), not carded or combed:		
	(A) Fine animals hair:		
	(1) Of goat	35	45
	(2) Of rabbit (E.T. 20%)	40	50
	(3) Of camel	35	45
	(4) Other	35	45
	(B) Coarse animal hair:		
	(1) Of goat	40	50
	(2) Other	35	45
53.03	Waste of sheep's or lambs' wool or of other animal hair (fine or coarse), not pulled or garnetted:		
	(A) Of sheep's or lambs' wool	15	20
	(B) Other	40	50

Import Tariffs

No.	Descriptions	Min. (%)	Ord. (%)
53.04	Waste of sheep's or lambs' wool or of other animal hair (fine or coarse), pulled or garnetted (including pulled or garnetted rags):		
	(A) Of sheep's or lambs' wool	15	20
	(B) Other	40	50
53.05	Sheep's or lambs' wool or other animal hair (fine or coarse), carded or combed:		
	(A) Sheep's or lambs' wool	20	30
	(B) Rabbits' hair (E.T. 20%)	50	70
	(C) Other	40	50
53.06	Yarn of carded sheep's or lambs' wool (woollen yarn), not put up for retail sale	50	70
53.07	Yarn of combed sheep's or lambs' wool (worsted yarn), not put up for retail sale	50	70
53.08	Yarn of fine animal hair (carded or combed), not put up for retail sale	50	70
53.09	Yarn of horsehair or of other coarse animal hair, not put up for retail sale	50	70
53.10	Yarn of sheep's or lambs' wool, of horsehair or of other animal hair (fine or coarse), put up'for retail sale	60	80
53.11	Woven fabrics of sheep's or lambs' wool or of fine animal hair	100	130
53.12/ 53.13	Woven fabrics of horsehair or of other coarse animal hair	100	130
54. Flax & Ramie			
54.01	Flax, raw or processed but not spun; flax tow and waste (including pulled or garnetted rags)	20	30
54.02	Ramie, raw or processed but not spun; ramie noils and waste (including pulled or garnetted rags)	20	30
54.03	Flax or ramie yarn, not put up for retail sale	40	50
54.04	Flax or remie yarn, put up retail sale	50	70
54.05	Woven fabrics of flax or of ramie:		
	(A) Fabrics containing 85% or more by weight of flax or ramie respectively:		
	(1) Of flax	60	80
	(2) Of ramie	60	80
	(B) Fabrics of flax or of ramie mixed with other textile materials:.		
	(1) Mixed with cotton	650	80
	(2) Other	70	90

Import Tariffs

No.	Descriptions	Min. (%)	Ord. (%)
55.	Cotton		
55.01	Cotton, not carded or combed	3	8
55.02	Cotton linters	20	30
55.03	Cotton waste (including pulled or garnetted rags), not carded or combed	20	30
55.04	Cotton, carded or combed	3	8
55.05	Cotton yarn, not put up for retail sale	30	40
55.06	Cotton yarn, put up for retail sale	40	50
55.07	Cotton gauze	50	70
55.08	Terry towelling and similar terry fabrics, of cotton	50	70
55.09	Other woven fabrics of cotton:		
	(A) Fabrics containing 85% or more by weight of cotton:		
	(1) Grey	50	70
	(2) Bleached or dyed	50	70
	(3) Printed	50	70
	(4) Other	50	70
	(B) Fabrics of cotton mixed with other textile materials, containing less than 85% by weight of cotton:		
	(1) Mixed with flax or ramie	60	80
	(2) Other	70	90
56.	Man-made Fibres (discontinuous), Not Carded, Combed or Otherwise Prepared for Spinning:		
56.01	Man-made fibres (discontinuous), not carded, combed or otherwise prepared for spinning:		
	(A) synthetic fibres:		
	(1) Acrylic fibre	25	35
	(2) Other	50	70
	(B) Regenerated fibres	25	35
56.02	Continuous filament tow for the manufacture of man-made fibres (discontinuous):		
	(A) Of synthetic fibres:		
	(1) Acrylic fibre	25	35
	(2) Other	50	70
	(B) Of regenerated fibres	25	35
56.03	Waste (including yarn waste and pulled or garnetted rags) of man-made fibres (continuous or discontinuous), not carded, combed or otherwise prepared for spinning	50	70

Import Tariffs

No.	Descriptions	Min. (%)	Ord. (%)
56.04	Man-made fibres (discontinuous or waste), carded, combed or otherwise prepared for spinning:		
	(A) Of synthetic fibres:		
	(1) Acrylic fibre	25	35
	(2) Other	50	70
	(B) Of regenerated fibres	25	35
56.05	Yarn of man-made fibres (discontinuous or waste), not put up for retail sale:		
	(A) Of synthetic fibres	70	90
	(B) Of regenerated fibres	50	70
56.06	Yarn of man-made fibres (discontinuous or waste), put up for retail sale	70	90
56.07	Woven fabrics of man-made fibres (discontinuous or waste)	100	130
57.	Other Vegetable Textile Materials; Paper Yarn & Woven Fabrics of Paper Yarn		
57.01	True hemp ("Cannabis sativa"), raw or processed but not spun; tow and waste of true hemp (including pulled or garnetted rags or ropes)	20	30
57.02	Manila hemp (abaca) ("Musa textilis"), raw or processed but not spun; tow and waste of manila hemp (including pulled or garnetted rags or ropes)	15	20
57.03	Jute and other textile bast fibres not elsewhere specified or included, raw or processed but not spun; tow and waste thereof (including pulled or garnetted rags or ropes):		
	(A) Jute	15	20
	(B) Other textile bast fibres	20	30
	(C) Tow and waste	20	30
57.04	Other vegetable textile fibres, raw or processed but not spun; waste of such fibres (including pulled or garnetted rags or ropes):		
	(A) Sisal and other fibres of the agave family, and waste of such fibres:		
	(1) Sisal	15	20
	(2) Other	20	30
	(B) Coir and coir waste	20	30
	(C) Other	20	30

Import Tariffs

No.	Descriptions	Min. (%)	Ord. (%)
57.05/ 57.06	Yarn of jute or of other textile bast fibres of No. 57.03:		
	(A) Of jute	25	35
	(B) Other	35	45
57.07	Yarn of other vegetable textile fibres; paper yarn:		
	(A) Yarn of other vegetable textile fibres	35	45
	(B) Paper yarn	50	70
57.08/ 57.10	Woven fabrics of jute or of other textele bast fibres of No. 57.03:		
	(A) Of jute	30	40
	(B) Other	40	50
57.11/ 57.12	Woven fabrics of other vegetable textile fibres; woven fabrics of paper yarn:		
	(A) Of other vegetable textile fibres	40	50
	(B) Of paper yarn	70	90
58.	Carpets, Mats, Matting & Tapestries; Pile & Chenille Fabrics; Narrow Fabrics; Trimmings; Tulle & Other Net Fabrics; Lace; Embroidery		
58.01	Carpets, carpetting and rugs, knotted (made up or not):		
	(A) Of wool or fine animal hair	100	130
	(B) Of man-made textile materials	100	130
	(C) Other	80	100
58.02	Other carpets, carpetting, rugs, mats and matting, and ''Kelem'', ''Schumacks'' and ''Karamanie'' rugs and the like (made up or not):		
	(A) Of wool or fine animal hair	100	130
	(B) Of man-made fibre textile materials	100	130
	(C) Other	80	100
58.03	Tapestries, hand-made, of the type Gobelins, Flanders, Aubusson, Beauvals and the like, and needle-worked tapestries (for example, petit point and cross stitch) made in panels and the like by hand:		
	(A) Of wool or fine animal hair	100	130·
	(B) Of silk or man-made textile materials	100	130
	(C) Other	80	100
58.04	Woven pile fabrics and chenille fabrics (other than terry-towelling or similar terry fabrics of cotton falling within No. 55.08 and fabrics falling within No. 58.05):		

Import Tariffs

No.	Descriptions	Min. (%)	Ord. (%)
	(A) Of silk	100	130
	(B) Of wool or fine animal hair	100	130
	(C) Of cotton	50	70
	(D) Of synthetic fibres	100	130
	(E) Of regenerated fibres	60	80
	(F) Other	60	80
58.05	Narrow woven fabrics, and narrow fabrics (bolduc) consisting of warp without weft assembled by means of an adhesive, other than goods falling within No. 58.06:		
	(A) Of wool or fine animal hair	100	130
	(B) Of cotton	50	70
	(C) Of silk or man-made textile materials	100	130
	(D) Other	60	80
58.06	Woven labels, badges and the like, not embroidered, in the piece, in strips or cut ot shape or size	80	100
58.07	Chenille yarn (including flock chenille yarn), gimped yarn (other than metallised yarn of No. 52.01 and gimped horsehair yarn); braids and ornamental trimmings in the piece; tassels pompons and the like:		
	(A) Chenille yarn and gimped yarn	50	70
	(B) Other	80	100
58.08	Tulle and other net fabrics (but not including woven, knitted or crocheted fabrics), plain:		
	(A) Of cotton	50	70
	(B) Of silk or man-made fibres	100	130
	(C) Other	70	90
58.09	Tulle and other net fibrics (but not including woven, knitted or crocheted fabrics), figured; hand or mechanically made lace, in the piece, in strips or in motifs:		
	(A) Of cotton	60	80
	(B) Of silk or man-made fibres	100	130
	(C) Other	80	100
58.10	Embroidery, in the piece, in strips or in motifs	100	130

59. Wadding & Felt; Twine, Cordage, Ropes & Cables; Special Fabrics; Impregnated & Coated Fabrics; Textile Articles of a Kind Suitable for Industrial Use

Import Tariffs

No.	Descriptions	Min.(%)	Ord.(%)
59.01	Wadding and articles of wadding; textile flock and dust and mill neps:		
	(A) Wadding and articles of wadding:		
	(1) Of cotton	40	50
	(2) Of silk	70	90
	(3) Of man-made fibres	80	100
	(4) Other	70	90
	(B) Other		
59.02	Felt and articles of felt, whether or not impregnated or coated:		
	(A) Felt	80	100
	(B) Articles of felt	100	130
59.03	Bonded fibre fabrics, similar bonded yarn fabrics, and articles of such fabrics, whether or not impregnated or coated:		
	(A) Bonded fibre fabrics and similar bonded yarn fabrics:		
	(1) Of cotton, flax or ramie	50	70
	(2) Of man-made fibres	100	130
	(3) Other	80	100
	(B) Articles	100	130
59.04	Twine, cordage, ropes and cables, plaited or not:		
	(A) Of bast fibres or leaf fibres	40	50
	(B) Of man-made fibres	80	100
	(C) Other	70	90
59.05	Nets and netting made of twine, cordage or rope, and made up fishing nets of yarn, twine, cordage or rope:		
	(A) Fishing nets	40	50
	(B) Other	80	100
59.06	Other articles made from yarn, twine, cordage, rope or cables, other than textile fabrics and articles made from such fabrics	80	100
59.07	Textile fabrics coated with gum or amylaceous substances, of a kind used for the outer covers of books and the like; tracing cloth; prepared painting canvas; buckram and similar fabrics for hat foundations and similar uses:		
	(A) Tracing cloth	20	30
	(B) Painting canvas	40	50
	(C) Other:		
	(1) Of cotton, flax or ramie	60	80
	(2) Of man-made fibres	100	130
	(3) Other	80	100

Import Tariffs

No.	Descriptions	Min. (%)	Ord. (%)
59.08	Textile fabrics impregnated, coated, covered or laminated with preparations of cellulose derivatives or of other artificial plastic materials:		
	(A) Electrical insulating cloth and tape	30	40
	(B) Imitation leather	50	70
	(C) Other	70	90
59.09/ 59.10	Linoleum and materials prepared on a textile base in a similar manner to linoleum, whether or not cut to shape or of a kind used as floor coverings; floor coverings consisting of a coating applied on a textile base, cut to shape or not	70	90
59.11	Rubberised textile fabrics, other than rubberised knitted or crocheted goods:		
	(A) Electrical insulating cloth and tape	30	40
	(B) Other:		
	(1) Of cotton, flax, ramie, hemp, jute and the like	60	80
	(2) Of man-made fibres	100	130
	(3) Other	80	100
59.12	Textile fabrics otherwise impregnated or coated; painted canvas being theatrical scenery, studio back-cloths or the like:		
	(A) Electrical insulating cloth and tape	30	40
	(B) Painted canvas	40	50
	(C) Other:		
	(1) Of cotton, flax, ramie, hemp, jute and the like	100	130
	(2) Of man-made fibres	100	130
	(3) Other	80	100
59.13	Elastic fabrics and trimmings (other than knitted or crocheted goods) consisting of textile materials combined with rubber threads:		
	(A) Of cotton, flax or ramie	60	80
	(B) Of man-made fibres	100	130
	(C) Other	80	100
59.14	Wicks, of woven, plaited or knitted textile materials, for lamps, stoves, lighters, candles and the like; tubular knitted gas mantle fabric and incandescent gas mantles	50	70
59.15	Textile hosepiping and similar tubing, with or without lining, armour or accessories of other materials	25	35

Import Tariffs

No.	Descriptions	Min. (%)	Ord. (%)
59.16	Transmission, coveyor or elevator belts or belting, of textile material, whether or not strengthened with metal or other material	25	35
59.17	Textile fabrics and textile articles, of a kind commonly used in machinery or plant	25	35
60.	**Knitted & Crocheted Goods**		
60.01	Knitted or crocheted fabric, not elastic nor rubberised:		
	(A) Of wool or fine animal hair	100	130
	(B) Of cotton	50	70
	(C) Of synthetic fibres	100	130
	(D) Of regenerated fibres	100	130
	(E) Other	100	130
60.02	Gloves, mittens and mitts, knitted or crocheted, not elastic nor rubberised:		
	(A) Of wool or fine animal hair	100	130
	(B) Of cotton	70	90
	(C) Of man-made fibres	100	130
	(D) Other	100	130
60.03	Stockings, under stockings, socks, anklesocks, sockettes and the like, knitted or crocheted, not elastic nor rubberised:		
	(A) Of wool or fine animal hair	100	130
	(B) Of cotton	70	90
	(C) Of man-made fibres	100	130
	(D) Other	100	130
60.04	Under garments, knitted or crocheted, not elastic nor rubberised:		
	(A) Of cotton	70	90
	(B) Of man-made fibres	100	130
	(C) Other	100	130
60.05	Outer garments and other articles, knitted or crocheted, not elastic nor rubberised:		
	(A) Of wool or fine animal hair	100	130
	(B) Of cotton	70	90
	(C) Of synthetic fibres	100	130
	(D) Of regenerated fibres	100	130
	(E) Other	100	130
60.06	Knitted or crocheted fabric and articles thereof, elastic or rubberised (including elastic knee-caps and elastic stockings)	100	130
61.	**Articles of Apparel & Clothing Accessories of Textile Fabric; Other Than Knitted or Crocheted Goods**		

Import Tariffs

No.	Descriptions	Min. (%)	Ord. (%)
61.01	Men's and boys' outer garments:		
	(A) Of silk	100	130
	(B) Of wool or fine animal hair	100	130
	(C) Of cotton	70	90
	(D) Of flax or ramie	70	90
	(E) Of man-made fibres	100	130
	(F) Of imitation leather	70	90
	(G) Other	80	100
61.02	Women's, girls' and infants' outer garments:		
	(A) Of silk	100	130
	(B) Of wool or fine animal hair	100	130
	(C) Of cotton	70	90
	(D) Of flax or ramie	70	90
	(E) Of man-made fibres	100	130
	(F) Of imitation leather	70	90
	(G) Other	80	100
61.03	Men's and boys' under garments, including collars, shirt fronts and cuffs:		
	(A) Of silk	100	130
	(B) Of cotton	70	90
	(C) Of synthetic fibres	100	130
	(D) Of regenerated fibres	100	130
	(E) Other	80	100
61.04	Women's girls' and infants' under garments:		
	(A) Of silk	100	130
	(B) Of cotton	70	90
	(C) Of synthetic fibres	100	130
	(D) Of regenerated fibres	100	130
	(E) Other	80	100
61.05	Handkerchiefs	70	90
61.06	Shawls, scarves, mufflers, mantillas, veils and the like:		
	(A) Of wool or fine animal hair	100	130
	(B) Of silk or man-made fibres	100	130
	(C) Other	70	90
61.07	Ties, bow ties and cravats	100	130
61.08/ 61.09	Corsets, corset-belts, suspender-belts, brassieres, braces, suspenders, garters and the like (including such articles of knitted or crocheted fabric), whether or not elastic:		
	(A) Of man-made fibres	100	130
	(B) Other	80	100

Import Tariffs

No.	Descriptions	Min. (%)	Ord. (%)
61.10	Gloves, mittens, mitts, stocking, socks and sockettes, not being knitted or crocheted goods:		
	(A) Of man-made fibres	100	130
	(B) Other	80	100
61.11	Made up accessories for articles of apparel (e.g. dress shields, shoulder and other pads, belts, muffs, sleeve protectors, pockets)	80	100
62.	Other Made Up Textile Article		
62.01	Travelling rugs and blankets:		
	(A) Electric blankets	80	100
	(B) Of wool or fine animal hair	100	130
	(C) Of cotton	70	90
	(D) Of synthetic fibres	100	130
	(E) Of regenerated fibres	100	130
	(F) Other	70	90
62.02	Bed linen, table linen, toilet linen and kitchen linen; curtains and other furnishing articles:		
	(A) Of silk	100	130
	(B) Of cotton	70	90
	(C) Of flax or ramie	70	90
	(D) Of man-made fibres	100	130
	(E) Other	80	100
62.03	Sacks and bags, of a kind used for the packing of goods:		
	(A) Of bast fibres or leaf fibres:		
	(1) Of jute	30	40
	(2) Other	40	50
	(B) Of man-made fibres	80	100
	(C) Other	70	90
62.04	Tarpaulins, sails, awnings, sunblinds, tents and camping goods:		
	(A) Of cotton	60	80
	(B) Of bast fibres or leaf fibres	60	80
	(C) Of man-made fibres	100	130
	(D) Other	80	100
62.05	Other made up textile articles (including dress patterns):		
	(A) Of silk	100	130
	(B) Of cotton	70	90
	(C) Of bast fibres or leaf fibres	70	90
	(D) Of man-made fibres	100	130
	(E) Other	80	100

Import Tariffs

No.	Descriptions	Min. (%)	Ord. (%)
63.	Old Clothing & Other Textile Articles; Rags		
63.01	Clothing, clothing accessories, travelling rugs and blankets, household linen and furnishing articles (other than articles falling within No. 58.01, 58.02 or 58.03), of textile materials, footwear and headgear of any material, showing signs of appreciable wear and imported in bulk or in bales, sacks or similar bulk packings	100	130
63.02	Used or new rags, scrap twine, cordage, rope and cables and worn out articles of twine, cordage, rope or cables	40	50

XII. Footwear, Headgear, Umbrellas, Sunshades, Whips, Riding-crops and Parts Thereof; Prepared) Feathers and Articles Made Therefore; Artificial Flowers; Articles of Human Hair

No.	Descriptions	Min. (%)	Ord. (%)
64.	Footwear, Gaiters & the Like; Parts of Such Articles		
64.01	Footwear with outer soles and uppers of rubber or artificial plastic material	80	100
64.02	Footwear with outer soles of leather or composition leather; footwear (other than footwear falling within No. 64.01) with outer soles of rubber or artificial plastic material	80	100
64.03	Footwear with outer soles of wood or cork	80	100
64.04	Footwear with outer soles of other materials	80	100
64.05	Parts of footwear (including uppers, in-soles and screw-on heels) of any material except metal	70	90
64.06	Gaiters, spats, leggings, puttees, cricket pads, shin-guards and similar articles, and parts thereof	80	100
65.	Headgear & Parts of Headgear		
65.01	Hat-forms, hat bodies and hoods of felt, neither blocked to shape nor with made brims; plateaux and manchons (including slit manchons), of felt	80	100
65.02	Hat-shapes, plaited or made from plaited or other strips of any material, neither blocked to shape nor with made brims	80	100
65.03	Felt hats and other felt hoods and plateaux falling within No. 65.01, whether or not lined or trimmed	100	130

Import Tariffs

No.	Descriptions	Min. (%)	Ord. (%)
65.04	Hats and other headgear, plaited or made from plaited or other strips of any material, whether or not lined or trimmed	100	130
65.05	Hats and other headgear (including hair nets), knitted or crocheted, or made up from lace, felt or other textile fabric in the piece (but not from strips), whether or not lined or trimmed	100	130
65.06	Other headgear, whether or not lined or trimmed:		
	(A) Of leather or fur	100	130
	(B) Other	80	100
65.07	Head-bands, linings, covers, hat foundations, hat frames (including spring frames for opera hats), peaks and chinstraps, for headgear	80	100
66.	Umbrellas, Sunshades, Walking-sticks, Whips, Riding Crops And Parts		
66.01	Umbrellas and sunshades (including walking-stick umbrellas, umbrella tents, and garden and similar umbrellas)	100	130
66.02	Walking-sticks (including climbing-sticks and seat-sticks), canes, whips, riding-crips and the like	100	130
66.03	Parts, fittings, trimmings and accessories of articles falling within No. 66.01 or 66.02	100	130
67.	Prepared Feathers & Down & Articles Made of Feathers or of Down; Artificial Flowers; Articles of Human Hairs		
67.01	Skins and other parts of birds with their feathers or down, and articles thereof, (other than goods falling within No. 05.07 and worked quills and scapes)	100	130
67.02	Artificial flowers, foliage or fruit and parts thereof; articles made of artificial flowers, foliage or fruit	100	130
67.03	Human hair, dressed, thinned, bleached or otherwise worked; wool, other animal hair and other textile materials, prepared for use in making wigs and the like	80	100
67.04/05	Wigs, false beards, eyebrows and eyelashes, switches and the like, of human or animal hair or of textiles; other articles of human hair (including hair nets)	100	130

	Import Tariffs		
No.	**Descriptions**	**Min.(%)**	**Ord.(%)**

XIII. Articles of Stone, of Plaster, of Cement, of Asbestos, of Mica and of Similar Materials; Ceramic Products; Glass and Glassware

No.	Descriptions	Min.(%)	Ord.(%)
68.	Articles of Stone, of Plaster, of Cement, of Asbertos, of Mica & Similar Materials		
68.01	Road and paving setts, curbs and flagstones, of natural stone (except slate)	50	70
68.02	Worked monumental or building stone, and articles thereof (including mosaic cubes), other than goods falling within No. 68.01 or within Section 69:		
	(A) Monumental or building stone:		
	(1) Marble	70	90
	(2) Other	50	70
	(B) Articles	70	90
68.03	Worked slate and articles of slate, including articles of agglomerated slate:		
	(A) Slate	50	70
	(B) Articles	60	80
68.04	Hand polishing stones, whetstones, oilstones, hones and the like, and millstones, grindstones, grinding wheels and the like (including grinding, sharpening, polishing, trueing and cutting wheels, heads, discs and points), of natural stone (agglomerated or not), of agglomerated natural or artificial abrasives, or of pottery, with or without cores, shanks, sockets, axles and the like of other materials, but without frameworks; segments and other finished parts of such stones and wheels, of natural stone (agglomerated or not), of agglomerated natural or artificial abrasives, or of pottery:		
	(A) Grinding wheels	12	17
	(B) Oil stones	12	17
	(D) Other	30	40
68.05/ 68.06	Natural or artificial abrasive powder or grain, On a base of woven fabric, of paper, of paperboard or of other materials, whether or not cut to shape or sewn or otherwide made up:		
	(A) On a base of woven fabric	15	20
	(B) On a base of paper or paperboard:		
	(1) Water-proof	15	20
	(2) Other	30	40
	(C) Other	30	40

Import Tariffs

No.	Descriptions	Min. (%)	Ord. (%)
68.07	Slag wool, rock wool and similar mineral wools; exfoliated vermiculite, expanded clays, foamed slag and similar expanded minerals materials; mixtures and articles of heat-insulating, sound-insulating, or sound-absorbing mineral materials, other than those falling in Section No. 68.12 or 68.13 or in Section 69:		
	(A) Mineral wools and expanded mineral materials	30	40
	(B) Other	40	50
68.08	Articles of asphalt or of similar material (e.g. of petroleum bitumen or coal tar pitch)	40	50
68.09	Panels, boards, tiles, blocks and similar articles of vegetable fibre, of wood fibre, of straw, of wood shavings or of wood waste (including sawdust), agglomerated with cement, plaster or with other mineral binding substances	30	40
68.10	Articles of plastering material	80	100
68.11	Articles of cement (including slag cement), of concrete or of artificial stone (including granulated marble agglomerated with cement), reinforced or not:		
	(A) For building purpose	30	40
	(B) Railway sleepers of cement	9	14
	(C) Other	50	70
68.12	Articles of asbestos-cement, of cellulose fibre-cement or the like	30	40
68.13	Fabricated asbestos and articles thereof (e.g. asbestors board, thread and fabric; asbestos clothing, asbestos jointing), reinforced or not, other than goods falling within No. 68.14; mixtures with a basis of asbestos and mixtures with a basis of asbestos and magnesium carbonate, and articles of such mixtures	30	40
68.14	Friction material (segments, discs, washers, strips, sheets, plates, rolls and the like) of a kind suitable for brakes, for clutches or the like, with a basis of asbestos, other mineral substances or of cellulose, whether or not combined with textile or other materials	30	40
68.15	Worked mica and articles of mica, including bonded mica splittings on a support of paper or fabric (e.g. micanite and micafolium)	25	35

Import Tariffs

No.	Descriptions	Min. (%)	Ord. (%)
68.16	Articles of stone or of other mineral sustances (including articles of peat), not elsewhere specified or included	50	70
69.	Ceramic Products		
69.01	Heat-insulating bricks, blocks, tiles and other heat-insulating goods of siliceous fossil meals or of similar siliceous earths (e.g. kieselguhr, tripolite or diatomite)	40	50
69.02	Refractory bricks, blocks, tiles and similar refractory constructional goods, other than goods falling within No. 69.01	20	30
69.03	Other refractory goods (e.g. retorts, crucibles, muffles, nozzles, plugs, supports, cupels, tubes, pipes,sheaths and rods), other than goods falling within No. 69.01	15	20
69.04	Building bricks including flooring blocks, support or filler tiles and the like)	70	90
69.05	Roofing tiles, chimney-pots, cowls, chimney-liners, cornices and other constructional goods, including architectural ornaments	70	90
69.06	Piping, conduits and guttering (including angles, bends and similar fittings)	70	90
69.07	Unglazed setts, flags and paving, hearth and wall tiles	70	90
69.08	Glazed setts, flags and paving, hearth and wall tiles	80	100
69.09	Laboratory, chemical or industrial wares; troughs, tubs and similar receptacles of a kind used in agriculture; pots, jars and similar articles of a kind commonly used for the conveyance or packing of goods:		
	(A) Laboratory, chemical or industrial wares	20	30
	(B) Other	70	90
69.10	Sinks, wash basins, bidets, water closet pans, urinals, baths and like sanitary fixtures	80	100
69.11	Tableware and other articles of a kind commonly used for domestic or toilet purposes, of porcelain or china (including biscuit porcelain and parian)	80	100
69.12	Tableware and other articles of a kind commonly used for domestic or toilet purposes, of other kinds of pottery	80	100
69.13	Statuettes and other ornaments, and articles of personal adornment; articles of furniture	80	100
69.14	Other articles	80	100

Import Tariffs

No.	Descriptions	Min. (%)	Ord. (%)
70.	Glass & Glassware		
70.01	Waste glass (cullet); glass in the mass (excluding optical glass)	40	50
70.02/ 70.03	Glass in balls, rods and tubes, unworked (not being optical glass)	40	50
70.04	Unworked cast or rolled glass (including flashed or wired glass), whether figured or not, in rectangles	40	50
70.05	Unworked drawn or blown glass (including flashed glass), in rectangles	40	50
70.06	Cast, rolled, drawn or blown glass (including flashed or wired glass), in rectangles, surface ground or polished, but not further worked	40	50
70.07	Cast, rolled, drawn or blown glass (including flashed or wired glass) cut to shape other than rectangular shape, or bent or otherwise worked (e.g. worked or engraved), whether or not surface ground or polished; multiple-walled insulating glass; leaded lights and the like	40	50
70.08	Safety glass consisting of toughened or laminated glass, shaped or not	40	50
70.09	Glass mirrors (including rear-view mirrors), unframed, framed or backed:		
	(A) Mirrors in sheets or plates	50	70
	(B) Other	80	100
70.10	Carboys, bottles, jars, pots, tubular containers and similar containers, of glass, of a kind commonly used for the conveyance or packing of goods; stoppers and other closures, of glass	30	40
70.11	Glass envelopes (including bulbs and tubes) for electric lamps, electronic valves or the like:		
	(A) For electronic valves and tubes	25	35
	(B) Other	60	80
70.12	Glass inners for vacuum flasks or for other vacuum vessels	80	100
70.13	Glassware (other than articles falling in No. 70.19) of a kind commonly used for table, kitchen, toilet or office purposes, for indoor decoration, or for similar uses	80	100
70.14	Illuminating glassware, signalling glassware and optical elements of glass, neither optically worked nor of optical glass	60	80

No.	Descriptions	Min. (%)	Ord. (%)
	Import Tariffs		
70.15	Clock and watch glasses and similar glasses (including glass of a kind used for sunglasses but excluding glass suitable for corrective lenses), curved, bent, hollow and the like; glass spheres and segments of spheres, of a kind used for the manufacture of clock and watch glasses and the like:		
	(A) Clock and watch glasses	50	70
	(B) Other	60	80
70.16	Bricks, tiles, slabs, paving blocks, squares and other articles of pressed or moulded glass, of a kind commonly used in building; multe-cellular glass in blocks, slabs, plates, panels and similar forms	70	90
70.17	Laboratory, hyglenic and pharmaceutical glassware, whether or not graduated or calibrated; glass ampoules:		
	(A) Laboratory, hygienic and pharmac- ceutical glassware	20	30
	(B) Glass ampoules	40	50
70.18	Optical glass and elements of optical glass other than optically worked elements; blacks for corrective spectacle lenses:		
	(A) Optical fibre	12	17
	(B) Blanks for corrective spectacle lenses	25	35
	(C) Other	30	40
70.19	Glass beads, imitation pearls, imitation precious and semi-precious stones, fragments and chippings, and similar fancy or decorative glass smallwares, and articles of glassware made therefrom; glass cubes and small glass plates, whether or not on a backing, for mosaics and similar decorative purposes; artificial eyes of glass, including those for toys but excluding those for wear by humans; ornaments and other fancy articles of lamp-worked glass; glass grains	80	100
70.20	Glass fibre (including wool), yarns, fabrics and articles made therefrom:		
	(A) Fibre and yarn	40	50
	(B) Fabrics:		
	(1) For industrial use	30	40
	(2) Other	50	70

No.	Descriptions	Min. (%)	Ord. (%)
	Import Tariffs		
	(C) Articles:		
	(1) For industrial use	30	40
	(2) Other	50	70
70.21	Other articles of glass:		
	(A) For industrial use	30	40
	(B) Other	80	100

XIV. Pearls, Precious and Semi-precious Stones, Precious Metals, Rolled Precious Metals, and Articles Thereof; Imitation Jewellery; Coins

No.	Descriptions	Min. (%)	Ord. (%)
71.	Pearls, Precious & Semi-precious Stones, Precious Metals Rolled Precious Metals, & Related Articles Imitation Jewellery		
71.01	Pearls, unworked or worked, but not mounted, set or strung (except ungraded pearls temporarily strung for convenience of transport) (E.T. 30%)	80	100
71.02	Precious and semi-precious stones, unworked, cut or otherwise worked, but not mounted, set or strung (except ungraded stones temporarily strung for convenience of transport):		
	(A) Industrial diamonds	9	14
	(B) Other diamonds:		
	(1) Uncut and unpolished	40	50
	(2) Other	70	90
	(C) Jadeite:		
	(1) Uncut and unpolished	40	50
	(2) Other	70	90
	(D) Other:		
	(1) Uncut and unpolished	40	50
	(2) Other	70	90
71.03	Synthetic or reconstructed precious or semi-precious stones, unworked, cut or otherwise worked, but not mounted, set or strung (except ungraded stones timporarily strung for convenience of transport):		
	(A) Industrial diamonds	9	14
	(B) Other:		
	(1) Uncut and unpolished	40	50
	(2) Other	70	90
71.04	Dust and powder of natural or synthetic		

Import Tariffs

No.	Descriptions	Min. (%)	Ord. (%)
	precious or semi-precious stones	12	17
71.05	Silver, including silver gilt and platinum-plated silver, unwrought or semi-manufactured:		
	(A) Unwrought	NIL	NIL
	(B) Semi-manufactured:		
	(1) Powder	NIL	NIL
	(2) Other	40	50
71.06	Rolled silver, unworked or semi-manufactured	40	50
71.07	Gold, including platinum-plated gold, unwrought or semi-manufactured:		
	(A) Unwrought	NIL	NIL
	(B) Semi-manufactured:		
	(1) Powder	NIL	NIL
	(2) Other	40	50
71.08	Rolled gold on base metal or silver, unworked or semi-manufactured	40	50
71.09	Platinum and other metals of the platinum group, unwrought or semi-manufactured:		
	(A) Unwrought	NIL	NIL
	(B) Semi-manufactured:		
	(1) Plates, sheets and powder	NIL	NIL
	(2) Other	6	11
71.10	Rolled platinum or other platinum group metals, on base metal or precious metal, unworked or semi-manufactured	6	11
71.11	Goldsmiths', silversmiths' and jewellers' sweepings, residues, lemels, and other waste and scrap, of precious metal	NIL	NIL
71.12	Articles of jewellery and parts thereof, of precious metal or rolled precious metal	100	130
71.13	Articles of goldsmiths' or silversmiths' wares and parts thereof, of precious metal or rolled precious metal, other than goods falling within No. 71.12	80	100
71.14	Other articles of precious metal or rolled precious metal:		
	(A) For industrial or laboratory use	6	11
	(B) Other	80	100
71.15	Articles consisting of, or incorporating, pearls, precious or semi-precious stones (natural, synthetic or reconstructed)	100	130
71.16	Imitation jewellery	100	130

72. Coin

No.	Descriptions	Min. (%)	Ord. (%)
72.01	Coin	NIL	NIL

Import Tariffs

No.	Descriptions	Min. (%)	Ord. (%)

X V . Base Metals & Articles of Base Metal

73.   Iron & Steel & Related Articles

No.	Descriptions	Min. (%)	Ord. (%)
73.01	Pig iron, cast iron and spiegeleisen, in pigs, blocks, lumps and similar forms:		
	(A) Pig iron and cast iron (E.T. 20%)	3	8
	(B) Other	3	8
73.02	Ferro-alloys:		
	(A) Ferro-manganese (E.T. 10%)	6	11
	(B) Ferro-tungsten (E.T. 20%)	6	11
	(C) Ferro-chrome (E.T. 10%)	3	8
	(D) Ferro-silicon (E.T. 30%)	6	11
	(E) Ferro-vanadium	20	30
	(F) Ferro-molybdenum (E.T. 20%)	6	11
	(G) Ferro-titanium (E.T. 10%)	6	11
	(H) Other (E.T. 10%)	6	11
73.03	Waste and scrap metal of iron or steel	3	8
73.04	Shot and angular grit, of iron or steel, whether or not graded; wire pellets of iron or steel	20	30
73.05	Iron or steel powders; sponge iron or steel:		
	(A) Sponge iron or steel	3	8
	(B) Other	12	17
73.06	Puddled bars and pilings; ingots, blocks, lumps and similar forms, of iron or steel	6	11
73.07	Blooms, billets, slabs and sheet bars (including tinplate bars), of iron or steel; pieces roughly shaped by forging, of iron or steel	6	11
73.08	Iron or steel coils for re-rolling	9	14
73.09	Univeral plates of iron or steel	12	17
73.10	Bars and rods (including wire rod), of iron or steel, hot-rolled, forged, extruded, cold-formed or cold-finished (including precision-made); hollow mining drill steel:		
	(A) Wire-rod	15	20
	(B) Bars and rods (other than wire rod)	15	20
	(C) Hollow mining drill steel	25	35
73.11	Angles, shapes and sections, of iron or steel, hot-rolled, forged, extruded, cold-formed or cold-finished; sheet piling of iron or steel, whether or not drilled, punched or made from assembled elements:		
	(A) Angles	12	17
	(B) Channels and joists	9	14
	(C) Z-bars, tees and girders	9	14
	(D) Sheet piling	15	20
	(E) Other	15	20

Import Tariffs

No.	Descriptions	Min. (%)	Ord. (%)
73.12	Hoop and strip, of iron or steel, hot-rolled or cold-rolled	20	30
73.13	Sheets and plates, of iron or steel, hot-rolled or cold-rolled:		
	(A) Rolled but not further worked	12	17
	(B) Electroplated (other than tinplated)	15	20
	(C) Tinplated:		
	(1) Plain	15	20
	(2) Decorated	20	30
	(D) Other	12	17
73.14	Iron or steel wire, whether or not coated but not insulated	40	50
73.15	Alloy steel and high carbon steel in the forms mentioned in Nos. 73.06 to 73.14:		
	(A) Ingots	6	11
	(B) Blooms, billets, slabs and sheet bars and roughly forged pieces	6	11
	(C) Coils for re-rolling	9	14
	(D) Wire rod	15	20
	(E) Bars and rods (other than wire rod):		
	(1) Of stainless steel	30	40
	(2) Other	15	20
	(F) Angles, shapes and sections	12	17
	(G) Hoop and strip	15	20
	(H) Sheets and plates:		
	(1) Of high carbon steel	12	17
	(2) Of high-speed steel	12	17
	(3) Of stainless or heat-resisting steel	30	40
	(4) Silicon-steel sheets	15	20
	(5) Other	12	17
	(I) Wire	15	20
73.16	Railway and tramway track construction material of iron or steel, the following; rails, check-rails, switch blades, crossings (or frogs), crossing pieces, point rods, rack rails, sleepers, fish-plates, chairs, chair wedges, sole plates (base plates), rail slips, bedplates, ties and other material specialised for joining or fixing rails:		
	(A) Rails and sleepers	9	14
	(B) Other	12	17
73.17	Tubes and pipes, of cast iron	30	40
73.18	Tubes and pipes and blanks therefor, of iron (other than of cast iron) or steel, excluding high-pressure hydro-electric conduits:		

No.	Descriptions	Min. (%)	Ord. (%)
	(A) "Seamless" tubes and pipes and blanks therefor:		
	(1) Boiler tubes and pipes	12	17
	(2) Drill tubes and pipes for oil drilling	12	17
	(3) Casing tubes and pipes for oil drilling	12	17
	(4) Drill and casing tubes and pipes for geological prospecting	12	17
	(5) Stainless steel tubes and pipes	30	40
	(6) Blanks for tubes and pipes	6	11
	(7) Other	9	14
	(B) Other	12	17
73.19	High-pressure hydro-electric conduits of steel, whether or not reinforced	12	17
73.20	Tube and pipe fittings (e.g. joints, elbows, unions and flanges), of iron or steel	15	20
73.21	Structures and parts of structures, (for example, hangars and other buildings, bridges and bridge-sections, lock-gates, towers, lattice masts, roofs, roofing frameworks, door and window frames, shutters, balustrades, pillars and columns), of iron or steel; plates, strip, rods, angles, shapes, sections, tubes and the like, prepared for use in structures, of iron or steel:		
	(A) Shutters, gates, doors, door and window frames and the like	40	50
	(B) Other	20	30
73.22	Reservoirs, tanks, vats and similar containers, for any material (other than, compressed or liquefied gas), of iron or steel, of a capacity exceeding 300l, whether or not lined or heat-insulated, but not fitted with mechanical or thermal equipment	25	35
73.23	Casks, drums, cans, boxes and similar containers, of sheet or plate iron or steel, of a description commonly used for the conveyance or packing of goods	30	40
73.24	Containers, of iron or steel, for compressed or liquefied gas	12	17
73.25	Stranded wire, cables, cordage, ropes, plaited bands, slings and the like, of iron of steel wire, but excluding insulated electric cables:		
	(A) New	15	20
	(B) Old	40	50

Import Tariffs

Import Tariffs

No.	Descriptions	Min.(%)	Ord.(%)
73.26	Barbed iron or steel wire; twisted hoop or single flat wire, barbed or not, and loosely twisted double wire, of kinds used for fencing, of iron or steel	50	70
73.27	Gauze, cloth, grill, netting, fencing, reinforcing fabric and similar materials, of iron or steel wire; expanded metal, of iron or steel:		
	(A) For industrial use	15	20
	(B) Other	50	70
73.28	Chain and parts thereof, of iron or steel:		
73.29	(A) Heavy chains for transmission, lifting etc.:		
	(1) New	15	20
	(2) Old	35	45
	(B) Other	60	80
73.30	Anchors and grapnels and parts thereof, of iron or steel	30	40
73.31	Nails, tacks, staples, hook-nails, corrugated nails, spiked cramps, studs, spikes and drawing pins, of iron or steel, whether or not with heads of other materials, but not including such articles with heads of copper	60	80
73.32	Bolts and nuts (including bolt ends and screw studs), whether or not threaded or tapped, screws (including screw hooks and screw rings), rivets, cotters, cotter-pins and similar articles, of iron or steel: washers (including spring washers) of iron or steel	60	80
73.33	Needles for hand sewing (including embroidery), hand carpet needles and hand knitting needles, bodkins, crochet hooks, and the like, and embroidery stilettos, of iron or steel	60	80
73.34	Pins (excluding hatpins and other ornamental pins and drawing pins), hairpins, curling grips and the like, of iron or steel	70	90
73.35	Springs and leavers for springs, of iron or steel:		
	(A) For railway locomotives and rolling stock	9	14
	(B) Other	40	50

Import Tariffs

No.	Descriptions	Min. (%)	Ord. (%)
73.36	Stoves (including stoves with subsidiary boilers for central heating), ranges, cookers, grates, fires and other space heaters, gas-rings plate warmers with burners, wash boilers with grates or other heating elements, and similar equipment, of a kind used for domestic purposes, not electrically operated, and parts thereof, of iron or steel	60	80
73.37	Boilers (excluding boilers of No. 84.01) and radiators, for central heating, not electrically heated, and parts thereof, of iron or steel; air heaters and hot air distributors (including those which can also distribute cool or conditioned air), not electrically heaated, incorporating a motor-driven fan or blower, and parts thereof, of iron or steel	60	80
73.38	Articles of a kind commonly used for domestic purposes, sanitary ware for indoor use, and parts of such articles and ware, of iron or steel; iron or steel wool; pot scourers and scouring or polishing pads, gloves and the like, of iron or steel:		
	(A) Enamelled ware	80	100
	(B) Other	60	80
73.39/40	Other articles of iron or steel:		
	(A) Crucibles for industrial use	12	17
	(B) Other articles for industrial use (other than crucibles)	30	40
	(C) Other	70	90
74.	Copper & Articles of Copper		
74.01	Copper matte; unwrought copper (refined or not); copper waste and scrap:		
	(A) Copper matte and cement copper	6	11
	(B) Unrefined copper	6	11
	(C) Refined copper, unwrought:		
	(1) Copper	6	11
	(2) Brass	9	14
	(3) White metal (German silver)	25	35
	(4) Other	12	17
	(D) Copper waste and scrap	9	14
74.02	Master alloys	12	17

Import Tariffs

No.	Descriptions	Min. (%)	Ord. (%)
74.03	Wrought bars, rods, angles, shapes and sections, of copper; copper wire:		
	(A) Copper	9	14
	(B) Brass	15	20
	(C) White metal (German silver)	30	40
	(D) Other	15	20
74.04	Wrought plates, sheets and strip, of copper:		
	(A) Copper	9	14
	(B) Brass	15	20
	(C) White metal (German silver)	30	40
	(D) Other	15	20
74.05	Copper foil (whether or not embossed, cut to shape, perforated, coated, printed, or backed with paper or other reinforcing material), of a thickness (excluding any backing) not exceeding 0.15mm:		
	(A) Copper	9	14
	(B) Brass	15	20
	(C) White metal (German silver)	30	40
	(D) Other	15	20
74.06	Copper powders and flakes:		
	(A) Copper	9	14
	(B) Brass	20	30
	(C) White metal (German silver)	30	40
	(D) Other	20	30
74.07	Tubes and pipes and blanks therefor, of copper; hollow bars of copper:		
	(A) Copper	9	14
	(B) Brass	15	20
	(C) White metal (German silver)	30	40
	(D) Other	15	20
74.08	Tube and pipe fittings (e.g. joints, elbows, sockets and flanges), of copper:		
	(A) Copper	9	14
	(B) Brass	15	20
	(C) White metal (German silver)	30	40
	(D) Other	15	20
74.09/ 74.10	Stranded wire, cables, cordage, ropes, plaited bands and the like, of copper wire, but excluding insulated electric wires and cables	9	14
74.11	Gauze, cloth, grill, netting, fencing, reinforcing fabric and similar materials (including endless bands), of copper wire:		
	(A) For industrial use	15	20
	(B) Other	50	70

Import Tariffs

No.	Descriptions	Min. (%)	Ord. (%)
74.12/ 74.15	Nails, tacks, staples, hook-nails, spiked cramps, studs, spikes and drawing pins, of copper, or of iron or steel with heads of copper; bolts and nuts (including bolt ends and screw studs), whether or not threaded or tapped, screws (including screw hooks and screw rings), rivets, cotters, cotter-pins and similar articles, of copper; washers (including spring washers) of copper	60	80
74.16	Springs, of copper	30	40
74.17	Cooking and heating apparatus of a kind used for domestic purposes, not electrically operated, and parts thereof, of copper	60	80
74.18	Other articles of a kind commonly used for domestic purposes, sanitary ware for indoor use, and parts of such articles and ware, of copper	60	80
74.19	Other articles of copper:		
	(A) For industrial use:		
	(1) Crucibles	12	17
	(2) Other	30	40
	(B) Containers:		
	(1) For compressed or liquefied gas	12	17
	(2) Other	30	40
	(C) Other	60	80
75.	Nickel & Articles of Nickel		
75.01	Nickel mattes, nickel speiss and other intermediate products of nicket metallurgy; unwrought nickel (excluding electro-plating anodes); nickel waste and scrap	6	11
75.02	Wrought bars, rods, angles, shapes and sections, of nickel; wite:		
	(A) Wire	12	17
	(B) Other	9	14
75.03	Wrought plates, sheets and strip, of nickel; nickel foil; nickel powders and flakes;		
	(A) Plates, sheets and strip	9	14
	(B) Other	12	17
75.04	Tubes and pipes and blanks therefor, of nickel; hollow bars, and tube and pipe fittings (e.g. joints, elbows, sockets and flanges), of nickel	12	17
75.05	Electro-plating anodes, of nickel, wrought or unwrought, including those produced by electrolysis	9	14

Import Tariffs

No.	Descriptions	Min.(%)	Ord.(%)
75.06	Other articles of nickel:		
	(A) For industrial use:		
	(1) Wire cloth	15	20
	(2) Crucibles	12	17
	(3) Other	30	40
	(B) Containers	30	40
	(C) Other	50	70
76.	Aluminium & Articles of Aluminium		
76.01	Unwrought aluminium: aluminium waste and scrap	9	14
76.02	Wrought bars, rods, angles, shapes and sections, of aluminium; aluminium wire;		
	(A) Wire	12	17
	(B) Other	20	30
76.03	Wrought plates, sheets and strip, of aluminium	20	30
76.04	Aluminium foil (whether or not embossed, cut to shape, perforated, coated, printed, or backed with paper or other reinforcing material), of a thickness (excluding any backing) not exceeding 0.20mm	25	35
76.05	Aluminium powders and flakes	20	30
76.06	Tubes and pipes and blanks therefor, of aluminim; hollow bars of aluminium	20	30
76.07	Tube and pipe fittings (e.g. joints, elbows, sockets and flanges), of aluminium	25	35
76.08	Structures and parts of structures, (e.g. hangars and other buildings, bridges and bridge sections, towers, lattice masts, roofs, roofing frameworks, door and window frames, balustrades, pillars and columns), of aluminium; plates, rods, angles, shapes, sections, tubes and the like, prepared for use in structures, of aluminium:		
	(A) Shutters, gates, doors, door and window frames and the like	40	50
	(B) Other	25	35
76.09	Reservoirs, tanks, vats and similar containers, for any material (other than compressed or liquefied gas), of aluminium, of a capacity exceeding 300l, whether or not lined or heat-insulated, but not fitted with mechanical or thermal equipment	25	35

Import Tariffs

No.	Descriptions	Min. (%)	Ord. (%)
76.10	Casks, drums, cans, boxes and similar containers (including rigid and collapsible tubular containers), of aluminium, of a description commonly used for the conveyance or packing of goods	25	35
76.11	Containers, of aluminium, for compressed or liquified gas	12	17
76.12	Stranded wire, cables, cordage, ropes, plaited bands and the like, of aluminium wire, but excluding insulated electric wires and cabies	15	20
76.13/ 76.15	Articles of a kind commonly used for domestic purposes, sanitary ware for indoor use, and parts of such articles and ware, of aluminium	70	90
76.16	Other articles of aluminium		
	(A) For industrial use	30	40
	(B) Other	60	80
77.	Magnesium & Beryllium & Related Articles		
77.01	Unwrought magnesium; magnesium waste (excluding shavings of uniform size) and scrap	15	20
77.02	Wrought bars, rods, angles, shapes and sections, of magnesium; magnesium wire; wrought plates, sheets ans strip of magnesium; magnesium foil; raspings and shavings of uniform size, powders and flakes, of magnesium; tubes and pipes and blanks therefor, of magnesium; hollow bars of magnesium; other articles of magnesium:		
	(A) Materials	20	30
	(B) Articles	50	70
77.03 77.04	Beryllium, unwrought or wrought, and articles of beryllium:		
	(A) Unwrought	20	30
	(B) Wrought	20	30
	(C) Articles	60	80
78.	Lead & Related Articles		
78.01	Unwrought lead (including argentiferous lead); lead waste and scrap:		
	(A) Unrefined lead	15	20
	(B) Refined lead, unwrought (other than lead alloys)	15	20
	(C) Lead alloys, unwrought:		
	(1) Type metal	20	30
	(2) Other	15	20
	(D) Waste and scrap	20	30

Import Tariffs

No.	Descriptions	Min. (%)	Ord. (%)
78.02	Wrought bars, rods, angles, shapes and sections, of lead; lead wire	20	30
78.03	Wrought plates, sheets and strip, of lead	20	30
78.04	Lead foil (whether or not embossed, cut to shape, perforated, coated, printed, or backed with paper or other reinforcing material), of a weight (excluding any backing) not exceeding 1,700g/m^2; lead powders and flakes	25	35
78.05	Tubes and pipes and blanks therefor, of lead; hollow bars, and tube and pipe fittings (for example, joints, elbows, sockets, flanges and S-bends), of lead	20	30
78.06	Other articles of lead:		
	(A) For industrial use	30	40
	(B) Containers	30	40
	(C) Other	60	80
79. Zinc & Related Articles			
79.01	Unwrought zinc; zinc waste and scrap:		
	(A) Unwrought zinc	15	20
	(B) Waste and scrap	20	30
79.02	Wrought bars, rods, angles, shapes and sections, of zinc; zinc wire	20	30
79.03	Wrought plates, sheets and strip, of zinc; zinc foil; zinc powders and flakes;		
	(A) Plates, sheets and strip	20	30
	(B) Foil	25	35
	(C) Powder and flakes	15	20
79.04	Tubes and pipes and blanks therefor, of zinc; hollow bars, and tube and pipe fittings (e.g. joints, elbows, sockets and flanges), of zinc	20	30
79.05/06	Other articles of zinc:		
	(A) For industrial use	30	40
	(B) Containers	30	40
	(C) Other	60	80
80. Tin and Related Articles			
80.01	Unwrought tin; tin waste and scrap:		
	(A) Babbitt metal	15	20
	(B) Ingots and slabs (E.T. 40%)	15	20
	(C) Other	20	30
80.02	Wrought bars, rods, angles, shapes and sections, of tin; tin wire	30	40
80.03	Wrought plates, sheets and strip, of tin	30	40

Import Tariffs

No.	Descriptions	Min. (%)	Ord. (%)
80.04	Tin foil (whether or not embossed, cut ot shape, perforated, coated, printed, or backed with paper or other reinforcing material), of a weight (excluding any backing) not exceeding 1kg/m²; tin powders and flakes	30	40
80.05	Tubes and pipes and blanks therefor, of tin; hollow bars, and tube and pipe fittings (e.g. joints, elbows, sockets and flanges), of tin	35	45
80.06	Other articles of tin:		
	(A) For industrial use	30	40
	(B) Containers	30	40
	(C) Other	60	80
81.	Other Base Metals Employed in Metallurgy & Related Articles		
81.01	Tungsten (wolfram), unwrought or wrought, and articles thereof:		
	(A) Unwrought	15	20
	(B) Wrought:		
	(1) Wire	15	20
	(2) Other	20	30
	(C) Articles	50	70
81.02	Molybdenum, unwrought or wrought, and articles thereof:		
	(A) Unwrought	15	20
	(B) Wrought:		
	(1) Wire	15	20
	(2) Other	20	30
	(C) Articles	50	70
81.03	Tantalum, unwrought or wrought, and articles thereof:		
	(A) Unwrought	9	14
	(B) Wrought	20	30
	(C) Articles	50	70
81.04	Other base metals, unwrought or wrought, and articles thereof; cermets, unwrought or wrought, and articles thereof:		
	(A) Unwrought:		
	(1) Bismuth	15	20
	(2) Cadmium	9	14
	(3) Cobalt	9	14
	(4) Germanium	15	20
	(5) Manganese	15	20
	(6) Antimony (E.T. 20%)	20	30
	(7) Titanium	9	14
	(8) Thorium, uranium depleted in U235	15	20

Import Tariffs

No.	Descriptions	Min. (%)	Ord. (%)
	(9) Other	15	20
	(B) Wrought	20	30
	(C) Articles	50	70
82.	Tools, Implements, Cutlery, Spoons & Forks' of Base Metals; & Related Articles		
82.01	Hand tools, the following: spades, shovels, picks, hoes, forks and rakes; axes, bill hooks and similar hewing tools; scythes, sickles, hay knives, grass shears, timber wedges and other tools of a kind used in agriculture, horticulture or forestry	40	50
82.02	Saws (non-mechanical) and blades for hand or machines saws (including toothless saw blades):		
	(A) Hand saws	40	50
	(B) Blades:		
	(1) For hand saws	40	50
	(2) For machine saws	15	20
82.03	Hand tools, the following: pliers (including cutting pliers), pincers, tweezers, tinmen's snips, bolt croppers and the like; perforating punched; pipe cutters; spanners and wrenches (but not including tap wrenches); files and rasps	40	50
82.04	Hand tools, including glaziers' diamonds, not falling within any other heading of this Section; blow lamps, anvils; vices and clamps, other than accessories for, and parts of, machine tools; portable forges; grinding wheels with frameworks (hand or pedal operated)	40	50
82.05	Interchangeable tools for hand tools, for machine tools or for power-operated hand tools (e.g. for pressing, stamping, drilling, tapping, threading, boring, broaching, milling, cutting, turning, dressing, morticing or screw driving), including dies for wire drawing, extrusion dies for metal, and rock drilling bits	15	20
82.06	Knives and cutting blades, for machines or for mechanical appliances	15	20
82.07	Tool-tips, unmounted, of sintered metal carbides (e.g. carbides of tungsten, molybdenum or vanadium)	15	20

Import Tariffs

No.	Descriptions	Min. (%)	Ord. (%)
82.08	Coffee-mills, mincers, juice-extractors and other mechanical appliances, of a weight not exceeding 10kg and of a kind used for domestic purposes in the preparation, serving or conditioning of food or drink	60	80
82.09	Knives with cutting blades, serrated or not (including pruning knives), other than knives falling within No. 82.06, and blades therefor	60	80
82.10/ 82.11	Razors and razor blades (including razor blade blanks, whether or not in strips)	60	80
82.12	Scissors (including tailors' shears), and blades therefor	60	80
82.13	Other articles of cutlery (e.g. secateurs, hair clippers, butchers' cleavers, paper knives); manicure and chiropody sets and appliances (including nail files):		
	(A) Manicure and chiropody sets and appliances	70	90
	(B) Other	60	80
82.14	Spoons, forks, fish-eaters, butter-knives, ladles, and similar kitchen or tableware	60	80
82.15	Handles of base metal for articles falling within No. 82.09, 82.13 or 82.14	60	80
83.	Miscellaneous Articles of Base Metal		
83.01	Locks and padlocks (key, combination or electrically operated), and parts thereof, of base metal; frames incorporating locks, for handbags, trunks or the like, and parts of such frames, of base metal; keys for any of the foregoing articles, of base metal	60	80
83.02	Base metal fittings and mountings of a kind suitable for furniture, doors, staircases, window, blinds, coachwork, saddlery, trunks, caskets and the like (including automatic door closers); base metal hatracks, hat-pegs, brackets and the like	60	80
83.03	Armoured or reinforced safes, strong-boxes, strong-rooms, strong-room linings and strong-room doors, and cash and deed boxes and the like, of base metal:		
	(A) Cash and deed boxes	60	80
	(B) Other	40	50

Import Tariffs

No.	Descriptions	Min. (%)	Ord. (%)
83.04	Filing cabinets, racks, sorting boxes, paper trays, paper rests and similar office equipment, of base metal, other than office furniture falling withint No. 94.03	60	80
83.05	Fittings for loose-leaf binders, for files or for stationery books, of base metal; letter clips, paper clips, staples, indexing tags, and similar stationery goods, of base metal	60	80
83.06	Statuettes and other ornaments of a kind used indoors, of base metal; photograph, picture and similar frames, of base metal; mirrors of base metal	80	100
83.07	Lamps and lighting fittings, of base metal, and parts thereof, of base metal (excluding switches, electric lamp holders, electric lamps for vehicles, electric battery or magneto lamps, and other articles falling within Section 85 except No. 85.22):		
	(A) Miners' safety lamps	15	20
	(B) Lamps for use as aids to navigation	12	17
	(C) Other	60	80
83.08	Flexible tubing and piping, of base metal	25	35
83.09	Clasps, frames with clasps for handbags and the like, buckles, buckle-clasps, hooks, eyes, eyelets and the like, of base metal, of a kind commonly used for clothing, travel goods, handbags or other textile or leather goods; tubular rivets and bifurcated rivets, of base metal; beads and spangles, of base metal:		
	(A) Beads and spangles	80	100
	(B) Other	60	80
83.10/11	Bells and gongs, non-electric, of base metal, and parts thereof of base metal	60	80
83.12/ 83.13	Stoppers, crown corks, bottle caps, capsules, bung covers, seals and plombs, case corner protectors and other packing accessories, of base metal:		
	(A) Tear tab ends	20	30
	(B) Other	60	80
83.14	Sign-plates, name-plates, numbers, letters and other signs, of base metal	60	80

Import Tariffs

No.	Descriptions	Min. (%)	Ord. (%)
83.15	Wire, rods, tubes, plates, electrodes and similar products, of base metal or of metal carbides, coated or cored with flux material, of a kind used for soldering, brazing, welding or deposition of metal or of metal carbides; wire and rods, of agglomerated base metal powder, used for metal spraying	20	30

XI. Machinery and Mechanical Appliances Electrical Equipment; Parts Thereof

No.	Descriptions	Min. (%)	Ord. (%)
84.	Boilers, Machinery & Mechancial Appliances & Related Articles		
84.01	Steam and other vapour generating boilers (excluding central heating hot water boilers capable also of producing low pressure steam); super-heated water boilers	25	35
84.02	Auxiliary plant for use with boilers of No. 84.01 (e.g. economisers, superheaters, soot removers, gas recoverers and the like); condensers for vapour engines and power units	25	35
84.03	Producer gas and water gas generators, with or without purifiers; acetylene gas generators (water process) and similar gas generators, with or without purifiers	20	30
84.04/ 84.05	Steam or other vapour power units, whether or not incorporating boilers	25	35
84.06	Internal combustion piston engines:		
	(A) For propelling locomotives	6	11
	(B) For propelling vehicles:		
	(1) Diesel engines	9	14
	(2) Other	25	35
	(C) Aircraft engines	6	11
	(D) Marine propulsion engines:		
	(1) Outboard marine engines	12	17
	(2) Other	6	11
	(E) Other:		
	(1) Diesel engines	9	14
	(2) Other	25	35
84.07	Hydraulic engines and motors (including water wheels and water turbines)	25	35
84.08	Other engines and motors:		
	(A) Aircraft engines	6	11
	(B) Other	25	35

Import Tariffs

No.	Descriptions	Min. (%)	Ord. (%)
84.09	Mechanically propelled road rollers:		
	(A) Vibration rollers	15	20
	(B) Other	30	40
84.10	Pumps (including motor pumps and turbo pumps) for liquids, whether or not fitted with measuring devices; liquid elevators of bucket, chain, screw, bank and similar kinds	20	30
84.11	Air pumps, vacuum pumps and air or gas compressors (including motor and turbo pumps and compressors, and free-piston generators for gas turbines); fans, blowers and the like:		
	(A) Air pumps and vacuum pumps	20	30
	(B) Air or gas compressors:		
	(1) Refrigerating compressors, of a motor rated capacity of more than	20	30
	(2) Refrigerating compressors, of a motor rated capacity of not more than 1.5KW	40	50
	(3) Free-piston generators for gas turbines	40	50
	(4) Other	20	30
	(C) Fans, blowers and the like	20	30
84.12	Air conditioning machines, self-contained, comprising a motor-driven fan and elements for changing the temperature and humidity of air:		
	(A) Of a refrigerating capacity of more than 4,000 kcal	40	50
	(B) Other	70	90
84.13	Furnace burners for liquid fuel (atomisers), for pulverised solid fuel or for gas; mechanical stokers, mechanical grates, mechanical ash dischargers and similar appliances	25	35
84.14	Industrial and laboratory furnaces and ovens, non-electric	25	35
84.15	Refrigerators and refrigerating equipment (electrical and other):		
	(A) Of a refrigerating temperature of —30C or lower, or of a capacity of more than 340 litres	30	40
	(B) Other	80	100
84.16	Calendering and similar rolling machines (other than metal-working and metal-rolling machines and glass-working machines) and cylinders therefor	20	30

Import Tariffs

No.	Descriptions	Min. (%)	Ord. (%)
84.17	Machinery, plant and similar laboratory equipment, whether or not electrically heated, for the treatment of materials by a process involving a change of temperature such as heating, cooking roasting, distilling, rectifying, sterilising, pasteurising, steaming, drying, evaporating, vapourising, condensing or cooling, not being machinery or plant of a kind used for domestic purposes; instantaneous or storage water heaters, non-electrical:		
	(A) Water heaters	80	100
	(B) Other	20	30
84.18	Centrifuges; filtering and purifying machinery and apparatus (other than filter funnels, milk strainers and the like), of liquids or gases:		
	(A) Centrifuges:		
	(1) Clothes-dryers, each of a dry linen capacity not exceeding 6 kg	50	70
	(2) Other	20	30
	(B) Filtering and purifying machinery and apparatus:		
	(1) For household use	80	100
	(2) Other	30	40
84.19	Machinery for cleaning or drying bottles or other containers; machinery for filling closing sealing, capsuling or labelling bottles, cans, boxes, bags or other containers; other packing or wrapping machinery; machinery for aerating beverages; dish washing machines:		
	(A) Dish washing machines	70	90
	(B) Other	25	35
84.20	Weighing machinery (excluding balances of a sensitivity of 5cg or better), including weight-operated counting and checking machines; weighing machine weights of all kinds	60	80
84.21	Mechanical appliances (whether or not hand operated) for projecting, dispersing or spraying liquids or powders; fire extinguishers (charged or not); spray guns and similar appliances; steam or sand blasting machines and similar jet projecting machines:		
	(A) Mechanical appliances for projecting, dispersing or spraying liquids or powder:		

No.	Descriptions	Min. (%)	Ord. (%)
	(1) For household use	60	80
	(2) Other	20	30
(B)	Fire extinguishers	50	70
(C)	Other	30	40
84.22	Lifting, handling, loading or unloading machinery, telphers and conveyors (for example, lifts, hoists, winches, cranes, transporter cranes, jacks, pulley tackle, belt conveyors and teleferics), not being machinery falling within No. 84.23:		
(A)	Pulley tackle and hoists; winches and capstans	20	30
(B)	Cranes:		
	(1) Ship's derricks and cranes	12	17
	(2) Caterpillar cranes	20	30
	(3) Tower cranes (other than ship's cranes)	20	30
	(4) Other	20	30
(C)	Other machinery	20	30
(D)	Parts:		
	(1) For ship's derricks and cranes	12	17
	(2) Other	20	30
84.23	Excavating, levelling, tamping, boring and extracting machinery, stationary or mobile, for earth, minerals or ores (e.g. mechanical shovels, coal-cutters, excavators, scrapers, levellers and bulldozers); pile-drivers; snow-ploughs, not self-propelled (including snow-plough attachments):		
(A)	Drilling machinery:		
	(1) Drilling depth of 6,000 metres and more	6	11
	(2) Other drilling machinery	12	17
	(3) Parts	6	11
(B)	Other oil-well machinery:		
	(1) Machinery	12	17
	(2) Parts	9	14
(C)	Mining machinery:		
	(1) Machinery	20	30
	(2) Parts	12	17
(D)	Bulldozers, graders, land-planers, excavators and scrapers, self-propelled:		
	(1) Machines with an engine of more than 320 H.P.	12	17

Import Tariffs

No.	Descriptions	Min. (%)	Ord. (%)
	Import Tariffs		
	(2) Other machines	20	30
	(3) Parts	12	17
	(E) Other:		
	(1) Machinery	20	30
	(2) Parts	12	17
84.24	Agricultural and horticultural machinery for soil preparation or cultivation (e.g. ploughs, harrows, cultivators, seed and fertiliser distributors): lawn and sports ground rollers:		
	(A) Agricultural and horticultural machinery for soil preparation or cultivation:		
	(1) Ploughs, seeders, planters and transplanters, fertiliser distributors and manure spreaders, scarifiers, cultivators, weeders, hoes and harrows	20	30
	(2) Other machines	20	30
	(3) Parts	12	17
	(B) Lawn and sports ground rollers	30	40
84.25	Harvesting and threshing machinery; straw and fodder presses; hay or grass mowers; winnowing and similar cleaning machines for seed, grain or leguminous vegetable and egg-grading and other grading machines for agricultural produce (other than those of a kind used in the bread grain milling industry falling within No. 84.29):		
	(A) Combined harvester-threshers	12	17
	(B) Egg grading and other grading machines for agricultural produce	30	40
	(C) Other	20	30
84.26	Dairy machinery (including milking machines):		
	(A) Milking machines	15	20
	(B) Other	20	30
84.27	Presses, crushers and other machinery, of a kind used in wine-making, cider-making, fruit juice preparation or the like	20	30
84.28	Other agricultural, horticultural, poultry-keeping and bee-keeping machinery; germination plant fitted with mechanical or thermal equipment; poultry incubators and brooders	20	30
84.29	Machinery of a kind used in the bread grain milling industry, and other machinery (other than farm type machinery) for the working of cereals or dried leguminous vegetables	20	30

Import Tariffs

No.	Descriptions	Min. (%)	Ord. (%)
84.30	Machinery, not falling within any other heading of this Section, of a kind used in the following food or drink industries; bakery, confectionery, chocolate manufacture, macaroni, ravioli or similar cereal food manufacture, the preparation of meat, fish, fruit or vegetables (including mincing or slicing machines), sugar manufacture or brewing	20	30
84.31	Machinery for making or finishng cellulosic pulp, paper or paperboard	20	30
84.32	Book-binding machinery, including book-sewing machines	25	35
84.33	Paper or paperboard cutting machines of all kinds; other machinery for making up paper pulp, paper or paperboard	20	30
84.34	Machinery, apparatus and accessories for type-founding or type-setting; machinery, other than the machine-tools of No. 84.45, 84.46 or 84.47, for preparing or working printing blocks, plates or cylinders; printing type, impressed flongs and matrices, printing blocks, plates and cylinders; blocks, plates, cylinders and lithographic stones, prepared for printing purposes e.g. planed, grained or polished):		
	(A) Machinery, apparatus and accessories for type-founding or type-setting and machinery for making printing plates, block or cylinders:		
	(1) Electronic colour scanners	15	20
	(2) Other machinery and apparatus	25	35
	(3) Parts	15	20
	(B) Other	25	35
84.35	Otherprinting machinery; machines for uses ancillary to printing:		
	(A) Machinery	25	35
	(B) Parts	15	20
84.36	Machines for extruding man-made textiles; machines of a kind used for processing natural or man-made textile fibres; textile spinning and twisting machines; textile doubling, throwing and reeling (including weft-winding) machines	15	20
84.37	Weaving machines, knitting machines and machines for making gimped yarn, tulle, lace, embroidery, trimmings, braid or net; machines for preparing yarns for use on such machines, including warping and warp sizing machines	15	20

Import Tariffs

No.	Descriptions	Min. (%)	Ord. (%)
84.38	Auxiliary machinery for use with machines of No. 84.37 (e.g. dobbies, Jacquards, automatic stop motions and shuttle changing mechanisms); parts and accessories suitable for use solely or principally with the machines of the present item or with machines falling within No. 84.36 or 84.37 (e.g. spindles and spindle flyers, card clothing, combs, extruding nipples, shuttles, healds and heald-lifters and hosiery needles):		
	(A) Auxiliary machinery	15	20
	(B) Parts and accessories for use with the machines of No. 84.36:		
	(1) Extruding nipples and rotors	9	14
	(2) Other	12	17
	(C) Other parts and accessories:		
	(1) Wire healds, reeds and shuttles	40	50
	(2) Spring-hook needles for knitting machines, above No. 2	12	17
	(3) Other spring-hook needles for knitting machines	40	50
	(4) Other	12	17
84.39	Machinery for the manufacture or finishing of felt in the piece or in shapes, including felt-hat making machines and hat-making blocks	20	30
84.40	Machinery for washing, cleaning, drying, bleaching, dyeing, dressing, finishing or coating textile yarns, fabrics or made-up textile articles (including laundry and dry-cleaning machinery); fabric folding, reeling or cutting machines; machines of a kind used in the manufacture of linoleum or other floor coverings for applying the paste to the base fabric or other support; machines of a type used for printing a repetitive design, repetitive words or overall colour on textiles, leather, wallpaper. wrapping paper, linoleum or other materials, and engraved or etched plates. block or rollers therefor:		
	(A) Clothes-washing machines for household use, each of a dry linen capacity not exceeding 6 kg	80	100
	(B) Other clothes-washing machines	50	70
	(C) Other machinery for textile industry	15	20
	(D) Other	20	30

Import Tariffs

No.	Descriptions	Min. (%)	Ord. (%)
84.41	Sewing machines; furniture specially designed for sewing machines; sewing machine needles:		
	(A) Sewing machines for industrial use	30	40
	(B) Sewing machines for household use	60	80
	(C) Furniture specially designed for sewing machines and sew machine needles	80	100
84.42	Machinery (other than sewing machines) for preparing, tanning or working hides, skins or leather (including boot and shoe machinery)	20	30
84.43	Converters, ladles, ingot moulds and casting machines, of a kind used in metallurgy and in metal foundries:		
	(A) Machines	25	35
	(B) Parts	15	20
84.44	Rolling mills and rolls therefor:		
	(A) Mills	25	35
	(B) Parts	15	20
84.45	Machine-tools for working metal or metal carbides, not being machines falling within No. 84.49 or 84.50:		
	(A) Operated by numerical control system	9	14
	(B) Other	20	30
84.46	Machine-tool for working stone, ceramics, concrete, asbestos-cement and like mineral materials or for working glass in the cold, other than machines falling within No. 84.49	20	30
84.47	Machine-tool for working wood, cork, bone, ebonite (vulcanite), hard artificial plastic materials or other hard carving materials, other than machines falling within No. 84.49	20	30
84.48	Accessories and parts suitable for use solely or principally with the machines falling within Nos 84.45 to 84.47, including work and tool holders, self-opening dieheads, dividing heads and other appliances for machine-tools; tool holders for any type of tool or machine-tool for working in the hand	12	17
84.49	Tools for working in the hand, pneumatic or with self-contained non-electric motor	20	30
84.50	Gas-operated welding, brazing, cutting and surface tempering appliances	20	30
84.51	Typewriters, other than typewriters incorporating calculating mechanisms; cheque-writing machines	30	40

Import Tariffs

No.	Descriptions	Min. (%)	Ord. (%)
84.52	Calculating machines; accounting machines, cash registers, postage-franking machines, ticket-issuing machines and similar machines, incorporating a calculating device:		
	(A) Electronic calculators	60	80
	(B) Other	30	40
84.53	Automatic data processing machines and units thereof; magnetic or optical readers, machines for transcribing data onto data media in coded form and machines for processing such data, not elsewhere specified or included:		
	(A) Analogue machines and hybrid machines	9	14
	(B) Digital data processing machines:		
	(1) Of a word length of 32 bits or more	9	14
	(2) Of a word length less than 32 bits	50	70
	(C) Peripheral equipment:		
	(1) For digital data processing machines of a word length less than 32 bits	30	40
	(2) Other	9	14
84.54	Other office machines (e.g. hectograph or stencil duplicating machines, addressing machines, coin-sorting machines, coin-counting and wrapping machines, pencil-sharpening machines, perforating and stapling machines)	30	40
84.55	Parts and accessories (other than covers, carrying cases and the like) suitable for use solely or principally with machines of a kind falling within No. 84.51, 84.52, 84.53 or 84.54		
	(A) Of the machines of No. 84.53:		
	(1) For digital data processing machine and peripheral equipment of a work length less than 32 bits	30	40
	(2) Other	9	14
	(B) Of electronic calculators	40	50
	(C) Other	25	35
84.56	Machinery for sorting, screening, separating, washing, crushing, grinding or mixing earth, stone, ores or other mineral substances, in solid (including powder and paste) form; machinery for agglomerating, moulding or shaping solid mineral fuels, ceramic paste, unhardened cements, plastering materials or other mineral products in powder or paste form; machines for forming foundry moulds of sand	20	30

Import Tariffs

No.	Descriptions	Min. (%)	Ord. (%)
84.57	Glass-working machines (other than machines for working glass in the cold); machines for assembling electric filament and discharge lamps and electronic and similar tubes and valves	20	30
84.58	Automatic vending machines (e.g. stamp, cigarette, chocolate and food machines), not being games of skill or chance	40	50
84.59	Machines and mechanical appliances, having individual functions, not falling within any other heading of this section:		
	(A) Nuclear reactors	3	8
	(B) Steering and rudder equipment and gyroscopic stabilisers for ships	9	14
	(C) Air humidifiers or de-humidifiers	50	70
	(D) Other	20	30
84.60	Moulding boxes for metal foundry; moulds of a type used for metal (other than ingot moulds), for metal carbides, for glass for mineral materials (e.g. ceramic pastes, concrete or cement) or for rubber or artificial plastic materials	15	20
84.61	Taps, cocks, valves and similar appliances, for pipes, boiler shells, tanks, vats and the like, including pressure reducing valves and thermostatically controlled valves:		
	(A) Valves	20	30
	(B) Other	40	50
84.62	Ball, roller or needle roller bearings	15	20
84.63	Transmission shafts, cranks, bearing housing, plain shaft bearings, gears and gearing (including friction gears and gear-boxes and other variable speed gears), flywheels, pulleys and pulley blocks, clutches and shaft couplings:		
	(A) Transmission shafts for ships	9	14
	(B) Other	20	30
84.64	Gaskets and similar joints of metal sheeting combined with other material (e.g. asbestos, felt and paperboard) or of laminated metal foil; sets or assortments of gaskets and similar joints, dissmilar in composition, for engines, pipes, tubes and the like, put up in pouches, envelopes or similar packings	20	30

Import Tariffs

No.	Descriptions	Min. (%)	Ord. (%)
84.65	Machinery parts, not containing electrical connectors, insulators, coils, contacts or other electrical features and not falling within any other heading in this section	20	30
85.	Electrical Machinery & Equipment & Related Articles		
85.01	Electrical goods of the following descriptions; generators, motors, converters (rotary or static), transformers, rectifiers and rectifying apparatus, inductors:		
	(A) Generators of 300,000 KW or more	6	11
	(B) Other generators	20	30
	(C) Motors	25	35
	(D) Transformers of 360 MVA or more	6	11
	(E) Other transformers	25	35
	(F) Convertors and rectifiers	20	30
	(G) Other	25	35
85.02	Electro-magnets; permanent magnets and articles of special materials for permanent magnets, being blanks of such magnets; electro-magnetic and permanent magnet chucks, clamps, vices and similar work holders; electro-magnetic clutches and couplings; electro-magnetic brakes; electro-magnetic lifting heads	15	20
85.03	Primary cells and primary batteries:		
	(A) Zinc-manganese dioxide dry cells	60	80
	(B) Other	30	40
85.04	Electric accumulators:		
	(A) Alkaline accumulators	30	40
	(B) Other	70	90
85.05	Tools for working in the hand, with self-contained electric motor	20	30
85.06	Electro-mechanical domestic appliances, with self-contained electric motor	80	100
85.07	Shavers and hair clippers, with self-contained electric motor	80	100
85.08	Electrical starting and ignition equipment for internal combustion engines (including ignition magnetos, magneto-dynamos, ignition coils, starter motors, sparking plugs and glow plugs); generators (dynamos and alternators) and cut-outs for use in conjunction with such engines:		

Import Tariffs

No.	Descriptions	Min. (%)	Ord. (%)
	(A) For locomotives	6	11
	(B) For aircraft	6	11
	(C) For ships	6	11
	(D) Other	20	30
85.09	Electrical lighting and signalling equipment and electrical windscreen wipers, defrosters and demisters, for cycles or motor vehicles	35	45
85.10	Portable electric battery and magneto lamps, other than lamps falling within No. 85.09:		
	(A) Miners' safety lamps	15	20
	(B) Flashlights	80	100
	(C) Other	50	70
85.11	Industrial and laboratory electric furnaces, ovens and induction and dielectric heating equipment; electric or laser-operated welding, brazing, soldering or cutting machines and apparatus	20	30
85.12	Electric instantaneous or storage water heaters and immersion heaters; electric soil heating apparatus and electric space heating apparatus; electric hair dressing appliances (e.g. hair dryers, hair curlers, curling tong heaters) and electric smoothing irons; electro-thermic domestic appliances; electric heating resistors, other than those of carbon:		
	(A) Soil heating apparatus and electric heating resistors	30	40
	(B) Other	80	100
85.13	Electricalline telephonic and telegraphic apparatus (including such apparatus for carrier-current line systems):		
	(A) Wave carriers and facsimile equipment	9	14
	(B) Stored program control switching systems	9	14
	(C) Teletype apparatus	9	14
	(D) Other	20	30
85.14	Microphones and stands therefor; loudspeakers; audio-frequency electric amplifiers.		
	(A) Audio-frequency electric amplifiers	25	35
	(B) Other	30	40

Import Tariffs

No.	Descriptions	Min. (%)	Ord. (%)
85.15	Radiotelegraphic and radiotelephonic transmission and reception apparatus; radio-broadcasting and television transmission and reception apparatus (including receivers incorporating sound recorders or reproducers) and television cameras; radio navigational aid apparatus, radar apparatus and radio remote control apparatus:		
	(A) Radiotelegraphic and radiotelephonic transmission and reception apparatus	9	14
	(B) Radio-broadcasting, television transmission and relay apparatus	9	14
	(C) Radio receivers, including receivers incorporating a sound recorder or reproducer, etc., but not including television sets incorporating a radio-broadcast receiver	100	130
	(D) Television sets, including receivers incorporating a radio-broadcast receiver, or a sound recorder or reproducer, etc.:		
	(1) Of colour	80	100
	(2) Other	60	80
	(3) Of colour (CKD and SKD)	70	90
	(4) Other (CKD and SKD)	50	70
	(5) Parts (of colour)	60	80
	(6) Other	40	50
	(E) Television cameras:		
	(1) Television cameras and parts thereof, for scientific use only	12	17
	(2) Other	80	100
	(3) Parts	60	80
	(F) Radio navigational aid apparatus and navigation radar apparatus	3	8
	(G) Other	9	14
85.16	Electric traffic control equipment for railways, roads or inland water-ways and equipment used for similar purposes in port installations or upon airfields	15	20
85.17	Electric sound or visual signalling apparatus (such as bells, sirens, indicator panels, burglar and fire alarms), other than those of No. 85.09 or 85.16:		
	(A) Burglar and fire alarms	30	40
	(B) Other	50	70

Import Tariffs

No.	Descriptions	Min.(%)	Ord.(%)
85.18	Electrical capacitors, fixed or variable:		
	(A) Power capacitors	15	20
	(B) Other	25	35
85.19	Electrical apparatus for making and breaking electrical circuits, tor the protection of electrical circuits, or for making connections to or in electrical circuits (for example, switches, relays, fuses, lightning arresters, surge suppressors, pluge, lampholders and junction boxes); resistors, fixed or variable (including poten-tiometers), other than heating resistors; printed circuits; switchboards (other than telephone switchboards) and control panels:		
	(A) Printed circuits	25	35
	(B) Other	30	40
85.20	Electric filament lamps and electric discharge lamps (including infra-red and ultra-violet lamps); arc-lamps:		
	(A) For scientific or medical purposes only	15	20
	(B) For use in railway or tramway locomotives and rolling-stock	15	20
	(C) For use in other vehicles	35	45
	(D) For use in aircraft or ships	15	20
	(E) Other	50	70
85.21	Thermionic, cold cathode and photocathode valves and tubes (including vapour or gas filled valves and tubes, cathode-ray tubes, television camera tubes and mercury arc rectifying valves and tubes); photocells; mounted piezo-electric crystals; diodes, transistors and similar semi-conductor devices; light emitting diodes; electric microcircuits:		
	(A) Electronic valves and tubes:		
	(1) Television camera tubes	25	35
	(2) Television picture tubes	30	40
	(3) Cathode-ray tubes for radar apparatus	9	14
	(4) Other	12	17
	(B) Electronic microcircuits:		
	(1) Large scale or very large scale integrated circuits	6	11
	(2) Other	20	30
	(C) Other	20	30

No.	Descriptions	Min. (%)	Ord. (%)
	Import Tariffs		
85.22	Electrical appliances and apparatus, having individual functions, not falling within any other heading of this Chapter:		
	(A) Particle accelerators	6	11
	(B) Metal or mine detectors	12	17
	(C) Signal generators	9	14
	(D) High or intermediate frequency amplifiers:		
	(1) Tuners	40	50
	(2) Other	12	17
	(E) Other	25	35
85.23	Insulated (including enamelled or anodised) electric wire, calbe, bars strip and the like (including co-axial cable), whether or not fitted with connectors:		
	(A) Electric wire	50	70
	(B) Electric cable	15	20
85.24	Carbon brushes, arc-lamp carbons, battery carbons, carbon electrodes and other carbon articles of a kind used for electrical purposes	25	35
85.25	Insulators of any material	25	35
85.26	Insulating fittings for electrical machines, appliances or equipment, being fittings wholly of insulating material apart from any minor components of metal incorporated during moulding solely for purposes of assembly, but not including insulators falling within No. 85.25	25	35
85.27	Electrical conduit tubing and joints therefor, of base metal lined with insulating material	40	50
85.28	Electrical parts of machinery and apparatus, not being goods falling within any of the preceding headings of this section		
	(A) Of electric motors	20	30
	(B) Other	30	40

XVII. Vehicles, Aircraft, Vessels and Associated Transport Equipment

No.	Descriptions	Min. (%)	Ord. (%)
86.	Railway & Tramway Locomotives, Rolling-stock & Parts Thereof; Railway and Tramway Track Fixtures & Fittings; Traffic Signalling Equipment of All Kinds (Not Electrically Powered)		
86.01/02	Electric rail locomotives, battery operated or powered from an external source of electricity	6	11
86.03	Other rail locomotives; tenders	6	11

Import Tariffs

No.	Descriptions	Min.(%)	Ord.(%)
86.04	Mechanically propelled railway and tramway coaches, vans and trucks, and mechanically propelled track inspection trolleys:		
	(A) For railway	6	11
	(B) For tramway	9	14
86.05	Railway and tramway passenger coaches and luggage vans; hospital coaches, prison coaches, testing coaches, travelling post office coaches and other special purpose railway coaches:		
	(A) For railway	9	14
	(B) For tramway	12	17
86.06	Railway and tramway rolling-stock, the following; workshops, cranes and other service vehicles	15	20
86.07	Railway and tramway goods vans, goods wagons and trucks:		
	(A) For railway	9	14
	(B) For tramway	12	17
86.08	Containers specially designed and equipped for carriage by one or more modes of transport	12	17
86.09	Parts of railway and tramway locomotives and rolling-stock:		
	(A) Of railway locomotives and rolling-stock	6	11
	(B) Of tramway locomotives and rolling-stock	9	14
86.10	Railway and tramway track fixtures and fittings; mechanical equipment, not electrically powered, for signalling or controlling road, rail or other vehicles, ships or aircraft; parts of the foregoing fixtures, fitting or equipment	12	17
87.	Vehicles, Other Than Railway or Tramway Rolling-stock, and Related Parts		
87.01	Tractors (other than those falling within No. 87.07), whether or not fitted with power take-offs, winches or pulleys	15	20
87.02	Motor vehicles for the transport of persons, goods or materials (including sports motor vehicles, other than those of No. 87.09):		
	(A) Sedan cars, jeeps and passenger vehicles with seats less than 30	120	150
	(B) Motor passenger vehicles with seats for 30 persons or more	70	90
	(C) Trolley buses	40	50

No.	Descriptions	Min. (%)	Ord. (%)
	(D) Motor trucks with loading capacity of 30 tons or more	9	14
	(E) Motor trucks with loading capacity of 8 to 30 tons (not including 30 tons)	30	40
	(F) Motor trucks with loading capacity less than 8 tons	50	70
87.03	Special purpose motor lorries and vans (such as breakdown lorries, fire-engines, fire-escapes, road sweeper lorries, snow-ploughs, spraying lorries, crane lorries, searchight lorries, mobile workshops and mobile radiological units), but not including the motor vehicles of No. 87.02:		
	(A) Fire engines and fire escapes	3	8
	(B) Mobile drilling derricks	12	17
	(C) Radio broadcasting and communication vans	9	14
	(D) Mobile clinics	20	30
	(E) Mobile radiological units	9	14
	(F) Mobile enviromental monitoring units	15	20
	(G) Mobile electric generator sets	20	30
	(H) Crane lorries	20	30
	(I) Other	25	35
87.04	Chassis fitted with engines, for the motor vehicles falling within No. 87.01, 87.02 or 87.03:		
	(A) For motor trucks:		
	(1) With loading capacity of 30 tons or more	9	14
	(2) With loading capacity of 8 to 30 tons (not including 30 tons)	20	30
	(3) Other	35	45
	(B) For trolleybuses	30	40
	(C) For motor passenger vehicles with seats for 30 presons more	50	70
	(D) Other	80	100
87.05	Bodies (including cabs), for the motor vehicles falling within No. 87.01, 87.02 or 87.03	60	80
87.06	Parts and accessories of the motor vehicles falling within No. 87.01, 87.02 or 87.03:		
	(A) Of tractors	9	14
	(B) Of motor trucks:		
	(1) With loading capacity of 30 tons or more	6	11
	(2) With loading capacity of 8 to 30 tons (not including 30 tons)	20	30
	(3) Other	35	45

Import Tariffs

No.	Descriptions	Min. (%)	Ord. (%)
	(C) Of trolley buses	30	40
	(D) Of motor passenger vehicles with seats for 30 persons or more	50	70
	(E) Other	80	100
87.07	Works trucks, mechanically propelled, of the types used in factories, warehouse, dock areas or airports for short distance transport or handling of goods (e.g. platform trucks, fork-lift trucks and straddle carries); tractors of the type used on railway station platforms; parts of the foregoing vehicles:		
	(A) Vehicles	20	30
	(B) Parts	12	17
87.08	Tanks and other armoured fighting vehicles, motorised, whether or not fitted with weapons, and parts of such vehicles	80	100
87.09	Motor-cycles, auto-cycles and cycles fitted with an auxiliary motor, with or without side-cars; side-cars of all kinds	120	150
87.10	Cycles (including delivery tricycles), not motorised	80	100
87.11	Invalid carriages, whether or not motorised or otherwise mechanically propelled	15	20
87.12	Parts and accessories of articles falling within No. 87.09, 87.10 or 87.11:		
	(A) Of motor-cycles and auto-cycles	80	100
	(B) Of cycles	60	80
	(C) Of invalid carriages	12	17
87.13	Baby carriages and parts thereof	60	80
87.14	Other vehicles (including trailers), not mechanically propelled, and parts thereof:		
	(A) Trailers:		
	(1) Tank trailers and van trailers	15	20
	(2) Trailers of the caravan type for housing or camping	25	35
	(3) Other	25	35
	(B) Other	60	80
88.	Aircraft & Related Parts; Parachutes; Catapults & Similar Aircraft Launching Gear; Ground Flying Trainers		
88.01	Balloons and airships	6	11
88.02	Flying machines, gliders, and kites; rotochutes	6	11
88.03	Parts of goods falling in No. 88.01 or 88.02	6	11
88.04	Parachutes and parts thereof and accessories thereof	6	11

No.	Descriptions	Min. (%)	Ord. (%)

Import Tariffs

No.	Descriptions	Min. (%)	Ord. (%)
88.05	Catapults and similar aircraft launching gear; ground flying trainers; parts of any of the foregoing articles	6	11
89.	Ships, Boats & Floating Structures		
89.01	Ships, boats and other vessels not falling within any of the following headings of this Section		
	(A) Motor vessels	9	14
	(B) Other	20	30
89.02	Vessels specially designed for towing (tugs) or pushing other vessels	9	14
89.03	Light-vessels, fire-floats, dredgers of all kinds, floating cranes, and other vessels the navigability of which is subsidiary to their main function; floating docks; floating or submersible drilling or production platforms:		
	(A) Dredgers	6	11
	(B) Floating docks	20	30
	(C) Drilling or production platforms	6	11
	(D) Other	6	11
89.04	Ships, boats and other vessels for breaking up	6	11
89.05	Floating structures other than vessels (e.g. buoys and beacons)	20	30

XVIII. Opitcal, Photographic, Cinematographic, Measuring, Checking, Precision, Medical and Surgical Instruments and Apparatus; Clocks and Watches; Musical Instruments; Sound Recorders or Preproducers; Television Image and Sound Recorders or Reproducers & Related Parts

No.	Descriptions	Min. (%)	Ord. (%)
90.	Optical, Photographic, Cinematographic, Measuring, Checking, Precision, Medical & Surgical Instruments & Apparatus & Related Parts		
90.01	Lenses, prisms, mirrors and other optical elements, of any material, unmounted, other than such elements of glass not optically worked; sheets or plates, of polarising material:		
	(A) Polished lenses for spectacles	35	45
	(B) Other	15	20
90.02	Lenses, prisms, mirrors and other optical elements, of any material, mounted, being parts of or fillings for instruments or apparatus, other than such elements of glass not optically worked:		

Import Tariffs

No.	Descriptions	Min. (%)	Ord. (%)
	(A) For photographic cameras:		
	(1) For process cameras	9	14
	(2) Colour filters	60	80
	(3) Other	60	80
	(B) Cinematographic cameras or projectors	30	40
	(C) Other optical instruments	9	14
	(D) Other	40	50
90.03	Frames and mountings, and parts thereof, for spectacles, pince-nez, lorgnettes, goggles and the like	50	70
90.04	Spectacles, pince-nez, lorgnettes, goggles and the like corrective, protective or other	60	80
90.05	Refracting telescopes (monocular and binocular), prismatic or not	20	30
90.06	Astronomical instruments (e.g. reflecting telescopes, transit instruments and equatorial telescopes), and mountings therefor, but not including instruments for radio-astronomy	3	8
90.07	Photographic cameras; photgraphic flashlight apparatus and flashbulbs other than discharge lamps of No. 85.20:		
	(A) Cameras, for scientific or medical purposes only	12	17
	(B) Process cameras	15	20
	(C) Other cameras	80	100
	(D) Photographic flashlight apparatus and flashbulbs	60	80
90.08	Cinematographic cameras, projectors, sound recorders and sound reproducers; any combination of these articles	30	40
90.09	Image projectors (other than cinematographic projectors); photographic (except cinematographic) enlargers and reducers:		
	(A) Image projectors:		
	(1) Microfilm or microfiche readers	12	17
	(2) Other	30	40
	(B) Photographic enlarges and reducers	60	80
90.10	Apparatus and equipment of a kind used in photographic or cinematographic laboratories, not falling within any other heading in this Section; photo-copying apparatus (whether incorporating an optical system or of the contact type) and thermo-copying apparatus; screens for projectors:		

Import Tariffs

No.	Descriptions	Min. (%)	Ord. (%)
	(A) Apparatus and equipment of a kind used in photographic or cinematographic laboratories:		
	(1) For ordinary photographic use	60	80
	(2) For cinematographic use	30	40
	(3) Other	15	20
	(B) Photo-copying and thermo-copying apparatus	50	70
	(C) Screen for projectors	40	50
90.11	Microscopes and diffraction apparatus, electron and proton	9	14
90.12	Compound optical microscopes, whether or not provided with means for photographing or projecting the image	9	14
90.13	Optical appliances and instruments (but not including lighting appliances other than searchlights or spotlights), not falling within any other number of this Section, lasers other than laser diodes:		
	(A) Searchlights and spotlights	50	70
	(B) Hand magnifying glasses and ''door eyes''	40	50
	(C) Lasers	6	11
	(D) Other	12	17
90.14	Surveying (including photogrammetrical survey-ing), hydrographic, navigational meteorological, hydrological and geophysical instrument; compasses; rangefinders:		
	(A) Navigational instruments and compasses	3	8
	(B) Other	9	14
90.15	Balances of a sensitivity of 5 mg or better, with or without their weights:		
	(A) Of a sensitivity of 0.1 mg or better	12	17
	(B) Other	30	40
90.16	Drawing, marking-out and mathermatical, calculating instruments, drafting machines, pantographs, drawing sets, slide rules, disc calculators and the like; measuring or checking instruments, appliances and machines, not fall-ing within any other heading of this Section (e.g. micrometers, callipers, gauges, measuring rods, balancing machines); profile projectors:		
	(A) Drawing, marking-our and mathematical calculating instruments; slide rules, disc calculators; measuring rods	50	70
	(B) Other	15	20

Import Tariffs

No.	Descriptions	Min. (%)	Ord. (%)
90.17	Medical, dental, surgical and veterinary instruments and appliances (including electro-medical apparatus and ophthalmic instruments):		
	(A) Electo-medical apparatus	12	17
	(B) Dental instruments and appliances	12	17
	(C) Hypodermic needles and syringes of all kinds	40	50
	(D) Other	12	17
90.18	Mechano-therapy appliances; massage apparatus; psychological aptitude-testing apparatus; artificial respiration, ozone therapy, oxygen therapy, aerosol therapy or similar apparatus; breathing appliances (including gas masks and similar respirators):		
	(A) Massage apparatus	30	40
	(B) Other	20	30
90.19	Orthopaedic appliances, surgical belts, trusses and the like; splints and other fracture appliances; artificial limbs, eyes, teeth and other artificial parts of the body; hearing aids and other appliances which are worn or carried, or implanted in the body, to compensate for a defect or disability	12	17
90.20	Apparatus based on the use of X-rays or of the radiations from radio-active substances (including radiography and radiotherapy apparatus); X-ray generators; X-ray tubes; X-ray screens; X-ray high tension generators; X-ray control panels and desks; X-ray examination or treatment tables, chairs and the like	6	11
90.21	Instruments, apparatus or models, designed solely for demonstrational purposes (e.g. in education or exhibition), unsuitable for other uses:		
	(A) For educational use	NIL	NIL
	(B) Other	15	20
90.22	Machines and appliances for testing mechanically the hardness, strength, compressibility, elasticity and the like properties of industrial materials (e.g. metals, wood, textiles, paper or plastics)	15	20
90.23	Hydrometers and similar instruments; thermometers, pyrometers, barometers, hygrometers, psychrometers, recording or not; any combination of these instruments:		

No.	Descriptions	Min. (%)	Ord. (%)
	(A) Thermometers and pyrometers:		
	(1) Pyrometers, thermometers for industrial use	15	20
	(2) Clinical thermometers	30	40
	(3) Other	60	80
	(B) Hydrometers and similar instruments, barometers, hygrometers, psychrometers	20	30
	(C) Combinations	20	30
90.24	Instruments and apparatus for measuring checking or automatically controlling the flow, depth, pressure or other variables of liquids or gases, or for automatically controlling temperature, (e.g. pressure gauges, thermostals, level gauges, flow meters, heat meters, automatic oven-draught regulators), not being articles falling within No. 90.14	12	17
90.25	Instruments and apparatus for physical or chemical analysis (such as polarimeters, refractometers, spectrometers, gas analysis apparatus); instruments and apparatus for measuring or checking viscosity, porosity, expansion, surface tension or the like (such as viscometers, porosimeters, expansion meters); instruments and apparatus for measuring or checking quantities of heat, light or sound (such as photometers (including exposure meters), calorimeters); microtomes:		
	(A) Instruments and apparatus for physical or chemical analysis	12	17
	(B) Instruments and apparatus for measuring or checking viscosity, porosity, expansion, surface tension or the like	12	17
	(C) Instruments and apparatus for measuring or checking quantities of heat, light or sound:		
	(1) Exposure meters	50	70
	(2) Other	12	17
	(D) Microtoms	12	17
90.26	Gas, liquid and electricity supply or production meters; calibrating meters therefor;		
	(A) Gas, liquid and electricity supply or production meters:		
	(1) For household use	40	50
	(2) Other	20	30
	(B) Other	20	30

Import Tariffs

No.	Descriptions	Min. (%)	Ord. (%)
90.27	Revolution counters, production counters, taximeters, mileometers, pedometers and the like, speed indicators (including magnetic speed indicators) and tachometers (other than articles falling within No. 90.14); stroboscopes:		
	(A) Revolution counters	40	50
	(B) Taximeters, mileometers and speed indicators for vehicles	25	35
	(C) Other	12	17
90.28	Electrical measuring, checking analysing or automatically controlling instruments and apparatus:		
	(A) Electronic navigational instruments	3	8
	(B) Other electronic measuring, checking, analysing or automatically controlling instruments and apparatus	9	14
	(C) Other	9	14
90.29	Parts or accessories suitable for use solely or principally with one or more of the articles falling within No. 90.23, 90.24, 90.26, 90.27 or 90.28;		
	(A) Of electronic navigational instruments	3	8
	(B) Of gas meters, water meters and watt meters for houehold use	35	45
	(C) Other	12	17
91.	Clocks & Watches & Related Parts		
91.01	Pocket-watches, wrist-watches and other watches, including stop-watches	60	80
91.02	Clocks with watch movements (excluding clocks of No. 91.03	80	100
91.03	Instrument panel clocks and clocks of a similar type, for vehicles, aircraft or vessels	80	100
91.04	Other clocks:		
	(A) Astronomical and observatory clocks	3	8
	(B) Other	80	100
91.05	Time of day recording apparatus; apparatus with clock or watch movement (including secondary movement) or with synchronous motor, for measuring, recording or otherwise indicating intervals of time	40	50
91.06	Time switches with clock or watch movement (including secondary movement) or with synchronous motor	40	50
91.07	Watch movements (including stop-watch movements), assembled	60	80

Import Tariffs

No.	Descriptions	Min. (%)	Ord. (%)
91.08	Clock movements, assembled	80	100
91.09	Watch cases and parts of watch cases	60	80
91.10	Clock cases and cases of a similar type for other goods of this Section, and parts thereof:		
	(A) Clock cases and parts thereof	60	80
	(B) Other	40	50
91.11	Other clock and watch parts:		
	(A) Clock parts:		
	(1) Springs	40	50
	(2) Other	60	80
	(B) Watch parts:		
	(1) For electronic type	25	35
	(2) Other	40	50
92.	Musical Instruments; Sound Recorders or Reproducers; Television Image & Sound Recorders or Reproducers; Parts & Accessories of Such Articles		
92.01	Pianos (including automatic pianos, whether or not with keyboards); harpsichords and other keyboard stringed instruments; harps but not including aeolian harps	50	70
92.02	Other string musical instruments	50	70
92.03	Pipe and reed organs, including harmoniums and the like	60	80
92.04	Accordions, concertinas and similar musical instruments; mouth organs	60	80
92.05	Other wind musical instruments	50	70
92.06	Percussion musical instruments (e.g. drums, xylophones, cymbals, castanets)	50	70
92.07	Electro-magnetic, electrostatic, electronic and similar musical instruments (e.g. pianos, organs, accordions)	50	70
92.08	Musical instruments not falling within any other heading of this Section (e.g. fairground organs, mechanical street organs, musical boxes, musical saws); mechanical singing birds; decoy calls and effects of all kinds; mouth-blown sound signalling instruments (e.g. whistles and boatswains' pipes)	60	80
92.09/ 92.10	Parts and accessories of musical instruments, including perforated music rolls and mechanisms for musical boxes; metronomes, tuning forks and pitch pipes of all kinds	50	70
92.11	Gramophones, dictating machines and other sound recorders or reproducers, including		

Import Tariffs

No.	Descriptions	Min. (%)	Ord. (%)
	record players and tape decks, with or without sound-heads; television image and sound recorders or reproducers:		
	(A) Gramophones and record players	100	130
	(B) Dictating machines and other sound recorders or reproducers	60	80
	(C) Television image and sound recorders or reproducers	80	100
92.12	Gramophone records and other sound or similar recordings; matrices for the production of records, prepared record blanks, film for mechanical sound recording prepared tape, wires strips and like articles fo a kind commonly used for sound or similar recording:		
	(A) Recorded:		
	(1) Gramophone records, tapes and the likes for teaching languages	free	free
	(2) Other	50	70
	(B) For recording		
	(1) Prepared record blanks, film for mechanical sound recording	50	70
	(2) Magnetic tapes and discs for electronic calculating machines	15	20
	(3) Sound-recording tapes	50	70
	(4) Video tapes	50	70
	(5) Other	50	70
92.13	Other parts and accessories of apparatus falling within No. 92.11:		
	(A) Of gramophones and record players	100	130
	(B) Of television image and sound recorders or reproducers	60	80
	(C) Other	60	80

XIX. Arms & Ammunition & Related Parts

No.	Descriptions	Min. (%)	Ord. (%)
93.	Arms & Ammunition & Related Parts		
93.01	Side-arms (e.g. swords, cutlasses and bayonets) and parts thereof and scabbards and sheaths therefor	60	80
93.02	Revolvers and pistols, being firearms	60	80
93.03	Artillery weapons, machine-guns, sub-machine-guns and other military firearms and projectors (other than revolvers and pistols)	60	80
93.04	Other firearms, including Very pistols, pistols and revolvers for firing blank ammunition only, line-throwing guns and the like	60	80

Import Tariffs

No.	Descriptions	Min. (%)	Ord. (%)
93.05	Arms of other descriptions, including air, spring and similar pistols, rifles and guns	60	80
93.06	Parts of arms, including gun barrel blanks, but not including parts of side-arms	60	80
93.07	Bombs, grenades, torpedoes, mines, guided weapons and missiles and similar munitions of war, and parts thereof; ammunition and parts thereof, including cartridge wads; lead shot prepared for ammunition	60	80

XX. Miscellaneous Manufactured Articles

No.	Descriptions	Min. (%)	Ord. (%)
94.	Furniture and Parts Thereof; Bedding, Mattresses, Mattress Supports, Cushions and Similar Stuffed Furnishings		
94.01	Chairs and other seats (other than those falling within No. 94.02), whether or not convertible into beds, and parts thereof	80	100
94.02	Medical, dental, surgical or veterinary furniture (e.g. operating tables, hospital beds with mechanical fittings); dentists' and similar chairs with mechanical elevating, rotating, or reclining movements; parts of the foregoing articles:		
	(A) Chairs for hairdressers	80	100
	(B) Other	20	30
94.03	Other furniture and parts thereof:		
	(A) Filing systems and cabinets for office use, designed for placing on the floor or ground	60	80
	(B) Other	80	100
94.04	Mattress supports; articles of bedding or similar furnishing fitted with springs or stuffed or internally fitted with any material or of expanded, foam or sponge rubber or expanded, foam or sponge artificial plastic material, whether or not covered (e.g. mattresses, quilts, eiderdowns, cushions, pouffes and pillows):		
	(A) Mattress supports	80	100
	(B) Articles stuffed with down or animal hair	100	130
	(C) Articles stuffed with silk or man-made fibre wadding	100	130
	(D) Other	80	100

Import Tariffs

No.	Descriptions	Min. (%)	Ord. (%)
95.	Articles & Manufacturers of Carving or Moulding Material		
95.01-05	Worked tortoisr-shell, mother of pearl, ivory, bone, horn, coral (natural or agglomerated) and other animal carving material, and articles of those materials:		
	(A) Worked animal carving materials	60	80
	(B) Articles	100	130
95.06-08	Worked vegetable or mineral carving material and articles of those materials; moulded or carved articles of wax, of stearin, of natural gums or natural resins (e.g. copal or rosin) or of modelling pastes, and other moulded or carved articles not elsewhere specified or included; worked, unhardened gelatin (except gelatin falling within No. 35.03) and articles of unhardened gelain:		
	(A) Worked vegetable or mineral carving materials	60	80
	(B) Articles of vegetable or mineral carving materials	100	130
	(C) Worked, unhardened gelatin and articles of unhardened gelain:		
	(1) Capsules for pharmaceutical use	30	40
	(2) Other	70	90
	(D) Other	100	130
96.	Brooms, Brushes, Powder-Puffs & Sieves		
96.01	Brooms and brushes, consisting of twigs or other vegetable materials merely bound together and not mounted in a head (e.g. besoms and whisks), with or without handles; other brooms and brushes (including brushes of a kind used as parts of machines); prepared knots and tufts for broom or brush making; paint rollers; squeegees (other than roller squeegees) and mops:		
	(A) Broom and brushes, consisting of twigs or other vegetable materials merely bound together and not mounted in a head	80	100
	(B) Other broom and brushes; paint rollers, squeegees and mops:		
	(1) Writing brushes	80	100
	(2) Painting brushes	80	100

Import Tariffs

No.	Descriptions	Min. (%)	Ord. (%)
	(3) Brushes of a kind used as parts of machines	25	35
	(4) Brushes of metal wire	40	50
	(5) Brushes of bristles (other than tooth brushes)	80	100
	(6) Tooth brushes	80	100
	(7) Other	80	100
	(C) Prepared knots and tufts for broom and brush making	80	100
96.02/ 96.05	Powder-puffs and pads for applying cosmetics or toilet preparations, of any material	100	130
96.06	Hand sieves and hand riddles, of any material:		
	(A) Standard sieves	20	30
	(B) Other	80	100
97.	Toys, Games & Sports Requisites & Related Parts		
97.01	Wheeled toys designed to be ridden by children (e.g. toy bicycles and tricycles and pedal motor cars); dolls' prams and dolls' push chairs	60	80
97.02	Dolls	60	80
97.03	Other toys; working models of a kind used for recreational purposes	60	80
97.04	Equipment for parlour, table and funfair games for adults or children (including billiard tables and pintables and table-tennis requisites):		
	(A) Table-tennis requisites	40	50
	(B) Other	60	80
97.05	Carnival articles; entertainment articles (e.g. conjuring tricks and novelty jokes); Christmas tree decorations and similar articles for Christmas festivities (e.g. artificial Christmas trees, Christmas stockings, imitation yule logs, Nativity scenes and figures therefor)	80	100
97.06	Appliances, apparatus, accessories and requisites for gymnastics or athletics, or for sports and outdoor games (other than articles falling within No. 97.04)	40	50
97.07	Fish-hooks, line fishing rods and tackle; fish landing nets and butterfly nets; decoy "birds", lark mirrors and similar hunting or shooting requisites	60	80
97.08	Roundabouts, swings, shooting galleries and other fairground amusements, travelling circuses, travelling menageries and travelling theatres	80	100

Import Tariffs

No.	Descriptions	Min. (%)	Ord. (%)
98.	Miscellaneous Manufactured Articles		
98.01	Buttons and button moulds, studs, cuff-links, and press-fasteners, including snap-fasteners and press-studs; blanks and parts of such articles	80	100
98.02	Slide fasteners and parts thereof	60	80
98.03	Fountain pens, stylograph pens and pencils (including ball point pens and pencils) and other pens, pen-holders, pencil-holders and similar holders, propelling pencils and sliding pencils; parts and fittings thereof, other than those falling within No. 98.04 or 98.05:		
	(A) For use in machines	30	40
	(B) Other	60	80
98.04	Pen nibs and nib points:		
	(A) Pen nibs	50	70
	(B) Nib points	40	50
98.05	Pencils (other than pencils of No. 98.03), pencil leads, slate pencils, crayons and pastels, drawing charcoals, and writing and drawing chalks; tailors' and billiards chalks	60	80
98.06	Slates and boards, with writing or drawing surfaces, whether framed or not	60	80
98.07	Date, sealing or numbering stamps, and the like (including devices for printing or embossing labels), designed for operating in the hand; hand-operated composing sticks and hand printing sets incorporating such composing sticks	60	80
98.08	Typewriter and similar ribbons, whether or not on spools; ink-pads, with or without boxes:		
	(A) Ribbons	25	35
	(B) Ink-pads	80	100
98.09	Sealing wax (including bottle-sealing wax) in sticks, cakes or similar forms; copying pastes with a basis of gelatin, whether or not on a paper or textile backing	80	100
98.10	Mechanical lighters and similar lighters, including chemical and electrical lighters, and parts thereof, excluding flints and wicks	100	130
98.11	Smoking pipes; pipe bowls, stems and other parts of smoking pipes (including roughly shaped blocks of wood or root); cigar and cigarette holders and parts thereof	100	130
98.12	Combs, hair-slides and the like	100	1130

Import Tariffs

No.	Descriptions	Min. (%)	Ord. (%)
98.13/14	Scent and similar sprays of a kind used for toilet purposes, and mounts and heads therefor	100	130
98.15	Vacuum flasks and other vacuum vessels, complete with cases; parts thereof, other than glass inners	100	130
98.16	Tailors' dummies and other lay figures; automata and other animated displays of a kind used for shop window dressing:		
	(A) Lay figures for educational use	NIL	NIL
	(B) Other	60	80

XXI. Works of Art, Collectors' Pieces & Antiques

No.	Descriptions	Min. (%)	Ord. (%)
99.	Works of Art, Collectors Pieces & Antiques		
99.01	Paintings, drawings and pasteis, executed entirely by hand, (other than industrial drawings falling within No. 49.06 and other than hand-painted or hand-decorated manufactured articles):		
	(A) Portraits of revolutionary leaders and works imparting educational ideas for revolutionary reconstruction	NIL	NIL
	(B) Other	40	50
99.02	Original engravings, prints and lithographs:		
	(A) Portraits of revolutionary leaders and works imparting educational ideas for revolutionary reconstruction	NIL	NIL
	(B) Other	40	50
99.03	Original sculptures and statuary, in any material	40	50
99.04	Postage, revenue and similar stamps (including stamp-postmarks and franked envelopes, letter-cards and the like), used or if unused not of current or new issue in the country to which they are destined	40	50
99.05	Collections and collectors' pieces of zoological, botanical, mineralogical, anatomical, historical, archaeological, paleontological, ethnographic or numismatic interest	NIL	NIL
99.06	Antiques of an age exceeding one hundred years	NIL	NIL

Appendix

Rules for Foreign-Investment Enterprises Applying for Import and Export Licenses

(Issued on January 24, 1987 by the Ministry of foreign Economic Relations and Trade)

Article 1 : The said rules are formulated in accordance with the ''Regulations for the Implementation of Law of the People's Republic of China on Joint Ventures Using Chinese and Foreign Investment'' and the ''Provisions of the State Council for the Encouragement of Foreign Investment'' to simplify the procedures for application of import and export licences so as to facilitate the business operations of enterprises with foreign investment.

Article 2 : Foreign-investment enterprises shall apply for import licences for equipment and other materials, which are imported as investment of the foreign partners and require import licences, in accordance with the list of imported equipment and materials approved for the enterprise concerned. Chinese Customs shall examine the imported goods which do not require import licences in accordance with the approved list of imported equipment and materials.

Article 3 : Foreign-investment enterprises may import, without import licences, machinery and other equipment (including those requiring import licenses), vehicles to be used in production (trucks for transportation, special vehicles and vehicles for both passenger and cargo transport purposes), raw materials, fuel, spare parts, accessories and components which are needed in their export-oriented production, and the Customs shall supervise and examine them in accordance with the documents approved for the establishment of the enterprises, contracts or import-export contracts. The imported equipment and materials can only be used by the importers for production and cannot be sold or transferred in China. In special cases, if the imported raw materials and parts or the products manufactured with imported raw materials and parts are sold in China, the enterprises shall have to go through the same import formalities in accordance with Article 4 of the present Provisions.

Article 4: Foreign-investment enterprises may apply, within the scope of their approved business operation, for their import licences every six months in accordance with the approved import plan if import licences are required for equipment and vehicles for use in production, raw materials, fuel, spare parts, accessories and components these enterprises need to import for the purpose of producing goods for domestic sales and business transactions in the domestic market. The Customs shall examine the import of those items that are not under the import license plan in accordance with documents and contracts approved for the establishment of the enterprises.

Article 5: Import licences are to be issued by the provincial-level departments of foreign economic relations and trade for the imports of reasonable amounts of those non-production goods needed for the foreign-investment enterprises own use (if such imports require import licences).

Article 6: If export licences are required for exporting those products the foreign-investment enterprises produce, the enterprises shall apply for export licences every six months in accordance with their approved annual export plan.

Article 7: If foreign-investment enterprises export the products they produce and the exports do not need export licences, the Customs shall examine them in accordance with signed export contracts and other relevant documents.

Article 8: If foreign-investment enterprises export products, which are not produced by themselves, in order to solve their foreign-exchange balancing problem, export licences will be issued in accordance with approved documents (if their products are under the export licence plan). The Customs will examine the products, (if the products are not under the export licence plan), only in accordance with signed export contracts.

Article 9: Enterprises with foreign investment may apply for import and export licences with the relevant authorities in charge of the issuing of licences in accordance with the licence categories announced by the Ministry of Foreign Economic Relations and Trade.

Article 10: The said rules come into force on the day of promulgation.

SECTION B: Travel & Mailing

Rules Governing The Levying of Import Duties on Articles of Passengers' Baggage & Personal Postal Parcels

(Issued on June 16, 1978.)

Article 1:   These rules have been drawn up with a view to implementing the policy of State control of foreign trade, protecting the country's socialist economy, and simplifying the procedures for the collection of Customs duties so as to facilitate regular traffic.

Article 2:   Import duties on dutiable articles carried by inbound passengers, imported by means of personal parcels, carried by crew members of inbound means of conveyance for personal use or imported by any other means for personal use (all hereunder referred to as "imported articles") are to be levied by Customs according to these rules.

The import duties referred to in these rules include both Customs duties and the industrial and commercial consolidated taxes.

Article 3:   The schedule of import duty rates is as follows:

Tariff No	Descriptions of Articles	Rate of Import Duty
1.	Cereals, cereal flours	20%
2.	Medical equipment, scientific instruments and electronic computers	20%
3.	Pharmaceutical products and preparations, medicinal and aromatic substances of animal or vegetable origin	50%
4.	Office or household machines, recorders, cutting tools, hand tools, hand farm implements, and parts or accessories thereof	50%
	Television sets and parts or accessories thereof	50%
	Sports equipment, musical instruments	50%
5.	Foodstuffs and beverages	100%
6.	Deer antlers, musk, ginseng	100%
7.	Cotton cloth, linen, clothing and other articles for personal wear made of cotton or linen, cotton or linen fabrics and other cotton products	100%
8.	Radio sets, record-players and parts or accessories thereof	100%
	Bicycles and other vehicles, and parts or accessories thereof	100%
9.	Fabrics of woollen, silk, artificial and synthetic fibres and clothing and other articles for personal wear made thereof, clothing and articles for personal wear made of other materials (such as leather, fur, plastics etc.)	150%
	Cameras, photographic supplies or materials, video recorders, and parts or accessories thereof	150%
10.	Birds' nests, sharks' fins, bechede-mer, awabi, compoy, fish maws, fish lips	200%
	Tobacco and products thereof, wine and spirits	200%
	Cosmetics and perfumes	200%
11.	Wrist-watches, pocket-watches and parts or accessories thereof	200%
12.	Duty-free articles: 1. Books, newspapers, periodicals, educational films and latern-slides, and language records which are allowed to be imported; 2. Contraceptive devices and medications; 3. Gold and silver, and articles made thereof.	
13.	Articles not otherwise provided for in the above tariff numbers	100%

Article 4: Articles not enumerated in the above schedule shall be classified by Customs under the most appropriate tariff number.

Import duty on an article is to be levied at the tariff rate in force on the date of issue of the Customs Duty Memorandum.

Article 5: Imported articles are liable to advalorem duties. An article's duty-paying value shall be assessed by Customs on the basis of its c.i.f. value. If the c.i.f. value cannot be ascertained, the duty-paying value shall be assessed by Customs in light of domestic prices.

Article 6: Should a duty-payer be dissatisfied with the tariff classification and/or the duty-paying values of the imported articles as determined by Customs, he shall first pay the import duty in full and then file an appeal in writing with Customs within 14 days of the date on which the duty is paid. On receipt of the written appeal, Customs shall reconsider the case within seven days. If the original decision is maintained, Customs shall, within 14 days of the date of receipt of the original appeal, transmit the appeal, together with its comments, to the Customs Administration of the People's Republic of China for consideration. If the original decision is modified, the duty-payer is to be duly notified and the duty adjusted accordingly. Should the duty-payer still be dissatisfied with the modified decision, he may file another appeal within seven days of the date of receipt of the notification of the modified decision. Customs shall, within seven days of the date of receipt of the second appeal, forward the case to the Customs Administration of the People's Republic of China for consideration. The decision of the Customs Administration of the People's Republic of China shall be final.

Article 7: After apprvoal by the State Council, these rules shall be promulgated and put into force by Ministry of Foreign Trade.

Provisional Customs Regulations for Inward and Outward Baggage of Overseas Chinese and Other Passengers

*(Promulgated by the Ministry of
Foreign Trade on March 23, 1978)*

(1)   To effectively implement foreign trade control policy as well as serve the needs of those passengers having relatives in China or abroad, viz. overseas Chinese, foreigners of Chinese origin, permanent alien residents in China and Chinese nationals on visits to relatives abroad, Customs shall deal with their inward and outward baggage according to the present regulation, subject to the "Rules for Customs Supervision and Control over Inward and Outward Passengers' Baggage."

Table of Import/Export Limits for Duty-free or Dutiable Articles

Category	Item	Import Limit	Export Limit
	1. Overcoats	3	3
	2. Underwear	20 pcs.	20 pcs.
	3. Other clothes	20 pcs.	20 pcs.
	4. Bedding	1 pc. of each kind	1 pc. of each kind
	5. Woollen yarn and manufactures made thereof	4 kg.	4 kg.
	6. Scarves	6 pcs.	6 pcs.
	7. Shoes/Socks	12 prs. for each	12 prs. for each
	8. Dress material	30 m. (single width)	15 m. (single width)
Duty-free	Woollen piece goods	5 m. (double width)	—
	9. Foodstuffs*	50 kg	25 kg
	10. Cigarettes	600	600
	11. Wine/spirits	4 bottles	4 bottles
	12. Pharmaceutical products	50 yuan	25 yuan
	13. Ginseng/deer antlers	50 g.	50 g.
	14. Daily necessities	100 yuan	50 yuan
	15. Watches	1	
	16. Bicycles	1	
	17. Radios**	1	any 2 of
	18. Sewing machines	1	these 6 items
	19. Electric fans	1	
	20. Pocket calculators	1	
	1. Watches	1	
	2. Recorders (including combinations)	1	
Dutiable	3. TV sets	1	
	4. Cameras	1	
	5. Musical instruments (accordions or violins)	1	
	6. Ginseng/deer antlers	150 g.	

* Luxuries are dutiable   ** Without recording facility

(2)   Baggage carried by the above-mentioned passengers, if within the prescribed limit set on the attached table, shall be released on entry or departure either free of duty or on payment of duty. In case the imported articles listed as items Nos. 1 to 14 of the table exceed the import duty-free limit, they may still be released on payment of duty, provided they are in reasonable quantities for personal use and their total value does not exceed 200 yuan.

Articles exceeding duty-free and dutiable limits shall be returned abroad or to places in China as the case may be, except watches, radios, cameras and other items necessary for the journey, which shall be registered with Customs and taken out of or brought back to China by the passengers at the time of exit or entry.

The provisions of this Article also apply to baggage carried by the accompanying spouse and children of passengers. For children under 16 years of age, not half of the quantities specified under items Nos. 1 to 14 shall be duty-free. For children between the ages of 12 and 15, one watch per person may also be released duty free.

(3)   The above-mentioned passengers shall be subject to the Customs Rules for Short-term Visitors from the second time of entry of departure if they enter or leave China more than once within a year.

(4)   The limits prescribed in the table attached to the present regulation do not apply to baggage carried by the above-mentioned passengers who are coming to China or going abroad for resettlement. Their baggage may be released free of duty on entry or departure provided it is in reasonable quantities for personal use.

(5)   New handicrafts bought at state-owned shops, cultural relics (ascertained by the authorities in charge of cultural relics as permissible for export), old handicrafts, jewelry, gold and silver ornaments, etc., bought at Friendship Stores or Relics Stores by overseas Chinese or foreigners of Chinese origin with Renminbi obtained by the exchanging of foreign currencies, shall be presented on departure to Customs together with the relevant invoices and foreign exchange certificates, on the strength of which Customs shall release the articles concerned.

(6)   The present regulation came into force on April 5, 1978.

Regulations For Customs Control Over Baggage of Passengers Coming From or Going To Hong Kong and Macao

(Promulgated by the Ministry of Foreign Trade on July 1, 1979)

Article 1: Baggage carried by passengers coming from or going to Hong Kong and Macao (hereinafter referred to as "passengers"), if in reasonable quantities for personal use and within the limit specified in the "Table of Duty-free and Dutiable Articles Carried by Passengers" (see Appendix 1), shall be released either free of duty or on payment of duty after Customs inspection.

Table of Limites for Duty-free and Dutiable Articles Carried by Passengers

Category	Item	Import Limite	Export Limit
Duty-free	Total weight in which:	30 kg.	30 kg.
	1. Clothes of all kinds	35 pcs. (in reasonable quantities)	Total value not exceeding 15 yuan for traditional Chinese medicines, in which the total weight of Chinese medicinal herbs shall not exceed 1 kg.; each kind of medicine 250g.; Yunnanbaiyao 12 g.
	2. Shoes/socks/scarves	10 prs./pcs. of	
	3. Bedding	each 1 pc. or pr. of each kind, but 3 pcs. or prs. in all	
	4. Dress material (single width)	10 m.	
	5. Foodstuffs	15 kg.	
	6. Wine and spirits (including medicated wine)	2 bottles (not exceeding 750 g. each)	
	7. Cigarettes	400 pcs.	
	8. Therapeutic medicines and home remedies	in reasonable quantities for personal use only	
	9. Daily necessities	RMB20 yuan (in reasonable quantities for each kind)	
Dutiable	1. Pocket calculators	1 pc.	
	2. Watches, radios, TV sets, recorders (including combinations), cameras, electric fans, bicycles, sewing machines, and accessories thereof	1 pc. per person a year with a readonable quantity of accessories.	
	3. Ginseng/Deer antlers	100 g. of each	
Remarks	1. For children under 16 years of age, only articles necessary for personal use shall be release free of duty. 2. Furniture or unsanitary old clothes shall not be allowed to be brought into China. 3. Musks, toad cake, cinnabar, eucommia, gastrodia elata, Chinese caterpillar fungus, Pianzihuang, Angongnuihuang pills, Liushen pills and unappraised cultural relics shall not be allowed to be taken out of China. 4. Articles bought with Renminbi obtained through the exchanging of foreign currencies may be taken out on the strength of the relevant commercial invoices.		

Article 2: Inward passengers carrying baggage which is within the import duty-free limit as specified in the attached table may pass through "Green Channel" where it is so provided by Customs. Should articles carried by such a "Green Channel" passenger be found exceeding the import duty-free limit, which is deemed a violation of Customs regulations, Customs shall inflict on the offender a fine not greater than 500 yuan according to the nature of the case. In addition the articles exceeding the import duty-free limit shall be returned to Hong Kong or Macao. Should dutiable articles be found in such a case, it shall be deemed an act of smuggling and dealt with accordingly.

Article 3: Inward passengers carrying articles which are dutiable and/or over the import duty-free limit as specified in the table shall pass through "Red Channel," where it is so provided by Customs, and declare their articles to Customs, who shall release the articles after inspection according to the present regulation.

Article 4: Baggage carried by outward passengers may be released at the time of exit provided it does not exceed the limit as specified in the attached table.

Article 5: For passengers who will return within 24 hours, only items necessary for their personal use on the journey shall be released.

Article 6: For passengers coming in or going out for resettlement in China or Hongkong or Macao, Customs shall, on the strength of the relevant papers, deal with their baggage according to the provisions of the "Rules for Customs Supervision and Control over Inward and Outward Passengers' Baggage."

Article 7: Articles carried by outward passengers, if found to be in excess of the prescribed export limit, shall not be permitted to be taken out whereas articles carried by inward passengers, if found to be in excess of the prescribed import limit, shall be detained articles may be reclaimed and returned to Hong Kong or Macao within a month. On expiration of the time limit, the Customs shall dispose of the articles and remit to the national treasury the proceeds, realized from their disposal. However, passengers may make a request to bring along articles necessary for the journey guaranteeing the re-importation or re-exportation of such articles. With Customs approval and registration, such articles shall be released but must be brought back to or taken out of China at the time of re-entry or exit.

Article 8: Passengers shall be forbidden to bring into or take out of China certain prohibited articles (see Appendix 2). However, jewelry and gold and silver ornaments brought in by passengers at the time of entry and registered with Customs may be taken out at the time of exit.

Article 9: Selling for profit the articles released by Customs for inward passengers' personal use shall be strictly forbidden.

Article 10: Offenders of the present regulation shall be dealt with according to the relevant provisions of the regulations.

Appendix

List of Prohibited Import/Export Articles of the People's Republic of China

Prohibited Import Articles

(1)   Arms, ammunition and explosives of all kinds;

(2)   Radio transmitter-receivers and principal parts;

(3)   Renminbi;

(4)   manuscripts, printed matter, films, photographs, phonograph records, cinematographic films, loaded recording tapes and video-tapes, etc. detrimental to Chinese political, economic, cultural and moral interests;

(5)   Deadly poison, addictive narcotics, opium, morphia, heroin, etc;

(6)   Animals, plants, and products thereof infected with or carrying harmful germs and insect pests;

(7)   Unsanitary foodstuffs and germ-carrying food-stuffs from infected areas;

(8)   Other articles the importation of which is prohibited by national regulations.

Prohibited Export Articles

(1)   Arms, ammunition and explosives of all kinds;

(2)   Radio transmitter-receivers and principal parts;

(3)   Renminbi and securities in Renminbi;

(4)   Foreign currencies, bills and securities in foreign currencies (with the exception of those allowed to be taken out);

(5)   Manuscripts, printed matter, films, photographs, phonograph records, cinematographic films, loaded recording tapes and video-tapes, etc. which contain state secrets or otherwise not permissible for export;

(6)   Valuable cultural relics and rare books relating to China's revolution, Chinese history, culture and art;

(7)   Rare animals, rare plants and their seeds;

(8)   Precious metals and articles made thereof, jewelry and ornaments made thereof (with the exception of those within the quantity allowed to be taken out by outward passengers);

(9)   Other articles the exportation of which is prohibited by national regulations.

Forms & Documentation

China Customs
Passengers' Baggages Declaration Form

1.   arms, ammunition, narcotics, deadly poison, radio transmitters and receivers, plants and their seeds should be given to the customs for handling according to the provisions.

2.   Gifts, samples brought into China should be filled in the blanks on declaration form.

3.   Except for the remaining amount of foreign exchange brought into China by the traveller, any foreign exchange brought out from China should have the Bank of China's permit for checking.

4.   Baggages declared by the travellers if a label " △ " added by the customs, should be re-brought out from the country's border.

5.   This form will be given back to the traveller after chopped by the customs. This form has to be returned to the customs at traveller's return journey. Lose or alternation of this form will be handled with reference to the provisions prohibiting any acts against the rules.

Name _____

Nationality _____

From/To _____

Hand baggage _____ piece;
baggage by consigned shipment _____ piece.

Baggage shipped separately _____, will be shipped from/to _____.

Items	Quantity		
Watch			
Camera			
Movie Camera			
Television Set			
Tape recorder (including multi-purpose set)			

Items	Import declaration	Export declaration
Valuable oraments		
Cultural Relics		

Signature: _____   Date _____

The Customs' notes:

SECTION C: Shipping

Provisional Procedures for Vessel Tonnage Duties

(Promulgated and enforced by the General Customs Office on September 29, 1952)

Article 1:   Vessel tonnage duties (hereinafter simply referred to as tonnages) shall be levied by the Customs in accordance with these Procedures on foreign registered vessels and Chinese registered vessels chartered by foreign firms and Chinese or foreign registered vessels used by Chinese-foreign joint ventures (including vessels exclusively sailing within the ports) sailing in the ports of the People's Republic of China.

It is not necessary for the said vessels paying tonnages to pay additional vehicle and vessel service licence fees to the tax authorities.

Article 2:   Tonnages are divided into two types: one to be paid once every three months and the other to be paid once every 30 days, which shall be chosen by the payers themselves when they apply for the payment of the tonnages. The scale and rate of the tonnages are as follows:

(1)   Those to be paid once every three months:

Category of Vessel		Ton			Tonnage per Ton		Remarks
Power- Driven Vessel	Steamships Motorboats Tugboats	below 50 tons			3 jiao		Tonnages to be calculated and levied by net weight. The odd amount less than ½ ton is exempted from taxation; ½ ton or more than ½ ton is considered as 1 ton. Small vessels less than 1 ton shall be taxed as 1 ton except for those authorized by the Genera Customs Office to be exempted from taxation.
		51 tons to	150 tons		3 jiao 5 fen		
		151 tons to	300 tons		4 jiao		
		301 tons to	500 tons		4 jiao 5 fen		
		501 tons to 1,000 tons			6 jiao		
		1,001 tons to 1,500 tons			7 jiao 5 fen		
		1,501 tons to 2,000 tons			9 jiao		
		2,001 tons to 3,000 tons			1 yuan 1 jiao		
		3,001 tons to 4,000 tons			1 yuan 3 jiao		
		4,001 tons to 5,000 tons			1 yuan 5 jiao		
		more than 5,001 tons			1 yuan 8 jiao		
Non- powered Driver Vessels	Various Man-driven Boats, Lighters and Junks	below 10 tons			1 jiao 5 fen		
		11 tons to	50 tons		2 jiao		
		51 tons to	150 tons		2 jiao 5 fen		
		151 tons to	300 tons		3 jiao		
		more than 301 tons			3 jiao 5 fen		

(2)   Those to be paid once every 30 days shall be levied by half of the rates in the above list.

The tonnage shall be levied on an incoming vessel as from the date of its declaration for import. If the vessel does not leave China at the expiration of the tonnage licence obtained, the levy shall be continued as from the second day of the expiration.

Article 3:   The Tonnage for a vessel which is registered in or belong to a foreign country which has entered into treaty or agreement with the People's Republic of China for mutual preferential treatment in tonnages or fees levied on vessels shall be levied at a preferential rate. The rates of tonnages to be levied once every three months are as follows: (Note: This article has been amended according to Notice No. MGH-221(74) of the Ministry of Foreign Trade.)

Category of Vessel		Ton		Tonnage per Ton	Remarks
		below 50 tons		3 jiao	The procedures for
		51 tons to	150 tons	3 jiao 5 fen	calculation and
		151 tons to	300 tons	4 jiao	levy are the same
		301 tons to	500 tons	4 jiao 5 fen	as in the preceding
Power-	Steamships	501 tons to	1,000 tons	5 jiao 5 fen	list.
Driven	Motorboats	1,001 tons to	1,500 tons	6 jiao 5 fen	
Vessel	Tugboats	1,501 tons to	2,000 tons	8 jiao	
		2,001 tons to	3,000 tons	9 jiao 5 fen	
		more than 3,001 tons		1 yuan 1 jiao	
	Various	below 10 tons		1 jiao 5 fen	
Non-	Man-driven	11 tons to	50 tons	2 jiao	
powered	Boats,	51 tons to	150 tons	2 jiao 5 fen	
Driver	Lighters	151 tons to	300 tons	3 jiao	
Vessels	and Junks	more than 301 tons		3 jiao 5 fen	

If a vessel paying the tonnage as stipulated by this article applies for the payment once every 30 days in accordance with the procedures in the preceding article, the tonnage shall be levied at half of the rates of the above list.

Article 4: A foreign registered vessel or a Chinese registered vessel chartered by a foreign firm shall submit the vessel tonnage licence and the declaration at the Customs house for examination and import or clearance purposes as stipulated by the Customs when it arrives at or leaves a port with a Customs house. If the original licence has expired at the time of import of the tonnage has not been paid before, it shall file a declaration at the time of import, make the declaration at the Customss house and pay the tonnage by submitting (1) the certificate of the vessel's registry (or the testimonial signed and issued by the port authorities to testify that this certifiate has been kept in their custody) and (2) the proof of the vessel's tonnage for examination.

Article 5: If the term of validity of the tonnage licence of the above vessel is expired after its declaration for import or if it sails exclusively within the port, it shall make a declaration at the Customs house, pay the tonnage and obtain a new licence as stipulated in the preceding article at the expiration of the original licence. If it fails to make a declaration and pay the tonnage within five days of the second day of the expiration, it shall be fined as stipulated in Article 14 of these Procedures.

Article 6: A foreign registered vessel specially permitted to sail to or from a place with no Customs house shall submit the vessel tonnage licence to the local port authorities for examination (it shall be submitted to the local frontier public security authorities or troops for examination in a place without port authorities) as stipulated in Article 4 of these Procedures when it arrives at or leaves the port. At the expiration of the original licence, it shall also make a declaration at the local tax bureau as stipulated in Article 4 and Article 5 of these Procedures and the bureau shall collect the tonnage and issue a new licence in lieu of the Customs according to these Procedures. If it fails to make a declaration within the time limit, it shall be fined in accordance with Article 14.

Article 7: The payer shall pay the tonnage within five days (Sunday and the statutory holidays excepted) from the second day of the issue of the Notice of Tonnage Payment by the Customs house (or the tax bureau) and the Customs house (or the bureau) shall issue the vessel tonnage licence. If the time limit is exceeded, the Customs house (or bureau) shall collect the fine for late payment of 1/1000 of the payable tonnage amount daily from the sixth day to the date of the full payment of the tonnage and pay it into the treasury as the Customs' fines.

Article 8: In the case of a Chinese registered vessel chartered by a foreign firm or a foreign registered vessel chartered by a Chinese public or private enterprise, the vehicle and vessel service licence tax or the vessel tonnage already paid shall remain valid if it has not expired at the beginning or termination of the charter. However, the vessel shall make a declaration at the Customs house and pay the tonnage or make the declaration at the tax bureau and pay the vehicle and vessel service licence tax upon its expiration on the basis of its usage at that time.

Article 9: The tonnage amount shall not be readjusted within the term of validity of the tonnage licence already obtained even if the net weight of a vessel is increased or reduced due to repair. However, at the time of the next payment of tonnage, an application shall be made for the adjustment of the tonnage amount on the basis of the certificate of tonnage after the change of its weight. If the increase of weight is not disclosed and declared with intention of evading tonnage payment, the vessel shall be fined as stipulated in Article 14 of these Procedures.

Article 10: If a vessel which has paid tonnage is in any of the following cases, the Customs shall annotate and comment on the extension of the term of the licence validity according to the actual number of days after examining the papers of the port authorities submitted:

(1) A vessel sailing into a port of our country for the purpose of refuge or repair;

(2) A vessel unable to handle goods or passengers as a result of an epidemic prevention isolation;

(3) A vessel having been commandeered or chartered by the central or a local people's government.

Article 11: The following foreign registered vessels shall be exempt from tonnages:

(1) The vessels engaged by the embassies, legations and consulates of the countries having established diplomatic relations with our country;

(2) The vessels with the papers of local port authorities to take refuge, undergo repairs, suspend service or be disassembled and not to carry goods or passengers for the time being;

(3) The mooring pontoons, floating-bridge pontoons and floating

ative Council on November 11, 1954 and were notified to become effective by the General Customs Office of the Ministry of Foreign Trade on November 30 of the same year

Provisional Customs Procedures for the Collection of Fees

(Issued on May 1, 1981)

Article 1:   These Procedures are formulated in the light of current conditions and in accordance with the provisions in Article 21 of the Provisional Law of the People's Republic of China on Customs in order to meet the needs of the development of foreign economic and trade relations and tourism, facilitate the enterprises or personnel concerned to go through Customs Formalities, and strengthen the Customs' supervision.

Article 2:   The Customs shall delineate the areas under its supervision according to the actual conditions of import or export of goods, the volume of travellers' luggage, postal matter and means of transport at the ports, stations, international airports, border passes and international postal matter exchange offices (or stations) where it is located. No fees shall be collected for the duties carried out within the supervised areas of the Customs.

Article 3:   When an enterprise, unit or person concerned requests Customs officers to handle Customs formalities and carry out supervision duties outside the supervised areas, a prior application shall be made to the Customshouse concerned for approval and fees paid in accordance with the following provisions:
(1)   Renminbi 10 yuan shall be paid for each officer for each working day. A working day shall be eight hours; less than four hours are calculated as half a working day, while the required time between for and eight hours is counted as one working day.

(2)   The fees shall be doubled on festivals and holidays stipulated by the state.

On duty outside the supervised areas, the applicants shall supply means of transport to and from the working area, board and lodging and pay all the expenses in volved.

Article 4:   Receipts shall be given by the Customs upon payment of the fees.

Article 5:   All fees collected by the Customs are regarded as central revenue and shall be paid into the state treasury under the heading of "Income of Fees" in accordance with relevant provisions.

Article 6:   These Procedures shall be put into effect as of May 1, 1981.

Procedures Of The Customs For The Supervision Of International Sailing Vessels And Goods On Board

*(Promulgated by the Ministry of Communications and
the Ministry of Foreign Trade on December 31, 1958)*

Chapter 1   General Rules

Article 1:   These Procedures are formulated for the purpose of ensuring the effective implementation of the foreign trade control system and facilitating the transportation of international sailing vessels (hereinafter simply referred to as "ships(s)").

Article 2:   With the exception of those specially permitted by the Ministry of Communications jointly with the Ministry of Foreign Trade, ships shall only be permitted to berth and carry goods and passengers in the ports provided with Customes houses.

Article 3:   The port authorities shall notify the Customs in advance of the time of arrival and departure of ships.

Article 4:   The port authorities shall designate jointly with the Customs the places for ships to berth and carry goods and passengers in the ports. The port authorities shall obtain the Customs' consent of ships' changes of berths in the ports.

Article 5:   Ships shall be put under the supervison of the Customs from their arrival in the ports till their departure from the ports. The Customs shall be entitled to examine them if it deems necessary to do so.
During the stay of a ship in a port, the ship shall be allowed to leave the port first if it is required by force majeure to do so temporarily and it is not possible to obtain the approval of the Customs; however, the captain shall report the cause and situation of the departure from the port upon returing to the port.

Article 6:   If a ship is to carry goods, travellers' luggage, international mailbags and other articles, these jobs shall have the prior approval of the Customs and shall be done under the supervison of the Cusoms.

Chapter II   The Customs Declaration, Examination and Clearance Of Ships

Article 7:   When a ship enters a port, the caption shall submit to the Customs a ship's import manifest (the form omitted) and the following documents:
(1)   An import loading list;
(2)   An incoming passenger list (including through transport travellers, but no submission is required if there are no passengers);
(3)   A list (the form omitted) of the articles, currencies, gold and silver for the crew's personal use and as the ship's spares;
(4)   A crew list;
(5)   Other documents and papers required by the Customs.
If a ship calls at two or more ports of our country in succession on the same voyage, with the exception of its arrival at the first port, it shall be exempted from submitting the ship's import manifest and the document listed in the above item (3) when it arrives at the other ports. (Note: This article has been amended in accordance with Notice No. GH-Hu-73(59) of the Ministry of Foreign Trade.)

Article 8:   When a ship applies for export or sails to other ports of our country, the captain shall submit the following documents to the Customs:
(1)   An export loading list;
(2)   An outgoing passenger list (no submission is required if there are no outgoing passengers);
(3)   A crew list (exempt from submission if there are no changes);
(4)   A list of Renminbi balance after use (see Article 18 of these Procedures);
(5)   Other documets and papers required by the Customs.

Article 9:   When a ship calls at two or more ports of our country in succession on the same voyage, the captain shall be responsible for carrying the Customs envelope given to him by the first Customs house intact to the Customs house in the next port. A ship shall not be allowed to sail to any foreign country on its voyage between the ports of our country.

Article 10:   The crew shall not be allowed to leave the ship without the permit of the Customs between its arrival the port and the completion of the Customs' examination of the ship and the crew's luggage and articles. When a seaman carries his personal articles, currencies, gold and silver aboard the ship or on shore, he shall declare them at the Customs house and the Customs shall examine and clear them.

Article 11:   When the Customs examines a ship, the captain shall dispatch personnel to be present and open the rooms, cabins and storage places on board as required by the Customs. The captain shall act upon the request as soon as the Customs thinks it necessary to open up the parts of the ship, which may be used to conceal smuggled goods.
When the Custom examines the crew's luggage and articles, the seamen concerned shall be present at the time as required by the Customs and open the luggage, packages and storage places.

When the Customs finishes examining the ship, the captain shall sign on the examination record prepared by the Customs.

Article 12:   With the exception of the personnel engaged in examination and piloting, others shall not be allowed to go on board ships without the permit of the Customs before the completion of the Customs' examination of arriving ships and after the completion of the Customs' examination of leaving ships.

Article 13:   The port authorities shall only permit a leaving ship or go out of the port after it has been cleared by the Customs.

Chapter III   The Supervision of Ship's Fuel, Materials, Currencies, Gold and Silver

Article 14:   During a ship's stay in a port, the ship's materials and the currencies, gold and silver in the possession of the ship and its crew shall be sealed if the Customs thinks it necessary to do so; the captain shall be responsible for keeping the Customs sealing marks intact.

Article 15:   If a ship is to replenish fuel or materials, the captain or his agent shall prepare and submit a list to the Customs (an oral declaration shall be made for the replenishment of catering materials) for the Customs' verification and clearance.

Article 16:   If an application is made for the mutual allotment and transfer of ship's fuel or materials between foreign ships or between foreign international sailing ships of Chinese registry, the captains or their agents shall prepare a list, submit it to the Customs for approval and carry out the allotment and transfer under the supervision of the Customs.
(Note: This article has been amended in accordance with Notice No. GH-Lin-463(63) of the Ministry of Foreign Trade.)

Article 17:   The captain or his agent shall submit a "list of borrowed Renminbi" to the Customs for any Renminbi borrowed by the ship when he carries the Renminbi aboard the ship.
If the ship or its crew exchange foreign currencies or gold or silver for Renminbi, a clear declaration shall be made at the Customs and the exchange memos from the bank shall be submitted for examination.

Article 18:   Before a ship sails out of port or to another port of our country, the captain shall prepare a "list of the Renminbi balance after use" and submit it to the Customs for verification (exempt from submission if there is no Renminbi borrowed or exchanged for).
If the ship sails directly to a port of a foreign country, the surplus Renminbi shall be handed over by the ship to its agent under the supervision of the Customs and he is prohibited from taking it abroad; if the ship sails to another port of our country, the surplus Renminbi shall be kept in the custody of the captain himself or the seamen themselvs.

Article 19:   [Omitted]
If a ship replenishes fuel or materials in our country, the Customs house at the place of exit shall make an examination according to the ship's record if necessary.
If an outgoing ship has to carry Renminbi, and intends to use the

same in the ports along the coasts of our country, it shall declare it at the Customs, while the Customs house shall seal th Renminbi and give it to the captain who shall be responsible for having the custody of the money. At the next time of import the money shall be declared at the Customs house in the place of entry for verification.

The provisions in Articles 14, 15, 16, 17 and 18 of these Procedures shall not apply to the ships of Chinese registry.

Chapter IV The Customs Declaration, Examination and Clearance of Goods

Article 20: The owner of import goods or his agents shall submit the import licence together with the bill of lading and invoice(s) the the Customs when orbefore they arrive in the port.

The owner or agents of export goods shall submit the export licence together with the shipping order to the Customs before the exports are loaded on board a ship.

For the import or export goods to undergo commodity inspection as stipulated by the law, the papers shall be submitted for examination in accordance with the relevant provisions of the commodity inspection authorities.

If there is a discrepancy with respect to exports, the shipper or his agent shall make a report to the Customs within the time fixed by the Customs.

Article 21: Import and export goods shall be examined by the Customs. When the Customs examines the goods, their owner or his agent shall be present at the time fixed by the Customs and handle such jobs as moving, measuring, opening and repacking as required by the Customs.

Article 22: When a ship handles goods, each lot of them shall be clearly differentiated in accordance with the shipping order or the bill of lading and the number of packages shall be correctly counted.

The Customs shall be entitled to verify the tally records of the ship and the port authorities at any time. If confusion of goods is found or the number of goods is not correct, the ship and the port authorities shall promptly check and correct the records as required by Customs.

Article 23: Upon completion of a ship's handling of goods, the prot authorities shall submit to the Customs a copy of th goods hand-over and take-over cetificate prepared by them and the ship; if there is surplus, shortage or damage of the goods, a copy of relevant record prepared shall be submitted to the Customs.

Article 24: The import or export goods under the supervision of the Customs shall be stored in the storage places agreed to by the Customs.

Article 25: The port authorities, goods owner (or his agent) and shall only deliver, take delivery of or ship the export or import goods after they are cleared by the Customs and a seal is impressed on the bill of lading or the shipping order.

Chapter V   The Supervision of Ship's Padding and Ballast

Article 26:   If a ship is to unload padding and ballast (excluding those including those included in the import loading list), the captain or his agent shall make a list and submit it to the Customs for approval. The padding and ballast declared to be re-exported later shall be transported abroad within six months of the date of unloading and the Customs shall check and clear them on the basis of the list declared at the time of import; with regard to the padding and ballast not to be re-exported, the consignee shall go through import formalities within two months of the date of unloading. Those which are not re-exported or which go through import formalities after the time limited is exceeded shall be sold by the Customs and all the proceeds shall be paid into the state treasury after the deduction of transport, custody and other expenses.

In respect of the padding, ballast and footing declared by the captain for disposal, the captain or his agent or the take-over unit shall make an oral declaration at Customs and the take-over unit shall dispose of them with the consent of the Customs.

Article 27:   If a ship is to replenish padding and ballast, the captain or his agent shall make a list and submit it to the Customs for approval. Another list shall be prepared for the padding and ballast required to be re-imported and returned by the Customs after signing and certification.

The above padding and ballast to be reimported shall be re-transported in within one year of the date of the Customs' signing and certification and the Customs house in the place of entry shall examine and clear them on the basis of the list signed and certified by the Customs.

Chapter VI   Supplementary Provisions

Article 28:   If a ship fails to reach a port with a Customs house but has to berth at another place in distress or due to other cases of force majeure, it shall report to the local port authorities or people's committee so that thy can supervise it on behalf of the Customs and notify the nearest Customs house. If necessary, the Customs house shall dispatch an officer to exercise supervision.

Article 29:   The power-driven ships with the register tonnage more than 300 tons coming from or sailing to Hong Kong and Macao shall be handled in accordance with these Procedures.

Article 30:   These Procedures shall be put into effect as of March 1, 1959.

The Provisional Customs Procedures for the Supervision of Import and Export Containers and the Goods Contained Therein

(August 1, 1981)

Article 1: These Procedures are formulated for the purpose of strengthening the supervision of containers and the goods contained therein (hereinafter simply referred to as "container goods") entering and leaving our country.

Article 2: The containers used to ship import and export goods shall be examined by the Customs and comply with the requirements of the Customs for their supervision.

Article 3: If an incoming or outgoing means of transport carries import or export container goods, the person in charge of the means of transport shall make a declaration to the Customs with an import or export waybill (a manifest) or a loading list, indicating such contents as the number of containers carried, container numbers, measurement(s), descriptions of the import or export goods, quantities (weight), shipper, consignee, number of the bill of lading or the shipping order, etc. and attach the loading list of each container to such a document in submission.

Article 4: Import or export container goods shall be stored in the bonded warehouses authorized by the Customs. The units assigned by the Customs for the custody of the containers shall be responsible for keeping the sealing marks on the container intact and shall not break the said sealing marks or load or unload the containers without authorization and consent of the Customs. When the Customs examines container goods and supervises the loading and unloading of goods, the owner of goods, the manager of the containers or their agent (hereinafter simply referred to as shipment declarer) shall be present and handle them as required by the Customs. Import and export container goods shall be cleared by the Customs before delivery or shipment.

Article 5:   With regard to the import or export container goods going through supervision and clearance formalities on the spot at the port of entry or exit, the shipment declarer shall go through declaration formalities at least 24 hours before opening import containers or loading export containers and submit an import or export goods declaration in duplicate and other related documents.

Article 6:   With regard to the import container goods to be directly transported from the Customs house at the place of entry to an inland Customs house for supervision and clearance, or the export container goods to be supervised by an inland Customs house at the port of the place of exit, these goods shall go through the formalities as "goods under the supervision of the Customs," the shipment declarer shall submit an import or export goods declaration in duplicate) to the Customs house at the destination so as to have the goods examined and cleared according to the declaration.

Article 7:   With regard to the import or export of container goods which required supervision and clearance beyond the areas under the control of the Customs (including the container goods transported door to door), the shipment declarer or the unit concerned shall make a prior written application to the Customs, in order that Customs officers may carry out the supervision after approval and collect fees. The applicant unit concerned shall supply the means of transport and bear the travelling expenses thereon.

Article 8:   All the container goods under the supervision of the Customs shall have customs sealing marks affixed at the Customs house and the declarer or the tallyig department shall affix commercial transport sealing marks at the same time.

Article 9:   All purchased containers duly approved and imported shall proceed to the Customs house for declaration and customs duties formalities.

Article 10:   All temporary imported containers shall be declared at the Customs by the container management unit by filing declaration forms and the said unit shall submit a written guarantee for their re-transport out of our country within 3 months. This time limit can be extended for a further 3 months with the prior approval of the Customs on grounds of special circumstances. If the containers cannot be re-transported abroad within the time limit, they shall make a fresh application for import duty formalities at the Customs.

Article 11:   With regard to the non-commercial goods or articles shipped in containers, the declaring unit shall go through declaration formatlities in accordance with these Procedures and other relevant provisions.

Article 12:   The Customs shall establish its setups at or dispatch its officers to be stationed at special container wharves, warehouses, or designated places for loading and unloading containers as the case may be and the units concerned shall provide them with working facilities and supply necessary offices gratis.

Article 13:   No one is allowed to use container cargo transportation for smuggling and other illegal activities.

Article 14: The violations against the provisions in these Procedure shall be dealt within accordance with the related clauses of the Provisional Law of the People's Republic of China on Customs.

Article 15: These Procedures shall be promulgated and put into effect from August 1, 1981.

Model Contracts

CHINA IMPORT AND EXPORT CORPORATION

SALES CONTRACT

No. ....

Kwangchow, ...

This is to confirm that the China Import & Export Corporation, ...
.... Branch, Cable Address .... (hereinafter called the Sellers) and
.... Cable address .... (hereinafter called the Buyers)
have agreed to close the following transactions according to the terms and conditions stipulated below:

1. Name of Commodity & Specifications	2. Quantity	3. Unit Price	4. Amount

With   % more or less both in amount and quantity allowed at the Sellers' option.

5. **Total Value**

6. **Packing**

7. **Shipping Marks**

8. **Time of Shipment**

9. **Loading Port & Destination**

    Partical Shipments and Transhipments Allowed

10. **Insurance**   To be effected by the Sellers for 110% of Invoice Value against   and War Risks.

11. **Terms of Payment:**   By Irrevocable, Transferable and Divisible Banker's Acceptance Letters of Credit to cover
    the total value of each monthly (or lot of) shipment as stipulated above, to be available by draft(s) at ....
    days sight, to reach the Sellers .... days before the respective time of Shipment stipulated above (or within
    .... days after receipt of the Seller's advice) and to remain valid for negotiation in China until the 15th day
    after the relative time of shipment.

SELLERS   BUYERS

China Import & Export Corporation

Address: Address:

The General Terms and Conditions of this Contract on the back page constitute an inseparable part to this Constract
and shall be equally binding upon both parties.

GENERAL TERMS AND CONDITIONS

1. **Amendments of Letter of Credit**:   Buyers shall open Letter of Credit in accordance with the terms of this Contract. If any discrepancy is found, amendments of Letter of Credit should be made immediately by the Buyers upon receipt of the Sellers' advice, failing which the Buyers shall be responsible for any losses thus incurred as well as for late shipment thus caused.

2. **Shipping Advice**:   Immediately after loading is completed, the Sellers or their branches shall notify by cable the number of credit, quantity and name of vessel to the Buyers.

3. **Force Majeure**:   Should the Sellers fail to deliver the contracted goods or effect shipment in time by reason of force majeure beyond their control, the time of shipment might be duly extended, or alternatively a part or whole of the contract might be cancelled without any liability attached to the Sellers, but the Sellers have to furnish the Buyers with a certificate attesting such event(s).

4. **Arbitration**:   All disputes in connection with this Contract or the execution thereof shall be amicably settled through negotiation. In case no amicable settlement can be reached between the two parties, the case under dispute shall be submitted to arbitration, which shall be held in the country where the defendant resides, or in a third country agreed by both parties. The decision of the arbitration shall be accepted as final and binding upon both parties. The Arbitration Fees shall be borne by the losing party.

5. **Claims**:   Should the quality, quantity and/or weight be found not in conformity with those stipulated in this Contract, aside from those usual natural changes of quality and weight in transit and losses within the responsibility of the shipping company and/or insurance company, the Buyers shall have the right within 30 days after the arrival of the goods at the port of destination, to lodge claims concerning the quality, quantity or weight of the goods. (Claims for perishable goods are to be put forward immediately after arrival of the goods at destination)

6. For the quality and weight of the goods shipped, the Inspection Certificate issued by the Commodity Inspection Bureau at the port of loading shall be taken as final.

7. **Remarks**

Model Contracts

CONTRACT

No. ....

Kwangchow, Date: ....

This Contract is made by and between the China Import & Export Corporation, 2 Hong Kong Road, Guangdong, China (Cable Address: "ABC"), hereinafter called the Buyers and the

(Cable Address:) hereinafter called the Sellers; whereby the Buyers agree to buy and the Sellers agree to sell the commodities on the terms and conditions stipulated below:

1. **Commodity, Specifications, Quantity and Unit Price:**

2. **Total Value:**
3. **Country of Origin and Manufacturers:**
4. **Packing:** To be packed in strong wooden case(s) or in carton(s), suitable for long distance ocean/parcel post/air freight transportation and to change of climate, well protected against moisture and shocks. The Sellers shall be liable for any damage of the commodity and expenses incident thereto on account of improper packing and/or improper protective measures taken by the Sellers in regard to the packing.
5. **Shipping Mark:** The Sellers shall mark on each package with fadeless paint the package number, gross weight, net weight, measurement and the wordings: "Keep Away from Moisture" "Handle with Care", etc., and the shipping mark;
6. **Time of Shipment:**
7. **Port of Shipment:**
8. **Port of Destination:**
9. **Insurance:** To be covered by the Buyers after shipment.
10. **Payment:** The Buyers, upon receipt from the Sellers of the delivery advice specified in Article 14 hereof, shall, in 15-20 days prior to the date of delivery, open an irrevocable Letter of Credit with the Bank of China, in favour of the Sellers, for an amount equivalent to the total value of the shipment. The Credit shall be payable against presentation of draft drawn on the opening bank and the shipping documents specified in Article 13 hereof. The Letter of Credit shall be valid until the 15th day after the shipment is effected.
11. **Guarantee of Quality:** The Sellers guarantee that the commodity hereof is made of the best materials with first class workmanship, brand new and unused, and complies in all respects with the quality and specifications stipulated in this Contract.
12. **Claims:** Within 90 days after the arrival of the goods at destination, should the quality, specifications, or quantity be found not in conformity with the stipulations of the Contract except those claims for which the insurance company or the owners of the vessel are liable, the Buyers shall, on the strength of the Inspection Certificate issued by the China Commodity Inspection Bureau, have the right to claim for replacement with new goods, or for compensation, and all the expenses (such as inspection charges, freight for returning the goods and for sending the replacement, insurance premium, storage and loading and unloading charges, etc.) shall be borne by the Sellers.
    The Certificate so issued shall be accepted as the base of a claim. The Sellers, in acordance with the Buyers' claim shall be responsible for the immediate elimination of the defect(s), complete or partial replacement of the commodity or shall devaluate the commodity accoding to the state of defect(s). Where necessary, the Buyers shall be at liberty to eliminate the defect(s) themselves at Sellers' expenses. If the Sellers fail to answer the Buyers within one month after receipt of the claim aforesaid, the claim shall be reckoned as having been accepted by the Sellers.
13. **Documents:** The Sellers shall present to the paying bank the following documents for negotiation:
    (1) In case by sea:
        3 negotiable copies of clean on board ocean Bill of Lading marked "Freight to Collect"/"Freight Prepaid", made out to order, blank endorsed, and notifying the China National Foreign Trade Transportation Corporation at the port of destination. In case by air freight:
        One copy of Air Waybill marked "Freight Prepaid" addressed to the China National Foreign Trade Transportation Corporation at the port of destination.
        In case by post:
        One copy of Parcel Post Receipt.
    (2) 5 Copies of Invoice with the insertion of Contract No. and the Shipping Mark (in case of more than one shipping mark, the invoice shall be issued separately).
    (3) 4 copies of Packing List issued by the Manufacturers.

(4) One copy of Certificate of Quantity and Quanlity issued by the Manufacturers.

(5) Certified copy of cable/letter to the Buyers, advising shipment immediately after shipment is made.

(6) The Sellers shall, within 10 days after the shipment is effected, send by air-mail three copies each of the above-mentioned documents (except Item 5) two sets to the Buyers and the other set to the China National Foreign Trade Transportation Corporation at the port of destination.

14. **Shipment:**

   (1) In case of FOB Terms:

   a. The Sellers shall, 30 days before the date of shipment stipulated in the Contract, advise the Buyers by cable/letter the Contract No., commodity, quantity, value, number of package, gross weight and date of readiness at the port of shipment for the Buyers to book shipping space.

   b. Booking of shipping space shall be attended to by the Buyers' Shipping Agents, China National Chartering Corporation, Peking.

   c. Peking or their Port Agents, (or Liners' Agents) shall send to the Sellers 10 days befoe the estimated date of arrival of the vessel at the port of shipment, a preliminary notice indicating the name of vessel, estimated date of loading, Contract No. for the Sellers to arrange shipment. The Sellers are requested to get in close contact with the shipping agents. When it becomes necessary to change the carrying vessel or in the event of her arrival having to be advanced or delayed, the Buyers or the Shipping Agency shall advise the Sellers in time.
   Should the vessel fail to arrive at the port of loading within 30 days after the arrival date advised by the Buyers' the Buyers shall bear the storage and insurance expenses incurred from the 31st day.

   d. The Sellers shall be liable for any dead freight or demurrage, should it happen that they have failed to have the commodity ready for loading after the carrying vessel has arrived at the port of shipment on time.

   e. The Sellers shall bear all expenses, risks of the commodity before it passes over the vessel's rail and is released from the tackle. After it has passed over the vessel's rail and been released from the tackle, all expenses of the commodity shall be for the Buyers' account.

   (2) In case of C&F Terms:

   a. The Sellers shall ship the goods within the shipment time from the port of shipment to the port of destination. Trans-shipment is not allowed. The carrying vessel shall not be the one of the nationality unacceptable to the Buyers and shall not call en route at any port in the vicinity of Taiwan.

   b. In case the goods are to be despatched by parcel post/air-freight, the Sellers shall, 30 days before the time of delivery as stipulated in Article 6, inform the Buyers by cable/letter the estimated date of delivery, Contract No., commodity, invoiced value, etc. The Sellers shall, immediately after despatch of the goods, advise the Buyers by cable/letter the Contract No., commodity, invoiced value and date of despatch for the Buyers to arrange insurance in time.

15. **Shipping Advice:** The Sellers shall, immediately upon the completion of the loading of the goods, advise by cable/letter the Buyers of the Contract No., commodity, quantity, invoiced value, gross weight, name of vessel and date of sailing, etc. In case the Buyers fail to arrange insurance in time due to the Sellers not having cabled in time, all losses shall be borne by the Sellers

16. **Force Majeure:** The Sellers shall not be held responsible for the delay in shipment or non-delivery of the goods due to Force Majeure, which might occur during the process of manufacturing or in course of loading or transit. The Sellers shall advise the Buyers immediately of the occurence mentioned above and within fourteen days thereafter, the Sellers shall send by airmail to the Buyers a certificate of the accident issued by the Competent Government Authorities where the accident occurs as evidence thereof. Under such circumstances the Sellers, however, are still under the obligation to take all necessary measures to hasten the delivery of the goods. In case the accident lasts for more than 10 weeks, the Buyers shall have the right to cancel the Contract.

17. **Arbitration** All disputes in connection with the execution of this Contract shall be settled through friendly negotiations, failing which, each Party shall appoint one arbitrator who will nominate one umpire thus to form an arbitration committee. Arbitration is to take place at
The award of the Arbitration Committee shall be accepted as final by both Parties for settlement. Artbitration fee, unless otherwise awarded, shall be borne by the losing party. The Arbitratiors and the umpire shall be confined to persons of Chinese or Nationality. In case the Arbitration is to be held in Peking, the case in dispute shall then be submitted for arbitration to the Foreign Trade Arbitration Commission of the China Council for the Promotion of International Trade, Peking, in accordance with the "Provisional Rules of Procedure of the Foreign Trade Arbitration Commission of the China Council for the Promotion of International Trade". The decision by the Commission shall be accepted as final and binding upon both parties.

18. **Penalty** If the Sellers fail to effect the delivery at the contracted time of delivery, the Buyers shall have the option to cancel this Contract and demand for all losses resulted therefrom, or alternatively, the Sellers may postpone delivery with the Buyers' consent, on the condition that the Sellers pay to the Buyers a penalty 1.5% of the goods value for a delay within 30 days and further 0.5% for every 15 days thereafter. The penalty shall be deducted by the paying bank during the negotiation of payment.

19. Remark:
IN WITNESS THEREOF, this Contract is signed by both parties on the date as above-mentioned in two original copies;
each party hold one copy.

THE SELLERS:

THE BUYERS:
China Import & Export Corporation

SELLERS

BUYERS

China Import & Export Corporation

Model Contracts

PURCHASE CONTRACT

Contract No.: ....

Peking: ....

The Buyers: China Chemicals Import & Export Corporation,   Tinonmin, Peking.

Telex: 11
Cable: China

The Sellers:

This Contract is made by and between the Buyers and the Sellers; whereby the Buyers agree to buy and the Sellers agree to sell the under-mentioned goods subject to the terms and conditions as stipulated hereinafter:
1. **Name of Commodity and Specification:**

2. **Quantity:**

3. **Unit Price:**

4. **Total Value:**

5. **Packing:**

6. **Country of Origin & Manufacturer:**

7. **Terms of Pyament:** After conclusion of business, the Buyers shall open with the Bank of China, , an irrevocable letter of credit in favour of the Sellers payable at the issuing Bank against presentation of the shipping documents as stipulated under Clause 3(A) of the Terms of Delivery of this Contract after departure of the carrying vessel. The said letter of credit shall remain in force till the 15th day after shipment.

8. **Insurance:**   To be covered by the Buyers.

9. **Time of Shipment:**

10. **Port of Loading:**

11. **Port of Destination**

12. **Shipping Mark(s):**   On each package shall be stencilled conspicuously; port of destination, package number, gross and nett weights, measurement and the shipping mark shown on the right side. (For dangerous and/or poisonous cargo, the nature and the generally adpoted symbol shall be marked conspicuously on each package).

13. **Other terms:**
    a. Other matters relating to this Contract shall b dealt with in accordance with the Terms of Delivery as specified overleaf, which shall form an integral part of this Contract.
    b. This Contract is made out in Chinese and English, both versions being equally authentic.

14. Supplementary Condition(s) (Should any other clause in this contract be in conflict with the following Supplementary Condition(s), the Supplementary Condition(s) should be taken as final and binding).

SELLERS   BUYERS

TERMS OF DELIVERY

1. Terms of Shipment: For C & F Terms: The Sellers shall ship the goods within the time as stipulated in Clause (9) of this Contract by a directvessel sailing from the port of loading to China Port. Transhipment en route isnot allowed without the Buyers' consent. The goods should not be carried by vessels flying the flags of the countries not acceptable to the Buyers. The carrying vessel shall not call or stop over at the port/ports of Taiwan Province and the port/ports in the vicinity of Taiwan Province prior to her arrival at port of destination as stipulated in the Clause (11) of this Contract.

    For FOB Terms:
    (A) The shipping space for the contracted goods shall be booked by the Buyers or the Buyers' shipping agent, China Chartering Corporation (Address: Tinonmin, Peking. Cable Address: CHONGHU PEKING). The Sellers shall undertake to load the contracted goods on board the vessel nominated by the Buyers on any date notified by the Buyers, within the time of shipment stipulated in the Clause (9) of this Contract.
    (B) 10-15 days prior to the date of shipment, the Buyers shall inform the Sellers by cable of the contract number, name of vessel, ETA of vessel, quantity to be loaded and the name of shipping agent, so as to enable the latter to contact the shipping agent direct and arrange the shipment of the goods. The Sellers shall cable in time the Buyers of the result thereof. Should, for certain reasons, it become necessary for the Buyers to replace the named vessel with another one, or should the named vessel arrive at the port of shipment earlier or later than the date of arrival as previously notified to the Sellers, the Buyers or their shipping agent shall advise the Sellers to this effect in due time. The Sellers shall also keep close contact with the agent of
    (C) Should the Sellers fail to load the goods, within the time as notified by the Buyers, on board the vessel booked by the Buyers after its arrival at the port of shipment, all expenses such as dead freight, demurrage, etc., and consequences thereof shall be borne by the Sellers. Should the vessel be withdrawn or replaced or delayed eventually or the cargo be shut out, etc., and the Sellers are not informed in good time to stop delivery of the cargo, the calculation of the loss for storage expenses and insurance premium thus sustained at the loading port should be based on the loading date noticfied by the agent to the Sellers (or based on the date of the arrival of the cargo at the loading port in case the cargo should arrive there later than the notified loading date). The above-mentioned loss to be calculated from the 16th day after expiry of the free storage time at the port should be borne by the Buyers with the exception of Force Majeure. However, the Sellers still undertake to load the cargo immediately upon the carrying vessel's arrival at the loading port at their own risks and expenses. The payment of the aforesaid expenses shall be effected against presentation of the original vouchers after being checked.
2. Advice of Shipment: Immediately after completion of loading of goods on board the vessel the Sellers shall advise the Buyers by cable of the contract number, name of goods, quantity or weight loaded, invoice value, name of vessel, port of shipment, sailing date and port of destination.

    Should the Buyers be made unable to arrange insurance in time owing to the Sellers' failure to give the above mentioned advice of shipment by cable, the Sellers shall be held responsible for any and all damage and/or loss attributable to such failure.
3. **Shipping Documents:**
    (A) The Sellers shall present the following documents to the paying bank for negotiation of payment: (a) Full set of clean on board, "freight prepaid" for C & F Terms or "freight to collect" for FOB Terms, ocean Bills of Lading, made but to order and blank endorsed, notifying the Branch of China National Foreign Trade Transportation Corporation at the port of destination. (b) Five copies of signed invoice, indicating contract number and shipping marks. (c) Two copies of packing list and/or weight memo with indication of measurement. (d) One copy each of the certificate of quality and quantity or weight, as stipulated in the Clause 5 of the Terms of Delivery. (e) One duplicate copy of the cable advice of shipment, as stipulated in the Clause 2 of the Terms of Delivery.
    (B) The Sellers shall despatch, in care of the carrying vessel, one copy each of the duplicate documents to the Buyers and two sets to the Branch of China National Foreign Trade Transportation Corporation at the port of destination.
    (C) Immediately after the departure of the carrying vessel, the Sellers shall airmail one set of the duplicate documents to the Buyers and two sets to the Branch of China National Foreign Trade Transportation Corporation at the port of destination.
4. Dangerous Cargo Instruction Leaflets: For dangerous and/or poisonous cargo, the Sellers must provide instruction leaflets stating the hazardous or poisonous properties, transportation, storage and handling remarks, as well as precautionary and first-aid measures and measures against fire. The Sellers shall airmail, together with other shipping documents, three copies each of the same to the Buyers and the Branch of China National Foreign Trade Transportation Corporation at the port of destination.
5. Inspection: It is mutually agreed that the certificates of quality and quantity or weight issued by the Manufacturer shall be part of the documents to be presented to the paying bank for negotiation of payment. However, the inspection of quality and quantity or weight shall be made in accordance with the following:
    (A) For General Cargo: In case the quality, quantity or weight of the goods be found riot in conformity with those stipulated in this Contract after re-inspection by the China Commodity Inspection Bureau within 60 days after arrival of the goods at the port of destination, the Buyers shall return the goods to or lodge claims against the Sellers for compensation of losses upon the strength of Inspection Certificate issued by the said Bureau, with the exception of those claims for which the insurers or owners of the carrying vessel are liable. All expenses (including inspection fees) and losses arising from the return of the goods or claims should be borne by the Sellers. In such case, the Buyers may, if so requested, send a sample of the goods in question to the Sellers, provided that sampling is feasible.

(B) For Pharmaceuticals: Pharmaceuticals imported into China are subject to laws and regulations of the People's Republic of China. Disqualified pharmaceuticals are prohibited to be imported. It is mutually agreed that for the quality of the contracted goods in this category, the Inspection Certificate issued by the China Commodity Inspection Bureau after inspecting the goods within 60 days from the date of arrival at the port of destination shall be taken as final and binding upon both parties. The Sellers shall take back all the disqualified goods and compensate the Buyers for the value of the goods plus all losses sustained due to return of the cargo, such as freight, storage charges, insurance premium, interest, inspection charges, etc. Should the quantity/wheight be found not in conformity with those stipulated in this Contract after inspection by the China Commodity Inspection Bureau, the Buyers shall have right to claim against the Sellers for compensation of losses within 60 days after the arrival of the goods at the port of destination on the basis of the Inspection Certificate issued by the said Bureau.

6. Force Majeure: The Sellers shall not be held responsible for late delivery or non-delivery of the goods owing to generally recognized "Force Majeure" causes. However, in such case, the Sellers shall immediately cable the Buyers the accident and airmail to the Buyers within 15 days after the accident, a certificate of the accident issued by the competent government authorities or the chamber of commerce which is located at the place where the accident occurs as evidence thereof. Win the exception of late delivery or non-delivery due to "Force Majeure" Causes, in case the Sellers fall to make delivery or failure to make delivery of the goods in accordance with the terms of the Contract. If the "Force Majeure" cause lasts over 60 days, the Buyers shall have the right to cancel the Contract or the undelivered part of the Contract.

7. Arbitration: All disputes in connection with this Contract or the execution thereof shall be amicably settled through negotiation. In case no settlement can be reached between the two parties, the case under dispute shall be submitted to the Foreign Trade Arbitration Commission of the China Council for the Promotion of International Trade for arbitrtion. The arbitration shall take place in Peking, China and shall be executed in accordance with the Provisional Rules of Procedure of the said Commission and the decision made by the Arbitration Commission shall be accepted as final and binding upon both parties. The fees for arbitration shall be borne by the losing Party unless otherwise awarded.

Model Contracts

<u>CONTRACT</u>

No.: ....

Date: ....

The Sellers: China Import & Export Corporation, Hong Kong

Cable Address:

The Sellers:

Cable Address:

The Sellers agree to sell and the Buyers agree to buy the undermentioned goods on the terms and conditions stated below:

	1. Name of Commodity, Specification,	2. Quantity	3. Unit Price	4. total Amount

Packing: In bundles of 70-120 kilos each and/or ion lift bundles of about 1000 kilos

Shipment 3%   The above price includes a more or less at Buyers' commission of   % to Sellers' option   be calculated on FOB value.

5. **Time of Shipment:**

6. **Port of Loading:** China Ports.

7. **Port of Destination:**

8. **Insurance:** To be effected by the Sellers for 110% of invoice value covering

9. **Terms of Payment:**   The Buyers shall open, with a bank to be accepted by both the Buyers and the Sellers, an Irrevocalble, Transferable and Divisible Letter of Credit, allowing partial shipments and transhipment, in favour of the Sellers, payable at sight against first presentation of the shipping documents to the Bank of China in China.

The covering Letter of Credit must be opened before ...... an to remain valid in China until the 15th day (inclusive) from the date of shipment.

10. **Documents:** The Sellers shall present to the negotiations bank, Clean On Board Bill of Lading, Invoice, Packing List/Weight Memo, and Transferable Insurance Policy or Insurance Certificate when this Contract is made on CIF basis.

11. **Terms of Shipment:**
    1. The carrying vessel shall be provided by the Sellers. Partial shipments and transhipment are allowed.
    2. After loading is completed, the Sellers shall notify the Buyers by cable of the contract number, name of commodity, quantity, name of the carrying vessel and date of shipment.

12. **Quality/Quantity Discrepancy and Claim:** In case the quality and/or quantity/weight are found by the Buyers to be not in conformity with the Contract after arrival of the goods at th port of destination, the Buyers may lodge claim with the Sellers supported by survey report issued by an inspection organization agreed upon by both parties, with the exception, however of those claims for which the insurance company and/or the shipping company are to be held responsible. Claim for quality discrepancy should be filed by the Buyers within 30 days after arrival of the goods at the port of destination. The Sellers shall, within 30 days after receipt of the notification of the claim, send reply to the Buyers.

13. **Force Majeure**: In case of Force Majiure, the Sellers shall not be held responsible for late delivery or non-delivery of the goods but shall notify the Buyers by cable. The Sellers shall deliver to the Buyers by registered mail. if so requested by the Buyers, a certificate issued by the China Council for the Promotion of Internaional Trade or any competent authorites.

14. **Arbitration**: All disputes in connection with this Contract or the execution thereof shall be settled by negotiation between two parties. If no settlement can be reached, the case in dispute shall then be submitted for arbitration in the country of defendant in accordance with the arbitration regulations of the arbitration organization of the defendant country. The decision made by the arbitration organization shall be taken as final and binding upon both parties. The arbitration expenses shall be borne by the losing party unless otherwise awarded by the arbitration organization.

15. **Remarks**:

SELLERS   BUYERS

China Import & Export Corporation

Forms & Documentation

China Import & Export Corportion

INVOICE

Invoice No.
Credit No.
Contract No.
To Messrs.
Shipped by Vessel
Destination

Marks & Nos.	Quantities & Descriptions	Unit Price	Amount

Certificate of Origin
This is to certify that the goods named herein are of Chinese Origin.

China Import & Export corporation

Forms & Documentation

China Import & Export Corpation

Packing List/Weight Note (List)

Date: _____

To Messrs.

Commodity:

Mark & Nos.	Quantity	Gross Wt.	Tare Wt.	Nett Wt.

China Import & Export Corporation

_____

Forms & Documentation

China Council for the Promotion of International Trade

Certificate of Origin

(Date _____)

(This is to certify that the under mentioned commodities were produced/manufactured in the People's Republic of China)

(Mark & No.)   (Commodity)   (Quantity)   (Weight)

SECTION D: Advertising

Customs Procedures for the Supervision, Taxation and Tax Exemption of Import and Export Samples and Advertising Materials

(Issued on October 1, 1981)

Article 1: With regard to all samples imported or exported exclusively for reference in placing orders, for analysis and examination, for quality tests and all advertising materials for commercial publicity, the samples shall be supervised, taxed or exempted from duties by the Customs as stipulated in these Procedures whether they are bought at current prices or supplied free.

Article 2: For samples or advertising materials imported or exported, the receiving or sending unit or its agent (or the carrier) shall go through import or export formalities at the Customs.

Article 3: If a sample bought from or sold abroad has a value of more than Renminbi 200 yuan, an import or export licence shall be obtained in accordance with the related provisions of the state administration authorities of foreign trade; a sample with a value of less than RMB 200 yuan shall be examined and approved by the Customs. Samples or advertising materials to be presented are exempt from obtaining a licence. No import or export licences are required for the import and export of samples on advertising matters.

Article 4: All samples and advertising materials which have no commercial value or only analytical purposes and are to be disposed of subsequently shall not be subject to Customs duties and Industrial and Commercial (Consolidated) Tax. All other samples and advertising materials, whether they are bought or supplied free, shall be subject to Customs duties and Industrial and Commercial (Consolidated) Tax as are other imported goods.

Article 5: If dutiable import samples or advertising materials are scheduled to be retransported out of our country within six months, they shall be declared at the Customs house at the place of entry and the Customs shall collect a sum equal to the amount of the duties as security, which shall be refunded when they are transported out, if they are not re-exported within the time limit, the Customs shall take the said security for duties and pay it into the state treasury.

Article 6:   Those acts in violation of these provisions shall be handled in accordance with the Interim Law on Customs and related provisions.

Article 7:   These Procedures shall become effective as of October 1, 1980.

Measures on the Supervision and Control of Taxation of Imported and Exported Samples and Advertisment Products

(Promulgated and enforced July 15, 1982)

Article 1: The Customs is, according to the stipulations of these measures, to exercise supervision and control over and levy customs duty and industrial and commercial (consolidated) tax on all samples imported and exported for the sole purpose of serving as samples for ordering goods, sales, production, economic and technical exchange with foreigners, analysis or laboratory testing and all advertisement products used by enterprises to promote the commodities they manufacture for distribute, regardless of whether they are purchased for a price or given free of charge or reciprocally provided.

Article 2: The units receiving or sending imported and exported samples and advertisment products or their agents (or carriers) shall handle the import and export formalities with the Customs.

Article 3: An import or export license shall be presented to the Customs for examination in cases of samples and advertisement products purchased from abroad or sold outside of the country whose value is RMB 500 or over. No import or export license need be obtained in cases of those whose value is RMB 500 or less and those given or provided free of charge.[1] Foreign trade corporations which, having obtained State Council approval, have the right to engage in import and export business do not have to apply separately for import or export licenses as regards imported and exported samples and advertisement products within their approved scope of operations.

---

1 *Despite the ambiguity in the text of the measures, the PRC Customs Administration has advised us that only those goods with a value less than RMB 500 may be exempted from the requirement of an import or export license.*

However, all units (including foreign trade corporations which have the right to engage in import and export business) shall handle matters in accordance with the state's relevant control stipulations in cases of imported and exported samples and advertisement products purchased for a price, sold for a price, or given or provided free of charge, that fall under categories of commodities of which the state prohibits or restricts the import or export.

Article 4:   The Customs, upon examination and determination that the quantity is reasonable, may permit exemption of levy of customs duty and industrial and commerical (consolidated) tax on imported and exported samples and advertisement products that conform to the following circumstances:

(1)   Those that are without commercial value and other use;

(2)   Those that are used for analysis, laboratory testing or measuring and testing the quality of the products and are expended;

(3)   Those that fall under the category of bringing in samples or sending out samples for processing;

(4)   Those that are reciprocally provided according to scientific and technical exchange agreements signed between the governments of two countries;

(5)   Those whose quantity is piecemeal, and whose total value each time is RMB 50 or less.

Article 5:   Customs duty and industrial and commercial (consolidated) tax shall be levied in accordance with regulations on all of the following imported and exported samples and advertisement products, regardless of whether they are purchased for a price, sold for a price or given or provided free of charge:

(1)   Those whose total value each time is RMB 50 or over;

(2)   All types of imported motorized vehicles, bicycles, watches, television sets, radios, tape recorders, recording machines, record players, cameras, refrigerators for household use, sewing machines for household use, washing machines, duplicating machines, air conditioners, electric fans, vacuum cleaners, acoustical combinations, video recording equipment, filming apparatus, enlargers, projectors, calculators, computers and the main spare parts for the above goods. (Those falling under the stipulation of Article 4(4) of these measures are exceptions).

Article 6:   If it is determined that taxable imported and exported samples and advertisement goods are to be reexported or reimported within six months, this shall be reported to the Customs at the place of import or export. The Customs is to collect a security deposit equivalent to the amount of tax due, to be refunded at the time of reexport or reimport.

Article 7:   If the relevant units require to sell or transfer samples or advertisement products that have been let pass free of tax by Customs, or to transfer them to another use, they shall first obtain the approval of the Customs and also make up the customs duty and industrial and commercial (consolidated) tax in accordance with regulations.

Article 8: It is prohibited illegally to import or export goods and personal articles in the name of samples or advertisement products.

Article 9: Conduct violating the stipulations of these measures shall be handled in accordance with the Provisional Customs Law and relevant stipulations.

Interpretation

Measures on the Supervision and Control of Taxation of Imported and Exported Samples and Advertisment Products

1.   How to declare the import and export sample and advertising products? The importer or exporter is requested to fill in the import/export declaration form in duplicate. If the value of the goods is more than Renminbi 200 yuan, the importer or exporter is requested to submit the import/export permit for inspection.

2.   What are the meanings of non commercial value and other usages for samples and advertising products?
They mean:

a)   single shoe, single sock
b)   cloth and paper which are scissored or cut into useless materials
c)   garment with a scissored hole or with the mark "sample" (not easily faded out) at obvious position.
d)   the pictorial of products, specifications and tourist guide books

3.   Is there any levy of tax on imported non commercial value samples which are used for processing, assembling or compensation trade?
If these samples are not re-exported during the fixed period, tax will be levied in accordance with the provisions.

4.   How to levy tax on advertising products which accompany the consignment products, at the time of importation of the latter?
If the accompany advertising products are of the same kind of consignment products, tax will be levied in accordance with the tax rate for consignment products.
If the accompany advertising products are of different kinds, they will be levied in accordance with the provisions of the regulations of import tariffs.

SECTION E: Transport

Provisional Customs Rules Governing the Supervision and Control Over Motor Vehicles and Cargo Carried Thereon While Entering or Leaving the Frontier.

*(The Ministry or Foreign Trade informed customs
offices all over the country on 29th August, 1963)*

Article 1:   This rules are drafted to ensure the effective implementation of foreign trade control system so as to facilitate motor vehicle transportation entering or leaving the frontier.

Article 2:   Motor vehicles entering or leaving the frontier shall pass through such places with customs establishment. Also, they have to stop for customs inspection and declaration at places decided by the customs. If they have to pass such places without customs establishment, prior permission from provincial (autonomous regions) People's committee is required.

Motor vehicle with import and export cargo carried thereon, its driver shall forward a copy of cargo loading list (or shipping list) to the customs personnel to inspect the cargo while declaring for entering or leaving the frontier.

Article 3:   Except with permission from both the customs and the authority concerned, motor vehicle shall enter or leave the frontier after sunrise and before sunset.

Article 4:   Motor vehicle driver and escort shall present at the vicinity while customs inspecting the motor vehicle. They should also open or break the necessary portions or remove cargo on the vehicle in accordance with the request of the customs.

Article 5:   Motor vehicles entering or leaving the frontier can only proceed to drive across the frontier after clearance by the customs.

Foreign vehicles engaging in passenger and cargo transportation business shall have their drivers filled in an "Internal Driving Vehicle Declaration List" in duplicate according to the forms required by the customs if they proceed driving domestically after entering the frontier. After inspection by the customs, a copy of the list shall be kept or record by the customs the other copy shall be returned to the drivers after signed and sealed by the customs. The list should be submitted to the customs for cancellation while leaving the frontier.

Article 6:   Before the entering frontier motor vehicle arrives at the inspection spot decided by the customs and during the period when the leaving frontier motor vehicle received clearance inspection by the customs and immediately before leaving the frontier, they cannot stop, allow passenger getting or off the vehicle, load and unload cargo and other articles, unless with the customs' permission.

Article 7:   Articles stored for use by the vehicle itself and personal articles carried by the driver and escort should declare to the customs. The amount of the above articles are limited to those which stored for use during the journey.

Article 8:   Cargo recover, deliver or their agents shall forward import and export permission documents, shipment bills and other documents concerning the import export cargo carried on the motor vehicle to customs for declaration during the time stipulated by the customs. The cargo can only be continuously navigated or be transported out of the frontier after inspection for clearance by the customs.

Article 9:   Cargo receiver, deliver and their agents shall present at the vicinity while the customs inspecting the cargo. They will, according to the request of the customs, handle the work of removal, evaluation, opening or breaking of the cargo.

Article 10:   Import cargo prior to the customs' inspection clearance and export cargo received customs' inspection clearance pending for shipment shall be stored at those warehouses consented by the customs.

Article 11:   Motor vehicle and cargo carried thereon travelling Hong Kong and Macao shall be controlled in accordance with these rules.

Article 12:   These rules shall be implemented from 29th August, 1963.

SECTION F: Exhibits

Procedures of the Customs Service for the Supervision of Import Exhibits

(Promulgated and enforced by the Ministry of Foreign Trade on November 3, 1975)

I	**General Provisions**

Article 1: These Procedures are to ensure the effective implementation of state policies in the control of foreign trade and to facilitate foreign countries, exhibitions of China.

Article 2: The import exhibits referred to in these Procedures include those transported into our country by foreign countries for the purpose of holding economic, cultural, scientific, technical and other exhibitions in China as well as publicity materials, decoration materials, service materials, small articles for sale and all other articles relating to the exhibitions.

Article 3: The unit which accommodates a foreign country in its holding of an exhibition in China shall send a duplicate of the relevant instrument of approval in advance to the Customs house at the place of exhibition.

Article 4: Import exhibits shall be put under the supervision of the Customs Services and go through the Customs formalities as stipulated in these Procedures.

Article 5: When the Customs dispatches officers to the place of exhibition to carry out the supervision duties, the exhibition or host organization shall provide them with offices and necessary office equipment.

II	**The Declaration and Examination of Exhibits**

Article 6: Before the import of the exhibits, the exhibition organization or its agent shall translate the exhibit list in duplicate into Chinese which

should include such contents as marks, numbers, number of packages, weight, names, specifications, quantities, prices, etc., and declare them at the Customs house.

Article 7:   When the exhibits are imported, the exhibition organization or its agent shall submit a foreign goods transfer permit, a bill of lading (or a waybill) and a loading list for further conveyance to the Customs house at the place of entry and after they are examined by the Customs, transfer them to the place of exhibition as "the goods under the supervision of the Customs."
Approval from the Customs is needed when the exhibits are required for some reason to be moved out of the place of exhibition.

Article 8:   The exhibition organization shall notify the Customs before opening the cases of the exhibits so that the Customs officers can be present for examination.
When the Customs officers examine the exhibits, the exhibition organization or its agent shall be present.

Article 9:   The exhibition organization shall submit in advance to the Customs house at the place of exhibition for examination and approval the publicity materials and technical data for exhibition or use, including movies, slides, sound recording tapes, video recording tapes, discs, photos, maps, manuals, advertisements, etc. and only after approval shall they be allowed to be exhibited or used.
The publicity materials and technical data which degenerate the politics, economy, culture, morality, etc. of the People's Republic of China shall not be exhibited or used and shall be confiscated, returned abroad or the exhibition organization shall be ordered to amend them before use as the case may be.

Article 10: If there are some articles in the exhibits which shall be controlled as stipulated by other decrees of the People's Republic of China, the exhibition organization or its agent shall go through examination or approval formalities in accordance with the provisons of those decrees concerned.

III   The Use, Presentation, Sale and Disposal of Exhibits

Article 11: The cigarettes, wine and food transported in by the exhibition organization used for serving in the exhibition shall be used duty-free after verification and approval by the Customs, but shall not be transferred, sold or used for other purposes.

Article 12: The odd souvenirs or demonstration articles presented by the exhibition organization to the spectators and working personnel shall be examined and approved by the Customs before presentation.

Article 13: If any exhibits are to be presented as gifts or samples, the exhibition organization shall report the objects of presentation to the Customs and go through exemption or taxation formalities in accordance with the Customs' provisions for the administration of import gifts. (Note: The provisions for the administration of imported gifts have become invalid.)

Article 14: For all small articles for sale in the exhibition, the exhibition organization shall submit the permit signed and issued by the administration authorities of foreign trade of the People's Republic of China to the Customs for examination and pay the Customs duties and industrial and commercial consolidated tax.

Article 15: The following principles shall be applied to the exhibits to be sold by the exhibition organization:

(1) If the exhibits are to be sold to foreign trade import and export corporations of oiur country, the corporations concerned shall conduct the import formalities at the Customs.

(2) If the exhibits are to be sold (or presented) to the embassy or consulate of other countries in China or their diplomats the embassy or consulate or diplomats, concerned shall conduct the import formalities at the Customs.

(3) If they are to be sold to other Chinese or foreign organizations or individuals, the exhibition organization shall apply to the administration authorities of foreign trade of the People's Republic of China for permits and they shall be examined, taxed and cleared by the Customs in accordance with the permits.

Article 16: For the exhibits to be waived, the exhibition organization shall report their categories, quantities and values to the Customs. If there is any take-over unit, the take-over unit shall go through Customs formalities; if there is no take-over unit, they shall be disposed of by the Customs according to directions.

Article 17: After the exhibition has closed, the exhibition organization shall submit a disposition list of exhibits in time to the Customs house at the place of exhibition, which should separately list the details of consumption, presentation, sale, disposal, re-export, etc.

IV The Transfer and Re-export of Exhibits

Article 18: If the exhibition organization is to transfer the exhibits to another part of our country for another exhibition, it shall go through transfer formalities at the Customs as provided in Article 20 of these Procedures.

Article 19: The exhibits to be re-exported shall be completed within 3 months from the date of the closing of the exhibition. If the exhibition organisation fails to carry out the re-export as scheduled, it shall apply to the Customs for extension of time. Those exhibits which are not re-exported abroad within the said time limit shall be disposed of by the Customs in accordance with the regulations.

The exhibits re-exported as scheduled shall be exempted from Customs duties.

Article 20: When the exhibits are transferred or re-exported, the exhibition organization or its agent shall submit to the Customs a foreign goods transfer permit and a loading list in duplicate and go through transfer formalities as "the goods under the supervision of the Customs."

Procedures of Customs Service for the Supervision of Export Exhibits

(Announced by the Ministry of
Foreign Trade on September, 20 1976)

Article 1:   Deleted by the Ministry of Foreign Trade

Article 2:   Export exhibits referred to in these procedures include those exported overseas for the purpose of participating in exhibitions on economy trade, culture and technology or foreign expositions. The exhibits also include the related strff for publicity, decoration, reception, counter sale and other stuff used by the public at large for the above exhibitions.

Article 3:   The units for organising exhibitions overseas (or the units appointed by them — hereinafter referred to the same) shall forward to the customs at the place of leaving the frontier; a check list in duplicate with contents on the mark number, item number, specifications, quantity and price, indicating the approval authority and the document permit number together with the related transportation documents, for declaration.

Article 4:   Upon the re-import of exhibits, a check list of exhibits in duplicate in accordance with the stipulations in Article 3 of these procedures, indicating the original date and place of leaving the frontier, the name of transportation tools, the country or district where the exhibits were displayed as well as situations about the sale, present as gift, abandon, utilization of the exhibits or retaining them for use by PRC organisations station overseas shall be furnished by the units for organising exhibitions overseas, together with relevant transportation documents, to the customs located at the place where the exhibits enter the country. If the units for organising exhibitions overseas request to transport the exhibits to the customs where they belong for customs procedures, the customs at the place of entering the country may handle the exhibits in accordance with the rules for goods supervised and controlled by the customs.

Article 5: Personal things or things not for exhibition are not permitted to be stored inside the vessels for exhibition while the exhibits are being transported for export or for re-import.

Article 6: Things, samples, gifts or other information purchased or received by the units responsible for organising exhibitions overseas during the period when the exhibition was held overseas, shall be packed separately and a detailed list shall be forwarded to the customs for declaration.

Except those cooking utensils and bedding purchased and for the use by the personnel overseas during the overseas exhibition period, approval documents from the Ministry of Foreign Trade for all the other purchased items shall be forwarded to the customs for inspection. The customs will levy import tariff or grant exemption for the above-mentioned items in accordance with relevant regulations.

Article 7: The customs shall execute necessary inspection on the exhibits for export, or re-import as well as the things which were purchased overseas or received by the organising units. The units for organising exhibitions overseas shall be present at the vicinity when the customs inspect the above things. They may be requested by the customs to open the packings of those things.

Article 8: In accordance with the check list as stipulated in Articles 3 and 4 of these procedures and after the indication of the situations of exhibits and dates, the customs at the places of entering or leaving the country shall keep a copy of the check list for record and send the other copy to the customs where the units for organising exhibitions overseas belong (if there is no customs at such place, the copy will be sent to the customs in Beijing) for evaluation and closing of the case.

Article 9: If anything against these procedures or other laws and regulations is discovered during the process of inspection for clearance and the handling of the evaluation and closing of the case, the customs may detain the things. Upon finding out the facts of the situations, the customs will implement measures according to the relevant regulations.

SECTION G: Oil

Interim Customs Procedures for the Supervision of Import and Export Goods and Other Materials Needed in the Cooperative Exploration and Exploiation of Sea Oil and Engineers' and Technicians' Luggage and Articles

(Issued on October 1, 1981)

Article 1:   These Procedures are formulated in accordance with the relevant provisions of the "Interim Law of the People's Republic of China on Customs" and according to the spirit of Document No. GF-211(1980) of the State Council in order to facilitate the import and export of goods and materials needed in the cooperative exploration and exploitation of the sea oil of our country.

Article 2:   The Customs shall exercise supervision over all kinds of goods and materials imported and exported by oil companies for the purpose of exploring and exploiting the sea oil of our country in accordance with the documents and contracts (including subcontracts — the same hereinafter) approved by the State Council or the authorities authorized by the Council.

After the determination of a certain project, the oil company concerned shall submit a list of approved planned import goods, equipment and materials (including supplementary lists) to the Customs house at the location of the project as well as at the port of entry and exit for examination before import in addition to the submission of the aforesaid spproved documents and contracts. The production goods and materials which are examined and proved to be within the range of the project shall be imported by means of the above approved list without another application for licence(s) (but prior applications shall be made to the correct examination and approval authorities for approval with regard to the machinery and equipment to be imported). The import licence signed and issued by the administration authorities of foreign trade shall be submitted for examination in respect of goods and materials beyond the range of the project, those incidentally imported by the oil company concerned and not for direct use in production, and those which shall require an application for the import licence.

Article 3: When goods and materials are imported or exported, the oil company or its agent shall file an import or export goods declaration in duplicate and go through import or export formalities by submitting it together with such relevant documents as invoice, packing list, etc. If the goods and materials are imported and exported via different places, the shipment declarer shall file an import or export goods declaration in triplicate and go through the transfer formalities at the Customs house in the place of entry or, if they are exported at the Customs-house, in its location. The shipment declarer shall be responsible for asking the carrier to carry the Customs envelope with the goods to the Customs house at the destination or at the place of exit as the case may be, and the carrier shall ensure the Customs sealing marks are intact on the goods or on the means of transport.

Article 4: When the Customs examines import or export goods or materials, the owner or his agent shall be present and responsible for opening their packages. If examination is required in a place outside the areas under the supervision of the Customs, a prior application shall be made to the Customs, a prior application shall be made to the Customs for approval and fees shall be paid as stipulated by the Customs.

Article 5: To import (including the imports on lease) goods and materials within the duty-free range approved by the state, the Customs shall clear the articles duty-free; with regard to the goods and materials beyond the above duty-free range, the Customs shall clear them after collecting Customs duties and industrial and commercial (consolidated) taxes in accordance with the regulations.

For goods and materials temporarily imported, the oil company concerned shall go through declaration formalities at the Customs house in its location guarantee to re-export them within six months; the articles shall be exempted from Customs duties, but a deposit equivalent to the payable duties shall be paid and a guarantee shall be given for the re-export of them within the fixed period. The deposit shall be refunded when the goods and materials are re-transported abroad. If the time limit for re-exporting the above goods and materials temporarily imported shall be extended due to particular reasons, an application shall be made to the Customs for approval for proper extension of the time limit. If they are not re-transported abroad within the said time, the import formalities shall be supplemented as stipulated by these Procedures and Customs duties and industrial and commercial (consolidated) taxes collected accordingly.

Article 6: Import goods and materials shall go through Customs formalities or be specially permitted by the Customs for clearance before delivery and forwarding; export goods and materials shall go through Customs formalities and be shipped abroad under the supervision of the Customs.

Article 7:   The consignment warehouses established by foreign firms in oil bases shall be handled by the Customs in accordance with the "Interim Procedures for the Supervision of Bonded Goods and Bonded Warehouses." But if goods and materials consigned and maintenance parts and components are turned for import, the taxation or tax exemption shall be conducted as stipulated in Article 5 of these Interim Procedures.

Article 8:   Import goods and materials shall be dealt with by the Customs as stipulated if they are not declared at the Customs or their taxes are not paid at the expiration of three months from the date of the declaration for import by the means of transport.

Article 9:   With regard to the foreign engineers and technicians who come to China to carry out the exploration exploitation duties, the authorities concerned shall supply the Customs a list in quadruplicate, sending the copies separately to the Customs houses at the place of entry, their location, Guangzhou Customs house and Jiulong Customs house. The Customs shall handle their luggage and articles on the basis of the list and in accordance with the provisions for the administration of the import and export of luggage and articles and the incoming and outgoing mailed articles of the foreign engineers and technicians who are invited to work in China.

The luggage and articles carried by the engineers and technicians of our country who cross the borders as required by their work shall be handled in accordance with the "Provisions on the Luggage and Articles of Our Exit Working Personnel Crossing the Borders" and the provisions in the document of Supplementary Notice No. MGH 517 (79) of the four Ministries of Foreign Trade, Foreign Affairs, Foreign Economic Relations and Finance.

Article 10:   Any of the following shall be dealt with by the Customs according to different conditions in accordance with the relevant clauses of the "Interim Law of the People's Republic of China on Customs:"

(1)   False declarations;

(2)   The delivery or shipment of the import or export goods and materials which have not been cleared by the Customs by a unit concerned without authorization;

(3)   Smuggling by making use of the import or export goods and materials;

(4)   Selling the goods which are cleared duty-free by the Customs without authorization;

(5)   The goods which are permitted by the Customs to import temporarily are not re-exported as scheduled and their Customs formalities are not supplemented as stipulated;

(6)   Opening Customs envelopes and sealing marks without authorization or losing the Customs envelopes;

(7)   Other violations against the provisions of the Customs.

Article 11:   According to the requirements of the work, the Customs shall establish offices or station officers in the cooperative exploration and exploitation bases of sea oil. Oil companies and their branches shall supply free working rooms and living facilities.

Article 12:   These Procedures shall be put into effect as of October 1, 1981.

III PORT CONTROL

SECTION A: Administration

Provisional Regulations of the People's Republic of China for the Administration of Ports

(Promulgated by the Government Administrative Council and enforced on January 23, 1954)

I General Rules

Article 1: All the ports along the coasts of the People's Republic of China shall be provided respectively with port administration bureaux, sub-bureaux and offices (hereinafter referred to as "port central office(s)") by the Ministry of Communications of the Central People's Government (hereinafter referred as the "MOC of the CPG") according to the demands of trade and transport and in light of the handling duties and equipment capacity of each port. With regard to the establishment or withdrawal of a port office, an application shall be made by the MOC of the CPG to the Government Administrative Council of the Central People's Government (hereinafter referred to as the GAC) for approval and promulgation.

Article 2: Port offices shall be responsible for the management of port and other affairs as required by these Regulations and each one shall be a business accounting unit in our enterprise economy.

Article 3: Port office shall be under the direct jurisdiction and be centrally coordinated by the Headquarters of Marine Transportation of the MOC of the CPG in administration, business, technology and finance. Port offices shall also be subject to the supervision and direction of local people's government.

Article 4: The director or chief of a port office shall be charged with the fulfillment of the port production and financial plans, the utilization and safeguard of the port property and equipment and the maintenance of the port safety, order and staff discipline. To carry out the above tasks smoothly, he shall maintain close contact and cooperation with the Navy, public security, public health, coustoms and other departments concerned.

Article 5:   The orders and instructions issued by the director or chief of a port office, provided these are within the limits of his statutory authority, shall be strictly observed and executed by the organizations, enterprises, vesels and by all personnel concerned.

Article 6:   All port equipment within the boundary of a port shall be under the unified management of the port office. The wharves, warehouses, subsidiary office builings, etc. which are still in the possession of other organizations and enterprises within the port boundary shall be handed over to the port office gradually for its unified management and administration as required under Article 13 of these Regulations.

Article 7:   Whenever any other organization or enterprise of the state has to carry out any engineering construction within the boundary of a port, application shall be made to the port office for approval.

Article 8:   In compliance with other decrees and regulations, a port office shall be charged with the supervision and direction of the private shipping companies' affairs which include the vessels, wharves and warehouses within the jurisdiction of the port.

II   The Delimitation of Port Boundary

Article 9:   The land boundary of a port includes the land occupied by the port and the coastline, wharves, warehouses, machinery, equipment, dangerous goods storage areas, fuel and material storage areas and oil-filling equipment, dockyard, docks, related port engineering structures, fresh water supply base, beacons, etc.

Article 10:   The water boundary of a port includes the surface and underwater areas occupied by the port, courses for vessels to enter or leave the port, all enchorages and berths, river branches connected with and needed by the port and adjacent waters with potentialities for the future development of the port.

Article 11:   To delimit the boundary of a port, each port office shall work out a scheme of the port boundary according to concrete conditions, draw a plan of the land and water boundaries and submit them together with the manual to the local people's government so that the units concerned can be called together to discuss them and make a decision, which shall be submitted to the MOC of the CPG for verification and then passed on to the GAC for approval before their execution.

Article 12:   The railway line within a port boundary used for the transfer of goods and passengers between the railway and a steamship is the business line of the railway authorities. The one used for the transfer of goods within the port itself is the exclusive line of the port office. The system of the division of labour between the railway and the port and the rules for the operation of trains and cars within the port area shall be handled on the basis of agreements or contracts signed by the railway administration office and the port office.

Article 13:   Other state organizations and enterprises shall continue to hold and use the wharves, warehouses, subsidiary office buildings, etc. in their present possession within the port boundary; their property rights should not be changed for the time being. They shall also continue to rent the wharves and warehouses they are renting within the port area, but these places shall be places under the unified management of the port office. To meet the needs for the development of internal and foreign trade, the port office shall, wherever appropriate, make applications to the local people's government for decision so that these premises should be regulated and regained and their leases terminated.

The Ministry of Agriculture and the Ministry of Commerce of the Central People's Government shall still enjoy the property rights of the fishing wharves, petroleum wharves and their special-use warehouses in their present possession within the port boundary and the stevedores assigned to these places shall also be under the leadership and administration of them respectively.

III   Authority of Port Offices

Article 14:   The duties of the port offices shall be to:

(1)   Supervised each party concerned in the observation of the state decrees relating to shipping and port affairs and take effective measures to prevent and stop all acts in violation of the aforesaid decrees;

(2)   Be charged with the safeguard of all equipment in port boundaries and waterways, maintain the depths and widths of courses and waterways, and guarantee the safety of vessels in entering or leaving ports and the improvement of their navigation efficiency;

(3)   Carry out various items of construction in ports in order to ensure the development of national economy,

(4)   Supervise stevedores, coordinate the handling, custody, receipt and delivery of goods, supervise goods and passenger transportation, coordinate such means of land and water communications as motor vehicles, carts, lighters, etc. and handle such business as the receipt, delivery or re-export of goods;

(5)   Manage and supply ships' fuel, materials and fresh water and other services for vessels;

(6)   Organize pilotage, administer and supervise the entries and exits of vessels;

(7)   Establish and supervise port radio stations to circulate meteorological information among sailing vessels and consult with them about maritime affairs;

(8)   Rescue vessels, lives, goods, etc. from distress and keep the salvaged property in good custody; investigate and handle all maritime affairs and average cases;

(9)   Administer examination of seamen and pilots; grant them certificates; handle the registry of vessels;

(10)   Assist ship registry offices in survey and measurement of vessels;

(11)   Supervise all projects, machinery and building equipment in ports and carry out technical examination and maintenance of them;

(12)   Supervise hygienic and fire prevention equipment in ports and carry out epidemic prevention examination and the jobs of safety and pubic health;

(13)   Supervise and maintain lighting, signal and security equipment which is under the jurisdiction of the ports;

(14)   Collect port charges and various fees as stipulated;

(15)   Supervise and direct all the affairs of private shipping companies, vessels, wharves, warehouses and holders of port tools which are under the jurisdiction of ports

Article 15:   The limits of the authority of port offices are as follows:

(1)   To be entitled to sign various relevant business contracts in the name of port offices in accordance with the laws, regulations, orders and instructions issued by the MOC of the CPG;

(2)   To promulgate various necessary rules, regulations and procedures as stipulated by the decrees after approval from the MOC of the CPG;

(3)   To investigate, charge or fine the organizations, enterprises, vessels and individuals who are found contravening the state decrees and regulations relating to shipping and port affairs;

(4)   To inflict such punishments as warning, demerit record, demotion or withdrawal of certificates from seamen, pilots, etc who have violated technical safety provisions;

(5)   To be entitled to take effective measures if necessary and to require the vessels staying in ports and the organizations, enterprises or individuals within the port boundaries to supply all first-aid tools or equipment immediately so as to prevent injury to human bodies, lives, vessels, goods and other property and to maintain unobstructed courses;

(6)   To be entitled to demand owners of sunken ships and things in port water or its vicinity to salvage the same within a specific time, and to salvage or remove the same without the consent of the owners if they obstruct waterways and are not disposed of within the specified time upon the issue of the announcements or written notices; the expenses required and other payable taxes according to regulations shall be compensated for with the proceeds from selling off the salvaged ships and things, the deficiency to be borne by the original owners or the surplus to be refunded to them;

(7)   For the sake of the safety of port boundaries and the needs of operation, the port office is entitled to require the owner(s) to remove or move out any properties or goods in port boundaries within a specified time; with regard to the removal of fixed structures, applications shall be made to local people's governments for disposition;

(8)   For goods not taken within the time limit, the port offices shall be entitled to dispose of the same in accordance with relevant decrees and regulations.

Article 16:   When a vessel is involved in any of the following cases, the port office shall be entitled to prohibit it from leaving the port:

(1) Contravening the provisions for the safety specifications relating to ship's certificates, ship's current state, supplies, equipment, etc. or the provisions of other decrees and regulations:

(2) Failing to pay the following sums:

1. Various port charges;
2. Fines for contravening decrees and regulations;
3. Reparations for the damage of port engineering structures, course marks and other property in the port.

Article 17: The port office shall clear the vessel which is prohibited from leaving the port due to the failure to pay the sums as stipulated in the preceding Article if it supplies sufficient guaranties to compensate for the sums.

Article 18: If the vessel damages any port project(s), structure(s), course mark(s) or other property in the port, but the responsibility has not been established, the port office shall be entitled to prohibit the vessel from leaving the port for not more than 3 days (to be counted from the time when the order reaches the opposite party until a full 72 hours have elapsed), and if the responsibility has not been established within the said time, the vessel shall be cleared.

Article 19: All expenses of the vessel during the time when it is prohibited from leaving the port (including examination, verification and other fees) shall be borne by the vessel.

Article 20: If a port office without authorization or any decrees prohibits a vessel from leaving the port, the vessel shall be entitled to claim compensation by the port office for the direct loss it has incurred due to the prohibition from leaving the port and has the right to sue the port office.

Article 21: The port office shall be entitled to sue the original claimant(s) if the office has prohibited a vessel from leaving the port upon request by any other organization, enterprise or individual but such a prohibition has been held by the court to be illegal.

Article 22: The affairs relating to wharves, warehouses and their subsidiary equipment within port areas which are not run by the state shall be dealt with in accordance with the current government decrees and they shall be under the unified administration and control of port offices.

IV Supplementary Provisions

Article 23: With regard to the corporate economic status and fixed capital of a port office, separate regulations shall be formulated and put into effect by the MOC of the CPG.

Article 24: The procedures for the Navy to use ports shall be separately formulated by the GAC.

Article 25: These Regulations shall be put into effect as from the date of approval of promulgation by the GAC.

Collection of Port Dues and Charges on the Import & Export of Cargo carried by Foreign Vessels & for International Trade

(Enforced on January 1972)

Article 1:   These regulations shall apply to port dues and charges levied and collected on ocean-going vessels engaged in international trade and on cargoes imported or exported foreign in ports of the People's Republic of China.

Article 2:   Rates in these regulations are fixed and collected in Renminbi Yuan. All disbursements for account of payer shall be settled in Renminbi or in foreign currency at official exchange rate published by the People's Bank of China.

Each ship or its agent shall submit to the Harbour Authorites in writing, not later than the date of ship's arrival, the terms and conditions stipulated in C/P and/or Contract of Affreightment in connection with the responsibility for the payment of port dues and charges, failing which the accounts shall be settled with the agent.

Article 3:   Charging mode and calculating unit:

(1)   For vessels chargeable according to NRT (or DWT if no NRT), part of one NRT shall be taken as one NRT or DWT; for vessels chargeable according to HP, part of one HP shall be taken as one HP.

(2)   For charges payable according to days used, part of one day shall be taken as one day; for charges payable according to hours used, part of one hour shall be taken as one hour.

(3)   Charge on cargoes shall be calculated by metric tons in gross weight.

Minimum weight of each kind of cargo on B/L calculatable is 10 kilos; any fraction over 5 kilos if it exceeds 10 kilos shall be taken as another 10 kilos, while the fraction below 5 kilos be dropped. The weight of more than two kinds of cargoes listed in same class shall be aggregated and its fractional weight shall be rounded up.

Minimum charge on each B/L collectable is RMB ￥0.10. Cargoes as fixed with converting weight rates shall be charged according to "Table of Converting Rates". (Table IV)

For import cargoes, the weight /measurement on B/L shall be taken; for export cargoes, the same shall be offered by the shippers/cargo-owners.

Article 4: Payers shall make all payments on the second day after receiving the notice of payment; should the second day fall on Sunday/holiday, it may be extended accordingly. In case dues and charges being undercharged or overcharged, both payee and payer may claim a refund from each other within 180 days after settlement. No claim against the refund shall be made at the expiry of this period.

Article 5: Both pilotage and shifting charge on vessels entering or leaving port and moving inside harbour with pilot on board shall be collected separately according to ship's NRT (or HP in case of a tug).

Pilotage:

Shanghai and Whampoa: RMB ￥0.30 per NRT (or HP)
Other ports: RMB ￥0.20 per NRT (or HP)

Shifting charge:

Tientsin: RMB ￥0.20 per NRT (or HP)
Other ports: RMB ￥0.10 per NRT (or HP)

The minimum tonnage of pilotage and shifting charge calculatable is 500 tons (or HP).

Pilotage or shifting charge on vessels under tow shall be calculated respectively on tug's HP and vessel's NRT. No charge shall be collected on boat used for pilot's communication.

Article 6: Charges shall be collected at the towage rate if tugs are used for towing vessels entering or leaving port and moving inside harbour.

Article 7: Harbour dues shall be levied on vessels at the rate of RMB ￥0.25 per NRT (or HP in case of a tug) for each entry or departure.

Vessels entering/leaving in ballast, for refuge and non-engagement in carriage of passengers/cargoes shall be exempted from payment of the harbour dues.

Article 8: Berthing charge shall be collected at the rate of RMB ￥0.10 per NRT (or HP)/day on following vessels berthing alongside wharf or at buoy:

(1) Remaining in berth 4 hours after completion of loading/unloading (that means the delivery of cargo has been completed).

(2) Without loading/unloading in harbour.

(3) Taking berth alongside wharf or at buoy waiting to be repaired or under repaid.

(4) Entering for refuge but remaining in berth 4 hours after release of alarm.

Note: Time used in cleaning and sweeping holds, time lost in waiting for tide and in waiting for loading/unloading caused by fault of the harbour shall be deducted from the berthing time without collection of the berthing charge.

Article 9: Charges for opening/closing hatches shall be collected per hatch (irrespective of decks) at the following rate.

2,000 NRT or under: RMB ￥50.00 per hatch

2,001 NRT upwards: RMB ￥100.00 per hatch

No charge shall be collected in case the opening/closing of hatches is operated during the period of loading/unloading.

Article 10: Loading/unloading charges and harbour dues on goods shall be collected on import/export cargoes at the rates fixed in "Loading/Unloading Charges for Import/Export Cargoes in International Trade". (Table I)

(1)   The loading/unloading charge shall be calculated as if the ship was not equipped with any handling devices in case the port handling devices have to be used for loading/unloading because: a) the ship is not equipped with at least one set of handling device per each hatch; b) the handling equipments fail to work for causes not due to the fault of the harbour; or c) the master refuses to let use of ship's handling equipments.

(2)   Rates of the loading/unloading charges from ship's hold to ship's side (including lighters) or vice versa shall be calculated at 50% of the rate on "cargo hold" from ship to warehouse, storing place, wagon, ship or vice versa.

(3)   The difference shall be borne by the ship between the rates of the loading/unloading charges on cargo operations carried out in "cargo hold" and in refrigerated cargo, holds deep-tanks, oil-tanks, water-tanks, small hatches, cabins or ship without handling devices.

(4)   The loading/unloading charges on heavy lifts, if the port handling devices are used shall be doubled at the rate of "heavy lifts" fixed in "Loading/Unloading Charges for Import/Export Cargoes in International Trade". The charges on floating crane shall be collected according to the hire actually paid in case it is hired by the harbour from other party while its loading/unloading charges collected at the corresponding rates.

(5)   In case cargoes in packages are loaded in bulk by means of cutting open its bags at ship's side, an additional charge for cutting and emptying the bags shall be collected at the rate of RMB ￥0.40 per ton. In case cargoes in bulk are discharged by means of bagging cargoes in ship's holds, an additional charge for bagging cargoes and sewing the bags shall be collected at the rate of RMB ￥0.40 per ton.

Article 11: Harbour dues on import/export goods in international trade shall be collected respectively in accordance with "Loading/Unloading Charges for Import/Export Cargoes in International Trade".

Mails, fuel and store as well as appliances for ship's own use, dunnaging and lashing materials, spare packing stuffs with the cargo, articles for embassys, gifts, and presents, exhibition goods and international transit goods shall be exempted from payment of the harbour dues.

Article 12: Winchman charge shall be collected according to tons of cargo actually loaded/unloaded at the rate of RMB ￥0.08 per ton.

Article 13: Other services as applied and hire of port's handling devices and boats shall be charged at the rates fixed in the "Rates for other Service and Hire of Handling Devices and Boats in Harbour". (Table

III)

Article 14: Charges for stevedores standing by on account of the ship shall be collected at the rate of RMB ¥1.00 per man/hour.

Article 15: Tallying charge on foreign vessels at various sea ports shall be collected in accordance with the following Regulations:

    (1) Tallying charge:

        1. Fertilizers, sugar, cereals, ore, ore powder, cement, soda ash and salt in bags: RMB ¥0.20 per ton.

        2. Other cargoes in packages: RMB ¥0.30 per ton.

        3. Cargoes in bulk (package uncounted): RMB ¥0.05 per ton.

    (2) Charge on distinguishing cargo's marks: RMB ¥0.10 per ton.

    (3) Re-tallying charge: RMB ¥0.20 per ton.

    (4) Charge for tallymen standing by: RMB ¥2.00 per man/hour.

    (5) Drawing Stowage Plan of a set of 4 copies for 50 lots or under of cargoes loaded: RMB ¥5.00.

Drawing Stowage Plan of a set of 4 copies for 51 lots or upward of cargoes loaded: RMB ¥10.00.

Each additional copy shall be charged at RMB ¥1.00.

    (6) The minimum tallying charge: RMB ¥10.00.

Article 16: International transit goods refer to goods from one foreign country to itself or to another transhipped at port(s) of the People's Republic of China by means of the following transhipment:

    (1) Ship to ship transhipment;

    (2) Ship to rail transhipment;

    (3) Rail to ship transhipment.

The transhipment charges for international transit goods shall be collected according to the rates fixed in the "Rates for International Transit Goods", in which the charges shall include those only for loading/unloading, conveying, lightering and tallying so incurred in the harbour. All other charges shall be collected separately according to the expenses actually incurred.

Note: No transhipment shall be made for bulk-oil, highly dangerous goods, fresh cargoes, livestocks and animals.

Article 17: The Ministry of Communications of the People's Republic of China is the authority for the interpretation of these Regulations.

Regulations on Border Inspection Procedures

*(Promulgated by the State Council and
enforced on April 30, 1965)*

Article 1:   With a view to safeguarding the sovereignty and national security of
the People's Republic of China and facilitating the entry and exit of
people and means of communication and transportation, border
inspection stations shall be set up at harbours, airports, boundary
railway stations and other outlets open to foreign countries and at
ports specially authorized for entry and exit.

Article 2:   Border inspection stations shall be responsible for inspecting people
entering and leaving the country, their passports and other entry and
exit documents and baggage, and means of communication and
transportation entering and leaving the country and the commodities
carried therein.

Article 3:   People and means of communication and transportation entering and
leaving the country shall pass through harbours, airports, boundary
railway stations and other outlets open to foreign countries and
through ports specially authorized for entry and exit.

People entering and leaving the country shall comply with the laws
and decrees of the People's Republic of China and with the border
inspection system.

Article 4:   People entering and leaving the country shall produce their passports
or other entry and exit documents to the border inspection stations for
inspection.

Border inspection stations shall prohibit the entry and exit of those
who refuse to produce their passports or other entry and exit
documents for inspection. Those whose passports or other entry and
exit documents are not in accordance with the entry and exit

regulations of our country shall be prohibited from entering or leaving the country and ordered to apply for proper entry and exit documents.

Article 5: People entering and leaving the country shall allow the border inspection stations to inspect their baggage.

The border inspection stations shall handle the baggage of foreign diplomats, consular officers and other personnel entitled to preferential treatment in accordance with the relevant stipulations laid down by the People's Republic of China.

Article 6: Captains of ships entering or leaving the country shall submit to the border inspection stations a list of their crew members and passengers and shall accept inspection by the inspection stations.

Crew members and other personnel when embarking on or disembarking from their ships shall produce valid documents to the border inspection stations for inspection. They shall not embark on or disembark from their ships without the permission of the border inspection stations.

Ships entering or leaving the country, when sailing within the territorial sea, harbours or rivers of the People's Republic of China, shall not drop off or take on people, or load or unload goods midway. Chinese ships and ships of other nationalities in distress, on being allowed to sail into harbours not open to foreign countries in the People's Republic of China, shall accept inspection by the local border defence forces or the public security organs. They shall leave the harbours immediately when the causes of their distress no longer exist.

Article 7: Captains of airplanes entering or leaving the country shall submit to the border inspection stations a list of their crew members and passengers and shall accept inspection by the border inspection stations.

Planes entering the country, before landing at the designated airports, and planes leaving the country, from the time they take off from the designated airports until they leave the border, shall not land midway or air-drop personnel and goods. If, in the event of distress or accident they are compelled to land or air-drop personnel and goods midway, the captains should immediately report the details and the causes to the border inspection stations or local public security organs through civil aeronautic stations.

Article 8: Chief conductors of train crews or conductors of cargo trains entering and leaving the country shall report to the border inspection stations the number of crew members and passengers and the marshalling activity of the train and shall accept inspection by the border inspection stations.

Trains entering or leaving the country, when running from the border to a railway station inside the People's Republic of China, shall not drop off or take on people, load or unload goods, or stop without reason midway.

Article 9: Responsible persons of automobiles or other motor vehicles entering or leaving the country shall report to the border inspection stations the number of crew members and passengers with a description of the goods carried therein. They shall accept inspection by the border inspection stations.

Non-mechanical vehicles or horse-drawn carts entering or leaving the country shall accept inspection by the border inspection stations.

Article 10:   If ships, airplanes, trains, automobiles and other means of communication and transportation carry people entering or leaving the country illegally or goods endangering the security of our country, the responsible persons of the means of communication and transportation must report to the border inspection stations immediately and await their action.

Article 11:   People violating these regulations shall be dealt with by the border inspection stations according to the circumstances of the cases and in accordance with the law.

Article 12:   These regulations shall take effect from the date of promulgation.

SECTION B: Ship

General Rules Governing Joint Inspection of Incoming and Outgoing Ships

(Approved by the State Council on September 8, 1961 and on October 24, 1961)

1.   These General Rules are enacted for the purpose of strengthening joint inspection of incoming and outgoing ships, crews of ships, passengers, baggage and cargo so as to insure safety of navigation, safeguard the security of the frontiers, stop smuggling, prevent epidemics from being brought into or out of the country, and facilitate the movement of ships entering into and leaving the harbours and foreign trade and transportation.

2.   The organs which shall take part in the joint inspection and the different spheres of inspection to be carried out on their responsibility are as follows:

a.   Harbour Bureau: to assume responsibility for examining the ship's documents and matters concerning the safety of navigation of ships.

b.   Customs: to assume responsibility for inspecting the ships, cargo, and the baggage and articles carried by crews of ships and passengers to see whether there is breaching of laws and smuggling.

c.   Frontier inspection organ: to assume responsibility for carrying out frontier inspection of the ships as well as the passports, related documents, baggage and articles of ships' crew and passengers.

d.   Frontier health and quarantine organ: to assume responsibility for carrying out medical inspection and health inspection and for giving the necessary health treatment to the ships, crews of ships, passengers, luggage and cargo.

Except with the special approval of the State Council, no other organ may carry out inspection.

3.   Permits for ships' entry into and departure from ports shall be handled by the Harbour Bureau, and no other organ may obstruct or detain the ships under any pretext. In case it is necessary to prohibit or delay a ship's entry into or departure from the port, the action must be taken through the Harbour Bureau.

4.   The Harbour Bureau shall assume responsibility for organizing the joint inspection and shall notify the relevant inspection organs in advance of the time at which a ship enters into and departs from the port and the place of its berth.

5.   When the ship is, according to regulations, subject to quarantine inspection at the time of entry into the port, all personnel taking part in joint inspection, except for the pilot and personnel approved by the frontier and quarantine personnel, should board the ship to carry out inspection after the ship is being examined by the quarantine personnel.

6.   Inspection of the baggage and personal effects of foreign diplomats and consular officials and other personnel entitled to preferential treatment shall be handled in accordance with the relevant regulations of the People's Republic of China.

7.   Unless otherwise provided for by the State, Chinese ships navigating in inland rivers and along the coast shall, in principle, not be subject to inspection. If necessary, inspection may be carried out by the relevant inspection organs through the Habour Bureau.

8.   Inspection of ships, crews of ships, passengers, baggage and cargo shall be limited to the port of departure, port of arrival and port of call. Unless under special circumstances, a ship may not be stopped for inspection while on its way.

9.   The Harbour Bureau at each port shall periodically call and chair a joint inspection conference attended by representatives of the Customs, frontier inspection organ and frontier helath and quarantine organ and, if necessary, may invite representatives from other organs concerned to attend the conference to discuss matters concerning joint inspection.

The joint inspection conference shall appoint a secretary to handle the routine affairs under the leadership of the Harbour Bureau.

10.   the term "inspection" in these General Rules refers to the items listed under Article 2. Where provisions have been made, other matters, such as control exercised by the harbour bureaus over ships, supervision and collection of duties by the Customs in respect of ships and cargo, and health supersvision exercised by the frontier health and quarantine organs in respect of ships shall still be handled by the competent organs in accordance with the relevant provisions.

11.   These General Rules shall be put into effect from the date of their promulgation.

Regulations Governing Supervision and Control of Foreign Vessels by the People's Republic of China

(Approved by the State Council on August 22, 1979)

General Provisions

Article 1: The purpose of these Regulations is to safeguard the sovereignty of the People's Republic of China, to maintain traffic order in port areas and coastal waters, to ensure safety of navigation and to prevent pollution of waters.

Article 2: These Regulations as well as relevant laws, statutes and rules issued by the Government of the People's Republic of China (all foreign vessels (hereinafter referred to as "vessels") navigating in port areas and coastal waters of the People's Republic of China) shall comply with. Vessels shall be subject to inspections by the Harbour Superintendency Administration set up in the port by the Government of the People's Republic of China where the latter deems such inspections necessay.

The term "coastal waters" mentioned in these Regulations means inland waters and territorial sea of the People's Republic of China as well as water areas officially defined as coming under the jurisdiction thereof.

Part 1 Entry, Departure and Navigation

Article 3: The master or owner of a vessel shall, a week prior to its expected arrival at the port, submit the required forms to the Habour Superintendency Administration through the vessel's port agent for completion of entry formalities, and shall report, 24 hours in advance of her arrival (or on her departure from the last port of call if the voyage takes less than 24 hours), the vessel's ETA, fore and aft drafts on arrival to the Harbour Superintendency Administration through the port agent. Should there be any change in the ETA, same shall be reported in time.

A report shall be submitted in advance to the Harbour Superintendency Administration in case of special circumstances, such as the vessel being in distress, the engines broken down or her crew or passengers suffered from acute disease, which necessitate the vessel to make an emergent entry into or to return to the port during the voyage.

Article 4:   No vessel shall enter or leave the port, or navigate or shift berths therein without a pilot being appointed by the Harbour Superintendency Administration. Matters regarding pilotage shall be dealt with according to the Regulations with respect to Sea-port Pilotage issued by the Ministry of Communications of the People's Republic of China.

Article 5:   Upon arrival at the port, vessels shall immediately submit the Entry Report and other relevant forms for check-up, besides,vessels shall submit ship's papers and relevant documents for examination and be subject to inspections. Prior to leave, vessels shall submit the Departure Report and other relevant forms for clearance examination and may only leave the port after port clearance has been obtained.

Article 6:   Upon arrival at the port, arms and ammunition on board are to be sealed up by the Harbour Superintendency Administration. Radio-telegraph transmitter, radio-telephone transmitter, signal rockets, flare signals and signal guns shall only be used in case of emergency, and a report shall be made to the Harbour Superintendency Administration immediately after such things have been used.

Article 7:   Shooting, swimming, fishing, setting off of firecrackers or fireworks and other actions calculated to endanger the order and security of the port shall be prohibited.

Article 8:   The Harbour Superintendency Administration is fully authorized to detain the vessel concerned, or to order the vessel to stop sailing, to change route or to return to the port under any of the following circumstances:
          (a)   unseaworthiness;
          (b)   violation of laws or regulations of the People's Republic of China,
          (c)   involvement in marine accident;
          (d)   non-payment of expenses to which the vessel is liable or failure to produce security required, or
          (e)   other cases prohibiting the vessel from sailing.

Article 9:   Vessels navigating in Chinese port areas and coastal waters shall comply with regulations governing straits, waterways, routes and areas closed to navigation and shall not be engaged in activities endangering the national safety, rights and interests of the People's Republic of China.

Article 10:   Vessels navigating within the port areas shall not proceed at a speed liable to endanger the safety of other vessels and port installations.

Article 11:   Boats (rafts) attached to vessels shall not be sailed within port areas except for life-saving purposes.

Article 12:   No vessel shall have its boats, derricks and gangways, etc., stretched outboard while navigating or shifting berths within port areas.

Article 13:   Vessels requiring to enter any of the Chinese ports open to foreign trade for shelter or temporary stay shall apply to the Harbour Superintendency Administration for permission. Such application shal state: name of the vessel, call-sign, vessel's nationality, name of the shipping company, port of sailing, port of destination, vessel's position, speed, drafts, colour of hull and colour and mark of funnel. Such vessels shall take shelter at places designated.

Vessels requiring to take shelter or to lie at anchor temporarily at places other than any of those Chinese ports open to foreign trade shall, in addition to the above formalities, observe the following regulations:

  (a)   reporting promptly to the nearest Harbour Superintendency Administration the time and position of anchoring and the time of departure;

  (b)   fulfilling the requirements of local authorities concerned and submitting to their inspections, inquires and instructions; and

  (c)   no one to be allowed ashore and no cargo loaded or discharged without permission of local authorities concerned.

Part 2   Berthing

Article 14:   While berthing in port, vessels shall have on board a sufficient member of men to ensure safe manoeuvring, and, in case of emergency such as typhoon warning, etc., all crew members shall return immediately aboard to take necessary precautions and urgent measures.

Article 15:   Gangways for access of crew members, passengers and other persons shall be properly secured and fitted with railing or manropes. Rope ladders shall be safe and strong. Sufficient illumination shall be available at night.

Article 16:   Vessels requiring to work propellers shall pay close attention to the surroundings at the stern, and shall only do so under the condition that the safety of other vessels and harbour installations has been ensured.

Article 17:   While berthing in port, all exhaust valves and discharge openings of the vessel which may give trouble to other vessels, harbour craft, the wharf or the access of persons shall be properly covered.

Article 18:   No light of any vessel shall be exhibited in such a manner as to impair the safe navigation of other vessels; strong lights directed at the fairway must be properly screened.

Article 19:   All vessels should be in safe and good working conditions for cargo operation as required. All cargo handling equipments should be maintained in good working order and certificate of fitness should be made available therefor.

Article 20:   Vessels shall apply in advance for and obtain permission from the Harbour Superintendency Administration before carrying out the

following operations:
    (a)   overhauling of any boiler, main-engine, windlass, steering gear or radio-station;
    (b)   trial trip or engine-test;
    (c)   lowering boat (raft) for life-saving drill;
    (d)   welding (except for repairing in shipyard) or working with naked light on deck; or
    (e)   decorating with colourful lights.

Article 21:   Vessels under fumigation shall take strict safety measures and exhibit appropriate signals prescribed by the Harbour Superintendency Administration.

Article 22:   In order to ensure the safety of the port and vessels, when ordered to shift berth or to sail ahead of or behind the schedule, vessels shall observe such orders as given by the Harbour Superintendency Administration.

Part 3   Signals and Communications

Article 23:   Vessels navigating or berthing in Chinese port areas or coastal waters shall by day hoist the national flag of the country or registry. On entering or leaving port or shifting berths, vessels shall in addition display signal-letters and relevant signals prescribed by the Harbour Superintendency Administration.

Article 24:   When entering or leaving port or at anchor, vessels shall pay close attention to the call and signals of the port signalstation. When visual signals are used, the Regulations with respect to Coastal Port Signals issued by the Government of the People's Republic of China shall be complied with. Where signals are not specified by Chinese coastal ports, the International Code of Signals shall be applicable.

Article 25:   Vessels shall not make sound signals at will within the port except when necessitated by safety of navigation. Vessels requiring to test whistles shall make an advance report to the Harbour Superintendency Administration.

Article 26:   Vessels making use of their VHF radio-telephone in port shall comply with the Provisional Regulations Governing the Use of VHF Radio-telephone by Foreign Vessels issued by the Ministry of Communications of the People's Republic of China.

Part 4   Dangerous Cargoes

Article 27:   Vessels carrying or handling dangerous cargoes shall exhibit the prescribed signals, comply with the regulations relating to the carriage of dangerous cargoes and take all necessary safety measures. Cargoes of contradictory nature, in particular, must be separately stowed. It is strictly forbidden to stow explosives with ignitable materials or inflammable cargoes in the same hold.

Article 28:   Vessels carrying grade I highly hazardous cargoes shall, 3 days prior to the ETA, apply to the Harbour Superintendency Administration through their port agent for endorsement, with their descriptive names, properties, packing, quantity, place of stowage stated in detail and a booklet of Description of Dangerous Materials attached, and shall not enter the port, discharge the cargoes or make transit unless permission has been obtained. Such cargoes being: explosives, highly poisonous articles, radio-active substances, compressed gases, liquefied gases, oxidizing agents, substances liable to spontaneous combustion, substances which, in contact with water, emit inflammable gases, inflammable liquids, inflammable solids, acidic corrosives, etc.

Vessels intending to carry the above-mentioned hazardous cargoes for export shall, 3 days prior to the loading thereof, apply for endorsement and shall not load until permission has been obtained.

Article 29: Vessels applying for Certificate of Safety Stowage of Export Dangerous Cargoes shall, 3 days prior to loading, submit a written application to the Harbour Superintendency Administration, stating, inter alia: descriptive names, properties, packing, quantity, place of stowage (accompanied by stowage plan), intermediate ports, port of destination, and shall load at the berths designated by the Harbour Superintendency Administration.

Part 5   Fairway Protection

Article 30: Vessels under way shall comply with the rules of navigation and maintain traffic order. In case of accidents involving the risk of sinking, a report shall immediately be made to the Harbour Superintendency Administration and all effective measures shall be taken to steer clear of the fairway to avoid impeding the traffic and endangering other vessels. If the vessel is sunk, a temporary signal shall promptly be marked by the parties involved at the place of the wreck.

Article 31: Salvage operations on shipwrecks or other objects in port areas or coastal waters shall be carried out in accordance with the Regulations Governing the Salvage of Shipwrecks or Sunken Objects issued by the Government of the People's Republic of China. The Harbour Superintendency Administration may, as it thinks fit, notify the owners thereof to carry out salvage and clear the fairway within a specified time, or to arrange an immediate salvage to refloat or demolish the sunken vessel or object and to clear the fairway, with all responsibilities and expenses incurred borne by the owners concerned.

Article 32: Where any sunken or floating object has been found by any vessel, a report thereon shall be made and the object salvaged handed over to the Harbour Superintendency Administration, whereupon, a reward may be given by the latter as appropriate.

Article 33: Where any vessel wishes to dispose of any refuse such as garbage in port, it shall exhibit signals prescribed by the Harbour Superintendency Administration to request ash boats (cars).

Article 34: Fairway installations and aids to navigation shall be well cared for. Vessels causing damages thereto or to harbour constructions or other facilities shall report immediately to the Harbour Superintendency Administration and shall be held responsible for the restoration made or the expenses incurred.

Part 6   Prevention of Pollution

Article 35:   No vessel shall discharge oils, oily mixtures or other harmful pollutants or refuse within port areas and coastal waters of the People's Republic of China.

Article 36:   If any ballast water, tank washings or bilge water is to be discharged from any vessel, an application shall be made to the Harbour Superintendency Administration for approval. Where a vessel has arrived from a plague-infested port, necessary sanitary treatment should been given by the Quarantine Authorities. Dirty water and hold washings from holds where dangerous cargoes or harmful pollutants have been stowed shall only be discharged at the designated place after their having been tested by and to the satisfaction of the sanitation departments concerned.

Article 37:   Oil tankers and vessels with oil as fuel shall carry the Oil Record Book on board and make appropriate entries as required.

Article 38:   Where a pollution has occurred within the port area or coastal waters, the vessel at fault shall have all relative particulars entered in the Oil Record Book and the Deck Log, and shall have the matter immediately reported to the Harbour Superintendency Administration. Meanwhile, all effective measures shall be taken to prevent the oil from spreading. Where any chemicals should be applied, an application together with a description of their compositions and properties shall be sent to the Harbour Superintendency Administration for approval.

Article 39:   Matters not provided for in this part shall be dealt with in accordance with the regulations relatings to the prevention of pollution of marine environment issued by the Government of the People's Republic of China.

Part 7   Fire-Fighting and Salvage

Article 40:   Smoking or making naked fire in the hold or elsewhere liable to cause fire hazard to the vessels is strictly prohibited.

Article 41:   Vessels bunkering oil or oil-tankers handling cargo oil shall take strict fire prevention measures for safety.

Article 42:   While welding in port, vessels shall clean up the surroundings beforehand, take strict precautionary measures, he provided with fire-fighting apparatus and examine the worksite before and after the operation. No welding can be done inside or near oil compartments, unless and until all the oil has been emptied, oil residues cleared out, the compartments sufficiently ventilated, the inflammable gases expelled, and a certificate of fitness obtained.

Article 43   Should any vessel be involved in a fire hazard or marine casualties, an immediate report shall be made to the Harbour Superintendency Administration. Such report must contain ship's position, tonnage, drafts, cargo on board, damages suffered and assistance required.

Article 44:   Where necessary, the Harbour Superintendency Administration may order and direct any vessel in port or in coastal waters to rescue the vessel in distress. The vessel so ordered and directed is obliged to do its utmost to render every possible assistance as long as its own safety will not be endangered.

Article 45: As soon as the officers from the Harbour Superintendency Administration or the salvage departments concerned have arrived, the master of the vessel in distress shall report the accident occurred and measures taken so far, provide all information and facilities required and make suggestions with regard to the salvage as appropriate. All decisions taken by the Harbour Superintendency Administration for maintaining safety and order shall be complied with by all parties concerned.

Part 8   Marine Accidents

Article 46: Should any vessel be involved in marine accident, the master shall give the Harbour Superintendency Administration a summarized report by telegram or radio-telephone soonest possible. In case the accident has occurred outside of port areas, the master shall, within 48 hours of the vessel's arrival at the first port of call, submit a marine accident report to the Harbour Superintendency Administration. Such report shall be submitted within 24 hours of the accident if the same has happened in port.

Article 47: Should any vessel be involved in marine accident causing death of or injury to persons or damages to properties in port areas or coastal waters of the People's Republic of China, the master of the vessel at fault shall render every possible assistance to the ship and persons in distress, make timely report to the Harbour Superintendency Administration and be prepared for investigation and settlement. Should the party at fault refrain from rendering any assistance in spite of the imminent danger or flee into hiding, severge punishment will be imposed.

Article 48: Should death happen to any person on board, an immediate report thereof shall be sent to the Harbour Superintendency Administration. Where any damage or death has caused to the port or its persons through the fault of the ship, or vice versa, the spot should be kept untouched and timely reports should be given to the Harbour Superintendency Administration by both Parties. In case of dispute either party may resort to the Harbour Superintendency Administration for investigation and settlement. Matters involving penal proceedings shall be dealt with by judicial organs of the People's Republic of China.

Article 49: Matters not provided for in this part shall be dealt with in accordance with the Regulations Governing Investigation and Settlement of Marine Accidents promulgated by the Ministry of Communications of the People's Republic of China.

Part 9   Penalties for Violation
of Regulations

Article 50:   Vessels violating these Regulations and all relevant laws, statutes and rules issued by the Government of the People's Republic of China shall, according to the seriousness of the case, be warned or fined by the Harbour Superintendency Administration. All offences of vicious or serious nature shall be handed over to the judicial organs.

Article 51:   Any offender not yielding to the conclusions made by the Harbour Superintendency Administration may, within 15 days of the receipt thereof, appeal to the Bureau of Harbour Superintendency of the People's Republic of China. The above said conclusions, however, shall remain valid before its being modified.

Part 10   Supplementary Provisions

Article 52:   Matters concerning prevention of collisions not provided for in these Regulations and relevant rules and regulations issued by the Government of the People's Republic of China shall be dealt with in accordance with the International Regulations for Preventing Collisions at Sea accepted by the Government of the People's Republic of China.

Article 53:   These Regulations shall become effective upon the approval by the State Council of the People's Republic of China. The Regulations Governing Entry and Departure of Foreign Vessels Into and From Ports of the People's Republic of China promulgated by the Ministry of Communications of the People's Republic of China on the 12th of March,, 1957 shall at the same time be repealed.

Regulations Governing Foreign Vessels Sailing in Yangtze River

(Enforced on April 20 1983)

Article 1: The Yangtze River is the inland waterway of the People's Republic of China. These Regulations have been formulated with a view to safeguarding the sovereignty of the People's Republic of China, to ensuring the safety of vessels and to maintaining the order of traffic in the Yangtze River waterway and its ports in accordance with the regulations governing supervision and control of foreign vessels by the People's Republic of China.

Article 2: These regulations and all relevant laws and administrative statutes issued by the government of the People's Republic of China shall apply to all motorized and non-motorized vessels and other water-borne means of transport of foreign registry (hereinafter referred to as "vessels") sailing in the Yangtze River waterway or berthing at its ports.

Article 3: For the purpose of these regulations, the ports referred to in these regulations are Nantong and Zhangjiagang, which are open to vessels of foreign registry in the Yangtze River waterway. The term "Yangtze River waterway" shall mean the main waterway extending from the line joining Liuheiwu (31°30'52"N, 121°18'54"E) at the lower reaches of the estuary of the Liu River, and the signal post (31°37'34"N, 121°22'30"E) at the lower reaches of the estuary of the Shiqiao River, Chongming Island, and upwards to the upper boundary of Zhangjiagang (a line joining point 31°59'35"N, 120°20'00"E and point 31°57'13"N, 120°20'00"E).

Article 4: These regulations shall be enforced by the Harbour Superintendency Administration of the People's Republic of China, and all vessels shall

	be subject to its supervision and control.
Article 5:	No vessels may enter the Yangtze River waterway or its ports without the permission of the Harbour Superintendency Administration of the People's Republic of China. Those permitted to enter the Yangtze River waterway shall be subject to inspection of the Quarantine Office, the Harbour Superintendency Administration, the Frontier Defence Office, the Customs and the Animal and Plant Inspection Office, and complete all relevant formalities. The above-mentioned authorities are entitled to exercise ship board supervision if it is necessary.
Article 6:	Vessels entering the Yangtze River waterway shall not engage in shipping business between the various ports along the Yangtze River and between these ports and the port of Shanghai, nor shall they engage in other unauthorised operations.
Article 7:	A vessel entering the Yangtze River ports shall:

    (a)   Apply one week prior to its expected time of passing through the port of Shanghai, to the Harbour Superintendency Administration at her expected port of arrival through the port agent for foreign ships to complete the entry formalities;

    (b)   Report, 24 hours in advance of her passing through the port of Shanghai (or on her departure from the last port of call if the voyage takes less than 24 hours), the vessel's expected time of passage and the vessel's ETA at her expected port of arrival along the Yangtze River, the vessel's size, fore and aft drafts, the maximum height above the actual waterline to the Harbour Superintendency Administration of Shanghai and of the expected port of arrival through the port agents;

    (c)   Give timely advice of any alteration in the ETA reported.

Article 8:	Vessels sailing in the Yangtze River waterway or berthing at its ports shall apply to the harbour Superintendency Administration at the port of arrival along the Yangtze River for pilotage, and for passing through the port of Shanghai, shall apply to the Shanghai Harbour Superintendency Administration for pilotage.
Article 9:	Upon arrival at the port, vessels shall immediately submit the entry report and other relevant forms, ship's papers and relevant documents for examination and be subject to inspection. Before leaving the port, vessels shall report the time of departure and the port of destination to the Harbour Superintendency Administration and complete the departure formalities through the port agent and may leave the port only after port clearance has been obtained.
Article 10:	Vessels sailing in the Yangtze River waterway or berthing at its port shall be day hoist the national flag of the People's Republic of China at the top of the front mast and the national flag of the country of registry at th stern; an "H" flag shall in addition be hoisted when there is a pilot on board. On entering or leaving ports or shifting berths, vessels shall moreover display signal-letters and other prescribed signals.
Article 11:	Vessels making use of their VHF radio-telephone in the Yangtze River waterway or its ports shall comply with the provisional regulations governing the use of VHF radio-telephone by foreign vessels issued by the Ministry of Communications of the People's Republic of China.

Article 12: In the Yangtze River, a vessel's radio-telegraph and radio-telephone transmitters can only be used to communicate with the river or coastal radio-stations of the People's Republic of China, and they can only be used in ports in case of emergency, and reports shall be made to the Harbour Superintendency Administration immediately afterwards.

In the Yangtze River waterway and its ports, a vessel's signal rockets, flare signals or gun signals can only be set off in case of emergency, and reports shall be made to te Harbour Superintendency Administration immediately afterwards.

Article 13: Vessels sailing in the Yangtze River waterway or berthing at its ports are prohibited from carrying out the following activities:

(a) Photographing, drawing, videotaping, surveying, military installations and militaryships or

(b) Shooting, swimming, fishing and setting off fire-crackers or fireworks; or

(c) Engaging in other activities threatening the national safety, interests and good order of the People's Republic of China

Article 14: Vessels sailing in the Yangtze River waterway shall anchor as near to the outer limit of the fairway as is practicable — but not the main fairway — under extra-ordinary circumstances such as bad weather, flood peaks, etc, which make temporary anchoring necessary. Such vessels shall have the position and time of anchoring and the time of departure promptly reported to the nearest harbour Superintendency Administration, and no one shall be allowed ashore without permission of the local public security authorities.

Article 15: Vessels sailing in the Yangtze River waterway shall not proceed at a speed that would threaten the safety of other vessels and installations ashore.

Article 16: With respect to the regulations on navigation, berthing and prevention of collisions, vessels in the Yangtze River waterway or berthing at its ports shall comply with the regulations governing prevention of collision in inland waterways promulgated by the Ministry of Communications of the People's Republic of China.

Article 17: While using signals, vessels shall comply with the regulations governing prevention of collision in inland waterways and other relevant signal regulations; signals not being specified therein shall be displayed in accordance with the relevant international regulations.

Article 18: No vessels sailing in the Yangtze River waterway or berthing at its ports shall discharge or dispose of oils, oily mixtures or other harmful pollutants or refuse into the water.

Aticle 19: Matters provided for in these regulations shall be carried out in accordance therewith, while those not being set forth herein shall be dealt with in accordance with the regulations governing supervision and control of foreign vessels by the People's Republic of China and other relevant laws and statutes.

Article 20: These regulations shall become effective upon the date of promulgation on April 20, 1983.

Forms & Documentation

Shipper

CHINA SHIPPING COMPANY

Consignee   or assigns.

BILL OF LADING
Notify   Direct or with Transhipment

Vessel   Voy.   S/O No.   B/L No.

Port of Loading: Port of Discharge

Nationality: THE PEOPLE'S REPUBLIC OF CHINA   Freight payable at

Particulars furnished by the Shipper

Marks and Numbers	No. of Packages	Description of Goods	Gross Weight	Measurement

Total Packages (in words)

Shipped on board the vessel named above in apparent good order and condition (unless otherwise indicated) the goods or packages specified herein and to be discharged at the above mentioned port of discharge or as near thereto as the vessel may safely get and be always afloat.
The weight, measure, marks, numbers, quality, contents and value, being particulars furnished by the Shipper, are not checked by the Carrier on loading.
The Shipper, Consignee and the Holder of this Bill of Lading hereby expressly accept and agree to all printed, written or stamped provisions, exceptions and conditions of this Bill of Lading, including those on the back hereof.

Freight and Charges: In witness whereof, the Carrier or his Agents has signed Bills of Lading all
of this tenor and date, one of which being accomplished, the others to
stand void.

Shippers are requested to note particularly th exceptions and
conditions of this Bill of Lading with reference to the validity   Dated .... at ....
of the Insurance upon their goods.

.... For the Master

See Clauses on the Back.

The following are the conditions and exceptions hereinbefore referred to:

1. **Defination.** Wherever the term "Shipper" occurs hereinafter, it shall be deemed to include also Receiver, Consignee, Holder of the Bill of Leading and Owner of the goods.
2. **Jurisdiction.** All disputes arising under and in connection with this Bills of Lading shall be determined in the People's Republic of China.
3. **Period of Responsibility.** The responsibility of the carrier shall commence from the time when the goods are loaded on board the ship and shall cease when they are discharged from the ship.
4. **Responsibilities.** The carrier shall be bound, before and at the beginning of the voyage, to exercise due diligence to make the ship sea-worthy; properly man, equip and supply the ship, and to make the holds, refrigerated and cool chambers and all other parts of the ship in which goods are carried fit and safe for their reception, carriage and preservation.
   The carrier shall not be liable for loss or damage arising or resulting from defects not discoverable though the carrier has exercised due diligence as aforesaid.
5. **Immunities.** Neither the carrier nor the ship shall be responsible for loss or damage, arising or resulting from:
   (a) force Mojeure;
   (b) Dangers or accidents of the sea or other navigable waters;
   (c) Fire;
   (d) Military activities;
   (e) Strikes, lock-outs, stoppage or restraint of labour from whatever cause, whether partial or general;
   (f) Orders or acts of government authorities (seizure, arrest, quarantine, etc.);
   (g) Act or ommission of the shipper, consignee or their agents;
   (h) Nature and latent defects of the goods;
   (i) Defects in packing not discoverable from outside;
   (j) Insufficiency, illegibility or inadequacy of marks;
   (k) Sickness or death of live animals;
   (l) Act, neglect or defcult of the Master, Mariner, Pilot or any other person in the navigation or management of the ship;
   (m) Saving or attempting to save life or property at sea;
   (n) Any other cause arising whithout the actual fault or neglect of the carrier or his agents.
6. **Packing and Marks.** The shipper shall have the goods properly packed accurately and clearly marked before shipment. The port of destination of the goods should be marked in letters of 5 cm high, in such a way as will remain legible until their delivery.
7. **Freight and Other Charges.** Advance freight together with other charges is due on shipment. If not prepaid, though stipulated, the freight and other charges shall be paid by the shipper or receiver, plus 5% interest per annum running from the date of notification for their payment.
   If the cargo shipped are perishables, low cost goods, live animals, deck cargo or goods for which there is no carrier's agent at the port of destination. The freight for such cargo and all related charges shall be paid at the time of shipment.
   Freight payable at destination is due on ship's arrival together with other charges. Advance freight and/or freight payable at destination shall be paid to the carrier in full, irrespective of whatever loss or damage may happen to ship and cargo or either of them.
8. **Penalty Freight.** The carrier is entitled, at port of shipment and/or port of destination, to verify the quantity, weight, measurement and contents of the goods as declared by the shipper. If the weight, measurement and/or contents of such goods as stated in the Bill of Lading turned out to be inconsistent with that of the goods actually loaded, and the freight paid falls short of the amount which would have been due if such declaration had been correctly given, the carrier is entitled to collect from the shipper double the amount of difference between the freight for the goods actually shipped and that mis-stated.
   The shipper shall be liable for loss and damage to the ship and/or cargo arising or resulting from inaccuracies in stating the description, quantity, weight, measurement or contents of the goods and shall indemnify the carrier for the costs and expenses in connection with weighing, measuring and checking such goods.
9. **Lien.** The carrier shall have a lien on the goods for freight, dead freight, demurrage and any other amount payable by the cargo, and shall be entitled to sell the goods by auction of otherwise at carrier's option. If, on the sale of the goods, the proceeds fail to cover the amount due and the cost and expenses incurred, the carrier shall be entitled to recover the difference from the shipper.
10. **Notice of Claim.** When the cargo is taken delivery of by the receiver against Bill of Lading, if notice of damage or partial loss be not given in writing to the carrier at the time of the removal of the goods by the receiver, such removal shall be prima facie evidence of the delivery by the carrier of the goods as described in the Bill of Lading. If the partial loss or damage of the goods cannot be discovered under the usual way of delivery, a notice of claim shall be given in writing within three days of the delivery. However, such notice of claim is not required in case the receiver has verified the goods jointly with the carrier.
    In all circumstances, the carrier and the ship shall be discharged from all liabilities in respect of loss or damage unless suit is brought within one year after delivery of the goods or the date when the goods should have been delivered.
11. **Indemnity.** The indemnity for loss of cargo shall be determined on the basis of its actual value, while the indemnity for damage to cargo shall be determined on the basis of the difference between the values of the goods before and after the damage. The value of the goods shall be determined on the basis of the market value of the port of destination on the day of ship's arrival, or, in case of nonarrival, on the day of expected arrival, or, at the carrier's option, on the basis of the market value of the goods at the port of loading on the day of departure plus other charges concerned.
    The duties and expenses saved shall be deducted from the indemnity for loss of or damage to the goods. The amount of indemnity for loss of or damage to cargo shall in no case exceed R.M.B. Y700 per package or freight unit, except special agreement besides Bill of Lading has been made and extro freight paid. Should the actual value of the goods per package or freight unit exceed the declared value stated in the aforesaid agreement, the carrier's liability, if any, shall not exceed the declared value, and any partial loss or damage shall be adjusted pro rata on the basis of such declared value. Under no circumstances shall the carrier make allowances for loss of profits or loss in market value.
12. **Loading, Discharging and Delivery.** The goods shall be supplied and taken delivery of by the owner of the goods as fast as the ship can take and discharge them, without interruption, by day and night, Sundays and

Holidays included, notwithstanding any custom of the port to the contrary and the owner of the goods shall be liable for all losses or damages incurred in default thereof.

Discharge may commence without previous notice. If the goods are not taken delivery of by the receiver from alongside the vessel without dalay, or if the receiver refuses to take delivery of the goods, or in case there are unclaimed goods, the carrier shall be at liberty to land such goods on shore or any other proper places at the sole risk and expense of the shipper or receiver, and the carrier's responsibility of delivery of cargo shall be deemed to have been fulfiled.

The carrier has the right to sell the goods by public auction, if they are not taken delivery of within one month after the ship's arrival at the port of destination. Goods liable to deteriorate or those under special conditions shall be sold earlier.

13. **Lighterage.**   Any ligherage in or off ports of loading or ports of discharge shall be for the account of the shipper or receiver.

14. **Forwarding, Substitute of Vessel, Through Cargo and Transhipment.**   If necessary, the carrier may carry the goods to their port of destination by other vessel or vessels either belonging to the carrier or other persons or by rail or other means of transport proceeding either directly or indirectly to such port, and to carry the goods or part of them beyond their port of destination, and to tranship, lighter, land and store the goods on shore or afloat and reship and forward same at carrier's expense but at shipper's or receiver's risk. The responsibility of the carrier shall be limited to that part of the transport performed by him on the vessel under his management.

15. **Deviation and Changing of Route.**   Any deviation in saving or attempting to save life or property at sea, or any reasonable deviation and changing of route shall not be deemed to be infringement or breach of the contract of carriage, and the carrier shall not be liable for any loss or damage resulting therefrom.

16. **Dangerous Cargo.**   If goods of an inflammable, explosive or dangerous nature are shipped without contents being previously declared or shipped under false description, they may at any time be landed at any place or thrown overboard or destroyed or rendered innocuous by the carrier without compensation. The shipper shall be liable for all damages caused by such goods to the ship and/or cargo on board.

If any such goods shipped with such knowledge and consent shall become a danger to the ship or cargo, they may likewise be dealt with by the carrier without liabilitiy on the part of the carrier except to general average, if only.

17. **Deck Cargo, Plants and Live Animals.**   Cargo on deck, plants and live animals are received, handled, carried, kept and discharged at shipper's or receiver's risk and the carrier shall not be liable for loss thereof or damage thereto.

18. **Refrigerated Cargo.**   Before loading cargo in any insulated space, the carrier shall, in addition to the Class Certificate, obtain the certificate of the Classification Society's Surveyor or other competent person, stating that such insulated space and refrigerating machinery are in the opinion of the surveyor or other competent person fit and safe for the carriage and preservation of refrigerated cargo. The aforesaid certificate shall be conclusive evidence against the shipper, receiver and/or any holder of Bill of Lading.

Receivers have to take delivery or refrigerated cargo as soon as the ship is ready to deliver, otherwise the carrier shall land the cargo at the wharf at receiver's risk and expense.

19. **Timber.**   Any statement in this Bill of Lading to the effect that timber has been shipped "inapparent good order and condition" does not involve any admission by the carrier as to the absence of stains, shakes, splits, holes or broken pieces, for which the carrier accepts no responsibility.

20. **Bulk Cargo.**   As the carrier has no reasonable means of checking the weight of bulk cargo, any reference to such weight in this Bill of Lading shall be deemed to be for reference only, but shall constitute in no way evidence against the carrier.

21. **Heavy Lifts and Awkward Cargo.**   Any one piece or package of cargo which weighs 2000 kilos or upwards and any awkward or over length cargo must be marked with the weight and/or dimensions and/or length clearly and boldly by the shipper and shall be loaded and discharged by shore crone or otherwise at the ship's option and at the risk and expense of the shipper or receiver. If any damage, loss or liability to the ship, lighter, wharf, quay, cranes, hoisting tackle, or whatsoever or to whomever occurs owing to the lack of statement or mis-statement of weight, measurement or length, the shipper or receiver shall be responsible for such damage, loss or liability.

22. **Optional Cargo.**   The port of discharge for optional cargo must be declared to the vessel's agents at the first of the optional ports not later than 48 hours before the vessel's arrival there.

In the absence of such declaration the Carrier may elect to discharge at the first or any optional port and the contract of carriage shall then be considered as having been fulfilled. Any option must be for the total quantity of goods under this Bill of Lading.

23. **Goods to More Than One Consignee.**   Where bulk goods or goods without marks or goods with the same marks are shipped to more than one cansignee the consignees or owners of the goods shall jointly and severally bear any expenses or loss in dividing the goods or parcels into pro rata quantities and any deficiency shall fail upon them in such proportion as the carriers, his servants or agents shall decide.

24. **General Average.**   General average, if any, shall be adjusted in the People's Republic of China.

25. **War, Quarantine, Ice, Strikes, Congestion, Etc.**   Should it appear that war, blockade, pirate, epidemics, quarantine, ice, strikes, congestion and other causes beyond the carrier's control would prevent the vessel from safely reaching the port of destination and discharging the cargo thereat, the carrier is entitled to discharge the cargo at the port of loading or any other safe and convenient port and the contract of cariage shall be deemed to have been fulfilled.

Any extra expenses incurred under the aforesaid circumstances shall be borne by the shipper or receiver.

Forms & Documentation

Loading/Unloading Charges and Harbour Dues for Import/Export Cargoes in International Trade (Table I)

No.	Kinds of cargo	From ship's hold to warehouse, storing place, wagon, ship or vice versa — Cargo holds	Refrigerated holds, deep-tanks, water-tanks, small hatches, cabins and ship without handling device	From ship's hold to lighter or vice versa — Cargo holds	Refrigerated holds, deeptanks, water-tanks, small hatches, cabins and ship without handling device	Inward	Outward
1.	Coal, Slack, Minerals, Ore, Ore powder, Phosphate, Cement, Soda ash, Cereals, Salt, Sand.	1.60	2.60	1.50	2.50	1.20	0.60
	Sugar	1.60	2.60	1.50	2.50	3.00	1.50
2.	Pig iron, Steel bar (excluding scrap (Steel ingots, Non-ferrous, Metal ingots, Coke, Semi-coke, Coal lump, Asphalt.	2.40	3.40	2.20	3.20	1.20	0.60
3.	Goods other than those listed	2.40	3.40	2.20	3.20	3.00	1.50
4.	Rubber, Tyre (including waste tyre), Paper in reels, Crated paper.	3.00	4.00	2.70	3.70	3.00	1.50
	Highly dangerous goods, Refrigerated goods, Light bulky cargoes, Wool.	3.00	4.00	2.70	3.70	6.00	3.00
Heavy Lifts	Each piece exceeding 3 tons but up to 5 tons	3.00	4.00	2.70	3.70	Collectable according to corresponding kinds of cargo.	
	Each piece exceeding 5 tons but up to 10 tons	4.00	5.00	3.50	4.50		
	Each piece exceeding 10 tons but up to 25 tons	6.00	7.00	3.50	6.50		
	Each piece 25 tons upwards	8.00	9.00	7.00	8.00		
Special rates	Loading/unloading Cereals into/from tankers	—	4.00	4.00	4.00	1.20	0.60
	Fertilizers	1.40	2.40	1.20	2.20	1.20	0.60
	Pasuo Port: Minerals, Ores	2.30	3.30	—	—	1.20	0.60

Charges / Loading/unloading charges / Harbour Dues. Operations. Cargo in/out. Rate per ton (Yuan).

Table for Light Bulky Cargoes
Cotton in man-made Packets, Wool in man-made Packets, Tobacco in man-made Packets, Barks, Coir fibre, Hemp Skins, Walnuts, Reeds, Bamboo, Bamboo leaves, Bamboo broom, Bamboo cases, Straw mats, Straw paper, Straw bags, Straw & Products, Coconut fibre, Shell, Cane dregs, Wood coal, Carbon black, Cork sheets & goods, All kinds of suit case, Bamboo & Wood & Ratten furnitures, Bamboo caps, Banana leave fans, Ground nuts, Sunflower seeds, Dried chillies, Dried dates, Dried fruits, Tea, Vermicelli, Shrimp bran, Wheat bran, Aluminium wares, Bulbs, Glass products, Lamp chinney, Flask vacuum containers, Sewing machines, Bicyles, Operating bed, Toys, Table tennis balls, Balls, Paper toilet, Clout, Scrap skins, Yarn waste, Wool, Pillow padding, Shoes, Exhibition goods, Scene property, Gypsum model, Clocks & watches, Radio sets, Bee honey, Enamel wares, Goods of 4 cubic metres or over in capacity per weight ton.

Forms & Documentation

Rates for International Transit Goods   (Table II)

No.		Rates ship to ship transhipment	Rates ship to rail transhipment	Storing Charges
1.	Coal, Slack, Minerals, Ores, Ore Powder, Phosphate, Cement, Soad ash, Cereals, Salt, Sugar, Fertilizers, Sand, Stone, Brick, Tile,	4.50	3.50	No storing charge shall be collected from the 1st day to the 10th day.
2.	Pig iron, Steel bar (excluding steelscrap) steel ingots, Non-ferrous, Metal ingots, Coke, Semi-coke, Coal lump, Asphalt.	5.20	4.00	Rate per ton/day from 11th day: Warehouse: RMBY0.15
3	Goods other than those listed	6.00	4.50	
4.	Rubber, Tyre (including waste tyre), Paper in reels, Crated paper, Wool, Light bulky cargoes.	7.50	6.50	Storing place: RMBY0.05 Period of charges collectable:
	Each piece exceeding 3 tons but up to 5 tons	11.00	7.50	From the time the whole
	Each piece exceeding 5 tons but up to 10 tons	16.00	12.00	lot of cargo being into the
	Each piece exceeding 10 tons but up to 25 tons	21.00	17.00	warehouse/storing place to the time the same having
	Each piece 25 tons upwards	31.00	23.00	left,
Notes		At Shanghai: Ship to rail transhipment service unavailable. At district within the port of Tientsin and at Canton port: No transhipment service available.		

Forms & Documentation

Rates for Other Service and Hire of Port Handling Devices and Boats (Table III)

Items	Charging Unit	Rates (Yuan)	Notes
Tug	HP/hour	0.15	1. Time used for boats hired chargeable: From the time when the boats leave their mooring spots to the time when they return there. In case of the boats unreturning to their employment, the time shall not be counted after the completion of the service.
Floating crane	ton/hour (lifting capacity)	4.00	
Shore crane	ton/hour (lifting capacity)	2.00	
Vacuator	set/hour	15.00	
Oil delivered by barge	per ton	6.00	
Oil delivered by pipe	per ton		
Fresh water supplied by barge	per ton	0.40	
Fresh water supplied ex wharf	per ton	2.50	
Sweeping holds	per hatch	0.50	
Dismantling (shifting board)	per hatch	70.00	
separation		300.00	2. Time used for handling devices hired chargeable: From the time when the handling devices reach the place where used to the time after the completion of use.
Special trimming	per ton (chargeable at 3% of tons actually loaded in each deck of hold)	0.60	
Fire boat	per HP	0.25	
Other services	man/hour	1.00	
Rain proof equipment for loading/unloading	hatch/day	30.00	
			3. Vessels without handling devices shall be charged according to the stipulation of Art. 10 in case of the port handling devices being used for cargo operation.
			4. The tug charge is comprised in the charges on hiring of floating crane and barges for supply/delivery or fresh water and oil.
			5. Materials in need of the services shall be supplied by the applicants.

Table of Converting Rates (Table IV)

Description of Cargo		Unit	Converting weight Kilo
Camels, Cattle, Horses, Mules, Asses		Per head	1000
Swine, Sheep, Dogs		Per head	200
Liverstocks, Animals, Poultry in cages		Per cubic metre	1000
Timber		Per cubic metre	1000
Packing empty container made of various materials (such as: tin, case, basket and cage with the exception of those folded) Furniture		Self-weight plus two folds	
Cigarettes	in packets outside	Per 10000 pcs.	15
	in cases (iron drums) outside	Per 10000 pcs.	20
Other cargoes impossible to be weighed		Per cubic metre	10000

Note: The calculations of self-weight plus two folds shall be taken in such a way that the self-weight is added to two folds, viz: 25 (a 25-ton-weight empty drum in self-weight) x 3 (two folds) = 75 Kilos.

Forms & Documentation

REPORT OF ENTRY FOR FOREIGN-GOING SHIP

Ship's Name _____

Nationality _____

Port of Registry _____

Ship's Owner or Charterer _____

Gross Tonnage _____

Net Tonnage _____

Deadweight Tonnage _____

Import Cargo _____ Tons

Through Cargo _____ Tons

Cargo Destined for Other Chinese Port(s) _____

Cargo Unmanifested or Without Bill of Lading: _____

First Port of Present Voyage _____

Date of Departure _____

Last Port _____

Date and Time of Arrival at This Port _____

Draft F. _____ m/ft

A. _____ m/ft

Forms & Documentation

Papers submitted herewith:

Report on Articles Restricted for Use in Port	1 Copy
Crew List	4 Copies
Passenger List — Inward and/or Through Passengers	4 Copies
(Not required if not carrying passengers)	
Import Manifest	1 Copy
List of Specified Articles, Foreign Currencies, Gold, Silver	
Belonging to Ship and/or Members of Crew	1 Copy
(Not required of ship arriving from Chinese port)	
Maritime Declaration of Health	1 Copy
(Not required of ship arriving from Chinese port)	
Other Papers	

Papers submitted herewith for examination:

1. Certificate of Nationality
2. Tonnage Certificate
3. Navigation Certificate
4. Passenger Certificate
5. International Loadline Certificate
6. Deratting or Deratting Exemption Certificate
7. Deck Log Book
8. Engine Log Book
9. Tonnage Dues Certificate
10. Manifest of Cargo Destined for Other Chinese Port(s)
11. Manifest of Cargo Shipped From and Destined for Foreign Port(s)
12. Other Papers

I hereby declare that the particulars entered on this form are true and correct.

To _____ Harbour Supervision Office
Customs   of the People's Republic of China
Frontier Defence Inspection Station
Quarantine Service

Captain (Signature) _____

Date

Forms & Documentation

REPORT OF CLEARANCE

Ship's Name _____   Nationality _____

Date and Time of Sailing _____   Crew Replacement _____

Draft F. _____ m/ft. A. _____ m/ft.   Laden Draft (mean) _____ m/ft.

Cargo Loaded at this Port _____ Tons,   Total of Cargo On Board_____Tons

Next Port _____   Destination_____

Papers submitted herewith:

(1) Crew List 4 Copies (Not required if already submitted on arrival and no crew replacement. In case of replacement, give names of persons replaced and recruited and reasons therefor:)

(2) Passenger List 4 Copies (Not required if no passenger or already submitted on arrival with no change on departure)

(3) Export Manifest 2 Copies (Only 1 copy is required if ship not applying for supervision of loading of danagerous cargo)

(4) List of JMP Balances 1 Copy

To   Harbour Supervision Office
                Customs   of the People's Republic of China
                Frontier Defence Inspection Station
                Quarantine Service

                                    Captain (Signature)_____

                                    Date_____

Forms & Documentation

MARITIME DECLARATION OF HEALTH

(To be rendered by the masters of ships arriving from ports outside the territory)

Port of arrival _____

Date and time of arrival_____

Name of ship_____

Nationality _____

Master's name _____

First port of present voyage and date of departure_____

port of destination_____

Net tons _____

Description of cargo_____

Deratting or deratting exemption certificate _____

Port and date of issue _____

Number of crew_____

Number of passengers_____

Ports of call with dates of arrival and dates of departure_____

HEALTH QUESTIONS   ANSWER YES OR NO

1.   Is there on board now or has there been during the voyage any case or suspected case of plague, cholera, yellow fever, smallpox, typhus or relapsing fever ? Give particulars in the schedule.

Note: In the absence of a surgeon, the master should regard the following symptoms as ground for suspecting the existence of infectious disease: high fever or fever persisting for several days or attended with glandular swelling; or any acute skin rash or eruption with or without fever; severe diarrhoea with symptoms of collapse; jaundice accompanied by fever.

2.   Is there any sick person on board now apart from the abovementioned cases ?

3.   Has any person died on board during the voyage otherwise then as a result of accident ? Give particulars in the schedule.

4.   Has plague occurred or been suspected among the rats or mice on board during the voyage, or has there been an abnormal mortality among them ?

Forms & Documentation

SCHEDULE TO THE MARITIME DECLARATION OF HEALTH

Name	Class or rank	Age	Sex	Nationality	Port and date of embark	Date of onset, history and disposal of the case

Master Signature _____

Ship's surgeon countersigned _____

Date _____

Forms & Documentation

International Sanitary Convention, 1944

MARITIME DECLARATION OF HEALTH

(INTERNATIONAL FORM)

(To be rendered by the Masters of ships arriving from ports outside the Territory)

Port of _____ Date _____
Name of Vessel _____ From _____ To
Nationality _____ Master's Name _____
Net Registered Tonnage _____
Deratisation or Certificate _____ Dated _____
Deratisation
Exemption   Issued at _____
No. of   Cabin _____ No. of Crew _____
Passengers   Deck _____
List of ports of call from commencement of voyage with dates of Departure:

_____

_____

**ANSWER
YES or NO**

HEALTH QUESTIONS

1.   Has there been on board during the vayage* any case or suspected case of Plague, Cholera, Yellow fever, Typhus fever, or Smallpox ? Give particulars in the Schedule. (overleaf)
      *If more than six Weeks have elapsed since the voyage began. it will suffice to give particulars for the six weeks.
      (NOTE — In the absence of a surgeon, the master should regard the following symptoms as ground for suspecting the existence of infectious disease. lever accompanied by prostration or persisting for several days. or attended with glandular swelling or any acute skin rash or eruption with or without fever, severe diarrhoea with symptoms of collapse, Jaundice accompanied by fever)
2.   Has plague occurred or been suspected among the rats or mice on board during the voyage, or has there been an unusual mortality among them ?
3.   Has any person died on board during the voyage otherwise than as a result of accident ? Give particulars in Schedule.
4.   Is there on board or has there been during the voyage any case of illness which you suspect to be of an infectious nature ? Give particulars in Schedule.
5.   Is there any sick person on board now ? Give particulars in Schedule.
6.   Are you aware of any other condition on board which may Lead to infection or the spread of infectious disease ?
      I hereby declare that the particulars and answers to the questions given in this Declaration of
Health (including the Schedule) are true to the best of my knowledge and belief.

                              Signed _____
                                MASTER
                              Countersigned _____
                                SHIP'SSURGEON
                                  P.T.O.

Date _____

Forms & Documentation

SCHEDULE TO THE DECLARATION

Paticulars of every Case of Illness or Death occuring on Board

Name	Class or Rating	Age	Sex	Nationality	Port of Embarkation	Date of Embarkation	Nature of Illness	Date of its onset	Results of Illness*	Disposal of case**

* State whether recovered, still ill, died.

** State whether still on board, landed at (give name of port) buried at sea

245

List of Specified Articles, Foreign Currencies, Gold, Silver belonging to Ship and/or Members of Crew.

Item		Watch		Camera		Recorder		Transistor Radio		Gold, Silver, and Articles made thereof, Jewelry, Diamond.	Exposed but Undeveloped Photographic Plates and/or Films	Foreign Currency and Draft.		
Number	Name	Brand	Pcs.	Brand	Pcs.	Brand	Pcs.	Brand	Pcs.			U.S.$	£St.	H.K.$
Belonging to ship (including articles for sale to Passengers and Crew).														

Ship's Name: _____

Captain (Signature): _____   Date: _____

Forms & Documentation

REPORT ON ARTICLES RESTRICTED FOR USE IN PORT

Ship's Name		Nationality	

No.	Items of Articles	Quantity	Remarks
1.	Arms		
2.	Ammunitions		
3.	Radio Transmitter		
4.	Radio Telephone		
5.	Radar		
6.	Radio Direction Finder		
7.	Echo sounding Machine		
8.	Range Finder		
9.	Course Recorder		
10.	Sextant		
11.	Signal Gun		
12.	Signal Rocket of All kinds		
13.	Flare Signal of All Kinds		

I hereby declare,

(1) Items No. 1,2,. are ready to be sealed up while in port and guarantee not to use the above articles in port according to the regulations.

(2) Items No. 3,4. are the articles including those for emergency use and lifeboats.

(3) private articles belonging to the crew and passengers are included in the above, and the contents of the report are true and correct.

To
Harbour Supervision Office,

The People's Republic of China
Captain (signature) _____
Date _____

Forms & Documentation

Ship's Name _____

Crew List

No.	Crew's Name	Sex	Age	Rank	Nationality	Nationality — Home Address	Seaman's Book No. or Passport No.	Remarks

Total of Crew _____

Captain (Signature) _____

Date _____

Forms & Documentation

THE PEOPLE'S REPUBLIC OF CHINA

_____ **HARBOUR SUPERINTENDENCY ADMINISTRATION**

PORT CLEARANCE FOR FOREIGN-GOING SHIP

The vessel _____ of _____ nationality cleared this port at _____ hours _____ day of _____ 19____ with _____ crews and _____ passengers and   tons of cargo including _____ passengers embarked at this port with _____ tons of cargo bound for _____

Date of Signature _____

SECTION C: Aircraft

Customs Procedures for the Supervision of International Civil Aircraft

(Revised, promulgated and enforced by the Ministry of Foreign Trade on October 1, 1974)

I	**General Rules**
Article 1:	These Procedures are formulated for the purpose of ensuring the effective implementation of the state policies and customs decrees in the control of foreign trade and to facilitate international civil air transportation.
Article 2:	The international civil aircraft referred to in these Procedures are all civil aircraft entering and leaving our country, excluding the special planes taken by the heads of states and governments.
Article 3:	Except those specially permitted, international civil aircraft shall be permitted to land or take off only at the international airports provided with Customs houses.
	International airports shall notify the Customs two hours before the landing or taking off of civil aircraft.
Article 4:	If an international civil aircraft is to handle passengers, goods, postal items, luggage and other articles, it shall have to be authorised by Customs and do the work under the Customs' supervision.
II	**The Declaration, Examination and Clearance of Aircraft**
Article 5:	After the landing of an international civil aircraft, the commander or his agent shall submit the following documents to the Customs immediatly:
	(1) A manifest of entering and transit passengers and luggage;
	(2) A manifest of import and transit goods, postal items and

other articles and a copy of the airway bill relating to the goods;

(3)   A list of the aircrew and their personal effects which include currencies, gold and silver.

Article 6:   Before an international civil aircraft takes off, the commander or his agent shall submit the following documents to the Customs:

(1)   A manifest of outgoing passengers and luggage;

(2)   A manifest of export goods, postal items and other articles and a copy of the airway bill relating to the goods;

(3)   A list of the aircrew and their personal effects which include currencies, gold and silver (which is exempt from submission if there is no change in the aircrew after entering the airport).

Article 7:   When an international civil aircraft lands and takes off at the second and third international airports in our territory in the same flight, the commander or his agent shall submit the declaration documents to the Customs as stipulated in Article 5 and Article 6 of these Procedures.

The commander or the person assigned by him shall be responsible for carrying the customs envelope given him by the Customs intact to the Customs house at the next airport.

Article 8:   If an international civil aircraft incidentally lands at a designated unscheduled airport with the consent of the civil aviation administration department because of the climate and other objective reasons, it shall be exempt from submission of declaration documents if it does not handle passengers and goods. However, the commander shall take necessary measures to keep all the goods and luggage on board intact.

Article 9:   An international civil aircraft shall be examined by the Customs after landing or before taking off.

When the Customs examines the aircraft, the commander or the person assigned by him shall be present. When the Customs considers it necessary to open up the relevant parts of the plane and look into the flight log and other documents, the commander or the person assigned by him shall act upon the request and submit the same for examination.

Upon completion of the Customs' examination of the aircraft, the commander shall sign the examination record compiled by the Customs.

Article 10:   An international civil aircraft shall only be permitted to take off after the Customs has finished examination, and signs and seals the export manifest for clearance.

III   The Supervision of Passengers, Goods, Postal Items and Luggage

Article 11:   Incoming or outgoing passengers and their luggage and articles shall go through customs formalities before going out of the airport or boarding the aircraft.

Article 12:   Import or export goods, postal items, luggage and other articles shall go through customs formalities and the Customs shall sign and seal the airway bill or other relevant documents for clearance before the airport delivers or receives them for shipment.

Article 13: The passengers, goods, postal items, luggage and other articles in transit in the original aircraft shall be examined if the Customs considers it necessary to do so.

Article 14: The passengers in transit who have to change aircraft shall go through transit formalities in accordance with the relevant provisions of the Customs.

Article 15: The goods, postal item, luggage and other articles in transit by changing aircraft shall be landed and stored in the storage places approved by the Customs, put under the supervision of the Customs and go through transit formalities in accordance with the relevant provisions of the Customs.

Article 16: If a military aircraft or a special plane carrying the head of a state or a government entering or leaving our country also carries general goods and/or passengers, the department concerned shall give a notice to the Customs and the Customs shall supervise them in accordance with these Procedures and other relevant provisions.

IV   The Supervision of Articles Carried by the Aircrew

Article 17: The articles, currencies, gold and silver carried by the aircrew for their own use shall be examined and cleared by the Customs when they enter or leave our country.

Article 18: The articles carried by the aircrew for import or export shall be restricted to the necessary or odd articles for their own use in the flight. The imported articles shall be prohibited from sale or transfer. When the aircrew of a foreign civil aircraft buy reasonable quantities of articles for their own use and carry them abroad, the aircrew shall submit the foreign currency exchange memos and the sales memos of the stores which sold them to Customs for examination.

Article 19: The aircrew shall be prohibited from carrying articles into or out of our country on behalf of other persons.

V   The Supervision of Aircraft's Fuel, Oil, Parts, and Supplies as well as Gold, Silver and Currencies

Article 20: The fuel, oil, parts, spares, normal equipment, and supplies as well as gold, silver and currencies shall be examined or sealed if the Customs thinks it necessary to do so. The commander shall keep the Customs sealing marks intact.

The above articles shall be prohibited from sale or transfer for other purposes during the aircraft's stay at the airport.

Article 21: The fuel, oil, parts, spares, normal equipment, supplies, etc. obtained from an aircraft for use by the other aircraft belonging to the same civil aviation enterprise shall be listed in a separate certificate for clearance without a licence, signed by the commander, submitted to the Customs for examination and the articles should be stored in the storage places approved by the Customs under the supervision of the

Customs. When they are to be used or transported out, a certificate for clearance without a licence shall be made, signed and submitted to the Customs for verification and cancellation.

The above articles are exempt from customs duties, but they shall be prohibited from sale or transfer for other purposes.

Article 22:   An application shall be made to the Customs for supervision when an international civil aircraft is to replenish fuel, oil, parts, spares, normal equipment and supplies.

VI   The Supervision of Import and Export Articles of International Civil Aviation Enterprises

Article 23:   An international civil aviation enterprise shall make a list of the common articles transported in for its own use and such business materials as publicity materials, souvenirs, documents, forms, tickers, etc. and declare them at the Customs. After approval, the Customs shall tax and clear the public articles and such other articles as publicity materials without taxation, but prohibit them from sale.

Article 24:   "Public postal items" received and sent by international civil aviation enterprises are confined to the letters between civil aviation listed in the manifest for the Customs examination and clearance when they are imported or exported.

VII   Supplementary Provisions

Article 25:   The captain or his agent or the civil aircraft is to replenish fuel, oil, parts, spares, a prompt notice to the Customs if an international civil aircraft is forced to drop passengers with parachutes and discard goods within our territory because of engine troubles or other reasons or if the airplane crashes in our country due to accidents.

Article 26:   Those acts in violation of the relevant provisions of these Procedures shall be dealt with by the Customs in accordance with related decrees.

SECTION D: Health & Quarantine

Procedures for The Collection of Border Health Quarantine Fees

(Issued on 1st March, 1979)

1.   These procedures are applied to the collection of fees by the border health quarantine authority from domestic and overseas personnal entering or leaving the border, transport vehicles luggage and cargo on the implementation of sanitation treatments and issurance of certificates.

2.   Fees stipulated by these procedures will be calculated in Renminbi (yuan) currency. If a payee pays in foreign exchange, it will be calculated in accordance with the official exchange rate of the Bank of China.

3.   The fees collected by the collection units can be cancelled out as expenses.

4.   Collection of fees on vessels will be calculated upon their dead weight tons. Other transport vehicles may use it as reference.

5.   Health items in service nature, used by personnel entering or leaving the border, transport vehicle, luggage, cargo, like visiting a patient at home, rescue, temporary treatment, ambulance (car and ship), fees will be collected in accordance with the "Medical treatment fee standard" for foreigners.

6.   Persons who disobey the procedures and the implementation details of the People's Republic of China for supervision of sanitation at Border ports, or incur serious risk on the spread of infections disease under quarantine shall be punished by paying a fine within the range of one thousand yuan to five yuan by viture of Article 7 of the procedures of the People's Republic of China for Supervision of sanitation at Border Ports.

7.   Domestic and overseas personnel, transport vehicle will be charged at the same fees in accordance with these procedures. Domestic overseas passengers, overseas Chinese, Chinese of Hong Kong and Macao who personally suffer financial difficulties may have their payment reduced or exempted after examination of their cases

8.   Official receipt for payment of Quarantee fees shall be given to payee.

9.   Interpretation rights of these procedures shall be with the ministry of Health of the People's Republic of China.

Editor's Notes

The Procedures will be executed from 1st March 1979 onward. Fees collection procedures stipulated in the code health and military control in year 1972(72) number 154 on the provisional regulations handle health quarantine are abolished with immediate effect.

Appendix

Fee Collection Standard for Border Health Quarantine

No	Items	Amount (Yuen)	Remarks
1	Issuance of inoculation certificate	2	50% deduction for signatory on the original certificate, Fee of charge for inoculation of bacteria vaccine.
2	Procedures fee for group inoculation on board	30	excluding transportation fees for working personnel
3	rat inspection and issuance of rat free immunity certificate	100-200	50% reduction for signatory on the certificate for extension
4	Pest control /sterlization procedure fees	50-200	50% for part of the areas
5	killing rat by using machinery or poision	100-200	medicine fee by killing rats by using steam and smoke, sterlization pest control will be calculated separately according to the market retail price
6	Issuance certificates for killing rats by steam, smoke, sterlization and pest control in vessels	0.3 per dead weight ton	
7	Issuance certificate for killing rat by steam, smoke, sterlization and pest control in aeroplanes	100-400 (small, medium, large size)	

8	Issuance certificate for killing rats by steam, smoke, sterlization and pest control in trains.	30 (each cargo, passenger truck)
9	Issuance certificate for killing rats by steam, smoke, sterlization and pest control in motor vehicles	10-20
10	Sterlization of ballast water	0.30 per ton
11	Inspection and issuance of certificate on coffins and corpses	30
12	Issuance of other quarantine certificates	10-50

Trial Procedures for Monitoring Infectious Diseases in Border Ports

(Issued by the Ministry of Public Health on June 18, 1980)

To prevent epidemic diseases from spreading in and out of our country, to safeguard the health of travellers and communications staff passing over the borders and the health of our people and to promote international friendly intercourse, we shall, in our health quarantine, strengthen the monitoring of diseases, pay attention to the collection and accumulation of both domestic and overseas information on epidemic situations, sum up and analyse these data conscientiously and identify the patterns of the spreading of diseases so as to put forward countermeasures to prevent them. Hence these Procedures are formulated.

I   General Rules

Article 1:   The infectious diseases monitored by health quarantine authorities include influenza, malaria, poliomyelitis, dengue fever, typhus and relapsing fever (hereinafter referred to as "monitored diseases") or other types of diseases designated by the Ministry of Public Health.

Article 2:   The incubation periods of the monitored diseases referred to in these Procedures are precribed as follows:

(1)   3 days for influenza;

(2)   Malaria: 12 days for malignant malaria; 14 days for intermittent or ovale malaria; 30 days for tertian malaria;

(3)   12 days for poliomyelitis;

(4)   6 days for dengue fever;

(5)   14 days for typhus;

(6)   8 days for relapsing fever.

Article 3:   The means of communications referred to in these Procedures include vessels, aircraft and vehicles; the examination ports stated include seaports, airports, stations and border crossings; the meaning of days is the same as in Article 2 of the Rules for the Implementation of the Regulations on Border Health Quarantine.

Article 4:   Health quarantine authorities implement the monitoring of infectious diseases in ports, airports, stations and crossings which are open to international navigation, traffic or air traffic and the means of transport stationed in these places.

Article 5:   The monitored subjects include personnel (including transit pesonnel) and means of transport entering or leaving the territory of our country, the people in ports, airports, stations and border crossings and the insect vectors, animals, food and drinking water which can spread the monitored diseases.

Article 6:   The monitoring shall cover the following:

(1)   The gathering and report of epidemic situations;
(2)   The individual investigation of primary cases;
(3)   The epidemiological investigation of sudden spreading;
(4)   The separation and identification of pathogens;
(5)   The investigation of insect vectors;
(6)   The observation of the use of vaccines and the evaluation of their effectiveness as well as the investigation of the levels of immunity of people;
(7)   The gathering and investigation of the local incidence and mortality of each monitored disease and other information relating to epidemiology;
(8)   The supervision of the patients, suspected patients and close contacts of monitored diseases;
(9)   The necessary hygienic treatment of the means of communications and luggage contaminated or suspected of being contaminated and the animals and insects infected or suspected of being infected.

Article 7:   The monitoring shall be centrally coordinated and administered. Quarantine sections shall be in charge of the monitoring of diseases; Health sections shall be in charge of the monitoring of mass communications and its hygienic treatment; examination sections (or laboratories) shall be in charge of the separation and identification of pathogens.

Article 8:   The control of the epidemic situations of the monitored diseases shall be handled by quarantine authorities in accordance with the "Regulations of the People's Republic of China for the Administration of Acute Infectious Diseases". The quarantine authorities shall collect standard fees, which are fixed by the state, for supplying medicines for prevention and treatment or applying hygienic treatment in the monitoring of diseases.

II   The Transmission of Epidemics

Article 9:   In case a monitored disease or a suspected monitored disease is found on the means of transport in a port, an airport, a station or a border crossing, the person(s) in charge of the said means of transport shall make a report to the quarantine authorities.

After the above report of the epidemic situation is received, the quarantine authorities shall in turn report it to the local health epidemic prevention authorities.

Article 10: In case a monitored disease or a suspected monitored disease is found among the crowds of people in a port, an airport, a station or a border crossing, or found in the personnel entering our country, the epidemic prevention or host or medical organization in the said place shall report the situation to the local health epidemic prevention authorities and notify the local quarantine authorities or those that provide clinic facilities cards.

Article 11: In case the primary or incident case(s) of a monitored disease is (are) identified by the health epidemic prevention authorities in their subordinate areas, they shall promptly give a notice to local health quarantine authorities and supply the information on local epidemic situations at regular intervals.

Article 12: The quarantine authorities shall, on their own initiative, get in touch with the epidemic prevention authorities in the districts where they are located, such as the epidemic prevention departments and other units concerned in seaports, airports, stations and border crossings in order to collect and find out the information on the epidemic situations of monitored diseases.

Article 13: Upon the discovery of any sudden spreading of a monitored disease within the limits of its monitoring area, the quarantine authorities shall report it as soon as possible to the public health authorities of the province, municipality or autonomous region and also report it to the Ministry of Public Health.

Article 14: The overseas epidemic situations of monitored diseases shall be gathered, translated, printed and distributed by the units assigned by the Ministry of Public Health; with regard to domestic epidemic situations, the Ministry of Public Health shall notify the units concerned to supply the information to the quarantine authorities.

Article 15: All reports of monitored diseases shall be filed and submitted in Infectious Diseases Report Cards.

III General Provisions for Monitoring

Article 16: Quarantine authorities shall conduct regular search and analyse both domestic and overseas epidemic situations of monitored diseases and know the epidemic areas and trends well.

Article 17: Quarantine authorities shall strengthen the epidemiological inquiries about monitored diseases in the examination of the means of transport and the personnel passing over the borders.

Article 18: Quarantine authorities shall try to discover patients contracted of monitored diseases or suspected monitored diseases in their exercise of sanitary supervision and their rounds of visits.

Article 19: Quarantine authorities shall carry out pathogenic examination and individual investigation of the patients contracted of monitored diseases or suspected monitored diseases so as to locate the infectious sources.

Article 20: If they deem it necessary, quarantine authorities shall require incoming travellers to file health declaration cards. The way to provide the cards is to distribute them in advance among incoming personnel on the way or before they arrive at their destination with the help of travel service agencies, airline companies or other units concerned so as to save the time of examination upon entering our country.

Article 21: Quarantine authorities shall individually or selectively provide the one with close contacts of any monitored disease or the personnel coming from the epidemic area of any monitored disease with clinic facilities cards.

Article 22: Quarantine authorities shall distribute the knowledge of prevention and treatment of monitored diseases among the travellers communications staff passing over the borders and provide them with necessary medicines for prevention and treatment.

Article 23: Quarantine authorities shall carry out investigation of insect vectors and animal hosts and that of the immunity levels of crowds at regular intervals in cooperation with epidemic prevention departments in ports, airports, stations and border crossings at any time. When there is a tendency of the sudden spread of an epidemic disease in any of the said places, they shall report it to higher epidemic prevention departments so as to take necessary precautions.

IV   The Administration of Monitored Diseases

influenza

Article 24: Quarantine authorities shall take the following measures if any patients or suspected patients of influenza are found in their sanitary supervision or rounds of examinations:

(1)   Collect throat gargle or pituitary membrane imprint specimens so as to separate viruses;

(2)   According to the patients' conditions, suggest to the patients that they be treated separately from other patients or provide them with medicines for prevention and treatment;

(3)   Carry out necessary sterilization or ventilation of the rooms where the patients or suspected patients stay;

(4)   Those with close contacts with patients should be kept under medical observation or provided with clinic facilities cards according to conditions.

Article 25: Quarantine authorities shall, jointly with animal and plant quarantines, carry out the epidemiological investigation of the poultry, birds, livestock and monkeys, etc. on the means of transport where influenza occurs and take appropriate and preventive action.

Article 26: During the period when the means of transport from an epidemic area of influenza or from where influenza has occurred within 3 days before its arrival stays in a port, an airport, a station or a border crossing, quarantine authorities shall keep constant sanitary supervision over said vehicle and inquire into the health condition of the personnel on it in a timely manner so as to begin their rounds of treatment.

malaria

Article 27: When quarantine authorities discover suspected malaria patients during their routine examination, sanitary supervision or rounds of treatment, they shall extract blood from them in good time in order to examine malaria protozoa and make enquiries into the following

(1)   The history of contact with a malaria epidemic area within one month before arrival;

(2)   Whether there is any occurrence of malaria within 2 years before arrival;

(3)   Whether there are such typical clinical symptoms as feeling cold and hot at the time;

(4)   Whether the liver or spleen is swollen.

Article 28: When any malaria patients are discovered aboard any means of transport or among the personnel passing over the borders, quarantine authorities shall:

(1)   Make blood smears in time for the patients and separate malaria protozoa;

(2)   Provide the patients with cures for malaria or send them to hospital for isolation treatment;

(3)   Provide malignant malaria patients coming from a malaria affected area with cures especially for malaria caused by drugfast protozoa.

Article 29: When any mosquitos are found aboard means of transport coming from a malaria epidemic area or carrying any malaria patient(s), quarantine authorities shall:

(1)   Examine the sanitary condition of the means of transport and exterminate the mosquitos in time if they are found hiding themselves in some parts of the same;

(2)   Collect specimens so as to identify the types of the mosquitos and to test their sensibility to drugs;

(3)   Urge the persons in charge of the means of transport to exterminate mosquitos thoroughly and direct them technically; and after exterminating mosquitos, examine the effects carefully.

Article 30: Quarantine authorities shall supply preventive cures for malaria to the personnel travelling from or to a serious epidemic area of malaria.

poliomyelitis

Article 31: If suspected poliomyelitis patients are discovered in the course of routine examinations, sanitary supervision or rounds of treatment, quarantine authorities shall gather the specimens of excrement, urine and blood of the patients for virus separation and serologic examination.

Article 32: When poliomyelitis patients are found in the course of routine examinations, sanitary supervision or rounds of treatment, quarantine authorities shall take the following measures:

(1)   Gather the specimens of patients' excrement, urine and blood in time for virus identification and serum classification;

(2)   Advise the patients to be treated separately from other patients or send them to a hospital especially equipped for infectious diseases;

(3)   Sterilize the environment, aritles and patients' excrement suspected of being contaminated;

(4)   Provide those in close contact with the affected patients with clinic facilities cards or carry out medical observation not exceeding 14 days after leaving the affected environment.

Article 33:   Quarantine authorities shall take samples from drinking water and food from the means of transport for examination on which a poliomyelitis case or a suspected poliomyelitis case has occurred within 3 weeks before its arrival and sterilize them if necessary; samples from the drinking water and food from a means of transport coming from the epidemic area of poliomyelitis shall also be examined or sterilized if necessary.

dengue fever

Article 34:   If quarantine authorities find any dengue fever patient(s) or any patient(s) suspected of contracting dengue fever in their examination, sanitary supervision or rounds of treatments, they shall take the following measures:

(1)   Send the patient(s) to hospital for isolation treatment and gather blood specimens for virus separation and serologic examination;

(2)   Gather the specimens of dengue-fever mosquitos for virus separation from the places where the patient(s) has(have) stayed;

(3)   Arrange the patients in a mosquito-free room to be separately treated for not less than 5 days from the date in which the disease was contracted;

(4)   Provided those in close contact with the disease with clinic facilities cards or carry out 14 days' health observation;

(5)   Promptly exterminate the mosquitos in ports, airports, stations or border crossings or aboard means of transport where dengue fever patient(s) is(are) found.

Article 35:   If quarantine authorities find any live mosquitos aboard means of transport from an epidemic area of dengue fever, they shall:

(1)   Examine the sanitary state of the means of transport and exterminate mosquitos which are found to conceal themselves in some parts of the means of transport;

(2)   Gather specimens of mosquitos for identification and separation of viruses;

(3)   Urge the person(s) in charge of the means of transport to exterminate mosquitos thoroughly and direct him (them) technically, and after eliminating them, check the results carefully.

Article 36:   Quarantine authorities shall exercise proper administration of animals such as monkeys from the epidemic area of dengue fever jointly with animal and plant quarantines.

typhus and relapsing fever

Article 37: When quarantine authorities discover any patient(s) suffering from typhus or relapsing fever in their examination, sanitary supervision or rounds of treatments, they shall take the following meansures:

    (1)   Eliminate lice from the patient(s), isolate him(them) and gather specimens for pathogenic separation;

    (2)   Eliminate insects from suspected patients and carry out medical observation for 14 days or 8 days;

    (3)   Provide those with contact of the patient with clinic facilities cards after the elimination of lice, or carry out health observation for 14 days or 8 days after the elimination of insects;

    (4)   Eliminate lice from patient's, suspected patients' and contacted's clothes, luggage and other articles and places which are prone to concealment of lice and sterilize them if necessary;

    (5)   Gather blood specimens from the patient(s) or suspected patients for laboratory examination;

    (6)   Gather lice specimens from the bodies of the patient(s), suspected patients and contacted for pathogenic separation and drug sensibility tests.

Article 38: When quarantine authorities find lice on the means of transport from the epidemic area of typhus or relapsing fever, they shall gather specimens for examination and eliminate the insects.

Article 39: These Procedures shall be put into effect from the date of issue.

Procedures of The People's Republic of China for Supervision of Sanitation at Border Ports

(Approved by the State Council on December 30, 1981 and issued on February 4, 1982)

I General Rules

Article 1: These Procedures are formulated as required under Article 3 of "The Regulations of the People's Republic of China on Border Health Quarantine." the purposes are to strengthen the supervision of sanitation at border ports and aboard international means of transport, to improve their sanitary conditions and to extinguish infectious sources, cut off channels of spreading, prevent infectious diseases from spreading into or out of our country and safeguard the health of the people.

Article 2: These Procedures are applicable to ports, airports, stations and passages open to foreigners (hereinafter generally designated as "border ports") and to international going vessels, aircraft and vehicles staying in these places (hereinafter referred to as "means of transport").

II Sanitary Requirments for Border Ports

Article 3: A sanitary cleaning system shall be established in border ports to eliminate the breeding places of flies and mosquitos, install litter bins and their regular cleansing so as to keep the environment clean and tidy.

Article 4: Daily refuse in border ports shall be removed every day and fixed refuse dumps provided for that purpose shall be regularly cleared;

daily sewage shall not be drained off indiscriminately and shall go through disinfecting treatment so as to prevent the environment and water sources from contamination.

Article 5: The departments concerned shall adopt feasible meansures to reduce the quantity of insect vectors and rodents to a harmless level in the buildings of border ports.

Article 6: All floors of waiting rooms in piers, airports, stations and customs houses shall be kept neat and clean, their walls dust-free and their windows and tables bright and clean. They shall be well ventilated and equipped with necessary sanitary facilities.

Article 7: A perfect sanitary system shall be established in restaurants, cafes, canteens, dining rooms, kitchens, buffets and small shops in border ports so as to regularly keep them clean and tidy and make their walls, ceilings, tables and chairs clean and dustfree. The areas shall be provided with equipment to ward off mosquitos, flies, rats and mice and with refrigeration equipment so as to eliminate these pests.

Article 8: Attendants shall be put in charge of the toilets and bathrooms in border ports, cleaning them regularly and keeping them clean and tidy so as to free them from flies and bad odours.

Article 9: The warehouses, godowns and goods yards in border ports shall be kept clean and tidy. When abnormal quantities of dead mice or rats are found, immediate reports shall be given to health quarantine autorities or local public health and epidemic prevention departments.

Article 10: The water sources for border ports shall be well protected and toilets, seepage wells, etc. which will pollute the water sources shall not be built within a distance of 30 meters in diameter from a water source.

III   Sanitary Requirements for Means of Transport

Article 11: Means of transport shall be equipped with first-aid medicines and equipment as well as disinfectants, insecticides and rodenticides. If necessary, provisional quarantine rooms shall be arranged aboard ships.

Article 12: The prevention and elimination of insect vectors and rodents from means of transport shall be as follows:

(1)   Ships, aircraft and trains shall be provided with adequate preventive measures against rodents so as to free them from rodents or to keep their quantity at a harmless level.

(2)   The means of transport shall be kept free from mosquitos, flies or other injurious insects, which shall be eliminated upon discovery.

Article 13: The toilets and bathrooms on means of transport shall be kept clean, tidy and free from unpleasant odours.

Article 14: the sanitary requirements for the disposition of excrement, urine, refuse and sewage on means of transport are as follows:

(1)   Daily refuse shall be put in containers with covers, prohibited from being dumped indiscriminately into port areas, airports or station areas and must be removed by means of special refuse vehicles (or vessels) to designated places for treatments. If necessary,

excrement, urine and sewage shall go through sanitary treatment before being disposed.

(2)   The refuse in solid form on means of transport from epidemic areas of plague shall be disposed of by incineration, while the excrement, urine, ballast water and sewage on means of transport from the epidemic areas of cholera shall be sterilized if necessary.

Article 15:   The sanitary requirements for cargo holds, luggage cars, postal cars and freight cars of means of transport as well as trucks are as follows:

(1)   Such insect vectors and harmful animals as mosquitos, flies, cockroaches and mice and their breeding conditions shall be eliminated from cargo holds, luggage cars, postal cars, freight cars and trucks which shall be thoroughly cleaned before goods are being loaded or unloaded so as to be free of excrement, urine and refuse.

(2)   The freight cars or trucks carrying poisonous articles and food shall be placed separately in different designated places for decontamination and shall be thoroughly cleaned after goods are completely unloaded.

(3)   The luggage and goods from epidemic areas shall be carefully examined to prevent the carrying of insect vectors and rodents.

Article 16:   The sanitary requirements for passenger cabins, lodging cabins and passenger cars of means of transport as well as other passenger vehicles are as follows:

(1)   Passenger cabins, lodging cabins, passenger cars and other passenger vehicles shall be cleaned whenever necessary, kept free of refuse and dust and well ventilated.

(2)   Bedding shall be replaced and washed after use each time and be free from lice, fleas, bedbugs or other insect vectors.

IV   Sanitary Requirements for Food, Drinking Water and Personnel Engaged in These Industries

Article 17:   The food supplied to border ports and on means of transport shall conform to the provisions in "The Regulations of People's Republic of China on Food Hygienic Administration" and food hygienic standards.

Article 18:   The drinking water supplied to border ports and on means of transport shall conform to "Hygienic Standards of Drinking Water" stipulated by our country. The drinking water supplied by means of transport as well as storage containers and water pipelines shall be cleaned regularly and kept clean.

Article 19:   The sanitary requirements for personnel engaged in the supply of food and drinking water are as follows:

(1)   The patients or carriers of infectious intestinal or sufferers from active tuberculosis diseases or suppurative exudative dermatosis shall not be engaged in work in the supply of food and drinking water.

(2)   Each of the personnel engaged in the supply of food and drinking water shall go through a medical check-up every year. Those newly engaged in this work shall first have a medical check-up and those proved up to standard shall be granted health certificates.

(3)   The personnel engaged in the supply of food and drinking water shall cultivate good hygienic habits, dress neatly and cleanly at work and strictly abide by the hygienic operation system.

V   The Duties of Persons in Charge of Border Ports and Means of Communications

Article 20:   The duties of the officers in charge of border ports and means of transport in the field of hygienic work are as follows:

(1)   To complete the hygienic work well and regularly subject themselves to the supervision and examination of the sanitary supervision personnel and provide them with facilities for their work.

(2)   To abide by these Procedures and other sanitary decrees, regulations and provisions.

(3)   To adopt immediate meansures to improve the unsanitary conditions of border ports and the means of transport in accordance with the advice of the sanitary supervision personnel.

(4)   To report the situation when a quarantine infectious disease or a monitored one is found to the border health quarantine authorities or local epidemic prevention department and immediately adopt epidemic prevention measurses.

VI   The Responsibilities of Sanitation Supervision Authorities

Article 21:   The health quarantine authorities in border ports shall exercise sanitary supervision over border ports and means of transport under the administration of local people's governments. Their major responsibilities are to:

(1)   Supervise and direct the officers in charge of the departments concerned in border ports and on means of transport in the prevention and elimination of insect vectors and rodents;

(2)   Examine the food and drinking water on the means of transport in border ports or crossings over the borders and exercise sanitary supervision over systems of transport, supply and storage facilities;

(3)   Carry out examination, supervision and hygienic treatment of persons who have died from causes other than accidents in border ports and on means of transport;

(4)   Supervise the officers in charge of the departments concerned in border ports and means of transport in the removal and treatment of excrement, urine, refuse and sewage;

(5)   Exercise sanitary supervision over environmental factors which are of epidemiological significance to quarantine and monitored infectious diseases;

(6)   Adopt measures to prevent mosquitoes from breeding in the vicinity of border ports;

(7)   Conduct hygienic propaganda and education, spread hygienic knowledge among people and heighten the consciousness of the personnel in border ports and on means of transport to abide

by and implement these Procedures.

Article 22: A border port health quarantine organ shall be provided with 1 to 5 border port sanitary supervisors to carry out the tasks of sanitary supervision and such posts shall be concurrently held by the professional personnel above the rank of leading cadre or quarantine doctor of the border port health quarantine organ, who are of good character and conscientious in their work. Border port sanitary supervisors shall be recommended by health quarantine authorities, certified by the public health administration authorities of provinces, municipalities and autonomous regions, and appointed by the Ministry of Public Health of the People's Republic of China and granted "Certificates of Border Port Sanitary Supervisors".

Article 23: With their certificate, border port sanitary supervisors shall be entitled to exercise sanitary supervision, examination and technical control over the officers in charge of border ports and means of transport; they could jointly with the departments concerned put forward proposals of improvement to the units or individuals concerned with unsatisfactory sanitary work and which resulted in the spread of infectious disease and to take necessary measures to deal with them in coordination with the departments concerned.

VII   Rewards and Punishments

Article 24: Border port qurantine authorities shall encourage and reward units and individuals that have made remarkable achievements towards the implementation of these Procedures and the state decrees, regulations and provisions relating to public health.

Article 25: Border port health quarantine authorities shall, according to different conditions, warn or fine the units and individuals that have contravened these Procedures and the decrees, regulations and provisions relating to public health and may submit the cases to judicial authorities for punishment according to law.

VIII   Supplementary Provisions

Article 26: These Procedures shall go into effect as of the date of issue.

Regulations of the People's Republic of China on the Guarantee of Imported and Exported Animals and Plants

(Issued by the State Council on June 4, 1982)

I   General Rules

Article 1:   These Regulations are formulated in order to protect the agriculture, forestry, animal husbandry and fishery of our country and the health of our people, safeguard our reputation in foreign trade, fulfil our international obligations, prevent diseases, insects, weeds and other harmful organisms which harm animals and plants from spreading into or out of our country and strengthen the quarantine of import and export animals and plants.

Article 2:   All commercial or non-commercial animals, plants, animal products, vegetable products and their means of transport which enter, leave or pass through territories of the People's Republic of China are within the quarantine range under these Regulations and particularly include the following:

(1)   Animals: Livestock, poultry, wild animals, bees, fish, silkworms, etc.

(2)   Animal products: Raw hides, hair, meat, viscera, fat, blood, eggs, semen, bones, hoofs, horns, etc.

(3)   Plants: Cultivated plants, wild plants and their seeds, nursery stock, propagating materials, etc.

(4)   Vegetable products: Grains, beans, peas, cotton, oils, hemp, flax, tobacco, kernels, dried fruits, fresh fruits, vegetables, raw medicinal materials, logs, fodder, etc.

(5)   Vehicles, vessels and aircraft carrying animals, plants, animal products and vegetable products as well as packing, bedding and

padding materials, breeding tools, etc.

The other goods and means of transport which may carry the objects of quarantine shall also be put in quarantine.

Article 3:   Animal infectious diseases and parasites, insects and weeds which are dangerous to plants as well as other harmful organisms (generally designated as insect vectors) shall be put in quarantine and divided into the objects of quarantine and quarantinable insect vectors.

(1)   The objects of quarantine mean the insect vectors which are prohibited from entering our country as stipulated by the state. The list of the objects of quarantine shall be promulgated by the Ministry of Agriculture, Animal Husbandry and Fishery of the People's Republic of China.

(2)   Quarantinable insect vectors include those put in quarantine as stipulated in relevant agreements and trade contracts with foreign countries and those for which the export units have applied for quarantine.

Article 4:   The animal and plant quarantines set up in the ports and airports of the People's Republic of China which are open to international navigation or air traffic as well as on land borders and border rivers, and the animal and plant quarantine stations set up in the capitals of provinces and autonomous regions concerned (hereinafter generally referred to as port animal and plant quarantine authorities) are the authorities concerned which conduct quarantine duties of import and export animals and plants on behalf of the state.

Article 5:   All animals, plants, animal products, vegetable products and their means of transport shall only be permitted to be imported or exported after passing the standard upheld by quarantine.

II   Import Quarantine

Article 6:   An application shall be made in advance to the Ministry of Agriculture, Animal Husbandry and Fishery for approval to import animals and animal products. However, an application shall be made in advance to the Ministry of Forestry for approval where the import of wild animals and their products are concerned.

To import seeds, nursery stock and propagating materials, import departments shall fill in "Examination and Approval Lists for Quarantine of Seeds and Nursery Stock Imported" for submission. For those to be imported by the departments concerned of the State Council, such lists shall be submitted separately according to the professional distribution works to the Ministry of Agriculture, Animal Husbandry and Fishery or the Ministry of Forestry respectively for examination and approval; for those to be imported by the departments of provinces, autonomous regions and municipalities directly under the Central Government, they shall be submitted to the Departments (or Bureaux) of Agriculture (Forestry or State Farm and Land Reclamation) of respective areas for examination and approval.

Article 7:   Any quarantine regulations which our country stipulated or agreed between governments should be indicated on the agreement for trade, technical co-operation, gift, exchange or assistance for the importation of animals, plants and their products. Also the said agreement shall contain the requirement of a quarantine certificate from the country of origin.

Article 8: Animals, plants, animal products and vegetable products imported shall be quarantined by port animal and plant quarantine authorities.

(1) Before or after the arrival of goods in a port, the consignee unit or its agent shall fill in the declaration for quarantine and submit it (or the waybill) together with such documents as the quarantine certificate from the export country to the port animal and plant quarantine authorities for quarantine.

(2) For trains or motor vehicles entering our country, the port animal and plant quarantine authorities shall carry out quarantine duties and inspection together with the border authorities concerned; for incoming vessels, quarantine duties shall be carried out on board after the joint inspection; for incoming aircraft, quarantine shall be implemented on the spot where goods are unloaded.

Article 9: A "Quarantine Clearance Notice" shall be signed and issued for all animals, plants, animal products or vegetable products imported in which no objects of quarantine or quarantinable insect vectors are found through quarantine, or such clearance shall be stamped on the waybill so as to permit them to be imported.

Article 10: For all imported animals or animal products in which the objects of quarantine and quarantinable insect vectors are found through quarantine, a "Quarantine Disposal Notice" shall be signed and issued according to different circumstances and the declarer(s) shall be notified to dispose of them separately as follows:

(1) The animal(s) which has (have) contracted a serious infectious disease and all others in the same flock shall be wholly returned or killed and its (their) remains shall be destroyed.

(2) The animal(s) which has (have) contracted a general infectious disease shall be returned or killed and its (their) remains shall be destroyed; the other animals in the same group shall be isolated and put under observation in the animal quarantine isolation yard or a designated place.

(3) The animal(s) which has (have) contracted a non-infectious disease shall be treated medically.

(4) Animal products shall be sterilized, returned or destroyed. If the animals which are isolated and observed as mentioned in Item (2) above and which are treated as mentioned in Item (3) do not have any disease found through quarantine, and if the animal products as mentioned in Item (4) passed the examination of quarantine after sterilization, they shall be allowed to be imported.

Article 11: For the import plants or vegetable products in which the objects of quarantine and quarantinable insect vectors are found through quarantine, a "Quarantine Disposal Notice" shall be signed and issued according to different circumstances and the declarer(s) shall be notified to dispose of the same separately in ways such as fumigation, sterilization, controlled use, return or destruction. They shall be allowed to be imported if they passed the examinations after such neutralizing treatments as fumigation, sterilization, etc.

Article 12: The quarantine and disposition of imported animals, plants, animal products and vegetable products shall be carried out in the ports of import.

All application shall be made to the Ministry of Agriculture, Animal Husbandry and Fishery for approval if they shall be transported to a designated inland place for disposition due to the limitation of the conditions in the port or other causes. In the course of transportation and handling, strict measures shall be adopted to prevent the epidemic situation from proliferating and a notice shall be given to the local quarantine department for supervision.

Article 13: The declarer(s) or consignee unit shall deal with the places, warehouses, means of transport, bedding and padding materials, breeding tools, etc. which are contaminated by the objects of quarantine and quarantinable insect vectors as required by the port animal and plant quarantine authorities.

Article 14: If any object of quarantine or quarantinable insect vector is found in imported animals, plants, animal products or vegetable products through quarantine, the port animal and plant quarantine authorities shall issue and sign quarantine certificates according to different circumstances.

Article 15: The following shall be prohibited from import:

(1) Daily injurious insects, animal or plant pathogenic micro-organisms (including cultures of bacteria, cultures of viruses, biological products) and other harmful organisms;

(2) The animals, seeds, nursery stock and propagating materials relating to a country or area in a serious epidemic situation as well as susceptible animal products and vegetable products;

(3) Soil.

The list of the aforesaid which are prohibited from import shall be promulgated by the Ministry of Agriculture, Animal Husbandry and Fishery. If it is necessary to import any of them for scientific research, an application shall be made in advance for the special approval for the Ministry of Agriculture, Animal Husbandry and Fishery.

III   Export Quarantine

Article 16: If export animals, plants, vegetable products or non-commercial animal products are required to be quarantined, the export unit or its agent shall file a declaration for quarantine in advance, submit the quarantine certificate from the place of production and declare the same at the port animal and plant quarantine authorities for quarantine. They shall be cleared by a quarantine certificate signed and signed and issued by the authorities concerned after passing the requisite examination.

The export quarantine of commercial animal products shall be handled by the import and export commodity inspection authorities.

Article 17: The animals, plants, animal products or vegetable products in which quarantinable insect vectors are found through quarantine shall be prohibited from the export or shall go through neutralizing treatments before export.

Article 18: The contaminated areas, warehouses, means of transport, bedding and padding materials, breeding tools, etc. shall be dealt with as stipulated in Article 13 of these Regulations.

IV The Quarantine of Articles Carried by Travellers

Article 19: The animals, plants, animal products or vegetable products carried or consigned by the travellers or communications staff entering our country shall be put in quarantine on the spot in port. They shall be cleared if no objects of quarantine are found through quarantine; those in which the objects of quarantine are found shall be prohibited from entering our country or released only after sterlization. If no quarantine results can be obtained, such articles shall be kept in custody pending further quarantine and the owners shall be informed of the final disposition of the articles after the quarantine results are obtained.

Article 20: The raw meat carried or consigned by the travellers or communications staff shall go through epidemic prevention check before being permitted to enter our country.

Article 21: The animals, plants, animal products or vegetable products carried or consigned by the travellers or communications staff leaving our country shall be put in quarantine and clearance certificates granted in appropriate cases.

V The Quarantine of International Mail Parcels

Article 22: The plants and vegetable products mailed into our country shall be quarantined by the port animal and plant quarantine authorities. A parcel without any objects of quarantine found through quarantine shall be cleared by putting a mailing clearance stamp on the parcel. A "Quarantine Disposal Notice" shall be signed and issued after the quarantine of a parcel in which the objects of quarantine are found and sent together with the parcel to the receiver by post. A parcel failing to go through quarantine shall be returned with a parcel retuen label to the sender by post. "Quarantine Disposal Notice" shall be signed and issued for a parcel to be destroyed and the notice shall be sent to the sender by post.
Raw animal products shall be prohibited from entering our country by post (a small number of samples excepted).

Article 23: The plants, animal products or vegetable products mailed out of our country shall be put in quarantine and clearance certificates shall be granted in appropriate cases.

Article 24: Permits shall be signed and issued by the Ministry of Agriculture, Animal Husbandry and Fishery for the importation of daily harmful injurious insects, animal or plant pathogenic micro-organisms (including the cultures of bacteria, the cultures of viruses, biological products) and other harmful organisms as well as the natural enemies of diseases and insect pests.

VI   Transit Quarantine

Article 25:   For the animals, plants, animal products or vegetable products in transit through our country, the carrier shall file a declaration or a waybill for quarantine and declare them at the port animal and plant quarantine authorities for quarantine at the port of entry. This shall be presented together with the quarantine certificate from the country of origin. They shall not be quarantined again at the port of exit.

Article 26:   If the plants, animal products or vegetable products carried by a train, truck or aircraft through our territory change means of transport in one of our ports, the exteriors of their packages shall be examined; if they pass through our territory in the original vehicle, the exterior of the vehicle shall be examined. If no objects of quarantine are found through quarantine, a "Quarantine Clearance Notice" shall be signed and issued or a quarantine clearance stamp shall be affixed on the waybill so as to permit them to go through. If any objects of quarantine are found, the articles shall be wholly returned. They contaminated places, tools, etc. shall be dealt with as stipulated under Article 13 of these Regulations.

Article 27:   If animals in transit have no objects of quarantine found through quarantine, they shall be permitted to pass through our territory. If any objects of quarantine are found in them, they shall be wholly returned. The contaminated places, tools, etc. shall be dealt with as stipulated under Article 13 of these Regulations.

The fodder, excrement, urine, padding grass, dirt, remains, etc. of the animals in transit shall be treated in designated places and shall not be abandoned indiscriminately.

If any objects of quarantine are found in the fodder of the animals in transit, the carrier shall be notified to replace the fodder and the original fodder shall be sterlized at the spot.

VII   Punishments

Article 28:   Those found in violation of these Regulations shall be criticized, disciplined or fined according to different circumstances. Serious cases shall be punished by judicial authorities according to law.

VIII   Supplementary Provisions

Article 29.   The units concerned shall render necessary assistance to the port animal and plant quarantine authorities when they are executing their duties in ports, airports, stations, post offices, warehouses, etc.

When the port animal and plant quarantine authorities execute field quarantine, the declarer(s) shall be present to render such assistance as moving, opening and repacking packages, etc.

A sampling certificate shall be issued and signed if the port animal and plant quarantine authorities take samples.

Article 30:   The departments in charge shall notify the port animal and plant quarantine authorities concerned in time of the quarantine clauses in any agreements or trade contracts entered into and signed with foreign countries.

Article 31: When port animal and plant quarantine officers are on quarantine duties, they shall wear quarantine uniform and insignia.

Article 32: The port animal and plant quarantine authorities shall collect quarantine fees in the execution of quarantine and the procedures for such collection shall be formulated by the Ministry of Agriculture. Animal Husbandry and Fishery.

Article 33: The detailed rules for the implementation of these Regulations shall be prescribed by the Ministry of Agriculture, Animal Husbandry and Fishery jointly with the Ministry of Forestry.

Article 34: These Regulations shall be put into effect from the date of issue.

IV SECURITY

SECTION A: Administration

Notice of The Ministry of Public Secuirty of The People's Republic of China

(Issued on March 15, 1981)

To ensure transportation safety in international civil aviation service, it has been decided that starting from April 1, 1981, technical security checks will be conducted on all Chinese and foreign passengers and luggage boarding international flights at all civil airports in the People's Republic of China.

1.   Weapons, tools for criminal purposes, ammunition, explosives, combustibles, extremely poisonous or radioactive materials and other dangerous items hazardous to safety of the flight are strictly prohibited on board.

2.   Except for those who have obtained special permission, all the passengers must pass through an inspection gate or detector check. Passengers' hand-carried items must pass the inspection of detectors. When necessary, bodily searches and open-luggage checks must be made. Passengers who refuse to go through inspection procedures are not allowed to board the plane and will be responsible for their own losses.

3.   The above-mentioned dangerous items discovered in the course of the inspection must be handled by the airport security inspection deepartment. Suspects of hijacking and other acts endangering safety of the flight must be turned over to the local public security organs.

The notice is hereby announced.

Notice of The Ministry of Public Security of The People's Republic of China

(Issued on October 15, 1981)

To ensure the safety of domestic civil flights, it has been decided to enforce a technical security inspection at all civil aviation airports in China of Chinese and foreign passengers on all regular domestic civil flights and their luggage and other belongings beginning from November 1, 1981.

1.   It is strictly forbidden for anyone to carry aboard or put inside unaccompanied luggage or pieces of cargo any weapon, tool used for criminal purposes, ammunition, any explosive, inflammable, lethally poisonous or radioactive article, or any other dangerous item threatening flight safety.

2.   Except where special exemption is granted, all passengers and their luggage and other belongings will be subjected to security inspection. When necessary, a body search may be conducted. Anyone who refuses the inspection will not be permitted to board the plane and will be solely responsible for any personal loss arising therefrom.

3.   Cases of passengers found to be carrying any one of the above-mentioned dangerous items will be handled by the airport security inspection department concerned. Anyone suspected of hijacking a plane or committing any other act endangering flight safety will be handed over for investigation to a public security organ.

   The notice is hereby announced.

The Decision of the Standing Committee of the National People's Congress on the setting up of the State Security Organization in the execution of the duties of public security on detection, detention, pretrial and exercise the power of arrest.

(promulgated on 2nd September, 1983)

In its first session, the Standing Committee of the Sixth National People's Congress has decided to set up a State Security Authority to be responsible for the investigation of spying and secret agent case which was originally the work of the public security authority. As its work is of the nature of public security, the State Security Authority can exercise a public security department's power of investigation, detention, pretrial and assist, as stipulated in the constitutions and the laws.

SECTION B: Control

Joint Notice on Smuggling and Speculation for Resale of Import and Export Articles.

(Issued by the General Administration of Industry & Commerce and General Administration of Customs on 30th September, 1980)

To protect the economic order of socialism the following regulations are stipulated to fight the activities of smuggling, speculation for resale at a profit import and export article in accordance with the instruction of the State Council of the People's Republic of China and the Military Commission of the Control Committee of the Chinese Communist Party, the Criminal Laws of the People's Republic of China as well as related laws and orders:

1.   Any person who violates the laws and regulations of customs by participation in the activities of smuggling and speculation for resale at a profit, the tools for smuggling will be confiscated by the customs in accordance with the customs laws and regulations. If the case is serious, a fine will be imposed on the person or the person will be sent to the judicial authority for punishment in accordance with the law.

2.   Any person who violates the regulations and orders of the State Monetary Control and the Management of Administration of Industry and Commerce by assisting in the resale for profit of those non-smuggled import or export articles, foreign currencies, foreign exchange certificates, gold, silver, jewelry, jade, ancient relics, perious herbs, his property will be confiscated if the situations is serious, a fine will be imposed or the person will be sent to the judicial authority for punishment according to the laws.

3.   Any person who sells the personal imported articles, shall sell them to the purchasing units appointed by the state. These articles are not allowed to be displayed for sale in the market place or traded in the black market. Any person who violates these rules, will, in view of the seriousness of the case, be ordered to pay an additional tax, accept compulsory purchase, have his articles conficated or have himself sent to the judicial authority for punishment in accordance with the law.

4.   Commercial units shall have the approval from the Administration Authority of Industry and Commerce of above county level before engaging in the import of the personal articles. Any unit which does not have such approval shall not engage in the business of importing articles from foreigners, overseas Chinese, overseas Chinese of Hong Kong, Macao and Taiwan. Disobedient units will have their illegal profit confiscated by the Administration Authority of Industry and Commerce for submission to the State Treasury or will be fined. The unsold articles will be confiscated by appointed commercial units. Serious offenders will be ordered to suspend business for inspection and the leader concerned will investigated and held responsible.

5.   A business unit which has been granted approval to engage in the business of importing articles for personal use is only permitted to purchase stock from appointed business units if it has to purchase its stock from any port or villages where overseas Chinese live. Any other state enterprises, group business enterprises or co-operative retailers are prohibited from purchasing stock by going into any port or village where overseas chinese live. They are also prohibited from engaging in the negotiation of sale and purchase.

6.   If it is necessary for the authorities, troops, organizations, schools, industrial enterprise units, people's communes, production main teams, production teams and individuals to purchase imported articles, they are prohibited from purchasing them from private individual or black markets. They must purchase them from business units appointed by the state. Offenders will be dealt with in accordance with the seriousness of the matter by paying compensated tax, compulsory purchase by the government, paying compensated price, paying a fine or having the articles confiscated. Those units whose matters are serious will have their leaders investigated for responsibility.

7.   Habitual offenders, capital offenders and keymen of offending groups who participate in smuggling, speculating of resale of import and export articles as well as crimials who disturb, object inspection, challenge the customs and the Administration Authority of Industry and Commerce, or involve in abusing assaulting and battering customs personnel will be punished heavily in accordance with the laws.

8.   All the cadres and the general public shall work together with the public security, the customs and the Administration Authority for Industry and Commerce in fighting the activities of smuggling and speculation of reselling. Commendation or material awards will be given to those personnel and units, who have the merit of reporting or disclosing smuggling and speculation for reselling activities, in accordance with the regulations.

Procedures for Customs Rewards in the Prohibition of Smuggling

(Promulgated by the General Customs Office On September 24, 1982)

Article 1: These procedures are formulated for the purpose of encouraging individuals and units (or organizations) to assist in preventing smuggling so as to contribute to the safeguard of the socialist economic order.

Article 2: In addition to political encouragement, rewards shall be given to the informants in smuggling cases and such units of collective ownership as rural people's communes and production brigades and teams helping to solve such cases after the cases concerned are dealt with according to law.

Article 3: The rewards for the informants shall not exceed 10 per cent of the total proceeds from the fines and confiscations in each case; the maximum amount in each case shall not exceed Renminbi 1,000 yuan.

Article 4: Reward shall be given to such units of collective ownership as rural people's communes and production brigades and teams assisting to solve smuggling cases in amounts not exceeding 10 per cent of the total proceeds from the fines and confiscations in each case. But the maximum amount in each case shall not exceed Renminbi 10,000 yuan.

Article 5: The rewards for the informants with special contributions shall not be limited to the maximum amount aforesaid if special approval of the General Customs Office is obtained.

Article 6: Political encouragement shall be given to the informants in the smuggling cases in which the offenders are acquitted from conviction but only required to pay the evaded duties; and if necessary, a reward of not more than Renminbi 100 yuan shall be given to an informant or a unit of collective ownership assisting in solving such cases.

Article 7:   A reward of not more than Renminbi 500 yuan shall be given, if necessary, in addition to political encouragement, to an informant or a unit of collective ownership asissting to solve the smuggling case in which the articles shall be destroyed or forfeited to the government authorities as stipulated and the offender(s) is (are) free from fines.

Article 8:   Rewards in foreign currency will be given to informants residing outside our territory in appropriate cases.

Article 9:   If a rewarded informant or unit fails to collect the reward within 6 months from the date of the Customs' issue of the Notice of Reward, the right of entitlement shall be regarded as forfeited and the reward shall be paid into the Treasury.

Article 10:   The identites of informants is smuggling cases should be kept strictly confidiential Customs.

Article 11:   These Procedures shall be implemented by the tax authorities handling smuggling cases on behalf of Customs in the places without customs houses.

Article 12:   These Procedures shall be put into effect as of October 1, 1982. "Procedures For Customs' Rewards in the Prohibition of Smuggling" issued by the original Ministry of Foreign Trade shall then be annulled.

Regulations on Firearms Control of the People's Republic of China

(Approved by the State Council on 5th January, 1981. Enforced by the Public Security Bureau on 25th April, 1981)

Article 1: These regulations are provided to maintain social order, secure public safety and prevent criminals from using firearms to carry out destroying activities.

Article 2: Firearms (including bullets used by the firearms) in these regulations are referred to the following firearms of non-military system: military firearms, rifles submachine guns and machine guns, all sorts of firearms used in shooting sports, firearms with refling, multi-bullets firearms, gunpowder firearms, injection guns for anaesthetizing animals and airguns that can fire metal bullets.

Military firearms used to equip the Chinese People Liberation Army, civilian soldiers and armed police troops will be controlled by the related provisions on military troops and civilian soldiers system.

The Wearing and Disposition of Firearms

Article 3: The following personnel may possess firearms.

(i) The People's Court, the People's Procuratorate' Public Security Authority Personnel who carry firearms for the need of their work.

(ii) The People's government at border areas, sea front areas, provinces and self autonomous regions and responsible officials of the Communist Party or central government at other remote areas who have the need to carry firearms.

(iii) Party or government authority's confidential messengers of above provincial level, border prefectures, municipal, party and governmental authority and postal and cable authority's confidential communication messengers who carry firearms for the need of their work.

(iv)   The customs personnel who carry firearms for the need of their work.

(v)   Guards and escorting personnel of military works.

Article 4:   The following units may have the disposition of firearms

(i)   The need for disposition of firearms for security departments of mining factories, enterprises, authorities school, science research institutes.

(ii)   The need for disposition of firearms for important financial or monetary units, important warehouses, broadcasting stations or science research institutes which locate at remote areas and without establishment of armed guards.

(iii)   The need for disposition of firearms for geological exploration terms or surverying terms which operate business at remote areas or at sea.

(iv)   Liners, cargoships or tankers which sail at China sea coast or high sea or other ships which operate business at sea.

(v)   The need for disposition of firearms for civil airports or civil aircrafts.

Article 5:   Sports committees at above county level which promote shooting sports may dispose firearms for the sports.

Article 6:   Hunting production professional personnel or units may carry and dispose hunting firearms non professional hunting personnel may possess hunting firearms if they are Chinese citizens at or above the age of 18 but each personnel cannot possess more than 2 firearms.

Article 7:   Hunting production and scientific research teaching units, wild life rearing and pastoral business units and veterinary hospitals which need to carry out narcotic injection may dispose injection guns.

Article 8:   For the need of film making, film production factory may purchase outdated old fashion firearms as tools. However, except for a limited quantity of guns for special effect, the machinary parts of other firearms should be undergone technical treatment in order to prevent them from geninue bullet shooting.

Manufacture and Purchase of Firearms

Article 9:   All sorts of firearms should be made and repaired at the state appointed factories. Any other units and individuals are prohibited to make repair or process firearms by themselves.

Article 10:   Before purchasing military firearms, all units should report to their local public security authority about the types, quantity, usauge, scope of wearing and disposition of the firearms, Having received the consent from their public security bureau, they may apply for allocation of fund from the state appointed authority.

In purchasing all sorts of firearms for shooting sports, permission from the immediate supervising Sports Committee and consent from local county or municipal public security bureau are necessary. A purchase certificate will be issued thereafter for purchasing the firearms at state appointed authority.

In purchasing hunting and injection firearms, permission from forestry department of above county level and consent from public security authority are necessary. A purchase certificate will be issued thereafter for purchasing the firearms at state appointed authority. Stores retail for sale of hunting firearms shall register at public security authority of above county and municipal level.

Except for units appointed by the state or permitted by the head office, any units or individual are prohibited to purchase or sell firearms and bullets.

Control of Firearms

Article 11:   Personnel possessing firearms should have prior consent from responsible person of their own unit and have him submitted the case for approval from control department of above county level. Units possessing firearms should have prior approval from People's government of above county level.

Any unit or individual are prohibited to possess firearms and bullets without approval from legal procedures. Unapproved possession of firearms, bullets should not be handled privately and should hand in to the local public security authority.

Article 12:   Personnel and unit possessing firearms should apply for firearms possession licence from local county or municipal public security bureau. The firearms possession licence will be issued after evaluation by the county or municipal public security bureau.

Possessing firearms personnel who wish to carry the firearms while going downtown should bring along with them the firearms possession licence for inspection. If they have to carry their firearms to areas outside their own county or municipal for official assignment, they have to apply for firearms possession permit from their local county or municipal public security bureau.

Article 13:   Firearms which are of historical significance and taken care of by exhibition hall or museum should be registered with local county and municipal public security bureau and should not be transferred for other usage.

Article 14:   It is strongly prohibited to fire with purpose in cities, towns, civilian habitation spots, holiday resorts, airports, traffic routes and other shooting forbidden areas. Fire for hunting are prohibited at non-hunting area.

Article 15:   In certain specific areas and meeting places where carrying of firearms is prohibited, the firearms possessing personnel should hand in the firearms to the public security bureau or assigned units for custody. The firearms will be returned upon the personnel's departure.

Article 16:   All sorts of firearms should be well taken care of to ensure safety. Firearms possessed by the mass should be specially responsible by assigned personnel or warehouse (shelf) for safe keeping. Firearms and bullets should be stored separately. Lose, theft of occurance of other incidents should be strictly avoided.

Any lose or theft of firearms should report to the public security authority immediately and the vicinity should be protected.

Article 17: Firearms possessing unit or personnel are prohibited to give or let the firearms or bullets for others' use. Units or personnel lost the right of possessing firearms should return the firearms to the firearms distributing units. Also, the firearms possession licence should be returned to the issuance public security authority for cancellation.

Persons, who possess a hunting gun, move out from his original living county or municipelity should cancell his firearms possession licence in return for a carrying transporation permit at the issuance public security authority. When he arrives at his destination, he may apply a new firearms possession licence from the local public security authority by showing his possessing and possession.

Article 18: Before the transportation of firearms and bullets, transportation licence should be applied from the county or municipal public security bureau at the place of destination. Upon arrival, the licence can be used as proof for record registration or firearms possession licence application at local public security bureau.

Article 19: Hunting firearms brought into the border from abroad should have approval from the county or municipal public security bureau (where the applicants normally inhabit). At the time of entering the border, the frontier inspection station will examine the firearms and issue a carrying transportation permit after declaration at the customs. Upon arrival at the destination, the permit should be submitted to the local public security authority for exchange of firearms possession licence. Hunting firearms brought out of the Chinese territories should have the firearms possession licence cancelled at the original issuance public security bureau in exchange for carrying transportation permit. At the time of leaving the border. The firearms should be declared at the customs and the possession and transportation permit should be presented to the frontier inspection station.

Article 20: Firearms which cannot be used anymore and reported for cancellation by all units, should be recorded in a register. It should be submitted to the leaders at headoffices of provinces, autonomous regions or direct administered municipalities for approval. The detailed register should be handed in for inspection at local county or municipal public security bureau. After the firearms are completely undergoing a disfiguring treatment, they will be sent back to a metallurgical factory, appointed by the provinces, autonomous regions or direct administered municipalities public security office or bureau, for multing down in furnaces under the supervision of personnel sending from the units which intend to have the firearms multed down.

Article 21: Airguns which can fire metal bullets, if used by sports departments should be controlled as to shooting sports firearms if used by hunting units in hunting, should be controlled as hunting firearms. Individual who purchases or possesses airgun which can fire metal bullets should have it registered. The concrete rules shall be provided by provinces, autonomous regions, direct administered municipalities, public security office or bureau.

Article 22: The ministry of public security will unify the provisions of firearms carrying licence, firearms permit, purchase permit for shooting sport gun, hunting gun and injection gun. (firearms and ammunition transportation permit and possession and transportation permit.) Provinces, Autonomous regions and direct administer municipalities public security office or bureau will unify the printing of the above matters and will be issued by county or municipal public security bureau.

Article 23: Public security authority of all levels should implement supervison and execute scheduled inspection on the wearing, usage, custody and alternation circumstances of those non-military system in their localities.

Control of Foreigners' Firearms

Article 24: Foreign displomatic representative offices consulate general offices and their personnel in China who bring firearms into China should make prior application to the Ministry of Foreign Affairs of the People's Republic of China. After the consent of the Ministry, they have to declare the firearms to the customs while entering the border. The frontier inspection station will issue firearms carrying permit to them. Upon arrival at the destination, they should declare the firearms to the public security bureau where their offices are located at for firearms registration.

Except for hunting firearms using in hunting areas, firearms possessed by foreign diplomatic representatative offices, consulate general offices and their personnel should not be brought outsides their respective diplomatic representative offices or consulate general offices in China.

Foreign diplomatic representatative offices, consulate general offices and their personnel in China who leave China by bringing firearms with them should give notice to the ministry of Foreign Affairs of the People's Republic of China. They should cancel the firearms registration and apply for the carrying transportation permit with the public security bureau where their offices are located at. At the time of leaving the border, they should declare the firearms to the customs and give the carrying transportation permit to the frontier inspection station.

Article 25: Delegates and guards from delegations of foreign party, politics, military or parliament who carry firearms with them to China should seek prior consent after declaration of the firearms to the Ministry of Foreign Affairs of the People's Republic of China or from the host units. The host units will inform the frontier inspection station and make a record at the Ministry of Public Security.

Article 26: Foreign sports representative teams who carry shooting sports firearms with them particupate in shooting sports race activities in China should have prior approval from the Athetic Sports Committee of the People's Republic of China. At the time of entering the border, they should declare the firearms to the customs. The frontier inspection station will issue carry transportation permit for the firearms. Upon arrival at the destination of the race, they should register the firearms in record with the county or municipal Public Security bureau. The record will be cancelled upon leaving China. The shooting sports firearms which are in transit in China should have prior approval from the Athetic Sports Committee of the People's Republic of China. The Athetic Sports Committee or the People's Republic of China will then inform the frontier inspection station and add a seal on those transit shooting sports firearms.

Article 27:   Firearms — gunpowder carried by foreign civil aircrafts and foreign vessels should, at the time when these aircrafts and vessels entering Chinese ports, be sealed for custody by the frontier, inspection station. The seal will be re-opened upon leaving the border.

Article 28:   Unless with the approval from the destined province, autonomous regions, direct administer municipalities and the state head office of People's Republic of China, foreigners are not allowed to carry firearms and gunpowder with them to China if they are outside the provisions stipulated in Article 24, 25, 26 of the present regulations. Such foreigner who carry the firearms and gunpowder with them should declare to the customs at the time of entering the border. The frontier inspection station will seal the firearms and gunpowder for custody at the port temporary and return them to their owner when such owner leaves the Chinese territories or the carrying person may re-ship the firearms and gunpowder from the Chinese border. Firearms and gunpowder which are permitted to enter or leave the border should be handled in accordance with the provisions stipulated in Article 19 of the present regulations. Firearms and gunpowder in transit should be declared to the customs. The frontier inspection station will examine the firearms and gunpowder and add a seal onto them for transit. Any firearms and gunpowder undeclared to the customs will be treated as illegal transportation of firearms and gunpowder.

Article 29:   Foreigners who purchase hunting firearms in China should have consent and certificate issued by the foreign affairs departments of province, autonomous regions and direct administer municipalities or host units. And then, apply for a purchase permit from public security bureau of county or municipality where they intend to purchase. Upon receiving the approval, they have to purchase them at assigned store by showing the permit.

Penalty

Article 30:   Any violation of the present regulations, the incharge responsible person and the direct responsible person will be, according to the seriousness of the case, given disciplinary punishment and social order control punishment respectively. The punishment will be enforced until legal action for criminal liability is instituted.

Article 31;   People government of all provinces, autonomous regions and direct administer municipalities and concerned ministries or committees of the State Council may provide concrete control rules and report to the Ministry of Public Security for record in accordance with the present regulations.

Article 32: The Ministry of Public Security will announce the implementation of the present regulations after the State Council's approval. The "Interim measures on Control of Firearms" approved by the state council on June 27, 1951 and implemented by the Ministry of Public Security is abolished simultaneously.

Amendments :

Adjustments on Scope of Export Licenses

*(Announced by the Ministry of Foreign
Economic Relations and Trade (MOFERT)*

MOFERT has lifted the export license control on 43 export commodities and has put 22 other commodities under the licensing system. After the adjustment, the number of export commodities under the licensing system is reduced to 212 now.

The 43 export commodities taken off the MOFERT export license control list are as follows: liquors and wines, cotton-seed oil, rapeseed oil, water melons, water chestnuts, potatoes, cabbages, magnesium, mercury, cobalt, bismuth, selenium, molybdenum concentrate and ammonium molybdate, phthalic anhydride, acetone, natural rubber, sebacic acid, fire fighting devices, grain and oil processing machinery, machine tools, AC motors and AC generators, straw products, wicker-work, rattanwork, bamboowork, furniture, artificial flowers, electric fans, wardrobes, flashlights, batteries, flashlight bulbs, cotton vests, spun rayon vests, cotton-wool clothes, cotton bathing towels, cotton bedsheets, woollen knitwear, lotus seeds, fennel oil, cypress oil, l-cystine and insulin.

The following 22 export commodities that are now put under license control are: heavy-water, aldose, fluorite, talc, magnesia alba levis and magnesia alba ponderosa, scale graphite, buckwheat, seawater crab, walnut, bitter almond, citric acid, penicillin, sulfamethazine, sulphadiazine, sulfapyridine, antibiotic synergist, analgin, caffeine, tetraimidazole, levorotatory imidazole, narcissus bulb, firearms and ammunition for civilian use.

Among the 212 export commodities under the licensing system, exports of the following 25 commodities to places other than Hongkong and Macao do not need export licenses: pigs, cattle, fresh eggs, mutton, live poultry, live pigeons, frozen poultry, processed eggs, live sheep, live finless eels, raw and processed salt, litchi, jiaogan orange, Tianjin pears, Shatian pomelos, hami melons, ginkgoes, dried sweet potato slices, dried cassava slices, detergent, corrugated paper, ceramic bricks, ceramic wall and floor tiles, toilet paper and pencils.

The ministry stressed that the following 37 export commodities are under the export licensing system regardless of where are those commodities exported to: cotton yarn, grey cloth, polyester cotton yarn, polyester cotton grey cloth, bleached cotton cloth, sewing thread for overalls, peanut oil, rapeseeds, vermicelli, sorghum, jellyfish, peanut products, canned pork, minks, walnut kernels, rapeseed cake, cotton-seed cake, beetroot cake, bran, feathers and down, feather products, candles, dried chillies, fireworks, Chinese anise, black fungus, melon seeds, heparin sodium, lincomycin,ephedrine, potassium permanganate, agnate steel tubes and parts, barite, alumina, tires, white oil and rare earths.

The above adjustments were put into force as from January 1, 1987.

CHAPTER TWO

BANKING
FOREIGN
EXCHANGE
&
JOINT VENTURE

Brief Introduction

This chapter is divided into 3 separate topics.

The first topic is banking, the contents of which include the policies of the control of currency, and the functions of the Banks in China, especially those of the Bank of China. Since the publication of the First Edition of this book, two important legislations have been promulgated, namely:

1.   Interim Banking Control Regulations of the People's Republic of China, and;
2.   Provisional Regulations on Administrative over Financial and Trust Investment Organs.

Readers may refer to the contents of this Chapter for details.

As regards Foreign Exchange, it is always a serious problem to foreign investors and traders. It is due to the fact that China has a very strict foreign exchange control. Since 1983, China has announced few measures to ease the problem, effect of which is not at all sigificance, especially when China promulgated the ''Provisional Regulations on Violation of Exchange Control of the PRC'' on April 5, 1985.

In view of poor response of foreign investors' in expanding their investment in China, the Chinese Government has announced New 10 Articles Scheme to solve Foreign Investor's Foreign Exchange Crunch (please refer to the Appendix of this topic for details). These new measures have, to certain extent, improved the situation since early 1987.

The last topic is Joint Venture.

In recent years, Joint Venture has become less popular, as it involves a lot of effort in joint administration with the Chinese party, conflicts will usually arise from this co-operation process. For this reason and other related matters, foreign investors as well as most of the Chinese parties prefer to do technology transfer on basis of licensing or ''complete buy-out''.

Because of this trend, I have left out certain new legislations on joint ventures and updated those most important one.

I BANKING

SECTION A: Organization

Bank of China Regulations

(Effective 22nd September, 1980)

Chapter 1. General

1.   Bank of China is a State enterprise founded upon the ideology of socialism. It is the bank of the People's Republic of China specialized in foreign exchange.
2.   The duties of the Bank of China are: organising, ultilizing, saving and managing foreign exchange and capital. Its business include all kind of foreign exchange, international monetary activities and serving the modernization of socialism.
3.   The headquarter of the Bank of China is in Beijing. Upon the need of its business the bank can set up branch offices or representative office inside and outside the country at important trading, monetary places.

Chapter 2 Capital

4.   The Capital of the Bank of China is 1.1 billion Renminbi.

Chapter 3. Business

5.   The Bank of China deals and accepts the following business:
   (1)   International calculation of foreign trade and non-trading.
   (2)   Intra international banks savings and loans.
   (3)   Overseas Chinese remittance and international exchange.
   (4)   Foreign currencies saving, loans and foreign exchange related to People's Bank of China's approval on Renminbi savings and loans.
   (5)   The buying and selling of foreign exchange (including foreign currencies).

(6)   The buying and selling of international gold.

(7)   Organizing of participating in international monetary holdings' loan.

(8)   To invest or joint venture with other organisations, to set up banks, financing corporations or any other enterprises in Hong Kong, Macau and Overseas.

(9)   According to the endorsement of the State, the bank can issue debts in foreign currencies and other valuable stocks and shares.

(10)   Trusteeship and consultancy.

(11)   Any banking business as permitted and appointed by the State.

6.   To take part in international monetary conference upon the approval of the State.

7.   The bank of China's office, organisations in Overseas, Hong Kong and Macau have to do those business as approved by respective local laws and orders.

Chapter 4.   Organization

8.   The bank of China consists of a board of directors formed by one honourable director, Chairman and Vice-Chairman of the board of directors, executive director and several directors. They have to be appointed by the State Council.

9.   The duties of the board of directors of the Bank of China:

(1)   To examine the bank's business method and planning.

(2)   To hear and examine the report submitted by the bank's manager on his work.

(3)   To examine and pass the bank's annual accounting report and the methods in using the surplus.

(4)   To appoint the bank's senior staff.

(5)   To examine and approve the establishment and cancellation of any offices or organizations under the management of the bank inside or outside the country.

(6)   To examine and discuss important methods related to the bank.

10.   The Bank of China consists of a board of supervisors which is formed by one Chairman of the board of Supervisors and several supervisors. They are appointed by the State Council.

11.   The duties of the board of supervisors are:

(1)   To supervise the execution on the Bank's duties in relation to State policies, laws and orders and its business method.

(2)   To examine the bank's annual accounting report.

(3)   To investigate important cases and suggest ideas to deal with them.

12.   The Bank of China consists of one manager, several deputy managers. They are all nominated by the Chairman and have to be approved by the board of directors. After that, the list will be submitted to the State Council for appointment.

13.   The manager of the Bank of China has to be responsible for the management and business for the Bank. He has to submit a report of his work to the board of directors regularly. The deputy manager has to assist the general manager in the execution of his work.

Chapter 5.   Meeting

14.   The Bank of China board of directors will hold meeting once a year. This meeting will be called by the Chairman of the board of directors. The Bank of China board of supervisors will be holding meeting once every year. This meeting will be

called by the Chairman of the board of supervisors. This meeting can be held earlier or delayed. And the Chairman of the board of directors can call a joint directors and supervisors meeting

15.   The Bank of China board of directors meeting, board of supervisors meeting or directors-supervisors joint meeting can only be held with a quorum of 2/3 (including appointed proxy who attend the meeting. Motion can only be passed by half or above of the number of the attendants.

Chapter 6.   Additional regulation

16.   These regulations as well as its amendments (if any) have to be approved and passed by the State Council.

Forms & Documentation

Date:
To:

BANK OF CHINA

ABCD Company Hong Kong

This Letter of Credit is forwarded through:

We open an irrevocable Letter of Credit No in your favour for account of China Export & Import Corporation, Peking, to the extent of RMB¥8,000.00 (Renminbi Eight thousand yuan only) available against your draft(s) drawn on us at sight 5% more or less allowed, for 100% of the invoice value, accompanied by the following documents marked with numbers:

(1)   Full set of clean "on board" "freight to collect" Ocean Bills of Lading, made out to order and blank endorsed, marked: "AB, at the port of destination."

(2)   Invoice in 5 copies, indicating Contract No. 123456

(3)   Weight Memo/Packing List in 2 copies, indicating gross and nett weights of each package.

(4)   Certificate of Quality, Quantity/Weight in 1 each copies issued by the manufacturer.

(5)   Your letter attesting that the extra copies of documents have been dispatched according to Contract terms.

(6)   Your certified copy of cable dispatched to the accountees within immediately after shipment advising name of vessel, date, quantity, weight and value of the shipment.

(7)   Certificate issued by the shipping agents certifying that the carrying vessel is chartered or booked by the China Corporation. (In case this document is called for, Charter-party Bills of Lading are acceptable.)

Evidencing Shipment of:

50,000 M/T (2% more or less allowed) of 2,000 kilos nett each of Ammonia Sulphate, Nitrogen content, 20% min., Moisture: 0.6% max., Free Acidity: 0.07% max., Free from harmful substances.

RMB¥41.40 per M/T nett F.O.B., Packing charges included.
Country of origin: Hong Kong
Manufactures: WXY
Packed in new single bags, each containing 100 kilos nett, tare weight not less than 1 kilo.

Shipment from Hong Kong to People's Republic of China port(s) not later than January 1, 1982

Partial shipments allowed. Transhipment not allowed.
This credit remains valid in Hong Kong until February 20, 1982 (inclusive) and all drafts must be marked that they are drawn under this letter of credit.
We hereby undertake to effect payment against presentation at this office of the above-mentioned draft(s) and shipping documents drawn under and in accordance with the terms of this credit. Under M/T advice.
Special Instructions:

    1.   Charter Party Bill(s) is (are) acceptable.

    2.   You should provide 2% of spare bags free of charges along with the shipment.

    3.   In case of goods being carried by liners, a deduction of £0.70 per metric ton for stowage should be made from the unit price.

    4.   Banking charges outside the People's Republic of China are for seller's a/c.

PARTICULARS OF DRAFTS NEGOTIATED UNDER THIS CREDIT

Date	
Name of Negotiating Bank	
Amount in Words	
Amount in Figures	

Drawn under _____
L/C or A/P No. _____
dated

Payable with interest _____ % per annum
No. _____
Exchange for _____ Kwangchow, China. _____ 197_____
At _____ sight of this FIRST of Exchange(Second of exchange being unpaid)
pay to the order of _____
the sum of _____
To _____

Forms & Documentation

Amount(s) negotiated under this credit must be marked below.

Date	Amount Negotiated		Negotiating Bank	Remarks
	In words	In figures		

Forms & Documentation

Bank of China

(INCORPORATED IN CHINA WITH LIMITED LIABILITY)

IRREVOCABLE LETTER OF CREDIT NO.   opened by mail, through Bank of China.

To:
                                           Date:

Dear Sirs,

We hereby open an IRREVOCABLE LETTER OF CREDIT in your favour for account of The Commercial Bank of Hong Kong Ltd., by order of Thai Wa Trading Co., Hongkong, to the extent of HD$24,300.00 (say, Hongkong Dollars Twenty Four Thousand and Three Hundred Only), subject to conditions herein contained and available by your draft(s) in duplicate drawn on Thai Wa Trading Co., Hongkong, at sight for 100% of invoice value accompanied by the following documents:

1.   Signed commercial invoice(s) in triplicate.
2.   Insurance policy(ies) or Certificate(s) in assignable form and endorsed in blank, covering Cargo Clauses (W.A.), for full invoice value plus   % and showing claims payable at Hongkong.
3.   Complete Set of Clean "Shipped on Board" Bills of Lading
     made out to order and endorsed in blank marked "freight prepaid" and notify Thai Wa Trading Co., Hongkong,
     purporting to evidence shipment of:

30 M/Tons.   (Nett Weight)
    @ HK$ M/Ton.
     Packing: In New, Used/or Repaired Gunny Bags.
     Details as per Contract No
     C.I.F. Hongkong

Shipment from Kwangchow to Hongkong   not later than
Partial shipments are permitted   Transhipment is permitted
OTHER TERMS AND CONDITIONS: (These shall prevail over all printed terms in case of any apparent conflict).

Amount of credit and quantity of merchandise 10% more or less acceptable.

Draft(s) drawn under this Credit must be marked "Drawn under BANK OF CHINA, HONG KONG L/C No. dated   with interest clause where applicable and must be presented for negoiation in China on or before   February, 19   on which date this Credit expires.

The Credit is subject to the Uniform Customs and Practice for Documentary Credits (1974 Revision) International Chamber of Commerce Publication No.

We hereby engage with the drawers, endorsers and bona fide holders of draft(s) drawn and presented in accordance with the terms of this Credit that the draft(s) shall be duly honoured on presentation.

INSTRUCTIONS TO NEGOTIATING BANK:

1.   Amount of draft(s) negotiated must be noted on the back hereof.
2.   Please despatch the first set of documents direct to us by registered airmail and the second set by following airmail, unless otherwise directed.
3.   Method of reimbursement:

                                     We will credit your account with
                                     us upon receipt of the documents
                                     in compliance with the terms and
                                     conditions of this Credit.

                                     FOR BANK OF CHINA,

Forms & Documentation

Bank of China

This Letter of Credit is forwarded through

We open an irrevocable Letter of Credit No   in your favour
for account of
to the extent of

available against your draft(s) drawn on us at sight
for   100% of the invoice value, accompanied by the following documents marked with numbers
( )   Full set of clean "on board" "freight   Ocean Bills of lading, made out to order and blank
        endorsed, marked "Notify China National Foreign Trade Transportation Corporation, at the port of
        destination"
( )   Invoice in   copies, indicating contract No
( )   Weight Memo/Packing List in   copies, indicating gross and nett weights of each package
( )   Certificate of Quality, Quantity/Weight in   copies issued by the manufacturer
( )   Your letter attesting that the extra copies of documents have been dispatched according to Contract terms
( )   Your certified copy of cable dispatched to the accountees within   after shipment advising name of
        vessel, date, quantity, weight and value of the shipment
( )   In case of F O B shipment
        Certificate issued by the shipping agents certifing that the carrying vessel is chartered or booked by the China
        National Foreign Trade Transportation Corporation, Peking or China National Chartering Corporation, Peking
        (Charter party Bills of Lading are acceptable)

        In case of C&F or C I F shipment
        Your letter attesting that the nationality of the carrying vessel has been approved by the Buyers

Shipment from   to   not later than
Partial shipments   Transhipment
This credit remains valid in   until (inclusive) and all drafts must be marked that they are drawn under this letter of
credit
We hereby undertake to effect payment against presentation at this office of the above-mentioned draft(s) and shipping
documents drawn under and in accordance with the terms of this credit

Special Instruction

All documents must be presented to as IN ONE LOT by first available airmail

Forms & Documentation

Amount(s) negotiated under this credit must be marked below.

Date	Amount Negotiated		Negotiating Bank	Remarks
	In words	In figures		

Forms & Documentation

Date:

To:

Bank of China

This Letter of Credit is forwarded through:

We open an irrevocable Letter of Credit No.   in your favour
for account of China National   Import & Export Corporation, Guangzhou
to the extent of

available for 100% of the invoice value against the following documents marked with (x):

( )   Full set of clean "on board" "freight   Ocean Bills of lading, made out to order and blank
       endorsed, notifying China National Foreign Trade Transportation Corporation, at the port of destination."
(x)   Invoice indicating L/C number, contract number, shipping marks and shipment number (in case of partial
       shipment), in 5 copies.
(x)   Weight memo/packing list, indicating contract number, shipping marks, gross and nett weights of each
       package, in 4 copies.
(x)   Certificate of Quality, Quantity & Weight in 4 copies issued by the manufacturer.
(x)   Your certified copy of cable advising buyers of shipment.
(x)   Your letter attesting that the extra copies of documents have been disposed of in compliance with the
       provisions as stipulated in the relative contract between you and accountees.

evidencing shipment of:

Packing: Packed in

Each package should be marked with serial number, gross and net weight and the following marks:
Shipment from   to
Not later than
Partial shipments are   allowed. Transhipment is not allowed. On deck shipment is not allowed.
This credit remains valid in   until   (inclusive).
We hereby undertake to effect payment against presentation at this office of the above-mentioned shipping
documents drawn under and in accordance with the terms of this credit.

Special Instructions:
In case of F.O.B. shipment only: Should the carrying vessel fail to arrive at the loading port three days before the
stipulated shipment date, both the shipment and validity dates of the Credit shall be automatically extended for one
month subject to your presention to the negotiating bank of a certificate issued by the accountees' shipping agent
attesting the actual arrival date of the carrying vessel.

For BANK OF CHINA,

All documents must be presented to us IN ONE LOT by first available airmail.

Forms & Documentation

A/C No. Assigned ....

APPLICATION FOR OPENING ACCOUNT

To: Bank of China, Peking.   Date:

I, the undersigned, wish to open an account with your bank in currency of   and hereby agree to operate on it in accordance with your regulations.

Drawings on the said account are to be made by cheque.

The name of the account is to be:

————————————————

(In block letters)

For your information, I would like to provide you with the following particulars about myself:

Nationality: Postal address:

Occupation: Cable address:

Position: Office telephone No.:

Passport No.   Telex No.:   Answer bank

Identification paper from Chinese authorities, if any:

    Name of document:
    Name of document:

       Applicant's Chinese name in document:

         Applicant
         Surname   Personal name

         Signature: ——————————

Forms & Documentation

NOTICE OF THE ALTERATION OF SIGNATURE

Date:

To: Bank of China, Head Office, Banking Dept.

I/We, the undersigned, hereby notify you that the signature(s) now being used for operating on my/our account No.   kept with your bank is/are shown overleaf and shall supersede the one(s) now in your file which you are requested to please cancel on my/our behalf.

Name of A/C _____

_____

in block letters

_____

SIGN & OR STAMP according to specimen(s)
previously registered with us.

Forms & Documentation

SPECIMEN SIGNATURE CARD

Name:	
Address:	
Valid as from:	
Tel. No.	
How to sign on account ? (strike out inapplicable below)	
one signature	
two joint signatures	
to be accompied by official seal	
Signatory's name in block letters:	

NOTICE OF THE ALTERATION OF SIGNATURE

Date:

To: Bank of China, Head Office, Banking Dept.

I/We, the undersigned, hereby notify you that the signature(s) now being used for operating on my/our account No.   kept with your bank is/are shown overleaf and shall supersede the one(s) now in your file which you are requested to please cancel on my/our behalf.

Name of A/C _____

_____

in block letters

_____

SIGN & OR STAMP according to specimen(s)
previously registered with us.

Forms & Documentation

SPECIMEN SIGNATURE CARD

Name:	
Address:	
Valid as from:	
Tel. No.	
How to sign on account ? (strike out inapplicable below)	
one signature	
two joint signatures	
to be accompied by official seal	
Signatory's name in block letters:	

Interim Banking Control Regulations of the People's Republic of China

(Promulgated by the State Council on January 7, 1986)

Chapter I: **General Provisions**

Article 1:   These. regulations are formulated with a view to strengthening the control over banks and other financial institutions, ensuring healthy development of financial undertaking and promoting socialist modernization construction.

Article 2:   Any bank or financial institution engaged in deposits, loans, individual savings, bills, foreign exchange, account settlements, trusts, investment, financial leasing or selling and buying of securities on other's behalf shall observe the provisions of these Regulations.

Article 3:   The Central Bank, specialized banks and other financial institutions shall carry out conscientiously the financial guiding principles and policies of the State and their financial activities shall be aimed at economic development, stabilization of currency and promotion of beneficial social and economic results.

Article 4:   Non-financial institutions are prohibited from engaging in financial business.

Chapter II: **The Central Bank**

Article 5:   The People's Bank of China (hereinafter referred to as the PBC) is the Central Bank of the State and the State organ, under the State Council, to lead and control national financial affairs and performs the following functions in an overall manner:

(1) to study and formulate national financial guiding principles and policies and to implement than upon their approval;

(2) to study and draft financial regulations;

(3) to formulate fundamental rules for financial operations;

(4) to control currency issuance, regulate its circulation and maintain currency stabilization;

(5) to control interest rates on deposits and loans, and to fix exchange rates of Renminbi against foreign currencies;

(6) to work out the national credit plan, to exercise centralized control over credit funds and to control working capital of state-owned enterprises in a unified way;

(7) to control foreign exchange, gold and silver, foreign exchange and gold reserves of the State;

(8) to examine and approve the establishment, abolition and merger of specialized banks and other financial institutions;

(9) to lead, control, co-ordinate, supervise and audit the financial operations of specialized banks and other financial institutions;

(10) to administer State Treasury, to issue Government bonds on the Government's behalf;

(11) to exercise control over value papers, such as enterprises' stocks, bonds as well as the financial market;

(12) participate in international financial activities on behalf of the Government.

Article 6: The PBC shall control insurance enterprises nation-wide in accordance with the stipulations of the State laws and administrative regulations.

Article 7: The PBC has a Council that serves as the decision-making body. The main tasks of the Council are as follows:

(1) to examine and consider the financial guiding principles and policies;

(2) to examine important matters concerning the annual plans of State credit, cash and foreign exchange;

(3) to determine the principles of establishment, abolition, merger and the division of operation of specialized banks and other financial institutions;

(4) to study other important matters related to the overall financial situation.

Article 8: The PBC shall establish branches and sub-branches in line with the necessities of economic development. The branches and sub-branches of the PBC shall exercise the central bank's relevant functions exercise leadership and control over the financial operations within the area under their jurisdiction.

Article 9: The PBC shall provide specialized banks and other financial institutions with the services of funds transfer, operation co-ordination, information supply and personnel training, in order to support their business development.

Article 10: The head office of the PBC and its branches and sub-branches are responsible to co-ordinating and arbitrating the disputes in operations among specialized banks and other financial institutions.

Article 11: The PBC shall not conduct direct business of granting loans to or accepting deposits from enterprises and individuals.

Chapter III: Specialized Banks

Article 12:   The State shall establish a number of specialized banks in line with the needs of the development of national economy. The specialized banks shall operate· deposits, loans, account settlements and individual savings in accordance with their respective stipulated scope of business.

Article 13:   All specialized banks are independent economic accounting entities. They shall exercise their functions and powers and engage in business operations independently in accordance with the stipulations of the State laws and administrative regulations.

Article 14:   Specialized banks shall perform the following fundamental functions:
    (1)   to formulate specific operating rules and methods in accordance with the basic financial regulations;
    (2)   to grant loans to enterprises in line with State policies and plans;
    (3)   to carry out interest rate floats within the prescribed range;
    (4)   to be responsible for funds management within their own system;
    (5)   to exercise supervision over credits and settlement of accounts;
    (6)   to exercise cash control over account-holding institutions in accordance with the State stipulation;
    (7)   to exercise supervision on payroll funds of its account-holding institutions in accordance with the State stipulation;
    (8)   to manage working capital of State-owned enterprises unde the authorization of the PBC;
    (9)   to hold and handle profit retention funds in accordance with stipulation;
    (10)   to engage in international financial operations upon approval of the State Council or the PBC head office.

Article 15:   Specialized banks may open branches providing the following conditions are met;
    (1)   The establishment of a branch is for the needs of economic development and its operation scale is paralleled with its size;
    (2)   It is within the limits of its business scope;
    (3)   There are qualified financial managerial personnel;
    (4)   Its establishment is in conformity with the principles of economic accounting;
    The head office of each specialized bank executes vertical leadership over its branches.

Article 16:   The following activities of the head offices of specialized banks must be submitted to the head office of the PBC for examination and approval:
    (1)   Activities related to the first item of Paragraph 1 of Article 5 of these Regulations;
    (2)   Activities beyond its prescribed business scope;
    (3)   Activities beyond the existing basic financial regulations or related to other specialized banks that needs unified formulated operation rules;
    (4)   Formulation and revision of institutional statutes;
    (5)   Opening branches abroad.
    Any aforementioned matters that go beyond the functions of the central bank stipulated in these Regulations shall be submitted by the head

office of the PBC to the State Council in a unified manner for examination and approval.

Article 17:   The following activities of branches of specialized banks shall be submitted to the provincial branches of the PBC for examination and approval:

(1)   Formulating major operating rules in the with the specific situation of the area under its jurisdiction;

(2)   Major changes in the emphasis of credit fund flows;

(3)   The operating rules related to other specialized banks in the area under its jurisdiction which need unified formulation.

Article 18:   Specialized banks must submit to the PBC their statements of credit plan performance, statistics, accounting and operations reports.

Article 19:   The establishment of specialized banks shall be approved respectively according to the following regulations:

(1)   The establishment of a head office of a specialized bank must be examined by the PBC and submitted to the State Council for approval;

(2)   The establishment of a provincial branch, the head office of a specialized bank shall submit an application to the head office of the PBC for approval;

(3)   The establishment of prefectural, municipal, and country branches shall be applied by the provincial branches of specialized banks to the provincial branches of the PBC for approval;

(4)   The establishment of operating units under the sub-branches of country level shall be applied by the prefectural and municipal branches to the prefectural and municipal branches of the PBC for approval.

Article 20:   The head offices, branches and sub-branches of specialized banks approved to be established shall be given a Certificate for Financial Operations by the head office or branches of the PBC. They shall register and obtain a business licence according to the Regulations for the Registration and Administration of Industry and Commerce and start operations.

Article 21:   The branches and sub-branches of specialized banks that intend to cancel their licences shall apply to the institutions which originally approved their establishment two months prior to their proposed termination. Upon approval, these branches shall be liquidated under the supervision of the approving institution. After liquidation, the certificate for financial operation and business licence shall be cancelled respectively.

Chapter IV: Other Financial Institutions

Article 22:   The financial institutions referred to in this chapter include trust and investment corporations, rural and urban credit cooperatives and other financial organizations approved by the PBC.

The provisions concerning specialized banks in these regulations are applicable to other financial institutions unless otherwise stipulated by the State or specially defined in this chapter.

Article 23:   The establishment of non-bank financial institutions, in addition to the conditions stipulated in Article 15 of these Regulations, shall have the minimum required capital subscribed by the PBC and organizational statutes.

Article 24: Big and medium-sized cities may establish trust and investment corporations when necessary. These corporations may operate capital funds, asset trust, capital and assets preservation, financial leasing, economic consultancies, security issuance and investments, etc. The business activities operated in accordance with the plan approved by the PBC.

Article 25: The application for the establishment of trust and investment corporations shall be submitted for approval according to the following rules:

(1) The establishment of national trust and investment corporations shall be examined and submitted to the State Council for approval by the head office of the PBC.

(2) The establishment of provincial trust and investment corporations shall be examined and submitted to the head office of the PBC for approval by the provincial branches of the PBC.

(3) The establishment of prefectural and municipal trust and investment corporations shall be examined and submitted to the provincial branches of the PBC for approval by prefectural and municipal branches of the PBC.

Article 26: The trust and investment corportations established by specialized banks in big and medium-sized cities shall be independent legal persons with independent accounting and shall be directed by the PBC in their business operations.

For specialized banks which operate trust business without their own independent trust and investment corporations, the sources and use of these funds must be wholly channeled into the credit plans of the banks and the income must be unitedly accounted for by the banks.

Article 27: Credit co-operatives may be set up in rural areas, big and medium-sized cities. Credit co-operatives are collective financial organizations, which exercise democratic management.

The rural credit co-operatives can operate deposits, loans, account settlements and individual savings in rural areas.

Urban credit co-operatives can operate deposits, loans, account settlements and individual savings in rural areas.

Urban credit co-operatives can operate deposits, loans and account settlements for neighbourhood collective organizations and individual industrial and commercial households and individual savings deposits. The measures of control over and approval of credit co-operatives shall be formulated separately by the PBC.

Article 28: Local governments at various levels are not permitted to establish local banks.

Individuals are not permitted to establish banks or other financial institutions and to engage in financial activities.

Chapter V: Currency Issuance Control

Article 29: Currency issuance must be subject to centralized and unified control. The head office of the PBC shall formulate the plan of currency issuance in light of the needs of national economic development and propose it to the State Council for approval. Upon approval of the plan, the head office of the PBC shall organize its implementation.

Article 30: The treasury departments are not allowed to make overdrafts with the PBC.

The PBC shall not purchase government bonds directly.

Article 31: The PBC vaults at all levels, when allocating and transferring uncirculated bank notes, shall operate according to the authorization issued by their respective superior organs. No unit or individual shall violate the provision here inabove and draw on the uncirculated bank notes in the vaults.

Article 32: When specialized banks make case-drawings on their accounts with the PBC, such drawings shall be restricted to the balance of their deposits maintained with the respective branches of the PBC. No overdrafts shall be allowed any case.

The case turned over by specialized banks to the PBC shall be handled according to the rules and regulations of the PBC's cashier system.

Article 33: Specialized banks shall carry out surveys and investigations over the performance of currency in circulation and make periodic reports accordingly to the PBC.

Article 34: Worn and torn RMB notes or coins shall be exchanged by specialized banks in accordance with the stipulations of the PBC. The offices of the PBC at respective levels are responsible for collection of these notes or coins and their destruction.

Chapter VI: Credit Funds Control

Article 35: The credit payments and receipts of specialized banks must be brought into the national credit plan according to regulations. The national credit plan shall be formulated by the head office of the PBC and submitted to the State Council for approval. Upon approval, the PBC head office is responsible for issuing and organizing its implementation.

Article 36: The treasury deposits are the source of credit funds of the PBC, and shall not be used and transferred by the banks handling the transactions.

The deposit rules of treasury deposits of government institutions, communities and military units shall be formulated by the PBC.

Article 37: The deposits absorbed by specialized banks shall satisfy the PBC's reserve requirement. The rate of reserve shall be stipulated by the PBC. The PBC shall adjust the rate according to the necessity of easy and tight money supply.

Article 38: The branches and sub-branches of the PBC shall grant loans to specialized banks upon the plans approved by the higher level banks and according to the credit policies plans.

Article 39: The funds of specialized banks can be utilized in inter-bank activities.

Article 40: Specialized banks shall have reserve for bad debts. The amount of reserve for bad debts shall be fixed by the PBC upon consultation with the Ministry of Finance.

Article 41: The foreign exchange credit funds of specialized banks shall be operated according to the Foreign Exchange Control Regulations of the State.

Chapter VII: Interest Rate Control

Article 42: The interest rate ceilings of various deposits and interest rate floors of various loans shall be drafted by the head office of the PBC and submitted to the State Council for approval, upon approval, the PBC shall stipulate differential rates in accordance with national economic policies and adjust them as the situation changes.

Head offices of specialized banks have certain rights to float interest rates. The floating range shall be stipulated by the head office of the PBC.

According to the regulations and authorization of the PBC, credit co-operatives may allow their interest rates on deposits and credits to float.

Article 43: Besides preferential term offered by banks, interest deduction may be given on loans granted to the trades and products which enjoy priorities in national economic development and have good economic results for the society but are losses for the enterprise itself. The interest deducted shall be paid by local authorities and government agencies which ratified the said deduction.

Article 44: The interest rates on deposits and loans between the PBC and specialized banks shall be stipulated by the head office of the PBC. The PBC shall adjust these rates in accordance with the necessities of tight or easy money supply.

Article 45: The interbank rates between specialized banks shall be negotiated and determined by the lender and borrower.

Chapter VIII: Deposits, Loans and Account Settlement Control

Article 46: The State protects the lawful rights and interests of depositors. The depositors can control and use their own deposits independently, other people cannot use these deposits.

Article 47: State protects the individual's savings deposits and adopts the principles of voluntary deposit, free withdrawal, deposits with interests and maintaining customer's confidentiality.

Article 48: In order to ensure the security and good economic results of loans, specialized banks shall tighten their screening procedures of granting loans and strengthen accoutability in granting such loans and shall abide by the credit policies and regulations concerned.

Specialized banks have the right to carry out inspection and supervision over the utilization of loans by the borrowing enterprises and to find out information concerning their plan implementation, operation and management, financial activities and stock.

Article 49: Specialized banks shall grant loans independently. Any unit and individual cannot force banks to grant loans and obstruct them to recall loans. Any unit shall not be exempted from repaying loans without approval of the State Council.

Article 50: In order to ensure that they meet their various liabilities, specialized banks shall maintain adequate liquidities.

Article 51: Specialized banks shall only accept and discount bills issued by legal commercial activities.

Article 52: Specialized banks must defend both receiver's and payer's legitimate rights and interests when they handle transfer account settlements. The regulations governing the settlements shall be formulated the PBC.

Chapter IX :   Violations Penalty

Article 53 :   The establishment of branches and sub-branches of specialized banks and other financial organizations in violating the provisions of these Regulations, the PBC shall order them to suspend operation, confiscate their illegal incomes in accordance with laws, investigate and affix the administrative responsibilities of persons directly responsible.

Article 54 :   In case violation of these Regulations by unauthorized withdrawal from the vaults of uncirculated bank notes occurs, the shall be recovered. The PBC shall investigate and affix the administrative duties of persons directly responsible.

Article 55 :   The administrative staff in banking and financial institutions, who promote their own interests by granting loans, shall be investigated and responsibility shall be affixed and the illegal income shall be confiscated.

Article 56 :   Staff in banking and financial institutions who neglect their duties and cause the loss of loans, shall be investigated and responsibilities affixed.

Article 57 :   Those who force the branches and sub-branches of specialized banks or other financial institutions to grant loans and cause the loss of loans shall be investigated and administrative and economic responsibilities affixed.

Provisional Regulations on Administration over Financial and Trust Investment Organs

(Promulgated by the People's Bank of China on April 26th, 1986)

Chapter I: General Provisions

Article 1:   The present Regulations are enacted in compliance with the provisions of the "Provisional Regulations on Bank Administration of the People's Republic of China", with a view to reinforcing the administration over the financial trust and investment organs and ensuring the healthy development of trust business.

Article 2:   All organs engaging in trust and investment shall observe the present Regulations.

Article 3:   The trust investment business of the present Regulations refers to the financial business in which the entrustee receives, manages or uses the trusted capital or trusted property according to the specific aim or requirement assigned by the entrustor.

Article 4:   Application must be submitted according to the prescribed procedure for the setting-up or revoking of financial trust investment organ. Without the due approval, no department or unit is allowed to engage in trust investment business.

It is forbidden for any individual to engage in trust investment business.

Article 5:   Financial trust investment organ shall work conscientiously to carry out and implement the financial policy and principle of the state; and the purpose of its business activities must be the development of economy, stabilization of currency and the enhancing of social economic efficiency.

Article 6:   The People's Bank of China shall give service to the financial trust investment organs and support their regular business activities in respect of transference of funds, coordination of work, supply of information, etc.

Chapter II: Administrative Organ

Article 7:   Financial trust investment organ shall only be set up in large and medium
               cities and shall satisfy the following conditions:
               (1)   In actual need by economic development;
               (2)   Equipped with qualified administrative personnel for the financial
                     business;
               (3)   In conformity to the principle of economic business accounting;
               (4)   With a constitution of organization;
               (5)   With the minimum capital of actual currency according to law.
               No financial trust investment organ is allowed to be set up in areas at or
               lower than the country level.

Article 8:   Financial trust investment organ must possess the minimum amount of
               actually received currency capital.
               (1)   Minimum amount of actually received renminbi capital is 50 million
                     yuan for setting up a national financial trust investment organ;
               (2)   The minimum amount of actually received Renminbi capital for a
                     province, autonomous region, city directly under the Central Govern-
                     ment, separately-listed city on plan, or a special economic zone to
                     set up a financial trust investment organ is 10 million yuan;
               (3)   The minimum amount of actually received Renminbi capital for a
                     prefecture or city directly under the provincial government to set
                     up a financial trust investment organ is 5 million yuan;
               (4)   The financial trust investment organ set up in the above-mentioned
                     areas, in case of also engaging in foreign-exchange business, must
                     at the same time possess a minimum amount of actually received
                     foreign-exchange down capital of 5 million, 2 million or 1 million
                     US dollars respectively.
               The capital fund of the financial trust investment organ shall be ensured
               intact, no department is allowed to draw therefrom.

Article 9:   The maximum registered capital of a financial trust investment organ may
               be three times the actually received currency capital fund.

Article 10:   The applicator for setting up a financial trust investment organ shall
               furnish the following material to the local People's Bank of China:
               (1)   An application form for the setting-up of financial trust investment
                     organ;
               (2)   Examination and approval paper from the responsible department;
               (3)   Organization constitution, the content of which includes the organ's
                     name, legal address, nature of enterprise, purpose of business,
                     amount of registered capital, range and kinds of business, form of
                     organization, administration, etc;
               (4)   Credentials-approving certificate issued by authoritative department;
               (5)   List of names of executive members of the organ and their resumes.

Article 11:   The application for setting up financial trust investment organ (including
               branch organ) shall be submitted for approval through the following
               stipulations:
               (1)   National organ shall be examined by the general ofice of the People's
                     Bank of China, and then be submitted to the State Council for
                     approval;
               (2)   The setting up of province-level (including separately listed city on

plan, special economic zone) organ shall be examined by the province-level branch of the People's Bank of China, and then be submitted to the general office of the People's Bank of China for the due approval;

(3) The setting-up of organ at the prefecture and province-direct-led city level shall be examined by the prefecture-or city-level branch of the People's Bank of China, and then be submitted to the province-level branch of the People's Bank of China for the approval, and concurrently be submitted to the general office of the People's Bank of China for the record;

(4) Trust investment organ engaging in foreign-exchange business shall unexceptionally be submitted to the general office of the People's Bank of China for approval, and shall apply with the State Foreign Exchange Administration Bureau for dealing with foreign-exchange business.

Article 12: The People's Bank of China shall issue the "Licence for Managing Financial Business" to the approved financial trust investment organ. The State Foreign Exchange Administration Bureau shall issue the "Licence Managing Foreign Exchange Business" to approved organ engaging in foreign exchange Business.

Financial trust investment organ shall, with the above-mentioned certificates, apply with the industrial and commercial administration department for registration.

Article 13: In case of merging of financial trust investment organs, another application procedure shall be undergone in accordance with the present Regulation and, after obtaining the due approval, the "Licence for Managing Financial Business" and "Licence for Managing Foreign Exchange Business" shall be replaced with new ones.

Article 14: The application for revoking a financial trust investment organ shall be submitted in the written form to the local People's Bank sixty days prior to the conclusion of business. And after the due approval, the financial trust organ shall, under the supervision of the local People's Bank of China and other related departments, conduct the check-up, pay the tax, clear the debts, cancel the Licence for Managing Financial Business and the Licence for Managing Foreign-Exchange Business; and apply with the industrial and commercial administrative department, with the notice from the People's Bank of China, for the handing back and revoking of the business licences.

Chapter III: Range of Business

Article 15: Financial trust investment organ may absorb the following trust deposits with the term of one year or over:

(1) Trust fund which the financial department entrusts to invest or loan out.

(2) Trust fund which the responsible authorities of enterprise entrust to invest or loan out.

(3) Labor insurance fund of labor insurance organ,

(4) Scientific research fund of scientific research institute,

(5) The funds of various academic associations and foundations.

Article 16: Trust investment organ managing Renminbi business may apply for the management of the following items of business:

(1)   Trust investment and trust loan business for which the entrustor has specified the particular items (Class A trust investment business for short);

(2)   Trust investment and trust loan business for which the entrustor has assigns the general requirement (Class B trust investment business for short);

(3)   Renting business of a solvency nature;

(4)   Agency for keeping and disposal of properties, agency for income and outgo, and agency for issuance of bonds;

(5)   Business for guaranteeing and witness for Renminbi debts, and the limit to the guarantee shall observe the prescription of the People's Bank of China;

(6)   Economic consultation business;

(7)   Business of issuing the negotiable securities approved by the People's Bank of China;

(8)   Other business approved by the People's Bank of China.

Article 17: The part of the Class B trust deposit absorbed by the trust investment organ managing Renminbi business used for the investment, loan and rent business of fixed assets shall observe the ratio stipulated by the People's Bank of China.

Article 18: The current-fund loan granted by the trust investment organ managing Renminbi business is limited to those in which the said organ invests; to the other enterprises, temporary circulating loan may be given with the maximum term not longer than three months.

Article 19: Trust investment organ managing foreign-exchange business may apply for the management of the following items of business:

(1)   Foreign-currency trust deposit at home and abroad;

(2)   Foreign-exchange loan abroad;

(3)   Issuing or as an agent to issue foreign-currency negotiable securities abroad;

(4)   Foreign-exchange trust investment business;

(5)   Lend foreign-currency loan to the enterprise in which the organ invests;

(6)   Renting business of a solvency nature internationally;

(7)   Guarantor and witness business for borrowing loans, contracting, tendering and carrying out agreement in foreign countries; the stipulations of the People's Bank of China;

(8)   Credential investigation and consultation business concerning the promotion of foreign economic and trade transactions;

(9)   Other items of business approved by the State Foreign-exchange Administration Bureau.

Article 20: The necessary corresponding Renminbi fund of the trust investment organ managing fore-exchange business may be raised, apart from the range stipulated by Article 15, through the issuance of Renminbi bonds with the approval of the People's Bank of China.

Article 21: Except for the mating Renminbi fund, the trust investment organ managing foren-exchange business is not allowed to engage in other Renminbi fund loan, renting and investment business without the due approval from the People's Bank of China.

Article 22: Except for approved by the State Council or the People's Bank of China, a financial trust investment organ is forbidden to engage in whatever way in industrial or commercial business and the business beyond the stipulations of the present Regulations in a direct manner.

Chapter IV: Business Administration

Article 23: The political administrative section and the enterprise section of the financial trust investment organ must be set up separately, and the said organ must adopt independent business accounting and take the sole responsibility for either profit or deficit, and become an enterprise legal person, and in respect of business is under the leadership, administration, coordination, supervision and inspection of the People's Bank of China.

Article 24: The source and application plan of the Renminbi funds of a financial trust investment organ shall be submitted, according to stipulations, to the People's Bank of China for due approval. As regards the one managing foreign-exchange business, its plan of income and outgo of foreign-exchange funds shall be submitted to the Stata Foreign-Exchange Bureau for due approval.

Article 25: The loan, investment and renting business used in fixed assets managed by financial trust investment organ shall be confined to the range of the fixed-assets plan officially approved by the state.

Article 26: Financial trust investment organ shall unexceptionally open its Renminbi account in the local People's Bank of China. The stipulated proportion of the Class B trust deposit it absorbs shall be deposited as the deposit reserve. As regards the organ managing foreign-exchange business, the foreign-exchange account shall be opened concurrently with the local Bank of China, and shall, according to the related provisions, deposit in the local foreign-exchange bureau the foreign-exchange deposit reserve.

Article 27: A financial trust investment organ shall, according to related provisions, put aside a certain proportion as the reserve for bad debt.

Article 28: The rate of interest on the deposit and loan, Renminbi and foreign-exchange, shall observe the provisions of the People's Bank of China.

Article 29: A financial trust investment organ shall, according to provisions, submit the following material to the People's Bank of China: annual work plan and summary, quarterly and monthly report of fund-source and execution of the plan of using fund, accounting report, financial report, annual final accounting report, final-accounting explanation, and the profit-loss report, and shall timely report the important business activities. The organ managing foreign-exchange business shall, according to related regulations, submit the above-mentioned material to the State Foreign-Exchange Bureau.

Article 30: Trust investment company set up by special banks in large and medium cities shall unexceptionally observe the present Regulations, adopt independent accounting, and become legal person; while its subordinate relation with the special bank can remain unchanged. The various special banks shall strengthen their leadership and administration over the subordinate trust investment companies.

The special bank which manages trust business without setting up independent trust investment company must observe the range of business division among the special banks in carrying out the business operation; its source and use of funds for trust business shall be brought in total sum into the credit plan of the special bank; and the loan and renting of fixed assets must be granted within the quota of loan for fixed assets approved for the special bank. The profit derived from trust business shall be unifiedly accounted by the special bank. Except for the special permission from the People's Bank of China, it is not allowed to manage investment business. It is not allowed to put up business shingle to the outside, nor to open separate bank account.

Article 31:   In case the financial trust investment organ violates the present Regulations, the People's Bank of China is entitled to order it to correct the mistake by a fixed deadline, and shall mete out such penalties, according to the seriousness of the case, as warning, circular of the violation, stopping business for rectification by order, revoking of licence for managing financial business and the licence for managing foreign-exchange business, etc.

Chapter V: Supplementary Provisions

Article 32:   The General Office of People's Bank of China is responsible for the formulation, revision, revoking and interpretation of the present Regulations.

Article 33:   The present Regulations shall enter into effect on the date of promulgation thereof.

SECTION B: Currency

Provisional Regulations of The Bank of China on the Control of Foreign Exchange Certificate

(Enforced on March 19, 1980)

1. With a view to strenthening exchange control, the State Council has authorized the Bank of China to issue "Foreign Exchange Certificates" (hereinafter referred to as "Exchange Certificates").

2. Exchange Certificates are in 7 denominations namely, 100 yuan, 50 yuan, 10, yuan, 5 yuan, 1 yuan, 5 jiao and 1 jiao. The yuan expressed in them is equivalent in value to the Renminbi yuan. No refund is allowed in case of loss.

3. Exchange Certificates are usable only in China for specific purposes. They are to be used by short-time visitors (foreigners, overseas Chinese, Hongkong and Macao compatriots), personnel of the diplomatic corps and foreign representative offices in China at the following places or for making the following payments:

    (a) at travel services dealing exclusively with foreigners, overseas Chinese, Hongkong and Macao compatriots, friendship stores, companies provisioning foreign ships, arts and crafts stores, curios shops, foreign trade centers and special shop counters for selling imported goods;

    (b) at guest houses, hotels and clubs accomodating exclusively foreigners, overseas Chinese, Hongkong and Macao compatriots;

    (c) payment of fares for through train or ship to Hongkong or Macao, and charges for transporting luggage or personal effects;

    (d) payment of fares for domestic or international flights and charges for transporting luggage or personal effects;

    (e) payment of international telecommunication charges and international parcel post;

    (f) at places where Exchange Certificates are required for payment as approved by the State General Administration of Exchange Control (or its branches) or according to afficial regulations.

4. Convertible foreign banknotes, bills of exchange or payment instruments in foreign currency that are immediately cashable or remittances from abroad may be used by the above-mentioned persons to exchange for Exchange Certificates at the Bank of China or its designated exchange centers throughout the country. When handing out the Exchange Certificates, the Bank of China (or its exchange center) shall issue to the customer an "exchange memo".

5. The holder may within 6 months and against the "exchange memo" convert the Exchange Certificates into Renminbi special deposits or foreign currency deposits with the Bank of China, or into foreign currency, or take them out of the country.

6. No private dealings in Exchange Certificates are permitted. Speculation in or counterfeit of the Exchange Certificate is strictly prohibited. Violators will be punished for undermining the socialist economic order according to Chapter 3 of the Criminal Law of the People's Republic of China.

Bank of China Regulations for Foreign Currency Deposits (Category A)

(Enforced on January 1, 1983)

Article 1:   Deposits under these regulations are handled by the Banking Department of the Head Office of the Bank of China and the bank's domestic branches and sub-branches.

Article 2:   An account for deposits may be opened by following bodies, enterprises and organizations:

(1)   Foreign diplomatic, consular and commercial missions, organs of international bodies and offices of non-governmental organizaions stationed in China;

(2)   Chinese and foreign enterprises and organizations set up in foreign countries or the Hongkong and Macao regions;

(3)   Enterprises operating in China with overseas Chinese capital or foreign capital or joint Chinese and foreign capital;

(4)   State organs, organizations, schools, state-owned enterprises and establishments and collective urban and rural economic bodies in China;

(5)   Others with the approval of the Bank of China.

Article 3:   Foreign exchange of the following kinds may be deposited in the aforesaid account:

(1)   Foreign exchange in convertible currency remitted, brought, or sent into China from abroad or the Hongkong and Macao regions. Where the foreign exchange is in foreign bank-notes, the bank-notes shall have to be first sold to the bank at its current buying rate and the proceeds converted into foreign currency at its current selling rate before the account can be credited. Where a foreign currency bill is not payable immediately, the amount can be credited to the account

only after collection by the bank;

(2) Foreign exchange funds of enterprises operating with overseas Chinese capital or foreign capital or joint Chinese and foreign capital;

(3) Foreign exchange kept by Chinese state organs, enterprises, establishments and organizations with the approval of the government department in charge of foreign exchange control;

(4) Other kinds of foreign exchange which the Bank of China has agreed to accept for deposit.

Article 4: Deposits are of two types, namely, fixed deposit and current deposit. Interest shall be paid at the rate published by the Head Office of the Bank of China.

(1) A fixed deposit takes the form of a deposit certificate issued in the name of the depositor and must be established and withdrawn in its entirety in one lump sum. Maturity may be of 3 months, half a year, 1 year or 2 years. The initial deposit must not be less than the equivalent of Rmb10,000. Where the interest rate changes prior to maturity, interest on the deposit shall still be paid at the rate originally fixed at the time of deposit. If the deposit is renewed after maturity, the interest rate ruling on the date of renewal is to apply.

(2) A current deposit takes two forms, namely, deposit book and current account. The intitial deposit must not be less than the equivalent of Rmb1,000. Withdrawals may be made at any time either by presentation of the deposit book or by a withdrawal slip, but no overdraft is allowed. Approval must be obtained from the bank in case the holder of a current account in China wishes to use cheques because of special need, but no interest is allowed for current accounts using cheques.

Deposits are restricted to 5 kinds of currencies, namely, the US dollar, Pound sterling, Hongkong dollar, Deutsche mark and Japanese yen. Deposits in other currencies shall be credited to the account only after the currency concerned has been converted into one of the aforesaid 5 currencies at the current exchange rate.

Article 5: A request for opening an account for deposits must be accompanied by an identification document, a letter of application and a specimen signature. If what is established is a fixed deposit, the bank shall issue to the depositor a fixed deposit certificate in the depositor's name, whereas if it is a current deposit, the bank shall issue to the depositor a deposit book or an advice notifying it of the opening of the account.

Article 6: The Use of Deposits:

(1) Funds in a deposit may be remitted to places within or outside China.

(2) Funds in a deposit may be converted into Renminbi at the current exchange rate.

(3) Funds in a deposit may be transferred to another foreign currency account kept with the bank.

(4) At the wise of the depositor and with the consent of the bank, withdrawals may be made in foreign bank-notes. In principle transfers abroad should be made in the same kind of currency as that deposited. If transfers are made in any other foreign currency, they

shall be dealt with as where foreign exchange is bought and sold by the bank.

Article 7: On maturity, a fixed deposit may be withdrawn against the deposit certificate and the specimen signature previously left with the bank or according to a pre-arranged procedure. A current deposit may be withdrawn against the deposit book and a withdrawal slip.

Article 8: A fixed deposit may be renewed on maturity by presenting the deposit certificate and furnishing the specimen signature to the bank or according to the pre-arranged procedure. In case a fixed deposit is not withdrawn on renewed on maturity, interest for the period after maturity shall be calculated at the rate for current deposits ruling on the date of maturity. Where a fixed deposit is withdrawn before maturity because of special need, the interest paid shall be that for current deposits ruling on the date of withdrawal.

Article 9: In case of loss of the deposit certificate, deposit book, cheques or signature stamp (seal), the depositor shall immediately file a written stop-payment request with the bank against a certificate issued by the depositor's unit or other documents originally agreed upon. Upon the bank's approval, a new deposit document may be issued to the depositor or a new specimen signature allowed to replace the old one. If a deposit has been withdrawn by fraud prior to receipt by the bank of the stop-payment request, the responsibility for loss shall be borne by the depositor.

Article 10: On closing an account, the depositor shall return to the bank the deposit book, certificate or unused cheques together with other related documents, if any.

Article 11: The bank has the responsibility for the confidentiality of the deposit of the depositor.

Article 12: These regulations are promulgated and put into force by the Head Office of the Bank of China.

Bank of China Regulations for Foreign Currency Deposits (Category B)

(Enforced on January 1, 1983)

Article 1:   Deposits under these regulations are handled by the Banking Department of the Head Office of the Bank of China and the bank's domestic branches and sub-branches.

Article 2:   An account for deposits may be opened in their own names by foreign nationals, foreign nationals of Chinese descent, overseas Chinese and Hongkong and Macao compatriots resident abroad or in the Hongkong and Macao regions, persons making short visits in China, foreign personnel of foreign diplomatic and consular missions and of foreign representations stationed in China, foreign technicians, correspondents, scholars, experts, seamen, students and trainees resident in the country, and Chinese nationals who are allowed by state regulations to retain foreign exchange for themselves.

Article 3:   Foreign exchange of the following kinds may be deposited in the aforesaid account:

(1)   Foreign exchange in convertible currency remitted or brought into China from abroad or from the Hongkong and Macao regions;

(2)   Where the foreign exchange brought in is in foreign bank-notes, the bank-notes shall have to be first sold to the bank at its current buying rate and the proceeds converted into foreign currency at its current selling rate before the account can be credited. Where a foreign currency bill is not payable immediately, the amount can be credited to the account only after collection by the bank;

(3)   Overseas Chinese remittances for buying houses but the purchase has not yet been finalized;

(4)   Other kinds of foreign exchange which the Bank of China has

agreed to accept for deposit.

Article 4:   Deposits are of two types, namely, fixed deposit and current deposit. Money can be freely credited to them. Interest shall be paid at the rate published by the Head Office of the Bank of China. The principal and interest may be remitted abroad on maturity.

(1)   A fixed deposit takes the form of a deposit certificate issued in the name of the depositor and must be established and withdrawn in its entirety in one lump sum. Maturity may be of 3 months, half a year, 1 year or 2 years. The initial deposit must not be less than the equivalent of Rmb50. Where the interest rate changes prior to maturity, interest on the deposit shall still be paid at the rate originally fixed at the time of deposit. If the deposit is renewed after maturity, the interest rate ruling on the date of renewal is to apply.

(2)   A current deposit takes the form of a deposit book. Withdrawals may be made at any time by presentation of the deposit book. The initial deposit must not be less than the equivalent of Rmb20.

(3)   Deposits are restricted to 5 kinds of currencies, namely, the US dollar, Pound sterling, Hongkong dollar, Deutsche mark and Japanese yen. Deposits in other currencies hhhali be credited to the account only after the currency concerned has been cover converted into one of the aforesaid 5 currencies at the current exchange rate.

Article 5:   A request for opening an account for deposits must be accompanied by a letter of application and a specimen signature If what is established is a fixed deposit, the bank shall issue to the depositor a fixed deposit certificate in the depositor's name, whereas if it is a current deposit, the bank shall issue to the depositor a deposit book. Persons resident abroad or in the Hongkong and Macao regions may contact the bank by post and an account for deposits will be opened for them according to arrangements. In such a case the deposit certificate or deposit book may be kept in the custody of the bank and a certificate of custody shall be issued to the depositor.

Article 6:   On maturity, a fixed deposit may be withdrawn against the deposit certificate and the specimen signature previously left with the bank or according to a pre-arranged procedure. A current deposit may be withdrawn against the deposit book or according to a pre-arranged procedure.

Article 7:   The Use of Deposits:

(1)   A deposit may be transferred abroad.

(2)   A deposit may be converted into Renminbi at the current exchange rate to be used in China or remitted to relatives in the country enjoying the special treatment accorded to overseas Chinese remittances.

(3)   A deposit may be used to pay the travelling expenses of visitors in China;

(4)   When leaving China, the depositor may, at his or her own wish and with the consent of the bank, withdraw his or her deposit in foreign bank-notes to be taken out of the country. The currency to be remitted abroad shall, in principle, be of the same kind as that deposited. If another kind of currency is remitted, the case shall be

	dealt with as where foreign exchange is bought and sold by the bank.
Article 8:	If a fixed deposit is not withdrawn on maturity, the bank may renew it for another similar period.
	Where withdrawal is made before maturity because of special need, the interest on the amount drawn shall be paid at the rate for current deposits ruling on the date of withdrawal, while the amount remaining undrawn shall continue to bear interest at the rate allowed at the time of deposit.
Article 9:	In case of loss of the deposit book, deposit certificate or signature stamp (seal) the depositor shall file a written stop-payment request with the bank against his identification certificate or other documents originally agreed upon. Upon the bank's approval, a new deposit deocument may be issued to the depositor or a new specimen signature allowed to replace the old one. If the deposit has been withdrawn by fraud prior to receipt by the bank of the stop-payment request, the responsibility for loss shall be borne by the depositor.
Article 10:	On closing an account, the depositor shall return to the bank the deposit book or deposit certificate together with other related documents, if any.
Article 11:	the bank has the responibility for the confidentiality of the deposit of the depositor.
Article 12:	These regulations are promulgated and put into force by the Head Office of the Bank of China.

Editor's Notes

the Bank of China will soon officially release its regulations for foreign currency deposits (Category A and B) and the regulations for special Renminbi deposits, which will be enforced form January 5, 1983. The regulations for various forms of deposits formerly issued by the head office of the Bank of China will be automatically annuled and replaced by the new sets of regulations, from January 1, 1983.

Bank of China Regulations for Special Renminbi Deposits

(Enforced on January 1, 1983)

Article 1:   Deposits under these regulations are handled by the Banking Department of the Head Office of the Bank of China and the bank's domestic branches and sub-branches.

Article 2:   An account for deposits may be opened by following bodies, enterprises, organizations and individuals:

(1)   Foreign diplomatic, consular and commercial missions, organs of international bodies and offices of non-governmental organizaions stationed in China;

(2)   Enterprises and organizations set up abroad or in the Hongkong and Macao regions;

(3)   Enterprises operating in China with overseas Chinese capital or foreign capital or joint Chinese and foreign capital;

(4)   Foreign nationals, overseas Chinese and Hongkong and Macao compatriots resident in or outside China;

(5)   Chinese nationals who are allowed by state regulations to retain foreign exchange for themselves.

(6)   Others with the approval of the Bank of China.

Article 3:   Foreign exchange of the following kinds may be converted into Renminbi at the current exchange rates and credited to the aforsaid account:

(1)   Remittances from abroad or the Hongkong and Macao regions in favour of a depositing unit or individual (exclusive of clearing foreign exchange);

(2)   Where the foreign exchange brought or sent into the country from abroad or from the Hongkong and Macao regions is in foreign

bank-notes, the account shall be credited only after the bank-notes have been converted into Renminbi at the current buying rate for foreign bank-notes. A foreign currency bill which is not payable immediately shall be credited to the account only after collection by the bank;

(3)　Other kinds of foreign exchange with the approval of the bank.

Article 4:　Deposits are kept in the name of the depositor and are of two kinds, namely, current deposit ane deposit book. Interest shall be calculated at the rate for current deposits published by the People's Bank of China. Where the depositing unit or individual requires the use of cheques because of special need, approval must be obtained from the bank, but no interest is allowed for current deposits using cheques. The initial deposit shall not be less than Rmb1,000 for representative bodies, enterprises and organizations, and Rmb20 for individuals.

Article 5:　To open an account, the depositor must provide the bank with an identification document or follow procedures already agreed upon.

Article 6:　The Use of Deposits:

(1)　The principal and interest of a deposit may be converted into foreign currency at the current exchange rate to be remitted abroad;

(2)　Funds in a deposit may be transferred to a Renminbi account or withdrawn in Renminbi bank-notes. The funds so transferred or withdrawn is not allowed to be re-deposited in the account.

(3)　A deposit may be transferred to another special Renminbi account kept with the bank.

Article 7:　In case of loss of the deposit book or signature stamp (seal), the depositor must notify the bank in writing to stop payment against an identification certificate or other pre-arranged evidential documents. Upon the bank's approval, a new deposit document may be issued to the depositor or a new speciamen signature allowed to replace the old one. If the deposit has been withdrawn by fraud prior to receipt by the bank of the stop-payment notice, the responsibility for loss shall be borne by the depositor.

Article 8:　On closing an account, the depositor shall return to the bank the deposit book and unused cheques together with other related documents, if any.

Article 9:　The bank has the responsibility for the confidentiality of the deposit of the depositor.

Article 10:　These regulations are promulgated and put into force by the Head Office of the Bank of China.

Interpretation

Bank of China Regulations for Special Renminbi Deposits

1.   The purposes of the revised regulations for foreign currency deposits and the special Renminbi deposits.

The new regulations are aimed at meeting the need arising from the implementation of China's open door policy. Foreign currency deposits in China had not been in huge amount until 1979. Following the rapid development of foreign trade and contacts with foreign countries after 1979, more and more enterprises and organizations now possess foreign exchange and the number of enterprises operating with overseas Chinese investment or foreign investment of joint Chinese and foreign investment increased. The number of visitors from foreign countries and Hongkong and Macao is also increased Enterprises and individuals in China are allowed, under current state policies, to possess foreign currencies. For these reasons, the regulations for foreign curency deposits currently in effect are incompatible for business development and hence the need for the revision. Therefore, BOC, a state bank that deals exclusively with foreign currency, now accepts foreign currency deposits and absorbs idle foreing currency for China's construction, making it, in the meantime, convenient for depositors earning inerest from their deposits.

2.   The characteristics of the new regulations

According to the new regulations, five foreign currencies — US dollar, British pound sterling, Hongkong dollar, German Deutsche mark and Japanese yen — will be accepted. The old regulations only accept the first three.

The new regulations provide that the initial deposit must be no less than the equivalent of Rmb20, as against Rmb100 previously.

A new article says, "The bank has the responsibility to keep secret the deposit of the depositor." It also stipulates that interest rates shall correspond to those on the world market.

All these are in the spirit of offering conveniences and good services to depositors.

3.   Will the new regulations be implemented in the Special Economic Zones ?

The new regulations will be implemented only outside the special economic zones. For the special economic zones, regulations compatible with their own conditions will be drafted and implemented by the Bank of China.

Forms & Documentation

Using Credit Cards in China

The Bank of China has handled the business of Credit Cards since 1979. The details of which are:

1.   **Cashing business**
A card holder may draw at most Renminibi 1500 yuan or the equivalent foreign exchange certificates at one time by producing the valid credit card to the authorized Bank of China or the specically arranged establishments (e.g. airports, hotels, guest houses, restaurants, arts and crafts shops and friendship stores), provided that the card holder has gone through the prescribed procedures and paid 4% of the amount drawn for service.
2.   **Direct purchasing business**
A card holder may directly purchase an agreed quantity of goods, without paying service charge, with valid credit card at the specially arranged establishments in China, provided that the card holder has gone through the prescribed procedures. These establishments will pay commission to the banks or corporations that issue the credit cards.
At present, this business is confined to a certain kind of shops in Beijing like Marco Polo Carpet Shop, Marco Polo Jewelry Shop, Marco Polo Shop, Yanjing Studio, Qingshanju, the Arts and Crafts Shop and the South Jade Carving Shop in Guangzhou.
3.   **Cashing personal cheques against credit cards business**
American Express Card holder may have their personal cheques cashed in the authorized Bank of China in accordance with the agreement between Amercian Express International and the Bank of China. The maximum amount against each cheque should not exceed US$1,000. But according to the same agreement, the

Bank fo China will not accept the cheque guaranteed by corporate card issued by American Internatonal.

Credit holders are reminded to note the followings when they use their cards in China.

1.   It is advisable for credit card holders to consult with local branches of the Bank of China for update information on appointed outlets before they use the cards.

2.   The Bank of China and the specially arranged etablishments will refuse to accept the following credit cards.

(1)   invalid credit cards

(2)   local credit cards (i.e. those cards which are only usable in certain localities.

(3)   credit cards listed in the cancellaton bulletin.

3.   Card holder is responsible for reporting the loss of his credit card to the authorized Bank of China if he loses the card during his stay in China. The Bank of China will notify immediately the departments concerned and the respective issuing bank.

Appendix

Chinese Cities where Credit Card can be used

Category of credit cards	Chinese cities where credit card can be used
American Express	Beijing, Shanghai, Tianjin, Nanjing, Wuxi, Suzhou, Hangzhou, Fuzhou, Xiamen, Quanzhou, Guangzhou, Shenzhen, Chengdu, Chongqing, Nanchang, Jiujiang, Jingdezhen, Nanning, Guilin, Kunming, Hankou, Changsha, Qingdao, Shijiazhuang, Qinhuangdao.
JCB card	Beijing, Shanghai, Tianjin, Nanjing, Zhenjiang, Yangzhou, Nanning, Guilin, Changsha, Dalian, Fuzhou, Wuxi, Suzhou, Guangzhou, Lanzhou, Quanzhou, Xiamen.
Federal Card	Beijing, Shanghai, Tianjin, Kunming, Hangzhou, Hefei, Nanjing, Lianyungang, Zhenjiang, Yangzhou, Suzhou, Wuxi, Changzhou, Nanchang, Jiujiang, Jingdezhenm, Chengdu, Chongqing, Guangzhou, Shenzhen, Haikou, Fanyu, Zhaoqing, Jiangmen, Zhongshan, Shantou, Qingdao, Jinan, Fuzhou, Xiamen, Quanzhou, Hankou, Dalian, Shenyangm, Changsha, Urumqi, Lanzhou, Shijiazhuang, Qinhuangdao, Yinchuan, Taiyuan.
Million Card	Beijing, Shanghai, Tianjin, Nanjing, Suzhou, Wuxi, Yangzhou, Kunming, Nanjing, Guilin, Fuzhou, Xiamen, Quanzhou, Dalian, Shenyang, Hangzhou, Guangzhou, Shenzhen, Dandong, Yingkou.
Master card	Beijing, Shanghai, Tainjin, Hangzhou, Kunming, Nanchang, Jiujiang, Jingdezhen, Nanjing, Lianyungang, Suzhou, Wuxi, Changzhou, Zhenjiang, Yangzhou, Chengdu, Chongqing, Changsha, Qingdao, Jinan, Fuzhou, Xiamen, Quanzhou, Dalian, Nanning, Guilin, Hankou, Guangzhou, Shenzhen, Urumqi, Shijiazhuang, Qinhuangdao, Taiyuan, Hefei, Bangfu, Wuhu.
Diner's Club	Beijing, Shanghai, Tianjin, Guangzhou, Nanjing, Kunming, Nanning, Guilin, Changsha, Fuzhou.

Forms & Documentation

The Reformation of the People's Bank of China

(Reported by the China Daily on October 2 1983)

As a major reform in China's banking system, the People's Bank of China will henceforth function exclusively as a national central bank, Liu Hongru, vice president of the People's Bank of China, said on Wednesday.

In a press interview the vice-president said that the reform will be of great significance in promoting the development of China's monetary undertakings.

The reform was made according to a recent decision by the State Council, which specified that the People's Bank of China should become a national central bank, and that an Industrial and Commercial bank should be set up to take over the commercial role originally exercised by the People's Bank of China.

As a national central bank, he said, the People's Bank of China will concentrate on the study and formulation of policies on national monetary affairs, strengthen the management of credit funds and maintain the stability of currency in circulation to stimulate the development of the national economy.

Liu Hongru said that the People's Bank of China will control 40 to 50 per cent of national credit funds to regulate and balances national credit payments.

He said Renminbi (people's currency) has become one of the stable currencies in the world, enjoying a high prestige internationally.

The relations established by the People's Bank of China with international monetary organizations will be further consolidated and developed, he assured. The reform will not in any way affect savings and deposits in China by overseas Chinese, Hongkong and Macao compatriots or foreign nationals.

The press interview went as follows:

New Needs

Question: Why is it necessary for the People's Bank of China to exclusively function as a national central bank?

Answer: This is dictated by the needs arising from the development of socialist construction. In the past the People's Bank of China functioned both as a central bank and as a commercial and savings bank. To better the role of the bank as an economic lever, concentrate social funds on national economic construction and change the present state of having funds managed by more than one department while the use of funds is over decentralized, it is necessary to strengthen the role of the central bank.

Q: What are the specific functions of the People's Bank of China as a central bank?

A: It will mainly study and formulate principles, policies, decrees and basic rules and regulations on national monetary affairs and have them implemented after approval by higher authorities. It will also issue currency and control circulation of currency on the market, exercise unified control over credit and deposits interest rates and the exchange rate, work out national credit plans and control credit funds, control State foreign exchange and gold, silver and foreign exchange reserves. It will act as the State treasury, examine and approve the establishment, merger and dissolution of monetary organizations, co-ordinate and examine the operations of all monetary organizations, control the monetary market and carry out monetary activities in the world on behalf of the Chinese government.

Q: What will be the tasks of the new Industrial and Commercial Bank?

A: It will control circulating funds and funds earmarked for technical transformation of enterprises according to State policies and credit plans approved by the People's Bank. It will handle bank deposits, loans, settlement of accounts and savings within the limits set by the State. It will also handle cash management and other operations as entrusted to it by the People's Bank of China.

Credit Funds

Q: How will the People's Bank strengthen the management of credit funds?

A: In order to change the over-decentralization of credit funds it is necessary for the People's Bank of China to control 40 to 50 per cent of credit funds for regulating and balancing credit payments. To this end the budgetary deposits of the State financial treasury, government offices and people's organizations will be incorporated into the credit funds controlled by the People's Bank of China. The various specialized banks will contribute to the People's Bank a certain percentage of the deposits they have absorbed, which will be used at the bank's own discretion. The People's Bank of China will re-evaluate the operational funds of various specialized banks.

At the same time the credit payments handled by various specialized banks will be incorporated into the national credit plan.

Monetary organizations in the country will have to work out annual plans for foreign exchange credit and foreign exchange investment.

Q: How will the People's Bank of China administer specialized banks and other monetary organizations?

A: It will exercise its authority over specialized banks and other monetary organizations chiefly by economic means with administrative measures as complement. The specialized banks and other monetary organizations must carry out the ecisions of the people's Bank and its council. Otherwise the People's Bank of China has the power to impose economic or administrative sanction.

The People's Bank of China will soon draft China's banking law and put out rules and regulations for the operation of the entire banking system.

Operating under the State Council, other specialized banks and financial organizations, including the new Industrial and Commercial Bank of China, the Agricultural Bank of China, the Bank of China, the People's Construction Bank of China and the People's Insurance Company of China, will function independently within the State-prescribed limits of operation in accordance with State laws, decrees, policies and plans.

Q: Will there be any changes in the function of the State General Administration of Exchange Control (SGAEC) for unified administration of State foreign exchange?

A: No change at all. SGAEC and its branches will still exercise unified management of State foreign exchange under the People's bank of China. The People's Bank of China shall improve SGAEC's work to meet the State's needs for foreign exchange control and business expansion. Apart from this the Bank of China's unified management of State foreign exchange will remain unchanged.

SECTION C: Loan

Provisional Regulations on Providing Loans for Capital Construction Projects

(Approved for Transmission by the State Council on August 28, 1979)

For the purpose of speeding up socialist modernization, upgrading the financial management of capital construction and making the most of the investmet capital, provisional regulations are hereby issued to provide loans for some capital construction projects.

I   The Lending Institution

Article 1:   The institution authorized to grant loans for capital construction projects is the People's Construction Bank of China (hereinafter called the Construction Bank).

II   The Eligible Borrowers and the Purposes for which the Loans are to be Used

Article 2:   The Construction Bank shall grant loans for investment capital to enterprises engaged in industry, transport, land reclamation, animal husbandry, marine products, commerce, tourism, etc. who have instituted an independent accounting system and are able to repay the loans.
Investment capital required by government organizations and non-profit institutions and for construction projects specified in the state plans shall be allocated by the Ministry of Finance.

Article 3:   The borrower must be an independent entity who assumes economic responsibility for production. Where loans are to be used for renovations or extension of existing plants, it is the responsibility of the existing enterprise to apply for and repay the loans; in case of establishing a new enterprise, it is the responsibility of the preparatory organ who will be in charge of production after the project is in operation. If the borrower has been incorporated into a specialized or regional enterprise, it is the responsibility of that specialized or regional enterprise.

III   Prerequisites for Borrowing

Article 4:   Before a project is financed by the Construction Bank, the borrower shall submit a target plan duly approved by the competent authorities and a preliminary design of the project that has been included in the state plans for capital construction for the current year.

The planning commissions at all levels and the departments in charge must invite the Construction Bank to join them in examining and approving the target plan for the project and in deciding on the current-year plan for capital construction. The capital construction commissions at all levels and the departments in charge must do likewise when examining and approving the preliminary design of the project.

When approved, a copy each of the target plan, the preliminary design and the current-year plan for capital construction shall be provided to the head office of the Construction Bank or its branch, whichever is involved in the financing.

Article 5:   The projects must meet the following conditions before they are financed:

(1)   The production technique is up to standard and the products in good demand;

(2)   Factors of production such as raw materials, fuel, power, water supply, transport are in place and ready to be used;

(3)   An acceptable estimate of the time it takes to generate enough returns to pay for the investmet, and an assurance that repayment of the loan will be made when due;

(4)   The construction site, equipment, materials and construction manpower have been duly arranged.

IV   Application, Examination and Approval of the Loan

Article 6:   After the approval of the target plan, the borrower may submit a preliminary application to the Construction Bank who shall, if agreeable, sign an agreement with the borrower. Funds needed for the preparatory stage before the start of the project may be borrowed from the Construction Bank, if the department in charge stands surety for the borrower.

Article 7:   After the preliminary design is approved, the borrower will ask the department in charge to include the project in the current-year plan for capital construction and simultaneously submit a formal application to the Construction Bank with supportive documents such as an estimate of the total cost for the preliminary design duly approved by the authorities higher up, a yearly construction plan and an agreement signed with other enterprises to work in cooperation during the construction of the project. When the documents are found in order, the Construction Bank shall sign a loan contract with the borrower.

Article 8:   The loan contract shall set forth the term of the loan, the total loan amount, interest rate and the purposes for which the loan is granted. The contract shall also include yearly plans for the drawdown and repayment. The contract specifies the responsibilities of both parties: the borrower undertakes to use the loan for the purposes as stated in th constract, to make repayment when due, and the Construction Bank undertakes to provide loanable funds according to the progress of the project.

The contract is legally binding on both parties. Either party in breach of the contract shall indemnify the other party for the losses incurred.

Article 9:   For the project in progress for which a loan contract has been signed, the planning commissions at all levels and the departments in charge shall guarantee the continuity in construction in the subsequent years so that the project will be completed on time or ahead of schedule. The materials and equipment needed for construction shall be provided by the departments in charge of supplies.

Article 10:   The Construction Bank may provide loans to finance small-size projects that do not take long to construct with all factors of production in place and ready for use, that will turn out products in urgent demand, and that will yield quick returns and large profits. Such loas are to be provided within the Bank's quota of freely disposable loanable funds.

V   Repayment and Supervision of the Loan

Article 11:   According to the progress of the project, the borrower shall make out an annual repayment plan up to the total amount of the loan and present it to the Construction Bank who shall, if agreeable, provide the funds according to the plan.

If the amount that needs to be drawn out in any one year exceeds the amount listed in the annual repayment plan, the matter is to be settled between the Bank and the borrower. In case the total repayment exceeds the total loan amount but comes within the estimate of the total cost of the project, a supplementary loan contract may be signed. For drawings in excess of the said estimate, consent must be obtained from the departments who have respectively approved the preliminary design and the target plan for the project.

Article 12:   The Construction Bank shall supervise the performance of the borrower and oversee how the loan is being utilized. Upon discovering that the borrower has diverted funds to unauthorized construction work, to aimless purchases of materials and equipment or has violated financial regulations, the Construction Bank shall give warnings and demand such mis-behavior be corrected within a specific period of time. If not heeded , the Bank has the right to suspend the loan before maturity and report to authorities higher up. The borrower shall provide financial statements and statistics to the Construction Bank. The Bank should be given access to materials it needs fore examination.

VI Repayment of the Loan

Article 13:   The borrower must repay the loan plus interest on maturity as set out in the loan contract.

The term of the loan is to be counted from the date of the loan contract to the date of full repayment. For enterprises in heavy industry, it shall be not longer than 15 years; for others no longer than 10 years, except those referred to in Article 10 for which the term shall not exceed five years. The term of the loan is to be determined according to the specific case and set out in the loan contract.

Article 14:   Interest shall be charged on an annual basis as of the date of the drawdown. Normally, the interest rate is 3% per annum. The specific rate is to be determined by the borrower's line of trade, its importance in the development of the national economy and according to the government economic policies.

Where the loan is not fully repaid on maturity, interest rate on the overdue loan shall be charged at double the rate. In case the loan is diverted to unauthorized projects, the interest rate on the diverted portion shall be tripled.

Article 15:   Sources of funds for repayment: During the period of repayment, newly established enterprises may repay the principal and interest out of the depreciation reserves for fixed assets, charges payable to the government for the use of the fixed assets and profits to be turned over to the government after the project is in operation. This shall also supply to existing enterprises that have borrowed from the Bank for renovations or extension of existing plants provided that they have instituted an accounting scheme to assess the economic gains from the borrowings. If not, they must repay out of profits to be turned over to the government corresponding to the proportion of the new fixed assets to the entire fixed assets as well as out of the depreciation reserves for the new fixed assets and charges payable to the government for the use o the new fixed assets.

For enterprises that have difficulty in repaying the loan out of the above-mentined funds because of heavy tax and low profits, the industrial-commercial tax may be exempted during the period of repayment, if recommended by the provincial internal revenue department and approved by the Ministry of Finance.

Prior to the completion of the project, interest may be paid out of the loan and the portion so used shall be free of interest.

Borrowers that have completed construction on time or ahead of schedule and are thus able to repay the loan before maturity may use the funds set aside for repayment to expand production and improve the welfare o their workers and staff. In case borrowers fail to make repayment when due, they shall repay out of funds earmarked for making technological innovations or from capital accounts. They are not permitted to make repayment by way of including the loan in the cost of products or out of profits previously accumulated.

VII   Supplementary Regulations

Article 16:   Where a dispute over the implementation of the loan contract cannot be settled between the borrower and the Bank, the case shall be submitted to an economic court for arbitration. If the court has not been established, the matter shall be dealt with by the Capital Construction Commission in their locality.

Article 17:   The present regulations are applicable to state-owned enterprises. Loans to collectively owned enterprises may be handled on the principle of these regulations.

Article 18:   The had office of the Construction Bank shall formulate and make public detailed rules for implementing these Provisional Regulations.

Article 19:   Loans granted by the Construction Bank before these regulations become effective shall continue to be handled according to the provisions previously issued.

Article 20:   The present regulations shall come into force on the date of issue.

Provisional Regulations on Granting Loans to and Opening Accounts by Unemployed Youth in cities and towns for the Purpose of Setting up Enterprises of Collective Ownership

(Issued by the People's Bank of China on October 12, 1979)

1. Enterprises of collective ownership that are in operation with the approval of the competent authorities at a level not lower than the country or district (part of city) under licences issued by the Administration of Industry and Commerce, that have a certain amount of working capital, that have instituted an independent accounting system and are responsible for their own profits and losses may open accounts with the People's Bank of China (hereinafter called "the Bank").

2. Industrial enterprises of collective ownership who have opened accounts with the Bank, and met the requirements mentioned in (1) above, and provided their products are of fine quality, in good demand and profit-yielding may apply for industrial loans to cover shortage of working capital to pay for the concentrated arrival of raw materials they ordered. The Bank shall extend credit facilities to such enterprises consistent with the regulations for granting loans to collective industrial enterprises in cities and towns.

Enterprises that need to buy machines and equipment to expand production or upgrade the quality of products may apply for loans for purchasing equipment, provided that their investments will bring economic returns and the borrowers are able to repay the loans when due. The Bank shall extend support to such enterprises consistent with the regulations for granting loans to collective industrial enterprises in cities and towns for buying equipment.

3. Commercial enterprises of collective ownership that have opend accounts with the Bank and met the requirements mentioned in (1) above may apply for marketing loans to cover a temporary shortage of funds to stock up for the busy seasons, festivals or for urgent needs. The accounts to be opened thereunder should be kept separate from the deposit accounts they have opened, i.e., transactions of loans and deposits should be passed to the respective loan and deposit accounts.

No loans will be granted by the Bank to commercial enterprises of collective ownership who are subsidiaries of the state commercial enterprises, or who act as sales/purchase agents of the supply and marketing cooperatives, or who have obtained from them initial capital to launch themselves.

4.   Colletively owned enterprises engaged in catering, services and repairs who have opened accounts with the Bank and met the requirements mentioned in (1) above, may obtain funds from the Bank to finance the purchases of raw materials they need. In addition, the Bank may provide a temporary credit facility, but once only, to finance the purchases of simple equipment and tools vital to their business operations. Applications for such loans should be submitted by the enterprises with the departments in change standing surety for them. The term of the loan is to be determnined by the specific circumstances but no longer than two years. Repayment is to be made by installments.

5.   To provide funds for production and business operations, the enterprises mentioned in (2), (3) and (4) above should improve their business management, make a sound distribution of profits and have an increasing accumulation of surplus. The surplus should be set aside first to repay the loans and replenish their working capital.

6.   Collectively owned enterprises failing to meet the requirements mentioned in (1) abvoe, must have their accounts opened en bloc with the Bank in the name of the street administrative office, neighbourhood committee or the business entity with which the enterprises are affiliated. Generally, no loans are to be granted to them.

7.   the Bank may provide loans to cooperative shops not only to stock up for the busy seasons or festivals but to cover temporary shortage of funds to keep the shops stocked in order to increase sales.

The Bank and its branches shall give active support to and exercise strict supervision over the collectively owned enterprises run by the unemployed youth in cities and towns. In providing loans, the Bank should stick to the principle of "three assessments" (i.e., to assess the credit worthiness of the borrowers, to assess their applications for loans and to assess the effectiveness of the loans after they are granted); the term of the loan must be set and repayment made when due, so as to ensure the healthy development of the enterprises.

No credit will be granted to those enterprises that operate at a loss. Interest for the loans is to be charged at the prevailing rates for industrial/commercial loans.

The Bank's branches in the provinces, cities and autonomous regions may grant loans within the quotas allocated to them for industrial/commercial loans.

Provisional Regulations on Providing Special Short- and Medium-Term Loans from the People's Bank of China to the Light and Textile Industries

(Issued on January 14, 1980)

For the purpose of carrying out the policy of "readjustment, restructuring, consolidation and improvement" and taking special measures to boost the light and textile industries so as to meet market demands at home and abroad, provisional regulations are hereby issued for the People's Bank of China and the Bank of China to provide special short- and medium-term loans and foreign-currency loans in the form of buyers' credits to the light and textile industries.

I Elegible Borrowers and the Purposes for Which Loans are to be Used

Article 1: Loans are to be granted to stateowned and collectively owned enterprises in the light and textile industries (including specialized companies responsible for their own profits and losses). The loans are to be used primarily for the purposes of tapping production potential (including raw material potential), making technological innovations and launching small-scale construction and renovation projects related to such purposes.

Article 2: No loans shall be granted for construction of new factories or for extension of existing factories.

II Prerequisities for Borrowing

Article 3: Applicants must meet the following requirements:
(a) They must be able to generate quick returns, more profits and more foreign exchange earnings in proportion to the money

borrowed.

(b) They must have the necessary materials, equipment, design and construction manpower in place and ready to be used for the project undertaken, and must be assured of the availability of raw materials, power and labour force once the project is in operation. They must be able to find markets to sell their products.

(c) Their production techniques must be up to standard.

(d) They must promuse economic yields and must be able to repay the loan with operating profits when due.

(e) They must be able to take effective measures to prevent environmental pollution.

III   Term and Repayment of Loans

Article 4:   A loan is normally available for one to two years but not longer than three years.

Article 5:   A borrower must institute a separate accounting system to monitor the economic gains from the loan. Repayment of the loan plus interest shall be made out of earnings attributed to the loan, not from previous earnings.

State-owned enterprises must repay loans out of the profits from new projects or from the depreciation reserves for fixed assets or from the charges payable to the government for the use of fixed assets. If the above-mentioned funds are not sufficient for repayment, the deficit may be covered by the industrial-commercial tax that would otherwise be collected by the government on the increased output attributed to the loan.

Collectively owned enterprises must repay loans out of the accumulated profits from the new project after tax (during the period of repayment, the department in charge is not allowed to collect profits or other funds from the borrower for tax purposes) or from the depreciation reserves for fixed assets. If these funds are inadequate for repayment, the deficit may be covered by the income tax and industrial-commercial tax that would otherwise be collected by the government on the increased output attributed to the loan.

Article 6:   If a loan cannot be repaid when it falls due, owing to suspension of the project in the course of construction or to failure of the borrower to generate the expected returns, repayment must be made out of the depreciation reserves for fixed assets and other reserves.

Article 7:   The interest rate to be charged for a loan is 4.2% per month and interest is to be paid as soon as the financed project is in operation.

IV   Applications for Loans, Examination and approval of Applications

Article 8:   Plans for borrowing shall be examined and approved as follows:
The Bureau of Light Industry, the Bureau of Light Industry No. 2 (handicrafts) and the Bureau of Textile Industry in the provinces, municipalities and autonomous regions (hereinafter called "local departments in charge") shall submit annual plans for borrowing on the basis of their programmes for tapping production potential and

for making technological innovations duly approved by the Economic commission in their locality. Plans for borrowing are to be examined by the local branches of the People's Bank of China (hereinafter called "bank branches"). They are to be submitted for re-examination by the head office of the People's Bank of China (hereinafter called "bank head office") and the ministries of light and textile industries (hereinafter called the "responsible ministries") who will, after adding their comments, submit the plans for further approval to a joint conference chaired by the State Economic commission and attended by the bank head office, the State Planning Commission, responsible ministries and the Ministry of Finance. Then, the responsible ministries and the bank head office shall send back to the local departments in charge the approved plans for borrowing involving maximum project financing of over two million yuan for the textile industry and over one million yuan for light industries, with copies sent to the bank branches, the local economic commissions, planning commissions and finance bureaus. As for loans below the said maximum amounts, the bank head office and responsible ministries shall send back the approved plans for borrowing to the bank branches with copies sent to the local departments in charge.

Article 9: Authority to deal with applications for loans: Borrowers shall submit their applications to the bank branch where they keep an account. If a loan is below the said maximum amount, the bank branch has the right to approve the application in consultation with the local departments in charge. A report shall be sent to the responsible ministries and bank head office and a copy sent to the local economic commission, planning commission and finance bureau. For a loan over the maximum amount, the application shall be examined by the bank branch together with the local departments in charge and then, if agreeable, submitted to the bank head office and the responsible ministries for approval. The bank head office and the responsible ministries shall send back the approved application to the bank branches and local departments in charge with copies sent to the State Economic Commission, State Planning Commission and Ministry of Finance and their respective organizations.

Article 10: After approval of the project to be financed, the borrower and the bank shall sign a loan agreement whereby the bank is to provide funds within the approved amount in accordance with the progress of the project.

Article 11: A loan that has not been completely drawn down in the current year may continue to be available in the next year. Repayment received during the current year may be used for lending by the bank within its jurisdiction.

V Supply of Materials for Projects to be Financed

Article 12: The planning commission and supply administration at different levels shall be responsible for the supply of materials such as steel, timber, cement, etc. needed by the projects to be financed. These materials shall first be supplied from the local stockpile. The State

Administration of Supplies will provide half of the necessary amount, which is then included in its distribution plans for tapping production potential nad technological innovation. The ministries of light and textile industries shall make suggestions on the allocations of materials to be provided by the State Administration of Supplies. Accordingly, the State Administration of Supplies will instruct its local branches to supply the materials on the spot. The remaining supplies are to be provided, in principle, by the local authorities.

Article 13: Special equipment shall be supplied by the ministries of light and textile industries; general equipment by the State Administration of Supplies and its local branches; and optional equipment by the local authorities.

VI   Periodic Review and Supervision of Loans

Article 14: The People's Bank of China and the departments in charge shall inquire into each project before financing it and oversee the performance of the borrower after the loan is granted. They must carefully check whether the project conforms to the provisions of Articles 1, 2 and 3 and see to it that all necessary measures have been taken, giving preference to those borrowers who promise good returns and have the ability to repay loans.

Article 15: The loan be used to finance the project for which it is granted. The bank has the right to suspend the loan before maturity in case the borrower changes its plans and raises its expenditure without the bank's consent or diverts the loan and construction materials to projects other than those agreed upon by the bank.

Article 16: The People's Bank of China and the departments in charge should work in close cooperation to help the borrower run its enterprise and regularly check the progress of the project and how the loan is being utilized so as to urge the enterprise to make the most of the loan with early returns.

Article 17: The borrower must submit to the departments in charge and the bank branch quarterly and annual reports on the progress of the project and how the loan is being used, with supporting statements and statistics. On the basis of these reports, the ministries of light and textile industries shall submit a quarterly consolidated report to the State Economic Commission and State Planning Commission with a copy sent to the bank head office.

VII   Loans in Convertible Foreign Currency

Article 18: When light and textile industrial enterprises require loans in foreign currency, such loans shall generally be in the form of buyers' credits. In addition to the funds from buyers' credits, the Bank of China may, if necessary, grant a supplementary loan in convertible foreign currency to cover down payment for imported equipment plus freight and insurance, or to import major components to fit the equipment to be manufactured by the borrower, or to import such things that are not covered by buyers' credits, thereby accelerating the development of light and textile industries.

Article 19: Foreign currency loans are to be applied for and granted according to the regulations issued by the Bank of China.

VIII Supplementary Regulations

Article 20: These regulatins are to be formulated and amended by the head office of the People's Bank of China. Branch banks in the provinces, municipalities and autonomous regions may issue supplementary rules to suit local conditions and submit a report to the head office for the record.

These regulatons shall come into force on the date of issue.

Regulations For Providing Short-Term Loans in Foreign Currency by the Bank of China

(Approved by the State Council on August 30, 1980)

With the funds it raises from abroad, the Bank of China is ready to provide loans in foreign currency to export-oriented industries and other enterprises in order to boost their foreign exchange earnings on the basis of self-reliance, thereby speeding up the socialist modernization of our country. It is for these purposes that the following regulations are formulated.

I   Eligible Borrowers and the Purposes for which Loans are to be Used

Article 1:   Loans are to be granted to export-oriented industries and other enterprises earning foreign exchange income directly or indirectly who can meet the prerequisites for borrowing. The loans are primarily for encouraging export-oriented industries to tap production potential and renovate obsolete plants and equipment.

Article 2:   The loans are to be used for:

(a)   financing imports of advanced technology, equipment and materials essential to upgrading the borrower's productivity and the quality, variety and packaging of export goods;

(b)   financing imports of raw materials and components to be processed for export;

(c)   developing transportation and tourism and carrying out engineering projects contracted with foreign firms;

(d)   supporting the processing of raw materials and assembling of parts supplied by foreign buyers, and supporting compensatory trade; and

(e)   providing short-term working capital to production that earns foreign exchange directly or indirectly.

II   Prerequisites for Borrowing

Article 3:   Applicants must meet the following requirements:

(a)   Effective productivity of the loan: Preference is given to borrowers who are able to earn more foreign exchange in proportion to the money invested and repay bank loans sooner. Borrowers should be able to run their enterprises efficiently, make the most of the imported advanced technology, equipment and raw materials, tap their production potential, renovate obsolete plants and equipment, enhance the competitiveness of their export goods in the international markets, thereby earning more foreign exchange for the country.

(b)   Assurance of repayment: Borrowers must give evidence of a reliable source of foreign exchange income and the ability to repay loans plus interest for which they are required to submit a schedule of repayment.

Where loans are granted to the export-goods industry, the increased output attributed to the loan should be primarily for export and not be included in the state domestic marketing plan. The income from the increased output and the export proceeds in foreign exchange should first be set aside for repayment of the bank loan. In case the goods are to be turned over to a foreign trade corporation for export, the borrower should sign a sales contract with this corporation which commits the latter to repay the bank loan in foreign exchnge for the borrower.

Enterprises not directly related to the export trade must submit a document of approval signed by the department in charge committing the latter to repay the loan from its own foreign exchange income. When necessary, the bank may demand that some organization that has a regular foreign exchange income stand surety for the borrower.

(c)   Readiness of domestic factors of production to make imported materials and equipment operational: Domestic factors of production refer to factory buildings, equipment, steam, water, electricity and fuel, raw materials, labour force, technological expertise and counterpart funds in Renminbi requisite to making the imported equipment and materials operational. These items must be duly arranged and approved by the Planning Commission or the authorities in charge who have to list them in their plans or sign contracts with the borrower.

(d)   With respect to the items mentioned above, borrowers should obtain prior approval of higher authorities for those items that require allotment of funds for capital construction or technological installations.

III   Applications for Loans, Examination and Approval of Applications and Drawdowns of the Loans

Article 4:   Applications for loans should be submitted to the Bank of China (or People's Bank of China where the Bank of china does not exist) together with the following supporting documents: a document evidencing the approval of the proposed project by the department in charge; a list of imports the loan is to finance; a schedule proving the domestic factors of production are in readiness or a copy of the relevant contract; a document approved by the department in charge showing that counterpart funds in Renminbi have been earmarked for repayment of the loan (if the borrower is not directly involved in the export trade); a copy of the sales contract signed with a foreign trade corporation which commits itself to repay the loan in foreign exchange for the borrower (if the borrower is to repay the loan with export proceeds).

Article 5:   Applications for loans by the departments under the State Council shall be examined item by item against the prerequisites for borrowing by the head office of the Bank of China. Applications by local departments and enterprises shall be reviewed by the Bank of China's regional branches in the provinces, municipalities and autonomous regions within the bounds of their respective loan quotas assigned by the head office. Cases that need to be reviewed by the head office or ministries concerned should be submitted to them for approval. In examining the applications, the bank should keep in touch with the departments in charge and work in cooperation with them.

Article 6:   After the application is approved, the borrower should sign a loan agreement, open a loan account with the Bank of China and place and order for imports. If the borrower fails to sign the loan agreement or submit a list of imports within the specified time, the bank may revoke its approval of the loan. The list of imports must be signed by the bank before the order is placed. Without the approval of the bank, neither the purpose for which the loan is to be used nor the descriptions and quantities of imports should be changed. The borrower should submit to the bank a copy of the contract signed with the foregn trader who provides the goods. The bank should help the borrower to make the most of the loan.

Article 7:   For a substantial loan, the borrower should submit a quarterly withdrawal plan according to which the bank will raise the funds. In case the plan needs to be adjusted because of miscalculation or unexpected changes of circumstances, the borrower should apply to the bank for adjustment a month before the end of the quarter. For failure to carry out the plan, the borrower shall bear additional bank charges on the amount of the withdrawal falling short of, or in excess of, the planned amounts so as to compensate the bank for losses in raising funds from abroad.

IV   Term of Loans and Rates of Interest

Article 8:   The term of the loan is to be counted from the day of the withdrawal to the day of repayment. Loans for importing raw materials and components to be processed for export are normally available for one year. Loans for importing equipment or materials to be used in making equipment, and loans for other purposes shall not exceed three years. Where loans take the form of buyers' credits, the maturity shall not exceed five years.

Article 9: The interest rates for loans are to be determined and made public by the head office of the Bank of China on the basis of the cost of raising funds on the international money markets plus its handling charges.

V Repayment of Loans

Article 10: Full repayment must be made on the due date specified in the loan agreement. If the borrower fails to repay, the surety is responsible for repayment. If necessary, the Bank of China or the People's Bank of China may force repayment by debiting the foreign currency deposit account of the borrower or the surety (or by writing off the foreign exchange quota alloted to the borrower and seizing his counterpart funds in Renminbi earmarked for the purchase of the foreign exchange quota).

Article 11: A borrower who has a regular foreign exchange income should repay the loan from foreign exchange earnings. A borrowr who is not directly involved in the export trade should repay the loan from export proceeds received through a foreign trade corporation. This corporation or some other organization which stands surety for the borrower should issue a certificate to "repay foreign exchange quota" against which the borrower may purchase foreign exchange with Renminbi from the Bank of China to repay the loan. Foreign exchange earnings from the processing of raw materials and assembling of parts provided by foreign buyers or earnings from compensatory trade must first be set aside for repayment of the loan.

Article 12: Loans made to finance a construction project by a state-owned enterprise may be repaid out of profits derived from the increased output, out of depreciation reserves for fixed assets, or out of charge payable to the government for the use of fixed assets. Enterprises that are authorized to retain a portion of their profits may make repayment from the retained profits after deductions for the staff's welfare fund and bonus funds. However, deductions for the production development fund and for retention of increased profits are not allowed. Loans to collectively owned urban enterprises may be repaid out of profits derived from the increased output (profits before tax) or from depreciation reserves for fixed assets. The department in charge is not allowed to collect profits or demand payment out of the project financed by the bank loan so long as the loan remains to be repaid. If the above-mentioned funds are sufficient to repay the loan and a surplus remains, income tax shall be paid on the surplus or a percentage of profits shall be turned over to the government as required. If not, the deficit may, with the consent of the Internal Revenue Bureau, be covered by the industrial and commercial tax on the increased output which would otherwise be collected by the Bureau. When applying for the loan, the borrower should send a copy of the application to the Bureau for its reference.

VI   Buyer's Credits

Article 13:   When loans are provided in the form of buyers' credits, the following rules shall apply, apart from other provisions in the regulations:

(a)   The borrower must abide by the provisions in the buyer's credit agreement tht the Bank of China has signed with a foreign bank and must place orders for imports from the country in which the foreign bank is located.

(b)   The borrower must indicate in the order for imports that the buyer's credit is to be used for payment. The sales contract signed between the Chinese foreign trade corporation and the foreign seller should indicate the name of the bank providing the buyer's credit.

(c)   At the time the sales contract is signed, the Bank of China shall negotiate with the foreign bank providing the buyer's credit and sign an agreement on the drawdown of the credit. The agreement shall be signed by the Bank of China head office or by one of its branches with its authorization.

VI   Bank Supervision

Article 14:   The Borrower must maximize the effective productivity of the loan by relying on cost accounting. Preference is given to the borrower who earns more foreign exchange in proportion to the amount of the loan granted and makes repayment sooner. The borrower who performs poorly or who is unable to repay his loan upon maturity, will not receive further loans until he shows improvement in management.

Article 15:   Both the bank and the borrower shall abide by the loan agreement: the Bank undertakes to provide the loanable funds; the borrower undertakes to draw on the loan and utilize its productive potential effectively. The bank shall raise the interest by 10-50% for overdue loans counting from the maturity date, and by 100% for loans diverted to use other than those authorized by the bank.

Article 16:   The bank shall inquire into each project before financing it, examine the borrower's application before approving it and oversee the performance of the borrower after the loan is granted. The bank has the duty to help the borrower achieve its economic goals. In this way the bank shall fulfil its role of promoting, regulating and supervising the economic activities of the borrower.

For large loans, the bank shall sit in on the negotiations between the borrower and the foreign supplier and make suggestions as to the preferred currency for making payment and the method of payment. The borrower must provide the bank with all necessary information, documents, statistics and a duplicate of the relevant contract.

The borrower shall be held accountable for violation of government decrees and policies; failure to abide by the regulations, the contract or the agreement; dissipation of foreign exchange; or failure to repay the loan when due. At the same time the bank may take such disciplinary actions as suspending or recalling the loan before maturity, raising the interest rate or even suing the borrower in a court of law.

VI Supplementary Regulations

Article 17: On the date the regulations come into force, "Regulations for Providing Short-term Loans in Foreign Currency," issued by the Ministry of Finance on September 29, 1978, shall no longer be valid except for loans and loan agreements previously approved and signed. Detailed rules for the enforcement of the regulations shall be formulated separately by the Bank of China.

Provisional Regulations for Providing Loans to Joint Ventures of Chinese and Foreign Ownership by the Bank of China

(Approved by the State Council
and enforced on March 13, 1981)

Article 1:   According to Article 8 of the Law of the People's Republic of China on Joint Ventures Using Chinese and Foreign Investment that a joint venture shall open an account with the Bank of China or a bank approved by the Bank of China, the provisional regulations are hereby issued to provide loans for financing business operations of joint ventures of Chinese and foreign ownership (hereinafter referred to "joint ventures").

Article 2:   **The Prospective Borrower**
Any joint venture that has been approved by the Foreign Investment Commission of the PRC according to the People's Republic of China on Joint Ventures Using Chinese and Foreign Investment, registered with the General Administration of Industry and Commerce of the PRC and granted a business licence is qualified to apply for loans.

Article 3:   **Types of Loans**
The Bank of China provides loans of the following types:
(1)   Self-liquidating loans: to meet the requirements of joint ventures in the process of production and marketing.
(2)   Accounts receivable financing: to provide financing to joint ventures before their accounts receivable are collected in China or abroad.
(3)   Loans for long-term investment: to finance the purchase of fixed assets for expanding business operations or for technological renovation.
The above-mentioned loans are granted in renminbi or foreign currency and are to be repaid in the currency in which the loans are

denominated. Interest on foreign-currency loans in payable in foreign currency.

Article 4: **Prerequisites for Borrowing**

The applicant must fulfil the under-noted requirements:

    (a)   to abide by the law of the People's Republic of China on Joint Ventures Using Chinese and Foreign Investment,

    (b)   to have opened a deposit account with the Bank of China or with a bank (hereinafter refer to "bank") duly approved by the Bank of China;

    (c)   a firm of good credit standing and sound management;

    (d)   to have enough resources to repay the loan plus interest. Loans are granted on collateral security or a surety bond acceptable to the bank.

Article 5: **Term of the Loan**

The maturity of the loan is to be determined between the borrower and the bank accoring to the purpose for which the loan is granted and the specific requirements of each case.

Article 6: **Rate of Interest**

The interest rate for loans in renminbi is determined by the People's Bank of China. The Bank of China shall fix the interest rate for loans in foreign currency with the approval of the People's Bank of China.

Article 7: **Application for, Documentation and Utilization of the Loan:**

    (a)   with the approval of its board of diretors, the qualified borrower may fill out an application form and submit to the bank together with the certified documents, supportive materials and a copy of the relevant contract.

    (b)   after the application is approved, the borrower should sign a loan agreement, open a loan acocunt with the bank and complete other for formalities as required by the agreement. For credit loans, a $\frac{1}{8}^{2}$ter of guarantee acceptable to the bank should be attached to the loan agreement; for collateral loans, the borrower should attach an act of mortgage agreed by the bank as security.

Article 8: **Repayment of Principal and Interest of the Loan**

    (a)   Full repayment must be made when due as set in the loan agreement. In the event of default the guarantor is responsible for full repayment in the case of a credit loan. The bank has the right to debit the account of the borrower or the guarantor for the repayment of principal and interest. In the case of a collateral loan, the bank has the right to sell the collateral property for the purpose of repayment. Interest on overdue loans shall be charged 20% to 50% over and above the original interest rate as from the due date.

    (b)   Successive interest payments shall be made as scheduled by the bank. When overdue, the bank shall take the initiative in debiting the payable interest to the borrower's loan account to be compounded.

Loan Service and Supervision

Article 9:   In pursuance of the government decrees and policies, the bank serves the needs of joint ventures by giving active support to their production and business management. The borrowers should accept the supervision and examination by the bank as to how the loan are being utilized. They should submit reports to the bank in respect of their programs for production, marketing, finance and capital construction and on how such programs are being carried out. In case of violation of the loan agreement, the bank may, according to the seriousness of the offence, take such disciplinary action as suspending or recalling the loan before maturity, so as to safeguard its own interest.

SECTION D: Treasury Bill

Regulations of the Treasury Bills
of the People's Republic of China

(Promulgated by the State Council on January 28, 1981)

Article 1:   The Treasury Bills of the People's Republic of China are determined to
be issued from the year 1981 in order to regulate and stabilize the
national economy, properly centralise financial resources from all
quarters, carry out the socialist modernization construction and
gradually raise the standards of the material and cultural life of the
people.

Article 2:   The Treasury Bills shall be mainly distributed and issued to state
enterprises, enterprises of collective ownership, competent
authorities of enterprises and local governments. They shall be
properly subscribed for by Party and government organizations,
bodies, units of armed forces, institutions and opulent rural people's
communes, production brigades and teams. Individuals shall also be
allowed to volunteer to subscribe for them.

Article 3:   The number of Treasury Bills to be issued each year shall be
determined by the State Council and the issue shall begin as of
January 1 of that current year. All payments must be made on or
before June 30 and the interest therein shall be calculated from July
1 of that current year.

Article 4:   The annual interest shall be fixed at 4% for the Treasury Bills. The
interest of the Treasury bills shall be paid in one lump sum when the
principal is repaid and no compound interest shall be calculated.

Article 5:   The Treasury Bills shall be calculated in Renminbi. The Treasury Bills
are of 8 different denominations: 10 yuan, 50 yuan, 100 yuan, 500
yuan, 1,000 yuan, 10,000 yuan, 100,000 yuan and 1,000,000 yuan.

Article 6:   From the sixth year of the issue of the Treasury Bills, lots shall be drawn at a time specified and the principal shall be repaid by 5 different payments in 5 years in accordance with the amount of issue, no less than 20% of the total amount to be repaid each time.

Article 7:   The issue of the Treasury Bills, the repayment of the principal and the payment of the interest shall be handled by the People's Bank of China and its subordinate organizations.

Article 8:   The funds raised by means of the Treasury Bills shall be used in a unified way by the State Council in accordance with the development and overall balance of the national economy.

Article 9":   The Treasury Bills shall not be circulated as money and shall not be freely bought and sold.

Article 10:   Those who forge the Treasury Bills or damage their reputation shall be punished according to law.

Article 11"   The Ministry of Finance shall be authorized by the State Council to handle the interpretation of the Regulations on the Treasury Bills.

Regulations on the 1982 Treasury Bills of the People's Republic of China

(Adopted by the State Council on January 8, 1982)

Article 1: The issue of the 1982 Treasury Bills of the People's Republic of China is determined in order to regulate and develop the national economy, properly centralise financial resources from all quarters, carry out the socialist modernization construction and gradually raise the standards of the material and cultural life of the people.

Article 2: The Treasury Bills shall be issued to: state enterprises, enterprises of collective ownership, competent authorities of enterprises and local governments, Party and government organizations, bodies, units of armed forces, institutions and opulent rural people's communes, production brigades and teams; individuals in urban and rural areas.

Article 3: The number of Treasury Bills to be issued each year shall be determined by the State Council and the issue shall begin from January 1 of that current year. All payments by units must be on or before June 30 and that by individuals on or before September 30.

Article 4: The interest rates of the Treasury Bills: the annual interest shall be fixed at 4% for those purchased by units; the annual interest shall be fixed at 8% for those purchased by individuals.

The interest for all the Treasury Bills shall be calculated from July 1 of that current year and no interest shall be paid for principal before its payments due day.

The interest of the Treasury Bills shall be paid in one lump sum when the principal is repaid and no compound interest shall be calculated.

Article 5: The Treasury Bills shall be calculated in Renminbi. The units purchasing them shall be given the receipts of the Treasury Bills and shall have their names on record or report the loss of the receipts in case of loss, the individuals purchasing them shall be granted the Treasury Bills proper. The Treasury bills are of 6 different denominations: 1 yuan, 5 yuan, 10 yuan, 50 yuan, 100 yuan and 1,000 yuan.

Article 6: The repayment of the principal and the payment of the interest of the Treasury Bills shall become payable from the sixth year of issue. For those purchased by individuals, lots shall be drawn at a time specified and the money shall be repaid by 5 different payments in 5 years in accordance with the amount of issue, no less than 20% of the total amount to be repaid each time; for those purchased by units, no lots shall be drawn and the money shall be repaid by 5 different payments in 5 years on the average in accordance with the total amount of the purchases by units.

Article 7: The issue of the Treasury Bills, the repayment of the principal and the payment of the interest shall be handled by the People's Bank of China and its subordinate organizations.

Article 8: The funds raised by means of the Treasury Bills shall be used in a unified way by the State Council in accordance with the needs of the development and overall balance of the national economy.

Article 9: The Treasury Bills shall not be circulated as money and shall not be freely bought and sold.

Article 10: Those who forge the Treasury Bills or damage their credit shall be punished according to law.

Article 11: The Ministry of Finance shall be authorized by the State Council to handle the interpretation of the Regulations on the Treasury Bills.

Regulations on the 1983 Treasury Bills of the People's Republic of China

(Promulgated by the State Council on September 27, 1982)

Article 1: The issue of the 1983 Treasury Bills of the People's Republic of China is determined for the purpose of properly concentrating financial resources from all quarters and carrying out the socialist modernization construction.

Article 2: The Treasury Bills shall be issued to: state enterprises, enterprises of collective ownership, competent authorities of enterprises and local governments; Party and government organizations, bodies, units of armed forces, institutions and opulent rural people's communes, production brigades and teams; individuals in urban and rural areas.

Article 3: The number of Treasury Bills to be issued shall be determined by the State Council and the issue shall begin from January 1 of that current year. The deadlines for payment: all payments by units shall be made on or before June 30 each year and those by individuals shall be made on or before September 30 each year.

Article 4: The interest rates of the Treasury Bills: the annual interest shall be fixed at 4% for those purchased by units; the annual interest shall be fixed at 8% for those purchased by individuals.

The interest for all Treasury Bills shall be calculated from July 1 of that year and interest shall not be allowed for the payments ahead of schedule.

The interest of Treasury Bills shall be paid in one lump sum when the principal is repaid and no compound interest shall be calculated.

Article 5: The Treasury Bills shall be calculated in Renminbi. The units purchasing them shall be granted the receipts of the Treasury Bills and entitled to have their names entered therein or report the loss of the receipts; the individuals purchasing them shall be granted the Treasury Bills. The Treasury Bills are issued in four denominations: 5 yuan, 10 yuan, 50 yuan and 100 yuan.

Article 6:   The repayment of the principal and the payment of the interest of the Treasury Bills shall be handled from the sixth year after issue. For those purchased by individuals, lots shall be drawn at a time specified and the money shall be repaid by five different annual payments in five years in accordance with the amount of issue, 20% of the total amount to be repaid each time; for those purchased by units, no lots shall be drawn and the money shall be repaid by 5 different annual payments in five years in equal terms in accordance with the total amount of the purchases by units.

Article 7:   the issue of the Treasury Bills, the repayments of the principal and the payment of the interest shall be handled by the People's Bank of China and its subordinate organizations.

Article 8:   The funds raised by means of the Treasury Bills shall be used in a unified way by the State Council in accordance with the needs of the development and overall balance of the national economy.

Article 9:   The Treasury Bills shall not be circulated as money and shall not be freely bought and sold except in the manner specified above.

Article 10:   Those who forge the Treasury Bills or damage their reputation shall be punished according to law.

Article 11:   The Ministry of Finance shall be authorized to handle the interpretation of the Regulations on the Treasury Bills.

II FOREIGN EXCHANGE

SECTION A: Overall policy

Provisional Regulations for Foreign Exchange Control of the People's Republic of China

(Issued on the State Council on December 18, 1980)

Chapter I. General provisions

Article 1: These provisional regulations are formulated for the purpose of strengthening foreign exchange control, enhancing national foreign exchange income and economizing foreign exchange expenditure so as to expedite the economic growth and sfeguard the rights and interests of the country. All foreign exchange income and expenditure, the issuance and circulation of all kinds of foreign exchange instruments and securities and the carrying of foreign exchange, precious metals and foreign exchange instruments and securities into or out of the People's Republic of China shall be governed by these regulations.

Article 2: Foreign exchange herein mentioned refers to:
    a. foreign currenies, inclusive of banknotes, coins, etc.
    b. Securities in foreign currency, inclusive of government bonds, treasury bills, bonds and debentures, shares, interest and dividend coupons, etc.
    c. Instruments payable in foreign currency, inclusive of bills, drafts, checks, bank deposit certificates, postal savings certificates, etc.
    d. Other foreign exchange assets.

Article 3: The People's Republic of China pursues the policy of centralized control and unified management of foreign exchange by the State. The administrative organ of the People's Republic of China in charge of foreign exchange control is the State General Administration of

Foreign Exchange Control (SGAFEC) and its branches. The specialized foreign exchange bank of the People's Republic of China is the Bank of China. No other financial institutions shall be allowed to engage in foreign exchange business, unless approved by the SGAFEC.

Article 4:   All Chinese and foreign organizations and individuals resident in the people's Republic of China must, unless otherwise stipulated by law, decree or in these regulations, sell their foreign exchange proceeds to the Bank of China. Any foreign exchange they equire is to be sold to them by the Bank of China in accordance with the plan approved by the State or with relevant regulations.

The circulation, usage and mortgage of foreign currency in the People's Republic of China are prohibited. Illicit sales and purchases of foreign exchange, and interception and flight of foreign exchange in whatever form, are prohibited.

Chapter II. Foreign exchange control relating to state organizations and collective economic units

Article 5:   All foreign exchange income and expenditure of state organs, armed forces, organizations, educational institutions, state enterprises, government undertakings, and urban and rural collective economic untics resident in China (hereinafter briefly called resident establishments) are controlled through planning.

Resident establishments are permitted to retain a proportion of their foreign exchange in accordance with regulations.

Article 6:   Resident establishments, unless approved by the SGAFEC or its branches, shall not be permitted to: hold foreign exchange without permission, keep foreign exchange abroad, offset foreign exchange expenditure against foreign exchange income, or use the foreign exchange belonging to non-resident state organs or enterprises and undertakings resident in foreign countries or Hongkong and Macao regions, by way of borrowings or transfer.

Article 7:   Unless approved by the State Council, resident establishments shall not be permitted to issue securities and certificates with foreign exchange value either inside or outside of China.

Article 8   Ministries of the State Council, and the people's governements of various provinces, municipalities and autonomous regions shall compile annual overall plans of credits to be accepted by resident establishments under their jurisdiction from banks or enterprises in foreign countries or in Hongkong and Macao regions, which shall be submitted to the SGAFEC and Foreign Investment Control Commission for examination and reported to the State Council for approval.

The procedure for examination and approval of loans and credits shall be prescribed sperately.

Article 9:   The retained foreign exchange of resident establishments, non-trade foreign exchange received in advance and reserved for later payments under compensatory trade, borrowed free foreign exchange and other foreign exchange held with the approval of the SGAFEC or its branches, must be deposited in foreign exchange deposit accounts or foreign exchange quota accounts to be opened in the Bank of China, and must be used within the prescribed scope and subject to the supervision of the Bank of China.

Article 10: When resident establishments import or export goods, the banks handling the transaction shall check up the foreign exchange receipts and payments either against the import or export licenses as examined by the customs or against the customs declaration forms for imports or exports.

Article 11: Non-resident state organs must use foreign exchange according to the plan apprvoed by the State. The operating profits of enterprises and undertakings resident in foreign countries or in Hongkong and Macao regions must, except the portion kept locally as working funds according to the plan approved by the State, be transferred back on schedule and be sold to the Bank of China.

All non-resident establishments are not permitted to keep foreign exchange for resident establishments without autorization.

Article 12: Delegations and work-groups sent temporarily to foreign countries or Hongkong and Macao regions must use foreign exchange according to their respective specific plans, and must upon their return promptly transfer back their surplus foreign exchange to be verified by and sold to the Bank of China.

Foreign exchange earned in their business activities by the delegations and work-groups referred to in the above paragraph and by memebers thereof, must promptly be transferred back, and must not, without the approval of the SGAFEC or its branches, be kept abroad.

Chapter III. Foreign exchange control relating to individuals

Article 13: Foreign exchange remitted from foreign countries or Hongkong and Macao regions to Chinese or foreign nationals or stateless persons residing in China must be sold to the Bank of China, except the retained portion as permitted by the State.

Article 14: Chinese and foreign nationals ans stateless persons residing in China are permitted to hold in their own custody foreign exchange kept by them inside China.

Foreign exchange referred to in the above paragraph may not be sent out of China illicitly either in person or through others or by post. In case of sale, the owners must sell the foreign exchange to the Bank of China and shall be permitted to retain a portion of the foerign exchange according to the ration prescribed by the State.

Article 15: When foreign exchange kept in foreign countries or Hongkong and Macao regions by Chinese residents prior to the founding of the People's Republic of China, by overseas Chinese prior to their returning to and settling down in China, and by Hongkong and Macao compatriots prior to their returning to and settling down in their native places, it transferred back to China, the owners are permitted to retain a portion of the foreign exchange according to the ration prescribed by the State.

Article 16: When foreign exchange belonging personally to individuals who are sent to work or study in foreign countries or in Hongkong and Macao regions is remitted or brought back or China, the owners are permitted to retain the entire amount of foreign exchange.

Article 17:   The rations of retention of foreign exchange permitted under Articles 13, 14 and 15 of these regulations shall be prescribed separaely. Foreign exchange retained by individuals as permitted under Articles 13, 14, 15 and 16 must be deposited in the Bank of China, remitted out of China through the Bank of China, or brought out of China against certification issued by the Bank of China. It is, However, not permitted to send deposit certificates out of China without authorization, either in person or through others or by post.

Article 18:   Foreign exchange remitted or brought into China from foreign countries or Hongkong and Macao regions by foreign nationals coming to China, by overseas Chinese and Hongkong and Macao compatriots returning for a short stay, by foreign expects, technicians, staff members and workers engaged to work in resident establishments, and by foreign students and trainees, may be kept in their own custody, sold to or deposited in the Bank of China, or remitted or brought out of China.

Article 19:   Chinese and foreign nationals and stateless person gresiding in China may apply to the local branches of the SGAFEC for the purchase of foreign exchange to be remitted or brought out of China. After approval, the foreign exchange will be sold to the applicants by the Bank of China.
When foreign expert, technicians, staff members and workers engaged to work in resident establishments require foreign exchange to be remitted or brought out of China, the Bank of China will act in accordance with the relevant stipulations in the contracts or agreements.

Chapter IV. Foreign exchange control relating to foreign organs stationed in China and their personnel

Article 20:   Foreign exchange remitted or brought to China from foreign countries or Hongkong and Macao regions by foreign diplomatic organs, consulates, commercial organs, organs of international organizations and non-governmental organizations stationed in China, diplomatic officials, cousuls as well as the permanent staff of the above organs, may be kept in their own custody, sold to or deposited in the Bank of China, or remitted or brought out of China.

Article 21:   The conversion into foreign exchange, if required, of visa and certification fees received in renminbi from Chinese citizens by diplomatic organs and consulates stationed in China, must be approved by the SGAFEC or its branches.

Chapter V. Foreign exchange control relating to enterprises with overseas Chines capital, enterprises with foreign capital, and Chinese and foreign joint ventures and their personnel

Article 22: All foreign exchange receipts of enterpises with overseas Chinese capital, enterprises with foreign capital and Chinese and foreign joint ventures must be deposited in the Bank of China, all their foreign exchange disbursements must be paid from their deposit accounts. Enterprises referred to in the above paragraph must submit periodic reports and statements of their foreign exchange business to the SGAFEC or its branches which are empowered to inspect their activities in respect of foreign exchange receipts and payments.

Article 23: Renminbi should be used in the settlement of accounts between enterprises with overseas Chinese capital, enterprises with foreign capital, Chinese and foreign joint ventures and other enterprises and individuals residing in the People's Republic China, in all cases except where otherwise approved by the SGAFEC or its branches.

Article 24: Enterprises with overseas Chinese capital, enterprises with foreign capital and foreign investors in Chinese and foreign joint ventures may apply to the Bank of China for remitting out the net profits after tax as well as other legitimate earnings by debiting their froeign exchange deposit accounts.

Enterprises and foreign investors referred to in the above paragraph should apply to the SGAFEC or its branches for transferring foreign exchange capital out of China by debiting their foreign exchange deposit accounts.

Article 25: An amount not exceeding 50% of the net wages and other legitimate earnings after tax may be remitted or brought out of China in foreign exchange by staff members and workers of foreign nationality and those from Hongkong and Macao regions employed by enterprises with overseas Chinese capital, enterprises with foreign capital and Chinese and foreign joint ventures.

Article 26: Enterprises with overseas Chinese capital, enterprises with foreign capital and Chinese and foreign joint ventures which are wound up or closed in accordance with legal procedure, should be reponsible for the liquidation on schedule of their outstanding liabilities and taxes due, under the joint supervision of the relevant departments in charge and the SGAFEC or its branches.

Chapter VI. Control relating to carrying foreign exchange, precious metals and foreign exchange instruments and securities into and out of China

Article 27: No restriction as to the amount shall be imposed on the carrying into China of foreign exchange, precious metals and their manufactures, but declaration ot the customs is required at the place of entry.

Foreign exchange carried or re-carried out of China shall be permitted by the customs against certification issued by the Bank of China or against the original declaration form on the date of entry.

Precious metals and their manufactures carried or re-carried out of

China shall be permitted by the customs according to the respective circumstances as prescribed by the State or against the original declaration form on the date of entry.

Article 28: Permission shall be given to carrying renmibi traveller's cheques, traveller's letters of credit and other convertible renminbi instruments and securities, when entering China against declaration to the customs, and when departing from China against certification issued by the Bank of China or against the original declaration form on the date of entry.

Article 29: The carrying out of China of bonds, debentures, share or stock certificates of non-resident establishments and title deeds for land and buildings situated abroad as well as certificates, agreements and contracts necessary in connection with the exercise of rights regarding creditor's rights, inheritance, land and buildings and other foreign exchange assets held by Chinese residing in China is not permitted either in person or through others or by post, unless otherwise approved by the SGAFEC or its branches.

Article 30: The carrying out of China of renminbi cheques, drafts, passbooks, deposit certificates and other renminbi instruments and securites held by Chinese or foreign nationals or stateless persons residing in China, is not permitted, either in person or through others or by post.

Chapter VII. Supplementary provisions

Article 31: All units and individuals have the right to inform against any violator of these regulations. Reward shall be given to such untis or in individuals according to the merit of the information. Violators shall be penalized by the SGAFEC, its branches, departments in charge of public security, departments in charge of administration and control or industry and commerce, or customs, on the merites of each case. The penalties may be compulsory conversion of the foreign exchange, or fine, or confiscation of the properties, or both fine and confiscation, or sentence by judicial organs according to law.

Article 32: The foreign exchange control regulations for special economic zones, for trade in border disticts, and for dealings among inhabitants along the border lines shall be enacted by the people's governments of the provinces, municipalities and autonomous regions concerned according to the provisions of these regulations and in the light of specific local conditions, and shall be enforced upon the approval of the State Council.

Article 33: Detailed rules for the enforcement of these regulations shall be enacted by the SGAFEC.

Article 34: These regulations shall come into force on March 1, 1981.

SECTION B: Corporation

Rules for the Implementation of Exchange Control Regulations Relating to Enterprises with Overseas Chinese Capital, Enterprises with Foreign Capital and Chinese — Foreign Joint Ventures

¹Approved by the State Council and promulgated by the State Administration of Exchange Control on August 1, 1983)

Article 1: These rules are formulated for implementing the provisions of Chapter V of the "Provisional Regulations for Exchange Control of the People's Republic of China".

Article 2: In Chapter V of the "Provisional Regulations for Exchange Control of the People's Republic of China", the term "enterprises with overseas Chinese capital" refers to corporations, enterprises or other economic entities registered in China with overseas Chinese capital or capital of compatriots in Hongkong and Macao areas, and managed independently or jointly with Chinese enterprises: the term "enterprises with foreign capital" refers to corporations, enterprises or other economic entities registered in China with foreign capital, and managed independently or jointly with Chinese enterprises; the term "Chinese- foreign joint ventures" refers to enterprises jointly established, owned and run in China by corporations, enterprises, other economic entities or individuals with overseas Chinese capital, capital of compatriots in Hongkong and Macao areas or foreign capital and Chinese corporations, enterprises or other economic entitles.

Article 3: For all business involving foreign exchange receipts and payments, enterprises with overseas Chinese capital, enterprises with foreign capital and Chinese-foreign joint ventures must act in accordance with the stipulations in "the Provisional Regulations for Exchange Control of the People's Republic of China" as well as those of the rules hereby stipulated.

Article 4: Enterprises with overseas Chinese capital, enterprises with foreign capital and Chinese-foreign joint ventures should open Renminbi deposit accounts and foreign exchange deposit accounts in China with the Bank of China or any other banks approved by the State Administration of Exchange Control (SAEC) or its branch offices, payments and receipts in these accounts being subject to the supervision of the bank with which the enterprises have established accounts. When applying for the opening of the accounts, the enterprises shall submit for verification their operating licenses issued by the State Administration for Industry and Commerce of the People's Republic of China.

Article 5:   The solely borne exploration fund and its cooperative development fund and cooperative production fund provided by the enterprises engaged in cooperative explitation of offshore petroleum resources in China are permitted to be deposited in banks situated in foreign countries or in Hongkong and Macao areas agreed upon by their Chinese partners.

Article 6:   Should they find it necessary to open foreign exchange deposit accounts with banks abroad or in Hongkong and Macao areas other than the accounts opened in accordance with Article 5 of these reules, enterprises with overseas Chinese capital, enterprises with foreign capital and Chinese - foreign joint ventures should apply to SAEC or its branch offices for approval. The enterprises concerned shall submit to SEAC or its branch offices quarterly statements of payments into and withdrawal from such accounts within 30 days after the end of each and every quarter.

Article 7:   All foreign exchange receipts of enterprises maintaining foreign exchange accounts with banks in China in accordance with Article 4 of these rules, must be deposited in the said accounts and all their foreign exchange disbursements incurred in normal business operations can be paid from these accounts.

Article 8:   For the implementation of the petroleum operations specified in their contracts, the enterprises with foreign capital engaged in cooperative exploitation of offshore petroleum resources may pay directly outside of China wages, salaries, cost of procurements, various labor costs and service charges to foreign workers and staff members, foreign subcontractors and suppliers. The foreign workers and staff members and foreign subcontractors shall pay taxes on the income earned in China in accordance with the provisions of the tax laws of the People's Republic of China.

Article 9:   Enterprises with overseas Chinese capital, enterprises with foreign capital, and Chinese - foreign joint ventures shall submit on or before the scheduled date to the SEAC or its branch offices the following statements with explanatory notes in detail:

(1)   Balance sheet as of December 31 of the previous year, profit and loss statement and statement of receipts and payments of foreign exchange for the previous calendar year, to be submitted before March 31 of each year, along with audit reports by auditors registered in the People's republic of China.

(2)   Budget of foreign exchange receipts and payments for the coming year, which should be submitted before December 1 of each

year (subsequent amendments, if any, must be reported immediately). The SAEC and its brach offices are authorized to request the enterprises to provide information about their business activities involving foreign exchange, and to inspect their foreign exchange income and expenditure.

Article 10: Enterprises with overseas Chinese capital, enterprises with foreign capital and Chinese and foreign joint ventures dealing in exchange between Renminbi and foreign currencies must make the currency conversion according to the offical rates of exchange published by the SAEC; their foreign exchange receipts from exports may be converted into Reminbi in conformity with the Chinese government regulations governing foreign trade exchange conversions.

Article 11: Except where otherwise approved by the SEAC or its branch offices, foreign exchange receipts realized from exports by the enterprises with overseas Chinese capital, enterprises with foreign capital and Chinese foreign joint ventures should be transferred back and credited to their foreign exchange deposits accounts with banks in China and the enterprises should also go through the procedure of cancelling their commitments for foreign exchange receipts from these exports.

Article 12: Except in the following cases, Renminbi should be used in the settlement of accounts between enterprises with overseas Chinese capital, enterprises with foreign captial, Chinese-foreign joint ventures themselves on the one hand and Chinese entities, enterprises, individuals residing in the People's Republic of China on the other.

(1) For products manufactured by these enterprises and sold to Chinese entities or enterprises engaged in foreign trade which would otherwise have to import, foreign currencies may be used in pricing and in settlement of accounts, provided that prior approval by Chinese foreign trade authorities has been obtained and that agreement on this arrangement has been reached between the seller and buyer; the prices of the products may be such as to be commensurate with those current in world markets.

(2) If enterprises with overseas Chinese capital, enterprises with foreign with foreign capital, and Chinese — foreign joint venture purchase, for the sake of production, the commodities exported or imported by Chinese entities engaged in foreign trade, foreign currencies may be used in pricing the said commodities commensurate with those current in world markets and in settlement of accounts, with the prior approval of Chinese foreign trade authorities and the arrangement between the seller and buyer.

(3) Foreign currencies may be used in payment for, and in the settlement of accounts related to, construction work performed by Chinese construction entities according to contracts, provided that prior approval from the SAEC or its branch offices ha been obtained.

(4) For other items eligible according to the State Council regulations or approved by the SAEC or its branch offices, foreign exchange may be used in pricing and in settlement of accounts.

For the foreign exchange transactions thus approved, receipts and payments may be entered into the foreign exchange deposit accounts of these enterprises.

Article 13: Overseas Chinese investors and foreign investors of enterprises with overseas Chinese capital, of enterprises with foreign capital, or of Chinese — foreign joint ventures may apply to the banks with which they have opened accounts for remitting abroad their net profits after tax deductions as well as other legitimate earnings, by debiting the foreign exchange deposit accounts of the enterprises concerned. At the time of application, the investors concerned should submit for examination a report on profit distribution passed by the board of directors or by other authorities with power similar to the board of directors, documentary evidence showing that all taxes have been duly paid, and the contracts containing stipulations in regard to the distribution of profits or earnings.

Overseas Chinese investors and foreign investors of enterprises with overseas Chinese capital, of enterprises with foreign capital, or of Chinese — foreign joint ventures should apply to the SAEC or its branch offices in transferring their foreign exchange capital abroad by debiting the foreign exchange deposit accounts of the enterprirses concerned.

Article 14: Enterprises with overseas Chinese capital, enterprises with foreign capital and Chinese and foreign joint ventures engaged in cooperative exploitation of such resources as offshore petroleum, coal, etc., and other co-operative and joint ventures, whose costs are recovered and profits are taken in kind in accordance with the stipulations provided in their contracts, may send the products thus taken out of China but such enterprises should remit the amount of tax due to the government of the People's Republic of China as well as other required payments. Should the products be sold within China, then it shall be handled in accordance with stipulations of Article 12 hereof, and the foreign exchange derived from these sales may be remitted out after tax and other payments are made.

Article 15: Staff members and workers of foreign nationality and those from Hongkong and Macao areas employed by entrprises with overseas Chinese capital, enterprises with foreign capital and Chinese — foreign joint ventures may remit abroad their wages and other legitimate earnings after tax deductions, the amounts being debited to the foreign exchange deposit accounts of the enterprises concerned for the remittance of amounts exceedings 50% of their wages and other earnings, they may apply to the SAEC or its branch offices.

Article 16: Foreign exchange expenses incurred in the business operations of the branches or offices abroad or in Hongkong and Macao areas set up with the approval of competent authorities by enterprises with overseas Chinese captial, enterprises with foreign capital and Chinese — foreign joint ventures may be remitted to these branches or offices; remitting to the foreign exchang deposit accounts of the enterprises concerned, with the approval of the SAEC or its branch offices.

Article 17: Enterprises with overseas Chinese capital, enterprises with foreign capital, and Chinese — foreign joint ventures may borrow foreign exchange from banks or enterprises located in foreign exchange from banks or enterprises located in foreign countries or in Hongkong and Macao area, but must report such borrowings to the SAEC or its branch offices for the record.

Article 18: Enterprises with overseas Chinese capital, enterprises with foreign capital, and Chinese — foreign joint venture winding up operations in accordance with legal procedure, should carry out liquidation within the scheduled period, under the joint supervision of the Chinese finance, taxation and foreign exchange control authorities. Overseas Chinese investors or foreign investors should be responsible for their outstanding liabilities and their taxes due in China. After completion of the liquidation, overseas Chinese investors and foreign investors may apply to the SAEC or its branch offices for remitting abroad from the foreign exchange deposit accounts of the closing enterprises the funds they own or receive as their share of apportionment.

Article 19: The reules to control foreign exchange receipts and payments of bank with overseas Chinese capital, banks with foreign captial, joint Chinese-foreign banks and other financial institutions shall be further regulated by the SAEC.

Article 20: Approved by the State Council, these rules are promulgated and put into effect by the SAEC.

Rules for the Implementation of Exchange Control Relating to Foreign Representations in China and Their Personnel

(Issued on August 10, 1981)

Article 1:   These rules are formulated for implementing the stipulations in articles 20 and 21 of the "provisional regulations for exchange control of the People's Republic of China."

Article 2:   Foreign exchange in convertible currency and payment instruments in convertible renminbi remitted or carried into China from foreign countries or from Hongkong and Macau by foreign diplomatic missions, consulates, official commercial offices, offices of international organisations and non-government bodies resident in China (hereinafter called foreign representations in China), diplomatic officials and consuls as well as members of the permanent staff of the above foreign representations, may be kept in their own possession, or sold to or deposited with the Bank of China, or remitted out of China. If they are to be taken out of China, the matter shall be handled according to the stipulations of the "Rules governing the carrying of foreign exchange, precious metals and payment instruments in convertible currency into or out of China."

Article 3:   In regard to countries which have signed payments agreements with China their representations in China and personnel thereof shall only receive payment in renminbi when remittances to them are effected through a clearing account.

Article 4:   Where foreign diplomatic missions and consulates in China with to convert into foreign currency visa and certification fees receiyed in renminbi from Chinese citizens, a written application has to be filed with the State General Administration of Exchange Control or its branch offices for approval.

Article 5:   When foreign representations of China and their personnel sell commodities and equipment they previously brought into China from abroad or from Hongkong and Macau, or bought in China, the Bank of China shall not provide them with foreign exchange for the renminbi proceeds they receive from the sale.

Article 6:   These rules are promulagted by the State General Administration of Exchange Control.

SECTION C: Individual

Rules Governing the Carrying of foreign Exchange, Precious Metals and Payment Instruments in Convertible Currency Into Or Out of China

(Issued on August 10, 1981)

Article 1:	These rules are formulated for implementing the stipulations in Aricles 27, 28, 29 and 30 of the "Provisional regulations for exchange control of the People's Republic of China"
Article 2:	No restriction is imposed on the quantity of foreign exchange, payment instruments in convertible renminbi, gold, silver, platinum and other precious metals and objects made from them which may be carried into China by persons entering the country, but they must be declared to the customs at the place of entry.
Article 3:	The carrying out of China of foreign exchange, payment instruments in convertible renminbi, gold, silver, platinum and other precious metals and objects made from them previously brought in shall be premitted by the customs against the original declaration form issued at the time of entry.
Article 4:	The unused portion of the renminbi which has been converted either from foreign exchange and payment instruments in convertible renminbi brought in or from foreign exchange remitted in by persons entering the country may be converted back into foreign exchange before their departure from China and the customs shall permit the taking out of China of the foreign exchange so obtained against the exchange memo issued by the Bank of China.
Article 5:	The carrying out of China of objects made from gold, silver, platinum and other precious metals bought in the country shall be permitted by the customs against certification by the sellers within the limit as prescribed by the state.
Article 6:	The carrying out of China of foreign exchange and payment

instruments in convertible renminbi shall be permitted by the customs against certification by the Bank of China. The carrying out of China of drafts, traveller's cheques and traveller's letters of credit in foreign currency, and renminbi bank-note and passbook custodian certificates issued or sold by the Bank of China shall be permitted by the customs after examination, and no certificatio by the Bank of China is required.

Article 7: Chinese, or foreign nationals, or stateless persons residing in China shall, when emigrating from the country, be permitted by the customs to carry out of China gold, silver, platinum and other precious metals and objects made from them within the limit as prescribed by the state.

Article 8: The carrying or sending out of China in person, or by others, or by post of renminbi cheques, drafts, passbooks and deposit certificates and other renminbi payment instruments held by Chinese, or foreign nationals, or stateless persons residing in the country is not permitted.

Article 9: Unless otherwise approved by the State General Administration of Exchange Control or its branch offices, it is not permitted to carry or send out of China in person, or by others, or by post documents and securities held by Chinese residing in the country, such as foreign bonds, debentures, shares and title deeds; certification and agreements relating to the settlement of creditor's right, inheritances, real estates and other foreign exchange assets abroad; and letters and instruments contained instructions of payment abroad.

Article 10: Where foreign enterprises which have terminated their business in China and foreign nationals who have left China wish to carry out of China foreign securities kept in the country, they shall be permitted to do so by the customs on the approval of the State General Administration of Exchange Control or its branch offices, but it is not permitted to carry out of the country Chinese securities and shares whether in person, or by others, or by post.

Article 11: Where bilateral agreements have been signed between China and foreign countries on the carrying of currencies into and out of each other's boundary, matters will be handled in accordance with the provisions thereof.

Article 12: These rules shall also apply where foreign exchange, payment instruments in convertible renminbi, gold, silver, platinum and other precious metals and objects made from them are carried into or out of China by compatriots from Hongkong and Macau.

Article 13: These rules are promulgated by the State general administration of exchange control.

Provisional Regulations on Violation of Exchange Control of the People's Republic of China

Approved by the State Council on March 25, 1985
Promulgated by the State Administration
of Exchange Control on April 5, 1985

Article 1:   These Provisional Regulations are formulated for the Implementation of Articles 31 and 33 of the Provisional Regulations for Exchange Control of the People's Republic of China.

Article 2:   The following cases shall be regarded as unlawful acquisition of foreign exchange (arbitrage):

    (1)   Payments in renminbi for imports or other items that should have been paid in foreign exchange, unless otherwise approved by the State Administration of Exchange Control or its branch offices (hereinafter referred to as SAEC), or decreed by the Chinese Government.

    (2)   Payments in renminbi by domestic organizations to defray the expenses in China for the following organizations; enterprises or persons in return for reimbursement in foreign exchange which is being retained and not sold to the state:

        (a)   Chinese organizations stationed abroad;

        (b)   foreign organizations stationed in China;

        (c)   overseas Chinese enterprises;

        (d)   foreign enterprises;

        (e)   joint ventures using Chinese and foreign capital;

        (f)   persons coming to China for a short stay.

    (3)   Payments in renminbi by Chinese organizations stationed abroad to defray expenses in China for others in return for reimbursement in foreign exchange;

    (4)   Payments in renminbi by foreign organizations stationed in China, overseas Chinese enterprises, wholly-owned foreign enterprises,

joint ventures using Chinese and foreign capital and the personnel thereof to defray expenses for others in return for reimbursement in foreign exchange or in other forms of a similar nature;

(5) Unless otherwise approved by SAEC, repayments in renminbi by delegations, work groups or members thereof sent abroad or to Hongkong and Macao, who put the foreign exchange allocated for the mission to other use, or spend it on their own shopping or likewise with the foreign exchange they earn from the official mission;

(6) Offsetting export proceeds or other foreign exchange earnings against import costs or other expenditures by domestic organizations.

Article 3: Penalties for unlawful acquisition of foreign exchange shall be imposed according to different circumstances as follows:

(1) For the arbitrageur who is the buyer of the unlawfully acquired foreign exchange, if still kept unused, he must repatriate within the set time limit and sell the foreign exchange to the state under compulsion. If it has been used up, the offender must repay either by selling to the state an equal amount of foreign exchange under compulsion or by deducting the amount from the foreign exchange quota allotted to him. In case the offender has no foreign exchange to repay, he is required to pay the difference between the domestic and international market price of the goods purchased with the unlawfully acquired foreign exchange.

In addition to the penalties listed for the above cases, the offenders may be fined a sum equivalent to 10% - 30% of the amount of the foreign exchange.

(2) For the arbitrageur, who is the seller of the unlawfully acquired foreign exchange, he shall be fined a sum equivalent to 10% - 30% of the amount of the foreign exchange according to the seriousness of the offence.

Article 4: The following cases shall be regarded as evasion of exchange control:

(1) Retaining, spending or depositing foreign exchange earnings abroad by domestic organizations without prior authorization by SAEC; Depositing foreign exchange earnings abroad in violation of the Regulations for Exchange Control Concerning Overseas Chinese Enterprises, Foreign Enterprises and Joint Ventures Using Chinese and Foreign Investment;

(2) Retaining or depositing abroad foreign exchange which is unlawfully acquired by domestic organizations, overseas Chinese enterprises, foreign enterprises and joint ventures using Chinese and foreign capital and which is acquired through such means as falsification by understating the export prices or commissions, or by overstating the import prices, expenses and commissions.

(3) Profits that should have been repatriated according to government regulations of the PRC have been retained for business operations or put to other use by the Chinese organizations stationed abroad or by the Chinese partners to joint ventures using Chinese and foreign capital stationed abroad:

(4) Misappropriation of funds by delegations or work groups and the members thereof sent abroad or to Hongkong and Macao, that is,

the foreign exchange allocated for the official mission or foreign exchange earned by the official mission, are, unless otherwise authorized by SAEC, deposited or put to other uses.

Article 5: Penalties for exchange control evasion shall be imposed according to the seriousness of the offences concerned as follows:

(1) The foreign exchange acquired through evasion, if still kept unused, must be repatriated by the offender or the organization he works with within the set time limit and sold to the state under compulsion; or the full amount of foreign exchange or part thereof shall be confiscated. In addition, the offender may be fined a sum equivalent to 10%-50% of the amount of foreign exchange acquired through evasion;

(2) If the foreign exchange acquired through evasion has been used up, the offender must repay an equal amount of foreign exchange which is to be sold to the state or confiscated. In addition, he may be fined a sum equivalent to 10%-50% of the amount of foreign exchange acquired through evasion;

(3) If the offender has no foreign exchange to repay, he shall be fined a sum equivalent to over 30% of but less than, the full amount of the foreign exchange acquired through evasion, or the goods purchased with the foreign exchange shall be confiscated, or both.

Article 6: The following cases shall be considered as disrupting financial stability:

(1) Engaging in foreign exchange operations without prior SAEC approval or on a scale beyond the limit set by SAEC;

(2) Issuing securities in foreign currencies in China or abroad, or accepting loans offered by banks or business enterprises in foreign countries or Hongkong and Macao by domestic organizations without prior approval of the State Council or the departments authorized by the State Council;

(3) Using foreign currency without prior SAEC approval as the monetary unit in settling accounts, signing loan contracts, making transfers or obtaining mortgages, or as a medium of exchange in business transactions;

(4) Buying and selling foreign exchange without authorization or in any disguised form, or at rates above those set by SAEC, or in unlawful operations of buying and selling at a profit.

Article 7: The following penalties shall be imposed on the offenders involved in the cases listed in Article 6:

(1) For cases referred to in (1) of Article 6, the offenders shall be ordered to stop that part of their foreign exchange operations that oversteps the authorized limit, or to wind up their foreign exchange business altogether. In addition, their unlawful foreign exchange earnings may be confiscated or a fine equivalent to less than the full amount of foreign exchange transactions may be imposed, or both.

(2) For cases referred to in (2) of Article 6, the offenders shall be ordered not to issue new securities or not to acquire new borrowings, and may also be fined a sum equivalent to less than 20% of the securities issued or loans accepted.

(3) For cases referred to in (3) and (4) of Article 6, the offenders must sell their unlawfully transacted foreign exchange to the state under

compulsion; in addition, their earnings shall be confiscated or a fine equivalent to less than the full amount of foreign exchange transacted may be imposed, or both.

Article 8: For offences not specifically listed in Articles 2, 4 and 6, penalties may be imposed according to the seriousness of offences by referring to most relevant cases listed in the present provisions.

Article 9: Minor offences or offenders who voluntarily confess to their unlawful activities to SAEC, show sincere repentance and demonstrate meritorious conduct by informing against other offenders shall be dealt with leniently or exempt from punishment. Offenders who refuse to confess, who try to cover up their offences or refuse to mend their ways despite repeated admonition shall be punished severely in accordance with Articles 3, 5 and 7 of the present provisions.

Article 10: Those who have committed such serious offences as unlawful acquisition of foreign exchange, evasion of exchange control or disrupting financial stability shall be prosecuted according to law.

Article 11: To prevent offenders from transferring their unlawfully acquired funds when a case is under investigation, SAEC is empowered to instruct the banks to freeze the funds for a period of no more than two months, after which the funds will be unfrozen automatically. If an extension of the period is necessary under special circumstances, SAEC must renotify the bank concerned. In case the offender refuses to pay the fine or the sum to be confiscated, SAEC is empowered to enforce the penalty by deducting the sum from the offender's bank account.

Article 12: At the end of investigating a case, SAEC shall notify the offender in writing of its decision on the penalty. If the offender does not agree with the decision, he may appeal to the immediate higher level of SAEC within fifteen days after the date of receipt of the written decision. If the offender still does not agree with the new decision, he may pursue legal proceedings in the local court.

Article 13: Cases involving violation of exchange control regulations shall be dealt with by SAEC; while cases involving unlawful acquisition of foreign exchange and evasion of exchange control that are of the nature of smuggling such as illegally getting the goods into or out of the country as part of luggage, by post or other means of transport, shall be dealt with by the Customs; and cases involving the use of foreign exchange or payment instruments in foreign currency for speculation and profiteering shall be dealt with by the Administration of Commerce and Industry.

Article 14: Provisions for violation of exchange control in the four special economic zones shall be separately formulated by Guangdong and Fujian provinces with reference to the present provisions.

Article 15: SAEC shall be responsible for interpreting the present provisions.

Article 16: The present provisions shall be in force on the day of promulgation.

Rules for the Implementation of The Examination and Approval of Applications by Individuals for Foreign Exchange

(Promulgated by the State General Administration of Exchange Contol December 31, 1981)

Article 1:   These Rules are formulated in order to implement the provisions of Article 19 of the Provisional Regulations for Exchange Control of the People's Republic of China.

Article 2:   The "individuals" mentioned in these Rules refer to Chinese, foreign nationals and stateless persons residing in China (hereafter referred to as "individuals").

Article 3:   The items for which individuals may apply for foreign exchange shall include: incidental remittances to be sent abroad; travelling and miscellaneous expenses needed when leaving China; the transfer abroad of investments and back deposits of overseas Chinese; and the transfer abroad of funds belonging to persons leaving China and emigrating abroad.

Article 4:   In cases of special circumstances (such as serious illness, death or other disaster) involving an individual's lineal relative abroad, the individual may apply for foreign exchange for incidental use, by presenting a certificate issued by his unit and a pertinent certificate issued by the locality where his relative is, and his application may be granted according to the circumstances.

Article 5:   An individual who has been given permission to leave China by the department of public security, and who has obtained a valid entry visa from the country of destination (in the case of a Chinese individual, an "exit receipt" must be obtained from the department of public security), may be provided with foreign exchange for travelling and miscellaneous expenses needed for the trip via the shortest route from the port of departure from China to his destination.

With respect to an individual who is leaving the country with a one-way exit visa in his passport, in addition to being provided with foreign exchange for travelling and miscellaneous expenses, his other requirements for foreign exchange shall be dealt with according to the following provisions:

1. Any retirement pay, severance pay, subsidies for leave of absence from work or pensions fort the disabled and for survivors that he has received from domestic institutions in accordance with relevant provisions may be permitted to be remitted abroad in tote, provided that he has obtained the certificate of his unit and the approval of the next higher department in charge, and subject to the examination and agreement of the Bank of China.

2. An individual who does not receive any retirement pay, severance pay, subsidies for leave of absence from work or pensions for the disabled and for survivors may be provided with foreign exchange according to the acual circumstances.

Foreign exchange shall not be provided to an individual who has been granted a two-way exit-entry visa and who has applied for permission to remit abroad his retirement pay, severance pay, subsidies for leave of absence form work or pensions for the disabled and for survivors.

Article 6: If an individual who has been granted permission to leave China by the department of public security has received foreign exchange remitted from abroad to use for his travelling and miscellaneous expenses when he leaves China and has made a request to retain the original currency before the bank effects payment to him, he may retain the money in the original currency and remit or take it abroad in person at the time he leaves the country.

Article 7: When Chinese living abroad and Hongkong and Macao compatriots have invested foreign exchange in national or local overseas Chinese investment corporations, they may be permitted to remit abroad the share capital and divdiends that they receive as due if, according to the corporation's articles of association, these are to be paid by the investment corporation in foreign exchange; foreign exchange shall not be provided if payment is to be made in Renminbi.

Article 8: When Chinese living abroad or Hongkong and Macao compatriots apply for permission to remit abroad the money that they have deposited in their own names in an Overseas Chinese Renminbi Savings Account in banks within our country, they may be provided with foreign exchange according to the circumstances.

Article: 9: When an individual and his entire family have been given permission by the been concluded between China and foreign counties on the movement of currencies into and out of each other's territory, matters will be handled in accordance with the provisions of the agreements.

Article 12: These Rules shall also apply where foreign exchange and Renminbi foreign exchange instruments, gold, silver, platinum or other precious metals and objects made from them are taken out of and brought into the country by compatriots from Hongkong and Macao.

Article 13: These Rules shall be promulgated and put into effect by the State General Administration of Exchange Control.

388   PRC Laws for China Traders & Investors

Interpretation

Detailed Rules Concerning Exchange Control Related to Individuals

(Enforce on January 1, 1982)

1.   These detailed rules are formulated for the purpose of implementing chapter III in the "Provisional Regulations for Exchange Control of the People's Republic of China".

2.   Foreign exchange remitted from foreign countries or from the Hongkong and Macao regions to Chinese and foreign nationals and stateless persons residing in China must be sold to the Bank of China. The recipients may retain a portion of 10% thereof as convertible foreign crrency when the foreign exchange in a single remittance is equivalent to Rmb3,000 or more.

Preferential treatment for overseas remittance will be applied to the renminbi acquired by selling the foreign exchange referred to in the above paragraph to the Bank of China.

3.   When foreign exchange kept in foreign countries or in Hongkong or Macao regions by Chinese nationals residing in China before te funding of the People's Republic of China, by overseas Chinese prior to their returning to and settling down in China and by Hongkong and Macao compatriots prior to their returning to and settling down in their native places, and foreign exchange acquire by inheriting propenty in foreign counties or in the Hongkong or Macao regions after the founding of the People's Republic of China or their returning and settling down in their native places or elsewhere in China is transferred to China through the Bank of China, the owners are permitted to retain a portion of 30% thereof as convertible foreign currency. Preferential treatment for overseas remittance will be applied to the renminbi acquired by selling the remaining 70% of the foreign exchange to the Bank of China.

The percentage for exchange retention prescribed in the above paragraph applies to forign nationals and stateless persons residing in China when their foreign exchange kept abroad or their foreign exchange acquired by inheriting property outside China is transferred to China through the Bank of China.

4. When foreign exchange is brought or remitted into China by overseas Chinese and Hongkong and Macao compatriots returning to and settling down in their native places or elsewhere in China, the owners are permitted to retain a portion of 30% thereof as convertible foreign currency against applications forwarded to the bank within two months after their entry into the country. Preferential treatment for overseas remittance will be applied to the renminbi acquired by selling the remaining 70% of the foreign exchange to the Bank of China. Applications for exchange retention as prescribed in the above paragraph shall be dealt with against declaration forms at the customs.

5. Personnel sent by the state to work in foreign countries or in Hongkong and Macao regins must, when returning upon the completion of their missions, bring or remit back into China their surplus wages and allowances in foreign exchange which belong to them personally; and must not keep them abroad. However, they are permitted to retain the entire amount thereof as convertible foreign currency, against certification of permanent offices of Chinese organizations stationed abroad.

6. Students, trainees, research students, scholars, teachers, coaches and other personnel sent to study in foreign countries or in the Hongkong and Macao regions must, when returning, promptly bring or remit back into China their surplus foreign exchange they receive abroad and must not keep it abroad. These personnel are permitted to retain the part thereof as convertible foreign currency that belongs to them personally, against certification of permanent offices of Chinese organizations stationed abroad.

7. Foreign exchange acquired by individuals as royalties, copyright fees, prizes, grant-in-aid subsidies and contribution fees for their inventions, creations and writings printed or published abroad, or for their speeches or lectures made abroad in their own names or for their contributions to newspapers, magazines and specialized journals outside China must be promptly transferred to China and must not be kept abroad. These individuals are permitted to retain thereof as convertible foreign currency the part of exchange that belongs to them personally, in accordance with the relevant regulations approved by the State Council and ministries or commissions under the State Council, or with the consent of the State General Administration of Exchange Control.

8. Foreign exchange that individuals are permitted to retain thereof as convertible foreign currency in the categories specified above must be deposited with the Bank of China. These foreign exchange deposits may be remitted or taken out of China, against certification of the Bank of China. Preferential treatment for overseas remittance applies to the renminbi acquired by selling such foreign exchange. It is, however, not permitted, without authorization, to carry or send deposit certificates out of China either in person or by others or by mail.

Disposal of foreign exchange retained by individuals must in no way violate the stipulation specified in the second paragraph of Article 4 of the "Provisional Regulations for Exchange Control of the People's Republic of China".

9. Chinese and foreign nationals and stateless persons residing in China are permitted to keep in their own possession foreign exchange already in China. It is, however impermissible to carry or send out of China such exchange either in person or by others or by post. If the owners wish to sell the exchange, they must sell it to the Bank of China in accordance with the stipulations prescribed in Article 2 of

those detailed rules.

10.   Foreign exchange remitted or brought into China from foreign countries or from the Hongkong and Macao regions by foreign nationals coming to China, by overseas Chinese and Hongkong and Macao compatriots returning for a short stay, by foreign experts, technicians, staff members and workers engaged to work in domestic organizations, and by foreign students and trainees may be kept in their own possession, or sold to or deposited with the Bank of China, or remitted or taken out of China against the original declaration forms to the customs upon their entry.

11.   When foreign experts, technicians, staff members and workers engaged to work in domestic organizations require foreign exchange to be remitted or taken out of China, the Bank of China will deal with their applications in accordance with the stipulations in the contracts or agreements.

12.   These detailed rules are approved by the State Council and promulgated by the State General Administration of Exchange Control for implementation.

III JOINT VENTURE

SECTION A: Overall policy

The Law of the People's Republic of China on Joint Ventures using Chinese and foreign Investment

(Adopted by the Second session of the Fifth National People's Congress on July, 1979)

Article 1:   With view to expanding international economic cooperation and technological exchange, the People's Republic of China permits foreign companies, enterprises, other economic entities or individuals (hereinafter referred to as foreign participants) to incorporate themselves, within the territory of the People's Republic of China, into joint ventures with Chinese companies, enterprises or other economic entities (hereinafter referred to as Chinese participants) on the principle of equality and mutual benefit and subject to authorization by the Chinese government.

Article 2:   The Chinese government protects, by the legislation in force, the resources inveted by a foreign participant in a joint venture and the profits due him pursuant to the agreements, contracts and articles of asssociation authorized by the Chinese government as well as his other lawful rights and interests.
All the activities of a joint venture shall be governed by the laws, decrees and pertinent rules and regulations of the People's Republic of China.

Article 3:   A joint venture shall apply to the Foreign Investment Commission of the People's Republic of China for authorization of the agreements and contracts concluded between the parties to the venture and the articles of association of the venture formulated by them, and the commission shall authorize or reject these documents within three months. When authorized, the joint venture shall register with the General Administration for Industry and Commerce of the People's Republic of China and start operations under license.

Article 4:   A joint venture shall take the form of a limited liability company.

In the registered capital of a joint venture, the proportion of the investment contributed by the foreign participant(s) shall in general not be less than 25 per cent.

The profits, risks and losses of a joint venture shall be shared by the parties to the venture in proportion to their contributions to the registered capital.

The transfer of one party's share in the registered capital shall be effected only with the consent of the other parties to the venture.

Article 5:   Each party to a joint venture may contribute cash, capital goods, industrial property rights, etc. as its investment in the venture.

The technology or equipment contributed by any foreign participant as investment shall be truly advanced and appropriate to China's needs. In cases of losses caused by deception through the intentional provision of outdated equipment or technology, compensation shall be paid for the losses.

The investment contributed by a Chinese participant may include the right to the use of a site provided for the joint venture during the period of its operation. In case such a contribution does not constitute a part of the investment from the Chinese participant, the joint venture shall pay the Chinese government for its use.

The various contributions referred to in the present article shall be specified in the contracts concerning the joint venture or in its articles of association, and the value of each contribution (excluding that of the site) shall be acertained by the parties to the venture through joint assessment.

Article 6:   A joint venture shall have a board of directors with a composition stipulated in the contracts and the articles of association after consultation between the parties to the venture, and each director shall be appointed or removed by his own side. The board of directors shall have a chairman appointed by the Chinese participant and one or two vice-chairmen appointed by the foreign participant(s). In handling an important problem, the board of directors shall reach decision through consultation by the participants on the principle of equality and mutual benefit.

The board of directors is empowered to discuss and take action on, pursuant to the provisions of the articles of association of the joint venture, all fundamental issues concerning the venture, namely, expansion projects, production and business programs, the budget, distribution of profits, plans concerning manpower and pay scales, the terminaton of business, the appointment or hiring of the president, the vice-president(s), the chief engineer, the treasurer and the auditors as well as their functions and powers and their remuneration, etc.

The president and vice-president(s) (or the general manager and assistant general manager(s) in a factory) shall be chosen from the various parties to the joint venture.

Procedures covering the employment and discharge of the workers and staff members of a joint venture shall be stipulated according to law in the agreement or contract concluded between the parties to the venture.

Article 7: The net profit of a joint venture shall be distributed between the parties to the venture in proportion to their respective shares in the registered capital after the payment of a joint venture income tax on its gross profit pursuant to the tax laws of the People's Republic of China and after the deductions therefrom as stipulated in the articles of association of the venture for the reserve funds, the bonus and welfare funds for the workers and staff members and the expansion funds of the venture.

A joint venture equipped with up-to-date technology by world standards may apply for a reduction of or exemption from incom tax for the first two to three profit making years.

A foreign participant who re-invests any part of his share of the net profit within Chinese territory may apply for the restitution of a part of the income taxes paid.

Article 8: A joint venture shall open an account with the Bank of China or a bank approved by the Bank of China.

A joint venture shall conduct its foreign exchange transactions in accordance with the forign exchange regulations of the People's Republic of China.

A joint venture may, in its business operations, obtain funds from foreign banks directly.

The insurances appropriate to a joint venture shall be furnished by Chinese insurance companies.

Article 9: The production and business programs of a joint venture shall be filed with the authorities concerned and shall be implemented through business contracts.

In its purchase of required raw and semi-processed materials, fuels, auxiliary equipment, etc., a joint venture should give first priority to Chinese sources, but may also acquire them directly from the world market with its own foreign exchange funds.

A joint venture is encouraged to market its products outside China. It may distribute its export products on foreign markets through direct channels or its associated agencies or China's foreign trade establishments. Its products may also be distributed on the Chinese market.

Where ever necessary, a joint venture may set up affiliated agencies outside China.

Article 10: The net profit which a foreign participant receives as his share after executing his obligations under the pertinent laws and agreements and contracts, the funds he receives at the time when the joint venture terminates or winds up its operations, and his other funds may be remitted abroad, through the Bank of China in accordance with the foreign exchange regulations and in the currency or currencies specified in the contracts concerning the joint venture.

A foreign participant shall receive encouragements for depositing in the Bank of China any part of the foreign exchange which he is entitled to remit abroad.

Article 11: The wages, salaries or other legitimate income earned by a foreign worker or staff member of a joint venture, after payment of the personal income tax under the tax laws of the People's Republic of China, may be remitted abroad through the Bank of China in accordance with the foreign exchange regulations.

Article 12:   The contract period of joint venture may be agreed upon between the parties to the venture according to its particular line of business and circumstances. The period may be extended upoon expiration through agreement between the parties, subject to authorization by the Foreign Investment Commission of the People's Republic of China. Any application for such extension shall be made six months before the expiration of the contract.

Article 13:   In case of heavy losses, the failure of any party to a joint venture to execute its obligations under the contracts or the articles of association of the venture, force majeure, etc. prior to the expiration of the contract period of a joint venture, the contract may be terminated · before the date of expiration by consultation and agreement between the parties and through authorization by the Foreign Investment Commission of the People's Republic of China and registration with General Administaration for Industry and Commerce. In cases of losses caused by breach of the contract(s) by a party to the venture, the financial responsibility shall be borne by the said party.

Article 14:   Disputes arising between the parties to a joint venture which the board of directors fails to settle through consultation may be setteld through conciliation or arbitration by an arbitral body of China or through arbitaration by an arbitral body agreed upon by the parties.

Article 15:   The present law comes into force on the date of its promulgation. The power of amendment is vested in the National People's Congress.

Regulations for the Implementation of the Law of the People's Republic of China on Joint Ventures Using Chinese and Foreign Investment

(Promulgated by the State Council on September 20, 1983)

Chapter I General Provisions

Article 1: The Regulations hereunder are formulated with a view to facilitating the implementation of the Law of the People's Republic of China on Joint Ventures Using Chinese and Foreign Investment (hereinafter referred to as "the Law").

Article 2: Joint ventures using Chinese and foreign investment (hereinafter referred to as "J.V.") established within China's territory in accordance with the Law are Chinese legal persons and are subject to the jurisdiction and protection of Chinese law.

Article 3: J.V. established within China's territory shall be able to promote the development of China's economy and the raising of scientific and technological levels for the benefit of socialist modernization. J.V. permitted are mainly in the following industries:

(1) Energy development, the building material, chemical and metallurgical industries;

(2) Machine manufacturing, instrument and meter industries and offshore oil exploitation equipment manufacturing;

(3) Electronics and computer industries, and communication equipment manufacturing;

(4) Light, textile, foodstuffs, medicine, medical apparatus and packing industries;

(5) Agriculture, animal husbandry and fish breeding;

(6) Tourism and service trades.

Article 4: Applicants to establish J.V. shall lay stress on economic results and shall comply with one or several of the following requirements:

(1)   They shall adopt advanced technical equipment and scientific management which enable the increase of the variety of products, the raising of quality and output, and the saving of energy and materials;

(2)   They shall provide benefits in terms of technical renovation of enterprises and result in less investment, quicker returns and bigger profits;

(3)   They shall enable the expanded production of products for export and result in increasing income in foreign currency;

(4)   They shall enable the training of technical and managerial personnel.

Article 5:   Applicants to establish J.V. shall not be granted approval if the project involves any of the following conditions:

(1)   Detriment to China's sovereignty;

(2)   Violation of Chinese law;

(3)   Nonconformity with the requirements of the development of China's national economy;

(4)   Environmental pollution;

(5)   Obvious inequity in the agreements, contracts and articles of association signed, impairing the rights and interests of one party.

Article 6:   Unless otherwise stipulated, the government department in charge of the Chinese participant in a J.V. shall be the department in charge of the J.V. (hereinafter referred to as "the J.V. in charge"). In case of a J.V. having two or more Chinese participants which are under different departments or districts, the departments concerned shall consult the district to ascertain one department in charge.

The in charge is responsible for guidance and assistance and exercising supervision over the J.V.

Article 7:   A J.V. has the right to do business independently within the scope of the provisions of Chinese laws, decrees, and the agreement, contract and articles of association of the J.V. The departments concerned shall provide support and assistance.

Chapter II Establishment and Registration

Article 8:   The establishment of a J.V. in China is subject to examination and approval by the Ministry of Foreign Economic Relations and Trade of the People's Republic of China (hereinafter referred to as the FERT). Certificates of approval aregranted by the FERT.

The FERT shall entrust the people's governments in the related provinces, autonomous regions, and municipalities directly under the central government or relevant ministries or bureaus under the State Council (hereinafter referred to as the entrusted office) with the power to examine and approve the establishment of J.V. that comply with the following conditions:

(1)   The total amount of investment is within the limit set by the State Council and the source of capital of the Chinese participants has been ascertained;

(2)   No additional allocations of raw materials by the state are required and do not affect the national balance of fuel, power,

transportation and foreign trade export quotas.

The entrusted office, after approving the establishment of a J.V., shall report this to the FERT for the record. A certificate of approval shall be issued by the FERT. (The FERT and the entrusted office will hereinafter be referred to as a whole as the examination and approval authority).

Article 9: The following procedures shall be followed for the establishment of a J.V.:

(1) The Chinese participant in a J.V. submit to its in charge a project proposal and a preliminary feasibility study report of the J.V. to be established with foreign participants. The proposal and the preliminary feasibility study report, upon examination and consent by the in charge, shall be submitted to the examination and approval authority for final approval. The parties to the J.V. shall then conduct work relevant to the feasibility study, and based on this, negotiate and sign J.V. agreements, contracts and articles of association.

(2) When applying for the establishment of a J.V., the Chinese participant is responsible for the submission of the following documents to the examination and approval authority:

(a) Application for the establishment of a J.V.;

(b) The feasibility study report jointly prepared by the parties to the J.V.;

(c) J.V. agreement, contract and articles of association signed by representatives authorized by the parties to the J.V.;

(d) List of candidates for chairman, vice-chairman and directors appointed by the parties to the J.V.;

(e) Written opinions of the in charge and the people's government of the province, autonomous region or municipality directly under the central government where the J.V. is located with regard to the establishment of the J.V.

The aforesaid documents shall be written in Chinese. Documents (b), (c) and (d) may be written simultaneously in a foreign language agreed upon by the parties to the J.V. Both versions are equally authentic.

Article 10: Upon receipt of the documents stipulated in Article 9 (2), the examination and approval and approval authority shall, within three months, decide whether to approve or disapprove them . Should anything inappropriate be found in any of the aforementioned documents, the examination and approval authority shall demand an amendment to it within a limited time. Without such amendment no approval shall be granted.

Article 11: The applicant shall, within one month after receipt of the certificate of approval, register with the administrative bureau for industry and commerce of the province, autonomous region or municipality directly under the central government in accordance with the provisions of the Procedures of the People's Republic of China for the Registration and Administration of Chinese-Foreign Joint Ventures (hereinafter referred to as "RA office"). The date on which it is issued its business license is regarded as the date of formal establishment of a J.V.

Article 12: Any foreign investor who intends to establish a J.V. in China but is unable to find a specific co-operator in China may submit a preliminary plan for his J.V. projects and authorize the China International Trust and Investment Corporation (CITIC) or trust and investment corporations of a province, autonomous region or municipality directly under the central government, or relevant government department or non-official organization, to introduce potential Chinese co-operators.

Article 13: The "J.V. agreement" mentioned in this chapter refers to a document agreed upon by the parties to the J.V. on some main points and principles governing the establishment of a J.V.

"J.V. contract" refers to a document agreed upon and concluded by the parties to the J.V. on their rights and obligations.

"Article of association" refers to a document agreed upon by the parties to the J.V. indicating the purpose, organizational principles and method of management of a J.V. in compliance with the principles of the J.V. contract.

If the J.V. agreement conflicts with the contract, the contract shall prevail.

If the parties to the J.V. agree to sign only a contract and articles of association, the agreement can be omitted.

Article 14: The J.V. contract shall include the following main items:

(1) The names, the countries of registration, the legal address of parties to the J.V., and the names, professions and nationalities of the legal representatives thereof;

(2) Name of the J.V., its legal address, purpose and the scope and scale of business;

(3) Total amount of investment and registered capital of the J.V., investment contributed by the parties to the J.V., each party's investment proportion, forms of investments, the time limit for contributing investment, stipulations concerning incomplete contributions, and assignment of investment;

(4) The ratio of profit distribution and losses to be borne by each party;

(5) The composition of the board of directors, the distribution of the number of directors, and the responsibilities, powers and means of employment of the general manager, deputy general manager and high-ranking management personnel;

(6) The main production equipment and technology to be adopted and their source of supply;

(7) The ways and means of purchasing raw materials and selling finished products, and the ratio of products sold within Chinese territory and outside China;

(8) Arrangements for income and expenditure of foreign currency;

(9) Principles governing the handling of finance, accounting and auditing;

(10) Stipulations concerning labor management, wages, welfare, and labor insurance;

(11) The duration of the joint venture, its dissolution and the procedure for liquidation;

(12)   The liabilities for breach of contract;

(13)   Ways and Procedures for settling disputes between the parties to the joint venture;

(14)   The language used for the contract and the conditions for putting the contract into force.

The annex to the contract of a J.V. shall be equally authentic with the contract itself.

Article 15:   The formation of a J.V. contract, its validity, interpretation, execution and the settlement of disputes under it shall be governed by the Chinese law.

Article 16:   Articles of association shall include the following main items;

(1)   The name of the J.V. and its legal address;

(2)   The purpose, business scope and duration of the J.V.

(3)   The names, countries fo registration and legal addresses of parties to the J.V., and the names, professions and nationalities of the legal representatives thereof;

(4)   The total amount of investment, registered capital of the J.V., each party's investment proportion, stipulations concerning the assignment of investment, the ratio of profit distribution and losses to be borne by parties to the J.V.;

(5)   The composition of the board of directors, its responsibilities, powers and rules of procedure, the term of office of the directors, and the responsibilities of its chairman and vice-chairman;

(6)   The setting up of management organizations, rules for handling routine affairs, the responsibilities of the general manager, deputy general manager and other high-ranking management personnel, and the method of their appointment and dismissal;

(7)   Principles governing finance, accounting and auditing;

(8)   Dissolution and liquidation;

(9)   Procedures for amendment of the articles of association.

Article 17:   The agreement, contract and articles of association shall come into force after being approved by the examination and approval authority. The same applies in the event of amendments.

Article 18:   The examination and approval authority and the registration and administration office are responsible for supervising and inspecting the execution of the joint venture contracts and articles of association.

Chapter III   Form of Organization and Registered Capital

Article 19:   A J.V. is a limited liability company.

Each party to the J.V. is liable to the J.V. within the limited of the capital subscribed by it.

Article 20:   The total amount of investment (including loans) of a J.V. refers to the sum of capital construction funds and the circulating funds needed for the J.V.'s production scale as stipulated in the contract and the articles of association of the J.V.

Article 21:   The registered capital shall generally be presented in total amount of investment registered at the registration and administration office for the establishment of the J.V. It should be the total amount of investment subscribed by parties to the J.V.

The registered capital shall generally be presented in Renminbi, or may be in a foreign currency agreed upon by the parties to the J.V.

Article 22:   A J.V. shall not reduce its registered capital during the term of the J.V.

Article 23:   If one party to the J.V. intends to assign all or part of his investment subscribed to a third party, consent shall be obtained from the other party to the J.V., and approval from the examination and approval authority is required.

When one party assigns all or part of his investment to a third party, the other party has pre-emptive right.

When one party assigns his investment subscribed to a third party, the conditions given shall not be more favourable than those given to the other party to the J.V.

No assignment shall be made effective should there be any violation of the above stipulations.

Article 24:   Any increase, assignment or other disposal of the registered capital of a J.V. shall be approved by a meeting of the board of directors and submitted to the orighinal examination and approval authority for approval. Registration procedures for changes shall be dealt with at the original registration and administration office.

Chapter IV   Ways of contributing Investment

Article 25:   Each participant to a joint venture may contribute cash or buildings, premises, equipment or other materials, industrial property, know-how, right to the use of a site as investment, the value of which shall be ascertained. If the investment is in the form of buildings, premises, equipment or other materials, industrial property or know-how, the prices shall be ascertained through consultation by the parties to the joint venture on the basis of fairness and reasonableness, or evaluated by the third party agreed upon by parties to the J.V.

Article 26:   The foreign currency contributed by the foreign participant shall be converted into Renminbi according to the exchange rate announced by the State General Administration of Foreign Exchange Control of the People's Republic of China (hereinafter referred to as the Foreign Exchange Control) on the day of its submission or be cross exchanged into a predetermined foreign currency.

Should the cash Renminbi contributed by the Chinese participant be converted into foreign currency, it shall be converted according to the exchange rate announced by the Foreign Exchange Control on the day of the submission of the funds.

Article 27:   The machinery equipment and other materials contributed as investment by the foreign participant shall meet the following conditions:

(1)   They are indispensable to the production of the joint venture;

(2)   China is unable to manufacture them, or manufactures them only at too high a price, or their technical performance and time of availability cannot meet the demand;

(3)   The price fixed shall not be higher than the current international market price for similar equipment or materials.

Article 28:   The industrial property or know-how contributed by the foreign participant as investment shall meet one of the following conditions:

    (1)   Capable of manufacturing new products urgently needed in China or products suitable for export;

    (2)   Capable of improving markedly the performance quality of existing products and raising productivity;

    (3)   Capable of notable savings in raw materials, fuel or power.

Article 29: Foreign participants who contribute industrial property of know-how as investment shall present relevant documentation on the industrial property or know-how, including photocopies of the patent certificates or trademark registration certificates, statements of validity, their technical characteristics, practical value, the basis for calculating the price and the price agreement signed with the Chinese participants. All these shall serve as an annex to the contract.

Article 30: The machinery, equipment or other materials, industrial property or know-how contributed by foreign participants as investment shall be examined and approved by the department in charge of Chinese participant and then submitted to the examination and approval authority for approval.

Article 31: The parties to the J.V. shall pay in all the investment subscribed according to the time limit stipulated in the contract. Delay in payment or partial delay in payment will be subject to a payment of interest on arrears or a compensation for the loss as defined in the contract.

Article 32: After the investment is paid by the parties to the J.V., a Chinese registered accountant shall verify it and provide a certificate of verification, in accordance with which the J.V. shall issue an investment certificate, which includes the following items: name of the J.V., date, month and year of the establishment of the J.V.; names of the participants and the investment contributed; date, month and year of the contriubtion of the investment; and date, month and year of issuance of the investment certificate.

Chapter V   Board of Directors and Management Office

Article 33: The highest authority of the J.V. shall be its board of directors. It shall decide all major issues concerning the J.V.

Aritcle 34: The board of directors shall consist of no less than three members. The distribution of the number of directors shall be ascertained through consultation by the parties to the J.V. with reference to the proportion of investment contributed.

The directors shall be appointed by the parties to the J.V. The chairman of the board shall be appointed by the Chinese participant and its vice-chairman by the foreign participant.

The term of office for the directors is four years. Their term of office may be renewed with the consent of the parties to the J.V.

Article 35: The board of directors shall convene at least one meeting every year. The meeting shall be called and presided over by the chairman of the board. Should the chairman be unable to call the meeting, he shall authorize the vice-chairman or other director to call and preside over the meeting. The chairman may convene an interim meeting based on a proposal made by more than one-third of the directors.

A board meeting requires a quorum of over two-thirds of the directors. Should the director be unable to attend, he shall present a proxy authorizing someone else to represent him and vote for him. A board meeting shall generally be held at the location of the joint venture's legal address.

Article 36: Decisions on the following items shall be made only after being unanimously agreed upon by the directors present at the board meeting:

    (1)   Amendment of the articles of association of the J.V.;

    (2)   Termination and dissolution of the joint venture;

    (3)   Increase or assignment of the registered capital of the J.V.;

    (4)   Merger of the J.V. with other economic organizations.

Decision on other items shall be made according to the rules of procedure stipulated in the articles of association.

Article 37: The chairman of the board is the legal representative of the J.V. Should the chairman be unable to exercise his responsibilities, he shall authorize the vice-chairman of the board or other director to represent the J.V.

Article 38: A J.V. shall establish a management office which shall be responsible for daily management.

The management office shall have a general manager and several deputy general managers who shall assist the general manager in his work.

Article 39: The general manager shall carry out the decisions of the board meeting and organize and conduct the daily management of the J.V. The general manager shall, within the scope empowered him by the board, represent the J.V. in outside dealings, have the right to appoint and dismiss his subordinates, and exercise other responsibilities and rights as authorized by the board within the J.V.

Article 40: The general manager and deputy general managers shall be engaged by the board of directors of the J.V. These positions may be held either by Chinese citizens or foreign citizens.

At the invitation of the board of directors, the chairman, vice-chairman or other directors of the board may concurrently be the general manager, deputy general managers or other high-ranking management personnel of the J.V.

In handling major issues, the general manager shall consult with the deputy general managers.

The general manager or deputy general managers shall not hold posts concurrently as general manager or deputy general managers of other economic organizations. They shall not have any connections with other economic organizations in commercial competition with their own J.V.

Ariticle 41: In case of graft or serious dereliction of duty on the part of the general manager, deputy general managers or other high-ranking management personnel, the board of directors shall have the power to dismiss them at any time.

Article 42: Establishment of branch offices (including sales offices) outside of China or in Xianggang or Aomen is subject to approval by the FERT.

Chapter VI   Acquisition of Technology

Article 43: The acquisition of technology mentioned in this chapter refers to the necessary technology obtained by the joint venture by means of technology transfer from a third party or participants.

Article 44: The techonology acquired by the J.V. shall be appropriate and advanced and enable the venture's products to display conspicuous social 'economic results domestically or to be competitive on the international market.

Article 45: The right of the J.V. to do business independently shall be maintained when making technology transfer agreements, and relevant documentation shall be provided by the technology exporting party in accordance with the provisions of Article 29 of the regulations.

Article 46: The technology transfer agreements signed by a joint venture shall be examined and agreed to by the department in charge of the J.V. and then submitted for approval to the examination and approval authority.

Technology tranfer agreements shall comply with the following stipulations:

(1) Expenses for the use of technology shall be fair and reasonable. Payments are generally made in royalties, and the royalty rate shall not be higher than the standard international rate, which shall be calculated on the basis of net sales of the products turned out with the relevant technology or other reasonable means agreed upon by both parties.

(2) Unless otherwise agreed upon by both parties, the technology exporting party shall not put any restrictions on the quantity, price or region of sale of the products that are to be exported by the technology importing party.

(3) The term for a technology transfer agreement is generally no longer than ten years.

(4) After the expiration of a technology transfer agreement, the technology importing party shall have the right to use the technolgy continuously.

(5) Conditions for mutual exchange of information on the improvement of technology by both parties of the technolgy transfer agreement shall be reciprocal.

(6) The technolgy importing party shall have the right to buy the equipment, parts and raw materials needed from sources they deem sutiable.

(7) No irrational restrictive clauses prohibited by Chinese law and regulations shall be included.

Chapter VII   Right to the Use of Site and its Fee

Article 47: J.V. shall practice economy in the use of land for their premises. Any J.V. requiring the use of a site shall file an application with local departments of the municipal (county) government in charge of land and obtain the right to use a site only after securing approval and signing a contract. The acreage, location, purpose and contract period and fee for the right to use a site (hereinafter referred to as site use fee), rights and obligations of the parties to J.V. and fines for breach of contract should be stipulated in explicit terms in the contract.

Article 48: If the Chinese participant already has the right to the use of site for the J.V. The Chinese participant may use it as part of its investment. The monetary equivalent of this investment should be the same as the site use fee otherwise paid for acquiring such site.

Article 49: The standard for site use fee shall be set by the people's governments of the province, autonomous region or municipality directly under the central government where the J.V. is located according to the purpose of use, geographic and environmental conditions, expenses for requisition, demolishing and resettlment and the J.V.'s requirements with regard to infrastructure, and filed with the FERT and the state department in change of land.

Article 50: Joint ventures engaged in agriculture and animal husbandry may, with consent of the people's government of the local province, autonomous region or municipality directly under the central government, pay a percentage of the J.V.'s operating revenue as site use fees to the local department in charge of land

Projects of a development nature in economically undeveloped areas shall receive special preferential treatment in respect of site use fees with consent of the local people's government.

Article 51: The rates shall not be subject to adjustment in the first five years beginning from the day the land is used. After that the interval of adjustment shall not be less than three years according to the development and changes in geographic and environmental conditions.

Site use fee as part of the investment by the Chinese participant shall not be subject to adjustment during the contract period.

Article 52: The fee for the right to the use of site obtained by a J.V. according to Article 47 of the regulations shall be paid annually from the day to use the land stipulated in the contract. For the first calendar year, the J.V. will pay a half-year fee if it has used the land for over six months; if less than six months, the site use fee shall be exempt. During the contract period, if the rates of site use fees are adjusted, the J.V. shall pay it according to the new rates from the year of adjustment.

Article 53: J.V. that have permission to use a site shall only have the right to the use of it but no ownership. Assignment of the right to use land is forbidden.

Chapter VIII   Planning, Purchasing and Selling

Article 54: A J.V. shall work out a capital consturction plan (including construction ability, building materials, water, power and gas suply) according to the approved feasibility study report, and the plan shall be included in the capital construction plan of the department in charge of the J.V. and shall be given priority in arranging supplies and be ensured to be carried out.

Article 55: Funds earmarked for capital consturction of a joint venture shall be put under unified management of the bank where the J.V. has opened an account.

Article 56: A J.V. shall work out a production and operating plan in accordance with the scope of operation and scale of production stipulated in the contract. The plan shall be carried out with the approval of the board of directors and filed with the department in charge of the J.V. Departments in charge of the J.V. and planning and administration departments at all levels shall not issue directive on production and operating plans to J.V.

Article 57: In its purchase of required machinery, equipment, raw materials, fuel, parts, means of transport and things for office use, etc. (hereinafter referred to as "materials"), a J.V. has the right to decide whether it buys them in China or from abroad. However, where conditions are the same it should give first priority to purchase in China.

Article 58: J.V. can purchase materials in China through the following channels:

   (1)   Those under planned distribution shall be brought into the supply plan of departments in charge of J.V. and supplied by materials and commercial departments or production enterprises according to contract;

   (2)   Those handled by materials and commercial departments shall be purchased from these departments;

   (3)   Those freely circulating on the market shall be purchased from production enterprises or their sale or commission agencies;

   (4)   Those export items handled by foreign trade corporations shall be purchased from the appropriate foreign trade corporations.

Article 59: The amount of materials needed for office and daily life use for J.V. purchased in China is not subject to restriction.

Article 60: The Chinese Government encourages J.V. to sell their products on the international market.

Article 61: Products of J.V. that China urgently needs or imports can be mainly sold on the Chinese market.

Article 62: A J.V. has the right to export its products itself or entrust sale agencies of the foreign participant or Chinese foreign trade corporations with sales on a commission or distribution.

Article 63: Within the scope of operation stipulated in the contract, a J.V. can import machinery, equipment, parts, raw materials and fuel needed for its production. A J.V. shall make a plan every year for items on which import licenses are required by the stipulation of the state, and apply for them every six months. for machines, equipment and other objects a foreign participant has contributed as part of his investment, the foreign participant can apply directly for import licenses with documents approved by examination and approval authority. For materials to be imported exceeding the stipulated scope of the contracts, separate application for import licenses according to state regulations is required.

A J.V. has the right to export its products by itself, for those export licenses are required by the stipulation of the State, the J.V. shall make an export plan every business year and apply for them every six months.

Article 64: A J.V. may sell its products on the Chinese market in the following ways:

(1)   For those items under planned distribution, J.V. in charge of J.V. will bring them into the distribution plan of the materials administration depatments, which sell them to designated users according to plan.

(2)   For those items handled by materials and commercial departments, the materials and commerical departments will sign purchase contracts with the J.V.

(3)   For excess portions other than those purchased by plan of the above two categories, and materials that do not belong to these two categories, the J.V. has the right to sell by itself or entrust sales to the organizations concerned.

(4)   For products of a J.V. that Chinese foreign trade companies need to import, the J.V. may sell to Chinese foreign trade companies, and foreign currency shall be paid.

Article 65:   Materials purchased and services needed in the China by J.V. shall be priced according to the following stipulations:

(1)   The six raw materials — gold, silver, platinum, petroleum, coal and timber — that are used directly in production for export shall be priced according to the international market prices provided by the Foreign Exchange Control or foreign trade departments, and paid in foreign currency or Renminbi.

(2)   When purchasing export or import commodities handled by Chinese foreign trade companies, the suppliers and buyers shall negotiate the price, with reference to the prices on the international market, and foreign currency shall be paid.

(3)   The prices for purchasing coal used as fuel and oil for motor vehicles, which are needed for manufacturing products to be sold domestically, as well as materials other than those listed in (1) and (2) of this article, and the fees charged for water, electricity, gas, heat, goods transportation, service, engineering, consultation service and advertisement etc, provided to J.V., shall be treated equally with state — owned enterprises and paid in Renminbi.

Article 66:   Prices of products of a J.V. for sale on the Chinese domestic market, except those items approved by the price control department for valuation with reference to the international market, shall correspond with state-set prices, be rated according to quality and paid for in Renminbi. Prices fixed by a J.V. for its products shall be filed with departments in charge of J.V. and of prices control.

Prices of export products of a J.V. will be fixed by the J.V. itself and shall be filed with J.V. in charge of J.V. and of price control.

Article 67:   A J.V. and other Chinese economic organizations shall, in their economic exchanges, undertake economic responsibilities and settle disputes over contracts in accordance with relevant law and the contract concluded between both parties.

Article 68:   A J.V. shall fill statistical forms on production, supply and marketing in accordance with relevant regulations, and file them with departments in charge, statistics departments and other departments concerned.

Chapter IX   Taxes

Article 69:   J.V. shall pay taxes according to the stipulations of relevant laws of the People's Republic of China.

Article 70:   Staff membersand workers employed by J.V. shall pay individual income tax according to the Individual Income Tax Law of the People's Republic of China.

Article 71:   J.V. shall be exempt from customs duty and industrial and commercial consolidated tax for the following imported materials:

(1)   Machinery, equipment, parts and other materials (materials here and hereinafter mean required materials for the J.V.'s construction on the factory site and for installation and reinforecement of machines), which are part of the foreign participant's share of investment according to the provisions of contract.

(2)   Machinery, equipment, parts and other materials imported with funds which are part of the J.V.'s total investment.

(3)   Machinery, equipment, parts and other materials imported by the J.V. with the additional capital under the approval of examination and approval authority on which China cannot guarantee production and supply.

(4)   Raw materials, auxiliary materials, components, parts and packing materials imported by the joint venture for production of export goods.

Taxes shall be pursued and payable according to regulations when the above-mentioned duty-free materials are approved for sale inside China or switched to the prodction of items to be sold on the Chinese domestic market.

Article 72:   Except for those export items restricted by the state, products of a J.V. for export will be exempt from industrial and commercial consolidated tax, subject to the approval by the Mininstry of Finance of the People's Repbulic of China.

A J.V. can apply for reduction or exemption of industrial and commercial consolidated tax for a certain period of time for products that are sold on the domestic market when it has difficulty to pay such tax in its intitial period of production.

Chapter X   Foreign Exchange Control

Article 73:   All matters concerning foreign exchange for J.V. shall be handled according to the Interim Regulations on Foreign Exchange Control of the People's Republic of China and relevant regulations.

Article 74:   With the business license issued by the General Administration for Industry and Commerce of the People's Republic of China, a J.V. can open foreign exchange deposit accounts and Renminbi deposit accounts with teh Bank of China, or some other banks designated. The bank handlng the account of the J.V. exercises supervision of receipts and expenditures.

All foreign exchange income of a J.V. must be deposited in the foreign exchange deposit account in the bank where an account has been opened; all payments by the joint venture in foreign exchange are to be made from its foreign exchange deposit account. The deposit interest rate shall be set as announced by the Bank of China.

Article 75:   A J.V. shall in general keep balance between its foreign exchange income and expenses. When a J.V. whose porducts are mainly sold on domestic market under its approved feasibility study report and contract has an unbalance of foreign exchange income and expenses, the unbalance shall be solved by the people's government of a relevant province, an autonomous region or a municipality directly under the central government or the department in charge under the State Council from their own foreign exchange reserves, if unable to be solved, it shall be solved through inclusion into plan after the examination and approval by the FERT together with the State Planning Commission of the People's Republic of China.

Article 76:   A J.V. shall get permission from the General Administration of Foreign Exchange Control or one of its branches to open a foreign exchange deposit account with an overseas bank or one in Xianggang or Aomen, and report to the Foreign Exchange Control or one of its branches its foreign exchange receipts and expenditures, and provide account sheets.

Article 77:   Sub-divisions set up by a J.V. in foreign countries or in Xianggang or Aomen shall open an account with the Bank of China wherever there is a branch. The sub-division shall submit its annual statement of assets and liabilities and annual profit report to the Foreign Exchange Control or one of its branches through the J.V.

Article 78:   A J.V. can apply to the Bank of China for foreign loans and Renminbi loans according to business needs and following the Provisional Regulations for Providing Loans to Joint Ventures Using Chinese and Foreign Investment by the Bank of China. Interest rates on loans to J.V. are as announced by the Bank of China. A J.V. can also borrow foreign exchange as capital from banks abroad or in Xianggang or Aomen, but shall file a report with the Foreign Exchange Control or one of its branches.

Article 79:   After foreign staff and workers and staff and workers from Xianggang and Aomen have paid income tax on their salaries and other legitimate incomes according to the law, they can apply to th Bank of China for permission to remit outside China all the remaining foreign exchange after deduction of their living expenses in China.

Chapter XI   Financial Affairs and Accounting

Article 80:   Procedures for handling financial affairs and accounting of J.V. shall be formulated in accordance with China's relevant laws and procedures on financial affairs and accounting, and in consideration of the conditions of the joint venture, and then being filed with local financial departments and tax authorities.

Article 81:   A J.V. shall employ a treasurer to assist the general manager in handling the financial affairs of the enterprise. If necessary a deputy treasurer can be appointed.

Article 82:   A J.V. shall (small J.V. may not) appoint an auditor to be responsible for checking financial receipts, payments and account, and to submit reports to the board of directors and the general manager.

Article 83: The fiscal year of a J.V. shall coincide with the calendar year, i.e. from January 1 to December 31.

Article 84: The accounting of a J.V. shall adopt the internationally used accrual basis and debit and credit accounting system in their work. All vouchers, account books, statistic statements and reports prepared by the enterprise shall be written in Chinese. A foreign language can used concurrently with mutual consent.

Article 85: Prinicpally J.V. shall adopt Renminbi as the standard currency. In keeping accounts, however, another currency can be used through consultation by the parties concerned.

Article 86: In addition to the use of standard currency to record accounts, J.V. shall record accounts in currencies actually used in payments and receipts, if such currencies in cash, bank deposits, funds of other currencies, creditor's right, debts, gains, expenses, etc. are inconsistent with the standard currency in recording accounts.

J.V. using a foreign currency in accounting shall work out a statement of accounts in Renminbi equivalents in addition to those in the foreign currency.

The actual amounts of losses and gains caused by differences in exchange rates in the course of remittances shall be recorded in the year's losses and gains accounts. No adjustments shall be made for recorded changes in exchange rates and remaining sum on the book of related foreign exchange accounts.

Article 87: Principles of profit distribution after payment of taxes in accordance with the Income Tax Law of the People's Republic of China concerning Joint Ventures with Chinese and Foreign Investment are as follows:

(1) Allocations for reserve funds, bonuses and welfare funds for staff and workers and expansion funds of the J.V. Proportion of allocations is decided by the board of directors.

(2) Reserve funds can be used to make up the losses of the J.V., and with the consent of examination and approval authority, to increase the J.V. capital for production expansion.

(3) After the funds described in (1) of this article have been deducted and if the board of directors decides to distribute the remaining profit, it should be distributed according to the proportion of each participant's investment.

Article 88: Profits cannot be distributed unless the losses of previous year's have been made up. Remaining profits from previous year (or years) can be distributed together with that of the current year.

Article 89: A joint venture shall submit quarterly and annual fiscal reports to parties to the joint venture, the local tax authority, department in charge of the J.V. and financial department at the same level to those departments.

A copy of the annual fiscal reports shall be submitted to the original examination and approval authority.

Article 90: Only after being examined and certified by an accountant registered in China can the following documents, certificates and reports be considered valid.

    (1)   Certificates of investment from all parties to a J.V. together with lists of assessed value, investments involving materials, site use rights, industrial property and know-how;

    (2)   Annual fiscal reports of the joint venture;

    (3)   Fiscal reports on liquidation of the joint venture.

Chapter XII   Staff and Workers

Article 91:   The employment, recruitment, dismissal and resignation of staff and workers, of J.V. and their salary, welfare benefits, labour insurance, labour protection, labour discipline and other matters shall be handled according to the Regulations of the People's Republic of China on Labour Management in Joint Ventures Using Chinese and Foreign Investment.

Article 92:   J.V. shall make efforts to conduct professional and technical training of their staff and workers and establish a strict examination system so that they can meet the requirements of production and managerial skills in a modernized enterprise.

Article 93:   The salary and bonus systems of J.V. shall be in accordance with the principle of distribution to each according to his work, and more pay for more works.

Article 94:   Salaries and remuneration of the general manager, deputy general manager(s), chief engineer, deputy chief engineer(s), treasurer and deputy treasurer(s), auditor and other high-ranking officials shall be decided upon by the board of directors.

Chapter XIII   Trade Union

Article 95:   Staff and workers of a J.V. have the right to set up grass-roots trade unions and carry on trade union activities in accordance with the Trade Union Law of the People's Republic of China (hereinafter referred to as "TUL") and the Articles of Association of Chinese Trade Union.

Article 96:   Trade unions in J.V. are representatives of the interests of the staff and workers. They have the power to represent the staff and workers to sign labour contracts with J.V. and supervise the execution of these contracts.

Article 97:   The basic tasks of the trade unions in J.V. are: to protect the democratic rights and material interests of the staff and workers pursuant to the law; to help the J.V. with the arrangement and rational use of welfare and bonus funds; to organize political, professional, scientific and technical studies, carry out literary, art and sports activities; and to educate staff and workers to observe labour discipline and strive to fulfil the economic tasks of the enterprises.

Article 98:   Trade union representatives have the right to attend as nonvoting members and to report the opinions and demands of staff and workers to meetings of the boards of directors held to discuss important issues such as development plans, production and operational activities of J.V.

Trade union representatives have the right to attend as nonvoting members of meetings of the board of directors held to discuss and decide on awards and penalties to staff and workers, salary systems, welfare benefits, labour protection an labour insurance, etc. The board of directors shall heed the opinions of the trade unions and win its co-opertaion.

Article 99: A J.V. shall actively support the work of the trade union, and, in accordance with stipulations of the TUL, provide housing and facilities for the trade union's office work, meetings, and welfare, cultural and sports activities. The J.V. shall allot an amount of money totalling 2 percent of all the salaries of the J.V.'s staff and workers as trade union's funds, which the trade union of the J.V. shall use according to the relevant managerial rules for trade union funds formulated by the All China Federation of Trade Unions.

Chapter XIV Duration, Dissolution and Liquidation

Article 100: The duration of a J.V. shall be decided upon through consultation of all parties to the joint venture according to actual conditions of the particular lines of business and projects. The duration of a J.V. engaged in an ordinary projects requiring large amount of investment, long construction periods and low interest rates on funds can be extended to more than 30 years.

Article 101: The duration of a J.V. shall be stipulated by all parties to the J.V. in the agreement, contract and articles of association. The duration begins from the day when the J.V. is issued a business license.

When all parties to a J.V. agree to extend the duration, the J.V. shall file an application for extending the duration signed by representatives authorized by the parties with the examination and approval authority six months before the date of expiration of the duration. The examination and approval authority shall give an official written reply to the applicant within one month beginning from the day it receives the application.

Upon approval of the extension of the duration, the J.V. concerned shall go through registration formalities for the alteration in accordance with the Procedures of the People's Republic of China for the Registration and Administration of Chinese-Foreign Joint Ventures.

Article 102: J.V. may be dissolved in the following situations:
(1) Termination of duration;
(2) Inability to continue operations due to heavy losses;
(3) Inability to continue operations due to the failure of one of the contracting parties to fulfil the obligations prescribed by the agreement, contract and articles of association;
(4) Inability to continue operations due to heavy losses caused by force majeure such as natural calamities and wars, etc.;
(5) Inability to obtain the desired objectives of the operation and at the same time to see a future for development;
(6) Occurence of other reasons for dissolution prescribed by the

contract and articles of association.

In cases described in (2), (3), (4), (5) and (6) of this article, the board of directors shall make an application for dissolution to the examination and approval authority.

In the situation described in (3) of this article, the party failed to fulfill th obligations prescribed by the agreement, contract and articles of association shall be liable to the losses thus caused.

Article 103: Upon announcement of the dissolution of a joint venture, its board of directors shall work out procedures and principles for the liquidation and nominate candidates for the liquidation committee. It shall report to the department in charge of the J.V. for examination, verification and supervision of th liquidation.

Article 104: Members of a liquidation committee are usually selected among directors of a J.V. In case the directors cannot serve or are unsuitable to be members of the liquidation committee, the J.V. may invite accountants and lawyers registered in China to do the job. When the examination and approval authority deems necessary, it may send personnel to supervise the process.

The liquidation expenses and remuneration to members of the liquidation committee shall be paid in priority from the existing assets of the joint venture.

Article 105: The tasks of the liquidation committee are: to conduct thorough check of the property of the J.V. concerned, its creditors' rights and liabilities; to work out the statement of assets and liabilities and 105 list of property; to put forward a basis on which property is to be evaluated and calculated; and to formulate a liquidation plan. All these shall be carried out upon approval of the board of directors. During the process of liquidation, the liquidation committee shall represent the joint venture concerned to sue and be sued.

Article 106: J.V. shall be liable to its debts with all of its assets. The remaining property after the clearance of debts shall be distributed among parties to the J.V. according to the proportion of each party's investment unless otherwise provided by agreement, contract and articles of association of the J.V.

At the time when a joint venture is being dissolved the value added to its net assets or remaining property that exceeds the registered capital is regarded as profit on which income taxes shall be levied according to law. The foreign participant shall pay income taxes according to law for the portion of the net assets or remaining property that exceeds his investment when he remits it abroad.

Article 107: On completion of the liquidation of a dissolved J.V., the liquidation committee shall submit a liquidation report approved by a meeting of the board of directors to the original examination and approval authority, go through formalities for nullifying its registration and· hand in its business license to the original registration authority.

Article 108: After dissolution of a J.V., its account bookds and documents shall be left in the care of the Chinese participant.

Chapter XV   Settlement of Disputes

Article 109: Disputes arising over the interpretation of execution of the agreement, contract or articles of association between the parties to the J.V. shall, if possible, the settled through friendly consultation or mediation. Disputes that cannot be settled through these means may be settled through arbitration or courts of justice.

Article 110: Parties to a J.V. shall apply for arbitration in accordance with the relevant written agreement. They may submit the dispute to the Foreign Economic and Trade Arbitration Commission of the China Council for the Promotion of International Trade in accordance with its arbitration rules. With mutual consent of the parties concerned, arbitration can also be carried out through an arbitration agency in the country where the sued party is located or through one in a third country in accordance with the arbitration agency's procedures.

Article 111: If there is no written arbitration agreement between the parties to a J.V., each side can file a suit with the Chinese People's Court.

Article 112: In the process of solving disputes, except for matters in dispute, parties to a J.V. shall continue to carry out other provisions stipulated by the agreement, contract and articles of association of the J.V.

Chapter XVI   Supplementary Articles

Article 113: The Chinese office in charge of visas shall give convenient service by simplifying procedures for staff and workers from foreign countries or from Xianggang and Aomen (including their family members) who frequently cross Chinese borders.

Article 114: Departments in charge of J.V. are responsible for handling applications and procedures for Chinese staff and workers going abroad for study tours, business negotiations or training.

Article 115: Staff and workers from foreign countries or from Xianggang and Aomen working for a J.V. can bring in needed means of transport and items for office use, paying regular customs duty and industrial and commercial consolidated tax on them.

Article 116: J.V. set up in the special economic zones shall abide by the provisions, if any, provided otherwise in the laws and regulations adopted by the National People's Congress, its Standing Committee or the State Council.

Article 117: The power to explain the Regulations is vested in the FERT.

Article 118: The regulations shall come into force on the day of promulgation.

Interpretation

Detailed Regulations for the Implementation of the Laws of the People's Republic of China on Joint Ventures Using Chinese and Foreign Investment

1.   Total amount of investment:
The total amount of investment of a J.V. refers to the sum (total) of the capital construction funds needed for the production scale specified in the contract and the articles of association of J.V. and the circulating funds for production. If the funds contributed by the parties to the J.V. fall short of the total amount of investment. The J.V. may, in its own name, obtain loans from the banks as its investment. Therefore, the total amount of investment of a J.V. may generally consist of two categories, funds provided by the parties to the J.V. themselves and loans obtained in the name of the J.V.
2.   Registered capital
The registered capital of a J.V. refers to the total amount of investment registered at the offices of the General Administration for Industry and Commerce for the establishment of the joint venture, and it should be the sum of investment subscribed by the parties to the J.V. The parties to the J.V. may, in accordance with the provisions of the J.V. contract, put in their subscribed investments to the J.V. in a lump sum or by installments.
3.   Investment subscribed
This refers to the amount of capital the parties to a J.V. the venture. The contribution to the J.V. by the parties is to be judged by the amount of investment subscribed and the responsibility of each party for the J.V. is limited to their respective share of investment subscribed.
4.   The Right to the use of site
The right to the use of site of a J.V. is the right to the use of a site obtained by the J.V. in accordance with the needs of its operation. The right may be obtained by the J.V. by concluding a leasing contract with te land department concerned of the local

government or it may be contributed by the Chinese participant as its investment by evaluating the right. Whichever way did the J.V. obtain the right to the use fo site, it should only have the right to use, but not the ownership. And transfer of the right to the use of site is prohibited.

5.   Investment certificates

Investment certificates are the certificates issued by J.V. to testify the share of investment subscribed by the parties to the J.V. They are issued to the J.V. after the parties to the J.V. have put in their repective subscribed investment and after the Chinese-registered accountant has verified the amount and issued the verification report. Without the consent of the other parties and the approval of the examination and approval authoirty of the J.V. party to the J.V. is prohibited to dispose of the certificate by transfer, mortgage or other ways.

6.   Reserve fund

The reserve fund of a J.V. is a special fund withheld from its profits to make up for the losses the J.V. may be subjected to and to guard against accidents. The proportion of the fund is to be decided by the board of directors, but it is not to exceed a certain amount. In general the reserve fund is not to be used for other purposes, but, with the approval of the J.V.'s examination and approval authority, may be used by the J.V. for increasing its capital or expanding production.

7.   Bonus and welfare fund for staff and workers

The bonus and welfare fund for the staff and workers of a J.V. is a special fund withheld from the profits of the J.V. to improve the welfare of the staff and workers and encourage individuals or groups who have made comparatively great contributions to the production and work. It can be used only for commending those who have made comparatively great contributions and providing collective welfare facilities for the staff and workers, medical and health service and financial aids.

8.   Enterprise expansion fund

The expansion fund of a J.V. is a special fund withheld from the J.V.'s profits to expand its production. It can be used for purchasing fixed assets, increasing circulating funds and expanding operation. It can also be used for the trial manufacture of new products, undertaking scientific research and running technical training for the staff and workers.

9.   Industrial property right.

It is the proprietary right acquired in accordance with the law for patented inventions, new designs and trade marks which will be protected according to the law, although such protection is strictly regional. Exclusive in character, the industrial property shall not be encroached upon by others. Use of such a right by others must have the consent of the owner of the right together with payment of loyalty. The Law on Joint Ventures Using Chinese and Foreign Investment stipulates that a J.V. may make its investment in industrial property, to which provision rules have been added in the Regulations for the Implementation of the Law on Joint Ventures Using Chinese and Foreign Investments.

10.   Knowhow

Knowhow, also known as technical secret, is technical knowledge which can be transferred or imparted and which is not known to the public and unpatented: Unlike the patent right whose effective period is limited, knowhow is monopolized by means of secrecy.

11.   Accrual basis

This is an accounting method of ascertaining the income and costs of a J.V. in a *fiscal period (a month, a season or a year). In other words, the income and costs of a current period should be dealt with as such, no matter if the sum is received or paid in that particular period. Conversely, the income and costs not of the current period shall not be dealt with as such, even if the sum is received or paid in that particular period. For instance, the rent of may should still be entered into the account book as the costs of that month, even if it was paid in April or June. The adoption of accrual basis makes it possible to accurately calculate a J.V.'s income, costs and profit or loss in various fiscal periods.*

12.   Debit-credit bookkeeping method

In accounting, the words "debit" and "credit" are used to record the increase and decrease of a J.V.'s application of funds (assets or costs) and its sources of funds (liabilities, capital or income). "Debit" signifies the increase in the application of funds or the decrease in the source of funds and "credit" denotes the decrease in the application of funds or the increase in the source of funds. In accordance with the principle that a J.V.'s application of funds must equal its sources of funds, each item of the economic activity that should be entered into the account book in accordance with the principle that "with debiting, there must be crediting and debiting and crediting must balance". In other words, the equivalent sums should be entered on both the debit side of one or several accounts and the credit side of one of several accounts. The sum total entered on the debit side of all accounts should equal that entered on the credit side of all accounts, and the total balance of the debit side of all accounts at the end of a period should equal that of the credit side of all accounts at the end of the same period. The account with debit balance is the account of the application of funds and the account with credit balance is the account of the source of funds.

13.   Statement of assets and liabilities

This is also known as "balance sheet". In Chinese-foreign J.V. it is an accounting report presenting in a summerized form the J.V. financial situation on a certain date (for instance, at the end of a month, season or year). There are usually two sides in the form, the left side listing the item of assets (including property, materials, receivables and rights, etc.) and the right side listing the item of liabilities (including short-term and long-term debts of different types) and the item of the investor's equity (including capital and retained earnings). The sum total of the items on the left side should equal that on the right side.

14.   Standard currency in bookkeeping

The standard currency, or standard money, is the legal tender of a country. For example, the Renminbi is the standard currency of China, the U.S. Dollar of the United States, the Pound Sterling of Britain, and the French Franc of France. The standard currency used in accounting is called standard currency in bookkeeping.

Interpretation

Introduction of the Law by a State Council Spokesman

I. The Object of Formultating the Regulations

The Article 18 of the Constitution of the People's Republic of China has stipulated explicitly that the People's Republic of China permits foreign enterprises, other foreign economic organizations or foreign individuals to invest in China or to undertake various forms of economic cooperation with Chinese enterprises or other Chinese economic organizations. This article also provides that the lawful rights and interests of the foreign enterprises and other economic organizations, as well as J.V. using Chinese and foreign investment located in China are protected by the laws of the People's Republic of China.

The Second Session of the Fifth Chinese National People's Congress held in July, 1979 adopted and promulgated the Law of the People's Republic of China on Joint Ventures Using Chinese and Foreign Investment, and thereafter has promulgated a series of seperate laws and regulations concerning joint ventures in accordance with that law, such as the Regulations of the People's Republic of China on the Registration and Administration of Joint Ventures Using Chinese and Foreign Investment Regulations of the People's Republic of China on Labour Management in Joint Ventures Using Chinese and Foreign Investment and the Income Tax Law of the People's Republic of China Concerning Joint Ventures Using Chinese and Foreign Investment, etc.

The Regulations promulgated are formulated in accordance with the open-door policy of China, the relevant provisions of the Constitution, the Law of the People's Republic of China on Joint Ventures Using Chinese and Foreign Investment and the practical experiences gained during these years. The Law of the People's Republic of China on Joint Ventures Using Chinese and Foreign Investment promulgated in 1979 is comparatively principled and simple. The present Regulations have further concretized those principles on the basis of that law, and clarified the issues that have not been involved in the joint venture law but put forward for solution by the practice of running J.V. Therefore, the formulation of the Regulations has made the laws of our country concerning Chinese and foreign joint ventures more concret and perfect.

The Chinese government intends that the formal promulgation and implementation of the Regulations shall not only enable the existing Chinese-Foreign joint ventures to be run more successfully and have a greater development on basis thereof, but also attract more foreign investors to cooperate with various departments concerned of our country to establish new J.V.

II   The Main Contents of the Regulations

The main contents provided by the Regulations are as follows:

1.   *The legal status of J.V. in China.* The Regulations stipulate explicitly that joint ventures are the Chinese legal persons, which are under the jurisdiction and protected by the Chinese law.

2.   *The industries in which J.V. are encouraged, the requirements to J.V. and the prohibited items.* The industries in which J.V. are encouraged by China are:

Energy development, the building material, chemical and metallurgical industries;

Machine manufacturing, instrument and meter industries and offshore oil exploitation equipment manufacturing;

Electronics and computer industries, an communication equipment manufacturing;

Light, textiles, foodstuffs, medicine, medical apparatus and packing industries;

Agriculture, animal husbandry and aquaculture.

Tourism and service trades.

From all these we can see that the field of J.V. are very broad.

The requirements set by the Regulations are mainly that the J.V. shall facilitate the construction of the four modernizations of our country and the acquisition of the advanced technologies which suit the needs of our country. The prohibited items are mainly that the J.V. shall not be detriment to China's sovereignty, in violation of Chinese law, unconformity with the requirements of the development of China's national economy, and impairment to the rights and interests of one of the parties to the J.V. All these are the minimum requirements of a soverign state, but not excessive demands, let alone any discriminations to J.V.

3.   *The procedure for establishment and approval of J.V., the agreement, contract, articles of association of J.V. and the main contents thereof, their organizational form and method of making investment as well as their operation rights.*

4.   *The board of directors and management organizations of J.V.* The Regulations stipulate explicitly that the board of directors composed of on basis of agreement by both parties to the J.V. is the highest authority of the venture and shall decide all the major issues thereof.

5.   *The relations between J.V. plan and the state plan, the marketing channel and price of J.V. products.* The Regulations stipulate that a J.V. shall work out its plan according to the scope of operation and production scale fixed in the contract, and carry it out upon approval by its board of directors. The Chinese department in charge and its planning and administrative departments at varios levels shall not assign the instructive plan to the J.V.

6.   *The foreign exchange matter and the financial and accounting system of J.V.*

The foreign exchange income and expenses of a J.V. is an issue that is concerned by foreign investors. All the matters concerning foreign exchanges of a J.V. shall be handled in accordance with the special laws and regulations on foreign exchange control of our country. And our country encourages J.V. to sell their products outside China, so as to solve their problems of foreign exchange expenditure. If their products are approved to be sold outside China but still have an unbalance in foreign exchange, the amount lacked will be solved by the department in charge of the enterprise. On the whole, the legitimate rights and interests of foreign investors are guaranteed.

7.   The departments in charge of J.V. and the regulations between these departments and J.V. The Regulations stipulate that departments in charge of J.V. are responsible for guidance, assistance and exercising supervision to J.V. That is to say the relation between these departments and joint ventures is not the leadership relation as that to the state-owned enterprises. This has reflected that the operation and management autonomy of J.V. are respected.

8.   The matters concerning labour management and trade union of J.V.

9.   Matters concerning consultation, conciliation and arbitration of the disputes arising between parties to J.V. The Regulations stipulate that the disputes between parties to a J.V. may be submitted for arbitration in China, or in the country where the party is being sued, or through the arbitration agency of the third country, if failed in friendly consultation or conciliation.

All these matters mentioned above are in common concern both at home and abroad, and needed to be clarified and resolved in practical work. It can be anticipated that J.V. are surely developed in a further step as all these issues have the laws to follow and been clarified.

III   The preferential Treatment to J.V.

The Regulations have permeated, from the beginning to the end, the principle of equality and mutual benefit. And at the same time stipulate some preferential treatments to J.V., such as:

1.   Certain goods imported by J.V. are exempt from customs duty and industrial and commercial consolidated tax. According to the stipulations of our country, the machinery, equipment and other goods as investment made by foreign participant or imported with the funds which are part of the total investment, and the raw materials which China cannot guarantee production and supply or those for production of export goods imported with the increased capital, are exempt from customs duty and industrial and commercial consolidated tax.

2.   J.V. may be granted a reduction or exemption, upon approval of their application, from industrial and commercial consolidated tax for exported products produced by them, except for those are prohibited to be exported by our country.

3.   The products produced by J.V., if are urgently needed in China or to be imported by China, may be sold mainly in Chinese domestic market.

All these are the preferential treatments favourable to foreign investors.

Provisions on the Purchase and Export of Domestic Products by Foreign Investment Enterprises to Balance Foreign Exchange Accounts

(Issued by the Ministry of Foreign Economic Relations and Trade on January 20, 1987)

Article 1 :   These provisions are hereby formulated in accordance with the relevant regulations of the State Council for the purpose of facilitating enterprises with foreign investment to balance their foreign exchange accounts. Subject to approval of their application, these enterprises are allowed to purchase and export products from other local sources (hereinafter referred to as non-resultant products) to make up for the shortfall in their foreign exchange accounts.

Article 2 :   In principle, these enterprises should balance their foreign exchange accounts by exporting the resultant products of their respective enterprises. But for those enterprises that have run into temporary difficulties in this regard may apply, within a certain period of time, for the purchase and export of non-resultant domestic products (except those subject to unified State control) so as to balance their foreign exchange accounts.

Article 3 :   An enterprise with foreign investment which complies with Article 2 of the provisions and which needs to purchase and export non-resultant domestic products to balance its foreign exchange accounts should first apply to the local provincial department of foreign economic relations and trade, stating the amount of foreign exchange and the corresponding amount of renminbi needed in the current year to purchase domestic products for export, and their names, specifications and quantities and their export channels.

Article 4 :   The approved quantity of non-resultant domestic products to be purchased by a foreign investment enterprise should be limited within the amount of foreign exchange needed to cover the shortfall in its production and operation, the foreign investor's profit repatriation or in its termination and liquidation.

Article 5: Foreign investment enterprises which are approved to purchase and export non-resultant domestic products to balance their foreign exchange accounts should mainly purchase products manufactured in the province, autonomous region or municipality where they are located. If they need to purchase them from other provinces, they should first have the approval of the provincial-level department of the foreign economic relations and trade of the relevant province, autonomous region and municipality.

Article 6: The domestic products purchased by an enterprise with foreign investment for export in order to balance its foreign exchange account must be shipped out of China and sold abroad, and must not be re-sold within China.

Article 7: Enterprises with foreign investment which are approved to purchase non-resultant domestic products to balance their foreign exchange accounts may export the products by themselves or by China's foreign trade corporations as their agents.

Article 8: Apart from approving enterprises with foreign investment to purchase domestic products for export, the people's governments of all provinces, autonomous regions, municipalities and cities with independent plans may, with the prerequisite of fulfilling State export targets, organize export of their local products through specialized foreign trade companies. Of the foreign exchange thus earned and locally retained in accordance with the relevant State regulations, part of the retained portion will go to the suppliers of the products according to the stipulated ratios and the remainder may be used by local people's governments to balance the foreign exchange accounts among the enterprises with foreign investment under the supervision of the local foreign exchange control departments.

Article 9: With regard to the products to be purchased and exported by enterprises with foreign investment as mentioned in Article 3 of the provisions, and those to be exported by people's governments of provinces, autonomous regions, municipalities and cities with independent plans as mentioned in Article 8, the purchase and export of those commodities which require State export licenses or are subject to export quotas should be approved by the Ministry of Foreign Economic Relations and Trade. That of other commodities should be approved by provincial-level departments of foreign economic relations and trade and then be submitted to the Ministry of Foreign Economic Relations and the Trade for the record.

The above-mentioned approval authorities (departments) should give replies to the respective applications within one month beginning from the date of their receipt. Among the approved export products, the export licenses required for those that should be exported with licenses should be issued in accordance with the procedures of the Ministry of Foreign Economic Relations and Trade on applying for export and import licenses by foreign investment enterprises.

Article 10: These provisions shall go into effect on the date of issue.

The Accounting Regulations of the People's Republic of China for the Joint Ventures Using Chinese and Foreign Investment

Promulgated on March 4, 1985 by the Ministry of Finance
of the People's Republic of China

Chapter I: General Provisions

Article 1:   The present regulations are formulated to strengthen the accounting work of the joint ventures using Chinese and foreign investment, in accordance with the provisions laid down in ''The Law of the People's Republic of China on Joint Ventures Using Chinese and Foreign Investment''. The Income Tax Law of the People's Republic of China Concerning Joint Ventures with Chinese and Foreign Investment'' and other relevant laws and regulations.

Article 2:   These regulations are applicable to all joint ventures using Chinese and foreign investment (hereinafter referred to as joint ventures) established within the territory of the People's Republic of China.

Article 3:   The public finance departments or business of provinces, autonomous regions and municipalities directly under the Central Government as well as the business regulatory departments of the State Council shall be permitted to make necessary supplements to these regulations on the basis of complying with these regulations and in the light of specific circumstances, and submit the supplements to the Ministry of Finance for the record.

Article 4:   The joint ventures shall work out their own enterprise accounting system in accordance with these regulations and the supplementary provisions made by the relevant public financial department or bureau of their provinces, autonomous regions or municipalities, or by the relevant business regulatory departments of the State Council, and in the light of their specific circumstances and submit their own system to their enterprise regulatory departments, local public finance department and tax authority for the record.

Chapter II: Accounting Office and Accounting Staff

Article 5:   A joint venture shall set up a separate accounting office with necessary accounting staff to handle its financial and accounting work.

Article 6:   A joint venture of large or medium size shall have a controller to assist the president and to take the responsibility in leading its financial and accounting work. A deputy controller may also be appointed when necessary.

A joint venture of relatively large size shall have an auditor responsible for review and examination of its financial receipts and disbursements, accounting documents, accounting books, accounting statements and other relevant data and those of its subordinate branches.

Article 7:   The accounting office and accounting staff of a joint venture shall fulfil their duties and responsibilities with due care, make accurate calculation, reflect faithfully the actual conditions, and supervise strictly over all economic transactions, protect the legitimate rights and interests of all the participants of the joint venture.

Article 8:   Accounting staff who are transferred or leaving their posts shall clear their responsibility and transfer procedures with those who are assuming their positions, and shall not interrupt the accounting work.

Chapter III: General Principles for Accounting

Article 9:   The accounting work of the joint ventures must comply with the laws and regulations of the People's Republic of China.

Article 10:   The fiscal year of a joint venture shall run from January 1 to December 31 under the Gregorian calendar.

Article 11:   The joint ventures shall adopt the debit and credit double entry bookkeeping.

Article 12:   The accounting documents, accounting books, accounting statements and the other accounting records of a joint venture shall be prepared accurately and promptly according to the transactions actually taken place, with all required routines done and contents completed.

Article 13:   All the accounting documents, accounting books and accounting statement prepared by a joint venture must be written in Chinese. A foreign language mutually agreed by the participants of the joint venture may be used concurrently.

Article 14:   In principle, a joint venture shall adopt Renminbi as its bookkeeping base currency. However, a foreign currency may be used as the bookkeeping base currency upon mutual agreement of the participants of a joint venture.

If actual receipts or disbursements of cash, bank deposits, other case holdings, claims, debts, income and expenses, etc., are made in currencies other than the bookkeeping base currency, record shall also be made in the currencies of actual receipts or disbursements.

Article 15:   The joint ventures shall adopt the accrual basis in their accounting. All revenues realized and expenses incurred during the current period shall be recognized in the current period, regardless of whether the receipts or disbursements are made. The revenues or expenses not attributable to the current period shall not be recongnized as current revenue or expenses, even if they are currently received or disbursed.

Article 16: The revenues and expenses of a joint venture must be matched in its accounting. All the revenues and relevant costs and expenses of a period shall be recognized in the period and shall not be dislocated, advanced or deferred.

Article 17: All the assets of a joint venture shall be stated at their original costs and the recorded amounts are generally not adjusted whether there is any fluctuation in their market prices.

Article 18: A joint venture shall draw clear distinction between capital expenditures and revenue expenditures. All expenditures incurred for the increase of fixed assets and intangible assets are capital expenditures. All expenditures incurred to obtain current revenue are revenue expenditures.

Article 19: Accounting methods adopted by a joint venture shall be consistent from one period to the other and shall not be arbitrarily changed. Changes, if any, shall be approved by the board of directors and submitted to the local tax authority for examination. Disclosure of the changes shall be made in the accounting report.

Chapter IV: Accounting for Paid-in Capital

Article 20: The participants of a joint venture shall contribute their share capital in the amount, ratio and mode of capital contribution within the stipulated time limit as provided in the joint venture contract. The accounting for paid-in capital by a joint venture shall be based on the actual amount contributed by each of its participants.

(1) For investment paid in cash, the amount and data as received or as deposited into the Bank of China or other banks where the joint venture has opened its bank account shall be the basis for recording the capital contribution.

The foreign currency contributed by a foreign participant shall be converted into Renminbi or further converted into a predetermined foreign currency at the exchange rates quoted on the day of the cash payment by the State Administration of Foreign Exchange Control of the People's Republic of China (hereinafter referred to as the State Administration of Foreign Exchange Control). Should the cash Renminbi contributed by a Chinese participant be converted into foreign currency, it shall be converted at the exchange rate quoted by the State Administration of Foreign Exchange Control on the day of the cash payment.

(2) For investment in the form of buildings, machinery, equipment, materials and supplies, the amount shown on the examined and verified itemization list of the assets as agreed upon by each participant and the data of the receipt of the assets shall be the basis of accounting according to the joint ventures contract.

(3) For investment in the form of intangible assets, i. e., proprietory technology, patents, trademarks, copyright and other franchises, etc.,

the amount and data as provided in the agreement or contract shall be the basis of accounting.

(4) For investment in the form of the right to use sites, the amount and data as provided in the agreement or contract shall be the basis of accounting.

The capital contributed by each participant shall be recorded into the accounts of the joint venture as soon as they are received.

Article 21 : The capital amount contributed by the participants of a joint venture shall be validated by certified public accountants registered with the government of the People's Republic of China, who shall render a certificate on capital validation, which shall then be taken by the joint venture as the basis to issue capital contribution certificates to the participants.

Chapter V : Accounting for Cash and Currency Accounts

Article 22 : A joint venture shall open its deposit accounts in the Bank of China or the other banks within the territory of the People's Republic of China and approved by the State Administration of Foreign Exchange Control or by one of its branches. All foreign exchange receipts must be deposited with the bank in the foreign currency deposit account and all foreign exchange disbursements must be made from the accounts.

Article 23 : A joint venture shall set up journals to itemize cash and bank transactions in chronological order. A separate journal shall be set up for each currency if there are several currencies.

Article 24 : The accounts receivable, accounts payable and other receivables and payables of a joint venture shall be recorded in separate accounts set up for different currencies. Receivables shall be collected and payables shall be paid in due time and shall be confirmed with the relevant parties periodically. The causes of uncollectible items shall be investigated and the responsibilities thereof shall be determined. Any item proved to be definitely uncollectible through strict management review shall be written off as bad debts after approval is obtained through reporting procedures specified by the board of directors. No ''reserve for bad debts'' shall be accrued.

Article 25 : In a joint venture using Renminbi as bookkeeping base currency, its foreign currency deposits, foreign currency loans and other accounts denominated in foreign currency shall be recorded not only in their original foreign currency of the actual receipts and payments, but also in Renminbi converted from foreign currency at an ascertained exchange rate (using the exchange rate quoted by the State Administration of Foreign Exchange Control).

All additions of foreign currency deposits, foreign currency loans and other accounts denominated in foreign currencies shall be recorded in Renminbi converted at their recording exchange rates, while deductions shall be recorded in Renminbi converted at their book exchange rates. Differences in the Renminbi amount resulting from the conversion at different exchanges rates shall be recognized as ''foreign exchange gains or losses'' (hereinafter referred to as ''exchange gains or losses'').

The recording exchange rates for the conversion of foreign currency to Renminbi may be the rate prevailing on the day of recording the transaction or on the first day of the month, etc. The book exchange rate may be calculated by the first-in-first-out method, or by the weighted average method, etc. However, for the decrease of accounts denominated in a foreign currency, the original recording rate may be used as book rate. Whichever rate is adopted, there shall be no arbitrary change once it is decided. If any change is necessary, it must be approved by the board of directors and disclosed in the accounting report.

The difference in Renminbi resulting from the exchange of different currencies shall also be recognized as exchange gains or losses.

The exchange gains or losses recognized in the account shall be the realized amount. In case of exchange rate fluctuation, the Renminbi balances of the foreign currency accounts shall not be adjusted.

Article 26:   If a joint venture using a foreign currency as its bookkeeping base currency, its Renminbi deposits, Renminbi loans and other accounts denominated in Renminbi shall be recorded not only in Renminbi but also in the foreign currency converted from Renminbi at the exchange rate adopted by the enterprise. Difference in the foreign currency amount resulting from the conversion at different exchange rates shall also be recognized as exchange gains or losses as stipulated in Article 25.

A joint venture using a foreign currency as bookkeeping base currency shall compile not only annual accounting statements in the foreign currency but also separate accounting statements in Renminbi translated from foreign currency at the end of a year. However, the joint venture's Renminbi bank deposits, Renminbi bank loans and the other accounts denominated in Renminbi shall still be accounted for in their original Renminbi amounts, and be combined with the other items converted into Renminbi from foreign currency. The differences between the original Renminbi amount of the Renminbi items and their Renminbi amount from currency translation shall not be recognized as foreign exchange gains or losses, but shall be shown on the balance sheet with an additional caption as ''currency translation difference''.

Chapter VI: Accounting for Inventories

Article 27:   The inventories of a joint venture refer to merchandise, materials and supplies, containers, low-value and perishable articles, work in process, semi-finished goods, finished goods, etc., in stock, in processing or in transit.

Article 28:   All the inventories of a joint venture shall be recorded at the actual cost.

(1)   The actual cost of materials and supplies, containers, low-value and perishable articles purchased from outside shall include the purchase price, transportation expenses, loading and unloading charges, packaging expenses, insurance premium, reasonable loss during transit, selecting and sorting expenses before taken into storage, etc. The cost of imported goods shall further include the customs duties and industrial and commercial consolidated tax, etc.

For merchandise purchased by a commercial or service-trade enterprise, the original purchase price shall be taken as the actual cost for bookkeeping.

(2)   The actual cost of self manufactured materials and supplies, containers, low-value and perishable articles, semi-finished goods and finished goods shall include the materials and supplies consum-

ed, wages and relevant expenses incurred during the manufacture process.

(3) The actual cost of materials and supplies, containers, low-value and perishable articles, semi-finished and finished goods completed through outside processing shall include the original cost of the materials and supplies or semi-finished goods consumed, the processing expenses, inward and outward transportation expenses and sundry charges.

The merchandise of the commercial or service-trade enterprises processed under contract with outside units shall be recorded at the purchase price after processing, including the original purchase price of the merchandise before processing, processing expenses and the industrial and commercial consolidated tax attributable.

Article 29: The receipt, issuance, requisition and return of the inventories of a joint venture shall be timely processed through accounting procedures according to the actual quantity and shall be itemized in the subsidiary ledger accounts with established columns for quantities and amounts, so as to strengthen the inventory control. The merchandise, materials, etc., in transit, shall be accounted for through subsidiary ledgers and their condition of arrival shall be inspected at all times. For those goods not arrived in due time, the relevant department shall be urged to take action. As to those goods that have arrived but not yet been checked or taken into storage, their acciptance test and warehousing procedures shall be carried out in a timely manner.

Article 30: The actual cost or original purchase price of inventories issued or requisitioned from the store of a joint venture may be accounted for by it under one of the following methods; first-in-first-out, shifting average, weighed average, batch actual, etc. Once the accounting method is adopted, no arbitrary change shall be allowed. In case a change of accounting method is necessary, it shall be submitted to the local tax authority for approval and disclosed in the accounting report.

Article 31: In the joint ventures using planned cost in daily accounting for materials and supplies, finished goods, etc., the planned cost of those issued from stock, shall be adjusted into actual cost at the end of each month.

For the commercial and service-trade enterprises using selling price in daily accounting for merchandise, the cost of goods sold shall be adjusted from selling price to original purchase price at the end of a month.

Article 32: A joint venture shall take physical inventory of its stock periodically, at least once a year. If any overage, shortage, damage, deterioration, etc., is found, the relevant department shall investigate the cause and write out a report. Accounting treatment shall be made as soon as the report is approved through strict management review and the reporting procedures specified by the board of directors. The treatment shall generally be completed before the annual closing of final accounts.

(1) The inventory shortage (minus inventory overage) and damage (minus salvage) of materials and supplies, work in process, semi-finished goods, finished goods, and merchandise, etc., shall be charged to the current expenses, except the amount, if any, that should be indemnified by the persons in fault.

(2) The net loss resulting from natural disasters shall be charged to non-operating expenses after deducting the salvage value recoverable

and insurance indemnity.

Article 33: If there is any inventory in a joint venture to be disposed of at a reduced price due to obsolescence, it shall be reported for approval according to the procedures specified by the board of directors, and the net loss on disposal shall be recognized as loss on sales. If the disposal is not yet done at the end of a year, disclosure shall be made in the annual accounting report for the actual cost per book, the net realizable value and the probable loss thereof.

Article 34: Disclosure shall be made in the annual accounting report of a joint venture on the actual cost per book, net realizable value and probable loss of its inventories of which the net realizable value is lower than the actual cost per book due to the decline of the market price.

Chapter VII: Accounting for Long Term Investment and Long Term Liabilities

Article 35: The investment of a joint venture in order units shall be accounted for at the amount paid or agreed upon at the time of the investment, and shall be shown in the balance sheet with a separate caption as "long term investment."

Income and loss derived from long term investment shall be recognized as non-operating income or non-operating expense.

Article 36: The bank loans borrowed by a joint venture for capital construction during its preparation period or for increasing fixed assets, expanding its business, or making renovation and reform of its equipment after its operation started, shall be accounted for at the amount and on the data of the loan and shall be presented in the balance sheet with a separate caption as "long term bank loans."

The interest expenses on the long term bank loans incurred during the construction period shall be charged to construction cost and capitalized as a part of the original cost of the fixed assets; but interest expense incurred after the completion of the construstion and the transfer of fixed assets for operation purpose shall be charged to current expenses.

Chapter VIII: Accounting for Fixed Assets

Article 37: A joint venture shall prepare a fixed assets catalog as the basis of accounting according to the criteria of fixed assets laid down in "The Income Tax Law Concerning Joint Ventures With Chinese and Foreign Investment" and in consideration of its specific circumstances.

Article 38: The fixed assets of a joint venture shall be grouped into five broad categories as follows: building and structures; machinery and equipment; electronic equipment; transport facilities (trains or ships, if any, shall be grouped separately); and other equipment. The joint venture may further group them into sub-categories according to the need of its management.

Article 39: The fixed assets of a joint venture shall be recorded at their original cost.

For fixed assets contributed as investment, the original cost shall be the price of the assets agreed upon by all the participants of the joint venture at the time of investment.

For fixed assets purchased, the original cost shall be the total of the purchase price plus freight, loading and unloading charges, packaging expenses and insurance premium etc. The original cost of the fixed assets that need installation work shall include installation expenses. The original cost of imported equipment shall further include the customs duties, industrial and commercial consolidated tax and etc. paid as required.

For fixed assets manufactured or constructed by the joint venture itself, the original cost shall be the actual expenditures incurred in the course of manufacture or construction.

Expenditures of a joint venture on technical innovation and reform that result in the increase of the fixed assets value shall be recorded as increments of the original cost of the fixed assets.

Article 40: Depreciation on the fixed assets of a joint venture shall generally be accounted for on an average basis under the straight line method.

(1) Depreciation on fixed assets shall be accounted for on the basis of the original cost and the group depreciation rate of the fixed assets.

Depreciation rate of the fixed assets shall be calculated and determined on the basis of the original cost, estimated residual value and the useful life of the fixed assets.

A joint venture shall determine the specific useful lives and depreciation rates for different groups of fixed assets according to the minimum depreciation period and the estimated residual value of the fixed assets as provided in the "Income Tax Law Concerning the Joint Ventures Using Chinese and Foreign Investment."

(2) In case where a joint venture needs accelerated depreciation or change of depreciation method for special reasons, application shall be submitted by the joint venture to the tax authority for examination and approval.

(3) Generally, depreciation of the fixed assets of a joint venture shall be accounted for monthly according to the monthly depreciation rates and the monthly beginning balances of the original cost per book of the fixed assets in use. For fixed assets put in use during a month, depreciation shall not be calculated for the month but shall be started from the next month. For fixed assets reduced or stopped to be used during the month, depreciation shall still be calculated for the month and be stopped from the next month.

(4) For the fixed assets fully depreciated but still useful, depreciation shall no longer be calculated. For the fixed assets discarded in advance, no retroactive depreciation shall be made either.

For the fixed assets declared scrap in advance or transferred out, the difference between the net proceeds obtained from disposal (less liquidation expense) and the net value of the fixed assets (original cost less accumulated depreciation) shall be recognized as non-operating income or non-operating expenses of a joint venture.

Article 41: For the purpose, sales, disposal, discarding and internal transfer, etc., of the fixed assets, a joint venture must execute accounting routines and set up foxed assets subsidiary ledger for the relevant accounting so as to strengthen the control of fixed assets.

Article 42: Physical inventory must be taken on the fixed assets of a joint venture at least once a year. If any overage, shortage or damage of the fixed assets is found, the cause shall be investigated and a report be written out by the relevant department. Accounting treatment shall be made as soon as the report is approved through strict management review and the reporting procedures specified by the board of directors. Generally, this work shall be finished before the annual closing of final accounts.

(1) For fixed assets overage, the replacement cost shall be taken as the original cost, the accumulated depreciation shall be estimated and recorded according to the existing usability and west and tear of the assets, and the difference between the original cost and the accumulated depreciation shall be credited to non-operating income.

(2) For fixed assets shortage, the original cost and accumulated depreciation shall be written off and the excess of original cost over accumulated depreciation shall be charged as non-operating expenses.

(3) For damaged fixed assets, the net loss after the original cost deducted by the accumulated depreciation, recoverable salvage value and the indemnity receivable from the person in fault or from the insurance company, shall be charged as non-operating expenses.

Chapter IX: Accounting for Intangible Assets and Other Assets

Article 43: The intangible assets and other assets of a joint venture include proprietary technology, patents, trademarks, copyrights, right to use sites, other franchise and organization expenses etc.

For intangible assets contributed as investment by the participants of a joint venture, the original cost shall be the value provided in the agreement or contract. The original cost of purchased intangible assets shall be the amount actually paid. Monthly amortization of the intangible assets shall be made over their useful life from the year when they come into use. Those without specified useful life may be amortized over a period of ten years. The amortization period shall not be longer than the duration of a joint venture.

Article 44: The expenses incurred by a joint venture during its preparation period (not including expenditures for acquiring fixed assets and intangible assets and the interest incurred during the construction period to be included in the construction cost), may be accounted for as organization expenses according to the provisions of the agreement and with the consent of all participants, and shall be amortized after the production or operation starts. The annual amortization shall not exceed 20 per cent of the expenses.

Article 45: The expenditures incurred by a joint venture on major repair and improvement of the leased-in fixed assets shall be amortized over the period benefited from such expenditures. However, the amortization period shall not be longer than the lease term of the fixed assets.

Chapter X: Accounting for Costs and Expenses

Article 46: The joint ventures shall maintain complete original records, practise norm control, adhere strictly to the procedures of measuring, checking, receiving, issuing, requisitioning and returning of goods and materials, strengthen the control of and accounting for cost and expenses.

Article 47: All expenditures of a joint venture related to production or operation shall be recognized as its cost or expenses.

Materials consumed by a joint venture in the course of production or operation shall be correctly calculated and charged to cost or expenses according to the quantity actually consumed and the price per book.

Wages and salaries of the staff and workers shall be calculated and charged to the cost or expenses according to the provisions in the contract and the decisions of the board of directors on the system of wage standard, wage form, bonus and allowance, etc., as well as the attendance records, time cards and production records. Payment as required on labor insurance, health and welfare benefits and government subsidies, etc., for the Chinese staff and workers, shall also be charged to cost or expenses as the same item as wages and salaries.

All other expenses incurred by a joint venture in the course of production or operation shall be charged to cost or expenses according to the amount actually incurred. The expenses attributable to the current period but not yet paid shall be recognized as accrued expenses and charged to the cost or expenses of the current period; however, the expenses paid but attributable to the current and future periods shall be recognized as deferred charges and amortized to the costs or expenses of the relevant periods.

Article 48: A joint venture shall summarize all the expenses incurred in the course of production or operation according to the specified cost and expense items.

(1) The production cost items of an industrial joint venture shall generally be classified into: direct materials, direct labor, and manufacturing overhead. A joint venture may set up additional items for fuel and power, outside processing cost, special instruments, etc., according to its actual needs.

Manufacturing overhead refers to those expenses arising from organizing and controlling production by workshop and factory administrative departments, including expenses for salaries and wages, depreciation, repairs and maintenance, materials consumed, labor protection, water and electricity, office supplies, travelling, transportation, insurance and so on.

Selling and general administrative expenses of an industrial joint venture shall be accounted for separately and shall not be included in the production cost of products.

Selling expenses refer to those expenses incurred in selling products and attributable to the enterprise, including expenses for transportation, loading and unloading, packaging, insurance, travelling, commission and advertising, as well as salaries and wages and other expenses of specifically established selling organs, etc.

General and administrative expenses include company headquarters expenses (salaries & wages, etc.), labor union dues, interest expense (less interest income), exchange loss (less exchange gains), expenses of board of directors' meetings, advisory fee, entertainment expenses, taxes (including urban building and land tax, license tax for vehicles and vessels, etc.), amortization of organization expenses for staff and workers' training, research and development expenses, fee for the use of site, fee for the transfer of technology, amortiza - tion of intangiable assets and other administrative expenses.

(2)   Expenses of the commercial enterprises incurred in the course of operation include purchasing expenses, selling expenses and administrative expense.

Purchasing expenses include those expenses incurred in the process of merchandise purchase, such as expenses for transportation, loading and unloading, packaging, insurance, reasonable loss during transit, selecting and sorting before warehousing.

Selling expenses include those expenses incurred in the course of merchandise sales and attributable to the joint venture, such as expenses for transportation, loading and unloading, packaging, insurance, travelling, commission, advertising, and salaries and wages and other expenses of sales organ, etc.

Administrative expenses include those expenses incurred in the course of merchandise storage, and the expenses of the enterprise administrative departments, such as expenses for salaries and wages, depreciation, repairs and maintenance, materials consumed, labor protection, office supplies, travelling, transportation, insurance, labor union dues, interest expense (less interest income), enchange loss (less exchange gains), expense of board of directors' meeting, advisory fee, entertainment, tax fee for the use of site, staff and workers' training and other administrative expense.

(3)   Expenses of the service - trade enterprises incurred in the course of operation include operating expenses and administrative expenses.

The operating expenses include various expenses incurred in business operation and may be summarized separately for different kinds of service.

The administrative expenses include various expenses incurred for the administration of the enterprise.

The joint ventures other than the above-mentioned types shall account for their expenses with reference to the above provisions.

Article 49:   A joint venture must distinguish the cost and expenses of the current period from that of the ensuing period. Neither accrual nor amortization shall be made arbitrarily. The cost and expenses of different internal depart- ments shall be distinguished from each other and shall not be mixed up. An industrial joint venture shall distinguish the cost of work in process from the cost of finished goods and the cost of one product from that of the other. Neither the cost of work in process nor the cost of finished goods shall be arbitrarily increased or decreased.

Article 50:   The joint venture shall select the methods of costing and of expense alloca- tion appropriate to the characteristics of its production and operation, its type of product and its purpose of service.

An industrial joint venture may select one or more than one of the following methods for its cost accounting: product type costing, process costing, job order costing, product category costing, norm costing and standard costing.

For the enterprises adopting the norm costing or the standard costing in accounting for product cost, the variances between actual cost and norm cost or between actual cost and standard cost shall generally be allocated according to the proportion of the products sold during a month and the products held at the end of the month.

Once the cost accounting method or the cost variance allocation method is adopted, no arbitrary change shall be allowed. If a change is necessary, it shall be approved by the board of directors, reported to the local tax authority for examination and disclosed in the accounting report.

Article 51: The joint ventures shall strengthen the control over cost and expenses, establish responsibility cost system, formulate plans on cost and expenses, control the expenditures at all times in accordance with the plans, evaluate the condition in implementing the plans periodically, analyze the cause of fluctuation in cost and expenses, take appropriate actions to reduce the cost and expenses and to improve the operation and administration of the enterprise.

Chapter XI: Accounting for Sales and Profit

Article 52: The sales of merchandise, products and services of a joint venture shall be regarded as realized after merchandise and products are shipped, services are rendered, invoices, bills and the bills of lading issued by shipping agency and all other shipping docuemtns are sent to the buyers or are accepted by the bank for collection.

Under the condition of delivery upon payment, if the sales proceeds are received, invoices and delivery orders are sent to the buyers, sales shall be regarded as realized whether the goods are actually issued or not.

Article 53: All the sales of a joint venture realized in a month shall be recognized in the month, and the relevant cost of the sales and expenses shall be transferred simultaneously. Revenue from sales must be matched with the cost of sales and expenses attributable. It is not allowed to recognize merely the sales revenue and disregard the relevant cost of sales and expenses. On the other hand, it is not allowed to charge the costs of sales and expenses without crediting the relevant revenue from sales.

Article 54: The sales returns of a joint venture occurred in a month shall reduce the sales revenue and cost of sales of the current month, regardless of to which year the returned sales belong.

Sales allowances given to the buyers through negotiation due to un-satisfactory quality of the merchandise or products sold or due to some other reasons shall be deducted from sales revenue of the current month.

Article 55: A joint venture shall account for its profit every month. The joint ventures in agriculture animal husbandry, aquaculture and other business that cannot account for profit monthly shall at least do their accounting for profit at the end of a fiscal year.

Article 56: The elements of the profit of a joint venture are as follows:

(1) The profit of an industrial joint venture includes profit from sales of the products, profit on other operations, non-operating income and expenses.

Profit from sales of the products refers to the profit derived from the products sold by the joint venture (including finished goods, semi-finished goods and industrial services).

Profit from other operation refers to those profits of a joint venture derived'from rendering non-industrial service (such as transportation etc.) and from sales of purchased merechandise and surplus materials, etc.

Non-operating income and expenses refer to the various gains and losses other than profit from sales of products and from other operations, including income from investment, loss on investment, income on disposal of fixed assets, loss on disposal of fixed assets, penalty and fines received, penalty and fines paid, donation contributed, bad debts, extraordinary losses etc.

(2)   The profit of a commercial enterprise includes profit from sales; profit from other operations and non-operating income and expenses.

Profit from other operations refers to those profit derived from operations other than sales of merchandise (such as occasional repairs, rental, etc.)

Non-operating income and non-operating expenses refer to various non-operating gains and losses other than profit from sales and profit from other operations, including income on investment, loss on investment, income from disposal of fixed assets, loss on disposal of fixed assets, penalty and fines received, penalty and fines paid, donations contributed, bad debts, extraordinary losses, etc.

(3)   Profit of a service-trade enterprise includes net operating income and non-operating income and expenses.

Article 57:   The profit distributable by a joint venture shall be the excess of its net profit over income tax payable and the required provisions of reserve fund, staff and workers' bonus and welfare fund and enterprise expansion fund. It shall be distributed to the participants of the joint venture in proportion to their shares of contributed capital if the board of directors decides to make the distribution.

The reserve fund may be used as provisional financial cushion against the possible loss of a joint venture. The staff and workers bonus and welfare fund shall be restricted to the payment of bonus and collective welfare for staff and workers. The enterprise expansion fund may be used to acquire fixed assets or to increase the working capital in order to expand the production and operation of the joint venture.

Article 58:   If a joint venture carries losses from the previous years, the profit of the current year shall first the used to cover the losses. No profit shall be distributed unless the deficit from the previous years is made up.

The profit retained by a joint venture and carried over from the previous years may be distributed together with the distributable profit of the current year, or after the deficit of the current year profit is made up therefrom.

Article 59:   A joint venture shall compile a profit distribution program at the end of a year, based on the profit or losses realized in the year and the retained profit or deficit carried over from the previous years, and submit the program to the board of directors for discussion and decision. The distribution shall be recorded in the books of account and recognized in the annual final accounts after the decision is made.

Chapter XII: Classification of Accounts and Accounting Statements

Article 60: The rules on the classification of accounts and accounting statements of joint ventures shall be formulated by the Ministry of Finance of the People's Republic of China, or by the relevant business regulatory departments and submitted to the Ministry of Finance for examination and approval.
A joint venture may supplement or omit the stipulated ledger accounts and the stipulated items of the accounting statements according to its specific circumstances, provided that it does not affect the accounting requirements and the summarization of the indexes in the accounting statements.

Article 61: The accounts of the joint ventures shall generally be classified according to the operation and management needs into four broad categories: assets, liabilities, capital, profit & loss. Profit and loss accounts may also be classified into income accounts and expenses accounts. For industrial joint ventures, another category may be added for cost accounts. The ledger accounts of a joint venture shall be coded according to their classification.

Article 62: The accounting statements of a joint venture shall include:
(1) Balance sheet;
(2) Income statement;
(3) Statement of changes in financial position;
(4) Relevant supporting schedules.
A joint venture may add additional information in its accounting statements after it is approved by all its participants, in order to meet the need of the foreign participant's head office in consolidation of financial statements.

Article 63: When a joint venture with subsidiary enterprises combines its accounting statements with those of its subsidiaries, its funds appropriated to end its current accounts with its subsidiaries shall be offset against the corresponding items in the accounting statements of the subsidiaries.

Article 64: On submitting its annual accounting statements, a joint venture shall attach a descriptive overview of its financial condition, primarily explaining:
(1) condition of production and operation;
(2) condition of realization and distribution of profit;
(3) condition of changes in capital and its turnover;
(4) condition of foreign exchange receipts and disbursements and their equilibrium;
(5) condition of the payment of industrial and commercial consolidated tax, income tax, fee for the use of site and fee for the transfer of technology;
(6) condition of overage, shortage, deterioration, spoilage, damage and write-off of different properties and supplies;
(7) other necessary issues to be explained.
On submitting quarterly statements, the joint venture shall also explain special conditions, if any.

Article 65: The quarterly and annual accounting statements of a joint venture shall be submitted to each participant of the joint venture, local tax authority, the relevant business regulatory department of the joint venture and the public finance department at the same level.
The quarterly accounting statements of a joint venture shall be submit-

ted within 20 days after the end of each quarter, and the annual accounting statements shall be submitted together with the audit report made by the certified public accountants within four months after the end of a year.

Article 66: The accounting statements of a joint venture shall be examined and signed by its president and controller and shall be under the seal of the joint venture.

Chapter XIII: Accounting Documents & Accounting Books

Article 67: A joint venture must acquire or fill out original documents for every transaction occurred. All the original documents must carry faithful contents, evidences of all the required procedures and accurate figures. Original documents from an outside unit must be signed and sealed by the unit. The original documents shall be verified and signed by the head of the department and the person responsible for handling the transaction. A joint venture shall check and inspect the original documents seriously. Any falsified or altered original document, or any fraudulent application or rquest or other similar events must be rejected and reported to the relevant party. The original documents with incomplete contents, insufficient evidences of required procedures or inaccurate figures shall be returned, amended or refilled. Only the original documents examined and proved correct can be taken as the basis for preparing accounting vouchers.

Article 68: The accounting vouchers of a joint venture include receiving voucher, disbursement voucher, and journal voucher. All vouchers must be filled out with required contents and can be taken as the basis in bookkeeping only after signed by the preparer, the designated verifier and the chief officer of the financial and accounting department. A receiving or disbursement voucher shall also be signed by the cashier.

Each kind of the accounting vouchers shall be filed according to its sequential number and bound into books monthly together with the original documents attached thereto, and shall be kept in safety without any loss or damage. For the important documents concerning claims and debts that need separate safe-keeping, cross reference shall be made on the original documents of the transaction and on the related vouchers.

Article 69: A joint venture shall number sequentially all documents issued to the outside, and retain its duplicate copy (or copies) or the stub. An original of such document with clerical error or withdrawn for cancellation shall be kept together with the duplicate or stub of the same sequential number. If the original copy is missing or unable to be recovered, the reason shall be noted on the duplicate or stubs.

Article 70: All the blank forms of important documents, such as check books, case receipts, delivery orders, etc., shall be registered in a special registration book by the financial and accounting department. Requisition of those blank forms shall be approved by the chief officer or a designated person of the financial and accounting department, and the person making the requisition shall sign the registration book for receiving the forms.

Article 71: A joint venture shall set up three kinds of primary accounting books, namely, journals, general ledger and subsidiary ledgers, as well as appropriate supplementary memorandum books.

All the books shall be kept with complete records, accurate figures, clear description and prompt registration, on the basis of the examined original documents and vouchers or summary of vouchers that are proved correct.

No record in the books of a joint venture shall be scraped, mended, altered or eliminated by correction fluid. When errors are made, they shall be amended by crossing off the error or by preparing additional vouchers according to the nature and circumstances of the error. When crossing method of amendment is used, the person making the correction shall sign on the place of amendment.

Article 72: A joint venture keeping its accounts by electronic computer shall maintain properly its accounting records stored in or printed out by the computer and shall regard such records as accounting books. The tapes, discs, etc., shall.be kept and no deletion shall be allowed unless the records in them are printed out in visible form.

Chapter XIV: Audit

Article 73: A joint venture shall engage the certified public accountants registered with the government of the People's Republic of China to audit its annual accounting statements and the books of account of the year and to issue an auditor's report, according to the provisions of "The Income Tax Law Concerning Joint Ventures with Chinese and Foreign Investment."

Article 74: Each participant of a joint venture may audit the accounts of the joint venture. The expenses thereon shall be paid by the participant making the audit. Any problem noted in the audit that needs to be resolved by the joint venture shall be submitted to the joint venture in a timely manner for discussion and resolution.

Article 75: The joint ventures shall furnish the auditors with all the documents, books and other relevant data as needed by them. The auditors shall be responsible for maintaining confidentiality.

Chapter XV: Accounting Files

Article 76: The accounting files of a joint venture including accounting documents, accounting books, accounting statements, etc., must be appropriately kept within the territory of the People's Republic of China. No loss nor spoilage shall be allowed.

Article 77: The annual accounting statements and all other important accounting files relevant to the rights and interests of all the participants of a joint venture, such as joint venture agreement, joint venture contract, articles of association of the joint venture, resolutions of the board of directors, investment appraisal list, certificate on capital validation, auditing report of the certified public accountants, long term economic contracts, etc., must be kept permanently. General accounting documents, accounting books and monthly and quarterly accounting statements shall be kept for at least 15 years.

Article 78: If the accounting files need to be destroyed after the expiration of the retention period, an itemized list of the files to be destroyed shall be prepared and reported to the board of directors, business regulatory department and tax authority for approval. No files can be destroyed unless such list is approved. The list of destroyed accounting files must be kept permanently.

Chapter XVI: Dissolution and Liquidation

Article 79: When a joint venture declares dissolution and goes into liquidation on or before the expiration of the joint venture contract, a liquidation committee shall be formed to conduct an overall check of the assets of the joint venture and its claims and debts, to prepare a balance sheet and a detailed list of assets, to suggest a basis for the valuation and calculation of the assets and to formulate a plan for liquidation. After the approval is obtained through submitting the liquidation plan to the board of directors for its discussion, the liquidation committee shall make disposal of the assets, collect the claims, pay taxes and clear debts, and resolve all remaining problems appropriately.

Article 80: The liquidation expenses of a joint venture and the remuneration to its liquidation committee members shall be given priority in making payments from the existing assets of the joint venture.

Article 81: The net liquidation income, i.e. the liquidation income in the process of the liquidation of a joint venture less the liquidation expenses and various liquidation losses, shall be dealt with as the profit of the joint venture.

Article 82: The assets of a joint venture left over after the clearance of all its debts shall be distributed among the participants of the joint venture according to the proportioin of each participant's investment contribution, unless otherwise provided by the agreement, contract or articles of association of the joint venture.

Article 83: The accounting statements on liquidation and dissolution of a joint venture shall be valid only after an examination is made and a certificate is issued by certified public accountants registered with the government of the People's Republic of China.

Article 84: After the dissolution of a joint venture, its accounting books and all other documents shall be left in the care of the Chinese participant.

Chapter XVII: Other Provisions

Article 85: The present regulations are formulated by the Ministry of Finance of the People's Republic of China. If there is any change in the laws, regulations and other relevant provisions of the People's Republic of China on which these regulations are based, the new provisions shall govern. If the present regulations need corresponding amendment, it shall be made by the Ministry of Finance of the People's Republic of China.

Article 86: For the joint ventures established in the special exonomic zones, if there are special provisions in the laws or regulations adopted by the National People's Congress of the People's Republic of China or its Standing Committee, or by the State Council, such provisions shall be followed.

Article 87: The right to interpret these regulations resides in the Ministry of Finance of the People's Republic of China.

Article 88: The present regulations shall be implemented on and after July 1, 1985.

Appendix

Procedures of the Customs of the People's Republic of China for the Administration of Materials and Parts that Enterprises with Foreign Investment Need to Import in order to Perform Product Export Contracts

(Announced by the general Administration of
customs on November 24, 1986)

Article 1:   These Procedures are formulated in accordance with the Provisional Customs Law of the People's Republic of China (now replaced by the Customs Law of the People's Republic of China 1987 — Author) and relevant provisions of the State Council for the encouragement of foreign investment in order to encourage the re-export of products that are processed (manufactured) by enterprises with foreign investment for which materials and parts need to be imported to perform their product export contracts and to expand exports to generate foreign exchange earnings.

Article 2:   Enterprises with foreign investment shall, in accordance with the provisions of these Procedures, injoy preferential treatment and perform the obligations in customs clearance and the paying of taxes. The goods imported and exported by them shall be declared to the Customs strictly according to the facts. Machinery and equipment, vehicles used in production and raw materials, fuel, knock-down parts, spare parts, components, sets of parts, auxiliary materials and packaging materials (hereinafter referred to as "Materials and Parts") that need to be imported by these enterprises for the execution of their product export contracts shall be categorized as bonded warehouse goods and shall be subject to supervision and control by the Customs.

Article 3:   The imported machinery, equipment, vehicles used in production, and Materials and Parts referred to in Article 2 of these Procedures shall be exempted from the requirement of obtaining import licenses. The Customs shall inspect and release such imports on the strength of the concerned enterprises's contract(s) or the import-export contract(s).

For products that are processed from Materials and Parts imported by enterprises with foreign investment and then re-exported, the Customs shall, at the time of re-export, handle the inspection and release of such products in accordance with the provisions of the Procedures of the Ministry of Foreign Economic Relations and Trade Concerning the Application of Import and Export Licenses by Enterprises with Foreign Investment. But if imported Materials and Parts are used in products to be sold domestically, the enterprise with foreign investment in question shall have to go through the import procedures retroactively in accordance with the relevant provisions of the State.

Where such products belong to the category of commodities subject to the control fo import licensing control, import licenses for the said imported goods shall be submitted to and inspected by the Customs.

Article 4:   As regards the imported Materials and Parts referred to in article 2 of these Procedures, exemption from import duties and the consolidated industrial and commercial tax applies only to that part of the imported Materials and Parts that is actually consumed in the processing of products for export.

The tax-free Materials and Parts referred to above shall include reasonable quantities of imported catalysts, catalytic agents, abrasives and fuel that are directly used in the processing products for export and that are consumed in the production process.

Imported Materials and Parts shall be restricted to use by the enterprise that processes products for export and such products may not be sold on the domestic market. But for those products that are, for one reason or another, approved for domestic disposal (sale), the imported Materials and Parts that are used for their manufacture shall be taxed retroactively in accordance with the relevant regulations. Taxes may be reduced or exempted for substandard and defective products and scrap materials that are left over in the course of production on the basis of their use value as the case may be.

Article 5:   Materials and Parts that enterprises with foreign investment need to import in order to manufacture products that are included in the List of Products to Substitute Imports approved by the department in charge as stipulated by the State shall, in light of these Procedures, be treated as bonded warehouse goods over which the Customs shall exercise supervision and control, thus obviating the need to go through the procedures for the payment of taxes at the time of import. When the product referred to above are supplied to domestic users, import duties and the consolidated industrial and commercial tax on the imported Materials and Parts used shall be paid to the Customs, and the import procedures required shall be completed retroactively in accordance with the relevant regulations.

If domestic users import similar types of products from abroad, they may enjoy preferential tax reduction or exemption. When enterprises with foreign investment supply the products referred to above to these users, preferential tax reduction or exemption may also be granted, provided that they shall, in accordance with the relevant provisions of the State submit for inspection the certificate of tax reduction or exemption that has been approved by the department in charge.

Article 6:   Materials and Parts that are purchased by enterprises with foreign investment from the bonded warehouse of the relevant departments or are
imported by other enterprises in the capacity of agents of the said enterprises with foreign investment shall be likewise treated at those imported
by the enterprises with foreign investment themselves, hence similarly
subject to the relevant provisions of these Procedures.

Article 7:   Enterprises with foreign investment that are engaged in processing operations for which materials must be imported must complete the registration
procedures with the Customs in the locality (or the appropriate administrative division of Customs) for the record, for which their relevant
contracts must be submitted, and, upon examination by the Customs,
a Manual of the Customs of the People's Republic of China for the Registration of Materials and Parts Needed to be Imported for Processing and
Re-export by Enterprises with Foreign Investment In Order to Perform
Product Export Contracts (hereafter referred to as the ''Registration
Manual'') shall be issued to the said enterprises with foreign investment.
Those enterprises that are qualified, upon vertification by Customs in the
locality, may be dealt with in accordance with the administrative provisions
of the Customs for bonded factories that import materials for processing
operations.

When the above-mentioned Materials and Parts are imported and, after
processing, the finished products are exported, an enterprise with foreign
investment shall make declarations to the Customs at the place of entry
and exit by submitting the Registration Manual, three copies of the
customs declaration form for imported and exported goods, the invoice
for the goods, packing lists and other relevant lists and certificates. The
Customs shall make annotations and comments, and them affix a seal
on the Registration Handbook, which shall then be returned to the enterprises with foreign investment, which shall use this to complete the
verification and cancellation procedures at the Customs in the locality (or
the appropriate administrative division of the Customs).

Article 8:   In respect of imported Materials and Parts imported under the items of
each import contract, within two months after completing the execution
(performance) of the relevant contracts, enterprises with foreign investment shall submit the Registration Manual, the customs declaration form
for imported and exported goods and other relevant documents to
Customs to complete the verification and cancellation procedures.

A record of the import, storage and care, allocation for use and passing
on to factories for processing of Materials and Parts, and the storage,
export and domestic sales of the finished products after processing, must
be kept by enterprises with foreign investment in specialized account books
and quarterly statements must be submitted to the Customs for examination. As for products that require a long production period, upon the
verification and approval of the Customs, such statements may be submitted every six months.

Article 9:   If products processed from imported and tax-exempted Materials and
Parts are, upon approval, sold domestically, the enterprise with foreign
investment concerned shall, within one month of the date of approval,
pay retroactively to the competent the Customs the customs duties and
consolidated industrial and commercial tax on the imported Materials and
Parts that were originally exempted from tax.

Article 10 : Except where the Customs has given approval because of special reasons, enterprises with foreign investment shall, within one year of the date of import of the tax-exempted imported Materials and Parts, process them into finished products and perform the relevant contracts.

Article 11 : When imported Materials and Parts after being processed into finished products are not exported directly but instead are transferred to another production enterprise, which also does processing on imported materials for re-export, for reprocessing and assembly, the enterprise that imported the Materials and Parts shall, together with this other production enterprise, complete the procedures with the Customs as regards transfer and verification and cancellation, for which the purchase and sales contract or production and processing contract signed by the two parties and other relevant documents must be submitted. Such production enterprise that carries on the business of reprocessing of imported materials for re-export shall, in accordance with the stipulations of these Procedures, apply for a new Registration Manual, and shall comply with the relevant stipulations of these Procedures, subject to the supervision and control of Customs.

Article 12 : In case of any alteration, transfer, suspension or cancellation of contracts that occurs after the importation of Materials and parts, the enterprise with foreign investment concerned shall complete as soon as possible the required procedures with the Customs for the said alteration, transfer, or cancellation.

Article 13 : In order to facilitate the business activities of carrying out processing and export by enterprises with foreign investment and by production enterprises that do reprocessing of imported materials for re-export, the Customs may, based on the actual situation, dispatch Customs officers to be stationed at the factories to carry out actual supervision and control, and may examine the relevant account books. The enterprises referred to above shall provide offices and the necessary facilities.

Article 14 : Enterprises with foreign investment may not, without authorization, transfer or sell domestically imported Materials and Parts and their processed products that are bonded warehouse goods. If an enterprise concerned is found to have made a transfer, or to have sold domestically without authorization, or to have acted illegally in violation of the stipulations of these Procedures, the matter shall be dealt with by the Customs in accordance with customs law and the relevant decrees and regulations of the State.

Article 15 : These Procedures shall be implemented as from December 1, 1986.

Regulations on the Registration of Joint Ventues Using Chinese and Foreign Investment

(Approved by the State Council on July 26, 1980)

Article 1:   The present regulations are worked out in accordance with stipulations laid down in the "Law of the People's Republic of China and Joint Ventures Using Chinese and Foreign Investment" and for the purpose of registering such ventures to protect their legitimate operations.

Article 2:   A joint venture using Chinese and foreign investment should, within one month after being approved by the Foreign Investment Commission of the People's Republic of China, register with the General Administration for Industry and Commerce of the People's Republic of China.

The Genreral Administration for Industry and Commerce authorizes the administrative bureaus for industry and commerce in the provinces, municipalities and autonomous regions to register joint ventures using Chinese and foreign investment in their localities. Licenses for operations shall be issued to the said joint ventures after examination by the General Administration for Industry and Commerce of the People's Republic of China.

Article 3:   In applying for registration, a joint venture using Chinese and foreign investment should produce the following documents:

(1)   The document of approval issued by the Foreign Investment Commission of the People's Republic of China.

(2)   The agreement on the joint venture reached by the various parties involved, the contract and the articles of association of the venture, in both Chinese and foreign languages and each in triplicates, and

(3) A duplicate of the license and other documents issued by the departments concerned under the government of the country (or region) from which the foreign participants in the joint venture come.

Article 4: In applying for registration of a joint venture using Chinese and foreign investment, a registration form, in triplicates shall be filled. Items to be registered include the name of the venture, its address, scope of production and business, forms of production and business, registered capital of the parties concerned, chairman and vice-chairmen of the board of directors, general director and deputy director of the plant, the number and date of approval on the document, the size of the entire staff, and the number of foreign workers and staff members.

Article 5: A joint venture using Chinese and foreign investment is regarded as having officially been established the day when a license for its operation is issued to it, and the legitimate production and business shall be protected by the law of the People's Republic of China.
An unregistered enterprise shall not be permitted to go into operation.

Article 6: A joint venture using Chinese and foreign investment shall, by producing the license for its operation, open an account with the Bank of China or another bank approved by the Bank of China, and register with the local tax bureau for payment of taxes.

Article 7: In cases where a joint venture using Chinese and foreign investment desires to move to a new site, shift its production, increase or cut or transfer the registered capital, or extend the contract period, the said venture shall, within one month after approval by the Foreign Investment Commission of the People's Republic of China, register the changes with the Administrative Bureau for Industry and Commerce in the province, municipality or autonomous region where it is located.
In cases where changes to other items are effected, the said venture shall have to forward at the end of the year a written report about these changes to the Administrive Burearu for Industry and Commerce in the province, municipality or autonomous region where it is located.

Article 8: In registering or getting its changes registered, a joint venture using Chinese and foreign investment shall pay the registration fee or the fee for getting its changes registered, the sum of which is to be fixed by the General Administration for Industry and Commerce of the People's Republic of China.

Article 9: A joint venture using Chinese and foreign investment, upon the expiration of the contract period of the venture or desirous of terminating the contract before its expiration date, shall upon production of the document of approval issued by the Foreign Investment Commission of the People's Republic of China register for the nullification of the contract with the Adminstrative Bureau for Industry and Commerce in the province, municipality or autonomous region where it is located. The license of the said venture shall be handed in for cancellation after examination by the General Administration for Industry and Commerce of the People's Republic of

China.

Article 10:   The General Administration for Industry and Commerce of the People's Republic of China and the Administrative Bureaus for Industry and Commerce in the provinces, municipalities and autonomous regions are authorized to supervise and inspect the joint ventures using Chinese and foreign investment in the areas they govern. In cases of violations of the present regulations, the violator shall be given a warning or be fined in accordance with the varying degrees of seriousness in each specific case.

Article 11:   The present regulations come into force on the date of its promulgation.

SECTION B: Labour

Regulations on Labour Management in Joint Ventures Using Chinese and Foreign Investment

(Approved by the State Council on July 26, 1980)

Article 1: Labour management problems concerning joint ventures using Chinese and foreign investment (hereinafter referred to as joint ventures) should be handled in accordance with the regulations, in addition to the pertinent stipulations in article 6 of the "Law of the People's Republic of China on Joint Ventures Using Chinese and Foreign Investment".

Article 2: Matters pertaining to employment, dismissal and resignation of the workers and staff members, tasks of production and other work, wage and awards and punishment, working time and vacation, labour insurance and welfare, labour protection and labour discipline in joint ventures shall be stipulated in the labour contracts signed.

A labour contract is to be signed collectively by a joint venture and the trade union organizaton formed in the joint venture. A relatively small joint venture may sign contracts with the workers and staff members individually.

A signed labour contract must be submitted to the labour management department of the provinical, autonomous regional or municipal people's government for approval.

Article 3: The workers and staff members of a joint venture either recommended by the authorities in the locality in charge of the joint venture or the labour management department, or recruited by the joint venture itself with consent of the labour management department, should all be selected by the joint venture through examination for their qualification.

Joint ventures may run workers' schools and training courses for

	training of managerial personnel and skilled workers.
Article 4:	With regard to the surplus workers and staff members as a result of changes in production and technical conditions of the joint venture, those who fail to meet the requirements after training and are not suitable for other work can be discharged. However, this must be done in line with the stipulations in the labour contract and the enterprise must give compensation to these workers.

The dismissed workers and staff members will receive assignments for other work from the authorities in charge of the joint venture or the labour management department.

Article 5:   The joint venture may, according to the degree of seriousness of the case, take action against those workers or staff members who have violated rules and regulations of the enterprise that result in certain bad consequences. Punishment by discharges must be reported to the authorities in charge of the joint venture and the labour management department for approval.

Article 6:   With regard to the dismissal and punishment of workers and staff members by the joint venture, the trade union has the right to raise an objection if it considers them unreasonable, and send representatives to seek a solution through consultation with the board of directors. Should the consultation fail to arrive at a solution, the matter will be handled in accordance with the procedures set forth in Article 14 of the present regulations.

Article 7:   When workers and staff members of a joint venture, on account of special conditions, submit resignation to the enterprise through the trade union in accordance with the labour contract, the enterprise should give its consent.

Article 8:   The wage level of the workers and staff members in a joint venture will be determined at 120 to 150% of the real wages of the workers and staff members of state-owned enterprises of the same trade in the locality.

Article 9:   The wage standards, the forms of wages paid, and bonus and subsidy systems are to be discussed and decided upon by the board of directors.

Article 10: The bonuses and welfare funds drawn by the joint venture from the profits must be used as bonuses, awards and collective welfare and should not be misappropriated.

Article 11: A joint venture must pay for the Chinese workers' and staff members' labour insurance, cover their medical expenses and various kinds of government subsidies in line with the standards prevailing in state-owned enterprises.

Article 12: The employment of foreign workers and staff members and their dismissal, resignation, pay, welfare and social insurances and other matters concerned should all be stipulated in the employment contacts.

Article 13: Joint ventures must implement the relevant rules and regulations of the Chinese government on labour protection and ensure safety in production and civilized production. The labour management department of the Chinese government is authorized to supervise and inspect their implementation.

Article 14: Labour disputes occurring in a joint venture should first of all be solved through consultation by both parties. If consultation fails to arrive at a solution, either party or both parties may request for arbitration by the labour management department of the people's government of the province, autonomous region or municipality where the joint venture is located. Either party that disagrees to the arbitration may file a suit at the people's court.

Article 15: The right of interpretation of the present regulations belong to the State Bureau of Labour of the People's Republic of China.

Article 16: The regulations come into force on the date of its promulgation.

SECTION C: Registration

Procedures for Registration, Examination and Approval of Joint Ventures between Chinese and Foreign Investors

(Printed and Distributed by the State Administration for Industry and Commerce on April 24, 1981)

1.   This Procedure for registration, examination and approval is formulated in accordance with "The Measures of Registration and Control of Joint Ventures Between Chinese and Foreign Investment" promulgated by the State Council of the People's Republic of China.
2.   Joint ventures between Chinese and foreign investors (hereinafter called joint ventures) must apply for registration with the administrations for industry and commerce in the provinces, municipalities or autonomous regions where they are located within 30 days of the approval by the Foreign Investment Control Commission of the People's Republic of China (hereinafter called the State Foreign Investment Control Commission) or the provincial, municipal and autonomous regional governments it entrusts.
3.   A joint venture, when applying for registration, must present the following certificates and materials:
     a.   A request for registration signed by the chairman and vice-chairman of the board of directors or the general manager and deputy general manager (one each from the Chinese and foreign sides).
     b.   The certificate of approval issued by the State Foreign investment Control Commission. Those approved by the provinces, municipalities and autonomous regions as entrusted by the State Foreign Investment Control Commission must present the certificates of approval issued by the provinces, municipalities and autonomous regions where the joint ventures are located.
     c.   The agreement, contract and regulations of the joint venture (both in Chinese and foreign languages in triplicate).
     d.   A feasibility study report of the joint ventures.
     e.   The legitimate business certificate issued by the competent government

department in the county (or region) where the foreign partner resides.

f. Verified documents concerning construction conditions such as environmental protection, urban construction, water and power supply, etc. issued by the relevant departments of the people's government in the city or country where the joint venture is located.

4. A joint venture applying for registration must fill out the application form in triplicate. The forms shall be printed and distributed in a unified way by the State Administration for Industry and Commerce. The joint venture must truthfully fill out the items listed in the form. The chairman and vice-chairman of the board of directors or the general manager and deputy general manager shall be held fully responsible for the contents filled therein.

5. The State Administration for Industry and Commerce shall reply within one month of receiving the registration application form of the joint venture and the related documents. Its procedure of examination and approval is as follows:

a. The provincial, municipal or autonomous regional administration for industry and commerce that handles the application shall examine the above-mentioned certificates and application form presented by the joint venture, and write an examination report. Where anything is found not in accordance with the stipulations, the applicant shall be promptly notified to make alterations.

b. The provincial, municipal or autonomous regional administration for industry and commerce that handles the application shall send to the State Administration for Industry and Commerce for approval all the documents and application forms together with the examination report, apart from keeping a copy of the agreement, contract and regulations of the joint venture and sending another copy to the administration for industry and commerce in the city or country where the joint venture is located.

c. The State Administration for Industry and Commerce, having approved the above documents, shall reply to the related provincial, municipal or autonomous regional administration for industry and commerce, instructing the latter to issue on its behalf "Notice of Approved Registration" and "Business License of the People's Republic of China."

d. The items "Examination, Approval and Comments by the State Administration for Industry and Commerce of the People's Republic of China" in the application form shall be signed by the General Director or the Deputy General Director-in-charge. Where the General Director authorizes the director of the provincial, municipal or autonomous regional administration for industry and commerce to sign on his behalf, he shall issue the certificate of authorization.

6. Where a joint venture moves site, switches to another line of production, adds or reduces or transfers its registered capital, or extends the term of the contract, it must, within one month of approval by the State Foreign Investment Control Commission, bring along the approval certificate to the administration for industry and commerce in the province, municipality or autonomous region where the joint venture is located, to change the registration. Where the chairman of the board of directors or the general manager of a joint venture is changed, it must immediately change the registration, fill out the registration change form and change the business license.

Where there is any change in respect of the contents of the registration, if must be reported at the end of the year to the administration for industry and commerce in the province, municipality or autonomous region where the said joint venture is located.

7.   Where a joint venture wishes to conduct business abroad and requests to obtain a "Business Certificate of the People's Republic of China." it must apply to the administration for industry and commerce in the province, municipality or autonomous region where it is located, and send a draft business certificate in duplicate to the State Administration for Industry and Commerce. The business certificate shall be issued by the department that handles the application on behalf of the State Administration for Industry and Commerce upon the latter's approval.

8.   A joint venture, during registration or when amending the registration, shall pay fees according to "The Temporary Regulations on the Standards of the Registration Fees Paid by the Joint Ventures Between Chinese and Foreign Investment" prepared by the State Administration for Industry and Commerce.

9.   A joint venture whose contract term expires or terminates ahead of time, must bring the approval documents of the State Foreign Investment Control Commission and the certificates of the Ministry of Finance and the Bank of China concerning the clearance of property to the department that handled its registration and go through the procedure to cancel the registration and hand in the business license.

10.   Upon the termination of the joint venture contract, if the Chinese party wishes to continue the business, it must register a new and obtain another business license.

11.   The procedure of applying for registration and its examination and approval regarding enterprises jointly run by overseas Chinese, compatriots in Hong Kong and Macao or their firms or enterprises together with other economic organizations in various localities or departments shall be handled with reference to this Procedure.

12.   Matters not included in this Procedure shall be amended or revised by the State Administration for Industry and Commerce.

SECTION D: Taxation

The Income Tax Law of the People's Republic of China Concerning Joint Ventures with Chinese and Foreign Investment

(Adopted by the Fifth National People's Congress on September 10, 1980)

Article 1:   Income tax shall be levied in accordance with this law on the income derived from production, business and other sources by any joint venture with Chinese and foreign investment (hereinafter called joint venture for short) int he People's Republic of China.

Income tax on the income derived from production, business and other sources by branches within or outside the territory of China of such joint ventures shall be paid by their head office.

Article 2:   the taxable income of a joint venture shall be the net income in a tax year after deduction of costs, expenses and losses in that year.

Article 3:   The income tax rate on joint ventures shall be 30 per cent. In addition, a local surtax of 10 per cent of the assessed income tax shall be levied.

The income tax rates on joint ventures exploiting petroleum, natural gas and other resources shall be stipulated separately.

Article 4:   In the case of a foreign participant in a joint venture remitting its share of profit from China, an income tax of 10 per cent shall be levied on the remitted amount.

Article 5:   A newly established joint venture scheduled to operate for a period of 10 years of more may, upon approval by the tax authorities of an application filed by the enterprise, be exempted from income tax in the first profit-making year and allowed a 50 per cent reduction in the second and third years.

With the approval of the Ministry of Finance of the People's Republic of China, joint ventures engaged in such low-profit operations as farming and forestry or located in remote, economically underdeveloped outlying areas may be allowed a 15-30 per cent reduction in income tax for a period of 10 years following the expiration of the term for exemptions and reductions mentioned in the preceding paragraph.

Article 6:   A participant in a joint venture which reinvests its share of profit in China for a period of not less than five years may, upon approval by the tax authorities of an application filed by the said participant, obtain a refund of 40 per cent of the income tax paid on the reinvested amount. A participant which withdraws its reinvested funds within five years shall pay back the tax amount refunded.

Article 7:   Losses incurred by a joint venture in a tax year may be carried over to the next tax year and made up with a matching amount drawn from that year's income. Should the income in the subsequent tax year be insufficient to make up for the said losses, the balance may be made up with further deductions against income year by year over a period not exceeding five years.

Article 8:   Income tax on joint ventures shall be levied on an annual basis and paid in quarterly instalments. Such provisional payments shall be made within 15 days after the end of each quarter. The final settlement shall be made within 3 months of the end of a tax year. Excess payments shall be refunded by the tax authorities or deficiencies made good by the taxpayer.

Article 9:   Joint ventures shall file their provisional income tax returns with the local tax authority within the period prescribed for provisional payments. The taxpayer shall file its final annual income tax return together with its final accounts within 3 months of the end of the tax year.

Article 10:   Income tax levied on joint ventures shall be computed in terms of Renminbi (RMB). Income in foreign currency shall be assessed according to the exchange rate quoted by the State General Administration of Exchange Control of the People's Republic of China and shall be taxed in Renminbi.

Article 11:   When joint ventures go into operation or when they change the nature of their business, change their address, close down, and make changes in or transfer registered capital, such joint ventures shall register with the General Administrative Bureau for Industry and Commerce of the People's Republic of China, and within 30 Days of such registration, present the relevant certificates to the local tax authority for tax registration.

Article 12:   The tax authorities have the right to investigate the financial affairs, account books and tax situation of any joint venture. Such joint venture must make reports according to the facts and provide all relevant information and shall not refuse to co-operate or conceal the facts.

Article 13:   A joint venture must pay its tax within the prescribed time limit. In cases of failure to pay within the prescribed time limit, the appropriate tax authority, in addition to setting a new time limit for tax payment, shall surcharge overdue payments at one-half of one per cent of the overdue tax for every day in arrears, starting from the first day of default.

Article 14: The tax authorities may, acting at their discretion, impose a penalty on any joint venture which has violated the provisions of articles 9, 11 and 12 of this law.

In dealing with any joint venture which has evaded or refused to pay tax, the tax authorities may, in addition to pursuing the tax, impose a penalty of not more than five times the amount of tax underpaid or not paid, according to the seriousness of the offence. Cases of gross violation shall be handled by the local people's courts according to law.

Article 15: In cases of disputes with tax authorities about tax payment, joint ventures must pay tax according to the relevant regulations first before applying to higher tax authorities for reconsideration. If they do not accept the decisions made after such reconsideration, they can bring the matter before the local people's courts.

Article 16: Income tax paid by a joint venture or its branch in other countries may be credited agianst assessed income tax of the head office as foreign tax credit.

Where agreements on avoidance of double taxation have been concluded between the government of the People's Republic of China and the government of another country, income tax credits shall be handled in accordance with the provisions of the related agreements.

Article 17: Detailed rules and regulations for the implementation of this law shall be formulated by the Ministry of Finance of the People's Republic of China.

Article 18: This law shall come into force from the date of promulgation.

Detailed Rules and Regulations for the Implementation of the Income Tax Law of the People's Republic of China Concerning Joint Ventures with Chinese and Foreign Investment

Article 1: These detailed rules regulations are formulated in accordance with the provisions of Article 17 of the Income Tax Law of the People's Republic of China Concerning Joint Ventures with Chinese and Foreign Investment (hereinafter called Tax Law for short).

Article 2: "Income derived from production and business" mentioned in Article 1 of the Tax Law menas income from the production and business operations in industry, mining, communications, transportation, agriculture, forestry, animal husbandry, fisheries, poultry farming, commerce, tourism, food and drink, service and other trades.

"Income from other sources" mentioned in Article 1 of the Tax Law covers dividends, bonuses, interest and income from lease or transfer of property, patent right, ownership of trade marks, proprietary technology, copyright, and other sources.

Article 3: "A local surtax of 10 per cent of the assessed income tax" in Article 3 of the Tax Law means a surtax to be computed and levied according to the actual amount of income tax paid by joint ventures.

Reduction or exemption of local surtax on account of special circumstances shall be decided by the people's government of the province, municipality or autonomous region in which the joint venture is located.

Article 4: A foreign participant in a joint venture, who wants to remit its share of profits from China, shall report to the local tax authorities, the remitting agency shall withhold an income tax of 10 per cent from the remittance. No tax shall be levied on that part of its share of profits which is not remitted from China.

Article 5: "The first profit-making year" mentioned in Article 5 of the Tax Law means the year in which a joint venture has begun making profit after its losses in the initial stage of operation have been made up in accordance with the provisions of Article 7 of the Tax Law.

Article 6: A participant in a joint venture, who reinvests its share of profit in this enterprise or in other joint ventures with Chinese and foreign investment for a period of not less than five years in succession, may receive a refund of 40 per cent of the income tax already paid on the reinvested amount upon the examination and approval of the certificate of the invested enterprise by the tax authorities to which the tax was paid.

Article 7: The tax year for joint ventures starts from January 1 and ends on December 31 on the Gregorian calendar.

Article 8: The amount of taxable income shall be computed by the following formulae:

1. Industry:
A. Cost of production of the year = direct material used in production of the year + direct wages + manufacturing expenses.
B. Cost of production of the year = inventory of semi-finished product at the beginning of the year and in-production product + cost of production of the year — inventory of semi-finished product at the end of the year and in-production product.
C. Cost of sale of product = cost of product of the year + inventory of product at the beginning of the year — inventory of product at the end of the year.
D. Net volume of sale of product = total volume of sale of product — (sales returns + sales allowance).
E. Profit from sale of product = net volume of sale of product — taxes on sales — cost of sale of product — (selling expenses + administrative expenses).
F. Amount of taxable income = profit from sale of product + profit from other operations + non-operating expenditure.

2. Commerce:
A. Net volume of sale = total volume of sale — (sales returns + sales allowance).
B. Cost of sales = inventory of merchandise at the beginning of the year + [purchase of the year — (purchase returned + purchase discount) + purchase expenses] — inventory of merchandise at the end of the year.
C. Sale profit = net volume of sale — sale tax — cost of sales — (selling expenses + overhead expenses).
D. Amount of taxable income = sale profit + profit from other operations + non-operating income — non-operating expenditure.

3. Service trades:
A. Net business income = gross business income — (business tax + operating expenses + overhead expenses).
B. Amount of taxable income = net business income + non-operating income — non-operating expenditure.

4. Other lines of operation:
For other lines of operations, refer to the above-mentioned formulae

for calculation.

Article 9:   The following items shall not be counted as cost, expense or loss in computing the amount of taxable income:

1.   expenditure on the purchase or construction of machinery, equipment, buildings, facilities and other fixed assets;

2.   expenditure on the purchase of intangible assets;

3.   interest on capital;

4.   income tax payment and local surtax payment;

5.   penalty for illegal operations and losses in the form of confiscated property;

6.   overdue tax payment and tax penalty;

7.   losses from windstorms, floods and fire risks covered by insurance indemity;

8.   donations and contributions other than those for public welfare and relief purposes:

9.   that part of the entertainment expenses for operating purposes above the quota of three per thousand of total sale income in the tax year or above the quota of ten per thousand of the total operational income and those entertainment expenses that are not relevent to production and operation.

Article 10:   Depreciation of fixed assets in use shall be calculated on an annual basis. Fixed assets of joint ventures cover houses, buildings, machinery and other mechanical apparatus, means of transport and other equipment for the purpose of production with useful life of more than one year. But items, with a per-unit value of less than Rmb 500 yuan and a short useful life can be itemized as expenses according to the actual number in use.

Article 11:   Fixed assets shall be assessed according to the original price.

Fixed assets used as investment, the original price shall be the price agreed upon by the participants at the time of investment.

For purchased fixed assets, the original price shall be the purchase price plus transport fees, installation expenses and other related expenses incurred before they are put to use.

For self-made and self-built fixed assets, the original price shall be the actual expenditures incurred in the course of manufacture or construction.

Article 12:   In depreciating fixed assets, the residual value shall be assessed first and deducted from the original price, the principle being making the residual value at 10 per cent of the original price; those requiring to retain a little or no residual value, shall be submitted for approval to the local tax authorities.

The depreciation of fixed assets shall generally be computed in average by the method of straight line.

Article 13:   The useful life for computing depreciation of fixed assets is as follows:

1.   the minimum useful life for houses and buildings is 20 years;

2.   the minimum useful life for trains, ships, machines and equipment and other facilities for the purpose of production is 10 years;

3.   the minimum useful life for electronic equipment and means of transport other than trains and ships is 5 years.

For cases where the fixed assets of joint ventures, owing to special reasons, need to accelerate depreciation or where methods of depreciation need to be modified, applications shall be submitted by the said ventures to the local tax authorities for examination and then relayed level by level to the Ministry of Finance of the People's Republic of China for approval.

Article 14: Expenditures arising from the increase of value of fixed assets in use as a result of technical reform shall not be listed as expense.

The fixed assets continuing in use after full depreciation shall no longer be depreciated.

Article 15: The balance of the gain of joint ventures derived from sale of fixed assets at the current price after the net sum of non-depreciated assets or the residual value is deducted shall enter the year's loss and gain account.

Article 16: Intangible assets such as technical know-how, patent right, ownership of trade marks, copyright, ownership of sites and other royalties used as investment shall be assessed by amortization according to the sums provided in the agreements or contracts from the year they begin in use; for the intangible assets that are bought in at a fixed price, the actual payment shall be assessed from the year they are put in use.

The above-mentioned intangible assets with provision of time limit for use, shall be assessed by amortization according to the provision of time limit for use; those without the provision shall be assessed by amortization in ten years.

Article 17: Expenses arising during the period of preparation for a joint venture shall be amortized after it goes into production or business, with the amount of amortization not exceeding 20 per cent each year.

Article 18: Inventory of merchandise, raw materials, in-production products, semi-finished products, finished products and by-products shall be computed according to the cost price. For the method of computation, the joint ventures may choose one of the following: first-in first-out, shifting average and weighted average. In those cases where a change in the method of computation is necessary, it shall be submitted for approval to the local tax authorities.

Article 19: Income tax to be paid in quarterly installments as prescribed in Article 8 of the Tax Law may be computed as one-fourth of the planned annual profit or the actual income in the preceding year.

Article 20: Joint ventures shall file their income tax returns and their final accounting statements with the local tax authorities within the prescribed period irrespective of profit or loss in the tax year and send the reports on auditing by the chartered public accountants registered in the People's Republic of China.

The accounting statements submitted by branches of joint ventures within China to their head offices shall be submitted to the local tax authorities at the same time for reference.

Article 21: Joint ventures shall file tax returns within the time limit set by the Tax Law. In case of failure to submit the tax returns within the prescribed time limit owing to special circumstances, application should be submitted in the said time limit, and the time limit may be appropriately extended upon the approval of the local tax authorities. The final day of the time limit for tax payment and filing tax returns may be extended if it falls upon an official holiday.

Article 22: Income of joint ventures in foreign currency shall be assessed according to the exchange rate quoted by the State General Administration of Foreign Exchange Control on the day when the tax payment certificates are made out and shall be taxed in renminbi.

Article 23: The accounting on the acrual basis shall be practised for revenue and expenditure of joint ventures. All accounting records shall be accurate and perfect and shall have lawful vouchers as the basis for entry account.

Article 24: The method of finance and accounting of joint ventures shall be submitted to local tax authorities for reference.
When the method of finance and accounting of joint ventures contradicts the provisions of the Tax Law, tax payments shall be computed according to the provisions of the Tax Law.

Article 25: Voucher for accounting books and reports used by joint ventures shall be recorded in the Chinese language or in both Chinese and foreign languages.
Accounting vouchers, accounting books and reports shall be kept for at least 15 years.

Article 26: Sales invoices and business receipts shall be submitted for approval to the local tax authorities before they are used.

Article 27: Officials sent by tax authorities shall produce identification cards when investigating the financial affairs, accounting book and tax situation of a joint venture and undertake to keep secret.

Article 28: Tax authorities may inpose a penalty of not more than Rmb 5,000 yuan on a joint venture which has violated the provisions of Articles 9, 11 and 12 of the Tax Law according to the seriousness of the case.

Article 29: Tax authorities may impose a penalty of not more than Rmb 5,000 yuan on a joint venture which has violated the provisions of paragraph 2 of Article 25, and Article 26 of these detailed rules and regulations.

Article 30: Tax authorities shall serve notices on cases involving penalty in accordance with the relevant provisions of the Tax Law and these detailed rules and regulations.

Article 31: When a joint venture applies for reconsideration in accordance with the provisions of Article 15 of the Tax Law, the tax authorities concerned are required to make decisions within three months after receiving the application.

Article 32: In Income tax paid abroad by joint ventures or its branches on their income earned outside China may be credited against the amount of income tax to be paid by their head offices upon presenting the foreign tax payment certificate. But the credit amount shall not exceed the payable tax on the income abroad computed according to the tax rate prescribed by China's Tax Law.

Article 33: Income tax returns and tax payment certificate used by joint ventures are to be printed by the General Taxation Bureau of the Ministry of Finance of the People's Republic of China.

Article 34: The right of interpretating the provisions of these detailed rules and regulations resides in the Ministry of Finance of the People's Republic of China.

Article 35: These detailed rules and regulations come into force on the same date as the publication and enforcement of the "Income Tax Law of the People's Republic of China Concerning Joint Ventures with Chinese and Foreign Investment".

The Decision of the Amendments to the Income Tax Law of the People's Republic of China on Joint Ventures Using Chinese and Foreign Investment

(Passed by the Standing Committee of the National People's Congress on 2nd September, 1983)

The Decree of the Chairmen of People's Republic of China No. 8

The decision of the amendments to "The Income Tax Law of the People's Republic of China on Joint Ventures Using Chinese and Foreign Investment" has been passed by the second session of the Standing Committee of the Sixth National People's Congress of the People's Republic of China on 2nd September, 1983. The amendments are now announced for implementation.

Chairman
The People's Republic of China

Li Zhinian

Amendments

The Second Session of the Standing Committee of the Sixth National People's Congress of the People's Republic of China has decided to amend "The Income Tax Law of the People Republic of China on Joint Ventures Using Chinese and Foreign Investment" as follows:

1. Paragrap 1 of Article 5 "A newly established joint venture scheduled to operate for a period of 10 years or more may, upon approval of the tax authorities for an application filed by the enterprise, be exempted from income tax in the first profitmaking year and allowed 50% reduction in the second and third years" will be amended as "Joint venture scheduled to operate for a period of 10 years or more may, upon approval of the tax authorities for an application filed by the enterprise, be exempted from income tax in the second and third years of the first profitmaking year and allowed 50% reduction in the third, fourth and fifth years.

2. In "Article 8 Income tax on joint ventures shall be levied on an annual basis and paid in quarterly instalments. Such provisional payment shall be made within 15 days after the end of each quarter. The final settlement shall be made within three months after the end of a tax year. Excess payments shall be refunded by the tax authorities or deficiencies made good by the taxpayer", "The final settlement shall be made within three months after the end of a tax year" will be amended as "The final settlement shall be made within five months after the end of a tax year."

3. In "Article 9 Joint ventures shall file their provisional income tax returns with the local tax authorities within the period prescribed for provisional payments. The taxpayer shall file its final annual income tax return together with its final accounts within three months after the end of the tax year", "within three month after the end of the tax year will be amended to "within four months after the end of the tax year.

Editor's Notes

The related Articles of the Income Tax Law of the People's Republic of China Concerning Joint Ventures with Chinese and Foreign Investment.

Article 5 A newly established joint venture scheduled to operate for a period of 10 years or more may, upon approval of the tax authorities for an application filed by the enterprise, be exempted from income tax in the first profitmaking year and allowed a 50% reduction in the second and third years.

In "Article 8 Income tax on joint ventures shall be levied on an annual basis and paid in quarterly instalments. Such provisional payment shall be made within 15 days after the end of each quarter. The final settlement shall be made within three months after the end of a tax year. Excess payments shall be refunded by the tax authorities or deficiencies made good by the taxpayer"

In "Article 9 Joint ventures shall file their provisional income tax returns with the local tax authorities within the period prescribed for provisional payments. The taxpayer shall file its final annual income tax returned together with its final accounts within three months after the end of the tax year"

Appendix

Provisional Regulations on China-foreign Cooperative Design Engineering Project

(Approved by the State Council on March 27th, 1986)
(Promulgated by the State Planning Commission and the Ministry
of Foreign Economic Relation & Trade on June 5th, 1986)

Article 1 : The present Regulations are enacted in order to strengthen the administration over the cooperative design engineering projects by Chinese designing institute and foreign designing institute (hereinafter referred to as "cooperative design") with a view to promoting the development of activity of cooperative design.

Article 2 : Chinese designing institute shall participate in the cooperative design for the designing of the engineering project with Chinese investment or with China-foreign joint investment and foreign loan, which needs to be entrusted to the foreign designing institute for the design thereof.

Engineering project with Chinese investment capable of being designed by Chinese designing institute is not allowed to be entrusted to foreign designing institute for the design thereof, but is allowed to import the part of designing technology related to the said engineering project or to derive technical and economic consultation from foreign designing institute.

The designing of foreign-invested engineering project in China shall on principle be entrusted to Chinese designing institute for the designing thereof. In case the investing party requires the engineering project to be entrusted to foreign designing institute for the designing thereof, Chinese designing institute shall participate in the cooperative design.

Article 3 : The responsible department or construction unit shall, simultaneously with the submission of the project proposal or task assignment, make the application for the engineering which needs cooperative design according to the limit of authority over the said project, and only after abtaining the approval thereof can the work begin. Small-scale project shall be approved by the responsible department or by the planning

Article 7: Cooperative design may include the whole process from the survey of the engineering project to the engineering design, or covers only a certain stage thereof for the cooperation.

Article 8: The major designing party shall propose the model-selection for equipment and the selection of material for the cooperative-designing project through the consultation between the two participants of the cooperative design; and preferential treatment shall be given to the candidancy of chinese equipment and material with the prerequisite of ensuring the production technique and technology or the requirement for the application thereof.

Article 9: Cooperative design shall adopt advanced and suitable standards and norms, and the both participants of cooperative design shall provide each other the model to be adopted.

Article 10: Both participants of the cooperative design shall have joint check up on the design conditions and be responsible for the quality of design. After the both participants of the cooperative design have completed the design, the said design shall be submitted to the entrusting party for examination and approval thereof.

Article 11: The entrusting party of the project shall provide with compensation, after going through the procedure of ratification with the various responsible departments according to different kinds, the foreign designing institute with the needed fundamental data, such as topography, geology, hydrology, climate, environment investigation, etc. in the course of cooperative design. The user of the said data is not allowed to transfer the data to the third party.

Article 12: In the course of cooperative design, the both participants thereof shall strictly observe their own obligations, and, in case of failure to reach the contracted requirement, shall undertake the responsibility according to the contract.

Article 13: Both participants of cooperative design shall pay due tax according to the related Chinese tax law for their income deriving from the designing.

Article 14: Cooperative design conducted between designing institute from Hong Kong or Macao and the designing institute in the interior of China shall be treated in light of the present Regulations.

Article 15: The State Planning Commission shall be responsible for the interpretation of the present Regulations.

Article 16: The present Regulations shall enter into force on July 1st, 1986.

commission of province, autonomous region or city directly under the Central Government according to the relation of auspices. As regards large or medium-scale projects, the responsible department or province, autonomous region or city directly under the Central Government, according to relation of auspices, shall put forward the opinion after examination thereof and then submit to the State Planning Commission for examination and approval thereof. As to the extraordinarily large project, the State Planning Commission shall organize the initial examination and put forward the opinion of the said examination, and then submit to the State Council for the approval thereof.

The responsible department or the construction unit of the engineering project, while selecting the optimum foreign designing institute, shall select the Chinese designing institute for the cooperative designing.

Article 4: Only the foreign designing institute which has passed the designing credential examination can undertake the design task of Chinese engineering project. The responsible department of the project shall conduct the examination for whether or not the credentials of the foreign designing institute are qualified.

The major content for the examination for the qualification of foreign designing institute includes the following:
(1) The designing credentials registry certificate issued by the country or region where the foreign designing institute is located;
(2) Technical level, technical force, and state of technical equipment;
(3) Qualifications and record of service in undertaking engineering designing and the state of management and administration;
(4) Social reputation.

Article 5: Both parties participating in the cooperative design must conclude the cooperative design contract to delimit the rights and obligations of each party.

The said cooperative-design contract shall cover the following content:
(1) Names, nationalities, major business offices, as well as the names, ranks, nationalities and addresses of the legal representatives of the both participants of the cooperative designing.
(2) Purpose, range and time limit of the cooperation;
(3) Form of cooperation as well as the requirement on the content, depth, quality and work progress of the said design;
(4) The currency composition, methods for distribution and ratio of distribution between the both participants concerning the fee of the said design;
(5) Method of liaison for work between the both participants of the cooperative designing;
(6) Liability on violation of contract;
(7) Method for solving the dispute arising with respect to the contract;
(8) Conditions for the contract to enter into force;
(9) Date and place of the concluding of the contract.

Article 6: Simultaneously with the conclusion of the contract for cooperative designing, the selected major designing party of the cooperative designing shall conclude the full-charge contract with the party which entrusts the project.

Interpretation

Circular of the Ministry or Finance Concerning Some Questions about the Income Tax of Joint Ventures Comprising Chinese and Foreign Investment

(Issued on June 8, 1981)

1.   *Concerning the refund of tax on reinvestment:*

   a.   *According to the provisions of Article 6 of the Income Tax Law Concerning Joint Ventures with Chinese and Foreign Investment, partners eligible to apply for a refund of tax paid on reinvestment should include Chinese partners as well as foreign partners. The scope of reinvestment to apply for tax refund should be confined to the reinvestment in the same joint ventures in China or other joint ventures using Chinese and foreign investment as well as the use of the profits shared to set up new joint ventures with Chinese companies or enterprises. Reinvestment in operations with one's sole investment or in cooperative production or cooperative operations is not eligible for tax refund.*
   b.   *When a joint venture draws from the reserve fund or enterprise development fund to pruchase fixed assets according to the provisions of the Law Concerning Joint Ventures involving Chinese and Foreign Investment, this means using statutory funds to expand reproduction and does not belong to the scope of reinvestment applying for the tax refund.*
   c.   *In applying for tax refund on reinvestment, a partner should obtain a certificate written by the enterprise that has accepted the investment. The said certificate must include the source of the investment fund, the amount of investment and the time limit of investment, and enclose a copy of the agreement or contract on the said investment. A partner who gains this share of profit from a joint venture in place A and invests it in a joint venture in place B or uses it to open a new joint venture in place B with a Chinese company or enterprise, may apply, on the strength of the above certificate, for tax refund on the reinvestment with the tax authorities at the place he has paid the tax.*

d.   The portion of income tax already paid on which a partner applies for refund as reinvestment out of his share of profit, does not include the local surtax levied on the assessed income tax. According to the provisions of Paragraph 2, Article 3 of the Detailed Rules and Regulations for the Implementation of the Income Tax Law Concerning Joint Ventures with Chinese and Foreign Investment, it is up to the People's government of the province, autonomous region or municipality where the joint venture is located to decide whether the local income tax should be reduced or exempted on special grounds.
The following are formulae for calculating the tax amount to be applied for a refund on reinvestment:

$$\text{Formula 1: } [\text{reinvestment amount} + (1 - \frac{33}{100})]$$
$$x\frac{30}{100} \times \frac{40}{100} = \text{tax refund amount}$$

$$\text{Formula 2: reinvestment amount} \times \frac{17.91}{100}$$
$$= \text{tax refund amount}$$

e.   If foreign partner remits aboard the amount of tax refund on reinvestment, it shall not be taxed as a remittance of profit.

2.   Concerning the taxation on profit remitted abroad:

When a foreign partner is goint to remit abroad his share of profit obtained from the joint venture, the remittance handling unit shall, without exception, withhold an income tax of 10% of the amount of profit to be remitted, according to the provisions of the Detailed Rules and Regulations for the Implementation of the Income Tax Law Concerning Joint Ventures with Chinese and Foreign Investment.

3.   Concerning the time limit for tax reduction
or remission for new joint ventures:

For a new joint venture to run for more than 10 years, if it starts operation in the middle of a tax year and makes a profit the same year, it should be regarded as the first profit-making year and is exempted from income tax. As for isolated, special cases, the enterprise may file a request and the local tax authorities shall deal with it in accordance with the actual circumstances.

4.   Concerning the calculation of credit limit:

According to the provisions of Article 16 of the Income Tax Law Concerning Joint Ventures with Chinese and Foreign Investment and Article 32 of the Detailed Rules and Regulations, the income tax paid abroad by a joint venture and its branches can be credited against the amount of tax income the head office is due to pay; but the credit amount must not exceed the amount of tax on the income obtained abroad calculated according to the tax rate stipulated in the Chinese tax law. This credit limit should be calculated on a country-by-country basis, that is, income derived from profits abroad such as interest and royalties can be calculated for credit limit by countries and not by categories; for a tax paid in a given country, the credit limit shall be calculated out of the amount of income earned from that country according to the tax rate stipulated in the Chinese tax law.

5.   Concerning the taxation on dividends and bonuses obtained by joint ventures:

The dividends and bonuses obtained outside China by a joint venture should be lumped together by the head office with the incomes from production and operation and be taxed. The tax already paid at the time of receiving the said dividends and bonuses abroad, can be credited against the assessed tax amount in China. For the dividends and bonuses obtained in China, such as those obtained by joint venture A for its investment in joint venture B, if the income tax is already paid at joint venture B according to the regulations of the tax law, then the sum shall not be included in the yearly profit of joint venture A for calculating the income tax.

6.   Concerning accelerated depreciation of fixed assets:

The minimum period for depreciation of fixed assets in joint ventures has been listed in three categories in the Detailed Rules and Regulations. These have taken into consideration the fast development of modern production technology and the universal practice of accelerated depreciation in various countries of the world, so they basically suit the actual needs of property renewal and capital recovery. Therefore, it is generally not allowed to be less than the depreciation period prescribed in the Detailed Rules and Regulations. Only in certain special cases is it permissable to apply for accelerated depreciation. In actual implementation, the following points can serve as reference for the time being, but must be strictly controlled:
    a.   The period of joint operation is shorter than the depreciation period of fixed assets as stipulated in the tax law and the property after the expiration of the joint operation period will become the property of the Chinese side (for instance, the period of the joint operation is generally 10 years for the cooperative construction and operation of a tourist hotel and, when the capital is recouped within this joint operation period, the hotel will be turned over to the Chinese side. In such circumstances, the enterprise can be allowed to apply for accelerated depreciation);
    b.   Strong acid, alkaline or corrosive equipment and factory buildings and structures subject to vibration and oscillation throughout the year;
    c.   Machinery or equipment operating around the clock year in and year out with a view to raising the utilization rate and stepping up utilization intensity.

Editor's Notes

Since the Income Tax Law Concerning Joint Ventures with Chinese and Foreign Investment and the Detailed Rules and Regulations for the Implementation of the Law were promulgated and enforced, various localities have raised a number of specific questions concerning policy matters and demanded clarification. These questions were discussed at a recent meeting on tax work involving foreigners, attended by representatives of six provinces (municipalities).

Interpretation

Tax Cuts for Joint Ventures

1.   The current industrial and commercial tax, instead of the former consolidated industrial and commercial tax, will be paid by joint ventures and such tax will be exemptd or reduced for joint ventures suffering a loss in manufacturing export products under normal operations.

2.   Import duties and business tax will be exempted for the following items: machinery and equipment and other materials imported by foreign investors as part of their share of capital, equipment and other materials imported by joint ventures with registered capital, or equipment and supplies which are not available in China and are imported as additional capital within the scope covered by contracts. Import duties and industrial and commercial tax will also be exempted on raw materials, auxiliary materials, parts and components and packaging materials imported for manufacturing export products.

3.   Income tax will be exempted for joint ventures in the first two profit-making years, and a 60% reduction will be allowed in the third year. The joint venture income tax law provides for income tax exemption for such enterprises in the first profit-making year and an allowance of a 50% reduction in the second year.

4.   The government has lifted restrictions on the proportion of joint venture products for domestic sale, the proportion for domestic sale of products urgently needed by the country may be increased or such products may be sold mainly on domestic markets. It is not necessary to ask the enterprises themselves to achieve a foreign exchange balance.

5.   If joint ventures buy raw and other materials in China, the price will be the same as for domestic manufacturers and be paid in Renminbi and the same applies to the supply of water, electricity, fuel and oil for transportation. But for precious metals used for manufacturing export products and petroleum, coal, timber and

other materials which have a big price difference between the domestic and international markets, the domestic prices will only apply to the portion that is used for producing products to be sold in China.
6.   The government has also decided to simplify the entry procedures for resident foreign employees of joint ventures and allow them to bring in the necessary means of transport and office equipment, but import duties will have to be paid according to regulations. Joint ventures' purchase of office equipment and daily necessities in China will not be subjected to restrictions as applied to domestic instituational purchasing.

Editor's Notes

The decision was announced on April 8 1982 by Li Hao, spokesman for the State Economic Commission, at a press conference attended by Chinese and foreign journalists.

Interpretation

Income Tax Law Concerning Joint Venture

The Finance Ministry, has recently made some statements among which, the Ministry has made its decision on tax related to those joint venture enterprises approved before the promulgation of the "Income Tax Law of the PRC concerning Joint Ventures with Chinese & Foreign Investment" (i.e. September 10 1980), hereinafter referred to as the new law).

The Finance Ministry said, before the promulgation of the new law, certain tax rates of those joint venture projects between Chinese authorities and foreign business are higher than the announced tax rate of the new law whereas, some of them are lower. In order to solve these matters, the Ministry has set up the following regulations.

1. In principle, the Finance Ministry will recognize the validity of any tax rate and conditions governing reduction or exemption or stipulated in joint venture agreements approved officially by the State Council (國務院), the Foreign Investments Commission (外資局), the Provincial People's Governments (省人民政府), even though those tax rates are not identical with the new law. The contracted parties to the respective joint venture projects, however must file all pertinent documents plus a copy of the contract with the local tax authority. The income tax rate for those contracts signed before the new law shall remain as it is, but not during any extension period that may be negotiated later, unless it is higher than the rate fixed by the new law, whereby, it can be adjusted from January 1, 1981 by following the new law.

2. If no local surtax was mentioned in contracts signed before the promulgation of the new law (i.e. September 10 1980), no such tax is payable over the duration of the contract period.

3. The new law shall apply to all joint venture protocols that had been

preliminarily agreed upon prior to the new law but were officially approved after the new law.
The new law shall apply to all other taxes, exemptions or taxes related to joint venture enterprises.

Interpretation

Notice of the State Council Concerning the Taxation of Chinese-Foreign Joint Ventures and Cooperative Projects

(September 21, 1982)

On September 10, 1980, the National People's Congress promulgated "The Income Tax Law Concerning Chinese-Foreign Joint Ventures" and "The Individual Income Tax Law;" on December 13, 1981, "The Income Tax Law Concerning Foreign Enterprises" was promulgated. Before the promulgation of these tax laws, some areas, departments or enterprises had entered into the contracts of joint ventures or cooperative projects with foreign or Hong Kong firms with the approval of the state authorities and some of the contracts contain clauses concerning tax liabilities. With this view, the Bureau of Revenue of the Ministry of Finance has given notice that the original clauses stipulated in the contracts concerning tax liabilities shall still be executed. But it is reported that some disputes still exist. For the sake of the proper implementation of policies, a notice is given as follows:

1   The original clauses stipulated in contracts shall be executed in the event that enterprise income tax liabilities under preferential clauses are listed, or when clauses for tax liabilities preferential treatment are clearly indicated for import materials required in the course of the construction of the projects contracted for by joint ventures or cooperative projects with foreign or Hong Kong firms with the approval of the state authorities before the promulgation of "The Income Tax Law Concerning Chinese-Foreign Joint Ventures" and "The Income Tax Law Concerning Foreign Enterprises."

2   The original clauses stipulated in contracts shall also be executed in case the above contracts contain the clauses of tax liabilities preferential treatment given to the income deriving from patent, copyright or other royalties obtained by foreign or Hong Kong firms.

3   The original clauses stipulted in contracts shall be executed in case the clauses of tax liabilities preferentcial treatment are included for individual income in the contracts approved by the state authorities before the promulgation of "The Individual Income Tax Law."

The above three clauses shall be executed until the expiration of the time limits originally stipulated in the contracts. If the time limits for the contracts are to be extended after the expiration, all taxes shall be paid in accordance with the provisions in "The Income Tax Law Concerning Chinese-Foreign Joint Ventures," "The Income Tax Law Concerning Foreign Enterprises" and "The Individual Income Tax Law." We hope the financial and tax departments shall execute them in accordance with this Notice. The Ministry of Finance shall be responsible for interpreting the specific problems in the course of execution.

Interpretation

Explanation Concerning the Scope of Fixed Asset

(Cui Shiu (81) No. 112)
(Issued by the Revenue Bureau of the Ministry of Finance on December 1 1981)

The categories of fixed assets listed in Article 10 of the "Detailed Rules and Regulations for The Implementation of The Income Tax Law of concerning Joint Ventures with Chinese and Foreign Investment" are referred to those assets including productive and unproductive assets which have a useful like of utilization period more than one year. But those objects with an utilization period of less than one year or value of not more than Renminbi 500 can be listed as fee according to practical usage.

Interpretation

Stipulations Concerning the Levy of Tax on Dividend & Bonus Gained by a Joint Venture Enterprises in China and Abroad

(Cui Shui (81) No. 188)
(Issued by the Ministry of Finance 8th June, 1981)

A Joint Venture enterprises shall have its head office combining dividend and bonus gained outside China with other profits gained by production and business in order to pay a grand total of its profit tax. If profit tax of these dividend and bonus have already been paid outside China, the amount can be set off from the tax which should be paid in China. With regard to the dividend and bonus gained in China, if joint venture enterprise A gains the dividend and bonus by investment in B's joint venture enterprise and B has already paid its profit tax according to the provisions of the tax law, A may exclude such dividend and bonus from the calculation of A's profits for the financial year.

Interpretation

Explanation Concerning the Levy of Profit Tax Remitted from China

(Cui Shui (81) No. 188)
(Issued by the Ministry of Finance 8th June, 1981)

When a foreign participant in a Joint Venture, who wants to remit its share of profits from China, the remitting agency shall, according to the provisions of the "Detailed Rules and Regulations for the Implementation of the Income Tax Law of the People's Republic of China Concerning Joint Venture with Chinese and Foreign Investment", withhold 10% from the remittance.

Interpretation

Stipulations Concerning the Tax Exemption for Remitting from China the Tax Refund of Profit Reinvestment.

(Cui Shui (81) No. 188)
(Issued by the Ministry of Finance 8th June, 1981)

A foreign participant in a joint venture who wants to remit from China its tax refund of profit re-investment will not be required to pay any tax because of the remittance of its share of profit.

Interpretation

Stipulation Concerning the Tax Reduction and Exemption Period for Newly Established Joint Business Enterprises

(Cui Shui (81) No. 188)
(Issued by the Ministry of Finance 8th June, 1981)

If a newly established Joint business enterprise which has a more than ten years joint business period commences business during the middle of the year and gains profits in the same year, then the year will be regarded as the first profit making year, tax exemption will be granted. Should there be any individual special situtation the enterprises may submit application and the local tax authority will consider the actual situation and deal with it.

Interpretation

Stipulations Concerning the Levy of Tax of those Joint Venture Enterprises Approved Before the Promulgation of the Law

(Cui Shiu (80) No. 187)
(Issued by the Ministry of Finance
5th November 1981)

1.   *Before the promulgation of the tax law, those joint venture contracts approved by official documents of the State council, Management Committee of Foreign Investment or People's Government at provincial level, the confirmed income tax rate, tax reduction and exemption contained therein, if inconsistent with the law, shall be acknowledged in principle. However, the unit to the contract shall file the related document and a copy of the contract with the tax authority via local tax authority. If the tax rate confirmed in the contract is lower than the rate stipulated in the law, the tax rate shall be executed in accordance with such rate confirmed in the contract during the period stipulated in the contract (excluding the entension of the contract period, hereinafter will refer the same)*

2.   *If the levy of local income tax is not confirmed in those joint venture enterprise with contracts approved before the promulgation of the tax law, such levy may be exempted in the execution of the contract during the stipulated period.*

3.   *Protocol of the joint venture enterprise contract signed previously and approved after the implementation date of the tax law, should be executed in accordance with the tax law.*

Interpretation

Stipulations Concerning the Levy of Individual Income Tax on Chinese Personnel Who Work for the Joint Venture Enterprises

(Cui Shui (80) No. 60)
(Issued on 9th December 1980 by the General Customs Bureau
of the Ministry of Finance)

In joint venture enterprises using Chinese and foreign Investment, working personnel, regardless they are Chinese or foreigner, will have to pay their individual income tax for the portion of income which exceed Renminbi 800 yuan. Since Chinese and foreign working personnel are treated equally, Chinese working personnel are requested to pay individual income tax if they are paid more than Renminbi 800 yuan monthly by the joint venture enterprises.

Forms & Documentation

Joint Venture Enterprise Using Chinese & Foreign Investment

Quarterly Tax Return
Filling Instructions

1.   This form is suitable for joint venture enterprise in the estimation of tax payment for a quarter of the year. This form should be filled in by joint venture enterprise within 15 days after the end of each quarter and submitted to the local tax authority, i.e. April 15, July 15, Oct 15 of each year and Jan. 15 of the next year will be the last dates for submission of the form. The last day for submission can be extended if it happens to be a public holiday.

2.   If, for some special reasons, a joint venture enterprise cannot submit this form within the stipulated period, it should, before the deadline of the submission period, apply to the local tax authority, which may give it approval to submit the form at a later date.

3.   Explanations of the columns in this form:

    a)   Date of Establishment: Fill in the date for the commencement of production and business of the joint venture enterprise

    b)   Kind of Business: Fill in the kind of business operated by the joint venture enterprise e.g. metallurgical industry, agricultural machines, electric power, pharmaceutical production, tourism, transportation, trust etc. A joint venture engaged in mining industry should list out the major items of its production.

    c)   Registered Capital: Fill in the amount of capital registered with the General Administration of Industry & Commerce. If the Capital is in foreign currency, the type and amount of this foreign currency should be filled in.

    e)   Capital actually received: Fill in the capital actually received in the account of this quarter. If the registered capital is in foreign currency, the type and amount of the foreign currency should be filled in.

f) License No: Fill in the License number issued by the General Administration of Industry and Commerce.

g) Number of employees: Fill in the number of ordinary staff members in the Column for "Staff members." Fill in the number of senior staff in the Column for "Others"

h) previous year income tax (losses): Fill in the income tax of the previous year by adjustment in accordance with the provisions of the tax Laws use red ink to fill in the losses.

i) Planned profit of this year: Fill in the planned profit of this year as scheduled by the joint venture enterprise.

j) Accumulation of tax already paid before this quarter: Fill in the accumulated amount of the estimated tax payment of the previous quarters of the year (Excluding the amount of this quarter). When submitting the estimated tax payment of the first quarter, this column can be left blank.

People's Republic of China
Ministry of Finance
General Taxation Bureau

Joint Venture Quarterly Income Tax Return

Form J-1

For....... Quarter of the Calendar Year 19 ....

Date of Establishment
.... , 19....................

Date Filed: ...., 19...... ....   Monetary Unit R.M.B.Y

Venture's Name		Address	City or County		Tel. No.
			Number and Street		

Kind of Business		Registered Capital		Paid-in Capital		License No.

Branch's Name	Address	Number of Employees							
		Total		Workers		Staff Members		Others	
		Number	Including Foreigners	Number	Including Foreigners	Number	Including Foreigners	Number	Including Foreigners

Last Year's Taxable Income (Loss)	Estimated Quarterly Tax Payments of Last Year		The Planned Profit for this Taxable Year	Cumulative Amount of Tax Paid for the Year Before this Quarter		Estimated Tax Payment for this Quarter	
	Amount	Including Local Income Tax		Amount	Including Local Income Tax	Amount	Including Local Income Tax

(J. V. Seal)   Responsible Officer   Accountant General
                     (Signature or Seal)   (Signature or Seal)

(Hereunder to be Filled by the Tax Authority):

Receiving Date		Inspection Date	
Inspection Record			
License No.		Tax Payment Date	

Tax Authority: Person in Charged:

Forms & Documentation

Joint Venture Enterprise Using Chinese & Foreign Investment

Annual Tax Return
Filling Instructions

1. This form is suitable for use by joint venture enterprise which has to pay its annual profit tax. The amount which should be declared for the year include the profit which it receives inside and outside Chinese territories.
2. This form should be filled in by joint venture enterprise within 3 months after the end of the year and submitted to the local tax authority i.e. before March 31 of the next financial year. The last day for submission can be extended if it happens to be a public holiday.
3. At the time of submitting this form, the joint venture enterprise should also file an account of its annual asset and debt, profit and loss, cost and other related items. Detailed explanation materials should be attached. If there is any foreign tax or credit previous years' losses to be covered.
4. A joint venture enterprise, regardless of its making profit or suffering loss in this financial year, should submit this form together with the necessary explanation materials to the local tax authority.
5. If, for some special reasons, a joint venture enterprise cannot submit this form within the stipulated period, it should, before the deadline of the submission period, apply to the local tax authority, which may give it approval to submit the form at a later date.
6. Explanations of the columns in this form:
   a)   Taxable year: Fills in the calender year
   b)   Business period: Fill in the business dates of this year, e.g. from January 1, to Dec. 31. If annual days are less than one year, then the actual business days

should be filled in.

   c)   Date of Establishment: Fill in the date for the commencement of production and business of the joint venture enterprise

   d)   Kind of Business: Fill in the kind of business operated by the joint venture enterprise e.g. metallurgical industry, agricultural machines, electric power, pharmaceutical production, tourism, transportation, trust etc. A joint venture engaged in mining industry should list out the major items of its production.

   e)   Registered Capital: Fill in the amount of capital registered with the General Administration of Industry and Commerce. If the capital is in foreign currency, the type and amount of this foreign currency should be filled in.

   f)   License No: Fill in the License number issued by the the General Administration of Industry and Commerce.

   g)   Number of employees: Fill in the number of ordinary staff members in the column for "staff members". Fill in the number of senior staff in the column for "Others".

   h)   Operating revenue: Fill in the annual income gained from sales or the total annual income gained from business.

   i)   Profit or Loss: Fill in the annual profit or loss of the enterprise any adjustment in accordance with the provision of the tax law (including the profit gained by branch offices). If there is a loss, use red ink to fill in. The materials for explaining after adjusted items should be filed together with the declaration form

   j)   Previous years loss to be covered: Fill in the previous years' loss to be covered by this year. The materials for explaining which previous year(s) and amount of losses to be covered should be filed as well.

   k)   Taxable Income = net profit − previous years losses

   l)   Income Tax = total income tax due x tax rate to be covered

   m)   Income Tax after Deduction = income tax − (income tax x reductive rate)

   n)   Total Annual Tax Due = Income tax after reduction + local income tax

   o)   Tax Due After Foreign Tax Credit = total annual tax due − foreign tax credit

   p)   Income Tax Due or Over Payment = tax due after foreign tax credit − estimated tax payment for the year

People's Republic of China
Ministry of Finance
General Taxation Bureau

Joint Venture Annual Income Tax Return

Form: J-2

Taxable Year: Calendar Year 19...........

Date of Establishment
................., 19......................

Business Period: Beginning............, Ending.............

Date Filed: ...., 19..................

Monetary Unit: R.M.B.¥

Venture's Name		Address	City or County			Tel. No.
			Number and Street			

Kind of Business		Registered Capital		Paid-in Capital		License No.	

Branch's Name	Address	Number of Employees							
		Total		Workers		Staff Members		Others	
		Number	Including Foreigners	Number	Including Foreigners	Number	Including Foreigners	Number	Including Foreigners

Computation of Tax	Operating Revenue	Profit or Loss	Previous Years Losses to be Covered	Taxable Income	Tax Rate	Income Tax	Reductive Rate	Income Tax after Reduction	Local Income Tax	Total Annual Tax Due

Computation of Tax Due or Over Payment	Total Annual Tax Due		Less: Foreign Tax Credit	Tax Due after Foreign Tax Credit		Less: Estimated Tax Payment for the Year		Income Tax Due or Over Payment	
	Amount	Including Local Income Tax		Amount	Including Local Income Tax	Amount	Including Local Income Tax	Amount	Including Local Income Tax

The return is accompanied by venture's balance sheet, profit and loss statement and other documents necessary for calculating income and income tax due thereon, including computation of tax abroad and previous year's losses to be covered.

(J. V. Seal)   Responsible Officer (Signature or Seal)   Accountant General (Signature or Seal)

(Hereunder to be Filled by the Tax Authority):

Receiving Date		Inspection Date	
Inspection Record			
License No.		Tax Payment Date	

Tax Authority: Person in Charged:

Forms & Documentation

Steps on How to Set up a Joint Venture in China

Step I

To decide whether the proposed project of a joint venture is feasible
Points to be decided upon:
1.   Projects requiring substantial capital investment
2.   Projects requiring advanced technology unavailable in China, for examples;
electronic, oil drilling
3.   Projects for the manufacture of goods that meet the demand of Chinese
market and which would otherwise have to be imported
4.   Export-oriented projects that upgrade Chinese goods
5.   Export-oriented projects that improve Chinese raw materials

Step II

Considerations in preparing the proposed project
1.   Purpose:
   A.   To define the objective of the venture
   B.   To identify and describe the partners' expected contribution of assets
   C.   To identify projected distribution markets
   D.   To provide preliminary estimates of costs for the venture
   E.   To allow your Chinese partner to estimate equivalent costs within local
pricing system

2. Complexity:
  A. Sufficient to delineate main parameters of the venture
  B. Simple as to be amenable to repeated revision requests

3. Flexibility:
  A. To allow for expansions or modernizations of existing facilities
  B. To allow for maximum domestic procurement
  C. To allow for possible utilization of used machinery
  D. To allow for countertrade obligations by the foreign partner
  E. To develop new export market

Step III

Select your Chinese prospective partner by identifying his strengths and limitations. Your Chinese prospective partner's strengths and limitations are conditioned by the following factors.

1. It depends very much on whether your Chinese prospective partner is a central organization or a provincial organization or a municipal organization.

2. Because of "A" above, except in the aspect of labour supply and local supplies or subcontracting Chinese organization on central, provincial or municipal level are different from one another in the provisions of financing sources, marketing outlets, and flexibility.

3. Before going into details about their differences, the followings are their similarities in the aspect of labour supply:
  A. Limited supply of skilled labour
  B. Low productivity and motivation (Except for those ventures which implement the policy of "renumberation by the number of work done")
  .C. Management is resistive to innovative and production level changes (situation has changed as the Chinese government implements the policy of "employment by contract" and ill behaved worker is liable to be sacked)

4. Similarities in the aspect of local supply or subcontracting:
  A. Regional, usually unreliable procurement
  B. The joint venture may be required to create its own capability or import option

5. Differences in financing sources:
  A. For central organization
    — potential access to national budget allocations
    — access to domestic loans
  B. For provincial organization
    — own discretionary financing
    — access to domestic loans
  C. For municipal organization
    — own discretionary financing
    — access to domestic loans

6. Differences in Marketing outlets:
  A. For central organization
    — Nationwide and/or regional
  B. For provincial organization
    — normally regional

C.   For municipal organization
— normally regional
7.   Differences in flexibility:
A.   For central organization
— confined by national development aims
B.   For provincial organization
— confined by regional marketing aims
C.   For municipal organization
— confined by regional marketing aims

Step IV

Negotiations — how are they usually operated
1.   The Chinese negotiators are straight-forward, thorough on details and excellent hosts
2.   Negotiation meetings cover normal business hours during the day, with a break for lunch.
3.   Because of their inexperience with equity joint venture arrangements, the lack of qualified management personnel and the small margin for economic or investment errors that can be afforded, the approach of Chinese negotiators to joint venture arrangements has been guarded and conservative.
4.   The Chinese negotiators expect the foreign partner to provide them with the basic information on the viability of the venture, inclusive of export projections, required supplies of raw materials, cost analyses based on Western production standard, these are used to estimate equivalent costs within the Chinese pricing system.
5.   The Chinese may use Western proposals as a technique for acquiring a "Free education" and for "brain-picking".
6.   When repeated visits by the Western company are necessary, the Chinese may use several of their negotiators in a sequential mode as a means to educate their technical personnel by compelling the Western party to restate and reexplain information to new groups of technical people.
7.   Foreign negotiators are advised to investigate at an early stage of the negotiations the availability of electric power and the contemplated sourcing of raw materials and supplies for the manufacturing joint venture plant.
8.   The Chinese expect to price the joint venture's products at "world-market price" levels based on estimated price levels in convertible currency for "typical" Western markets, and not reflecting the real social, material and labor costs of production. Export goals may be set by the government.
9.   In pricing the foreign partner's technology contribution to the joint venture, the Chinese negotiators may argue that the technology costs have been previously recovered in prior sales, and therefore, should be provided to the joint venture at a substantial discount.
10.   The general guidelines for pricing the Chinese equity contribution for any rights to rent real estate, buildings, for labor, equipment and utilities to be utilized by the joint venture will reflect "world-market" (I.E. Hong Kong) prices discounted so so to attract foreign investment.
Escalation costs will be provided for in the joint venture contract.
11.   The return on foreign investment is fixed by contract. It may be set at a flat percentage of profits over the entire period of joint ownership or it may be time-

varying, with higher paybacks occurring over the first few years of operation. In another variant, the foreign investor is guaranteed a certain amount of the joint venture's production at agreed upon price formulations for a period of years.

Step V

Preparation of Joint Venture Documents (In sequence)
1.   Letter of Intention
It is optional, legally non-binding and non-exclusive (as to other parties) statement recording reciprocal interest in a joint undertaking (see attached sample of a joint letter of Intention).
2.   Contract of Association
It is legally binding document which defines the objectives and economic justifications (as outlined in the feasibility study) of the venture as well as the responsibilities of the partners.
3.   Statutes
Document which details financial, management, accounting, depreciation, personnel handling and other procedures related to the day-by-day operations of the venture.

Forms & Documentation

List of Suggested Steps for the Formation of a Production and Marketing Joint Venture Contract

Introduction

Proclamation of intention and purpose

Chapter 1 — Fundamental information
1.   Purpose of the co-operation or joint venture
2.   Partners of the joint venture
3.   Legal aspects of the company formation
4.   The duration of operation
5.   The area of business of the joint venture
6.   The details of the goods to be manufactured
7.   The technical assistance, technological know how, documentation, licenses, quality control and guarantees
8.   The supply of raw materials, partical-finished commodities, spare parts, etc.
9.   Accessibility of site location, provisions of utilities
10.   Pollution control
11.   Transportation network
12.   The built in potential or capacity of production
13.   The dynamics of annual production
14.   Prelimary costs such as needs for fixed assets, working capital and installation cost.
15.   Investment of the joint venture
Chapter 2 — Markets of the production
1.   Price of goods, and projected
2.   Agreements on marketing assistance, advertising

3.   Distribution markets, existing and projected — subdivision of market
4.   Means for avoiding competition
5.   After-sale servicing assurance.
Chapter 3 — Planning of the steps
1.   Setting up the joint venture
2.   Attainment of the capacity and that of the project parameters
3.   Implementation (in stages, if necessary) and investment achievement
4.   Subsequent expansions
Chapter 4 — Taxation and customs duties
1.   Taxation and customs duties — existing and projected
2.   Duties on investment and on production
3.   Facilitations, rebates, exemptions for export of goods
4.   Insurance
Chapter 5 — Requirement for capital
1.   Composition and determination of fixed asset
2.   The necessary working capital
3.   Distribution of the capital requirements over the years (correlated with the investment achievement and the production development)
4.   Financing plan — value of capital, assets
Chapter 6 — Self capitalization
1.   Proportion and value of the partners' participation
2.   Asset contribution, proprietary industrial rights, cash of the subscribed capital
3.   Initial deposit
4.   Guarantees on the deposit of capital
5.   Installments scheduling
Chapter 7 — The acquisition of the loaned capital
1.   Conditions of credit, terms, interests
2.   Obligations of the partners for the acquisition of credit
3.   The method of guarantees granted by the company
4.   Scheduling of the needed credits and repayments
Chapter 8 — The company's administrative structure
1.   Management
2.   Research and development personnel
3.   Marketing personnel
4.   Labour
5.   Salary tariffs
6.   Training of the Chinese personnel
Chapter 9 — Assessment of economic ability
1.   Agreed currency for the operation of the company
2.   Allocation of the general expenditure
3.   Setting up of funds and provisions
4.   Cost and pricing structure
5.   Structure of the price of sale to the factory
6.   Structure of the price of sale to the consumer
7.   Estimation of the general utilization
8.   Viability, method of calculation — Minimum acceptable viability, recovery of capital from profits
9.   Method of calculation of the returns, related to the capital, related to the volume of business

Chapter 10 — Relations with other companies
1.   With subcontractors of the foreign partner
2.   With Chinese subcontractors
3.   With other subcontractors
Chapter 11 — Guarantees granted to foreign investors
1.   Necessity to conclude other agreements
     —   for political risks
     —   for avoiding double taxation
     —   e.g. possible with holding tax
2.   Reference to present agreements
Chapter 12 — Implementation of the preliminary operations
1.   Establishment of working groups and their responsibilities
2.   Nomination of the coordinating group and directors of the project
3.   Indication of the consultants to be used
Chapter 13 — Documentation to be prepared
1.   Technical studies
2.   Techno-economic studies
3.   Market studies
4.   Financing plan
5.   Accounting — viability, statement of general utilization, balance sheet and income statement, indices of viability, etc.
6.   Valuation of investments
7.   Various understandings, agreements, etc.
8.   Formulation of the association contract
9.   Formulation of the company's statutes
10.   Other documents
Chapter 14 — Work plan prior to the establishment of the company
1.   Detailed plan of projections for each assignment
2.   Possible programming
Chapter 15 — Miscellaneous
Chapter 16 — Period of validity of the agreement
1.   Announcements and necessary approvals for the signing of the contract and its implementation
2.   Period of validity, extension, conditions
3.   Termination of validity of the frame agreement (due to the signing of documents for the establishment of the company, by agreement of the parties, by other conditions)
4.   Solution of any problems that may arise during the implementation of the agreement

Appendix 1
Description of issues dealt with by the following working groups:
— *Working group for marketing*
— *Working group for technical matters*
— *Working group for economic and viability aspects*
— *Working group on legal matters*
— *Working group for the projection*
— *Working group on financial and bank related matters*
— *Coordinating working group*
— *Working group for the evaluation of the investments*
— *Other working groups of specialists*

Appendix 2 or other Appendixes (if necessary)

Model Contracts

Joint Letter of Intention
(Joint Venture Electronic Factory)

Tai Fat Company Limited of Hong Kong (hereinafter referred to as "Party A") conducted several friendly electronic factory with the great China Electronic Corporation (hereinafter referred to as "Party B"). Both Party A and Party B have reached mutual understanding and signed this joint venture contract hereunder. Whereas;

1.   Both parties unanimously held that in accordance with the Law of the People's Republic of China on Joint Venture Using Chinese and Foreign Investment, and in conformity with the Principle of equality, mutual benefit and co-operation, it may be feasible to build a large, modernized electronic factory in Shanghai.

2.   Both parties agree that the contribution of capital investment from each party shall be in equal share. The construction of the electronic factory is to be carried out in phases. In accordance with the needs of business development, it is estimated that the total amount of investment will gradually reach one billion Renminbi yuan.

3.   The investment from Party B will include land, factory building, workers' hostel, a part of equipment, necessary public utilities and necessary funds in Renminbi yuan; the investment from Party A may include the provision of equipment and necessary funds in foreign exchange, and will also include the value of Party A's unique Contributions — such as market study, engineering and technical know how — the value of which shall be fairly determined.

4.   Both parties agree that:

   (a)   the machines and equipment need for the inital stage shall not only represent the level of modern electronic technology in the world, but shall also be adaptable to current conditions in China.

   (b)   All expenditures in foreign exchange such as disbursement of profit and importation of necessary materials are to be covered by exporting finished electronicc products. Party A will try its best efforts to procure export orders.

5.   Both parties agree that the joint venture should proceed in three phases — planning, construction and operation.

6.   Both parties agree that during the first-stage construction of the proposed factory, personnel computer can be turned out. To achieve this, adequate machines and equipment should be used. Both parties shall consider using new technology to keep abreast with the constant progress in electronic industry.

7.   Party A will within three months by 1st November, 1982, prepare a market study to determine whether there is a good opportunity to manufacture computer in Chinese and English languages in China for export to other countries.

8.   Party B will provide to Party A by 1st August 1982 detailed specification of products planned to be produced in the joint venture electronic factory for domestic distribution, and will also provide to Party A by 20th August, 1982 detailed information of the costs required to produce computer manufactured for domestic distribution. The above mentioned information is to be used for reference by Party A only, Party B will also provide to Party A before 1st November 1982 a drawing of the factory site. The drawing will show the dimension of the site, the location of highways (existing and proposed), the location of highways (existing and proposed), the location of railways (existing and proposed) — the location of utilities (power, water, gas), and the location of workers' hostels.

9.   Both parties agree that after the results and conclusions of the market study are known to both of them, and only if the results of that study show that a good and sufficient export market exist, a delegation from Party B is to be invited to Hong Kong by Party A to conduct detailed discussions with the latter, so as to work out the specific provisions for the joint-venture agreement and enable both parties to sign a formal contract in Shanghai within 1983.

10.   This joint letter of intention is signed in Chinese and English tests; both texts are equally authentic.

Dated 1st July, 1982.

(signed)   (signed)

Wang Qiang   Tai Fat
Great China Electronic Corporation   Tai Fact Company Limited

Model Contracts

Joint Venture Agreement between Yellow River Confectionery (China) Limited and China Dragon Construction Corporation

Joint Venture Agreement

THIS AGREEMENT is made and entered into this 10th day of November, 1983, by and between YELLOW RIVER COMPANY CONFECTIONERY (CHINA) LIMITED, (hereinafter referred to as "YR" a corporation organized and existing under the laws of Japan and CHINA DRAGON CONSTRUCTION CORPORATION, (hereinafter referred to as "CD"), an entity oranized and existing under the laws of the People's Republic of China:

Witnesseth:

WHEREAS, CD has responsibility for the manufacture of confectionery products, including candies, in and for the People's Republic of China; and

WHEREAS, YR and its affiliated companies have experience, knowledge and capabilities in all aspects of production of candies, and

WHEREAS, CD and YR have previously cooperated successfully in a venture for the manufacture, distribution and sale of SNAKE brand candies in the People's Republic of China; and

WHEREAS, CD and YR desire to form a joint venture in the People's Republic of China for the purposes of producing high quality candies in the People's Republic of China for export and domestic sale;

NOW, THEREFORE, CD and YR agree to form a joint venture corporation in accordance with the following terms and conditions:

Article 1   Definitions

1.1   Unless the terms or context of this Agreement otherwise provides, the following terms shall have the following meanings:

1.1.1   "Jointly Owned Brand" ("JOB") shall mean the brand of 100 gm candies to be manufactured at the Factory.

1.1.2   "Factory" shall mean that certain factory, [name], located in Yellow River, Dragon Province, in the Territory, used by the JVC for production of the JOB.

1.1.3   "Territory" shall mean the People's Republic of China.

1.1.4   "JVC" shall mean YR CHINA CANDY CORPORATION, the joint venture company formed by CD and YR.

1.1.5   "Technology and Know How" shall mean the YR advanced and up-to-date technology, know-how, formulas, techniques and methods, provided in written or oral form, to be utilized by the JVC in producing the JOB.

1.1.6   "Feasibility Study" shall mean a written analysis prepared by either CD, YR or both conerning the economic and practical feasibility of the JVC.

1.1.7   "Joint Venture Law" shall mean the Law of the People's Republic of China on Joint Ventures Using Chinese and Foreign Investment, and the Regulations promulgated thereunder, as presently in effect.

1.1.8   "Company Operating Procedures" shall mean those philosophies, concepts and procedures agreed by CD and YR as the operating procedures for the JVC.

1.1.9   "Force Majeure" shall mean all events which are beyond the control of the parties to this Agreement of JVC, and which are unforeseen, or if foreseen, unavoidable and which arise after date of signature of this Agreement and prevent total or partial performance by either party or by the JVC.

Article 2:   Structure of the Joint Venture

2.1   The JVC shall be formed in accordance with the Joint Venture Law.

2.2   The Articles of Association and By-Laws of the JVC shall be those attached as Appendices A and B, respectively, to this Agreement.

2.3   The Articles of Association and By-Laws are hereby incorporated into and made part of this Agreement.

2.4   CD's interest in the JVC may be owned by GREAT WALL CORPORATION, a corporation organized and existing under the laws of the People's Republic of China, and wholly owned or controlled by CD.

2.5   YRs' interest in the JVC may be owned by SINO-TIGER INC., a corporation organized and existing under the laws of Japan.

2.6   The JVC will be organized with CD holding a 50% interest and YR's holding a 50% interest.

Article 3:   Scope of the Joint Venture

3.1   The JVC will produce the JOB for sale within the Territory and for export.
3.2   The JOB produced by the Factory will be sold 60% for export, at prevailing international prices for comparable products, and 40% within the Territory, for Renminbi and for Foreign Exchange Certificates, at prices comparable to similar products in the Territory, to ensure profits to the JVC.
3.3   The principal activities of the JVC will include:
   3.3.1   Development of a high quality 100 gm candy to be manufactured as the JOB.
   3.3.2   Development of a package design and packaging for the JOB.
   3.3.3   Conceptual design, detailed engineering, and layout of the Factory.
   3.3.4   Establishment and operation of the Factory in the Territory for production of the JOB.
   3.3.5   Sales of the JOB produced in the Factory for export and in the Territory.
   3.3.6   Development of a marketing, advertising and distribution system, and other services, to ensure maximum sales of the JOB.
3.4   Establishment of the Factory will be undertaken by the JVC following:
   3.4.1   The completion of a Feasibility Study regarding the economic viability of the JVC; and
   3.4.2   Determination, through the Feasibility Study, that the Factory will provide an equitable return on investment to the JVC.
   3.4.3   Issuance of any licenses or approvals which the governments of Japan or the Territory may require as a condition precedent to the execution of this Agreement.

Article 4:   Obligations of the Members

4.1   Each party will be responsible for its own costs incurred in connection with the formation of the JVC.
4.2   Initial operating capital required by the JVC after it is formed will be contributed ____% by CD and ____% by YRs, provided, however, that it is the intention of CD and YR that:
   4.2.1   Initial capital contributions of CD and YRs will be the minimum necessary to begin preliminary operations of the JVC and shall not exceed Pound Sterling 80,000 for each party, unless otherwise mutually agreed; and
   4.2.2   Additional operating funds and income will be obtained primarily from revenues generated by sales of the JOB by JVC pursuant to orders from third parties.
   4.2.3   Further necessary contributions by CD and YR to operating capital will be in accordance with cash flow projections established by Feasibility Studies.
4.3   CD and YR will make available to the JVC equipment, facilities, technical assistance and manpower on a reimbursable contract basis.
   4.3.1   CD will make available, for example:
      4.3.1.1   Management and labor personnel as may be required in establishing the JVC and the Factory.

4.3.1.2   Land, buildings, supplies, equipment, labour, and raw materials as may be required and available in the Territory for the establishment of the Factory and the production of the JOB.

4.3.1.3   Liaison services with relevant government authorities of the Territory.

4.3.2   YR will make available, for example:

4.3.2.1   Management, technical, engineering, production and quality control personnel and services as the JVC may require;

4.3.2.2   Technology and Know-How as may be required for the establishment and operation of a modern and up-to-date Factory;

4.3.2.3   Equipment, supplies and raw materials as may be required by the JVC and not otherwise available in the Territory;

4.3.2.4   Technical assistance, including technical, management and production training in the Territory and elsewhere, as may be required for personnel engaged in operation of the JVC or the Factory; and

4.3.2.5   Business and market development assistance in and outside the Territory to enable the JVC to establish a market for the JOB to be produced in the Factory.

4.3.3   The foregoing services, equipment and other items will be provided by CD and YR to the JVC and the Factory to enable them to achieve the purposes of this Agreement.

4.3.4   Payments by third parties to the JVC for the JOB will be used first to reimburse CD and YR for providing the services, equipment, personnel and other items referred to in Articles 4.3.1 and 4.3.2 of this Agreement.

4.3.5   Reimbursement shall be at costs or rates agreed by the parties in advance, and shall include each party's direct and indirect costs, without profit.

4.3.6   Revenues to the JVC in excess of such costs or rates will be used to cover any other costs of the JVC, and the remainder will be shared 50% to CD and 50% to YR.

Article 4:   Meeting of the JVC

4.1   CD and YR as the parties of the JVC, in meetings held or decisions taken in accordance with the terms of the Articles of Association and By-Laws, and the Company Operating Procedures, shall have supreme authority with respect to the management of the affairs of the JVC.

4.2   The parties reserve for themselves the exclusive determination, in accordance with the terms of this Agreement, the Articles of Association and the By-Laws of the following matters:

4.2.1   To elect and remove the members of the Board of Directors;

4.2.2   To review and approve the annual financial statements an disposition of the net income of the JVC;

4.2.3   To establish the overall policy and annual operating plan of the JVC;

4.2.4   To authorize the contracting of any loans by the JVC;

4.2.5   To approve any suit or claim of the JVC in any court of law or in any arbitration, whether as plaintiff or defendant, and any settlement agreement resulting therefrom;

4.2.6   To approve any purchase, sale or other disposition of a capital asset of the JVC;

4.2.7   To establish the terms and conditions of employment of officers, staff members and workers of the JVC; and

4.2.8   In all matters set forth in this Article 4, the resolutions and decisions for the Meetings of Members of the JVC shall be adopted by unanimous vote of the Members, except as otherwise provided by the Articles of Association and By-Laws.

Article 5:   Board of Directors and Officers of the JVC

5.1   Directors of the JVC

5.1.1   The Board of Directors of the JVC shall consist of five (5) persons.

5.1.2   Three Directors shall be nominated by the CD and two Directors shall be nominated by YR, and these five persons shall be elected by unanimous vote of the Members.

5.1.3   The following persons shall be nominated and elected at the first Meeting of Members:

5.1.3.1   Nominated by CD:

_____
(Name)

_____
(Title)

_____
(Name)

_____
(Title)

_____
(Name)

_____
(Title)

5.1.3.2   Nominated by YR:

_____

(Name)

_____

(Title)

_____

(Name)

_____

(Title)

5.1.4   If a Board Member dies, resigns or is removed from office, the party which originally nominated such Board Member shall nominate his successor, and that person shall be elected by unanimous vote of the Members.

5.1.5   The following functions shall be the exclusive prerogative of the Board of Directors of the JVC;

5.1.5.1   To elect officers of the JVC;

5.1.5.2   To establish management policies and business objectives of the JVC, including annual operating production and sales plans of the JVC;

5.1.5.3   To review the annual financial statements of the JVC; and

5.1.5.4   To make distribution of the net income of the JVC, such distribution to YR in all cases to be in Pound Sterling.

5.1.6   The resolutions of the Board of Directors shall be adopted in accordance with the Articles of Association and By-Laws, and all resolutions shall be adopted by unanimous vote.

5.1.7   No resolution of the Board of Directors shall be effective if any Director votes against the adoption of such resolution.

5.1.8   The Board of Directors shall not be precluded from adopting resolutions without a meeting pursuant to a unanimous written consent resolution of the Board of Directors.

5.2   Officers of the JVC

5.2.1   The Board of Directors shall elect as officers of the JVC a President, a Vice President (or more than one Vice President), a Secretary and a Treasurer.

5.2.2   Officers may, but need not, be members of the Board of Directors.

5.2.3   The President shall be nominated by CD and the Vice President (or, if there is more than one Vice President, then the senior-ranking Vice President) shall be nominated by YR and these officers nominated shall be elected by the Board of Directors.

5.2.4   The Secretary shall be nominated by CD and the Treasurer shall be nominated by YR, and these officers nominated shall be elected by the Board of Directors.

5.2.5   The Board of Directors shall by unanimous vote decide whether the JVC should have more than one Vice President, and which party shall nominate such additional Vice President(s) for election.

5.2.6   The following persons shall be nominated and elected as the initial officers of the JVC at the first meeting of the Board of Directors to serve in the positions set forth after their names:

Teng Ta _____ President, to be nominated by CD

Tai Fok _____ Vice President, to be nominated by YR

Koo Yi _____ Secretary, to be nominated by CD

Yi Min _____ Treasurer, to be nominated by YR

5.2.7   The Officers shall perform their functions until their death, resignation or removal by the Board of Directors.

5.2.8   Upon the death, resignation or removal from office of any Officer, the party who originally appointed such officer shall nominate a successor who shall be elected by the Board of Directors without delay.

Article 6:   Management Committee and Plant Managers

6.1   The President and Vice President (or, if there is more than one Vice President, the senior ranking Vice President) shall, with the approval of the Board of Directors, appoint a Management Committee consisting of themselves and such other persons as they mutually agree upon, to serve as a Management Committee of the JVC.

6.2   The President shall serve as Chairman of the Management Committee and the (senior ranking) Vice President shall serve as Vice Chairman of the Management Committee.

6.3   The Management Committee shall submit to the first and each annual meeting of the Board of Directors the following plans:

    6.3.1   An overall Policy Plan;

    6.3.2   An annual Operating Plan; and

    6.3.3   An annual production and Sales Plan.

6.4   The Plans shall be submitted to the Board of Directors annually not later than the 31st day of December of each year.

6.5   The Management Committee shall submit a monthly production and sales report to the members of the Board of Directors, and such report shall also contain recommendations for business to be undertaken by the JVC.

6.6   The Management Committee shall submit a monthly financial report to the members of the Board of Directors, and such report shall be submitted within ten (10) following the close of the month reported.

6.7   The initial Management Committee shall be composed of:

    6.7.1   Chairman (and JVC President)

6.7.2   Vice Chairman (and JVC Vice President)

6.7.3   Director

6.7.4   Chief Engineer

6.8 The Management Committee, with the approval of the Board of Directors, shall appoint a Manager and Deputy Manager for the Factory.

6.9 The Manager shall be nominated by YR and the Deputy Manager shall be nominated by CD.

6.10 The first managers, to serve for two years from the commencement of operations of the JVC, shall be:

      Weng Tai   Manager

      Tai Fook   Deputy Manager

6.11 The Manager and Deputy Manager shall be skilled in supervision and management of a factory established for production of candies, and they shall serve full-time at the location of the Factory.

6.12 Compensation and other terms of employment for the Manager and Deputy Manager shall be fixed by the Board of Directors.

6.13 The Manager shall be responsible for the design and lay-out of the Factory, the day-to-day management of the Factory, and, subject to overall supervision by the Management Committee, the management of the Factory, equipment, staff and workers employed in the Factory.

6.14 The Manager shall also be responsible for establishing and supervising procedures for quality control and production standards, and such other duties as may be specified by the Management Committee.

6.15 The JVC shall bear the full costs of the Manager, including his salary, suitable housing for him and his family, full-time services of a qualified interpreter/translator, automobile, round trip business class air fare between Hong Kong and the Factory in the Territory, and reasonable moving costs for him and his family to and from the Factory.

6.16 The Manager shall be entitled to six (6) weeks annual paid home leave for himself and his family with the cost of business class air fare to and from the Factory to be paid by the JVC.

6.17 Shall have the right at any time, upon thirty (30) days written notice to the Board of Directors, to recall the Manager, provided that YR shall have provided a qualified replacement prior to the departure of the said Manager.

Article 7:   Technology and Know-How

7.1 The JVC may request YR to render to it Technology and Know-How for the operation of the Factory, through consultations at the JVC office at Blue River, at the Factory, or by correspondence or other means, or through visitation by JVC technical personnel at YR facilities in Japan or elsewhere, or through the assignment of one or several YR technical experts to locations in the Territory.

7.2 YR shall be entitled to a fee for Technology and Know-How rendered by it or its personnel to the JVC at an established mutually agreed rate in H.K. Dollars per man-day.

7.3 The JVC shall reimburse to YR the reasonably necessary travel and living expenses of such personnel for the period during which such assistance is being rendered.

7.4   In the event that the compensation derived by technical experts and other persons temporarily assigned by YR to the JVC to impart Technology and Know-How is subject to individual income taxes in the People's Republic of China, such amounts shall be reimbursed to those persons by the JVC.

7.5   CD shall assist YR or non-Chinese JVC personnel to comply with all Chinese Government visa, travel permit and work permit formalities and other local laws and regulations, but all costs for transportation and lodging shall be borne by CD or the JVC, each for its own personnel.

7.6   YR shall assist CD and Chinese JVC personnel travelling to JAPAN with respect to visa requirements, and will assist in obtaining lodging and transportation in JAPAN for such personnel, but the cost of transportation to and within the   country   , and lodging shall be borne by CD or the JVC, each for its own personnel.

7.7   Technology and Know-How disclosed by YR to CD or the JVC shall at all times remain the property of YR and shall not be disclosed by CD, the Factory or the JVC, or any of their personnel, to third parties, and CD, the JVC and the Factory shall abide by such safeguards against unauthorized disclosure as YR may reasonably require.

Article 8:   Supply of Equipment and Raw Material to and Purchase of Local Components by the JVC

8.1   CD and YR shall enter into an Equipment and Raw Material Supply Agreement with the JVC setting forth the general policy, and the terms and conditions, under which the JVC will purchase or lease certain equipment from .either party necessary for the Factory.

8.2   YR and CD undertake to cause their respective Boards of Directors, subject to governmental approvals, if any required, to execute the Equipment and Raw Material Supply Agreement upon the approval of this Agreement and its Appendices by the relevant authorities in the Territory.

8.3   The JVC shall be encouraged to procure domestically in the Tertitory and machinery, equipment, components, parts, raw material, technical information, assistance or services from parties other than YR, provided such procurement does not jeopardize the achievement or maintenance of the quality standards required in the operation of the Factory of the production of the JOB.

Article 9:   Operation of the Joint Venture

9.1   Upon the approval by the relevant authorities in the Territory of the Joint Venture Agreement, including the Articles of Association any By-Laws, Company Operating Procedures, and other Appendices, the JVC will establish an office at CD for the following purposes:

9.1.1   To prepare such advertising, marketing or other information as may be necessary or desirable to inform customers and other third parties about the availability of the JOB from the JVC; and

9.1.2   To establish a plan for the preparation of Feasibility Studies or marketing and distribution proposals in response to orders or inquiries from third parties in or outside the Territory for the JOB;

and
9.1.3 To develop further Feasibility Studies for production of new confectionery products in the Territory.

9.2 Upon the agreement that an economically viable market for the JOB exists in and outside the Territory, the JVC shall commence operations in accordance with this Agreement and the Company Operating Procedures.

Article 10: Use of Land, Equipment, Technology

10.1 The real property, buildings, equipment, Technology and Know-How, and other items to be supplied by CD and YR shall be used by the JVC and the Factory only in the performance of this Agreement.

10.2 To minimize start-up costs of the JVC, facilities and equipment may be initially leased at mutually agreed rates from the parties, or from third parties.

10.3 The ownership and title to each of the items listed in this Article 10 shall at all times remain with the party providing the same.

10.4 In the future it may be mutually agreed that the JVC will construct, develop or purchase such real property, buildings, equipment, Technology and Know-How, and other items, such investment by the JVC being contingent on economic studies of future business conditions and the relevant laws and regulations of the Territory.

Article 11: Mutual Exclusivity

11.1 CD and YR agree that neither will undertake to establish individually or with other parties any other joint venture, co-production or similar enterprise for the production of the JOB in the Territory.

Article 12: Performance by Subsidiaries or Affiliates

12.1 Equipment, services or other items to be provided by YR to the JVC may be provided by YR or an affiliated or subsidiary company or YR

12.2 Equipment, services or other items to be provided by CD to the JVC may be provided by CD or an affiliated or subsidiary company of CD.

Article 13: Term

13.1 The term of the JVC shall be Twenty (20) years, commencing on the date of approval of this Joint Venture Agreement and its Appendices, by the appropriate government authorities of the Territory.

13.2 The term of the JVC may be renewed by the mutual agreement of the parties hereto, subject to approval of the appropriate authorities of the Territory.

13.3 Either party may, for any reason, give notice of termination of this Agreement or the JVC at any time upon 100 days notice to the other party.

13.4 Upon termination under this Article, YR shall be entitled to reimbursement of its costs hereunder, and any profits due, in Pound Sterling.

Article 14:   Arbitration

14.1 All disputes of any kind arising out of or in relation to this Agreement, including the existence or continued existence of this Agreement, which cannot be settled by the parties, shall be submitted to arbitration.

Article 15:   Force Majeure

15.1 If the conditions of Force Majeure shall prevail for a period in excess of nine (9) months, then either party, or either Member of the JVC, may cancel this Agreement, the JVC, and all other related agreements, by notice by registered airmail to the other party without any other formality.

15.2 The party claiming Force Majeure shall promptly inform the other affected party or parties and shall furnish appropriate proof of the occurrence and duration of such Force Majeure.

Article 16:   Taxes and Duties

16.1 The JVC shall be subject to the Joint Venture Income Tax Law of the Territory as presently in effect.

16.2 The JVC shall reimburse to personnel of YR such amounts, if any, as such personnel may be required to pay as personal income taxes in the Territory for JVC or other income received under this Agreement.

16.3 The JVC shall reimburse to personnel of CD such amounts, if any, as such personnel may be required to pay as personal income taxes in the Territory for JVC or other income received under this Agreement.

16.4 The JVC shall, with the assistance of CD, apply to the relevant authorities of the Territory for exemption of all import duties or similar charges on equipment, supplies or raw materials imported by or through YR, or the JVC, for the JVC for use in the Factory or otherwise in conection with this Agreement. To the extent such exemptions are not obtained on such equipment supplied by or through YR, such duties or similar charges, if any, imposed on YR shall be reimbursed to YR by the JVC.

16.5 CD shall assist the JVC in making such applications to the relevant authorities of the Territory to obtain the maximum tax exemptions for the JVC as are permitted under the Joint Venture Law and the Joint Venture Income Tax Law.

16.6 To the extent, if any, that YR or the JVC office in the Territory are subject to the Foreign Enterprise Income Tax Law of the Territory, the JVC shall be responsible for reimbursement or payment of such taxes as the case may be.

Article 17:   Labour Relations

17.1 The JVC shall establish all terms and conditions of employment, including wages and benefits, or managment, staff members and workers of the JVC, including terms and conditions of employment of persons employed in or for the Factory.

17.2 In establishing terms and conditions of employment of management, staff and workers of the JVC, the JVC shall be guided, but not bound, by the provisions of the Labor Management Regulations for Joint Ventures in the Territory as presently in effect.

Article 18: Trademarks

18.1 All trademarks, service marks or copyrighted material properly registered by YR or any of its subsidiaries or affiliates anywhere in the work shall at all times remain the sole property of YR or such subsidiaries or affiliates.
18.2 Any disputes under sub-Article 19.1 are not subject to arbitration and shall be resolved solely by YR in its own discretion.
18.3 The trademarks or service marks of the JOB shall be owned and registered by the JVC and, upon termination of the JVC, such trademarks or service marks shall be owned by CD.
18.4 If after the termination of the JVC, CD or any other entity continues to manufacture the JOB, CD or such other entity shall pay to YR a royalty of 10% of the wholesale selling price of the JOB for a period of 20 years.

Article 19: Miscellaneous provisions

19.1 Waiver. Failure or delay on the part of either party hereto to exercise any right, power or privilege hereunder, or under any other agreement relating thereto, shall not operate as a waiver thereof; nor shall any signle or partial exercise of any right, power or privilege preclude any other future exercise thereof.
19.2 Assignability. Subject to Article 2.4, 2.6, 12.1 and 12.2 hereof, this Agreement may not be assigned in whole or in part by any party without the prior written consent of the other party hereto.
19.3 Binding Effect. This Agreement is made for the benefit of YR and CD and may be enforced by either of them. This Agreement may not be changed orally, but only by a written instrument signed by CD and YR and approved, if required, by the relevant authorities in the Territory.
19.4 Severability. The invalidity of any provision of this Agreement shall not affect the validity of any other provision.
19.5 Language. The Agreement is executed in English language original and a Chinese language translation thereof.
19.6 Entire Agreement. This Agreement and the Appendices 1 & 2 hereto constitute the entire agreement and only understanding of and between CD and YR with respect to the subject matter hereof and supercedes all prior discussions, negotiations and agreements between them.
19.7 Notices. Any notice or written communication provided for herein by either party to the other, including but not limited to any and all offers, writings, or notices to be given hereunder, shall be made by telegram or telex, and confirmed by registered airmail letter, property transmitted or addressed to the appropriate party. The date of receipt of a notice or communication hereunder shall be deemed to be twelve (12) days after its postmark in the case of an airmail letter and two (2) working days after dispatch in the case of a telegram or telex. All notices and communications shall be sent to the

address hereinbelow set forth, until the same are changed by notice given in writing to the other party or the Members, as the case may be:

CD:

_____

_____

_____

Telex No.:_____

YR:

_____

_____

_____

Telex No.:_____

21.8 Appendices : The Appendices attached hereto are hereby made and integral part hereof. The Appendices are as follows:
    21.8.1   Articles of Association of Yellow River China Candy Corporation. (Appendix A)
    21.8.2   By-Laws of Yellow River China Candy Corporation. (Appendix B)

IN WITNESS WHEREOF, each of the parties hereto have caused this Agreement to be executed in three (3) counterparts on its behalf, and its corporate seal, if any, to be hereto affixed by its duly authorized officer as of the date hereinabove provided.

**China Dragon Construction
Corporation**

By: Oumin (Signed)
Title: Chairman

**Yellow River Confectionery Company
(China) Limited**

By: Tai King (Signed)
Title: Managing Director

Model Contracts

Articles of Association of the Yellow River China Candy Corporation

**Articles of Association
of the
Yellow River China Candy Corporation**

Article 1:   Name

1.1   The name of the Corporation is Yellow River China Candy Corporation.

Article 2:   Location of Registered Office

2.1   The registered office of the Corporation will be located in Yellow River, Dragon Province, People's Republic of China.

Article 3:   Duration

3.1   The Corporation is established for a period of Twenty (20) years from the date upon which the Corporation is licensed to do business by the General Administration for Industry and Commerce by the People's Republic of China.

3.2   The existence of the Corporation may be extended upon agreement of its Members and the approval of the relevant authorities of the People's Republic of China.

Article 4:   Status and Nature of the Corporation

4.1   The Corporation is a limited liability company established pursuant to the Law of the People's Republic of China on Joint Ventures using Chinese and Foreign Investment of July 1, 1979, and the Regulations thereunder, as presently in effect.

4.2   The Members of the Corporation are Yellow River Confectionery Company (China) Limited, ("YR"), a corporation organized and existing under the laws of Japan, and the China Dragon Construction Corporation ("CD"), organized and existing under the laws of the People's Republic of China.

Article 5:   Objects of the Corporation

5.1   To produce candies for sale within and outside of the People's Republic of China.

5.2   To establish production facilities in the People's Republic of China for the production of candies including:

    5.2.1   Conceptual design, layout and detailed engineering of production facilities;

    5.2.2   To undertake marketing, advertising and sales of candies manufactured in the production facilities.

    5.2.3   To do all such other things as may be necessary, incidental or conducive to the above objects, consistent with the laws and regulations of the People's Republic of China

Article 6:   Limitation of Liability

6.1   The Members have no liability for the debts or obligations of the Corporation.

Article 7:   Registered Capital

7.1   The Members shall contribute investments in the registered capital of the Corporation, and share in the profits (or losses) of the Corporation, in the following proportions:

    7.1.1   CD — 50%

    7.1.2   YR — 50%

7.2   Investments by the Members to the registered capital of the Corporation may be in the form of cash, capital goods, industrial property rights, or otherwise.

7.3   The initial investments of the Members shall be made as follows within 60 days after the Corporation is licensed to do business:

    7.3.1   CD   :Cash RMB: 10,000,000.00

    7.3.2   YR   :Cash US: 7,000,000.00

These Articles are hereby agreed to on this 10th day of November, 1983, by the following Members:

China Dragon Construction Corporation

By: _____Signed_____
                (Signature)

        _____Oumin_____
                (Name)

        _____Chairman_____
                (Title)

Yellow River Confectionery Company (China) Limited

By: _____Signed_____
                (Signature)

        _____Tai King_____
                (Name)

        _____Managing Director_____
                (Title)

Model Contracts

By-Laws of the Yellow River China Candy Corporation

**By-Laws of the
Yellow River China Confectionery Corporation**

Article 1:   Offices

1.1   The principal office of the Corporation shall be in the City of Yellow River, Dragon Province, People's Republic of China.
1.2   The Corporation may also establish offices at such other places as the Board of Directors may from time to time determine.

Article 2:   Meetings of Members

2.1   All Meeting of Members shall be held at such places as Board of Directors may determine.
2.2   An Annual Meeting of Members shall be held in the City of Yellow River during the month of May at a time and place to be determined by the Board of Directors.
2.3   Special Meetings of Members may be called either by the Chairman or the Vice Chairman of the Board of Directors.
2.4   Notice of the date, time and place of any meeting of Members shall be given by cable or telex to Members at the addresses provided at Article 11 of these By-Laws at least ten (10) days prior to such meeting.
2.5   A representative of each Member present at any meeting shall constitute a quorum.

2.6 The Chairman of the Board of Directors shall preside at all meetings of Members.

Article 3: Board of Directors

3.1 Unless and until otherwise resolved by resolution of the Members, there shall be five Directors of the Corporation.
3.2 China Dragon Construction Corporation ("CD") shall appoint three Directors, one of whom shall be named Chairman of the Board of Director.
3.3 Yellow River Confectionery Company (China) Limited ("YR") shall appoint two Directors, one of whom shall be named Vice Chairman of the Board of Directors.
3.4 Directors shall serve until replaced by the Member appointing them, and either Member may remove and replace a Director at any time.

Article 4: Powers and Duties of Board of Directors

4.1 The Management of all the affairs, property and interests of the Corporation shall be vested in the Board of Directors.
4.2 In addition to the powers and authorities conferred by the Articles of Association and these By-Laws, the Board of Directors shall exercise all powers of the Corporation and do all things as are not prohibited by law.
4.3 Regular or special meetings of the Board of Directors may be held upon notice to all Directors at the principal offices of the Corporation or at such other place as the Directors may designate.
4.4 Meetings of the Board of Directors may be called by the Chairman or the Vice Chairman.
4.5 The presence of at least four Directors is necessary to constitute a quorum for the transaction of business.
4.6 The Chairman of the Board or, in his absence, the Vice Chairman, shall preside at all meetings of Directors.
4.7 No salary or other compensation shall be paid to Directors, as such, for their services but, by resolution of the Board of Directors, a fixed sum and expenses of attendance, if any, may be allowed for attendance at each regular or special meeting of the Board of Directors; provided, that nothing herein contained shall be construed to preclude any Director from securing the Corporation in any other capacity and receiving compensation therefor.

Article 5: Officers

5.1 The Officers of the Corporation shall be a President, one or more Vice Presidents, a Secretary and a Treasurer.
5.2 Officers shall be elected by the Board of Directors for terms determined by the Board of Directors.
5.3 The Board of Directors shall fill vacancies among the officers occurring by death, resignation or removal promptly after such vacancies occur.
5.4 The President shall be the Chief Executive Officer of the Corporation and shall have general supervision of the affairs of the Corporation, shall sign or countersign all certificates, contracts, and other instruments of the

Corporation as authorized by the Board of Directors, and perform all such other duties as are incident to his office or as are properly required of him by the Board of Directors.

5.5 Each Vice President shall have such powers or discharge such duties as may be assigned to him from time to time by the Board of Directors. During the absence or disability of the President, the Vice Presidents, in the order designated by the Board of Directors, shall exercise all the functions of the President.

5.6 The Secretary shall issue notices of all meetings, keep minutes of all meetings, shall have charge of the seal and the corporate books, and shall make such reports or perform other duties as may be properly required of him by the Board of Directors.

5.7 The Treasurer shall have the custody of all monies and securities of the Corporation, and shall keep regular books of account. He shall disburse the funds of the Corporation in payment of the just demands of the Corporation, or as may be ordered by the Board of Directors, taking proper vouchers for such disbursements. He shall render to the Board of Directors from time to time as may be required of him an account of all his transactions as Treasurer and of the financial condition of the Corporation. He shall perform all duties incident to his office, or as are properly required of him by the Board of Directors.

5.8 The Board of Directors may appoint such other officers or agents as it shall deem necessary, who shall hold their offices for such terms, and shall exercise such powers and perform such duties, as shall be determined by the Board of Directors.

5.9 The salaries of all officers and agents of the Corporation shall be fixed by the Board of Directors.

Article 6: Books and Records of the Corporation

6.1 The books, accounts and records of the Corporation shall be kept, in the English and Chinese languages, at such place or places as the Board of Directors may from time to time appoint.

6.2 The books, accounts and records of the Corporation shall be open for inspection by either member or its authorized representative at any reasonable time.

6.3 The Board of Directors shall, by unanimous vote, appoint outside auditors for the Corporation, requesting such auditors to provide semi-annual audited statements, according to accepted international practices, on the financial condition of the Corporation.

6.4 Either Member of the Corporation may at any time and at the expense of the Corporation request and obtain an independent audit of the financial records or books of account of the Corporation and, upon receipt of such request the Corporation shall afford all reasonable facilities and disclose all relevant information in its possession to such Member or the persons appointed by it to make such audit.

Article 7: Fiscal Year

7.1 The fiscal year of the Corporation shall be the calendar year.

Article 8: Bank Account

8.1 The Corporation shall open an account with, and conduct its banking business principally with, the Bank of China.

Article 9: Distribution of Profits

9.1 After deduction of expenses and payment of taxes, profits of the Corporation shall be distributed to the Members as follows:
To   CD   :50%
To   YR   :50%

Article 10: Disputes

10.1 In the event of any dispute arising between the Members, or among the Board of Directors, which cannot in the opinion of any party be resolved through friendly consultation, any party may refer the matter to arbitration, in Hong Kong. The Appointing Authority for the arbitration shall be the China Arbitration Association, and the arbitration shall be conducted in both Chinese and English language.

Article 11: Notices

11.1 Notices required or permitted to be given hereunder shall be given personally in writing or by telex to the Members at the following addresses:
To CD:
Address:

To YR:
Address:

Article 12: Seal

12.1 The Company Seal of the Corporation shall be designed in a manner approved by the Board of Directors, and shall contain the name of the Corporation and the words "Company Seal," all in the English and Chinese languages.

Article 13: Amendments

13.1 Amendments to these By-Laws may be made by unanimous vote of the Board of Directors or otherwise in accordance with the applicable laws and regulations of the People's Republic of China.

Amendment to Article 100 of the "Regulations for the Implementation of the Law of the PRC on Joint Ventures Using Chinese and Foreign Investment"

Issued by the State Council on 15 January 1986

Article 100 of the "Regulations for the Implementation of the Law of the PRC on Joint Ventures Using Chinese and Foreign Investment" promulgated by the State Council on 20 September 1983 which reads: "The duration of a joint venture shall be decided upon through consultation of all parties to the joint venture according to the actual conditions of the particular lines of business and projects. The duration of a joint venture engaged in an ordinary project is usually from 10 to 30 years. Duration for those engaged in projects requiring large amounts of investment, long construction periods and low interest rates on funds can be extended to more than 30 years." shall be amended as follows:

"The duration of a joint venture shall be decided upon through consultation of all parties to the joint venture engaged in an ordinary project is from 10 to 30 years. Duration for those engaged in projects requiring large amounts of investment, long construction periods and low interest rates on funds, in projects which are aimed at producing sophisticated products and involve advanced or key technology to be provided by foreign partners, or in projects which are aimed at producing products with strong competitive power on the internatioinal market can be extended to 50 years or, upon the special approval by the State Council, to more than 50 years."

CHAPTER THREE

OIL &
OTHER ENERGY
RESOURCES

Brief Introduction

Due to the changed policies on the development of energy in China's modernization, many articles I quoted in the First Edition become either obsolete or less important, In view of these, I have deleted the following materials:

"Interim Regulations on Bonuses for Saving Specially Designated Fuels & Raw Materials in State-owned Industrial & Transport Enterprises."

"State Council Order for the Reduction of Oil Burning in Various Boilers and Industrial Kilns and Furnaces."

"The State Council Order for the Conservation of Electricity."

"The Policy for Coal Industry."

To update the information, I think, is no better than quoting the words of Mr. Wang Qingyi, Deputy President of the China Energy Research Society. Mr. Wang revealed the issue of China's energy in his Article.

"The Role Energy Plays in China's Modernization", published by the "Industrial Equipment & Materials" journal. He said ... between 1949 and 1984, the production of raw coal rose from 32 Mt to 789.2 Mt; petroleum from 0.12 Mt to 114.6 Mt; natural gas has amounted to 124.2 x $10^8 m^3$; and electric power output from 4,300 GW·h, to 377,000 GW·h of which 86,800 GW·h were generated by hydropower. In 1984, China's aggregate production of commercial energy (coal, petroleum, natural gas and hydroelectricity) was 778.5 Mtce, ranking third in the world.

China has also made considerable progress in the technology for energy development. It is fully capable of designing and constructing large coal mines, oil fields, oil refineries and power plants as well as providing complete sets of equipment for them. Today, when energy problems the world over are getting more and more acute, such achievements are undoubtedly significant to China in its pursuit for economic independence and development.

Characteristics of Energy Development in China

- **Industry.** Before the turn of this century. China's economic growth will remain dependent on the development of energy-intensive industries.
- **Transportation.** China is a vast country with a large population. To alleviate the pressure exerted on the country by its backward transportation, the demand for energy of the transport sector will certainly increase drastically.
- **Agriculture.** With only 7% of the world's arable land but 22% of its population, China needs a tremendous amount of energy for modernization of its agricultural activities.
- **National Defence.** Energy is seen as an essential prerequisite for the modernization of national defence.
- **Civil Consumption.** People's living standard is best reflected in society's energy consumption pattern. By the end of this century, in order to raise the standard of living of all Chinese to a comparatively well-off level, the average per capita consumption of energy will have to at least double that at present.

It can therefore be aptly said that China's modernization depends largely on the supply of energy and its effective utilization.

In view of the above, the Chinese government has attached great importance to solving its energy problems. Energy, recognized as the major force in China's economic advancement, has been given top priority for development.

The energy problems of China must be looked at in the Chinese context. While it is inappropriate to apply the existing mode of developed countries, it is essential to distinguish China from other developing countries. Given below are the factors that make China unique in its energy development.

1. China abounds in a variety of energy resources. The latest figures show that China has a proven coal reserve of 749,600 Mt and exploitable hydropower of 380 GW. Prospective oil reserves are estimated at 30,000 60,000 Mt, but at present, general survey and geological exploration work is still in an initial stage. In addition, China has also verified a considerable amount of uranium deposits. However, the average per capita energy reserve is low and prospecting for the scattered resources has so far been limited in scale. This gives rise to a series of problems in the development of China's energy resources, their transportation and the overall industrial layout of the country.

2. The economic structure of China is built upon domestic energy. Even in the days when petroleum had to be imported, 97% of the energy China needed was supplied domestically. In 1984 China exported 28.3 Mt of crude oil and petroleum products, and 6.9 Mt of coal. This only represented about 6% of China's domestic consumption. Future growth in energy output will basically be offset by the increasing demand of the domestic market. It is unlikely that China will need to import energy on a large scale.

3. China is one of the few countries in the world that relies on coal as the major source of energy. In 1984, coal accounted for 75.1% of the aggregate consumption of commercial energy in China. It constituted 75% of the fuel and power required by industry, 65% of industrial chemicals, and 85% of the fuel for civil use in the urban areas. Coal will remain predominant for a long time to come. The drastic increase in coal output and its utilization is expected to bring further demand on the country's transportation network and threats to the environment.

4. About 800 million of China's population live in the rural areas. At present, 85% of the energy consumed for daily purposes in rural China relies on non-commercial

energy. It is estimated that 180 Mt of firewood and 230 Mt of straws, totalling 230 Mtce, are burnt annually. Since it is not possible to increase on a large scale the supply of commercial energy for the rural areas within this century, there has arisen the need to develop a variety of small scale energy technologies based on local conditions.
5.   The average per capita energy consumption in China is quite low. In 1984, the average per capita consumption of commercial energy came to a mere 700 kgce, which was only ⅓ of the world's average per capita. By the year 2000, the figure is expected to rise to about 1 tce. So, an energy consumption structure and a modern life style that are in tune with the traditional low energy consumption pattern of the Chinese society must be sought.
6.   The energy utility rate in China is very low but wastage is alarmingly high. The unit GNP energy consumption is double the average of that of other developing countries. This shows that there is still much room for energy conservation.

Strategy and Policy of Development

Just as in many other developing countries, energy shortage has been a major obstacle to the economic development of China. The problems most urgently in need of solution are the lack of facilities for the production and transportation of primary energy, particularly coal, severe shortage of electricity supply, and insufficient energy sources for daily consumption in the rural areas. It is estimated that over 20% of China's industrial production facilities are left idle as a result of insufficient power supply. In rural areas energy for daily consumption is 20% short by the minimum standard of demand. The quantity of firewood burnt annually is twice the acceptable amount, resulting in severe destruction of vegetation, soil erosion and deterioration of the ecological environment. The arduous, pressing task of finding a solution to such energy problems is therefore one that demands much attention from the Chinese authorities.

According to a preliminary forecast by energy experts and government departments concerned, by 2000 the total output of commercial energy might reach 1,300 Mtce, which is slightly more than double the 1980 figure. But if the total industrial and agricultural output in 2000 is to quadruple that in 1980, the demand for energy will be 1,400 - 1,700 Mtce, which means that there will be a considerable discrepancy between supply and demand.

China's energy industry has a reasonably sound foundation. Where expansion of energy output is concerned , resources should not be a limiting factor in the long run. The most pressing matter at present is to devise with care and foresight a long-term strategy for energy development, to formulate scientific policy and planning, and to ensure their gradual implementation with resolution.

The ultimate goal of China's energy development plan by 2000 will be:

- to increase energy output and simultaneously practise strict energy saving. Efforts will be made to meet growing demands brought about by economic growth and rising standard of living:
- to establish a system which involves the co-ordinated development of different energy sources, a sensible energy layout and higher output and utility rate:
- to seek an initial solution to the problem of atmospheric pollution caused by large-scale coal burning in the urban areas while further destruction of the ecology caused by the excessive burning of firewood and straws in the rural areas will be checked.

Given below is a general picture of the present situation of China's energy sources, their conservation and the relevant policies adopted by the state:

1. Coal

In the foreseeable future, coal will remain the major source of energy in China. The output of raw coal is estimated at over 1,200 Mt for the year 2000.

Of the 789.2 Mt of raw coal produced in China in 1984, 394.7 Mt was produced by state-controlled mines which practise centralized distribution of products. The rest was produced by locally operated state-owned mines in provinces, municipalities and countries and by minor mines owned by local townships and villages and by individuals. Of these mines, 60,000 in the rural areas turned out 216.9 Mt. Coal produced by such small mines is usually for local consumption it is therefore significant to the development of rural industries and sideline production and to the improvement of rural life. The coal industry is one of the most labour intensive industries and at present mines above country level employ a total of 5.02 million workers. Only 4% of China's coal output comes from opencast mines. Underground mining remains dependent on manual labour. Up to 1984, about 42.6% of the state-run mines have been mechanized.

The average calorific value of raw coal produced in China is 21 MJ/kg. At present only 20% of China's raw coal is washed before it is sold. The domestic coal consumption of China in 1984 was as follows: power generation 21.8%, coking 8.2%, other industries 43.7%, railway 3.5%, and civil and commercial consumption 22.8%.

Among the problems faced by the coal industry of China are:

- insufficient investment and limitation in the scale of mine construction;
- primitive equipment and out-dated management method; low productivity and poor safety monitoring;
- low washability of raw coal and singularity of product mix.

To speed up growth of the coal industry, investment must be increased and the scale of development expanded. Future efforts will concentrate on the west with Shanxi as centre (including Inner Mongolia, western part of Henan and Hebei, Shaanxi and Ningxia); the Northeast (including eastern Inner Mongolia); East China (comprising Jiangsu, Shandong and Anhui); and Guizhou. The annual coal output of these regions at present totals 500 Mt and is expected to rise to 1,000 Mt by the end of this century. Efforts will also be made to mechanize the production process at the pits and to improve underground working conditions. Coal washing and the comprehensive utilization of coal will be upgraded. Research and development of such technologies as coal combustion, fluidized bed combustion and coal slurry combustion will also be strengthened. Coal mines in the future will follow the policy of comprehensive management. Study on new gasification and liquefaction technology will also be given priority.

2. Petroleum and natural gas

The petroleum industry is comparatively new in China. In the early 1960s, China successfully constructed the Daging Oilfield without foreign assistance. Since then, the Shengli Oilfield in Shandong, Dagang Oilfield in Tianjin, Liaohe Oilfield in Liaoning and Jizhong Oilfield in Hebei have been discovered and developed. New oilfields have also been discovered in Jiangsu, Henan, Hubei, Shaanxi, Gansu and Ningxia. Up to now, 133 oil-gas fields have been exploited in the whole country and 16 oil-gas production bases have been established. Daging, China's largest oil-producing zone, employs the technique of early injection to monitor the internal pressure in the oil-bearing strata. In 1984, Daging turned out 53.56 Mt of oil while Shengli turned out 23.01 Mt. In the oil-gas zone in Sichuan, 51 gas fields are in operation. Their output in 1984 amounted to $52 \times 10^8 m^3$. At present, there are 33 medium to large-sized refineries in the whole country, with a total annual crude oil processing capacity of 100 Mt. To date, China has laid 11,500 km of pipelines for the transportation of oil and gas.

The major problems encountered by the petroleum industry are low proven oil reserves, high percentage of oil burning, insufficient deep processing and backward natural gas prospecting and exploitation. To increase the proven reserves is the key to the successful development of the petroleum industry. In recent years, China has made tremendous progress by applying advanced technologies to oil prospecting. In 1984, geological reserves of 700 Mt were found. A breakthrough was made in the exploration of the Gugianshan oil deposit in the East China region, and 11 high-yielding wells with a daily capacity of 1,000 were sunk in the Shengli Oilfield. The exploration of the oil-bearing strata of the carboniferous system at the northern edge of the Junggar Basin in Xinjiang has made notable advances. Exploration work carried out in the Tarim Basin in Qinghai and Er-Lian Basin in Inner Mongolia also reported promising prospects for oil-gas exploitation.

The exploration of offshore oil and gas in China is only in an elementary stage but already a total of 11 oil-gas bearing structure have been discovered in the Bohai Sea and Beibu Bay. Development of the Chengbei Oilfield in the Bohai Sea and the Wei 10-3 Oilfield in Beibu Bay will begin in 1987. The annual output is estimated at 1 Mt. A large gas field discovered in the Yinggehai Basin is also ready for development. A marked increase in China's petroleum output can be expected in the 1990s.

China has abundant potential reserves of natural gas but so far proven reserves have been limited. The ratio of natural gas output to petroleum output in the world, calculated according to their calorific value, is 1.0 to 1.7. But in China, the ratio is only 1 to 10. Natural gas is widely distributed in China. In addition to gas-reservoir type gas and associated gas, there is also a rich reserve of coal-generated gas. To step up the exploration and exploitation of natural gas and to progressively increase its output is significant to the improvement of the energy structure and economic benefits of China. While every effort is made to speed up the exploitation of petroleum, much importance is also attached to the effective utilization of the 100 Mt of petroleum now produced annually. Heavy oil and crude oil directly consumed by power stations and industrial furnaces and kilns constitute some 30% of the total crude oil production. This high percentage causes reduction in the yield of light oil and restricts the deep processing and comprehensive utilization of petroleum. China has already adopted a policy to cut down the amount of oil used as fuel for boilers and furnaces by gradually replacing oil with coal. From now on, China's petroleum products will be mainly used as fuel for diesel engines and as industrial chemicals and lubricants. Advanced deep processing technology and high-strength catalysts will be applied to raise the yield and quality of light oils and increase the output of asphalt and other pertrochemical raw materials.

With a verified reserve of 31,100 Mt, China's oil shales are another important source of energy. First developed half a century ago, the Chinese oil shale industry has by now mastered sophisticated production technology. At present, the shale oil refineries at Fushun (Liaoning) and Maoming (Guangdong) produce 0.3 Mt of shale oil annually. Although production cost is high, the end product is cheaper than the petroleum sold on the international market. In view of this, shale oil may become an important supplement to natural oil.

3. Electricity

The power industry in China has been growing at a remarkable rate. The average annual growth rate between 1949 and 1984 was 13.6%. In 1984, the total installed capacity amounted to 80.12 GW and output 377,000 GW·h. There are altogether 12 power grids at GW level, of which four have a capacity of over 10 GW.

In 1984, 64.1% of the electricity generated in China was consumed by industry, 13.7% by the rural population, 0.7% by transportation, 6.9% by the urban population and 6.3% by factories. The remaining 8.3% was lost during distribution and transmission. A total of 398 gce/kW·h of coal was consumed by coal-fired power plants.

The major obstacles to the development of the power industry in China are: small construction scale; low exploitation and utilization of hydropower resources; poor technology and equipemtn; over-reliance on thermal power generating equipment; and a weak power grid structure.

Short power supply has been a serious problem in China for 16 years, resulting in a low average power consumption per capita. To cope with the foreseeable sharp increase in the demand for electricity by industry, agriculture and daily activities, the power industry must develop at an even more rapid pace. By the year 2000, power demand is expected to reach 1.2×10^{12} kW·h if it is to increase at the same speed as the national economy. To meet this demand, China must make use of advanced technology to step up the construction of the power industry; develop hydropower to replace coal-fired power; and construct nuclear power stations in regions suffering from severe shortage of energy.

In future, major thermal power stations will be built as close to the mining regions as possible. Large coal-fired power bases will be built in regions such as Shanxi, Inner Mongolia, Shaanxi, Ningxia, Henan and Anhui where coal reserves are rich and load centres are near.

China's hydropower resources possess huge potential for exploitation. A number of large hydropower stations will be constructed at the upper reaches of the Yellow River, the mainstream and tributaries of the Yangzi River at its upper and middle reaches, the Hongshui River, and the middle and lower reaches of the Lancang River. Several medium-sized hydropower stations will also be constructed in East China, South China and Northeast China where energy is in short supply.

China possesses not only nuclear fuel resources but also nuclear technology. Construction of a 300 MW nuclear power plant designed by Chinese experts is now underway. At the same time, the government has planned to import large GW-level commercial nuclear power plants. Advanced nuclear power technology will be imported so that by the end of this century, nuclear power plants of 10 GW will be built.

In order that the large amount of hydro-electricity generated at the upper reaches of the Yangzi River and Yellow River can be transmitted over long distances to consumption centres, technology of ultra-voltage transmission and direct current transmission will be developed.

4. Energy for the rural areas and new energy sources

In 1983, a total of 370 Mtce of energy was consumed in the rural areas of China. Of this amount, 140 Mtce was commercial energy of which production accounted for 65% and daily consumption 35%; the remaining 230 Mtce was non-commercial energy such as firewood and straws of which over 90% was for daily consumption. The rural areas of China suffer from severe shortage of energy and today, still about 40% of the rural population has no electricity supply at all.

A practical policy formulated according to local conditions and embracing the comprehensive utilization of energy must be adopted in the rural areas to improve their energy structure. Where agricultural production is concerned, an energy system in line with the actual conditions of the rural areas has to be established to prevent China from following the path of 'petroleum agriculture'. The present excessive consumption of firewood and straws must be checked and coal produced by small collieries should be made full use of as the main source of energy. In remote rural areas, new sources of energy must be developed and used.

China possesses 78 Mha of wasteland suitable for afforestation. If afforestation is carried out now, by the end of this century the acceptable amount of firewood that can be felled for fuel will provide ⅓ of the energy demand by the rural population. The conventional firewood-burning stoves commonly in use all over rural China have a heat efficiency of only about 10%. New firewood-saving stoves created in different parts of China use about half the fuel required by conventional stoves. As much as 100 Mt of firewood and straws can be saved each year if 90% of the rural households are to switch to the new firewood-saving stoves by the end of this century.

Vigorous development of small collieries and small hydropower stations is the solution to energy shortage in rural China. China's exploitable hydropower resources for small-sized hydropower stations (generating capacity under 12 MW) amount to 70 GW. Up to 1984, China had constructed 76,000 small hydropower stations. These stations, with a combined installed capacity of 8,670 MW and an annual output of 19,400 GW·h, provide about 2/5 of the electricity supply to the rural areas. Further development of such stations is to be expected.

The exploitation of new energy sources such as biogas, solar, geothermal, wind and tidal energy is regarded as an effective solution to the problem of energy shortage in the rural areas. These new energy sources will have an important role to play in remote regions such as high-lands, islands and pastoral areas. By 1985, initial progress made in the research and development of new energy sources include: 4.5 million of biogas tanks in rural China providing gas for 20 million people; a total 250,000 sq m of solar heat collecting areas for water heating; a 10 MW geothermal power station in Yangbajing, Tibet; 100,000 solar cookers in use throughout the country; solar cells with a generating capacity of 100 kW; 10,300 small wind-power generators; as well as numerous tidal power station with an aggregate capacity of 7,000 kW.

5. Energy Conservation

Energy conservation is of immense significance to China's economic development. The low utility rate of energy in China is due not only to its economic and technological backwardness but also to the high proportion of coal to other energy sources in the energy consumption structure of the country. It is unlikely that either will be changed within a short time, besides, the development of energy conversation technology will also require enormous investment of both time and capital. It is therefore impractical to estimate China's potentiality for energy conservation within a certain period on the basis of the energy utility rate of developed countries such as Japan.

As mentioned earlier, China has great potential for energy conservation. Since 1979, much had been achieved in this area. The moderate increase in energy consumption has brought about rapid growth of the country's economy. However, energy conservation in China is still in its infancy. Between 1981 and 1984, the amount of energy saved all over China was 100 Mtce, over 60% of which is the result of restructuring of the country's industry and the strict enforcement of energy conservation. In future, a gradual increase in the amount of energy saved by technological advancement can be expected.

In view of the importance of energy conservation, the Chinese government has set up specialized departments to embark on the formulation of policies, plans and regulations regarding energy saving. Research in energy conservation technology is also encouraged. Recent efforts made to conserve energy place special emphasis on improving energy management. Technological reforms, which have short investment recovery period, are encouraged. Adjustment of energy prices will also be made in line with the reform in the present system of economic management. Economic incentives such as tax exemption, credit loans and financial rewards are also provided to encourage energy conservation.

Energy is a major challenge to China in its struggle for modernization. Fortunately, China, with its comparatively abundant energy resources, has now established a dynamic energy system after more than 30 years' hard work. And what is more, the Chinese government is giving full attention to all the problems related to energy. This is manifested in such acts as constantly revising its energy policies and expanding the development of energy rescources by co-operating with foreign countries. The future of China's energy industry is full of promises.

From Mr. Wang's discussion, we can see that the data used for his discussion was collected around 1984. In order to have a clear picture of China's energy development, it is advisable to refer to the Seventh Five-year Plan 1986-1990.

I OIL EXPLOITATION

SECTION A: Overall policy

The Regulations of the Peoples's Republic of China on the Exploitation of Offshore Petroleum Resources in Cooperation with Foreign Enterprises

(Promulgated by the State Council on 30th January 1982)

Chapter I General Principles

Article 1: In order to develop the national economy, expand international economic and technological cooperation and safeguard national sovereignty and economic interests, these regulations are formulated to permit foreign enterprises to take part in the cooperative exploitation of offshore petroleum resources of the People's Republic of China (PRC).

Article 2: All petroleum resources in the internal waters, territorial waters and continental shelf of the PRC and the maritime resources in all waters within the limits of national jurisdication of the PRC are owned by the PRC.

All buildings and structures installed in the said sea areas to exploit petroleum and vessels serving the petroleum operations, as well as the corresponding onshore oil and/or gas terminals and bases are under the PRC jurisdiction.

Article 3: The PRC Government protects, in accordance with the legislations in force, investments by foreign enterprises participating in the exploitation of offshore petroleum resources, their share of profit and other legitimate rights and interests, and their activities in cooperative exploitation.

all cooperative activities to exploit offshore petroleum resources within the scope of the regulations shall comply with the laws and decrees of the PRC and the relevant stipulations by the state. All persons and enterprises taking part in the petroleum operations shall be bound by the laws of PRC and shall accept inspection and supervision by the competent authorities of the Chinese Government.

Article 4: The Ministry of Petroleum Industry of the PRC is the chief managing authority in charge of the exploitation of offshore petroleum resources in cooperation with foreign enterprises. The ministry determines the forms of cooperation and demarcates areas for cooperative exploitation in accordance with the zones and surface area dsignated by the state. It works out plans for the exploitation of offshore petroleum resources in cooperation with foreign enterprises in accordance with the long-term state economic program, formulates operational and management policies, examines and approves the overall development program for offshore oil and/or gas fields.

Article 5: The China National Offshore Oil Corporation (CNOOC) is in full charge of the work of exploiting offshore petroleum resources in the PRC in cooperation with foreign enterprises.

CNOOC is a state corporation, having the status of a legal person which has the exclusive right to explore for petroleum within the areas of cooperation and to develop, produce and market it.

CNOOC may establish regional subsidiaries, specialized companies and overseas offices to carry out the tasks entrusted by the head office as the work may require.

Article 6: CNOOC is, by calling for bids and entering into petroleum contracts with foreign enterprises, to exploit offshore petroleum resources in cooperation with foreign enterprises in accordance with the zones, surface area and area demarcated for cooperative exploitation.

Petroleum contracts referred to in the preceding paragraph shall come into force after approval by the Foreign Investment Commission of the PRC.

All documents signed by CNOOC in other forms of cooperative exploitation of petroleum utilizing technology and funds provided by foreign enterprises shall also be subject to approval by the Foreign Investment Commission of the PRC.

Chapter II Right and Obligations of the Parties to Petroleum Contracts

Article 7: CNOOC shall exploit offshore petroleum resources in cooperation with foreign enterprises by entering into petroleum contracts. Unless otherwise specified by the Ministry of Petroleum Industry or in the petroleum contract, the foreign enterprise that is one party to the contract (hereinafter "foreign contractor") shall provide exploration investment, undertake exploration operations and bear all exploration risks. After a commercial oil and/or gas field is discovered, both the foreign contractor and CNOOC shall make investment in the cooperative development. The foreign contractor shall be responsible for the development and production operations until CNOOC takes over the production operations when conditions permit under the petroleum contract. The foreign contractor may recover its investment and expenses and receive remuneration out of the petroleum produced according to the provisions of the petroleum contract.

Article 8:   The Foreign contractor may export the petroleum it receives as its share and/or purchases and remit abroad the investment it recovers, its profit and other legitimate income according to law.

Article 9:   All Chinese and foreign enterprises involved in the exploitation of offshore petroleum resources shall pay taxes in accordance with the tax laws of the PRC and pay royalties.

Any employee of the said enterprises in the preceding paragraph shall pay individual income tax according to law.

Article 10:   The equipment and material imported for the implementation of the petroleum contract shall be exempt from customs duties, or levied at a reduced rate, or given other preferential treatment in accordance with state regulations.

Article 11:   The foreign contractors shall a bank account in accordance with the stipulations of the provisional regulations for exchange control of the PRC.

Article 12:   In implementing the petroleum contract, the foreign contractor shall use appropriate and advance technology and managerial experience and is obliged to transfer the technology and pass on the experience to the personnel of the Chinese side involved in the implementation (hereinafter "Chinese personnel"). In the course of petroleum operations, the foreign contractor must give preference to the Chinese personnel in employment, keep the percentage of Chinese employed steadily rising, and train them in a planned way.

Article 13:   In the course of implementing the petroleum contract, the foreign contractor must accurately report the petrouleum operations to CNOOC in due time; and during the operations it must acquire complete and accurate data, records, samples, vouchers and other original data, and regularly submit to CNOOC the necessary data and samples as well as technological, economic, financing and accounting and administrative reports.

Article 14:   For the implementation of the petroleum contract, the foreign contractor shall establish its subsidary or branch or representative office within the territory of the PRC and fulfil and registration formalities according to law.

The domiciles of teh subsidiaries, branches and representative offices mentioned in the preceding paragraph shall be determined through consultation with CNOOC.

Article 15:   The provisions of Articles 3, 8, 9, 10 and 14 of the regulations shall apply to foreign subcontractors which render services to the petroleum operations.

Chapter III Petroleum Operations

Article 16:   In order to achieve the highest practicable ultimate oil recovery, the operator shall work out an overall development plan for each oil and/or gas field and conduct the production operations in accordance with the regulations and relevant rules promulgated by the Minsitry of Petroleum Industry on exploitation of petroleum resources and with reference to international practice.

Article 17:   For the implementation of the petroluem contract, the foreign contractor shall use the existing bases within the territory of the PRC. If a new base is needed, it shall be established within the territory of the PRC.

The location of the new base and such arrangements as may be necessary in special circumstances shall be subject to prior written approval from CNOOC.

Article 18: CNOOC has the right to send personnel to join the foreign operator in making master designs and engineering designs for the implementation of the petroleum contract. Design corporations within the territory of the PRC shall have priority in entering into subcontracts for the master designs and engineering designs, provided that the terms offered by these design corporations are competitive.

Article 19: The operator must give preference to manufacturers and engineering companies within the territory of the PRC in concluding subcontracts for all facilities to be built in implementing the petrolum contract, including artificial islands, platforms, buildings and structures, provided that they are competitive in quality, price, delivery schedules and services.

Article 20: As for the equipment and materials required to implement the petroleum contract, the operator and subcontractors shall give preference to procuring and using equipment and materials manufactured and supplied by the PRC, provided that these are competitive.

Article 21: As for the services required to implement the petroleum contract, including services for geophysical prospecting, well drilling, diving, helicopters, vessels and onshore bases, the operator and subcontractors shall enter into subcontracts and service contracts with the relevant enterprises within the territory of the PRC, provided that these services are competitive in price, efficiency and service quality.

Article 22: All assets purchased and built by the foreign contractor for implementation of the petroleum contract in accordance with the plan and budget shall be owned entirely by CNOOC when the foreign contractor has fully recovered its investment for those assets (but the rental equipment for any third party is excluded). Within the term (duration) of the petroleum contract, the foreign contractor may continue to use those assets in accordance with the provisions of the contract.

Article 23: CNOOC is the owner of all the data, records, samples, vouchers and other original data obtained in the course of the petroleum operations, as provided in Article 13 of the regulations.

The utilization, transfer, donation, exchange, sale and publication of the afore-mentioned data, records, samples, vouchers and other original data and their delivery and transmission to outside the PRC shall be conducted in accordance with the rules on the control of data and information formulated by the Ministry of Petroleum Indutry.

Article 24: The operator and subcontractors shall carry out the petroleum operations in compliance with the laws and rules on environmental protection and safety of the PRC, and with reference to international practice to protect fishery and other natural resources and prevent the air, seas, rivers, lakes and the land from being polluted or damaged.

Article 25:   The petroleum produced within the petroleum contract area shall be landed in the territory of the PRC or may be exported from oil and/or gas metering points of offshore terminals.

In case such petroleum has to be landed outside the territory of the PRC, approval must be obtained from the Ministry of Petroleum Industry.

Article 26:   In case of war, threat of war or other emergency circumstances, the PRC Government is to have the right to requisition a portion or all of the petroleum obtained and/or purchased by the foreign contractor.

Chapter IV Supplementary Provisions

Article 27:   Any dispute arising between foreign and Chinese enterprises during the cooperative exploitation of offshore petroleum resources shll be settled amicably through consultations. If the parties to the dispute fail to arrive at a solution through consultation, the dispute mau be settled through mediation or arbitration by an arbitration body of the PRC, or through arbitration by another arbitration body agreed upon by both parties.

Article 28:   In case an operator or subcontractor violates the regulations while conducting petroleum operations, the Ministry of Petroleum Industry is authorized to warn the operator or subcontractor and demand remedy within a limited time. Should the operator or subcontractor fail to remedy the violation within the specified time, the ministry shall have the right to take the necessary steps, even to the extent of suspending its right to conduct the petroleum operations. All economic losses so incurred shall be borne by the party responsible. The party responsible for serious violation of the regulations shall be fined or even be sued before juridical authorities by the Ministry of Petroleum Industry.

Article 29:   The terms used in the regulations shall be defined as follows:

(1)   "Petroleum" means crude oil or natural gas deposited underground and produced or being produced therefrom.

(2)   "Exploitation" means, in general, activities related to exploration, development, production and marketing of petroleum as well as other related activities.

(3)   "Petroleum contract" means the contract for the exploration for, and development and production of petroleum for, and development and production of petroleum signed, under the legislation in force, between CNOOC and foreign enterprises for the cooperative exploitation of offshore petroleum resources of the PRC.

(4)   "Contract area" means an offshore area demarcated by geographical coordinates for the exploitaion of petroleum resources under the petroleum contract.

(5)   "Petroleum operations" means all exploration, development and production operations carried out in the implementation of the petroleum contract, and other related activities.

(6)   "Exploration operations" means all the work done in locating

the petroleum-bearing traps by means of geological, geophysical and geochemical methods and exploratory drilling, and all work to determine the commerciality of the discovered petroleum traps, including appraisal drilling, feasibility studies and preparation for the overall development plan of any oil and/or gas field.

(7) "Development operations" means all the work of designing, construction, installation, drilling and other relevant research work carried out for petroleum production from the date of the approval of the overall development plan of an oil and/or gas field by the Ministry of Petroleum Industry, including production activities carried out before the commenement of commercial production.

(8) "Production operations" means all the operations carried out after the date of commencement of the commercial production of an oil and/or gas field for producting petroleum and related activities, such as extraction, injection, stimulation, processing, stroage, transportation and lifting of petroleum, etc.

(9) "Foreign contractor" refers to a foreign enterprise which may be a company or consortium entering into the petroleum contract with CNOOC.

(10) "Operator" refers to an entity, which is responsible for performing the operations under the petroleum contract.

(11) "Subcontractor" refers to an entity which renders services to the operator.

Article 30: The detailed rules and regulations for the implementation of the regulations shall be worked out by the Ministry of Petroleum Industry.

Article 31: The regulations shall come into force on the date of its promulgation.

SECTION B: Taxation

The Levy & Exemption of Customs Duties & Consolidated Industrial & Commercial Tax on Imports & Exports for the Chinese-Foreign Cooperative Exploitation of Offshore Petroleum Regulations

(Approved by the State Council on February 28, 1982 & promulgated by the General Administration of Customs & Ministry of Finance)

In order to encourage the Chinese-foreign cooperative exploitation of offshore petroleum, the levy and exemption of customs duties and consolidated industrial and commercial tax on imports and exports for offshore petroleum exploitation regulation are as follow:

Article I.   The following imported goods are shall be exempt from duties and tax:

1.   Machinery, equipment, spare parts and materials verified and approved for direct use in exploration operations.

2.   Machinery, equipment, spare parts and materials verified and approved as necessary imports for direct use in development operations in accordance with the provisions of Article 19 through Article 21 of the "Regulations of the People's Republic of China on the Exploitation of Offshore Petroleum Resources in Cooperation with Foreign Enterprises."

3.   Spare parts and materials verified and approved as necessary imports for manufacturing machinery and equipment in China for the purposes of offshore petroleum exploitation operations (including exploration, well drilling, well cementing, well testing, well logging, oil extraction, well repair, etc.).

4.   Machinery and other engineering equipment, temporarily imported by foreign contractors for the purposes of offshore petrileum exploitation and guranteed to be reexport is to be exempt from duties and tax when imported or reexported.

Article II.   In accordance with the stupulations of contracts, crude oil received by

	foreign contractors is to be exempt from export duties when exported.
Article III.	Customs duties and consolidated industrial and commercial tax is to be levied on import and export goods beyond the scope stipulated in Article I and Article II above according to the "The Import and Export Customs Tariff Rules of the People's Republic of China" and the "Consolidated Industrial and Commercial Tax Regulations of the People's Republic of China (Draft)."
Article IV.	All goods imported free of duties and taxes should not be used for other purposes without the Customs' approval. Violators are to be dealt with by Customs in accordance with "The Provisional Customs Law of the People's Republic of China".

Appendix

List of Imported Goods for the Chinese-Foreign Cooperative Exploitation of Offshore Petroleum Exempt from Duties and Tax

I.   Goods verified and approved as necessary imports for direct use in exploration:

(1)   Geophysical Exploration Vessels and their Accessories
       1.   Geophysical exploration vessels and their accessories.
       2.   Seismographs, components and their accessories, gravimeter and magnetometers and their accessories.
       3.   Hydrophone streamers and their accessories.
       4.   Computers specially for data processing and their accessories.
       5.   Seismic tapes.
       6.   On-land navigation and positioning equipment and their accessory facilities.

(2)   For well drilling:
       1.   Various offshore drilling installations including jack-ups and semisubmersible drilling rigs, floating drilling vessels and drilling platforms as well as tender vessels and service vessels.
       2.   Drills and their components, attachments or accessories.
       3.   Well cementing equipment and auxiliary equipment, including cement mixer and feeding equipment.
       4.   Well logging equipment and auxiliary equipment including electricial logging instruments, gas logging instruments, directional survey instruments and other logging insruments.
       5.   Petroleum testing equipment, well-repair equipment and their components, attachments or accessories.
       6.   Tools specially for well drilling, including drill bits, drill collars, drill rods, deviating and deviation control tools, fishing tools and other tools.
       7.   Drilling mud treating equipment and chemical materials.
       8.   Materials specially for oil wells, including tubing, casing, wellhead equipment and underwater equipment and tools.
       9.   Oil well cements and various additives.

(3)   For safety and lifesaving:
       1.   Various kinds of installations, spare parts and materials for blowout prevention.
       2.   Various kinds of installations and materials for fire prevention and fire fighting.
       3.   Various kinds of equipment, accessories and tools for lifesaving.
       4.   Special labor protection items for personnel working offshore.

    5.   Equipment and materials for diving operations.

(4)   For transportation and communications:

    1.   Helicopters and helipad equipment.

    2.   Vessels for transportation and convoy and their accessories.

    3.   Various kinds of equipment and accessoriws for wire and radio communication.

(5)   For fuels and oils:

Special fuels, lubricating oils and cooling fluid necessary for offshore operations.

II.   Goods verified and approved as necessary imports for development, i.e., oil field construction:

(1)   For oil extraction:

    1.   Production platforms, including oil extraction platforms, processing platforms, production platforms and flare platforms.

    2.   Offshore oil loading facilities, including single-point moorings, single articulated leg moorings, oil storage vessels, underwater oil storages and landing stage quays.

    3.   Ships for offshore construction operations.

    4.   Power generating equipment and accessories, including internal combustion engines, steam turbines, gas turbines, steam engines, generators and electric motors as well as control equipment and installation.

    5.   Injection equipment and accessories including water and gas injection equipment as well as facilities for water and gas treatment.

    6.   Downhole packers and downhole blowout preventors.

    7.   Hoisting equipment and tools.

    8.   Oil (gas) transportation equipment, line pipes, and their valves and pipe accessories, equipment for pumping and boosting stations and onshore terminals and their valve and pipe accessories, including various kinds of pumps for liquid separating, heat-exchanging, purifying, and compressing, various kinds of meansuring, monitoring and parameter indicating meters, various kinds of valves and pipe fittings, various kinds of electric instruments and cables.

(2)   For automation, remote controlling and telemetering:

    1.   Including various kinds of installation and meters.

    2.   Air-conditioning installations.

III.   Parts, components and materials verified and approved as necessary imports for the manufacture of machinery and equipment in China for offshore petroleum explotiation.

IV.   The Ministry of Petroleum is to have the responsibility to examine whether or not the above-mentioned goods need to be imported from abroad and to give approvals.

Interpretation

Interpretations on Certain Articles of the Tax Laws & Regulations related to the Joint Exploitation of Petroleum Resources
(Issued on March 20, 1982 by the Ministry of Finance)

1. *Foreign enterprises which are engaged in the cooperative exploitation of offshore petroleum resources are permitted, in accordance with the provision of Article 12 of the Detailed Rules & Regulations for the Implementation of the Income Tax Law Concerning Foreign Enterprising, to list as expenses the interest payments at reasonable rates on the loans which are borrowed from their affiliated companies on condition that the loans and interest payments are backed up by certifying documents and, after being examined by the relevant tax authorities, the loans are considered as being of normal terms and used as working capital in production or as capital investments in construction.*

Reference:
Article 12:   Foreign enterprises are permitted to list as expenses the interest payments on loans at reasonable rates on the condition that the loans and interest payments are backed up by certifying documents and, after beig examined by the local tax authorities, are considered as beig of normal terms.

2. *The taxable income derived by foreign enterprises from the cooperative expoitation of offshore petroleum resources shall be subject to the income tax and the local income tax at the income tax rates as stipulated in Article 3 and Article 4 of the Income Tax Law Concerning Foreign Enterprises, but the income after the income taxes, which is to be remitted abroad by foreign enterprises as dividends of the investing companies or as their share of profit shall not be subject to the income tax as stipulated in Article 11 of the Income Tax Law Concerning Foreign Enterprises.*

Reference:
Article 3:   Income tax on foreign enterprises shall be assessed at progressive rates for the parts in excess of a specific amount of taxable income.

The tax rates are as follows:

Range of income	Tax Rate (percent)
Annual income below 250,000	20%
That part of annual income from 250,000 to 500,000 yuan	25%
That part of annual income from 500,000 to 750,000	30%
That part of annual income from 750,000 to 1 million yuan	35%
That part of annual income over 1 million yuan	40%

Article 4:   In addition to the income tax levied on foreign enterprises in accordance with the provisions of the preceding article, a local income tax of 10% of the same taxable income shall be levied.
Where a foreign enterprise needs reduction in or exemption from local income tax on account of the small scale of its production or business, or its rate of profit, this shall be decided by the people's government of the province, municipality or autonomous region in which that enterprise is located.

Article 11:   A 20% income tax shall be levied on the income derived from dividends, interests, rentals, royalties and other sources in China by foreign companies, enterprises and other economic organizations which have have no establishments in China. Such tax shall be deducted by the paying unit in each of its payments of dividends, etc.
For the payment of income tax according to the provisions in the preceding paragraph, the foreign companies, enterprises and other enconomic organizations earning the income shall be the taxpayer, and the paying unit shall be the deduction agent. Taxes deducted on each payment by a deduction agent shall, within five days, be turned over to the State Treasury and the income tax return submitted to the tax authorities.
Income from interest on loans given to the Chinese Government or China's state banks by international finance organizations shall be exempted from income tax. Income from interest on loans given at a preferential interest rate by foreign banks to China's state banks shall also be exempted from income tax.
Income derived from interest on deposits of foreign banks in China's state banks and on loans given at a normal interest rate by foreign banks to China's state bnaks shall be taxed. However, exemption from income tax shall be granted to those foreign banks in whose countries income from interest on deposits and loans of China's state banks is exempted from income tax.

3.   *In accordance with the provision of Article 26 of the Detailed Rules & Regulations for the Implementation of the Income Tax Law Concerning Foreign Enterprises, the amount of income of foreign enterprises which are engaged in the cooperative exploitation of offshore petroleum resources may be computed on the basis of the volume of crude oil lifted (at the delivery point and handed over for export. If the crude oil pricing method determined in a cooperative exploitation pertroleum contract, after being examined by the relevant tax authorities, conforms to the principle of pricing method stipulated in Article 26 of the Tax Regulations, the corresponding pricing method in the petroleum contract will be allowed to compute the amount of income.*

Reference:

Article 26:   Foreign enterprises engaged in cooperative production with Chinese enterprises on the basis of prorating of products are considered as receiving income when such products are distributed, and the amount of their income shall be computed according to the prices at which the products are sold to the third party or with reference to the prevailing market prices of the products.

Foreign enterprises engaged in cooperative exploitation of offshore petroleum resources are considered as receiving income when they receive their shall of crude oil, and the amount of their income shall be computed according to the prices which are regularly adjusted with reference to the international market price of crude oil of equal quality.

4.   *If a foreign enterprise which is engaged in the cooperative exploitation of offshore petroleum resources holds two (2) contract areas, the loss incurred in one contract area, owing to the termination of operations or other causes, will be allowed to be offset from the proceeds receive of the other contract area. The taxable income of two contract areas shall be computed on the consolidated basis.*

5.   *The reasonable exploration expenses referred to in Article 22 of the Detailed Rules & Regulations of the Income Tax Law Concerning Foreign Enterprise include the geophysical survey expenses pertaining to the blocks granted through bidding, which were incurred in conducting converant the geophysical survey agreements signed by both parties prior to the signing of the contracts for the cooperative exploitation of petroleum contracts.*

The reasonable exploration expenses incurred by a foreign enterprise wihtin a contract area shall be accumulated and treated as capital expenditure, without being classified into tangible assets or intangible assets, and shall be amortized from the revenues derived from any oil (or gas) field within the same contract area that has gone into commercial production, but the time limit of such amorization shall not be less than one (1) year. For the exploration expenses which continued incurred after the commencement of commercial production, the exploration expenses incurred during the current tax year shall year by year be accumlated on yearly basis and shall be amortizrd starting from the following year in chronological order, but the time limit of such amortization of annual exploration expenses shall not be less than one (1) year. The reasonable exploration expenses incurred in any contract area within which commercial production has not yet commenced may be amortized from the revenues of oil (or gas) fields within a contract area that has gone into commercial production according to the above-mentioned method. Any loss which results from the termination of production within the above contract area may be amortized from the revenues of oil (or gas) fields within another contract area that has gone into commercial production and is operated by the same foreign enterprise.

Reference:

Article 22:   Expenses arising during the period of preparation for a foreign enterprise shall be amortized after it goes into production or business in a period not less than five years.

easonable exploration expenses incurred by foreign enterprises engaged in exploiting offshore petroleum resources may be amortized from the revenues derived from the oil (or gas) field that has gone into production for commercial purposes, but the time limit of such amortization shall not be less than one year.

6.   For used equipment, that is acquired from affiliated companies and shipped in from abroad by foreign enterprises engaged in the cooperative exploitation of offshore petroleum resources, if both parties to the contract agree to purchase the used equipment at a negotiated price, the original value of the equipment, being examined and approved by the relevant tax authorities, and the depreciation or amortization of the said equipment shall be calculated in accordance with the provisions of Article 18 and Article 22 of the Detailed Rules & Regulations of Income Tax Law Concerning Foreign Enterprises.

Reference:

Article 18:   The depreciation period for various kinds of fixed assets is set as follows:

1.   The minimum depreciation period for houses and buildings is 20 years;

2.   The minimum depreciation period for trains, ships, machines and equipment and other apparatus for the purpose of production is 10 years;

3.   The minimum depreciation period for electronic equipment, means of transport other than trains and ships, as well as appliances, tools and furniture relevant to production and operation is five years.

For cases where the depreciation on fixed assets of foreign enterprises, owing to special reasons, needs to be accelerated or to be computed under modified methods, applications may be submitted to the local tax authorities for exmaination and then relayed level by level to the Ministry of Finance for approval.

Depreciation of various kinds of fixed assets resulting from the investments of enterprises engaged in exploiting offshore petroleum resources, during and after the stage of development, may be calculated in accordance with a composite life method. The depreciation period shall not be less than six years.

For enterprises engaged in exploiting coal mineral resources, the provisions of the preceding paragraph may also be applied.

7. *For enterprises engaged in the exploitation of offshore petroleum resources all investments at the development period shall be aggregated and treated as capital expenditures with an oil (or gas) field as the unit, and depreciation shall be calculated starting from the month when the oil (or gas) field begins to go into commercial production, for purposes, but the time limit of such depreciation shall not be less than six (6) years. For the development investments which are made after commencement of commercial production of the oil (or gas) field, development investments made in same oil (or gas) field during the current tax year shall year by year be accumulated on an annual basis and shall be depreciated from the following year in chronological order, but the time limit of such depreciation shall not be less than six (6) years.*

For an oil (or gas) field in which development investments have already been made but commercial production has not yet commenced, the depreciation of development investments in the oil (or gas) field shall not be calculated until the commercial production of the oil (or gas) field commences.

For an oil (or gas) field which is abandoned in the middle of the contract, the development investments which have not been depreciated or the balance of development investments which have not been duly recovered through depreciation shall be recovered through depreciation in accordance with the remainding depreciation period from the revenue of other oil (or gas) fields that have gone into commercial production.

8. *The applicability of the time limits of depreciation and amortization stipulated in the third paragraph of Article 18 and the second paragraph of Article 22 of the Detailed Rules & Regulations of Income Tax Law Concerning Foreign Enterprises is not only to enterprises which are engaged in the exploiation of offshore petroleum resources. Depreciation of divisement investment in the form of various kinds of fixed assets made by enterprises engaged in exploiting coal mineral resources may also be calculated in accordance with a composited life method, but such depreciation period shall not be less than six (6) years.*

9. *No additional expenses shall be allowed as deductions in calculating the taxable income of a foreign enterprise if the deemed profit method is used to the calculate of its taxable income according to Article 24 of the Detailed Rules & Regulations of Income Tax Law*

Concerning Foreign Enterprises, owing to the resson that the deductions of necessary expenses are already taken into account in determining its profit rate.

Reference:

Article 24:   If a foreign enterprise cannot provide accurate evidence of costs and expenses and cannot correctly work out its taxable income, the local tax authorities shall appraise and determine its profit rate with reference to the profit level of other enterprises of the same or similar trade, and then calculate its taxable income on the basis of its net sales or its gross business income.

The taxable income of a foreign enterprise engaged in contracted projects for exploring and exploiting offshore petroleum resources shall be calculated according to the profit rate appraised and determined in relation to its gross income of the contract.

Interpretation

Stipulations Concerning the Levy of Income Tax on Personnel Who are Paid from the Joint Account of Joint Petroleum Exploitation

(Cui Shiu (82) No. 18)
(Issued on 26th February 1982
by the Ministry of Finance)

Questions were raised by the Tax Bureau of Zhanjiang City or Guangdong province for clear instructions concerning salary, income and method of paying indicidual income tax of those personnel who work for the joint oil exploitation venture of the Branch Office of China South Sea Petroleum Corporation and Total Exploration of France are paid by the joint account.
According to Article 6 of the Individual Income Tax Law, the income earner shall be the tax payer, the paying unit shall be the withholding agent. The income earner shall be the tax payer means that a person who receives the income in his own name or have the paying authority pays him the salary and income. As regard to the handling methods, the situation is complicated and has to be decided by the authority concerned after the paying of tax. Therefore the personnel, who work for both the Chinese and French petroleum company in the joint exploitation of petroleum and paid by the joint account, are requested to pay individual income in accordance with the stipulation of the tax.

Reference:
Article 6 of the Individual Income Tax of the People's Republic of China.
"For individual income tax, the income earner shall be the tax payer and the paying unit shall be the withholding agent. Tax payers not covered by withholding are required personally to file declarations of their income and pay tax themselves."

SECTION C: Environmental Protection

Marine Environmental Protection Law of the People's Republic of China

(Passed by the 24th Meeting of the Standing Committee of the Fifth National People's Congress, on August 23, 1982, effective March 1, 1983)

Chapter I: General Provisions

Article 1:   This law is specially legislated in order to protect the marine environment and resources, to prevent damage from pollution, to protect the ecological balance, to guarantee human health and to promote the development of marine undertakings.

Article 2:   This law is applicable to the inland seas and territorial seas of the People's Republic of China (P.R.C.) and to all other sea areas within the jurisdiction of the P.R.C..

Any vessels, platform, aviation instrument, underwater instrument, enterprise or institution unit and individual which engages in navigation, exploration, development, production, scientific research and other activities within the jurisdictional sea areas of the P.R.C. must observe this law.

This law is also applicable to cases of the discharge of harmful substances and the dumping of waste materials outside the jurisdictional sea areas of the P.R.C. which cause damage from pollution in the jurisdictional sea areas of the P.R.C..

Article 3:   All units and individuals entering the jurisdictional sea areas of the P.R.C. have responsibility for protecting the marine environment, and also have the duty to carry on supervision of and to inform on conduct involving harm from pollution of the marine environment.

Article 4:   The relevant departments of the State Council, the people's governments of the coastal provinces, autonomous regions and directly-administered municipalities may, according to the requirements of protecting the marine environment, delineate marine special protection districts, maritime nature protection districts and seashore scenic tourist districts, and adopt appropriate protective measures. The State Council is to approve the determination of marine special protection districts and maritime nature protection districts.

Article 5: The environmental protection department of the State Council shall be in charge of the marine environmental protection work for the entire country.

The state marine control departments shall be responsible for organizing the investigation, testing, and overseeing of the marine environment and the development of scientific research, and shall also be in charge of environmental protection work to prevent harm from pollution from the exploration and development of offshore petroleum and from the offshore dumping of waste.

The harbour superintendencies of the P.R.C. shall be responsible for handling the supervision and investigation of vessels' discharge of waste, and for the monitoring of harbour waters, and shall also be in charge of the environmental protection work of preventing harm from pollution from vessels.

The state fishing administrations and organs of supervision and control of fishing ports shall be responsible for the supervision of ships' discharge of waste in fishing ports and for the overseeing of the waters of fishing port districts.

The environmental protection departments of the military shall be responsible for the supervision of military vessels' discharge of waste and for the overseeing of the waters of military harbours.

The environmental protection departments of the coastal provinces, autonomous regions and directly-administered municipalities shall be responsible for organizing the coordination, supervision and inspection of the marine environmental protection work for their own administrative district, and shall also in charge of the environmental protection work of preventing harm from pollution from coastal engineering projects and from pollutants with land sources.

Chapter II: Prevention of Harm from Pollution of the Marine Environment from Coastal Engineering Projects

Article 6: Units in charge of coastal engineering construction projects must, before compiling a report on the planned tasks, conduct a scientific investigation of the marine environment, and according to the natural conditions and social conditions, must reasonably select the location, and also compile and submit an environmental impact report in accordance with the relevant state regulations.

Article 7: In building harbours or oil jetties and in constructing hydropower and tide power electric generation projects at estuaries and river mouths, measures must be adopted to protect aquatic product resources. In building dams across the migration channels of fishes and crabs, appropriate facilities must be built for fish passage.

Article 8: Facilities for receiving and handling residue oil, waste oil, foul water containing oil, and waste materials shall be set up in harbours and oil jetties and the necessary anti-pollution equipment and installations for monitoring and warning shall be provided.

Article 9: The development and use of coastal wastelands shall be comprehensively planned, and control strengthened. Blocking off the sea to build up land or other engineering projects involving blocking off of the sea, as well as the excavation of sand stones, shall be strictly controlled. Construction which actually needs to be carried on must be based upon investigative research and the comparision of economic results, and an environmental impact report on the engineering project must be submitted to the environmental protection departments of the province, autonomous region or directly-administered municipality for examination and approval. Large-scale engineering projects involving blocking off of the sea must also be reported to the environmental protection department of the State Council for examination and approval.

Destruction of coastal protective forests, scenic forests, scenic rock and mangrove forests or coral reefs is prohibited.

Chapter III: Prevention of Harm from Pollution of the Marine Environment from the Exploration and Development of Offshore Petroleum

Article 10: Enterprises developing offshore petroleum, or their unit in charge, before compiling a report on the planned tasks, are to submit an environmental impact report, including effective measures for preventing harm from pollution to the marine environment, and submit this to the environmental protection department of the State Council for examination and approval.

Article 11: When exploration for offshore petroleum and other maritime activities require explosive operations, effective measures are to be adopted to protect fishery resources.

Article 12: Control shall be strengthened with regard to the oil materials used in the exploration and development processes. The occurrence of oil leakage incidents shall be prevented. Residue oil and waste oil shall be retrieved to discharge them into sea is prohibited.

Article 13: Foul water containing oil and oil-based mixtures from offshore petroleum well drilling ships, well drilling platforms and oil extraction platforms should not be directly discharged; with regard to the stuff which is to be discharged after retrieval and processing, its oil content should not exceed the standards as required by the state.

Article 14: Offshore petroleum well drilling ships, well drilling platforms and extraction platforms should not place industrial garbage containing oil in sea areas. In placing other industrial garbage, harm from pollution should not be caused to fishery waters or navigation channels.

Article 15: In testing oil on the sea, oil and oil-based mixtures should not be discharged into the sea, and it shall be ensured that oil and gas are fully burned off, [so as to] prevent the pollution of the sea.

Article 16: Maritime pipelines for transport of oil and oil storage facilities shall conform to anti-seepage, anti-leakage and anti-rotting requirements and always be maintained in good condition, in order to prevent oil leakage incidents.

Article 17: In exploration and development of offshore petroleum, it is required that appropriate anti-pollution facilities and equipment be provided and that effective technical measures be adopted, in order to prevent the occurrence of oil-leakage incidents.

The occurrence of well blowout or oil leakage incidents shall be immediately reported to the state marine control departments and effective measures adopted to control and remove the oil pollution, and accepted the investigation and handling of the matter by the state marine control departments.

Chapter IV: Prevention of Harm from Pollution of the Marine Environment from Pollutions with Land Sources

Article 18: With regard to the discharge of harmful substances into the sea areas by coastal units, waste discharge standards and relevant regulations promulgated by the state, provinces, autonomous regions or directly-administered municipalities of the People's Government must be strictly carried out.

In maritime nature protection districtions, aquatic product breeding farms, and scenic seashore tourist districts, new waste discharge outlets are not to be built. Those waste discharge outlets that already existed before the promulgation of this law, which discharge pollutants not conforming to the state's waste discharge standards, shall be brought under control within a stated period of time.

Article 19: Waste water of a strongly radioactive nature is prohibited to be discharged into sea areas.

Waste water of a weak radioactive nature which is actually required to be discharged into sea areas, the state's radioactivity protection regulations and standards must be executed.

Article 20: Medical waste water and industrial waste water containing antigens of infectious diseases must be processed and strictly sterilized. It can only be discharged into sea areas after the disease antigens are eliminated.

Article 21: The discharge of industrial waste water and domestic waste water containing organic matters or nutritive substances into bays, half-sealed seas or other sea areas which have relatively poor self-cleaning capacities shall be controlled, in order to prevent the rich nutrition f sea waters.

Article 22: With regard to the discharge of waste water containing heat into sea areas, measures shall be adopted to guarantee that the water temperature of the neighbouring fishery areas conforms to the state's water quality standards, in order to avoid heat pollution endanger aquatic product resources from heat pollution.

Article 23: Coastal farms utilizing agricultural chemical pesticides is to carry out the state's safety usage regulations and standards for agricultural pesticides.

Article 24: Unit not having received approval from the environmental protection departments of the coastal provinces, autonomous regions or directly-administered municipalities, is not permitted to cast off or pile up on the coastal beach tailings, slag, coal ash slag, garbage or other waste materials. With regard to waste material piling sites nd treatment sites approved according to law and set up on coastal beaches, protective embankments is to be built in order to prevent waste material from washing away into the sea.

Article 25: To prevent pollution, and enable the water quality at estuaries and river mouths to be in good condition, the environmental protection departments and water system control departments of the coastal provinces, autonomous regions and directly-administered municipalities shall strengthen the control of rivers that enter the sea.

Chapter V: Prevention of Harm from Pollution of the Marine Environment from Vessels

Article 26: All vessels are prohibited from discharging oils, oil-based mixtures, waste materials and other harmful substances in the jurisdictional sea areas of the P.R.C. in violation of the stipulations of this law.

Article 27: Oil-tankers of 150 gross tonnage or above and non-oil tankers of 400 gross tonnage or above are to be equipped with appropriate anti-pollution equipment and materials.

Oil tankers of under 150 gross tonnage and non-oil tankers of under 400 gross tonnage shall be equipped with specialized containers for retrieving residue oil and waste oil.

Article 28: Oil tankers of 150 gross tonnage or above and non-oil tankers of 400 gross tonnage or above are required to keep record books for oils. Vessels carrying 2000 tons or above of bulk oil cargo shall carry an effective "Certificate of Insurance for Civil Liability for harm from Oil Pollution or other Financial Guaranty" or a "Credit Certificate for Civil Liability for Harm from Oil Pollution", or shall provide other financial credit guaranties.

Article 29: In discharging foul water containing oil, oil tankers for 150 gross tonnage or above or non-oil tankers of 400 gross tonnage or above must proceed in accordance with the state's discharge standards and regulations regarding vessel's foul water, and make accurate entries in the record books for oils.

Article 30: Vessels carrying toxic goods or those of a corrosive nature, in discharging water from washing of storehouses and other residue materials, must proceed in accordance with the state's regulations regarding vessels' discharge of foul water, and make accurate entries in the sea navigation log.

Article 31: In discharging radioactive substances, nuclear-powered vessels and vessels carrying radioactive substances must observe the stipulations of Article 19 of this law.

Article 32: To prevent the occurrence of oil leakage incidents, vessels must observe operational rules and adopt effective preventive measures when carrying on oil-filling and oil loading and unloading operations.

Article 33: Ship-building, ship-repair, ship-wrecking and ship-salvaging units shall all be equipped with anti-pollution material and equipment. In carrying on their work, they shall adopt preventive measures in order to prevent the pollution of sea areas from oils, oil-based mixtures and waste materials.

Article 34: When vessels have abnormal discharges of oils, oil-based mixtures and other harmful substances, or when toxic goods or those of a corrosive nature fall into the water and cause pollution, measures shall be immediately adopted to control and eliminate the pollution, and a report made to the nearby harbour superintendency, and investigation and handling of the matter accepted.

Article 35: In cases where the occurrence of incidents of marine damage by vessels causes or could cause major harm from pollution to the marine environment, the harbour superintendencies of the P.R.C. have the right to compel the adoption of measures to avoid or reduce this harm from pollution.

Article 36: All vessels have the duty to monitor maritime pollution. If conduct violating regulations and facts of pollution are discovered, they shall be immediately reported to the nearby habour superintendency. When fishing boats are concerned, reports may also be made to the nearby fishing administration and organ of supervision and control of fishing ports.

Article 37: With regard to vessels navigating through, anchoring in or conducting operations in the jurisdictional sea areas of the P.R.C., when facts of pollution occur, the harbour superintendency of the P.R.C. is to board the vessels to investigate and handle the matter. State personnel of the relevant government organizations authorized by the harbour superintendencies may also board the vessels to investigate and report the results of the investigation to the harbour superintendencies for handling.

Chapter VI: Prevention of Harm from Pollution of the Marine Environment from Dumping of Waste Materials

Article 38: No unit should dump any waste materials into the jurisdictional sea areas of the P.R.C before receiving the approval of the state marine control departments.

Units which require to dump waste materials must submit applications to the state marine control departments, and may only dump after having received the approval after examination of the state marine control departments and been issued a license.

Article 39: Units that have received approval to dump waste materials shall carry on the dumping in accordance with the time limit and conditions and in the designated area(s) indicated on the license. After waste materials have been loaded, verification shall be done by the approving department. In cases of the use of vessels to dump waste materials, the verification is to be done by the harbour superintendency of the harbour out of which [the ships] sail.

Article 40: Units that have received approval to dump waste materials shall record in detail the circumstances of the dumping, and, after the dumping, make a written report to the approving department. Vessels that dump waste materials must make a written report to the harbour superintendency of the harbour out of which they sail.

Chapter VII: Legal Liability

Article 41: In any cases of violation of this law that cause or could cause harm from pollution of the marine environment the relevant development in charge stipulated in Article 5 of this law may order that the matter be brought under control within a stated period of time, the payment of a pollutant discharge fee, the payment of the costs of eliminating the pollution, and compensation for the state's losses. It may also give warnings or impose fines. If a party dose not agree, he can bring suit in the people's courts within fifteen days of the date of receipt of the decision. In cases where the period is completed and suit has not been brought and the party also has not performed, the relevant department in charge is to apply to the people's courts for compulsory execution.

Article 42: Units of individuals that have suffered harm as a result of pollution of the marine environment have the right to demand compensation for their losses from the party that caused the harm from pollution. Disputes concerning liability for compensation and the amount of compensation may be handled by the relevant department in charge. If a party does not agree, the matter is to be resolved in accordance with the procedures stipulated in the "Civil Procedure Law of the People's Republic of China (for trial application)". Suit may also be brought directly in the people's courts.

Article 43: In cases entirely covered by one of the following circumstances, in which after the timely adoption of reasonable measures the harm from pollution of the marine environment still could not be avoided, is to be exempted from bearing liability for compensation:
    (1)   war conduct;
    (2)   irresistable natural disasters;
    (3)   carelessness or other negligent conduct in carrying out their duties on the part of the departments in charge of lighthouses or other navigation aiding equipment.
In cases where harm from pollution of the marine environment was completely caused by the intent or negligence of a third party, the third party is to bear the liability for compensation.

Article 44: In any cases of violation of this law, and harm from pollution of the marine environment, that cause serious losses to public or private property or injury or death to persons, the criminal responsibility of the directly responsible person(s) may be investigated according to law by the judicial organs.

Chapter VIII: Supplementary Provisions

Article 45: The meanings of the following terms in this law are:
    (1)   "Harm from pollution of the marine environment" refers to the direct or indirect introduction of substances or energy into the marine environment, engendering harmful influences such as harm to marine biological resources, danger to human health, hindrance to fisheries and other lawful maritime activities, or damage to the usage quality of sea water and lowering of and harm to the quality of the

environment.

    (2) "Fishery waters" refers to egg-laying sites, bait-gathering sites, sites for weathering the winter or migrating channels for fish and shrimp varieties and breeding grounds for fish, shrimps, shellfish and algae.

    (3) "Oils" refers to any type of oils and their refined products.

    (4) "Oil-based mixtures" refers to any mixtures which contain a portion of oil.

    (5) "Discharge" refers to the conduct of ejecting pollutants into the sea, including pumping out, spilling out, leaking out, spraying out and dumping out.

    (6) "Dump" refers to the conduct of placing waste materials or other harmful substances into the sea by means of ships, aviation instruments, platforms or other means of transport, including the conduct of the discarding of ships, aviation instruments, platforms or other means of flotation.

Article 46: In the case of any regulations regarding marine environmental protection currently in effect which conflict with this law, this law is in all cases to prevail.

Article 47: The environmental protection department of the State Council may formulate detailed implementing regulations according to this law and report them to the State Council for approval and enforcement.

The relevant departments of the State Council and the standing committees of the people's congresses and the people's governments of the coastal provinces, autonomous regions and directly-administered municipalities may formulate specific implementation measures according to this law and in line with the actual situation of the department or district in question.

Article 48: This law is to take effect on March 1, 1983.

The Provisional Law of Environmental Protection of the People's Republic of China

(Adopted in Principle at the 11th Meeting
of the Standing Committee of the
Fifth National People's Congress
on September 13, 1979)

Chapter I: General Provisions

Article 1:   This law is established in accordance with Article 11 of the Constitution of the People's Republic of China which provides that "the State protects the environment and natural resources and prevents and eliminates pollution and other hazards to the public."

Article 2:   The function of the Environmental Protection Law of the People's Republic of China is to ensure, during the construction of a modernized socialist state, rational use of the natural environment, prevention and elimination of environmental pollution and damage to ecosystems, in order to create a clean and favourable living and working environment, protect the health of the people and promote economic development.

Article 3:   For the purposes of this law, "environment" includes: the atmosphere, water, land, mineral resources, forests, grassland, wildlife, wild plants, aquatic plants and animals, famous spots and historic sites, scenic spots for sightseeing, hot springs, health resorts, nature conservation areas, residential districts, etc.

Article 4:   The guidelines governing environmental protection work are: overall planning, rational layout, comprehensive utilization, conversion of harm into good, reliance upon the masses with everybody taking part in the protection of the environment for the benefit of the people.

Article 5:   The State Council and its subordinate bodies, and the local people's governments at all levels shall endeavour to carry out environmental protection work in earnest and do a good job of it. They shall make overall plans for the protection and improvement of the environment in planning for national economic development and take practical measures for its implementation. Where pollution of the environment and other hazards to the public have already been caused, plans should be worked out to eliminate such in a systematic and orderly manner.

Article 6: All enterprises and institutes shall pay adequate attention to the prevention of pollution and damage to the environment when selecting their sites, designing, constructing and planning production. In planning new construction, reconstruction and extension projects, a report on the potential environmental effects shall be submitted to the environmental protection department and other relevant departments for examination and approval before designing can be started. The installations for the prevention of pollution and other hazards to the public should be designed, built and put into operation at the same time as the main project. Discharge of all kinds of harmful substances shall be in compliance with the criteria set down by the State.

The units which have caused pollution and other hazards to the environment shall, according to the principle of "whoever causes pollution shall be responsible for its elimination," make plans to actively eliminate such, or alternatively submit an application to the competent authorities for approval to transfer the property or move to some other place.

Article 7: In rebuilding old cities or building new ones, assessments shall be made of the potential environmental effects in industrial and residential areas, public utility facilities, and green belts by reference to the meteorological, geographical, hydrological and ecological conditions; and overall planning and rational layout shall be made to prevent pollution and other hazards to the public so as to build a clean modern city in a planned way.

Article 8: The citizen has the right to supervise, accuse and bring a complaint before the court against the unit or the individual who has caused pollution and damage to the environment. The unit or the individual thus accused and charged shall not take any retaliatory action.

Article 9: Foreigners or foreign aircraft, ships, vehicles, goods, plants and animals, etc. entering or passing through Chinese territory, territorial waters, or airspace shall be subject to the present law and other regulations and rules relating to the protection of the environment.

Chapter II: Protection of the Natural Environment

Article 10: Use the land rationally according to local conditions, improve the soil and increase the vegetation to prevent soil erosion, hardening, alkalinization, desertification, and water losses.

Comprehensive scientific surveys shall be carried out before going ahead with plans to reclaim wasteland, put up dykes along the seacoast or lakes, and conservancy facilities. Practical measures for protection and improvement of the environment shall be taken to prevent damage to the ecosystems.

Article 11:   Keep bodies of water such as rivers, lakes, seas, reservoirs, etc., from being polluted so as to preserve the quality of water in a good state. Protect, develop and utilize aquatic flora and fauna in a rational way. Fishing to the extent of threatening extinction of, and damage to, living resources is prohibited.

Exercise tight control over, and economize, use of water in industry, agriculture, and in daily life. Exploit rationally the subsoil waters to prevent exhaustion of water resources and surface subsidence.

Article 12:   In exploiting mineral resources, comprehensive surveying, evaluation and utilization should be carried out. Excavating and mining at random is strictly forbidden, and tailings and slags should be appropriately disposed of, to prevent damage to resources and pollution of the natural environment.

Article 13:   Strictly adhere to the National Forestry Law; protect and develop forest resources; fell trees in a rational way; tend trees and reforest at the appropriate time. Destroying forest to reclaim land and arbitrary cutting and felling are strictly forbidden. Preventive measures should be taken against forest fires.

Efforts should be made to plant trees everywhere and make barren hills, wasteland, desert areas and semi-desert areas green; tree planting should be vigorously carried out in villages, towns, and industrial and mining districts. Make good use of all available scattered open spaces inside and outside factory compounds, mining districts, school campuses, office compounds, along roadsides, river banks, and around villages and houses by planting trees and grass so as to turn the whole country into a big park.

Article 14:   Protect and develop forage resources. Actively plan and carry out the grassland development programme; herd sheep and cattle rationally; maintain and improve the regenerating capacity of the grasslands, and prevent the grasslands from deteriorating. Abusive exploitation of grassland is strictly forbidden. Efforts should be made to prevent grassland fires.

Article 15:   Protect, develop, and utilize rationally wildlife and wild plant resources. National regulations forbid hunting of rare animals and felling of precious trees.

Chapter III: Prevention and Elimination of Pollution and Other Hazards to the Public

Article 16:   Actively prevent and control noxious substances from factories, mines, enterprises and urban life, such as waste gas, waste water, waste residues, dust, garbage, radioactive material, etc., as well as noise, vibration, and bad odours from polluting and damaging the environment.

Article 17:   Enterprises or institutions that will cause pollution of the environment shall not be set up in the residential areas of the cities and towns, water resource protection zones, places of historic interest and scenic beauty, scenic "spots for sightseeing, hot springs, health resorts and nature conservation areas. Where such units have been established, a target date shall be set for elimination and control of the pollution, or

	making necessary adjustments, or removal.
Article 18:	Actively conduct experiments and adopt new technology, techniques and devices which are pollution-free or will reduce pollution.

Strengthen business management and carry out civilized production; make comprehensive use of such environment-pollution substances as waste gas, waste water and waste residues, and transform them into useful things. Discharge of such substances where necessary shall be in compliance with the criteria laid down by the State. Where such national criteria cannot be met for the time being, a later date will be set for compliance; if national standards still cannot be met by the dealine, a limit shall be set to production.

In cases where release of pollutants goes beyond the limits of the specified national standards, a fee shall be charged towards dealing with the release of such pollutants according to the quantities and concentrations of the pollutants released as specified in the relevant regulations.

Article 19: All smoke-discharging devices, industrial furnaces, motor vehicles, ships, etc. shall take effective measures to eliminate smoke and dust, and discharge off noxious gas shall be in compliance with the standards laid down by the State.

Develop and use on a large scale coal gas, liquefied petroleum gas (LPG), natural gas, marsh gas, solar energy, terrestrial heat and other non-polluting or less polluting energy sources. In the cities, district central heating should be promoted.

Article 20: Dumping garbage and waste residues into the waters is prohibited. Discharge of sewage shall be in compliance with the standards set down by the State.

Ships are prohibited from discharging substances containing oil, poison, and other harmful wastes into the waters protected by the law of this country.

It is strictly prohibited to discharge poisonous and harmful waste water by way of seepage pits, crevices, lava holes, or dilution methods. Prevent seepage of water containing industrial filth to ensure that subsoil water is not contaminated.

Take strong measures to protect soures of drinking water from contamination and gradually perfect the sewage discharge piping system and sewage purification facilities.

Article 21: Actively develop effective, low-toxin and low-residue agricultural pesticides. Promote comprehensive and biological methods of prevention and control; use rationally sewage for irrigation so as to prevent pollution of the soil and crops.

Article 22: Step up control of noise and vibration in urban and industrial districts. All kinds of noisy machines, motor vehicles, aircraft, etc. with heavy vibrations are required to install noise suppressors and antivibration devices.

Article 23: The units which emit harmful gases or dust should actively adopt sealed production equipment and technology, and install ventilating, dust collecting and purifying, and recovery facilities. The amount of harmful gases and dust in the working environment must conform with the standards for industrial hygiene specified by the law of this country.

Article 24: Registration and control of toxic chemicals must be strictly carried out. Highly toxic substances should be tightly sealed to prevent leakage during storage and transportation.

Radioactive materials, electro-magnetic radiation, etc. should be strictly monitored and controlled according to the applicable law of this country.

Article 25: Strict precautions shall be taken to prevent pollution of food in the course of production, processing, packing, transportation, storage, and marketing. Food inspection shall be strengthened, and the sale, export and import of foods not meeting the requirements of national hygienic standards shall be prohibited.

Chapter IV: Environmental Protection Office and its Functions

Article 26: The State Council has established an Environmental Protection Office whose main functions are:

(a) To implement and supervise the carrying out of national guidelines, policies, laws and acts relating to environmental protection;

(b) To draft regulations, rules, standards, economic and technical policies relating to environmental protection in conjunction with relevant departments;

(c) To develop long-term programmes and annual plans for protection of the environment in conjunction with relevant departments and to encourage and supervise their implementation;

(d) To make unified plans for organizing the monitoring of the environment; carry out investigations and keep under review the environmental situation and development trends of the whole country, and recommend improvement measures;

(e) To organize and coordinate, in conjunction with relevant departments, research and educational programmes in environmental science, actively promote foreign as well as domestic advanced experiences and techniques in the field of environmental protection;

(f) To direct the environmental protection work of all the departments under the State Council, and of the provinces, autonomous regions, and municipalities directly under the central government;

(g) To organize and coordinate international cooperation and communication in the field of environmental protection.

Article 27: The people's government of the provinces, autonomous regions, and municipalities directly under the central government shall establish environmental protection bureaus in their respective areas. The people's governments of the municipalities, autonomous prefectures, counties, and autonomous counties may establish environmental protection organizations as required.

The main functions of the local environmental protection organizations at every level are: To supervise and urge the implementation of the national guidelines, policies, laws and acts relating to the protection of environment in the various departments and units within their jurisdictions; to draft applicable local standards and specifications concerning environmental protection; to organize monitoring of the environment and keep under review the local environmental situation and development trends; to develop long-term programmes and annual plans applicable locally for the protection of the environment in conjunction with the relevant departments, and supervise their implementation; to organize local research and educational programmes in environmental science in conjunction with relevant departments; to actively promote foreign as well as domestic advanced experiences and techniques in the field of environmental protection.

Article 28: The relevant departments under the State Council, the local people's governments at all levels, large- and medium-size enterprises, and relevant instituions shall establish, as required, environmental protection offices separately responsible for the protection of the environment within their own system of affiliated organizations, departments, and units.

Chapter V: Scientific Research, Propaganda and Education

Article 29: China Environmental Science Research Institute, relevant scientific institutes, universities and colleges should devote major efforts to research in the following areas: fundamental principles of environmental science, environmental management, environmental economics, comprehensive control techniques, environmental quality evaluation, environmental pollution and human health, rational use and protection of the natural environment, etc.

Article 30: Cultural and publicity departments should actively carry out publicity and educational programmes to disseminate the knowledge of environmental science so as to enhance the understanding of the general public about the significance of environmental protection work and to raise the scientific and technical standards in the environmental field.

Environmental protection specialists should be trained in a planned way. The educational departments should establish a required course or speciality in environmental protection in the relevant departments of the universities and colleges. Middle and primary school textbooks should include appropriate texts relating to environmental protection.

Chapter VI: Rewards and Punishments

Article 31: The State will give commendations and rewards to units and individuals who have made outstanding achievements and contributions to the work of environmental protection.

The State will grant tax reductions or exemptions on, and apply a preferential pricing policy to, products manufactured by utilizing waste gas, waste water, and waste residues as main material, and the profits originating there from need not be turned over to the higher authorities but will be used by the manufacturers concerned to

	control pollution and improve the environment.
Article 32:	Units which have violated this law and other environmental protection regulations and rules by polluting and damaging the environment and causing hazards to the people's health shall, according to the merit of each case, be criticized, warned, fined, or ordered to pay damages and stop production and control and eliminate such pollution, by the environmental protection organizations at various levels subject to the approval of the people's government of the corresponding level.
	Unit leaders, persons directly responsible or other citizens who have caused serious pollution and damage to the environment resulting in casualties or substantial damage to farming forestry, animal husbandry, side-line production and fishery shall be held responsible administratively, economically, and even criminally, as the case may be, according to law.

Chapter VII: Supplementary Articles

Article 33:	The State Council may establish regulations and rules relating to environmental protection according to the present law.

Provisional Procedures for the Collection of Pollutant Discharge Penalties

(Issued on February 5, 1982)

Provisional Procedures for the Collection of Pollutant Discharge Penalties

Article 1: These Procedures are formulated on the basis of the provisions in Article 18 of the "The Environmental Protection Law of The People's Republic of China (Provisional)" that pollutant discharge penalties shall be collected as stipulated on the pollutants discharged in excess of the standards stipulated by the state in accordance with the numbers of quantities and concentrations or densities of the discharged pollutants.

Article 2: The collection of pollutant discharge penalties is aimed at urging enterprises and institutions to give more effective management and administration, save and put resources to comprehensive use, bring pollution under control and improve the environment.

Article 3: All enterprises and institutions shall observe such relevant standards as the "Provisional Standards of the Discharge of the Three Industrial Wastes (i.e., waste water, waste gas and industrial residue)" promulgated by the state. If the people's government of a province, an autonomous region or a municipality directly under the Central Government has approved and promulgated regional standards of discharge, the enterprises and institutions in the locality shall observe the regional standards of discharge.

Pollution discharge penalties shall be collected from the enterprises and institutions which discharge pollutants in excess of the above standards; heating boiler smoke and dust discharge penalties shall be collected from other pollutant discharge units.

Although a pollutant discharge unit pays pollutant discharge penalties, it shall not be exempted from the responsibilities of bringing pollution under control and compensating for damages which shall be borne by it and from other responsibilities stipulated by the law.

Article 4: A pollutant discharge unit shall report the kinds, numbers or amounts and concentrations or densities of the pollutants discharged as circumstances are to the local environmental protection department and register them with it, which shall serve as the grounds for the collection of pollutant discharge penalties after being examined and ratified by the environmental protection department or the monitoring unit assigned by it.

Article 5: The standards for the collection of pollutant discharge penalties shall be implemented as stipulated in the attached lists of these Procedures. A very few large or medium cities which have concentrated industries and are particularly seriously polluted shall properly readjust the standards of the charges with the approval of the Environmental Protection Leading Group of the State Council.

The penalties shall be calculated in accordance with the highest rate if the waste water or waste gas or industrial residue discharged by a pollutant discharge unit contains more than two harmful substances in the same discharge outlet.

The standards of the collection for the additional items to regional standards of discharge shall be prescribed by the people's government of a province, an autonomous region or a municipality directly under the Central Government in light of the attacted lists of these Procedures.

Article 6: If a pollutant discharge unit is below the standards of discharge after payment of pollutant discharge penalties, the standards of collection shall be increased by 5% every year from the third year of the beginning of collection. If the pollutant discharge unit has observed the standards of discharge or has remarkably reduced the numbers or quantities and concentrations or densities of pollutants discharged through control and strengthened administration, it shall make an application to the local environmental protection department and the collection shall be stopped or the penalties shall be reduced after it is proved to be true through monitoring.

The penalties shall be doubled if the pollutants discharged by newly-built, extended, rebuilt, productivity-enhanced, improved or transformed projects exceed the standards after the promulgation of the The Environmental Protection Law of the People's Republic of China (Provisional) or if they have pollutant treatment facilities but fail to put them into operation or if the pollutants discharged exceed the standards again after the removal of the treatment facilities without authorization.

Each province, autonomous region or municipality directly under the Central Government shall make other provisions for the increase or reduction of penalties according to actual conditions.

Article 7: Pollutant discharge penalties shall be paid monthly or quarterly. Regardless of its relations of jurisdiction and ownership, any pollutant discharge unit shall pay the pollutant discharge penalties to the specified bank within 20 days in accordance with the notice of payment from the local environmental protection department. If the payment is not made within the time limit, a fine for one thousandth of the amount in default shall be additionally collected every day.

The pollutant discharge penalties paid by the pollutant discharge units under the jurisdiction of the ministries of the Central Government and of provinces (autonomous regions and municipalities directly under the Central Government) shall be turned over to the provincial revenue and those paid by other pollutant discharge units shall be turned over to local revenue. In the cities where the enterprises under the jurisdiction of the central ministries and provinces are concentrated, the pollutant discharge penalties shall be turned over to the local revenue with the approval of the provincial people's governments.

Article 8: The pollutant discharge penalties paid by an enterprise shall be included in the cost of production. Those above the standards of collection shall be paid from the profit reserves or business funds or an enterprise of the whole people's ownership; they shall be paid from the profits after the payment of the income tax in the case of an enterprise of the whole people's ownership or of collective ownership which practises "paying taxed instead of turning over profits, independent accounting and assuming sole responsibility for its profits or losses." The pollutant discharge penalties paid by an institution shall be paid from the balance after completion of unit payments and extra-budgetary funds, and if they are still insufficient, the penalties shall be paid from the unit operating expenses.

Article 9: The pollutant discharge penalties collected shall be brought into the budget as environmental protection subsidies which shall be administered as special funds and shall not take part in the system division of net gains.

The environmental protection subsidies shall be planned and arranged for use in a unified way by the environmental protection departments jointly with the financial departments. The departments shall adhere to earmarking funds for their specified purposes only, collecting first and using later, keeping expenditures within the limits of income and guarding against overspending or diversion. Any surplus shall be carried forward for use in the next year.

Article 10: Environmental protection subsidies shall be mainly used to subsidize key pollutant discharge units for the control of the sources of pollution and for the comprehensive control measures of environmental pollution.

When a pollutant discharge unit takes measures to bring pollution under control, it shall first make use of its own financial resources and if they are really insufficient, it shall report the case to the authorities in charge. The authorities shall examine it, gather the same cases from the units concerned under their jurisdiction and then make an application to the environmental protection department and the financial department for the granting of a certain amount of subsidies out of the environmental production subsidies. In general, these subsidies shall not be more than 80 percent of the pollutant discharge penalties paid. It shall also be allowed to grant 80 percent of the environmental protection subsidies to every bureau in charge to arrange for use to subsidize enterprises and institutions to bring pollution under control under the supervision of the environmental protection department and the financial department. The units in the case as stated in Clause 2 of Article 6 shall not be subsidized.

Environmental protection subsidies shall be appropriately used to subsidize and environmental protection department for the purchase of the monitoring instruments and equipment, but shall not be used for administrative outlays and such non-business expenses as building offices, dormitories, etc.

Article 11:   Environmental protection subsidies shall be allocated under the supervision of the Construction Bank.

Article 12:   The people's government of each province, autonomous region and municipality directly under the Central Government shall formulate specific procedures for implementation on the basis of these Procedures.

Article 13:   These Procedures shall be put into effect as of July 1, 1982.

Appendix

Standards of Collection of Pollutant Discharge Penalties: Waste Gas

Names of Harmful Substances

Discharge Amout above Standard (per kg.)

Concentration above Standard (per 10 cu.m.)

Unit: Yuan

sulfur dioxide, carbon disulfide, hydrogen sulfide, fluorides, nitrogen oxides, chlorine, hydrogen chloride, carbon oxide.

sulfuric acid (mist), lead, mercury, beryllides

production dust

industrial & heating boiler smoke & dust

glass wool, slag wool, rock wool, aluminides

power station coal dust, cement dust

steel-making furnace dust, other dust

multiple more than standard Rimgelman density charge per ton fuel

0.04   *0.10*   *0.02*   *0.04*

less than 4 Scale 2 3.00

0.03 — 0.10

4.1 — 6   *6.1 — 9*   *over 9*
Scale 3   *Scale 4*   *Scale 5*
4.00   *5.00*   *6.00*

Notes:
(1) No penalties shall be charged for the time being for the smoke discharged from steam locomotives and other mobile sources of pollution.
(2) Pollutant discharge penalties for the waste gas from thermal power stations, industrial and heating boilers shall now termporarily be charged as smoke and dust. No penalties shall be charged for other harmful substances for the time being.

Appendix

Standards of Collection of Pollutant Discharge Penalties: Waste Water

Names of harmful Substances or Items   *Unit: Yuan/Ton Water*

Multiple of Concentration More than Standard

below 5   5 — 10   10 — 20   20 — 50   over 50

mercury, cadmium, arsenic, lead and their inorganic compounds, 6-valence chromium compounds

sulfides, petroleum and the like, volatile phenol, cyanides, organic phosphorus, copper, zinc, fluorine and their compounds, nitrobenzene, phenyl amines

suspended substances, COD, BOD, PH value

pathogens

0.15—	0.20—	0.30—	0.45—	0.90—
0.20	0.30	0.45	0.90	2.00
0.10—	0.15—	0.20—	0.35—	0.60—
0.15	0.20	0.35	0.60	1.00
0.04—	0.06—	0.10—	0.15—	0.20—
0.06	0.10	0.15	0.20	0.30
0.08				

Editor's Notes

If the PH values are beyond 6 — 9, one value above or below those values shall be calculated as one-fold of the base (0.04 — 0.06 yuan) for the multiple below 5 exceeding standard.

Appendix

Standards of Collection of Pollutant Discharge Penalties: Residue

Names of Harmful Substances   *Unit: Yuan*

residues containing mercury, cadmium, arsenic, 6-valence chromium, lead, cyanides, yellow phosphorus and other soluble deadly poisons

power plant powdered coal ash

other industrial residues

	Dumped or Discharged into Water Bodies (per ton)	*Piled without Precautions against Water or Seepage (per ton/month)*	*Piled without Specially provided Piling Places (per ton/month)*
	36.00	*2.00*	*1.20*
	5.00	*0.10*	*0.30*

Editor's Notes

(1)   Such acts as discharging, dumping or piling deadly poisonous residues without any precautions against water or seepage shall be promptly checked and the offenders shall be ordered to remove them in addition to the penalties.
(2)   The item of "power plant powdered coal ash" is only applicable to the coal-burning power plants which have been completed and put into production before the promulgation of the "The Environmental Protection Law (Provisional)" and are not provided with ash yards with the ash discharged into water bodies. The standard for "other industrial residues" is applicable to the powdered coal ash discharged by other power plants (including the above ones which have been extended).
(3)   No penalties shall be charged for the time being for the residues piled in such facilities as tailing dams, ash yards, residues (including gangue), special-purpose piling yards, etc.

II INSURANCE

SECTION A: Overall policy

Articles of Association of the People's Insurance Company of China

Chapter I   General Provisions

1.   The People's Insurance Company of China is a state-owned enterprise of the People's Republic of China and a specialized company transacting insurance business.

2.   The People's Insurance Company of China shall have its head office in Beijing, and may set up branches, sub-branches or subsidiaries both at home and abroad to meet the needs of business.

3.   The scope of business of the People's Insurance Company of China and its branches and sub-branches shall be:

   (1)   To underwrite different types of property insurance, life insurance, liability insurance, credit insurance, agricultural insurance and other insurances;

   (2)   To transact different types of reinsurance;

   (3)   To act on behalf of foreign insurance companies in the certification of losses and settlement of claims as well as in the conduct of related affairs;

   (4)   To purchase, rent, hire or exchange personal or real property having relation to business of the company;

   (5)   To transact such other business as entrusted and approved by the state;

   (6)   To do all matters for transacting the aforesaid business.

Chapter II   Capital

4.   The capital of the People's Insurance Company of China shall be Rmb500 million.

Chapter III   Organization

5.   The People's Insurance Company of China shall have a board of directors

consisting of 17 to 23 directors, all to be nominated by the Competent Department of the state. The board of directors shall elect 7 to 9 directors as managing directors and shall nominate among them a chairman and 1 to 2 vice-chairmen, to be reported to the State Council for appointment.

6. The powers and functions of the board of directors shall be:

(1) To examine and decide business policies and development plans of the company in accordance with the policy of the state;

(2) To decide the establishment or closing down of or change in branches, sub-branches or subsidiaries;

(3) To examine and decide annual budgets and final accounts and the plan for the allocation of the company's surplus each year as well as such matters as the board of directors deems important;

(4) To listen to reports by the general manager or the deputy general manager.

7. The People's Insurance Company of China shall have a board of supervisors consisting of 7 to 9 supervisors, to be nominated by the Competent Department of the state. The board of supervisors shall elect 3 managing supervisors and shall nominate among them a chief supervisor, to be reported to the State Council for appointment.

8. The powers and functions of the board of supervisors shall be:

(1) To examine annual budgets and final accounts;

(2) To inspect all accounts;

(3) To investigate important cases.

9. A meeting of the board of directors shall be held once every year, to be convoked by the chairman, who shall preside at the meeting. In case the chairman is, for any reason, unable to be present, the meeting shall be convoked by the vice-chairman, who shall act as the interim chairman.

A meeting of the board of supervisors shall be held once every year, to be convoked by the chief supervisor, who shall preside at the meeting.

A joint meeting may be held by the board of directors and the board of supervisors, and the chairman shall preside at the meeting.

10. When the meeting of the board of directors is adjourned, the chairman, vice-chairman, or the managing director under the entrustment of the former shall take charge of the day-to-day work of the board of directors.

11. The People's Insurance Company of China shall have a general manager and a number of deputy general managers, to be nominated by the chairman an appointed by the board of directors. The general manager of the People's Insurance Company of China shall be responsible for all daily affairs of the company, and the deputy general manager shall assist the general manager in his work.

Chapter IV Financial Affairs

12. The fiscal year of the People's Insurance Company of China shall be from January to December of each year. At the end of each fiscal year a balance sheet, business report, profit and loss account, inventory list and plan for allocation of surplus shall be complied and presented by the general manager to the board of supervisors for verification and to the board of directors for examination before submitted to the Competent Department of the state for the record.

Chapter V   Addendum

13.   Anything not expressly provided for herein shall be dealt with in accordance with pertinent laws and statues of the state and supplemented or revised by the board of directors.

Forms & Documentation

THE Insurance Company of China

Head office: Beijing   Established in 1949

OFFSHORE OIL EXPLORATION AND DEVELOPMENT INSURANCE POLICY

Policy No. _____

NOW THIS POLICY OF INSURANCE WITNESSES that THE INSURANCE COMPANY OF CHINA, at the request of the ASSURED and in consideration of the ASSURED having paid to the Company the premium agreed upon undertakes to insure the following risks subject to the terms and conditions contained in the clauses, additional clauses and/or endorsements attached hereto and in the Schedule printed overleaf.

Risk/Risks to be insured:

FOR THE INSURANCE CO. OF CHINA

Date _____

Forms & Documentation

SCHEDULE			
APPLICANT:		**POLICY NO.**	
ASSURED:			
PROPERTY INSURED			
SUBJECT INSURED:	INSURED VALUE:		INSURED AMOUNT:
TRADING AREA			
COVERAGE			
PERIOD OF INSURANCE:			
LIMIT OF LIAB.			
INSURANCE CONDITIONS			
DEDUCTIBLE:			
PREMIUM:	RATE:		TOTAL PREMIUM:
	PAYABLE:		
REMARKS:			

Forms & Documentation

COST OF CONTROL INSURANCE

1. **Named Assured(s)**:

2. **Period of Insurance**: For and during the space of twelve calendar months commencing at and ending at

3. **Co-ventures**: It is understood and agreed that this Insurance shall be deemed to insure the interest of the Named Assured and of any or all non-operators, co-venturers, co-owners, mining partners, partners, or other party/ies (all hereinafter referred to as "Co-Venturer(s)" for whom the Named Assured is responsible to provide insurance, in the expenses hereinafter defined.
    The cover granted under the immediate preceding paragraph in respect of Co-Venturers shall be limited to those wells in which a Co-Venturer has a common interest with the Named Assured(s) and shall be subject in all respects to the terms, conditions and rates specified herein.
    A Co-Venturer shall be deemed to be named as an additional Assured hereunder for the periods(s) of time that their interest is insured hereunder.

4. **Loss(es)**, if any, shall be adjusted with and payable to the Named Assured(s) and the Co-Venturer(s), if any, as their respective interests may appear.

5. The Underwriters agree, subject to the terms and conditions of this Policy to reimburse the Assured for expenses incurred by Assured in regaining control of all well(s) covered by this Policy located within the areas specified in the attached schedule.

6. (a) The Underwriters shall reimburse the Assured under this Policy for expenses as hereinafter defined, incurred by the Assured in regaining control of oil or gas well(s) covered hereunder, and/or any other well(s) which get out of control, during the period from the beginning of drilling, recompletion, completion, reworking, testing, cleaning out, repairing, reconditioning operations or other operations of any nature on well(s) of Assured or in which Assured owns an interest, until completion or abandonment of such operations as set forth in Paragraph 7 of this form, and other coverages as set out in Paragraph 6 (e) below.
    (b) In the event the well(s) insured gets out of control the Underwriters will reimburse the Assured for the costs of materials and supplies required, contractors equipment and services, and equipment and services of individuals or firms specializing in controlling wells, including directional drilling, and other operations necessary to bring the well(s) under control.
    (c) A well(s) shall be deemed out of control when there is a continuous flow of drilling fluid, oil, gas or water above the surface of the ground (or water-bottom in the case of a well(s) located in water) which is uncontrollable.
    (d) In any circumstances Underwriters liability for expenses of regaining control of well(s) shall cease when the well(s) is controlled above the surface of the ground (or waterbottom in the case of a well located in water).
    (e) It is understood and agreed that coverage afforded by this Policy also applies to:—
      (1) a producing well
      (2) a shut-in well or a well temporarily abandoned.
      and any other well or hole that gets out of control as a direct result of a well insured under this Policy getting out of control.

7. **Attachment and Termination of Coverage**: Such Insurance as is provided hereunder shall attach on new wells at the time of "spudding-in" and on all other wells not otherwise insured hereunder upon the commencement of deepening, reworking, reconditioning or other similar operations.
    Except in respect to completed wells insured hereunder, the insurance as is provided hereunder shall terminate upon either total and/or completed abandonment or completion of the wells, which shall include the setting of the "Christmas Tree", pumping equipment or well head equipment or the dismantling or removal of the drilling equipment from the location whichever shall occur later. Provide that, if removal of the drilling equipment from location occurs first, the period of time between complete removal of such equipment and the commencement of completion operations does not exceed 30 days or h.c.

8. **Limit of Liability**: It is the intent of this Policy to make available to the Assured(s) insurance up to but not exceeding
    any one occurrence subject to deductile as Paragraph 10 and co-insurance as Paragraph 11.

9. **Partial Interest Clause**: The limit(s) of liability, the deductible and the rates expressed herein apply when the interest insured here-under is 100%. In the event that the interest in any one operation insured hereunder does not amount to 100%, then the limit of liability, the deductible and the rates applicable to that operation shall be reduced proportionately and shall apply in the same proportion as the total interest insured hereunder bears to 100%.

10. **Deductible Clause:**
    Areas
    Assured to bear the first   3 of each claim.
    Areas
    Assured to bear the first   of each claim.

11. **Coinsurance**:   It is a condition of this Insurance that the Assured shall be a Co-insurer with Underwriters hereon as follows:
% coinsurance

It is further a condition that this coinsurance remains uninsured.

12. **Exclusions**:
    (a) The Underwriters shall have no liability for expense in connection with Bodily Injury, illness, disease, death, workmen's compensation, loss of hole, loss of drill stem, damage to any part of contractors drilling rig and equipment, loss or damage to property, loss of production, all fishing costs, all expense of conditioning well(s) to resume drilling operations.
    (b) Any wells insured underthe Continuation Clause (if any) of the expiring Policy are excluded.
    (c) Excluding claim or expenses resulting from
        (1) hostile or warlike action in time of peace or war, including action in hindering, combating or defending against an actual, impending or expected attack, by any government or sovereign power (de jure or de facto), or by any authority maintaining or using military, naval or air forces; or by military, naval or air forces or by any agent of any such government, power, authority or forces.
        (2) any weapon of war employing atomic fission or radioactive force whether in time of peace or war.
        (3) insurrection, rebellion, revolution, civil war, usurped power, or action taken by governmental authority in hindering, combating or defending against such an occurrence, destruction under quarantine or Customs regulations, confiscation by order of any government or public authority or trade.
    Notwidthstanding the above, this Insurance shall cover loss directly caused by acts committed by an agent of any government, party or faction engaged in war hostilities or other warlike operations, provided such agent is acting secretly and not in connection with any operation of the armed forces (whether military, naval or air forces) in the country where the property is situated. Nothing in the foregoing shall be construed to include any loss or expense caused by or resulting from any of the risks or perils excluded above excepting only the acts of certain agents expressly covered herein but in no event shall this Insurance include any loss or expense caused by or resulting from any weapon of war employing atomic fission or radioactive force whether in time of peace or war.

13. **Relief Wells**:   It is agreed that Relief Wells are automatically held covered hereunder subject to prior advice to Underwriters hereon, except that in the case of Relief Well(s) drilled by the Unit conducting the original drilling operation advice to Underwriters shall be as soon as possible, at an additional premium to be agreed, if any. However, this provision shall not apply in respect of the cost of drilling a Relief Well, coverage for which is as provided elsewhere herein.

14. In the event the Assured is the operator of the Well, the amount of Insurance deductible and rates stated herein shall be limited to Assured's percentage of ownership as stated in the contractual agreement made between the joint venturers before the loss occurred, but if said agreement requires coverage of a greater percentage of ownership than Assured's percentage, then this Policy shall cover such greater percentage and the joint operation as required by said agreement. This clause shall not increase the limit of liability in Paragraph 8 stated above.

15. **Premium**:   This Insurance is subject to an annual minimum and deposit premium of which shall be paid at inception. The actual premium shall be determined at the rates set forth herein, subject always to the earned premium being not less than the minimum and deposit premium stated herein.
The Assured to furnish to a report over his signature within   days after the end of each day period of this policy setting forth a statement of the entire operations carried on during the period and shall pay earned premium as determined adding thereto State Tax, if applicable.
The earned premium as determined shall be applied against the minimum and deposit premium until exhausted and thereafter the Assured shall pay the additional premium as indicated:

16. **Continuation Clause**:   Drilling, testing, deepening, reworking and reconditioning operations which commence during the period of this Policy to be covered hereunder until successful completion of the operation or until complete abandonment of the well irrespective of the expiry date of this Insurance.

17. **Warranty**:   It is warranted that all oil and/or gas wells for which Named Assured is operator and those wells where Named Assured has a non-operating interest but is responsible for insurance shall be insured hereunder for not less than the Named Assured's percentage interest as follows:—

18. **Other Insurance**:   Warranted no additional Control of Well Insurance in existence on the wells insured hereunder during the currency of this Insurance for the account of the Assured, unless the Underwriters hereon agree thereto in writing.

GENERAL CONDITIONS

A. It is made a condition of this Insurance that a blowout preventer of standard make will be set on the surface casing of the well(s) being drilled, same to be installed and tested in accordance with the usual practice.

B. Any of the Underwriters or their authorized representatives shall have the right and opportunity, whenever the Underwriters so desire, to inspect and examine any books or records so far as they relate to the premium computation hereon.

C. There can be no abandonment to the underwriters of any property.

D. No loss shall be paid hereunder if the Assured has collected the same from others.

E. It is the duty of the Assured and his agents, in all cases to take such measures as may be reasonable for the purpose of averting or minimising a loss.

F. It is understood and agreed that any loss hereunder shall not reduce the limits of liability as set forth in Paragraph No.8 of this form.

G. The Assured upon knowledge of an accident or occurrence likely to give rise to a claim hereunder, shall give, as soon as practicable, immediate written notice thereof to for transmittal to Underwriters.

H. In case the Assured and the Underwriters shall fail to agree as to the amount of loss, the same shall be ascertained by two competent and disinterested appraisers, the Assured and Underwriters each selecting one, and the two so chosen shall first select a competent and disinterested umpire: the appraisers together shall then estimate and appraise the loss, and failing to agree, shall submit their differences to the umpire: and the award in writing of any two shall determine the amount of the loss: the parties hereon shall pay the appraisers respectively selected by them and shall bear equally the expense of the appraisal and umpire.

I. All disputes arising between the Assured and the Underwriters shall be settled by friendly negotiation on the principles of seeking truth from facts and of fairness and reasonableness. Where a settlement fails after negotiation and it is necessary to submit to arbitration or take legal actions, such arbitration or legal actions shall be carried out in China.

J. The Underwriters may require from the Assured an assignment of all rights of recovery against any party for loss or damage to the extent that payment therefor is made by the Underwriters.

K. Privilege is granted to the Assured to release from liability any person, firm or corporation for whom the Assured is performing operations or who is performing operations for the Assured under contract or otherwise, provided the loss or damage subject to said release and indemnification arises out of or in connection with such operations.

L. **Cancelation Clause:** This Policy may be cancelled by either the Named Assured or Underwriters giving thirty days notice. Such cancellation shall become effective on the expiry of thirty days from Midnight of the day on which notice of cancellation is issued by or to Underwriters, but shall not apply to the Insurance of any oil or gas well being drilled, tested, deepened, reworked or reconditioned at the effective time of cancellation: such operations being covered hereunder until the total or complete abandonment of the well or the successful completion of the operation.

Notice of cancellation may also be given by a Co-Venturer of the Named Assured(s) or Underwriters in accordance with the foregoing clause in respect of that Co-Venturer's interest only, without affecting the insurance afforded hereunder to the Named Assured(s) or to the then Co-Venturers.

M. The above clauses and conditions are in addition to those clauses and conditions contained in the Policy to which this form is attached and insofar as they are inconsistent therewith are to supersede same.

Forms & Documentation

SEEPAGE POLLUTION AND CONTAMINATION INSURANCE

SCHEDULE

A) Insured:
B) Address of Insured:
C) Period of Policy:
D) Minimum and Deposit Premium:
E) Operations:

1. **Insuring Agreement:**   Whereas the Insured has agreed to pay the premium as stated in the Schedule, Underwriters, subject to the limitations, terms and conditions of this Policy, agree to indemnify the Insured against or pay on behalf of Insured:
    (a) all sums which the Insured shall by law be liable to pay as damages for bodily injury (fatal or non-fatal) and/or loss of, damage to or loss of use of property caused by or alleged to have been caused directly or indirectly by seepage, pollution or contamination arising out of the operations stated in the Schedule.
    (b) the cost of removing, nullifying or cleaning up seepage, polluting or contaminating substances emanating from the operations stated in the Schedule, including the cost of preventing the substances reaching the shore.
    Provided always that such Seepage, Pollution or Contamination results in a claim being made during the period of Policy as stated in the Schedule and of which immediate notice has been given in accordance with Clause 5 hereof except that any claim subsequently arising out of the circumstances referred to in such notice shall for the purpose of this Policy be deemed to have been made during the currency of this Policy.

2. **Limit of Liability:**   The Underwriters' limit of liability hereunder shall be Ultimate Net Loss in respect of any one claim and/or series of claims arising out of one event and in the aggregate during the Policy Period.

3. **Retention of the Insured:**   It is understood and agreed that the Insured shall bear the first Ultimate Net Loss of any claim and/or series of claims arising out of one event.

4. **Definitions:**
    (a) The unqualified word "Insured" includes the Named Insured, and any partner, executive officer, director or stockholder or employee thereof while acting within the scope of his duties as such.
    (b) The term "Ultimate Net Loss" shall be understood to mean the sums paid in the settlement of claims covered by this Policy (after making deductions for all recoveries, salvages and other insurance) and shall include Costs and expenses incurred in the defence of any claim or claims, and also Costs and expenses of litigation awarded to any claimant against the Insured.
    (c) The word "Costs" shall be understood to mean interest on judgements, investigation, adjustment and legal expenses (excluding, however, all expenses for salaried employees and retained counsel of and all office expenses of the Insured).

5. **Notice of Loss:**   The Insured upon knowledge of any event likely to give rise to a claim hereunder shall give immediate written notice thereof to Underwriters.
    APPLICATION OF SALVAGE:

6. All salvages, recoveries or repayments recovered or received subsequent to a loss settlement under this Policy, shall be applied as if recovered or received prior to such

Forms & Documentation

DRILLING BARGE INSURANCE

ALL RISKS (Except as hereunder excluded)

1. **Assured**:

2. **Period of Insurance**: If this insurance expires while an accident or occurrence giving rise to a loss is in progress, Underwriters shall be liable as if the whole loss had occurred during the currency of this insurance.

3. **Property Insured Hereunder**: This insurance covers the hull and machinery of the drilling barge(s), as scheduled herein, including all their equipment, tools, machinery, caissons, lifting jacks, materials supplies appurtenances, drilling rigs and equipment, derricks, drill stem, casing tubing while aboard the said drilling barge(s) and/or vessels moored alongside or in the vicinity thereof and used in connection therewith (but not such barges and/or vessels themselves) and including drill stem in the well being drilled, and all such property as scheduled herein, owned by or in the care custody or control of Assured, except as hereinafter excluded.

SCHEDULE OF PROPERTY INSURED

DESCRIPTION OF DRILLING BARGE	RATE	INSURED VALUE	HERETO AMOUNT

Each deemed to be separately insured.
Any loss paid hereunder shall not reduce the amount of this insurance except in the event of actual or constructive or compromised or arranged total loss.

4. **Navigation Limits**:
    (a) Privilege is granted to be towed within the above Navigation Limits.
    Also to cover in port, while going on or off, and while in docks and graving docks and/or wharves, ways gridirons and pontoons, subject to the terms and conditions of this insurance.
    (b) This insurance covers up to 25% of the scheduled amount of insurance hereunder on property insured herein (as described in Clause 3 above) when separated from the property insured hereunder whilst in temporary storage at, or in local transit to or from, ports or drilling barges within the Navigation Limits, provided in Paragraph (a). It is expressly understood and agreed, however, that this extended coverage is included within and shall not increase the total amount of insurance hereunder.

5. **Coverage**: Subject to its terms, conditions and exclusions this Insurance is against all risks of direct physical loss or damage to the property insured, provided such loss or damage has not resulted from want of due diligence by the Assured, the Owners or Managers of the property insured, or any of them.

6. **Collision Liability**:
    And it is further agreed that:
    (a) if the Vessel shall come into collision with any other ship or vessel, and the Assured or the Surety in consequence of the Vessel being at fault shall become liable to pay and shall pay by way of such damages to any other person or persons any sum or sums in respect of such collision, the Underwriters will pay the Assured or the Surety, whichever shall have paid, such proportion of such sum or sums so paid as their respective subscriptions hereto bear to the Agreed Value, provided always that their liability in respect of any one such collision shall not exceed their proportionate part of the Agreed Value;
    (b) in cases where, with the consent in writing of a majority (in amount) of Hull Underwriters, the liability of the Vessel has been contested, or proceedings have been taken to limit liability, the Underwriters will also pay a like proportion of the costs which the Assured shall thereby incur or be compelled to pay.
    When both vessels are to blame, then, unless the liability of the owners or charterers of one or both such vessels becomes limited by law, claims under the Collision Liability clause shall be settled on the principle of Cross-Liabilities as if the owners or charterers of each vessel had been compelled to pay to the owners or charterers of the other vessels such one-half or other proportion of the latter's damages as may have been properly allowed in ascertaining the balance or sum payable by or to the Assured in consequence of such collision.
    The principles involved in this clause shall apply to the case where both vessels are the property, in part or in whole, of the same owners or charterers, all questions of responsibility and amount of liability as between the two vessels being left to the decision of a single Arbitrator, if the parties can agree upon a single Arbitrator, or failing such agreement, to the decision of Arbitrators, one to be appointed by the Assured and one to be appointed by the majority (in amount) of Hull Underwriters interested; the two Arbitrators chosen to choose a third Arbitrator before entering upon the reference, and the decision of such single Arbitrator, or of any two of such three Arbitrators, appointed as above, to be final and binding.
    Provided that this clause shall in no case extend to any sum which the Assured or the Surety may become liable to pay or shall pay in consequence of, or with respect to:
    (a) removal or disposal of obstructions, wrecks or their cargoes under statutory powers or otherwise pursuant to law;
    (b) injury to real or personal property of every description;

    (c) the discharge, spillage, emission or leakage of oil, petroleum products, chemicals or other substances of any kind or description whatsoever;

    (d) cargo or other property on or the engagements of the Vessel;

    (e) loss of life, personal injury or illness.

Provided further that exclusions (b) and (c) above shall not apply to injury to any other vessel with which the Vessel is in collision or to property on such other vessel except to the extent that such injury arises out of any action taken to avoid, minimise or remove any discharge, spillage, emission or leakage described in (c).

7. **Deductible:** It is understood and agreed that each claim (including claims under the Sue and Labour Clause and the Collision Liability Clause) shall be reported and adjusted separately and from the amount of each claim the sum   of shall be deducted.

This clause shall not apply to a claim for Actual or Constructive or Compromised or Arranged Total Loss.

For the purpose of this Clause each occurrence shall be treated separately, but it is agreed that a sequence of losses or damages arising from the same occurrence shall be treated as one occurrence.

8. **Exclusions:** Notwithstanding anything to the contrary which may be contained in this insurance there shall be no liability under this insurance in respect of:—

    (a) Loss, damage or expense caused by or attributable to earthquake or volcanic eruption, or fire and/or explosion and/or tidal wave consequent upon earthquake or volcanic eruption.

    (b) Loss, damage or expense which arises solely from the intentional sinking of the barge for operational purposes; such sinking shall not constitute a collision, stranding, sinking or grounding within the meaning of this insurance.

    (c) Loss, damage or expense caused whilst or resulting from drilling a relief well for the purpose of controlling or attempting to control fire blowout or cratering associated with another drilling barge, platform or unit unless immediate notice be given to Underwriters of said use and additional premium paid if required.

    (d) Any claim, be it a Sue and Labour Expense or otherwise, for moneys materials or property expended or sacrificed in controlling or to control blowout or cratering or in fighting fire associated with blowout.

    (e) Loss, damage or expense caused by or resulting from delay detention or loss of use.

    (f) Wear and tear, gradual deterioration, metal fatigue, machinery breakdown, expansion or contraction due to change in temperature, corrosion, rusting, electrolytic action, error in design; nor does this insurance cover the cost of repairing or replacing any part which may be lost, damaged, or condemned by reason of any latent defect therein.

    (g) Loss of or damage to dynamoes, exciters, lamps, motors, switches and other electrical appliances and evices, caused by electrical injury or disturbance, unless the loss or damage be caused by a peril not excluded hereunder originating outside the electrical equipment specified in this clause. Nevertheless this clause shall not exclude claims for physical loss or damage resulting from fire.

    (h) Liabilities to third parties except as specifically covered under the terms of the Collision Liability Clause contained herein.

    (i) Claims in connection with the removal of property, material, debris or obstruction, whether such removal be required by law, ordinance, statute, regulation or otherwise.

    (j) Loss of or damage to drill stem located underground or underwater unless directly resulting from fire, blowout, cratering, or total loss of the Drilling Barge caused by a peril insured hereunder. There shall be no liability in respect of drill stem left in the well and through which an oil or gas well is completed.

    Blowout: The term "Blowout" shall mean a sudden, accidental, uncontrolled and continuous explosion from a well and above the surface of the ground of the drilling fluid in an oil or gas well, followed by continuous and uncontrolled flow from a well and above the surface of the ground of oil, gas or water due to encountering subterranean pressures.

    Cratering: The term "Crater" shall be defined as a basin-like depression in the earth's surface surrounding a well caused by the erosion and eruptive action of oil, gas or water flowing without restriction.

    (k) Well(s) and/or hole(s) whilst being drilled or otherwise.

    (l) Drilling mud cement chemicals and fuel actually in use, and casing and tubing in the well.

    (m) Unrefined oil or gas or other crude product.

    (n) Blueprints, plans, specifications or records, personal effects of employees or others.

    (o) Scraping or painting the bottom of the hull of the drilling barge.

9. **Blowout Preventer Warranty:** Warranted that (a) in all drilling operations

    (b) In all operations which require the removal of the christmas tree the well and/or hole will be equipped with a minimum of three pressure operated blowout preventers, which shall be installed and tested immediately after installation. Two of the aforesaid blowout preventers shall be of the pipe ram and blind ram type and the third shall be of the annular full closing type.

10. **Limit of Liability:** In no event, except as provided for in the Sue and Labour Expese Clause and Collision Liability Clause herein, shall the Underwriters' liability arising from any one accident or occurrence exceed the amount insured hereunder as set forth in Clause 3 in respect of the items subject to claim in such accident or occurrence.

In respect of the property insured hereunder Underwriters shall not be liable for more than their proportion of the cost of repairing or replacing the property damaged or lost with materials of like kind and quality to a condition equal to but not superior or more extensive than its condition prior to the loss; nevertheless in respect of the hull of the Drilling Barge covered hereunder all costs of repair and replacement for which Underwriters may be liable shall be on the basis of new for old with no deduction for depreciation.

In no event shall Underwriters be liable for any increased cost of repair of reconstruction by reason of law, ordinance, regulation, permit or license regulating construction or repair.

11. **Coinsurance:** The Assured shall maintain contributing insurance on terms no more restrictive than this insurance on the property insured hereunder of not less than 100% of the new reproductive cost less a reasonable depreciation. Failing to do so, the Assured shall be an insurer to the extent of such deficit and bear such proportionate part of any claim. If this insurance be divided into two or more items the foregoing conditions shall apply to each item separately.

12. **Constructive Total Loss:** There shall be no recovery for a Constructive Total Loss hereunder unless the expense of recovering and repairing the insured property shall exceed the actual insurance value.
In no case shall Underwriters be liable for unrepaired damage in addition to a subsequent Total Loss sustained during the period covered by this insurance.

13. **Sue and Labour Expense:** It is further agreed that should the property insured hereunder suffer loss or damage covered under the terms of this insurance, it shall be lawful and necessary for the Assured, their Factors, Servants and Assigns, to sue, labour and travel for, in and about the Defence, Safeguard and Recovery of the said property, or any part thereof, without prejudice to this insurance, and subject always to the terms conditions limitations and exclusions of this insurance, the charges thereof shall be borne by the Underwriters. And it is especially declared and agreed that no acts of the Underwriters or Assured in recovering, saving or preserving the property insured shall be considered as a waiver or acceptance of abandonment.
The Underwriters' liability for Sue and Labour Expenses shall not exceed 25% of the insured value of the item(s) in the Defence, Safeguard or Recovery of which such expense is incurred.

14. **Lay up and Cancellation:** To return daily pro rata of rates to be agreed by Underwriters for any period of 30 or more consecutive days the vessel may be laid up in port unemployed. Provided always that:—
    (a) the location shall be approved by surveyor appointed by Lloyd's Agent or approved by Underwriters.
    (b) there shall always be a watchman on board.
    (c) no return shall be allowed in the event of the vessel becoming an actual or constructive or compromised or arranged total loss during the currency of this insurance.
    (d) there shall be no shifts during the lay up period.
    (e) there shall be no movement of legs or variation in buoyancy during the lay up period.
    (f) in the event of any amendment of the annual rate, the rates of return shall be adjusted accordingly.
    The return for a laid-up period of 30 or more consecutive days which fall on two policies effected for the same Assured shall be apportioned over both policies on a daily pro rata basis.
    This insurance may be cancelled:—
    (a) by the Assured at any time by written notice subject to a return of premium to be agreed;
    (b) by Underwriters subject to 30 days written notice, in which event a pro rata daily return of premium shall be payable;
    (c) by Underwriters in respect of the perils of strikers locked-out workmen or persons taking part in labour disturbances or riots or civil commotions subject to 7 days written notice without return of premium.
    Cancellation by either party is subject to the retention by Underwriters of any minimum premium stipulated in the Policy.

15. **Release Agreements and Waivers of Subrogation:** The Assured may grant release from liability with respect to loss of or damage to property insured hereunder to any person firm or corporation for whom the Assured is operating under specific contract, provided:—
    (a) the said release is granted prior to the commencement of the operations;
    (b) the loss or damage subject to said release arises out of or in connection with such operations.
    Underwriters agree to waive their rights of subrogation against such person firm or corporation having been so released from such liability.

16. **Discovery of Records:** During the currency of this insurance or any time thereafter within the period of the time provided for in Clause 17 for bringing suit against these Underwriters, these Underwriters shall have the right of inspecting the Assured's records pertaining to all matters of cost, repairs, income and expenditures of whatsoever nature relating to the properties insured hereunder, such records to be open to a representative of these Underwriters at all reasonable times.

17. **Treatment of Disputes:** All disputes arising between the Assured and Underwriters shall be settled by friendly negotiation on the principles of seeking truth from facts and of fairness and reasonableness. Where a settlement fails after negotiation and it is necessary to submit to arbitration or take legal actions, such arbitration or legal actions shall be carried out in China.

18. **Loss Payable:** Loss, if any, (except claims required to be paid to others under the Collision Liability Clause), payable to

19. **Free of Capture and Seizure:** Notwithstanding anything to the contrary contained in this insurance, there shall be no liability for any claim caused by, resulting from, or incurred as a consequence of:—
    (a) Capture, seizure, arrest, restraint or detainment, or any attempt thereat; or
    (b) Any taking by requisition or otherwise, whether in time of peace of war and whether lawful or otherwise; or
    (c) Any mine, bomb, torpedo or other engine of war; or
    (d) Any weapon of war employing atomic or nuclear fussion and/or fusion or other like reaction or radioactive force or matter; or
    (e) Civil war, revolution, rebellion, insurrection, or civil strike arising there from or piracy; or

(f) (i)   the detonation of an explosive
     (ii) any weapon of war
     and caused by any person acting maliciously or from a political motive; or

(g) Any act for political or terrorist purposes of any person or persons, whether or not agents of a Sovereign Power, and whether the loss, damage or expense resulting there from is accidental or intentional; or

(h) Hostilities or warlike operations (whether there be a declaration or war or not) but this subparagraph (h) not to exclude collision or contact with aircraft, rockets or similar missiles, or with any fixed or floating object, or stranding, heavy weather, fire or explosion unless caused directly by a hostile act by or against a belligerent power which act is independent of the nature of the voyage or operation which the vessel concerned, or in the case of a collision or contact, any other vessel involved therein, is performing. As used herein, 'power' includes any authority maintaining naval, military or air forces in association with a power.

Forms & Documentation

PLATFORM DRILLING RIG INSURANCE

ALL RISKS

(Except as hereinafter excluded)

1. **Assured:**

2. **Period of Insurance:** If this insurance expires while an accident or occurrence giving rise to a loss in progress, Underwriters shall be liable as if the whole loss had occurred uring the currency of this insurance.

3. **Property Insured Hereunder:** This insurance covers Platform Drilling Rig(s), as scheduled herein, which includes all equipment, tools, machinery, materials, supplies, appurtenances, derricks, sub-structures and drill stem used in connection therewith and all property as scheduled herein, owned by or in the care custody or control of the Assured located on Platform Installation(s) except as hereinafter excluded.

SCHEDULE OF PROPERTY INSURED

DESCRIPTION OF DRILLING BARGE	RATE	INSURED VALUE	HERETO AMOUNT

Each deemed to be separately insured.
Any loss paid hereunder shall not reduce the amount of this insurance except in the event of a total loss and/or constructive and/or agreed and/or arranged total loss.

4. **Territorial Limits:**
   (a)
   (b) This insurance covers the property insured hereunder (as described in Clause 3 above) when separated from the platform installations whilst in storage at, or in local transit to or from, ports or platform installations within the Territorial Limits provide in Paragraph (a).

5. **Coverage:** Subject to its terms, conditions and exclusions this Insurance is against all risks of direct physical loss of or damage to the property insured, provided such loss or damage has not resulted from want of due diligence by the Assured, the Owners or Managers of the property insured, or any of them.

6. It is understood and agreed that each claim (including claims under the Sue and Labour Clause) shall be reported and adjusted separately and from the amount of each claim the sum of   shall be deducted. This clause shall not apply to a claim for Total or Constructive Total Loss.
   For the purpose of this Clause each occurrence shall be treated separately, but it is agreed that a sequence of losses or damages arising from the same occurrence shall be treated as one occurrence.

7. **Exclusions:** Notwithstanding anything to the contrary which may be contained in this insurance there shall be no liability under this insurance in respect of or resulting from:—
   (a) Named windstorm and/or hurricane within the U.S. Gulf or the Gulf of Mexico.
   (b) Loss, damage or expense caused by or attributable to earthquake or volcanic eruption, or fire and/or explosion and/or tidal wave consequent upon earthquake or volcanic eruption.
   (c) Loss, damage or expense caused whilst the insured property is being used to drill a relief well for the purpose of controlling or attempting to control fire, blowout or cratering unless immediate notice be given to Underwriters of said use and additional premium paid if required.
   (d) Any claim, be it a Sue and Labour Expense or otherwise, for moneys materials or property expended or sacrificed in controlling or attempting to control blowout or cratering or in fighting fire associated with blowout.
   (e) Loss, damage or expense caused by or resulting from delay detention or loss of use.
   (f) Wear and tear, gradual deterioration, metal fatigue, machinery breakdown, expansion or contraction due to change in temperature, corrosion, rusting, electrolytic action, error in design; nor does this insurance cover the cost of repairing or replacing any part which may be lost, damaged, or condemned by reason of any latent defect therein.
   (g) Loss of or damage to drill stem located underground or underwater unless directly resulting from fire, blowout, cratering, or total loss of the Platform Installation on which the Drilling Rig is mounted, caused by a peril insured hereunder. There shall be no liability in respect of drill stem left in the well and through which an oil or gas well is completed.
   (h) Loss of damage to dynamoes, exciters, lamps, motor switches and other electrical appliances and devices, caused by electrical injury or disturbances, unless the loss or damage be caused by a peril not excluded hereunder originating outside the electrical equipment specified in this clause. Neverthelss this clause shall not exclude claims for physical loss or damage resulting from fire.
   (i) Liabilities to third parties.
   (j) Claims in connection with the removal or property, material debris or obstruction whether such removal be required by law, ordinance, statute, regulation or otherwise.

    (k) Loss of or damage to platform installation(s), vessel(s), barge(s) or craft.
    (l) Well(s) and or hole(s) whilst being drilled or otherwise.
    (m) Drilling mud cement chemicals and fuel actually in use, and casing and tubing in the well.
    (n) Unrefined oil or gas or other crude product.
    (o) Blueprints, plans, specifications or records, personal effects of employees or others.

8. **Blowout Preventer Warranty:** Warranted that blowout preventer(s) of standard make will be set on the surface casing, such blowout preventer(s) to be installed and tested in accordance with the usual pratice.

9. **Limit of Liability:** In no event, except as provide for in the Sue and Labour Expense Clause herein, shall the Underwriters' liability arising from any one accident or occurrence exceed the amount insured hereunder as set forth in Clause 3 in respect of the items subject to claim in such accident or occurrence.
In respect of the property insured hereunder Underwriters shall not be liable for more than their proportion of the cost of repairing or replacing the property damaged or lost with materials of like kind and quality to a condition equal to but not superior to or more extensive than its condition prior to the loss.
In no event shall Underwriters be liable for any increased cost of repair or reconstruction by reason of law, ordinance, regulation, permit or license regulating construction or repair.

10. **Coinsurance:** The Assured shall maintain contributing insurance on terms no more restrictive than this insurance on the property insured hereunder of not less than 100% of the new reproductive cost less a reasonable depreciation. Failing to do so, the Assured shall be an insurer to the extent of such deficit and bear such proportionate part of any claim. If this insurance be divided into two or more items the foregoing conditions shall apply to each item separately.

11. **Constructive Total Loss:** There shall be no recovery for a Constructive Total Loss hereunder the expense of recovering and repairing and repairing the insured property shall exceed the actual insured value, or the new reproductive cost less a reasonable depreciation. Whichever shall be the greater. In no case shall Underwriters be liable for unrepaired damage in addition to a subsequent Total Loss sustained during the period covered by this insurance.

12. **Sue and Labour Expense:** It is further agreed that should the property insured hereunder suffer loss or damage covered under the terms of this insurance, it shall be lawful and necessary for the Assured, their Factors, Servants and Assigns, to sue, labour and travel for, in and about the Defence, Safeguard and Recovery of the said property, or any part thereof, without prejudice to this insurance, and subject always to the terms conditions limitations and exclusions of this insurance, the charges thereoff shall be borne by the Underwriters. And it is especially declared and agreed that no acts of the Underwriters or Assured in recovering, saving or preserving the property insured shall be considered as a waiver or acceptance of abandonment.
The Underwriters liability for Sue and Labour Expenses shall not exceed 25% of the insured value of the item(s) in the Defence, Safeguard or Recovery of which such expense is incurred.

13. **Cancellation:** This insurance may be cancelled:
    (a) by the Assured at any time by written notice subject to a return of premium to be agreed.
    (b) by Underwriters subject to 30 days written notice, in which event a pro rata daily return of premium shall be payable.
    (c) by Underwriters in respect of the perils of strikers locked-out workmen or persons taking part in labour disturbances or riots or civil commotions subject to 7 days written notice without return of premium.
Cancellation by either party is subject to the retention by Underwriters of any minimum premium stipulated in the Policy.

14. **Release Agreements and Waivers of Subrogation:** The Assured may grant release from liability with respect to loss of or damage to property insured hereunder to any person firm or corporation for whom or with whom the Assured is performing operations or who is performing operations for the Assured, under contract or otherwise, provided:—
    (a) the said release is granted prior to the commencement of the operations.
    (b) the loss or damage subject to said release arises out of or in connection with such operations.
Underwriters agree to waive their rights of subrogation against such person firm or corporation having been so released from such liability.

15. **Discovery of Records:** During the currency of this insurance of any time thereafter within the period of the time provided for in Clause 16 for bringing suit against these Underwriters, these Underwriters shall have the right of inspecting the Assured's records pertaining to all matters of cost, repairs, income and expenditures of whatsoever nature relating to the properties insured hereunder, such records to be open to a representative of these Underwriters at all reasonable times.

16. **Treatment of Disputes:** All disputes arising between the Assured and Underwriters shall be settled by friendly negotiation on the principles of seeking truth from facts and of fairness and reasonableness. Where a settlement fails after negotiation and it is necessary to submit to arbitration or take legal actions, such arbitration or legal actions shall be carried out in China.

17. **Loss Payable:** Loss, if any, payable to

18. **Free of Capture and Seizure:** Notwithstanding anything to the contrary contained in this insurance. there shall be no liability for any claim caused by, resulting from, or incurred as a consequence of:
   (a) Capture, seizure, arrest, restraint or detainment, or any attempt thereat; or
   (b) Any taking by requisition or otherwise, whether in time of peace or war whether lawful or otherwise; or
   (c) Any mine, bomb, torpedo or other engine of war; or
   (d) Any weapon of war employing atomic or nuclear fission and/or fusion or other like reaction or radioactive force or matter; or
   (e) Civil war, revolution, rebellion, insurrection, or civil strife arising there from or piracy; or
   (f) (i) The detonation of an explosive
       (ii) Any weapon of war and caused by any person acting maliciously or from a political motive; or
   (g) Any act for political or terrorist purposes of any person or persons, whether or not agents of a Sovereign Power, and whether the loss, damage or expense resulting there from is accidental or intentional; or
   (h) Hostilities or warlike operations (whether there be a declaration of war or not) but this subparagraph (h) not to exclude collision or contact with aircraft, rockets or similar missiles, or with any fixed or floating objects, or stranding, heavy weather, fire or explosion unless caused directly by a hostile act by or against a belligerent power which act is independent of the nature of the voyage or operation which the property insured hereunder, or in the case of a collision or contact, any other vessel involved therein, is performing. As used herein, 'power' includes any authority maintaining naval, military or air forces in association with a power.

III COAL

SECTION A: Overall policy

Interim Regulations on the Administration of Energy Conservation

(Promulgated by the State Council on January 12,1986)

Chapter I: **General Provisions**

Article 1: The Regulations are formulated for the purpose of implementing the state principle of placing equal stress on the development of energy resources and energy conservation, utilizing energy resources in a rational way, lowering energy consumption, improving economic efficiency and ensuring the sustained, steady and coordinated development of the national economy.

Article 2: All enterprises, institutions, offices, army units, organizations and individuals in town and country shall abide by these Regulations.

Article 3: Energy as described in these Regulations refers to coal, crude oil, natural gas, electric power, coke, gas, steam, petrol, kerosene, diesel, fuel oil and firewood.

Energy conservation as described in these Regulatiions refers to the achievement of the greatest economic efficiency at the lowest energy consumption through such means as technological progress, rational utilization, scientific management and the rationalization of the economic structure.

Chapter II: **The Administration System of Energy Conservation**

Article 4: The State Council shall institutionalize administrative meetings on the work of energy conservation. These meetings shall study and examine principles, policies, laws and regulations, plans and reform measures relating to energy conservation and they shall define and coordinate tasks for energy conservation. The day-to-day work on energy conservation shall be taken care of by the State Planning Commission and the State Economic Commission with a division of labour between them.

Article 5: The people's governments of provinces, autonomous regions and municipalities under the central authorities and related departments under the State Council shall place a principal responsible member in charge of energy conservation and they may institute the practice of having administrative meetings on the work of energy conservation. The day-to-day work shall be taken care of by the administrative agencies of energy conservation.

Departments, bureaux, prefectures and cities in provinces, autonomous regions and municipalities under the central authorities that are major energy users shall have principal responsible members take care of energy conservation and identify appropriate administrative agencies for energy conservation.

The administrative agencies of energy conservation in localities and departments are primarily concerned with implementing the state principles, policies, laws and regulations and standards relating to energy conservation, formulating policies on energy-saving technologies and such planning in their own localities, industries and departments, organizing and guiding the technological development and technological transformation of energy conservation, checking and overseeing improvement in the administration of energy conservation in enterprises and other units in their own localities, industries and departments, and making overall plans for and coordinating the fulfillment of the tasks of energy conservation.

Article 6: Enterprises whose annual overall energy consumption exceeds the equivalent of 10,000 tons of standard coal (hereafter referred to as key energy-consuming enterprises) shall designate a principal responsible member to be in charge of the work of energy conservation, and specify appropriate administrative agencies. With regard to enterprises whose annual energy consumption is less than 10,000 tons of standard coal the localities and departments shall formulate regulations in the light of the above-mentioned provisions and specific conditions.

The administrative agencies of energy conservation in enterprises shall be chiefly, responsible for implementing the state principles, policies, laws and regulations, and standards relating to energy conservation in their own enterprises, for implementing the regulations on energy conservation issued by the localities and departments, devising technical measures for energy conservation and seeing to their implementation in their own enterprises, making the administration of energy conservation more scientific, lowering the energy consumption of per unit product and fulfilling the tasks of energy conservation.

Article 7: The responsibility system must be practised in the work of energy conservation in localities, departments and enterprises.

The administrative agencies of energy conservation at all levels shall be fitted out with cadres and technical personnel who have the professional knowledge, and the vocational competence and who are dedicated to the work of energy conservation.

Article 8: The administrative agencies of energy conservation of the local people's governments and of the relevant departments in the State Council shall be at the same time the supervisory organs for the implementation of these Regulations in the localities they govern or in the enterprises they administer.

Aside from discharging the responsibility of supervision defined in Article 5 of these Regulations, the administrative organs of energy conservation in the localities and departments may ask technical service centres for energy conservation or other relevant units to monitor and check energy consumption in production and in daily life in the localities they govern or in the enterprises they administer.

Chapter III: The Fundamentals of the Administration of Energy Conservation

Article 9:   The State Statistical Bureau shall set up a sound system of statistics on energy. The statistical departments at all levels shall work in collaboration with the competent departments in the enterprises in doing a good job in the statistics on energy.

Enterprises shall establish and improve the keeping of initial records on energy consumption and the statistical records. They shall send statistical reports on energy to statistical departments; administrative agencies of energy conservation and their supervisory departments at regular intervals in accordance with the "Statistical Law of the People's Republic of China" and other regulations of the state relating to statistical work.

Article 10:   Enterprises shall be fitted out with energy-measuring instruments and shall improve the metrological management of energy in accordance with the "Metrological Law of the People's Republic of China" and other regulations of the state relating to metrological work.

Article 11:   The State Standards Bureau shall pool efforts and work out the basic standards for various kinds of energy, standards for energy management and standards for the energy consumption of products. The localities and departments shall formulate their own standards for energy consumption in the light of the national standards and the specific conditions in the localities and departments. Enterprises shall conscientiously meet all the standards for energy conservation.

Article 12:   The supervisory departments in enterprises shall work with energy supplies and regularly set advanced and reasonable energy consumption quotas for principal energy-consuming products made by enterprises in accordance with the overall energy consumption quotas for appraisal and the energy consumption quota for a single product set by the supervisory department in the State Council and checks shall be made in earnest. Enterprises shall have the energy consumption quotas broken down to workshops, teams and groups and machines and equipment and the responsibility system for the use of energy shall be set up.

Article 13:   Enterprises shall make an analysis of energy consumption and if necessary shall take up the work of energy balance. Key energy-consuming enterprises shall conduct checks on the overall energy consumption and the energy consumption of a single product.

Chapter IV: The Management of Energy Supply

Article 14: The administrative agencies of energy consumption in the localities shall work with energy suppliers and supervisory departments is enterprises and get enterprises to do a good job in energy supply and energy conservation. Priority in energy supply shall be determined by the performance of enterprises in energy management, energy consumption of products and overall economic efficiency. With regard to enterprises that rely basically on the state for energy supply, they shall be assigned a fixed amount or a quota according to their different conditions and they may keep whatever amount they have saved for their own use.

Article 15: The coal industry shall develop coal screening and coal washing so as to improve the quality of coal for use and ensure in a planned way that coal supply meets the different needs of users.

Coal-producing and transport departments shall organize the supply of coal with clear requirements for quality and quantity in accordance with the state distribution plan and the purchasing and marketing contracts and the transport contracts of enterprises. Coal needed by large enterprises in the metallurgical, electric power, chemical and building materials industries and by locomotives shall be supplied according to their technical requirements and supply by fixed places shall be gradually introduced.

Urban fuel companies shall supply coal for power generation in accordance with the needs of small and medium-size enterprises.

Article 16: The principle of fixing prices according to quality shall be implemented in coal supply. Coal used as fuel shall be priced according to its heat value.

As to coal measuring, the system of measuring in terms of commodity coal and the equivalent of standard coal shall be gradually instituted.

Article 17: Regulations on the planned supply and use of power shall be strictly observed. As for the rights and obligations of both the supplier and the user, they shall be exercised and fulfilled in accordance with the "National Regulations on the Supply and Use of Power" formulated by the supervisory department in the State Council.

Different rates of tariff for power shall be introduced. Enterprises shall be encouraged to use power when excessive water is relieved in a period of over-abundance and when the power load is at its lowest point. The determination of the different rates of tariff for power refers to the "Interim Regulations on Encouraging the Pooling of Resources for Power Generation and on the Introduction of Multiple Rates of Tariff for Power" approved by the State Council and transmitted to the State Economic Commission and other departments for implementation.

Article 18: Oil-burning shall be kept under strict control. New oil-burning enterprises shall follow the procedures of examination and approval as required by the relevant regulations of the state. Enterprises that have been singled out to replace oil-burning must be so remodelled within a definite period of time.

A special tax on oil burning shall be levied in accordance with tax regulations on boilers and industrial furnaces that burn crude oil and other fuels at bargain prices.

Article 19:   Oil used by diesel-engine generators shall be kept under strict control. Supply of oil to diesel-engine generators shall not be guaranteed except for those used to generate power for production in areas where there is no power supply or in border regions and pastoral areas and for stand-by power-generating units required by hospitals, broad-casting stations, postal and tele-communications departments and research institutions.

Article 20:   Oil-supplying departments shall work with relevant departments in mapping out a rational layout of gas stations in the urban and rural areas so as to reduce loss and waste of processed oil in storage and transportation.

Chapter V: The Management of Energy for Industrial Use

Article 21:   Industrial enterprises shall be rationally laid out when they are constructed by taking into consideration availability of energy resources, energy balance between production and marketing in the region and the rational flow of energy. No energy-guzzling industrial projects shall be located in energy-deficient regions except for those specially needed by the state.

Production of small blast furnaces, small converters, small electric furnaces, small rolling mills, small thermal power stations and small smelters and electrolyzers of non-ferrous metals that consume large amounts of energy shall not be rehabilitated, much less developed except in areas where energy resources are rich or transportation facilities are lacking and except for those approved by the people's governments of provinces, autonomous regions and municipalities under the central authorities or by the departments they have designated.

Article 22:   On the precondition that the needs of society are met, the structure of production, the structure of enterprises and the product mix shall be readjusted in accordance with the principle of the rational use of energy.

Article 23:   Enterprises shall act in accordance with the principle of the rational use of energy and go about production in a balanced, stable centralized and coordinated way so as to avoid loss or waste of energy.

Article 24:   The operation and management of the heat-supplying system in enterprises and the use of residual heat shall be governed by the pertinent provisions defined in the "Technical Guidelines for the Assessment of the Rational Use of Heat by Enterprises" of the State Standards Bureau.

Article 25:   The non-authorized expansion of the capacity of boilers shall be forbidden. Enterprises cannot add new boilers or revamp old ones, thus necessitating an increase in the volume of steam, unless they report to the higher authorities in advance and their requests are examined and approved by the administrative agencies of energy conservation in their localities in collaboration with the supervisory departments of enterprises, labour departments and fuel-supplying departments.

Article 26:   The supervisory departments of enterprises shall conduct regular checks on and comparison and appraisal of the principal furnaces in the enterprises they supervise and upgrade them in rating in accordance with the standards for rating furnaces in their own industry.

Article 27:   The making of coke by indigenous methods shall be kept under strict control. It may be retained where special conditions so warrant and with the approval of the people's governments of the provinces, autonomous regions and municipalities under the central authorities where the enterprises are located or with the approval of the departments they have designated.

Article 28: The power departments shall have a rational structure of power grids and transform the existing one towards this end so as to enhance the capacity of power supply and also to improve the quality of power supply. Measures shall be taken to use in a rational way hydropower and thermal power-generating units of high efficiency for power generation and to strengthen the rational despatching by power grids so as to lower the consumption of water and coal and save fuel.

The technical requirements for the supply of power to enterprises and for the use by them shall be enforced in accordance with the pertinent provisions defined in the "Technical Guidelines for the Assessment of the Rational Use of Power by Enterprises" of the State Standards Bureau.

Article 29: The combined generation of heat and power shall be encouraged. The power department and the local authorities shall combine heat generation with power generation in accordance with the principle of "where there is heat, there should be power generation" when the amount of steam required for production by heat users reaches a certain level and when there is a steady heated load all year around.

Enterprises shall encouraged to use residual heat and residual pressure for power generation. When power is sold through the power grid by the themal power stations enterprises have for themselves or by the small thermal power stations built by localities, power departments shall adopt a policy by providing support in line with states regulations.

Article 30: In regions with a relatively high degree of concentration of industries, local economic management departments shall organize in a planned way the specialized production of heat treatment, electroplating, casting, forging and oxygen-making so as to raise the utilization rate of energy.

Article 31: Combustible gases released by metallurgical petroleum and chemical enterprises shall be vigorously recovered and put to rational use.

Coal mines and industrial enterprises close to them shall seek to achieve the comprehensive utilization of gangue on the condition of economic viability. In regions where resources of bone coal, poor quality coal and oil shale are abundant, a comprehensive approach shall be adopted towards utilizing local fuels of low heat value while taking into consideration what economic benefits they will yeild.

Chapter VI: The Management of Energy for Urban and Rural Life

Article 32: Coal for use in daily life shall be gradually patternized and the use of the honey-comb briquet shall be vigouously popularized. Earnest efforts must be made to develop the technology which will remove the smoke when burning bituminous coal and to increase the varieties of coal for civilian use.

Article 33: Vigorous efforts shall be made to develop fuel forests and popularize the use of firewood and coal-saving cooking stoves. Regions which have the requisite conditions shall actively tap and exploit energy resources such as biogas, solar energy, wind power and geo-thermal energy.

Article 34:   The use of gas in cities shall be further promoted by utilizing multiple gas resources. Departments of urban and rural construction and environmental protection shall map out plans with relevant departments for a gradual increase in the coverage of cities by gas supply.

Article 35:   In designing buildings, on condition that interior comfort is reasonably provided, a comprehensive approach shall be adopted towards properly determining the building configuration and facing, improving cladding, selecting installations low in energy consumption and making adequate use of natural light so as to reduce energy consumption in lighting, heating and cooling.

Article 36:   Central heating shall be developed. Central heating shall be introduced through unified planning for newly-built apartment buildings with heating systems and for public buildings. Vigorous measures must be taken to gradually phase out boilers of low efficiency and replace the existing decentralized heating systems with central heating.

Heating installations in buildings shall adopt or switch to the use of hot water heating in accordance with the principle of economic rationality.

Article 37:   Residents in town and country shall have meters installed and pay charges for electricity, water and gas. The practice of paying a fixed sum and charging no fee for their supply shall be done away with.

Chapter VII: Promoting Technological Progress

Article 38:   When undertaking the construction of a new project and revamping or expanding an old one, advanced technology and equipment that ensure the rational use of energy must be used and the energy consumption of a newly built project or a revamped or expanded one shall not be higher than the domestic advanced standards for energy consumption. There should be specific requirements for energy conservation when design standards, criteria and regulations of a given industry are formulated or revised by the relevant departments. The feasibility study and initial design of an industrial project must include an assessment of the rational use of energy. Industrial projects that do not meet the requirements for energy conservation defined in the design standards, criteria and regulations not be approved for construction by the screening departments.

Article 39:   Localities, departments and enterprises shall make medium and long-range plans and annual plans for revamping for the purpose of energy conservation in accordance with the policy on energy-saving technology pursued in industries and they shall see to the implementation of these plans. The principal energy-consuming industries shall build in a planned way a number of projects of energy conservation that are tecnologically advanced, and economically reasonable and can be easily popularized.

Article 40:   Funds for energy-saving revamping undertaken by enterprises shall come primarily from their depreciation funds and their retained funds for production. Key energy-consuming enterprises whose main products have a higher rate of energy consumption than the average in their own industry must focus on energy conservation in their remodelling, energy conservation must have priority in their planning and funds must be made available.

Localities and departments shall earmark a fixed proportion of the depreciation funds at their disposal for energy-saving measures by enterprises. Such proportion should not be lower than 20% in regions which rely on the outside for energy supply and in key energy-consuming departments.

Article 41: Loans for energy conservation that are included in the state credit plan shall charge a preferential interest rate and a discount may be given by the supervisory department concerned in accordance with state regulations. Enterprises which have taken out loans shall be allowed to repay them with new earnings before the payment of income tax.

As for energy-saving projects which bring large benefits to society but small benefits to enterprises and which were originally financed by allocation of funds for capital construction but are now financed by loans, the supervisory department concerned may exempt such enterprises partially or totally from the payment of the principle and the interest.

As for projects of capital construction for energy conservation planned by the state, the state shall provide part of the investment and encourage localitics, departments and enterprises to pool their financial resources in undertaking the construction of energy-saving projects.

In the construction of energy-saving projects the method in inviting bids and submitting bids shall be used.

Article 42: For all major projects of energy conservation, an analysis of techno-economic feasibility or a feasibility study must be done by designing and consultancy units approved by the administrative agencies of energy conservation. The designing and consultancy units shall bear due legal responsibility for the technical soundness and economic viability of a construction project in accordance with the provisions in the contract.

Article 43: Important projects for the development of energy-saving technology shall be brought into line with the state plan for key scientific research projects. The administrative agencies in localities and departments shall energetically pool forces in the research into and popularization of applied technology for energy conservation.

Article 44: Products that yield marked results in energy conservation and have a big demand on the market shall be so priced that a good-quality products fetches a good price after the examination and approval of the supervisory department in the State Council.

New products of energy conservation appraised and approved by the department concerned shall be exempt from income tax and value-added tax within a specified period of time in accordance with the "Interim Provisions on Policy Aspects of the Promotion of Technological Progress in State-Owned Enterprises" approved and transmitted by the State Council to the State Economic Commission and other departments.

Article 45: When importing technologies and equipment, their technical conditions, economic benefits and level of energy consumption shall be taken into overall consideration. Priority shall be given to importing technologies and equipment that yield good results in energy conservation while limiting the importation of energy-guzzling technologies and equipment.

Article 46: Energy-saving machinery and equipment and surveying and testing instruments and meters which enterprises find it necessary to import for technological transformation shall enjoy the reduction of and exemption from import tariffs and product tax (or value-added tax) in accordance with the tax laws and regulations of the state.

Article 47:   Enterprises that manufacture machines and electronic products which are to be phased out by the announcement of the state must suspend their production and marketing within the specified period of time.

When enterprises use machines and electronic products which are to be phased out by the announcement of the state and when they use equipment whose energy consumption is higher than the standards, they must suspend their use within a definite time or revamp them — in accordance with the regulations of their supervisory departments. Such machines, electronic products and equipment shall be prohibited from being transferred to other places for other users.

Article 48:   Localities and departments shall actively develop the market for energy-saving technologies and technology transfer shall be carried out with remuneration. If necessary and when conditions are available, technical service centres for energy conservation may be set up and they may undertake activities such as providing consultancy services and information to enterprises and conducting energy surveys and tests.

Chapter VIII: Rewards and Penalties

Article 49:   The state shall regularly select advanced units of energy conservation through public appraisal and reward units which have achieved marked successes in energy conservation.

Article 50:   The state shall encourage the masses of the people to pitch in the effort for energy conservation. People who come up with outstanding proposals for energy conservation shall be rewarded in accordance with state regulations by the beneficiaries in a way commensurate to the economic benefits and proposals have yielded upon implementation. The state shall guarantee the lawful rights of people who criticize cases of energy waste, and forbid any retaliation against them.

Article 51:   State-owned industrial and communications enterprises which meet the provisions of Article 9, 10, 11 and 12 shall be entitled to bonuses of energy conservation in accordance with the relevant regulations of the state on rewards for saving specified fuels and raw and semi-finished materials and with the approval of the administrative agencies of energy conservation and other departments concerned.

Article 52:   As for rewards for water conservation in cities and in hydro-power generation, the Ministry of Urban and Rural Construction and Environmental Protection and the Ministry of Water Resources and Electric Power shall respectively devise measures, make it public and put into implementation when having examined and approved.

Article 53:   Minor cases of violatiions of these Regulations by units and individuals shall be dealt with by administrative agencies of energy conservation in the spirit of criticism and education; while major ones shall be dealt with in the following way on a case-by-case basis.

   (1)   Enterprises which continue to burn oil beyond the time limit in violation of Article 18, Section 1 shall have their oil supply terminated. The decision on the remination of oil shall be made by the agencies responsible for cutting down on oil burning and then it shall be referred to the oil-supply departments for implementation.

   (2)   The local administrative agencies of energy conservation shall

terminate the supply of energy to enterprises which have rehabilitated and expanded the use of small blast furnaces, small converters,
small electric-arc furnaces, small rolling mills, small thermal power
stations and small smelters and electrolyzers of non-ferrous metals,
which are all energy-guzzling, and enterprises which continue to
make coal by indigenous methods in violation of the provisions of
Article 21, Section 2 and Article 27, Administrative offices for
industry and commerce shall revoke their business licenses.

(3)   Local administrative agencies of energy conservation shall impose
fines on enterprises which have expanded the capacity of boilers
without authorization in violation of the provisions of Article 25.
Departments of fuel supply shall not supply energy for those which
have illegally expanded capacity of boilers.

(4)   Banks shall suspend loans to enterprises which, in violation of the
provisions of Article 47, continue to produce, market, use and
transfer, beyond the time limit, machines, electronic products and
equipment referred to in that article. Local administrative agencies
of energy conservation shall decide whether to terminate energy
supply or impose fines on them.

(5)   In addition to dealing in the way described above with enterprises
which violate the provisions of the foregoing relevent articles and
have caused gave consequences resulting from energy waste,
administrative agencies of energy conservation shall help relevant
departments look into these cases and find out who among the
responsible persons in the enterprises and who among those directly
involved hold administrative liability.

Units and individuals shall not be exempt from continuously performing the obligations specified in these Regulations after the above-
mentioned penalties are met out to them.

Article 54:   Enterprises, of which energy consumption exceeds the fixed quota shall
be charged extras. The extra charge must not go into the cost and must
not be covered by non-operational expenses. The income derived from
extra charges by localities shall be put at the disposal of the local
administrative agencies of energy conservation and be used for energy
conservation measures.

Having paid the extra charges, enterprises shall also have the obligation
of paying fines when violating the provisions of these Regulations.

Chapter IX: Propaganda and Education

Article 55:   Propaganda departments shall actively publicize principles, policies and
scientific and technical knowledge of energy conservation and adequately
use such forms of publicity as broadcasting, television, newspapers,
publications and lectures with a view to improving the people's understanding of the work of energy conservation and raising their scientific and
technical level.

Article 56:   Educational departments shall step up the training of energy conservation
personnel at different levels. Universities and technical secondary schools
shall train high and medium-level personnel of energy management in
a planned way.

Middle schools and primary schools shall take care that energy-related knowledge and consciousness of energy conservation should be inculcated in young people and teenagers.

Article 57: Directors responsible for energy conservation in enterprises, management personnel in energy conservation agencies and related operators shall receive planned training in energy conservation shall be part of the overall assessment or workers and staff.

Chapter X: Supplementary Provisions

Article 58: The people's governments of provinces, autonomous regions and municipalities under the central authorities, relevant departments of the State Council and army units may in line with these Regulations and their own specific conditions formulate rules for their implementation.

Article 59: The State Economic Commission is responsible for the interpretation of these Regulations.

Article 60: These Regulations shall go into effect on April 1, 1986.

From the day these Regulations come into force "Directive of the State Council on Cutting Down on Oil-Burning of All Types of Boilers and Industrial Furnaces", "Directive of the State Council on Saving Electric Power", "Directive of the State Council on Saving Processed oil", "Directive of the State Council on Saving Coal for Industrial Boilers" and "Directive of the State Council on Promoting Coal Washing and Coal Beneficiating and on the Rational Utilization of Energy Resources" shall be invalidated.

SECTION B: Safety

Safety Directive Nos 1-5

(Issued by the Ministry of Coal Industry on September 16, 1980 through August 20, 1981)

NO 1: Set up and Improve the Safety Supervisory Organs & Strengthen the work of Safety Supervision

1. The work of safety supervision must be strengthened conscientiously in order to ensure the implementation of the principle "safety first" and the strict implementation of "Coal Mine Safety Regulations" and to promote the development of coal production. The coal bureaus and coal mining administrations of various provinces and autonomous regions must have safety supervisory organs set up within the year. The directive lays down definite stipulations on the tasks, organizations and staffing of safety supervisory organs, competence of safety supervisors and ways of handling cases with people neglecting their duties.

2. The tasks of safety supervisory organs: The safety supervisory organs should supervise and examine work safety according to the safety regulations, the rules of operaton and the rules of production. If they find any problems and unsafe factors against the set rules and regulations, they should urge relevant departments to get a timely correction. They should supervise and examine the rational use of funds allocated for projects to strengthen safety and the progress of these projects. They should make statistics and analysis on accidents, promptly study developing trends of accidents, raise suggestions for the improvement of safety work, examine what precautions should be taken against accidents, urge leading cadres of the enterprises to organize prompt investigation into accidents, analyse reasons and

find out the persons responsible for the accidents, and make reports to higher authorities. They should assist departments concerned in conducting education on safety techniques and relevant legislations, give guidance to masses in the operation of the safety examination network, cooperate with the trade union to organize workers in safety examination, and accept and hear cases in which pressure is applied against those people who adhere to acting in accordance with regulations and rules.

3.   The directive called on coal bureaus and coal mining administration of various provinces and autonomous regions to set up their own safety supervisory bureaus. Each coal mine should set up a safety supervisory station. The post of director of the safety supervisory bureau director, and this bureau must be staffed with a chief engineer. The post of head of the safety supervisory station should be held by a cadre with a chief engineer. The post of head of the safety supervisory station should be held by a cadre with the grade of mine director, and this station must be staffed with an engineer in charge. Besides, the safety supervisory departments at various levels should contain a certain number of personnel in specific fields, such as mining, ventilation, machinery, electricity, transport, etc.

4.   The directive stipulates that the safety supervisors, within areas of their responsibility, have the right to enter any work place for safety examination; to stop any order or operation which would be against regulations and suggest on how to deal with regulation violators; to participate in the examination of designs and safety measures; and to demand a solution to problems of safety within a certain time limit as well as to stop the work in progress and evacuate people from the work-site if they see any danger of an accident.

NO 2:   Make Full Use of the Projects for Strengthening Safety & Emsure Safety in Production

1.   All those projects for strengthening safety scheduled to start this year, particularly those safety projects in connection with ventilation, gas, fire prevention and extinguishment, dust prevention and water control, must be up to the quality standard and completed on schedule.

2.   Priority should be given to those projects for strengthening safety in allocation of funds, the supply of equipment and materials and the arrangement of construction labour force.

3.   The funds, equipment and installations earmarked for safety projects must be used specially for these projects, and no one may divert them to any other purposes.

4.   Those safety projects turned over by other units should be kept in the hands of technically and academically qualified staff and workers, who can take good care of them and make the best use of them.

5.   A system of making regular reports should be instituted.

NO 3: Institute the System of Holding Office Meetings on Safety Work

1. This directive is used to call on coal bureaus, coal mining administrations and mines of various provinces and autonomous regions to institute the system of holding office meetings on safety work so as to study and solve in time safety problems existing in production and construction. The directive sets certain stipulations and specific requirements for the tasks of these kinds of meetings and also describes how to make these meetings fruitful.
2. The tasks of these meetings are to study and carry out the principles, policies, stipulations and instructions of higher authorities on safety in production, hear reports made by various units and safety supervisory departments on implementaion of coal mine safety regulations, rules of production, rules of operation, technical measures for safety and administratioin work for safety; study and analyse existing problems, work out solutions and make sure that relevant departments and personnel are responsible for solving those problems; analyse major accidents in their own departments, hold discussions on how to deal with personnel who are responsible for the accidents and those who seriously violate regulations and rules; draw up preventive measures to avoid recurrence of accidents of the same kind, examine whether the work decided on during previous meetings has been carried out; commend those staff who have performed their tasks well, investigate and affix responsibility of those who have failed to perform their tasks well.

NO 4: Strengthen the Management of Explosive & Detonations

1. Authorities concerned should take up seriously the management of explosives and detonators.
2. Strict demands should be set on the safety management of explosives factories.
3. Reliable safety measures must be taken for the transport of explosives and detonators.
4. Storage of explosives and detonators in coal bureaus and mines must be up to the safety standards.
5. Users of explosives and detonators should strictly follow the system of getting only what is needed and returning what is left over to the storehouse.
6. The system of reward and punishment should be strictly followed.
7. A thorough examination on the management of explosives and detonators must be carried out immediately.

NO 5: Strengthen Dust Prevention Work in Coal Mines & Eliminate Dust Hazards

1. Leading group for dust prevention work should be set up in every coal bureau and mine with a deputy director of the bureau (or a deputy head of the mine) and chief engineer assigned to be group

leaders. The leading group should include the responsible personnel in the departments of production, capital construction, safety, public helath, trade union, etc. Under the leading group there should be an office in charge of day-to-day work.

2.   Strictly follow the system of management of dust prevention.

3.   Stick to the comprehensive dust prevention measures.

4.   Make sure that dust prevention projects are ready as planned.

5.   Do a good job of prevention and control of occupational diseases.

Model Contracts

Co-operation Protocol

The following agreements were reached during friendly meetings between representatives of Speed Engineers & Construction Inc. (hereinafter referred to as Party A) and China Midland Coal Corporation (hereinafter referred to as Party B)
Whereas:

1.   Both parties agree to cooperate closely on the des construction and initial operation of the slurry pipeline from C C southeast Midland province to D City in Highland Province cooperation will begin with conceptual engineering, followed by basic engineering, procurement, construction, startup, training of personnel, and operation of the completed system, Party B authorizes Party A to perform joint design with Party B technical personnel, to provide direction and guidance to construction, to provide assistance for training personnel, and operational management, etc. Party A commits its full technical resources to Party B to ensure the successful completion and operation of this very important project.

2.   Both parties agree to speedily organize specialist groups to proceed with cooperation to initiate conceptual engineering as soon as possible in order to complete final design, prepare the construction schedule, and to start construction as soon as possible.

3.   It is anticipated the work will be performed in five phases:

Phase I: Conceptual engineering and coal sample test work.
Phase II: Basic engineering and initial procurement.
Phase III: Detail engineering, procurement, construction advisory

services and guidance.

Phase IV: Operational and managerial personnel training and start-up.

Phase V: Operation of the complete system.

During the above five phases, based on Party B requirements, Party A is willing to provide all assistance and be responsible for its suggestions and assistance provided until the technical, operational and managerial personnel of Party B have mastered all techniques and are able to manage the project.

Both parties agree to enter into one or more contracts for the above phases with the scope of work and all conditions for each phase being mutually agreed.

4.   Party A agrees in principle to become a participating partner in this project to ensure Party B's full commitment to the successful completion and operation of the pipeline. Details of Party B's financial participation will be worked out and agreed by both parties during performance of design. Party B's understands that the magnitude of Party B's financial participation is not especially significant but rather the principle of firm commitment and cooperation through the entire period of participation in accordance with Party A's request.

5.   Fluor has offered its proposal and quotation to Party A dated Oct 18, 1983 regarding the content, level, and cost for conceptual and basic engineering. Both sides are willing to reach agreement as soon as possible through friendly consultaion with a sincere sprit of cooperation in order to enable the joint work to start.

6.   This protocol prepared by representatives of Party A and Party B through friendly consulation reflects the good faith intent of both parties and it comes into force immediately as of the date of signing. However, no liability shall arise by virtue of this protocol since the contracts for the phases of the work shall alone establish the liability and responsibility of each party.

7.   This protocol is agreed and entered into this first day of Oct 30, 1983.

IV ENERGY CONSERVATION

The State Council Order for the Conservation of Electricity

(Energy-saving Order No. 2, April 15, 1981)

At present, the electric energy of our country is both short of supply and used very wastefully. The following order is issued for the purpose of strengthening the administration of power consumption, economizing on electricity and increasing the utilization ratios of the electric energy in order to suit the needs of the four-modernizations construction and the life of the people:

1. The controlled power consumption in quantity shall strictly be put into practice. The economic commission of each area shall regularly check and ratify the unit product electric consumption quotas and power consumption norms and supervise the implementation of them jointy with the power department and the authorities in charge of the users. They shall implement the procedures that "those who use power excessively shall be restricted; the excess shall be deducted from subsequent consumption in return; the quantity saved shall belong to the units themselves" for the purpose of restricting the units which consume power above quota and encouraging economy of electricity so as to use the saved electric energy for the increase of the units' production.

Newly-built and extended projects shall go through the formalities of the examination and approval of power consumption before construction, otherwise no power shall be supplied.

2. The use of electrical heating equipment shall be strictly controlled. All equipment originally heated with such primary energy as coal, oil, gas, etc. shall not be switched over to heating with electric energy from now on with the exception of the units approved by the authorities jointly with the power supply departments due to particular needs; the equipment which was irrationally transformed in the past shall be switched back within a definite time and if it is not transformed back when the time limit is exceeded, the power supply shall be discontinued.

3.   Preferential power supply shall be put into effect. Production power supply shall be preferred to the products with low energy consumption, good quality and suitable for sale. The enterprises shall reduce its product power consumption exceeding the quotas to less than the quotas within a definite time through rectifications and transformations and if some of them still fail to reduce the consumption by the end of 1982, the power supply departments shall restrict the power supply or raise the power charges. The power consumption quotas for various products are as follows:

Technological unit consumption for synthetic ammonia:　　　　　1,600 kwh/ton
Technological unit consumption for calcium carbide:　　　　　3,650 kwh/ton
Direct current unit consumption for caustic soda:　　　　　2,450 kwh/ton
Alternating current unit consumption for electrolytic aluminium　　20,000 kwh/ton
Technological unit consumption for silicon iron (containing 75% silicon):　9,500 kwh/ton
Technological unit consumption for electric steel (in metallurgical industry):　700 kwh/ton
Technological unit consumption for electric steel (in machinery industry):　800 kwh/ton

4.   Power consumption loads shall be regulated and balanced power consumption shall be put into effect. Non-continuous production shall be urged to keep clear of the peak-load power consumption and low-trough preferential power charges shall be implemented. In balancing power consumption, the economic commission of each area shall arrange the regular overhauls of large enterprises as far as possible in the peak periods of power consumption. In the places where hydropower is aailable, products with big power consumption such as iron alloys, electric steel, electrolytic aluminium, calcium carbide, silicon carbide, yellow phosphorus, etc, shall be arranged for more yields by making use of hydro-power in the water-abundant periods. Preferential power charges shall be put into effect for the units which only consume power in the water-abundant seasons.

5.   Living power consumption shall be saved. Power-undertaking and charge-undertaking systems shall be cancelled for the living power consumption of the residents in the families' dormitories of Party and government organizations, troops, enterprises and institutions. Annual plans shall be formulated in the light of the specific conditions of each area and they shall require that all users shall have electric meters installed and pay electricity charges according to the actual power consumption. Under the present circumstances, where electric meters still fail to satisfy the needs, the charges shall be settled by the provisional means of the calculation of charges on the basis of the actual wattages of the electrical appliances used.

6.   Power-consuming equipment shall be renewed or transformed. The scientific research, designing and building departments of the machinery industry shall speed up the research and manufacture of energy-saving and high-efficiency power-consuming equipment and the replacement of energy-wasting and low-efficiency power-consuming equipment. The State Commission of Machine Building Industry and the State Bureau of Standardization jointly with departments concerned such as the First Ministry of Machine Building Industry, shall prescribe, promulgate and put into effect the efficiency standards for major power-consuming equipment before 1982.

7.   Jointly with the departments in charge of enterprises, the Bureau of Standardization and the power department of each province, municipality or

autonomous region shall make a general survey of the electric energy utilization efficiency of such existing universal machines and tools as ventilators, blowers, centrifugal pumps, axial flow pumps, rectifiers, electric heaters, etc. Those with actual utilization efficiency lower than the following provisions shall be included in energy-saving plans and replaced or transformed by stages and in groups:

Ventilators, blowers:	70%
Centrifugal pumps, axial flow pumps:	60%
Rectifiers:	90%
Electric heaters:	40%

8. The First Ministry of Machine Building Industry shall be responsible for organizing the production units of mechanical and electrical products in each province, municipality or autonomous region to stop the production of the following old products with high power consumption and low efficiency before the end of 1982 at the latest:

Plug-in salt bath furnaces;

Low-temperature electric heating equipment without the use of remote infrared heating technology;

AC contactors of more than 100 A without the use of noiseless operating technology.

9. Electrical equipment shall be rationally deployed so as to remove the pratice of "the abusable use of energy." The electric motors with normal operating load rates lower than 40% and the transformers with the same lower than 30% shall be regulated or replaced by the power-using units before the end of 1983 at the latest.

10. In order to reduce idle power consumption, all the medium and small electric motors and various arc-welding transformers with idle rates more than 50% shall be additionally fitted with idling restricting devices by the power-using units before the end of 1983.

11. In the places where industries are concentrated, the local economic commissions shall gradually organize and economic commissions shall gradually organize and establish heat treatment, electroplating, casting and oxygen-producing centres on the principle of extensive cooperation among specialized departments so as to increase the effect of the utilization of electric energy.

12. The economic management of power networks shall be strengthened. Water energy and high-efficiency coal-burning generator sets shall be put to full use to generate more power. The problems such as the imbalance between power transmission, transformation and generation and the imbalance between the idle and working proportions shall be solved step by step. The transformation of city power networks shall be speeded up so as to ensure the quality of power supply. Power departments shall be required to reduce the average power line damage rates of the whole country to between 8.2% and 8.5% by 1985 on the existing basis.

13. Idle potentialities shall be exploited with great efforts. Power supply and power user departments shall jointly take measures to compensate for idling so as to increase power factors and achieve the on-site balance of idle power and the grading balance of power transmission, transformation and distribution networks. The current system of rewards and punishments for power factors shall continue to be in force.

14. Rural power networks shall be rectified and transformed. In general, the radius of power supply of a rural power network shall not exceed the following provisions:

10 kilovolts — 15 kilometres
15 kilovolts — 40 kilometres
Power departments shall, jointly with local departments concerned, be responsible for rectifying and transforming the networks in excess of the above provisions or which supply power in a roundabout way. Iron cables shall be prohibited from use as newly-built rural power lines. The transformation of the original iron cables shall be completed by stages and in groups before 1984. It shall be required to reduce the line damage rates of rural power supply lines to less than 12%.

Power supply departments shall organize people's communes, production brigades and teams to transform the low-voltage power supply lines which endanger safety and incur serious loss of electric energy so as to ensure safe and economic operation.

15.   With regard to the army's industrial and living power consumption, specific procedures for the implementation of power-saving shall be formulated in the spirit of power saving in this Order.

The State Council Order
for the Saving of Refined Oils

(Energy-saving Order No. 3 April 17, 1981)

Petroleum is a short supplied product in the economic construction of our country
and refined oils are strategic materials of even greater importance; therefore the
saving of refined oils shall be put in an important place. At present, refined oils are
consumed in large quantities in ou country and there is too much waste of them
because they are not strictly administered. The following order is issued for the
purpose of reducing the consumption of oils conscientiously so as to serve the
needs of the four-modernizations construction.

1. The system that refined oils are distributed in a unified manner, supplied in
fixed quantity and used within the limits shall strictly be implemented. The
economic commission at each level shall regularly examine and ratify the oil
consumption of each oil user unit jointly with the departments concerned, ration
them for use within the limits, supply them with coupons and shall not supply any
excessive quantity.

Refined oils shall be supplied by local oil companies in a unified manner in
accordance with the fixed quotas. Oil fields, oil refineries and the like shall not sell
refined oils themselves. The refined oils used by oil departments themselves shall
also be brought into the state distribution plans by accounts and in items and
similarly the oils used shall be provided for in fixed quantity and used within the
limits.

2. The oils used by motor vehicles shall conscientiously be controlled and
reduced. Oils shall be supplied to specialized transportation companies in
accordance with the transportation plans transmitted to lower levels by the state.
With regard to the lorries of industrial and mining enterprises, the economic
commissions at each level shall, jointly with the departments concerned, re-
examine and re-ratify the number of lorries used by each unit in accordance with the

current condition where social transport capacity is greater than the transport volume and in the spirit of giving full play to the transport capacity of specialized transport departments and supplying oils in accordance with the newly-fixed number of lorries used. The lorries not in use and in surplus as a result of the regularized production and construction tasks shall be reserved in stock and the supply of oils stopped. A small number more of the lorries of Party and government organizations, bodies and institutions shall be reserved in stock; during reservation, they shall be exempt from road tolls and their licences and oil books returned. Oils shall be supplied for the cars of each unit in accordance with the establishment of cars. The quantity of oils for a special car used by senior cadres shall not exceed 100 kilogrammes a month and that for a public car shall not exceed 70 kilogrammes a month, both of which shall be used within the limits.

3. There shall be standards for the allocation of cars. The cars used by the leading cadres of central organs, state organizations and of each province, municipality and autonomous region shall be allocated in accordance with the document No. 83 (1979) issued by the Central Committee of the CPC, i.e. "A Number of Provisions of the Central Committee of the CPC and the State Council for the Living Remuneration of Senior Cadres."

A car shall be allocated to three to five cadres at the rank of director or vice-director of a department, a bureau or an office under a ministry (including the cadres at the same rank of a prefecture, a city directly under the jurisdiction of a province or an enterprise or an institutuion at the prefectural level).

Two to three additional cars for communication shall be allocated according to the volume of official business to each department of a central organ or a state organization or to each province, municipality or autonomous region. One to two cars shall be allocated to each bureau under a prefecture or a city directly under the jurisdiction of a province.

Three to six cars shall be allocated to each county for common use by the county Party committee, county people's government and county people's political consultative conference. One to three cars shall be allocated to an independent enterprise or institution at the county level. A certain number of jeeps shall be allocated as required by the work to a geological, oil field, mine or field capital construction unit and the specific numbers shall be checked and ratified by local planning commissions and business authorities. In principle, no cars shall be allocated to a unit below the county level.

All foreign affairs departments shall use taxis whenever possible. A certain number of cars shall be allocated to each foreign affairs department of a central organ or a state organization or to another department with relatively more affairs and duties and the specific numbers shall be examined and ratified by the Bureau of Administration for Organ Affairs. The business cars used by the foreign affairs departments of each province, municipality or autonomous region shall be examined and determined by the people's government of the province, municipality or autonomous region.

The business cars used by procuratorates, courts and banks in every area shall be examined and determined by the people's government of each province, municipality or autononomous region and reported to the State Council for record. With regard to the business cars used by public security departments, the Ministry of public security departments, the Ministry of Public Security shall formulate the establishment of cars used for public security business, in the spirit of oil saving, submit it to the State Council for approval and then put it into effect.

The allocation of cars to each unit, including those purchased through various channels and with various outlays in the past, shall not exceed the total of the establishment as stipulated above. From now on, the allocation of cars to each administrative unit shall be under the unified administration of the Bureau of Administration for organ affairs at each level, while the planning commission in each area shall, jointly with the financial department and business authorities, be responsible for arranging and examining the allocation of cars to each enterprise or institution. Oils shall be supplied in accordance with the new establishments as of July 1, 1981. The units which do not have enough cars presently shall be gradually provided with more up to the stipulated establishments. The present surplus cars shall be gradually provided with more up to the stipulated establishments. The present surplus cars shall first be redistributed in accordance with the establishments within the same organization or the same province, municipality or autonomous region and if there are still surplus ones, they shall be submitted to the State Planning Commission for unified distribution.

4. From now on, the distribution quotas for cars (including sedans, jeeps, pick-up trucks, station wagons) shall be transmitted by the State Planning Commission in a unified manner to lower levels in accordance with the provisions for the establishments of cars and the requirements for the renewal of vehicles. All units shall go through the formalities of examination and approval as stipulated. Financial departments shall not reimburse for the cars purchased without examination and approval; banks shall not pay and transfer accounts for them, public security and communications supervision and administration departments shall not issue licences for them, commercial oil supply departments shall not supply oils for them, the office for the control of social group purchasing power at each level shall be entitled to confiscate them and turn them over to the departments in charge of supplies and then the departments shall otherwise redistribute them in accordance with the state plans.

5. Four-wheel-drive jeeps shall no longer be allocated to the units without tasks in the countryside in the capital of each province or each autonomous region or in a city with a population of more than one million. The original four-wheel drive jeeps shall gradually be replaced by sedans or two-wheel-drive jeeps and transferred for use by prefectures, counties or fieldwork units.

6. The long-distance transportation of lorries across provinces, municipalities and autonomous regions shall strictly be controlled and the transportation at a distance of more than two hundred kilometres shall be approved by the economic commissions of provinces, municipalities and autonomous regions. The formalities of approval shall be handled quarterly or yearly for the reasonable transportation with long-term fixed cooperative relations. Each communications administration station on the way shall be responsible for the examination.

The cars of local Party and government organizations at each level shall run within the area under their jurisdiction. Each unit along a railway shall go out on official business by train with the exception of urgent cases.

7. Various motor vehicles which have been used for many years and which consume oils for more than 20 per cent above the standards shall be rejected through the appraisal of local public security and communications departments, their fixed assets shall be checked and cancelled and they shall be recovered in a unified manner by the supplies department of each province, municipality or autonomous region for disposal and shall not be transferred for further use.

8. Social vehicles shall be organized for rational transportation. The economic

commissions in each area shall be responsible for the organization of cooperative transportation in various forms on the principles of voluntary participation and mutual benefit. The stress ahead of the distribution of lorries shall be laid on communications and transport departments and generally lorries shall no longer be distributed among state organizations, mass bodies and institutions.

9.   The supply of diesel oil shall be reduced with great efforts. The oil used by agricultural tractors shall be examined, ratified and supplied in fixed quantity for use within the limits in accordance with the annual volume of operations of the tractors actually started. The oil used for non-agricultural transportation shall be deducted from the fixed quantity. Commercial, agricultural and highway supervision and administration departments shall strictly control the non-agricultural business transportation of tractors.

From now on, the vehicles refitted with diesel engines shall be prohibited from carrying on business transportation. Higher authorities in charge shall make technical appraisals of existing vehicles refitted with diesel engines and stop the use of those which consume oil in excessive quantities and are unsafe. Local public security and communications departments shall put the execution of the aforesaid under their conscientious supervision.

10.   In order to save oil for agricultural irrigation and drainage power, the farming machinery departments shall organize the technical tests and appraisals of the water pumps produced by the existing water pump factories, issue production licences to those with their products up to standard and stop the production of and rectify those whose products are not up to the standard. The water conservancy and agricultural departments in each area shall organize people's communes, production brigades and teams to regulate irrigation and drainage machines which do not form complete sets and it shall be required to eliminate the phenomenon of "big horses drawing small carts" in respect of irrigation and drainage power before 1984. In the first half of 1982, the State Agricultural Commission shall, jointly with the Ministries of Water Conservancy and Electric Power Industry, prescribe the rational lift norms for agricultural irrigation and drainage and the cost limits for draught relief and flood drainage and those in excess of the norms or limits shall not be permitted to use oils or electricity.

11.   Urban and rural residents shall strictly be prohibited from burning diesel oil for rice cooking or heating. Commercial departments shall control the supply of civil kerosene stoves and generally they shall not supply them, with the exception of the appropriate supply to suit the particular needs of the patients in hospitals and for field operation.

12.   The oil used by the existing diesel generators shall be examined by commercial departments jointly with the departments concerned. Generally no oil shall be supplied except that coupons shall be issued and oil shall be supplied in accordance with the rated hours actually required for such operations as mining, exploration, construction, reclamation, pastoral area well drilling, etc. in the border and open country areas without power sources or for power source sets which shall be made ready for hospitals or for broadcasting, posts and telecommunications, scientific research, etc.

13.   If the designed oil consumption of the oil-consuming machines and tools now in production exceeds the following limits, they shall be improved before the end of 1982 at the latest so as to reduce the oil consumption to below the limits and their production shall be stopped for reduced at the expiration of the time limit, the execution of which shall be arranged for by the State Commission of Machine

Building Industry.

Commission of Machine Building Industry.
The Oil Consumption of a Motor Vehicle:—

4-ton lorry	29 litres/100 kilometres
2-ton lorry	17 litres/100 kilometres
common sedan	12 litres/100 kilometres
4-wheel-drive jeep	17 litres/100 kilometres
2-wheel-drive jeep	15 litres/100 kilometres
station wagon (less than 15 seats)	17 litres/100 kilometres

The Oil Consumption of a Diesel Engine:
1. Swirl-chamber or prechamber
    (1) 65 to 85 mm cylinder bore, 2,000 to 3,000 r.p.m. rotation speed 220g./hp-hr
    (2) 90 to 125 mm cylinder bore, 1,400 to 2,000 r.p.m. rotation speed 195g./hp-hr
    (3) more than 130 mm cylinder bore, 400 to 1,500 r.p.m. rotation speed 195g./hp-hr
2. Direct-injection-chamber
    (1) 90 to 125 mm cylinder bore, 1,400 to 2,000 r.p.m. rotation speed 185 g./hp-hr
    (2) more than 130 mm cylinder bore, 400 to 1,500 r.p.m. rotation speed 175 g./hp-hr

Red Flag brand high-grade sedans consume more oil, so their production shall be stopped as of June 1981.

14. The new increase of oil-consuming machines and tools shall strictly be controlled. The balance of supply and demand of oils shall be used as an important ground for the formulation of the plans to produce and import oil-consuming machines and tools. Production units and import units shall strictly act according to the state plans and strictly control the overfulfilment of production quotas and import plans.

It shall strictly be forbidden to refit, assemble or process various motor vehicles with supplied materials beyond the state plans. The import of cars shall strictly be controlled and that of various cars with state foreign currencies or with the foreign currencies owned by each unit itself shall be examined and approved by the State Commission of Machine Building Industry.

15. The system that old lubricating oil shall be turned over before supplying new oil shall be put into effect. The industrial and communications authorities and other departments concerned of each province, municipality or autonomous region shall transmit used lubricating oil recovery quotas down to each enterprise or institution and it shall strictly be forbidden to burn off, pour away or wash away used lubricating oil. The equipment which leaks shall be repaired within a definite time and the supply of lubricating oil shall be deferred or periodically stopped if the waste is serious. The supply shall be deferred or stopped until the defects are put right.

16. Commercial departments shall gradually build more oil-filling stations in large and medium cities and vital communications lines and urban construction and public security departments shall give them active support so as to reduce the wastage due to the scattered self-storage and long-distance oil filling of the oil user

units.

17.   The army shall formulate the specific procedures for the implementation of the establishments of cars and the saving of refined oils in the spirit of oil saving of this Order.

The State Council Order for the Conservation of Coal used by Industrial Boilers

(Energy-Saving Order No. 4 July 24, 1982)

Industrial boilers constitute heating power equipment which is indispensable to the development of the national economy and the improvement of people's life. Most of the existing boilers in our country are rather backward in equipment and rather low in the levels of management of their operation, resulting not only in much waste of fuel but also in serious pollution of the environment. The following order is issued for the purpose of improving the equipment situation of industrial boilers and strengthening the management of their operation so as to increase their thermal efficiency, save fuel and reduce pollution.

1. The fuel rationing system shall be put into effect for industrial boilers (excluding the boilers of power stations, locomotives and ships). Fuel supply departments shall, jointly with the authorities in charge of the users, regularly examine and ratify the fuel consumption quotas and the quantity of supply for boilers and the fuel supply departments shall isue fuel supply oupons accordingly. The fuel rationing by coupons shall be put into effect as of January 1, 1983, the saved part to be left to the users' disposal, and the excessive part shall not be supplied or shall be supplied at a higher price. Each user shall strengthen the management of the coal used by boilers by means of measurement and assessment.

2. Coal production departments and fuel supply departments shall jointly be responsible for the gradual achievement of the relative stability in respect to the variety and quality of coal supplied to each area. Key enterprises shall be selected in 1983 to begin the experiments of the fixed-point supply of coal. For the large and medium cities with coal supplied in a greater variety, the fuel supply departments shall be responsible for processing and supplying the power coal of sizes less than 15 mm in accordance with the situation of coal resources and the demands of

enterprises.

3.   The heat energy utilization ratios of heat-generating equipment shall be increased so as to save steam. Each industrial or mining enterprise shall set up a perfect system of the administration of the technological steam-consuming quotas so as to gradually achieve the planned, rated and measured steam consumption. The backward steam-consuming technology and equipment shall be transformed in a planned manner. The management of the heat power networks shall be made more effective and the heat preservation of the equipment piping networks shall fulfill the designed requirements. The total rate of leakage of pipelines, valves, drainages, etc. shall not exceed 0.2 per cent. When the steam is indirectly consumed, the recovery rate of condensation water shall not be lower than 60 to 80 per cent.

4.   Heating with steam shall be switched over to heating with hot water. The heating systems to be built in future shall make use of hot water for heating. The existing steam heating systems shall be switched over to hot water heating ones before the heating season of 1984 except for those approved by the energy-saving authorities. The fuel supply departments shall reduce the supply of coal if they are not transformed when the time limit is exceeded.

5.   The blind expansion of boiler capacity shall strictly be restricted. If a newly added or renewed or transformed boiler is to have its evaporative capacity expanded, it shall be examined and approved in advance by the local energy-saving department jointly with the fuel supply department and the department in charge of the user to review the procedure of the capacity expansion for the boiler, otherwise no coal shall be supplied.

6.   Low-efficiency boilers shall be renewed or transformed within a definite time. The renewal of such old-type boilers as Lancashire ones shall be completed before the end of 1986 at the latest. Other boilers with the operating thermal efficiency lower than the following minimum requirements shall be transformed; if the transformed ones still fall short of the requirements, or if their transformation expenses exceed 65% of the costs of purchase although they can fulfill the requirements, they shall be renewed. The transformation and renewal shall be completed before the end of 1990 at the latest. If they are neither renewed nor transformed when the time limit is over, the supply of fuel shall be stopped. All boilers not in use as a result of renewal shall be rejected, and sold to the material recovery companies in each area for disposal and strictly prohibited from being transferred for further use.

The minimum requirements (under the conditions of burning bituminous or brown coal Class 2 or 3) for the operating thermal efficiency of industrial boilers are as follows:

50% in the case of boilers with the capacity less than 1 t/h;

55% in the case of boilers with the capacity in the range of 1 t/h to 1.5 t/h;

60% in the case of boilers with the capaicty of 2 t/h;

65% in the case of boilers with the capacity in the range of 4 t/h to 6.5 t/h;

72% in the case of boilers of 10 t/h and of more than 10 t/h.

The plans and projects of the renewal or transformation of boilers shall be examined and determined by the energy-saving departments of provinces, municipalities and autonomous regions jointly with fuel supply, machine building, labour and environmental protection departments and submitted to the state and then the state shall entrust the State Bureau of Supplies with the verification of them jointy with the departments concerned so as to bring them into the state energy-saving plans. The State Bureau of Supply shall organize their implementation. The boilers required for renewal shall be included in state plans and arranged for their production by the machine-building industrial departments. The advanced techniques for the transformation of boilers shall go through the technical appraisals of the authorities above the prefectural or city level before being popularized or put to use.

7.   Necessary meters and water treatment or other devices shall be installed. Before the end of 1985, heating process monitoring or measuring meters and dust removers shall be fitted in each industrial boiler room which shall be equipped with soot blowing and with water treatment devices or in which effective water treatment measures shall be adopted.

8.   The renewal and transformation of boilers shall be arranged for in combination with the focused development of centralized heat supply or the combined production of heat and electricity. The planning and economic commissions of each province, municipality or autonomous region shall, jointly with the production, energy-saving, electric power and urban construction departments, do the overall planning well on the basis of city overall plans and combine them with the switching of oil burning and gas burning over to coal burning so as to put energy-saving funds to effective use.

Local people's government shall be responsible for organizing the departments concerned in the good planning and design of the industrial and residential areas to be built in the future so as to carry out centralized heat supply. Otherwise, urban construction departments shall not start construction and fuel supply departments shall not supply fuels.

9.   Users shall select and buy appropriate boilers according to the categories of coal locally supplied, boiler manufacturing enterprises shall produce them according to the needs of users and supplies distribution departments shall supply them according to the users' requirements. The new boilers ordered in the future which do not suit the categories of burned coal shall not be used; they shall be returned to the suppliers or returned for repairs and economic losses shall be compensated for in accordance with the provisions in the purchase contracts. If a boiler manufacturing enterprise does not produce it or them as stipulated in the contract, it shall compensate for the economic losses; if a user does not order an appropriate boiler according to the category of coal locally supplied, he shall compensate for the economic losses.

10.   No unit shall build any boilers without the examination and approval of the Ministry of Machine Building Industry and the Ministry of Labour and Personnel and without the issue of boiler manufacture licences by them. The boilers which do not conform to the standards of the product quality stipulated by the state shall not be delivered out of the plants. All hand-operated boilers of 1 t/h or more than 1 t/h shall not be built. Boiler products shall be supplied as stipulated in "The Supply Range of Industrial Boilers in Complete Sets" and equipped with necessary heating process measuring and recording meters.

11.   Boiler users shall carry out the technical operations training and examination of their operating personnel. A fireman shall pass an examination and obtain a certificate of qualification from the local safety supervisory organization for boilers and pressure containers before his independent operation. Each user shall strengthen the maintenance and management of boilers and establish a perfect overhauling system and a routine assessment system so as to ensure the good equipment condition and safe operation of boilers.

12.   The funds required for the renewal and transformation of boilers shall mainly be raised and settled by localities and enterprises ther ¬elves. If they really have difficulty, they shall apply to banks for seller's loans or bι ;bsidized by the state as it thinks fit.

13.   The army shall formulate the specific procedures for the saving of the coal used by boilers in the spirit of this Order.

CHAPTER FOUR

TRADE MARK
&
PATENT

Brief Introduction

The Trade Mark Law of The People's Republic of China was adopted at the 24th Session of the Standing Committee of the 5th National Congress on August 23, 1982 and was promulgated as the 10th Decree of the Committee. This law has been put into force since March 1, 1983.

For major contents of the Trade Mark Law, readers may refer to the materials listed in this Chapter.

Foreigner and foreign enterprises applying for trade mark registration in China shall be treated by reference to the agreements signed between the state of the applicants and the People's Republic of China, or by reference to the international treatries participated by both countries, or by reference to the principle of reciprocity. Here are some of the examples:-

1. Exchange Notes Between China, Belgium, the Netherlands and Luxembourg on the Mutual Benefit of Trade Mark Registration and Protection (April 10, 1975)
2. Exchange Notes Between China and Greece on the Mutual Protection of Trade Mark (April 19, 1975)
3. Exchange Notes Between China and France on the Mutual Benefit of Trade Mark Registration (July 15, 1975)
4. Exchange Notes Between China and New Zealand on the Mutual Benefit of Trade Mark Registration (July 18, 1975)
5. Exchange Notes Between China and The Federal Republic of Germeny on the Mutual Benefit of Trade Mark Registration (August 8, 1975)
6. Exchange Notes Between China and Iran on the Mutual Benefit of Trade Mark Registration (December 15, 1975)
7. Exchange Notes Between China and Thailand on Licensing Rights of Trade Mark Registration (January 18, 1977)
8. Exchange Notes Between China and Austria on the Mutual Benefit of Trade and Service Marks Registration (April 4, 1977)
9. Exchange Notes Between China and Spain on the Agreement of Trade Mark protection (June 10, 1977)
10. Exchange Notes Between China and Japan on Trade Mark Protection Agreement (September 29, 1977)

I FOR INVESTORS

SECTION A: Pre 1982

Regulations Governing Trade Marks

Article 1: The present Regulations are established for the purpose of strengthening trade mark administration and encouraging enterprises to ensure and improve the quality of their products.

Article 2: For all trade marks used by any enterprise, application for registration shall be made to the Central Administrative Bureau for Industry and Commerce.

For goods using no trade marks, the name and address of the enterprise concerned shall be clearly indicated on the goods or on their packings, if necessary and feasible, with a view to facilitating verification.

Article 3: A trade mark is distinctive sign representing the quality of the goods bearing it. The industrial and commercial administrations shall, in co-operation with other authorities concerned, exercise supervision and control over the quality of the goods.

Article 4: A trade mark must have a definite name. The words and/or design forming the trade mark must be simple and clear so as to facilitate identification.

Article 5: The following words or designs shall not be used as trade marks or in trade marks:

(1)   Those identical with or similar to the national flag, national emblem, military flag or decorations of the People's Republic of China;

(2)   Those identical with or similar to the national flags, national emblems or military flags of foreign countries;

(3)   Those identical with or similar to the emblems or names of the

Red Cross or the Red Crescent;

(4)   Those having a politically undesirable influence.

Foreign words shall not be used in trade marks, but trade marks for export goods may have explanatory foreign wording added.

Article 6:   A trade mark the registration of which is applied for, must not be identical with or confusingly similar to any trade mark already registered in the name of another enterprise for the same or similar goods.

Article 7:   Where two or more enterprises apply for the registration of identical or similar trade marks, the registration shall be accorded to the first applicant.

Article 8:   Where application for the registration of a trade mark is rejected, and the applicant objects to the decision, he may request for a re-examination of the case within one month from the date of receipt of the notice of rejection. If the application is again rejected after re-examination, the refusal shall be considered final and conclusive.

Article 9:   When a trade mark is approved for registration, the registration shall be published and a certificate of registration be issued by the Central Administrative Bureau for Industry and Commerce.

Article 10:   The term of validity of the registration of a trade mark begins from date of its approval and ends on the date when the enterprise concerned applies for its cancellation.

Article 11:   After a trade mark has been approved for registration, the Central Administrative Bureau for Industry and Commerce shall give public notice of cancellation of the registration in any of the following cases:

(1)   Where the quality of the goods concerned is lowered through roughness or carelessness in manufacture;

(2)   Where the name and/or the design of the trade mark are altered by the enterprise on its own accord;

(3)   Where the registered trade mark has ceased to be used for a year without approval of the competent authorities for its retention;

(4)   Where after examination, cancellation is deemed well-founded and justified in the light of the demands and proposals raised by masses of people, government organs, public associations or enterprises.

Article 12:   Where registration of a trade mark is applied for by any foreign enterprise, the following two conditions must be met:

(1)   An agreement on reciprocal registration of trade marks has been previously concluded between the People's Republic of China and the home country of the applicant;

(2)   The trade mark under application for registration has already been registered in the name of the applicant in his home country. The term of validity of the registration of a trade mark in China in the name of a foreign enterprise shall be determined by the Central Administrative Bureau for Industry and Commerce.

Article 13:   The Implementing Rules under the Regulations Governing Trade Marks shall be adopted and published by the Central Administrative Bureau for Industry and Commerce.

The People's Committees of the provinces, autonomous regions and municipalities directly under the central authority may, by virtue of the provisions of the Regulations Governing Trade Marks and the Implementing Rules under the Regulations, work out specific measures for trade mark administration.

Article 14: The Regulations shall enter into force as from the date of publication. The Provisional Regulations on Trade Mark Registration promulgated by the Government Administration Council on August 28, 1950 shall be abrogated on the same date.

Implementing Rules under the Regulations Governing Trade Marks

(Promulgated by the Central Administrative Bureau for Industry and Commerce on April 25, 1963)

Article 1:	These Rules are established in accordance with Article 13 of the Regulations Governing Trade Marks.
Article 2:	Only duly registered enterprises may apply for registration of trade marks.
Article 3:	An enterprise applying for registration of trade marks shall file a separate application with respect to each trade mark, accompanied by a quality specification form for the goods, 20 representations of the trade mark and a registration fee of RMB 20 yuan.
	The application shall first be submitted to the competent authorities in the field within which the enterprise falls, for examination and preliminary approval.
	The quality specification form for the goods concerned shall be filled out according to the prescribed technical criteria for the products, and examined and certified by the competent authorities in the field within which the enterprise falls.
Article 4:	Any enterprise applying for registration of a trade mark for a medicinal and pharmaceutical product shall attach to the application a certificate of authorisation to manufacture such products, issued by the public health department or bureau of a province, autonomous region or municipality directly under the central authority.
	In applying for the registration of trade marks intended for export goods, the enterprise shall attach to the application a certificate issued by the foreign trade authorities.
Article 5:	Where the same enterprise is using an identical trade mark for goods in different classes, a separate application for registration shall be

filed for each class in accordance with the annexed table for Classification of Goods.

Article 6: Where the application for registration of a trade mark is rejected, the registration fee paid by the applicant shall be refunded.

Article 7: Where after the registration of a trade mark, the appellation or design of the trade mark is to be altered, a new registration shall be applied for.

Article 8: Where after the registration of a trade mark, the enterprise needs to use the trade mark for other goods in the same class, it must seek the approval of the competent authorities.

Article 9: Where after the registration of a trade mark, the name or address of the enterprise is changed, an application for the alteration must be submitted within one month after such change.

Article 10: Where after the registration of a trade mark, it is assigned by the enterprise concerned to another enterprise, an application for the registration of the assignment shall be filed by the assignor and assignee jointly. For each trade mark, a separate application for registration of the assignment shall be filed together with an assignment registration fee of RMB 20 yuan; and the original certificate of registration of the trade mark shall be returned.

Article 11: Where a registered trade mark is cancelled at the request of the enterprise or by notice under Article 11 of the Regulations Governing Trade Marks, the enterprise shall return the certificate of registration for invalidation.

Article 12: Where a certificate of registration of a trade mark has been lost or damaged, a new certificate to replace it shall be applied for. The application must be accompanied by 5 representations of the trade mark and a replacement fee of RMB 5 yuan.

Article 13: Any application for the registration of a trade mark, for the alteration, assignment or cancellation of a trade mark registration or for the issue of a replacement of registration certificate shall first be submitted by the enterprise concerned to the administrative authorities for industry and commerce of the municipality or district where the enterprise is located. These authorities shall examine the application and transmit it to the Central Administrative Bureau for Industry and Commerce.

The applicant shall lodge with these local authorities a copy of the application and copies of other related documents.

Article 14: Where the administrative authorities for industry and commerce have notified the applicant concerned to fulfill the registration formalities not yet completed and other related requirements, the applicant must comply with this within the prescribed period of time. If the applicant fails to do so, the application shall be considered abandoned.

Article 15: Foreign enterprises shall entrust the China Council for the Promotion of International Trade with applications on their behalf for the registration of trade marks.

Article 16: Where a foreign enterprise applies for trade mark registration, an application shall be filed for each trade mark, accompanied by, besides the certificate of nationality, a power of attorney, a copy of the certificate of registration in the applicant's home country, 20 representations of the trade mark and the registration fee of RMB 20 yuan.

Article 17: Where a foreign enterprise desires to renew the registration of a trade mark at its expiration, the application for renewal must be filed before the expiration. A separate application shall be filed for each trade mark, accompanied by a power of attorney, a copy of the certificate of the renewal of registration in the applicant's home country, 20 representations of the trade mark and a registration fee of RMB 20 yuan. At the same time, the original certificate of registration shall be returned.

Article 18: Where a foreign enterprise applies for the alteration of the registration of a trade mark, a separate application shall be filed for each trade mark, accompanied by a power of attorney and documentary evidence for the alteration of the registration in the applicant's home country; and the original certificate of registration shall be returned.

Article 19: A foreign enterprise applying for the registration of the assignment of trade marks, shall, apart from the certificate of nationality of the assignee, file a separate application for each trade mark, accompanied by a power of attorney, documentary evidence for registration of the assignment in the applicant's home country, and an assignment registration fee of RMB 20 yuan; and at the same time, the original certificate of registration shall be returned.

Article 20: The application for registration of trade marks and various related documents submitted by a foreign enterprise shall be in the Chinese language. The certificate of nationality and documentary evidence for the registration of the trade marks in the applicant's home country shall each be accompanied by a Chinese translation. All evidential documents shall be duly notarised and legalised.

Article 21: The present Rules shall enter into force on the date of publication.

Interpretation

Notes to Some Articles of the Regulations Governing Trade Marks and the Implementing Rules under the Regulations Governing Trade Marks

Notes to some Articles of the "Regulations Governing Trade Marks" and the "Implementing Rules under the Regulations Governing Trade Marks" (hereinafter called the Regulations and the Rules):

1.   Pursuant to the decision of our Government, the implementation of Article 12 of the Regulations concerning the signing of agreement on reciprocal trade mark registration and the filing of copy of home registration shall, as from January 1, 1978, be based on the principle of reciprocity.

2.   The following Articles are not applicable to foreign enterprises:

(1)   Paragraph 2 of Article 5 of the Regulations. Foreign enterprises can use foreign words in their trade marks when applying for their registration in China.

(2)   Article 10 of the Regulations. The term of validity of a trade mark registration in the name of a foreign enterprise is ten years and its renewal shall be effective for another ten years.

(3)   Article 11 (3) of the Regulations. When a registered trade mark of a foreign enterprise has not been used for one year, the registration of the said trade mark shall not be cancelled and shall continue to be effective.

(4)   Article 3 of the Rules. When applying for trade mark registration, it is not necessary for a foreign enterprise to accompany its application with a quality specification form.

(5)   Article 2 and last paragraph of Article 13 of the Regulations as well as Articles 2, 4 and 13 of the Rules are not applicable to foreign enterprises.

Interpretation

Rules for Foreign Enterprises Applying for Trade Mark Registration in China

(Revised by the China Council for the Promotion of International Trade on December 12, 1980)

In accordance with Article 15 of the Implementing Rules under the Regulations Governing Trade Marks, foreign enterprises shall entrust the Trade Mark Registration Agency of the China Council for the Promotion of International Trade with applications on their behalf for registration of trade marks in China. The following rules are hereby established to facilitate foreign applications:

1.   The Trade Mark Registration Agency of this Council shall act on behalf of foreign applicants in matters relating to application for trade mark registration, renewal, assignment and change of name or address of the registered proprietor as well as other relevant services.

2.   For a trade mark application, the following documents shall be required:
   (1)   Power of Attorney in duplicate;
   (2)   Application in duplicate;
   (3)   Nationality certificate of the applicant in duplicate (for one or more than one trade marks);
   (4)   Copy of home registration in duplicate;
   (5)   Twelve prints.

3.   For a renewal application, the following documents shall be required:
   (1)   Power of Attorney in duplicate;
   (2)   Application in duplicate;
   (3)   Copy of home registration in duplicate;
   (4)   Original Chinese registration certificate;
   (5)   Twelve prints;

4.   For an assignment application, the following documents shall be required:
   (1)   Power of Attorney in duplicate;
   (2)   Application in duplicate;

(3)   Nationality certificate of assignee in duplicate (for one or more than one trade marks);

(4)   Copy of home registration in the name of assignee in duplicate;

(5)   Original Chinese registration certificate.

5.   *For an application for change of name or address of the registered proprietor, the following documents shall be required:*

(1)   Power of Attorney in duplicate;

(2)   Application in duplicate;

(3)   Copy of home registration showing charge of name or address in duplicate;

(4)   Origianl Chinese registration certificate.

6.   *The originals of Power of Attorney, nationality certificate and certificate of home registration shall be duly legalized by the Chinese Embassy or Consulate in the country in which the applicant or the agent is domiciled.*

7.   *Where a trade mark covers several classes of goods, a separate application shall be filed for each class accompanied by twelve prints of the mark.*

8.   *Nationality certificate may be filed in any form so long as it identifies the nationality of the applicant. Certificate of incorporation or extracts from the Commercial Register may also be accepted as nationality certificate.*

9.   *On the basis of the principle of reciprocity, copy of home registration shall not be required from enterprises of foreign countries which do not require a similar certificate from Chinese enterprises.*

10.   *For a word mark, indication of its meaning shall be required. If the word mark is in plain block letters, prints shall not be needed.*

11.   *Where the Chinese equivalents of a word mark are to be required, this Agency may offer, on request, its services as to translation, transliteration, hand-writing and preparation of prints.*

12.   *Literature or sample brochures shall be furnished in case the goods covered by the mark are not commonly known.*

13.   *Fees for services rendered by this Agency shall be scheduled separately.*

Trade Mark Registration Agency

SECTION B: Post 1982

The Trademark Law of the People's Republic of China

*(Passed August 23, 1982 by the 24th Meeting
of the Standing Committee of the Fifth National
People's Congress, effective March 1, 1983.)*

Chapter I: General Provisions

Article 1:   This law is specially formulated in order to strengthen trademark control, to protect the right of exclusive use of trademarks, to impel producers to guarantee the quality of commodities and uphold the reputation of trademarks, thereby safeguarding the interests of consumers and promoting the development of the socialist commodity economy.

Article 2:   The Trademark Bureau of the State Council department of administration of industry and commerce is in charge of the work of trademark registration and control for the entire country.

Article 3:   A trademark approved for registration by the Trademark Bureau is a registered trademark; the registrant of the trademark enjoys the right of exclusive use of the trademark and receives legal protection.

Article 4:   Enterprises, institutions, and individual industrialists or merchants who require the obtaining of the right of exclusive use of the trademarks of the commodities they produce, manufacture, process, select or distribute shall apply to the Trademark Bureau for registration.

Article 5:   In the case of commodities which the state stipulates must use registered trademarks, trademark registration must be applied for; before approval for registration is obtained [these commodities] should not be sold on the market.

Article 6:   Users of trademarks shall bear responsibility for the quality of the commodities with the trademarks they use. The departments of administration of industry and commerce at various levels shall, through trademark control, supervise the quality of commodities and stop conduct that deceives consumers.

Article 7:   The words and figures used in trademarks, or their composition, shall have notable characteristics and be easy to distinguish. In cases where registered trademarks are used, they shall in addition be marked with "registered trademark" or the symbol of registration.

Article 8:   Trademarks should not use the following words and figures:

(1)   Those that are the same as or similar to the state name, national flag, national emblem, military flag, or medals of the People's Republic of China;

(2)   Those that are the same as or similar to the state names, national flags, national emblems, or military flags of foreign countries;

(3)   Those that are the same as or similar to the banners, emblems or names of intergovernmental international organizations;

(4)   Those that are the same as or similar to the signs or names of the "Red Cross" or the "Red Crescent";

(5)   The commonly used name or figure of the commondity in question;

(6)   Those that directly indicate the quality, main raw materials, functions, uses, weight, quantity and other characteristics of the commodity;

(7)   Those that contain [material of] a racially discriminatory nature;

(8)   Those that promote in an exaggerated manner and contain [material of] a deceptive nature;

(9)   Those that are harmful to the customs of socialist morality or have other bad influences.

Article 9:   Foreigners or foreign enterprises, in applying for trademark registration in China, shall proceed in accordance with agreements their countries have signed with the People's Republic of China or international conventions to which both are party, or proceed in accordance with the principle of reciprocity.

Article 10:   In applying for trademark registration in China and handling other trademark matters, foreigners or foreign enterprises shall entrust the state's designated organization to be their agent.

Chapter II: Application for Trademark Registration

Article 11:   In applying for trademark registration, [applicants] shall fill in and submit a form with the class and name of the commodity using the trademark in accordance with the stipulated commodity classification table.

Article 12:   In cases where the same applicant uses the same trademark on commodities of different classes, he shall file separate applications for registration in accordance with the commodity classification table.

Article 13:   In cases where it is required to use a registered trademark on another commodity in the same class, a separate application for registration shall be filed.

Article 14   In cases where it is required to change the words or figures of a registered trademark, a new application for registration shall be filed.

Article 15:   In cases of registered trademarks where it is required to alter the registrant's name or address or other registration matters, an application for alteration shall be filed.

Chapter III: Examination and Approval of Trademark Registration

Article 16:   Any trademark for which registration is applied which conforms to the relevant stipulations of this law is to be preliminarily approved after examination by the Trademark Bureau and public announcement made.

Article 17:   In the case of any trademark for which registration is applied which does not conform to the relevant stipulations of this law or which is the same as or similar to a trademark for the same type of commodity or a similar commodity which is already registered or which has been preliminarily approved after examination, the application is to be rejected by the Trademark Bureau and no public announcement made.

Article 18:   In cases of two or more applicants applying for registration of the same or similar trademarks on the same type of commodity or a similar commodity, preliminary approval is to be granted after examination and public announcement made of the trademark applied for first. In cases where the applications are made on the same day, preliminary approval is to be granted after examination and public announcement made of the trademark first used; the applications of others are to be rejected and no public announcement made.

Article 19:   Anyone may raise objections to trademarks preliminarily approved after examination within three months of the date of public announcement. In cases where there are no objections or it is ruled that an objection is untenable, approval of registration is to be granted, a registered trademark certificate issued, and public announcement made. In cases where it is ruled that an objection is tenable, approval of registration is not to be granted.

Article 20:   The State Council department of administration of industry and commerce is to establish a Trademark Review Committee to be responsible for handling matters of dispute regarding trademarks.

Article 21:   The Trademark Bureau shall notify applicants in writing in cases of trademarks for which applications are rejected and no public announcement made. In cases where the applicant does not agree, he may apply for reexamination within fifteen days of receiving the notification. The Trademark Review Committee is to render a final decision and notify the applicant in writing.

Article 22:   In cases where an objection is raised to a trademark which has been preliminarily approved after examination and public announcement made, the Trademark Bureau shall hear the facts and reasons stated by the objector and the applicant and render a decision after investigation and verifiction. If a party does not agree, he may apply for reexamination within fifteen days of receiving notification. The Trademark Review Committee is to render a final ruling and notify the objector and the applicant in writing.

Chapter IV: Extension, Assignment and Licensing of Registered Trademarks

Article 23: The period of validity of a registered trademark is ten years, counted from the date of approval of registration.

Article 24: In cases where after the completion of the period of validity of a registered trademark it is required to continue its use, application for extension of registration shall be made within six months before the completion of the period. In cases where the application cannot be made within this period, a grace period of six months may be granted. In cases where application has still not been made by the completion of the grace period, the registered trademark in question is to be cancelled.

The period of validity for each extension of registration is ten years. After approval of an extension of registration, public announcement is to be made.

Article 25   In cases of assignment of registered trademarks, the assignor and the assignee shall jointly file an application to the Trademark Bureau. The assignee shall guarantee the quality of the commodities using the registered trademark in question.

After approval of an assignment of a registered trademark, public announcement is to be made.

Article 26: The registrant of a trademark may, through the signing of a trademark licensing contract, license another person to use his registered trademark. The licensor shall supervise the quality of the commodities on which the licensee uses his registered trademark. The licensee shall guarantee the quality of the commodities on which he uses the registered trademark in question.

Trademark licensing contracts shall be reported to the Trademark Bureau for the record.

Chapter V: Rulings on Disputes Regarding Registered Trademarks

Article 27: In cases where there is a dispute about an already registered trademark, application for a ruling may be made to the Trademark Review Committee within one year from the date of the registration after approval of the trademark in question.

The Trademark Review Committee, after receiving an application for a ruling, shall notify the relevant parties and [advise them to] put forward their reply arguments within a stated period.

Article 28: For trademarks in regard to which an objection had already been raised and ruled upon before approval of registration, applications for rulings with respect to the same facts and reasons should not be made again.

Article 29: After rendering a final ruling to uphold or revoke the registered trademark in dispute, the Trademark Review Committee shall notify the relevant parties in writing.

Chapter VI: Control of Trademark Use

Article 30:   In cases where in the use of registered trademarks there is one of the following types of conduct, the Trademark Bureau is to order rectification within a stated period or revocation of the registered trademark in question:
(1)   Changing on one's own of the words or figures on registered trademarks, or their composition;
(2)   Changing on one's own of the name or address of the registrant of a registered trademark or other registration matters;
(3)   Assignment on one's own of a registered trademark;
(4)   Cessation of use for three consecutive years.

Article 31:   When registered trademarks are used, in cases where the commodities in question are manufactured in a rough and slipshod way, the inferior being passed off as good, deceiving consumers, the departments of administration of industry and commerce at various levels are, differentiating among different circumstances, to order rectification within a stated period, and may also circulate a notice on the matter or impose fines, or the Trademark Bureau may revoke the registered trademark in question.

Article 32:   In cases where a registered trademark is revoked or not extended after the completion of the period, the Trademark Bureau is not, within one year of the date of revocation or cancellation, to approve applications for registration of trademarks which are the same as or similar to the trademark in question.

Article 33:   In cases of violation of the stipulation of Article 5 of this law, the local departments of administration of industry and commerce are to order application for registration within a stated time and may also impose fines.

Article 34   In cases where in the use of unregistered trademarks there is one of the following types of conduct, the local departments of administration of industry and commerce are to put a stop to it, [order] rectification within a stated period, and may also circulate a notice on the matter or impose fines:
(1)   Passing off as a registered trademark;
(2)   Violation of the stipulations of Article 8 of this law;
(3)   Manufacturing in a rough or slipshod way, passing off the inferior as good, deceiving consumers.

Article 35:   In cases where a party does not agree with the decision of the Trademark Bureau to revoke a registered trademark, he may apply for reexamination within fifteen days of receiving notification. The Trademark Review Committee is to render a final decision and notify the applicant in writing.

Article 36:   In cases where a party does not agree with a decision on fines rendered by the departments of administration of industry and commerce according to the stipulations of Article 31, 33 or 34 of this law, he may bring a suit in the people's courts within fifteen days of receiving notification. In cases where the period is completed and suit has not been brought and [the party] also has not performed, the relevant department of administration of industry and commerce is to apply to the people's courts for compulsory execution.

Chapter VII: Protection of the Right of Exclusive Use of Registered Trademarks

Article 37: The right of exclusive use of a registered trademark is limited to the trademark of which registration is approved and to the commodity of which use is approved.

Article 38: All cases where there is one of the following types of conduct belong to the category of infringement upon the right of exclusive use of registered trademarks:

(1) Without obtaining the license of the registered trademark owner, using on the same type of commodity or a similar commodity a trademark the same as or similar to his registered trademark;

(2) Unauthorized manufacture or sale of another's registered trademark sign;

(3) Causing other damage to another's right of exclusive use of a registered trademark.

Article 39: In cases where there is one of the types of conduct infringing upon the right of exclusive use of registered trademarks listed in Article 38, the person whose rights have been infringed upon may request the department of administration of industry and commerce at the county level or above in the infringer's locality to handle the matter. The relevant department of administration of industry and commerce has the right to order the infringer immediately to cease the infringing conduct, and to compensate the person whose rights have been infringed upon for his losses, the amount of compensation to be the profits gained by the infringer during the period of the infringement as a result of the infringement or the losses suffered during the period of infringement by the person whose rights have been infringed upon as a result of the infringement. In cases where the circumstances are grave, fines may also be imposed. In cases where a party does not agree, he may bring a suit in the people's courts within fifteen days of receiving notification. In cases where the period is completed and suit has not been brought and [the party] also has not performed, the relevant department of administration of industry and commerce is to apply to the people's courts for compulsory execution.

With regard to infringement upon the right of exclusive use of registered trademarks, the person whose rights have been infringed upon may also bring suit directly in the people's courts.

Article 40: In cases of counterfeiting of another's registered trademark, including the unauthorized manufacture or sale of another's registered trademark sign, in addition to compensation of the person whose rights have been infringed upon for his losses, and the possible additional imposition of fines, the criminal responsibility of the directly responsible person(s) is to be investigated according to law by the judicial organs.

Chapter VIII: Supplementary Provisions

Article 41:   Fees shall be paid in applying for trademark registration and handling other trademark matters, the specific fee standards to be fixed separately.

Article 42:   Detailed implementing regulations for this law are to be formulated by the State Council department of administration of industry and commerce and reported to the State Council for approval and enforcement.

Article 43:   This law is to be enforced from March 1, 1983. The "Trademark Control Act" promulgated by the State Council on April 10, 1963 is to become void at the same time. Any other regulations regarding trademark control that conflict with this law are to lose effect at the same time.

Trademarks already registered before the enforcement of this law are to continue to be effective.

Interpretation

The Trademark Law of the People's Republic of China

1. *Articles 1 and 3 protect the rights and interest of registered trademark owners. The law also defines infrigements on such rights and specifies penalties for them. Articles 38 and 39 stipulate that administrative control authorities of industry and commerce have the power to stop such infrigements immediately and demand compensations for the losses inflicted upon the victims. Fines will be imposed at the same time for more serious cases. The victims may directly file their cases to people's courts. Article 40 provides that persons directly responsible for counterfeiting registered trademarks of others shall be punished according to the criminal code.*

2. *The law contains specific provisions on trademark registration in China by foreign nationals and legal persons. Articles 9 and 10, trademark registration will be handled according to (A) agreements signed between the People's Republic of China and the countries to which the applicants belong. Or (B) international treaties which both China and the applicants' countries signed. Or (C) the principle of reciprocity, and (D) the Trademark Agency of the China Council for the Promotion of International Trade (CCPIT).*

3. *Article 16 stipulates that the Trademark Office will give a preliminary examination of trademarks for which applications for registration are filed, and publish them in its trademark bulletins. These trademarks are subject to challenge by any person within three months from the date of publications Article 19. If there is no challenge during this period or the challenge is adjudicated invalid, the trademarks will be approved for registration upon which certification shall be issued. If the challenge is adjudicated valid, the trademarks will not be approved for registration.*

4. *The trademark control authorities will set up trademark review and*

adjudication boards to handle disputes over trademarks whose publication is rejected or whose registrations have been turned down owing to challenge by a third party or over trademarks that have been approved for registration or trademarks on the register that have been cancelled for violating the trademark law. The review and adjudication boards will re-examine the cases and pass the final decisions.

5.   Article 24 provides that the owner of a registered trademark may authorize another person to use his trademark on the register by signing a trademark license contract and submit it to the Trademark Office for the record. The new provisions are added to meet the needs of the development of license trade in the world.

6.   The term of validity for a registered trademark shall be 10 years from the date of approval Article 23. An application for renewal may be filed six months before the expiration date. The period of validity for a renewal is 10 years.

7.   If a registered trademark is not used within three years after its registration, Article 30 stipulates that the competent authorities will demand the use of the trademark within a prescribed time limit, otherwise, the registered trademark will be cancelled. China's competent authorities will regard foreign trademarks as being in use when they are advertised or contained in commodity catalogs, sample copies or displayed at exhibitions. Owners of registered trademarks can, within three years after registration, adopt any of the above-mentioned measures to show that their trademarks are in use.

8.   Articles 1 and 6 stipulate that the owner of a registered trademark should be responsibe for the quality of goods as advertised, departments in charge of the administration of industry and commerce should, by way of trademark registration, supervise merchandise quality and prevent or stop cheating.

9.   Articles 31 and 34 also provide that for cases where goods to which a registered trademark is attached are manufactured in a rough and slipshod way or goods of inferior quality are offered for sale as up to standards, departments of administration of industry and commerce shall order corrections to be made within a prescribed time limit, or circulate a notice of criticism, or impose a fine, or have the trademarks revoked by the Trademark Office.

Detailed Rules for Implementation of the Trade Mark Law of the PRC

(Issued by the State Council on March 10, 1983)

Article 1 : These Detailed Rules are formulated in accordance with Article 42 of the Trade Mark Law of the People's Republic of China (hereinafter called the Trade Mark Law)

Article 2. Applicants for trade mark registration must be enterprises, institutions and self-employed industrial and commercial businesses registered according to law, or foreigners or foreign enterprises as specified in Article 9 of the Trade Mark Law.

Article 3 : Trade mark registration shall be applied for separately following the categories listed in the commodity catalogue. Each application must be accompanied by written application for trade mark registration and ten copies for the trade mark design (for those in fixed colour, a coloured design and a black-and-white trade mark).

The trade mark design shall be printed on glossy durable paper of not more than ten centimetres in length and width. Designs on plastic or other material resistant to glue, should be substituted for by designs printed or drawn on paper or photos.

Article 4 : Pharmaceuticals shall use registered trade marks.

Applications for pharmaceutical trade mark registration should be accompanied by certificates of approved production from health departments in the provinces, autonomous regions and municipalities.

Article 5 : The date of trade mark registration application is based on the date when the Trade Mark Bureau receives the application papers. Papers without sufficient procedures shall be returned, and the original date of application shall not be effective.

When two or more applicants apply on the same day for identical or similar trade marks on the same or similar commodity, each applicant shall send in a certificate of the date of the first use of the said trade mark upon notice from the Trade Mark Bureau. If the trade mark has been used on the same day or not yet used, the parties involved shall enter into consultation; if they fail to reach agreement in 30 days, it is the responsibility of the Trade Mark Bureau to make a ruling.

Article 6 : The Trade Mark Bureau shall establish a Trade Mark Registry to record the registered trade marks and related matters.

Article 7:   In changing the name of trade mark registerer each application shall be accompanied by a written application for changing the name of the trade mark registrant and a copy of the certificate of the change of the name of the registrant, and the original registration certificate shall be returned. Upon verification by the Trade Mark Bureau, the original certificate bearing additional remarks shall be issued and the change announced.

In changing the address of the registerer, a written application for changing the address of the trade mark registrant shall be sent in.

Article 8:   In use of the registered trade mark, the characters of ''Registered Trade Mark'' or marks of   ®   shall be used.

Article 9:   In case of rejection of a trade mark, the Trade Mark Bureau shall issue a notice of rejection to the applicant, and a copy shall be sent to the vertification unit.

Article 10:   In case of request for a re-examination of a rejected trade mark, a written application for re-examination of the rejected trade mark shall be submitted to the Trade Mark Assessment Committee.

Article 11:   In case of objection to a trade mark announced by the Trade Mark Bureau after preliminary examination, two copies of the written objection shall be submitted to the Trade Mark Bureau.

If the litigant contests the ruling of the Trade Mark Bureau with regard to the objection and applies for a re-examination by the Trade Mark Assessment Committee, two copies of the written application for re-examination of the objection to the trade mark shall be submitted.

Article 12:   In disputing a registered trade mark, two copies of the written application for a ruling concerning a disputed registered trade mark shall be sent to the Trade Mark Assessment Committee.

Article 13:   In applying for extension of registration of a trade mark, each application shall be accompanied by a written application for extension of registration of a trade mark and five copies of the trade mark design, and the original registration certificate shall be returned. Upon verification by the Trade Mark Bureau, the original certificate shall be issued with additional remarks, and the matter shall be announced.

Article 14:   In applying for transfer of a registered trade mark, each application shall be accompanied by a written application for transferring a registered trade mark, and the original registration certificate shall be returned. Upon vertification by the Trade Mark Bureau, the original certificate shall be issued to the receiver with additional remarks, and the matter shall be announced.

Article 15:   In applying for re-issue of a trade mark registration certificate which is missing or destroyed, an application shall be accompanied by a written application for re-issuing the trade mark registration certificate and five copies of the trade mark design.

Article 16:   Matters related to applying for trade mark registration, transfer of registration, extension of registration, change of the name or address of the registrant, and re-issuance of registration certificate, shall be verified by the local administration for industry and commerce. The applicant shall submit a copy of his application to the verification department.

Article 17:   The documents and fees required for applying for trade mark registration and other matters related to trade marks shall be submitted at the time of application in accordance with the provisions of the Detailed Rules. Otherwise, the case shall not be accepted.

Article 18: When a trade mark registerer permits others to use his registered trade mark and signs a contract for this purpose, he shall send a copy of the contract to the Trade Mark Bureau for the record and another copy to the administration for industry and commerce at the place of the two parties for possible check.

Article 19: In supervising commodity quality through the control of trade marks, administrations for industry and commerce shall act together with the related departments mainly in the sphere of commodity circulation. Where commodities using trade marks are crudely made or substandard ones are passed off as good ones to cheat consumers, those responsible shall be dealt with in accordance with Articles 31 and 34 of the Trade Mark Law.

Article 20: In case of any of the acts listed in Items (1), (2) and (3) of Article 30 of the Trade Mark Law, the local administration for industry and commerce shall notify the trade mark registrant to remedy the situtation; if the latter refuses to do so, the matter shall be reported to the Trade Mark Bureau for handling.

In case of acts listed in Item (4) of Article 30 of the Trade Mark Law, the local administration for industry and commerce shall ask the Trade Mark Bureau to revoke the registered trade mark. The use of trade marks includes advertising and exhibiting.

Article 21: Where commodities using registered trade marks are crudely made or sub-standard ones are passed off as good ones to cheat the consumers. as specified in Article 31 andItem (3) of Article 34 of the Trade Mark Law, the local administration for industry and commerce may deal with them as follows:

(1)   In minor cases, enjoin them to correct the situation within a time limit after criticism and education;

(2)   In serious cases, enjoin them to make self-criticism, issue a circular on this matter, or impose a fine of less than 2,000 yuan. For those using registered trade marks, the administration may also request the Trade Mark Bureau to revoke the registered trade marks.

Article 22: In case of a violation of Article 5 of the Trade Mark Law, the local administration for industry and commerce shall ban the sale of the commodities involved, stop advertising, seal up or take away the remaining unregistered trade mark signs, enjoin the party concerned to apply for registration within a time limit, and may also impose a fine of less than 1,000 yuan.

Article 23: For any of the acts listed in items (1) and (2) of Article 34 of the Trade Mark Law, the local administration for industry and commerce shall ban the sale of the commodities involved, stop advertising, seal up or take away the remaining trade mark signs and enjoin the party concerned to correct the situation within a time limit; the administration may issue a circular on the matter or impose a fine of less than 2,000 yuan according to the seriousness of the case.

Article 24: If the proprietary of a registered trade mark is encroached upon, the victim may ask the administration for industry and commerce at the country level and above at the place of the violation to deal with the matter or may file a suit directly with the court with local jurisdiction, in accordance with Article 39 of the Trade Mark Law.

In handling cases of encroaching upon the proprietary of a registered trade mark, the local administration for industry and commerce shall enjoin the party, whose act has been proven to constitute and encroachment upon the proprietary, to cease encroachment at once, to seal up to take away the trade mark signs; to remove the trade mark for commodities or packages; to issue a circular according to the seriousness of the matter; to order an indemnity according to law if the victim so demands; and may also impose a fine of less than 5,000 yuan for a serious case.

Article 25: Litigants contesting a decision of fines made by the local administration for industry and commerce in accordance with Item (2) of Article 21, and Articles 22, 23 and 24 of the Detailed Rules, may fine a suit with a people's court within 15 days of receiving the notice; if no suit is filed or the decision is not carried out at the end of the period, the local administration for industry and commerce shall request forced execution of the case by the court.

Article 26: Where serious imitation of other's registered trade mark, including producing and selling other's registered trade mark signs without permission, constitutes an offence, the victim or any government office, organisation, enterprise, institution or citizen may bring up the matter directly with a procuratorial organ, giving the latter responsibility to deal with the case. If the matter is brought up with a local administration for industry and commerce, the latter shall transfer it to a procuratorial organ for handling.

Article 27: In accordance with Articles 21, 22, 35, 36 and 39 of the Trade Mark Law, the litigants shall handle the matter within the time limit; those with extraordinary reasons may ask for two postponements, each not exceeding 30 days.

Article 28: Where the trade mark registrant applies for cancelling his registered trade mark or it should be revoked in accordance with Article 29, 30 and 31 of the Trade Mark Law, the Trade Mark Bureau shall do so and make announcement.

Where the trade mark registerer contests the decision of the Trade Mark Bureau to revoke his registered trade mark and requests re-examination by the Trade Mark Assessment Committee, he shall send in a written application for re-examining the revocation of a registered trade mark.

Article 29: Foreigners or foreign enterprises wishing to apply to register trade marks and pursue other matters related to trade marks, shall entrust the China Council for Promotion of International Trade to act on their behalf.

Article 30: Foreigners or foreign enterprises applying for registering trade marks, transferring trade marks, and extending registration, shall submit a document of power of attorney in addition to the application papers and fees.

The power of attorney document shall indicate the scope of the proxy and the nationality of the entrustor.

Article 31: Foreigners of foreign enterprises applying for registering trade marks and pursuing other matters related to trade marks, shall use the Chinese language.

The power of attorney document and related certificates shall go through notarial procedures, and authentication shall be handled under the principle of reciprocity. Documents in a foreign language shall be accompanied by a Chinese translation.

Article 32: Pending the enforcement of the trade Mark Law, the verified valid period for the trade marks already registered shall remain unchanged; the valid period for the registered trade marks whose valid period is not verified shall be calculated as from the date of enforcement of the Trade Mark Law.

Article 33: Standards of fees charged for application for registeration of trade marks and other matters related to trade mark, shall be worked out by the state Administration for Industry and Commerce.

Article 34: The Detailed Rules come into force on the date of publication.

The Statute of the Chinese AIPPI Group

(Set up in August 20 1983)

Chapter I: Name, Objects and Address

Article 1:   The official name of the group is the Chinese Group of the International Association for the Protection of Industrial Property.

Article 2:   The Group aims at promoting proper protection of industrial property both nationally and internationally as well as promoting economic, trade and technological cooperation between China and foreign countries. Major scope of work:

(1)   To fine out through study the industrial property system suitable to the conditions in China and to make proposals in this respect to the competent authorities concerned;

(2)   To propagate and pursue the Chinese industrial property system with a view to promoting the protection of industrial property and promoting China's modernizations of industry, agriculture, national defence and science and technology;

(3)   To investigate and study problems in the field of industrial property arising from among foreign countries and to make suggestions in this respect to the government and organizations concerned;

(4)   To promote the development of the system of protection of industrial property in the world on the basis of reforming the international economic order; to improve the international cooperation with legal circles of industrial property and to strengthen extensive contact and business relations with related organizations, industrial property lawyers in various countries and other persons

concerned.

Article 3: The address of the group is in the China Council for the Promotion of International Trade.

Chapter II. Membership

Article 4: Upon approval by the Board any person, enterprise or organization who deals with in his work or studies industrial property may become a member or collective member of the group.

Article 5: Any collective member may appoint one representative to participate in relevant activities of the group.

Article 6: Any member has the right to make suggestions and criticism as to the work of the group, to vote on issues discussed at general meetings, to elect and be elected leading member of the group.

Article 7: Any member is duty-bound to abide by the statutes and pay subscription.

Chapter III. General Meeting

Article 8: A general meeting is to be held every year. The board may determine to convene a temporary general meeting whenever needed.

Article 9: A general meeting shall examine the following matters:
(1) To examine the group's work report and expenditure and give necessary instructions to the board;
(2) to determine the group's annual plan and to approve its budget;
(3) To elect members of the board;
(4) To determine any other matters that the board may deem necessary to examine at a general meeting.

Chapter IV. Board

Article 10: The board shall be composed of 5 to 9 persons.

Article 11: The president, the vice presidents, and the secretary general of the group shall be elected by the board.

Article 12: The board shall examine important matters of the group.

Article 13: The term of office of each member of the board is three years. Any member of the board may remain in office after the three-year period upon being re-elected.

Chapter V. Subscriptions

Article 14: The subscriptions shall be paid by the members of the group, and the amount of each subscription shall be determined by the board according to annual expenditure.

Chapter VI. Supplementary Article

Article 15: The statutes shall come into force upon being endorsed at the meeting for the establishment of the Chinese group. Any amendment to the statutes must be approved by the general meeting.

Interim Rules on Applications for Prior Registration of Trademark in China

Approved by the State Council on March 15, 1985
Published by the State Administration for Industry
and Commerce on March 15, 1985

In accordance with Article 9 of the Trademark Law of the People's Republic of China and Article 4 of the Paris Convention for the Protection of Industrial Property, Rules regarding applications for prior registration of trademarks in China by nationals of the Paris Convention Member Countries are made as follows:

1. Beginning March 19, 1985, the Administration for Industry and Commerce of the People's Republic of China handles applications for priority on registration of trademarks in China, submitted by the nationals of the Paris Convention member countries.
2. Commencing March 19, 1985, nationals of the Paris Convention member countries, may, after filing an application for a trademark in any other member country, file another application for priority on registration of the same trademark for the same product in China within six months after the first filing, in accordance with the Paris Conventions.
3. When filing an application for priority on registration of the same trademark for the same product in China, the applicant should, at the same time, submit a duplicate of the first application. The duplicate should be certified by the department in charge of trademarks of the applicant's country and the application number should be clearly stated. The duplicate does not have to be authenticated, but the other documents required to be submitted to the Trademark Office should be authenticated. When applying for prior registration, the applicant may, in case the duplicate and the related documents are not available, submit them within three months following the date of second filing. If a written declaration or the duplicate and the related documents are not submitted within three months of the date of filing, the application will be regarded as null and void.
4. When the written declaration is approved, the date the application for the trademark is filed in the first member country may be adopted as the application date in China.

Provisional Regulations of Administration over Printing of Trademark

Promulgated by the State Industry and Commerce
Administration Bureau on December 21st, 1985

Article 1:   These Regulations are enacted to carry out and implement the Trademark Law of the People's Republic of China, to strengthen the administration over the printing of trademark, to maintain the socialist economic order, to protect the patent right of registered trademark and to safeguard the interest of the consumer.

Article 2:   Enterprise holding the ''business licence'' issued by industry and commerce administrative authorities and has been ratified to undertake such related business as the trademark printing, printing & dyeing, plate making, word engraving, work knitting, etching, printing on iron, mould casting, punching, gilding and applique is entitled to print and make trademark.

It is strictly forbidden to print trademark without business licence or beyond the range of business.

Article 3:   Enterprise, institution or individual industrial or commercial labourer who needs to print and make label of his registered trademark shall take the ''trademark registry certificate'' to the local industry and commerce administration bureau at prefecture or country level to obtain the ''certificate for printing registered trademark'' (CPRT hereinafter) and, with the said CPRT, to entrust trademark printer for the printing thereof.

One who makes use of other's registered trademark by concluding a due contract for using the said trademark and needs to print the said trademark label shall take the said contract for using the said trademark to the local industry and commerce administration bureau at prefecture or country level to obtain the CPRT and, with the said CPRT, to entrust the trademark printer for the printing thereof.

One who needs to print unregistered trademark label shall take the business licence to the local country-level industry and commerce administration bureau to obtain the ''certificate trusting the printing of unregistered trademark'' (CTPUT hereinafter) and then entrust the trademark printing unit for the printing thereof.

Article 4:   When issuing a CPRT, the industry and commerce administrative authorities shall carefully check the trademark registry certificate. For the registered trademark label which needs printing, it shall be checked whether or not it is clearly marked with the words of ''registered trademark'' or the sign of "注" or ''R'', whether or not the name or address of the manufacturer is clearly indicated, and whether or not relevant certificate has been furnished and checked in case it needs to be printed with the words or marks of ''high-quality'', ''famous brand'', etc. The CPRT shall remain valid for not longer than three months.

When issuing the CTPUT, the industry and commerce administrative authorities shall carefully study and check the business licence. As regards the unregistered trademark label needing to be printed, the said authorities shall check whether or not the said unregistered trademark violates the provisions laid down in Items 1, 2, 3 and 4 under Article 8 of the PRC Trademark Law.

Industry and commerce administrative authorities may collect the fee of cost of CPRT and CTPUT.

Article 5:   When a trademark-printing unit undertakes the business of printing a trademark, it shall collect the CPRT or CTPUT. The trademark label printed shall be identical with the trademark attached to the CPRT and CTPUT. The printing unit of trademark shall set up a registry system for the printing of trademark, according to which the CPRT or CTPUT and the sample of printed trademark label shall be filed in good order for possible future check thereon. The registry book and the collected documents for certification shall be kept for no shorter than one year.

Article 6:   In case one of the following occurs, trademark-printing unit shall refuse the printing of trademark label:

(1)   Print trademark label without submitting the CPRT or CTPUT;

(2)   Registered trademark label going to be printed is not identical with the trademark label attached to the CPRT;

(3)   Alter the CPRT without due authorization, or the CPRT is beyond the expiry date;

(4)   Print unregistered trademark label by using the sign of ''registered trademark'' or the sign of "注" or ''R'', or without indicating the name or address of the manufacturer, or the said name and address of the manufacturer are not identical with what are listed on the certificate furnished; or stamp on the works or sign of ''high-quality'' or ''famous brand'' without furnishing the corresponding certificate for due check.

Article 7:   It is strictly forbidden to buy or sell trademark label. The rejected or substandard trademark label resulting in the course of production or use must be totally destroyed.

Article 8:   Industry and commerce administrative authorities shall from time to time inspect what is going on in the business of trademark printing in various local regions. As regards the acts of violation of the provisions stipulated in Article 2, 5, 6 and 7 of the present Regulations, the industry and commerce administrative authorities at or above the country level are entitled to mete out such penalty as criticism, circular of warning, or taking back trademark labels and the printing plates and moulds therefor. As to serious cases, the penalty may be the confiscation of illegal income and a fine of less than 2,000 yuan. For such violation as having caused economic loss on the others, the said economic loss shall be compensated for by the violator. Those who are directly responsible for manufacturing or illegally selling other's registered trademark label without due authorization and hence commit the crime of passing off other's registered trademark shall be transferred to judicial organ for investigating and fixing the criminal responsibility.

Article 9: Foreign enterprise or individual who needs to print and make his registered trademark label shall bring the trademark registry certificate or the Chinese version of the certificate for trademark registration issued by the trademark administrative authorities of his own country to China's province-level industry and commerce administration bureau to which the printing unit belongs for obtaining the CPRT and, with the said CPRT, to entrust the printing unit for the printing thereof.

Those who need to entrust the printing of other's registered trademark label in China shall furnish the translated version in Chinese of the certificate which has been notarized and therefore is allowed for use, to China's province-level industry and commerce administration bureau to which the printing unit belongs for obtaining the CPRT and, with the said CPRT, to entrust the printing unit for the printing thereof.

Those who need to entrust the printing of unregistered trademark label in China shall furnish the translated version in Chinese of the business licence which is issued by their own country (region) and has been notarized to China's province-level industry and commerce administration bureau for obtaining the CTPUT and, with the said CTPUT, entrust the said printing unit of trademark for the printing thereof.

Article 10: Article 9 shall be referred for enterprise or individual from Hong Kong, Taiwan and Macao to entrust the printing of trademark labels.

Article 11: The present Provisional Regulations shall enter into force on the date of promulgation.

The Regulations for Administration over Trademark Printing promulgated by the State Industry and Commerce Administration Bureau on March 23rd, 1983 shall be revoked simultaneously.

Interim Provisions for Claims of the Right of Priority of the Payment by Individual Applicants

Approved by the State Council and promulgated by the State Administration for Industry and Commerce of the People's Republic of China on March 15, 1985.

In accordance with Article 9 of the Trademark Law of the People's Republic of China and Article 4 of the Paris Convention for the Protection of Industrial Property (hereinafter referred to as Paris Convention), the Provisions which regulate the claiming of right of priority with respect to applications for the registration of trademarks by nationals of the countries party to the Paris Convention are as follows:

1. From March 19, 1985, the Trademark Office of the State Administration for Industry and Commerce of the People's Republic of China shall receive and handle matters concerning claims of the right of priority with respect to applications for the registration of trademarks filed in China by nationals of the countries party to the Paris Convention.

2. Where any national of the countries party to the Paris Convention files, from March 19, 1985, an application for the registration of a trademark in one of the countries party to the Paris Convention, and subsequently files another application for the registration of the identical trademark with respect to the same goods in China, he may, according to the provisions of the Paris Convention, claim the right of priority within six months from the date of the first filing.

3. Any applicant who claims the right of priority under the preceding paragraph shall make a written declaration at the time of filing the application, and submit a copy of the first application for the registration of the trademark in the country party to the Paris Convention. The copy shall be certified by the trademark authority of that country and the date and number of the first filing shall be indicated. The copy shall not require any authentication, but the other documents required by the Trademark Office shall be authenticated.

    Where the copy of the application and the relevant evidential documents are not completed at the time of claiming, the applicant shall submit them within three months from the date of filing in China. If the applicant fails to make the written declaration or to meet the deadline for submitting the above-mentioned copy and the relevant documents, the claim to the right of priority shall be deemed nonexistent.

4. After the declaration claiming the right of priority has been accepted, the date of filing the first application for the registration of the trademark in the other country party to the Paris Convention shall be regarded as the date of filing in China.

Forms & Documentation

Copy of Home Registration

Pursuant to the decision of our Government, the implementation of Article 12 of the Regulations Governing Trade Marks concerning the filing of copy of home registration shall, as from January 1, 1978, be based on the principle of reciprocity. Consequently, copy of home registration will not be required from legal persons and natural persons of foreign countries which do not require a similar certificate from Chinese corporations and enterprises.

Forms & Documentation

Requirements for Filing Trade Mark Applications in China

I.   Application for Registration

1.   Application in duplicate for each trade mark (If one mark is to be registered in several classes, a serparate application is necessary for each class);
2.   Power of Attorney in duplicate for each trade mark;
3.   Copy of home registration;
4.   Certificate of nationality (no prescribed form). Certificate of a corporation's nationality should show that the corporation is organised under the laws of the applicant's country;
5.   Twelve prints for each application (The meaning and/or derivation of trade mark word must be clearly explained).
Of the above-mentioned documents, the original copy of Power of Attorney, the copy of home registration and the certificate of nationality must be legalised by Chinese Embassy. If the copy of home registration and the certificate of nationality are not written in English, their English versions are required.

II.   Renewal

1.   Application in duplicate for each class;
2.   Power of Attorney in duplicate for each trade mark;
3.   Copy of home-registration;
4.   Original Chinese registration certificate;
5.   Twelve prints for each application.
Of the above-mentioned documents, the original copy of Power of Attorney and the copy of home registration must be legalised by Chinese Embassy. If the copy of

home registration is not written in English, its English version is required.

III.   Change of Name of Address

1. Application in duplicate for each class;
2. Power of Attorney in duplicate for each trade mark;
3. Copy of home registration showing change of name or address;
4. Original Chinese registration certificate.

Of the above-mentioned documents, the original copy of Power of Attorney and the copy of home registration must be legalised by Chinese Embassy. If the copy of home registraion is not written in English, its English version is required.

IV.   Assignment

1. Application in duplicate for each class;
2. Power of Attorney in duplicate for each trade mark;
3. Copy of home registration in the name of assignee;
4. Certificate of nationality of assignee;
5. Original Chinese registration certificate.

Of the above-mentioned documents, the original copy of Power of Attorney, the copy of home registration and the certificate of nationality must be legalised by Chinese Embassy. If the copy of home registration and the certificate of nationality are not written in English, their English versions are required.

Forms and Documentation

Classification of Goods

Class 1.   Power generating equipments and electric power station equipments.
Class 2.   Agricultural machinery, farm tools, machines for animal husbandry; component parts and spare parts thereof.
Class 3.   Machines for lumbering, timber-sawing, wood-processing, match-making, paper-making and printing; component parts and spare parts thereof.
Class 4.   Machines for cotton-processing, spinning, weaving, printing, dyeing and chemical-fibre industries; component parts and spare parts thereof.
Class 5.   Machines for food industry; component parts and spare parts thereof.
Class 6.   Machines for tanning, sewing, shoe-making and machines for light industry not included in other classes; component parts and spare parts thereof.
Class 7.   Machines for pharmaceutical, rubber, glass, plastic and other chemical industries; component parts and spare parts thereof.
Class 8.   Machines for geological prospecting, mining and metallurgical and petroleum industries and machines for heavy industry not included in other classes; component parts and spare parts thereof.
Class 9.   General machines and machines not included in other classes; component parts and spare parts thereof.
Class 10.   Machine tools; accessories and spare parts thereof.
Class 11.   Equipments, apparatus, tools and materials for welding.
Class 12.   Grinding tools and supplies.
Class 13.   Cutting tools, measuring and weighing apparatus, industrial hand-tools.
Class 14.   Wire and wireless telegraphic equipments; wireless sets; phonographs; photographical, cinematorgraphical, optical, thermal, testing and surveying apparatus, instruments and supplies.
Class 15.   Electric illuminating installations; electrical apparatus and supplies.

Class 16.   Calculating and sorting devices, office machines and other computing apparatus.

Class 17.   Medical and veterinary apparatus and instruments.

Class 18.   Equipments for heating, cooking, refrigerating, drying, ventilating, water-supply and sanitary purposes.

Class 19.   Aircrafts, vessels, vehicles and other means of transportation.

Class 20.   Knives, scissors, pins, needles, tweezers and sharp-edged and pointed implements not included in other classes.

Class 21.   Metals and their manufactures not included in other classes.

Class 22.   Natural and articficial stones, cement, asphalt, asphalted felt, bricks and tiles, fireproof articles and building materials not included in other classes.

Class 23.   Glass, glass products for building, quartz products, glassware for everyday use.

Class 24.   Petroleum, petroleum products, industrial oils and greases.

Class 25.   Minerals not included in other classes.

Class 26.   Chemicals.

Class 27.   Fertilizers.

Class 28.   Dyestuffs, paints, pigments, distempers, printing inks, glazes.

Class 29.   Rubber, rubber manufactures, asbestos articles.

Class 30.   Natural resin, synthetic resin, plastics, plasticizers and plastic articles not included in other classes.

Class 31.   Medicines.

Class 32.   Medical and sanitary articles.

Class 33.   Meat, eggs, wild game, sea-food and manufactures thereof.

Class 34.   Milk, dairy products and substitutes thereof.

Class 35.   Canned foods.

Class 36.   Beer, wines, spirits and liquors.

Class 37.   Tea, coffee, cocoa, aerated water, fruit juice, ice products and soft drinks not included in other classes.

Class 38.   Sugar, sweets, honey, cakes, confectionary.

Class 39.   Fresh fruits, dried fruits, preserved fruits, jams and other fruit products.

Class 40.   Edible oils, soy sauce, sauces, vinegar, gourmet's powder and other condiments.

Class 41.   Preserved vegetables and vegetable products.

Class 42.   Cereal products and foods not included in other classes.

Class 43.   Tobacco and tobacco manufactures.

Class 44.   Silkworm eggs and cocoons.

Class 45.   Silk, silk wadding, cotton, flax, hemp, jute, feather and imitations thereof.

Class 46.   Yarns and threads.

Class 47.   Cotton piece goods.

Class 48.   Silk piece goods.

Class 49.   Woollen piece goods.

Class 50.   Flax, hemp and jute piece goods,

Class 51.   Ropes, strings, nets, bags, tents, felts, tarpaulin and waterproof articles not included in other classes; harness for horse and mule

Class 52.   Furs, hides and skins, leather, imitation leather; articles made of leather and imitation leather not included in other classes.

Class 53.   Clothing.

Class 54.   Headwear, shoes.

Class 55. Socks, stockings towels, neckwear, gloves, handkerchiefs and hair nets.
Class 56. Buttons, hairpins, ornament made of gold, silver and jewels.
Class 57. Embroidered articles, laces, ribbons, braids, curtains, tablecloths, beddings, carpets and indoor articles not included in other classes.
Class 58. Furniture, infants' carriages, articles made of bamboo, wood, rattan, palm, straw and grass.
Class 59. Paper and paper products.
Class 60. Pens, pencils, brushes for painting or writing; ink-sticks, inks; oil-colours for painting, advertising and stage purposes.
Class 61. Copying and printing apparatus.
Class 62. Drawing instruments and articles; stationery not included in other classes.
Class 63. Models, specimens, pictures, photographs, cinema films, books, newspapers and periodicals.
Class 64. Articles for cultural entertainment, sport goods and toys.
Class 65. Musical instruments and accessories thereof.
Class 66. Clocks, watches, timers.
Class 67. Daily-used enamelware and aluminum products, porcelains and earthenwares.
Class 68. Tooth paste, tooth powder.
Class 69. Cosmetics.
Class 70. toilet soap, other soap, detergents and polishing materials.
Class 71. Tooth-brushes, brushes, combs and other articles for cleaning.
Class 72. Matches, cigarette lighters and smokers' articles.
Class 73. Umbrellas, fans walking-sticks.
Class 74. Lacquerware, cloisonne; arts and crafts not included in other classes.
Class 75. Candles, kerosene lamps (lanterns) and illuminating appliances not included in other classes.
Class 76. Incense and anti-mosquito incense.
Class 77. Fireworks and crackers.
Class 78. Goods not included in other classes.

Forms and Documentation

Certification of Corporate Nationality

People's Republic of China

Certificate of Corporate Nationality

United States of America   )
State of   ) SS.
County of   )

    I hereby certify that ....
is a corporation duly under the laws of ....
and that ....
is ....
of the corporation and is duly qualified to sign on behalf of said corporation.

Signed on this .... day of .... 19......

                               _____
                                   Notary Public

My Commission Expires: _____

(to be legalized by the Embassy of the People's Republic of China)

Forms and Documentation

Application for Trade Mark Registration

To   General Administrative Bureau for
Industry and Commerce of the
People's Republic of China

We hereby apply for the registration of the trade mark ....
.... in Class ....
in respect of * ....
....

Name of applicant ....

Address ....

Signature of authorized
officer of enterprise ....

On the ...., 19.....

* Here specify the goods. If the goods are not commonly known, please indicate
the purposes and main materials thereof.

Forms and Documentation

Power of Attorney

To   General Administrative Bureau for
     Industry and Commerce of the
     People's Republic of China

     I/We, * ....
....
hereby entrust the Trade Mark Registration Agency of the China Council for the
promotion of International Trade with applying in the People's Republic of China
          registration
          renewal of registration
for   alteration of the registered proprietor's   of the trade mark(s) ..
          name/address
          registration of assignment

....

Signature of authorized
officer of enterprise ....

On the ...., 19.....

* Here fill in the name and address of applicant.

(To be legalized)

Forms and Documentation

Application for Alternation on the Entries in the Register

To   General Administrative Bureau for
       Industry and Commerce of the
       People's Republic of China

      We hereby apply for the alteration of the registered proprietor's
name/address of the trade mark ....
.... No. ....
from ....
to ....

Name of applicant ....

address ....

Signature of authorized
officer of enterprise ....

On the ...., 19.....

Forms and Documentation

Objects to be Altered

Objects	Original Registration	Alteration of Registration
Change of Scope of Business	_____	
Increase/Decrease of Transfer of Registered Capital	_____	_____
Change of Address	_____	_____
Extension of Contract Term	_____	_____
Change of the Chairman of the Board	_____	_____
Remarks of Approval	_____	_____

Date _____

Forms and Documentation

Application for Renewal of Registration of Trade Mark

To   General Administrative Bureau for
     Industry and Commerce of the
     People's Republic of China

     We hereby apply for the renewal of the registered of the trade mark ....
.... No. .... which will expire on
.... 19.....

Name of applicant ....

address ....

Signature of authorized
officer of enterprise ....

On the ...., 19.....

Forms and Documentation

Schedule of Charges for Trade Mark Matters

(effective from January 1, 1980)

	Official Fee RMB yuan	Agency Fee RMB yuan	Total RMB yuan
Application for registration in each class	20.00	230.00	250.00
Registration fee	80.00	—	80.00
Application for renewal	20.00	230.00	250.00
Registration fee for renewal	80.00	—	80.00
Application for registration of assignment	20.00	130.00	150.00
Registration fee for assignment	80.00	—	80.00
Recording change of name or address	—	130.00	130.00
Replacement fee for registration certificate	20.00	40.00	60.00

Editor's Notes

The fees for other services, such as preparing prints, choosing Chinese equivalent for foreign words in trade marks, requesting re-examination, etc. will be charged according to the amount of work involved.

II INTRA COUNTRIES

SECTION A: Protection

Exchange Notes Between China & Japan on Trademark Protection Agreement

(1)   The Letter from Japan

29th September, 1977

Mr. Wang Yaoting,
Director of the China Council for the Promotion of International Trade Committee.
Dear Mr. Wang
In connection with the enforcement of the Trademark Protection Agreement between Japan and China, please give us your opinions on the following points.
1.   When appling for trademark registration in China, a Japanese national may submit documents issued by the government of Japan certifying that application for trademark registration has been made in Japan and that a public notice of such an application will, it has been decided, be released or that the application has been accepted for consideration, and the government of the People's Republic of China will accept his case. Under these circumstances, in order to have a trademark registered in the People's Republic of China, a Japanese national should submit to the government of the People's Republic of China documents issued by the government of Japan certifying that his application for trademark registered has been accepted for consideration in Japan. Is the above understanding acceptable?
2.   According to the stipulations in Article 1 of Trademarks Protection Agreement between Japan and China, the agreement will not include the preferential treatments given to trademark registration, as stipulated by any multilateral industrial property rights agreement, if only one of the contracted parties (either Japan or China) has participated in the multilateral industrial property rights agreement. Is the above understanding acceptable?
3.   According to the stipulations of Japanese Trademark Laws, 10 years is the effective period for a trademark which is newly registered. And the registration can

be renewed several times. Please inform us what kind of measures will be imposed on Japanese nationals in respect of the effective period of a trademark and application for renewals.

4.   Please inform us what conditions and terms in the Trademark Control Regulations as well as the Implementation Details of the Trademark Control Regulations are not suitable for foreigners (including Japanese nationals).

Foreigners, including Japanese nationals, think that a trademark with only a pattern but no characters can also be accepted by China for registration. Is it possible?

(Signed)
Officer,
Patent Office,

(2)   The Letter from China

29th September, 1977

Officer,
Patent Office,
Japan.

With reference to your letter of 29th September, 1977, we would like to answer your questions as follows:

1.   In consideration of the actual situation of Japan, we agree that, when applying for trademark registration in China, a Japanese may submit documents issued by the government of Japan certifying that application for trademark registration has been made in Japan. Once the Japanese government approves the registration of that trademark, the registration certificate has to be re-submitted to the Chinese government.

2.   The preferential treatments given under the stipulations of Article 1 of the Trademark Protection Agreement between the People's Republic of China and Japan do not include the special preferential treatments as enjoyed by either party who participates in multilateral agreements concerning trademark registration with other countries.

3.   Certain parts of the Trademark Control Regulations of our country (announced by the State Council on 10th April, 1963) and its implementation details (announced by the Central Administration Bureau of Industry and Commerce) are not suitable for foreign countries, including Japan as specified below:

Trademark Control Regulations:
Clause 2 of Article 2,
Clause 2 of Article 5 (i.e. the last paragraph),
Article 10,
Clause 1 Item 2 of Article 11,
Implementation Details:
Article 2
Article 3
Article 4
Article 13

Our country will accept the application for registration of a Japanese trademark with only a pattern but no specified name.

4.   In view of the fact that a Chinese trademark newly registered in Japan will have an effective period of 10 years and can be renewed several items, the same treatment will be given to Japanese trademarks applying for registration in China.

(Signed)
Wang Yaoting,
Director,
China Council for the
Promotion of
International Trade.

The Trademark Protection Agreement between China and Japan

In accordance with the spirit that lay behind the joint declaration issued by the government of the People's Republic of China and the government of Japan on September 29, 1972, the two governments have, after friendly negotiations, come to the following agreement with a view to protecting trademarks so as to give a further boost to the trade relations between the two countries.

Article 1:   The corporate persons (including foreign trade institutions) and natural persons of either of the signatory parties should be able to enjoy, in the territory of the other signatory party, no less rights than the corporate persons (including foreign trade institutions) and natural persons of any third country with regard to the application for trademarks and other matters pertaining to the registration of trademarks.

Article 2:   1.   This agreement will come into force in either country on the 30th day after the necessary legal arrangements have been made in the country concerned and notices of confirmation exchanged. This agreement will be valid for a period of three years, after which it will continue to be valid until a declaration of termination is issued according to the second item of this clause.

2.   Upon or after the expiry of th first three years, either of the two signatory parties may at any time terminate the agreement by notifying the other party in writing three months in advance. This agreement is to be signed in Beijing on September 29, 1977. There will be two original copies, written in both Chinese and Japanese, which are equally effective.

(Signed) Government of the
Representative of People's
Republic of China Li Qiang

(Signed) Representative of
the Government of Japan

*Editor's note:This agreement came into effect on March 1, 1978 after the two
signatory parties had informed each other of the completion of the
necessary legal procedures in their own countries.*

Exchange Notes Between China & Spain on the Agreement of Trademark Protection

(1) Letter from Spain

10th June, 1977
Beijing

Mr. Li Qiang
Ministry of Foreign Trade
People's Republic of China
Dear Mr. Li,

I have the pleasure to propose a trademark protection agreement between the government of the Kingdom of Spain and the People's Republic of China.

In order to maintain intimate friendship and promote the development of trade between our two countries the agreements are made hereinafter:

Article 1:   The natural persons and corporate persons of either of the signatory parties shall be able to enjoy, in the territory of the other signatory party, the same rights given to the natural persons and corporate persons of that other signatory party with regard to the enjoyment given by law in the aspect of trademark contents and effects of factory or commerce during the effective period of their registration.

Article 2:   In order to enjoy the rights as stipulated in this agreement, either of the signatory parties is not allowed to put forward the condition of living or opening business in the country where trademark protection is being applied for.

Article 3:   Personnel involved in this agreement who would like to have their factory or commerce trademark registered in the other signatory country, shall fulfill the laws, regulations and procedures of that country.

Article 4: This agreement will be effective all the time unless either party serves a written notice on the other party indicating the intention to terminate this agreement.

I have the pleasure to suggest, if the above suggestions are accepted by the People's Republic of China, that this letter and your reply letter will together consititute an agreement of this issue and it will be effective two months after the date when you send your reply letter.

Best regards

(Signed)
Special Envoy in
People's Republic of China
Spain

(2) Letter from China

10th June, 1977
Beijing

Special Envoy of Spain in the People's Republic of China
Sir,

I have the pleasure to receive your letter of 10th June, 1977, the contents of which are as follows (deleted)*

I have the pleasure to inform you that the government of the People's Republic of China has accepted the contents of your letter. It is also confirmed that your letter and this reply letter will constitute an agreement between the People's of China and Spain. This agreement will come into effect two months after today.

Best regards

(Signed,)
Minister,
Foreign Trade Ministry,
People's Republic of China

Editor's note:— * — the contents are deleted by the editor as they are exactly the same as the letter from spain.

— The agreement became effective on 10th August, 1977.

Exchange Notes Between China & Greece on the Mutual Protection of Trademark

(1)   Note from China

Beijing
19th April, 1975

The Ambassador
Greece Embassy in China
Sir,
I have the pleasure to receive your note of 19th April, 1975, the contents of which are as follows:
"Sir,
I have the pleasure to inform you that the Government of Greece would like to reach a mutual protection agreement of Trademark with the People's Republic of China, in order to strengthen the friendly relationship and promote the development of trade between the two countries. The clauses are as follows:
1.   Natural persons or corporate persons having the nationality of either of the signatory countries shall, no matter whether they are living in the territory of the other signatory country or not, enjoy the same trademark protection rights as are already enjoyed by the natural persons or corporate persons having the nationality of the other signatory country, provided that it is within the effective period and the trademark registration has have been granted by the other signatory country.
2.   Natural persons or corporate persons having the nationality of either of the signatory countries shall obey the present laws and regulations of the country where they wish to seek trademark protection rights.
3.   The term "Trademark" shall be interpreted as the marks for the commercial goods of commercial enterprises and the marks for the products of industrial enterprises.

4. This agreement shall maintain its effect unless either party requests to terminate this agreement by serving a written notice on the other party six months in advance. If the People's Republic of China accept the above mentioned suggestions, may I have the pleasure to suggest further that this note together with your reply note shall constitute an agreement on this matter. This agreement shall come into effect two months from the date of you reply note."

I have the pleasure to inform you that the Government of the People's Republic of China agrees to the contents of you note. It is also confirmed that your note together with this reply note, shall constitute an agreement between our two countries and shall come into effect two months from today.

Li Qiang
Minister
Ministry of Foreign Trade
The People's Republic of China

Editor's note: *Letter from Greece and letter from China deleted.*

SECTION B: Registration

Exchange Note between China & Iran on the mutual benefit of Trademark Registration

(1)   Note from China

15th December, 1975
Beijing

Embassy of the Kingdom of Iran in The People's Republic of China:

The Ministry of Foreign Affairs of the People's Republic of China sends its regards to the Embassy of the Kingdom of Iran in China, and should that to raise the following points:

In order to strengthen the friendship and trade relationship between the People's Republic of China and Iran, the government of the People's Republic of China suggests on the basis of mutual benefit that the Government of the People's Republic of China accepts the application for trademark registration submitted by the natural persons and corporate persons of Iran in accordance with the laws and regulations of China, and that the Government of Iran accepts the application for the registration of trademark submitted by companies and enterprises from China in accordance with the laws and regulations of Iran.

Please confirm by return note if you agree to the above-mentined suggestions.

Our best regards

(Stamped)
Ministry of Foreign Affairs
The People's Republic of China

(2) Note from Iran

15th December, 1975

The Ministry of Foreign Affairs,
The People's Republic of China.
The Embassy of the Kingdom of Iran sends its regards to the Ministry of Foreign Affairs of the People's Republic of China, and is pleased to confirm the receipt of the number 258 note issued by the Ministry of Foreign Affairs on 15th December, 1975. The contents are as follows:
(contents deleted)*
It is also confirmed that the Government of the Kingdom of Iran agrees to the contents of the above note.
Our best regards.

(Stamped)
Embassy of the Kingdom of Iran
in the People's Repbulic of China.

Editor's note: **The contents are deleted by the editor as they are exactly the same as the note from China.*

Exchange Notes Between China & France on the Mutual Benefit of Trademark Registration

(1)   Note from China

15th July, 1975
Beijing

The Ambassador
Embassy of France in the People's Republic of China
Dear Mr. Ambassador,
With regard to the exchange of favoured nation status between the People's Republic of China and the Republic of France, I write on behalf of the Government of the People's Republic of China to inform you that, if the Republic of France will accord to the companies & enterprises of the People's Republic of China the rights of trademark & the enjoyment of trademark licensing rights in the Republic of France according to French laws, the government of the People's Republic of China will also grant the rights of trademark and the enjoyment of trademark licensing rights to natural persons and corporate persons of the Republic of France in the People's Republic of China in accordance with the laws of China.
If the government of the Republic of France agrees to the above suggestions and confirms by return note, this note together with your note will constitute an agreement between the governments of the two countries. The agreement will become effective sixty days after your reply.
Best regards.

(Signed)
Ma Wenbo
Vice Minister
The Ministry of Foreign Affairs

(2) Note from France

Mr. Ma Wenbo
Vice Minister
The Ministry of Foreign Affairs
The People's Republic of China.
Dear Mr. Vice Minister,
I have the pleasure to receive your note of 15th July, 1975, the contents of which are as follows
(contents deleted)*
I have the pleasure to inform you that the government of the Republic of France accepts all the proposals in your note. It is also agreed that your note, together with this reply note, will constitute an agreement between the governments of the two countries. The agreement will become effective from the date of this reply note.
Best regards

(signed)
Ambassador
Embassy of France in the
People's Republic of China

Exchange Notes Between China & New Zealand on the mutual benefit of Trademark Registration

(1)   Note from New Zealand

18th June, 1975

Mr. Li Qiang
Minister,
The Ministry of Foreign Trade
The People's Republic of China
Sir,
I have the pleasure to refer to the discussions held recently between the representtives of our two countries about trademark registration on the basis of mutual benefit. The purpose of these discussions is to strengthen the friendly relationship and promote the development of trade between New Zealand and the People's Republic of China.
I have the pleasure to suggest hereby an agreement to be reached by the governments of the two countries. According to the one signatory party's enterprises and nationals may apply for trademark registration as well as licensing rights of a registered trademark in the other party's territory, in accordance with the existing laws of the other party.
If the Government of the People's Republic of China accepts this proposal, I would like to have the pleasure to suggest that this letter together with your reply letter in the same exact wording, will constitute an agreement between our two governments. The agreement will become effective from the date of your reply letter.

(signed)
Minister
The Ministry of Trade and Industry

(2)   Note from China

18th June, 1975
Beijing

Minister,
The Ministry of Trade and Industry New Zealand.
Sir,
I have the pleasure to receive your letter of 18th June, 1975, the contents of which are as follows:
(contents deleted)*
I have the pleasure to confirm that the Government of the People's Republic of China accepts the proposal that your letter, together with this reply letter, will constituted an agreement between the governments of our two countries. This agreement will be effective from today.
Best regards.

(signed)
Li Qiang
Minister
The Ministry of Foreign Trade
The People's Republic of China

*Editor's Note: * Contents deleted by editor as it is exactly the same as the note from New Zealand.*

Exchange Notes between China & The Federal Republic of Germany on the mutual benefit of Trademark Registration

(1)   Note from China

8th August, 1975
Beijing

Embassy of the Federal Republic of Germany in the People's Republic of China
The Ministry of Foreign Affairs of the People's Republic of China sends its regards to the Federal Republic of Germany. The Governments of our two countries have held discussions on trademark registration between the two countries on the basis of mutual benefit, in order to strengthen the friendly relationship and the development of trade between the People's Repbulic of China and the Republic of West Germany. It has been agreed on principle that an agreement should be drafted, under which each of the signatory countries may, subject to the effective period aproved by the other signatory country receive the same degree of legal protection of trademark in the other signatory country as available domestically in that other signatory country. Such an agreement is to the interest of both countries. The Ministry of Foreign Affairs of the People's Republic of China confirms, on behalf of the Government of the People's Republic of China, the following agreements have been reached by reason of mutual that benefit of trademark registration between the two countries: The two governments agree on the basis of equality and mutual benefit that trading companies and enterprises from each of the signatory countries may apply for trademark registration and licensing rights of a registered trademark in the other signatory country in accordance with th laws of the latter.
This agreement, as it is, is also suitable for use in Berlin (Wests)
The agreement will be effective from the date when the embassy of the Federal Republic of Germany in the People's Republic of China sends the reply note of confirmation.

The Ministry of Foreign Affairs of the People's Republic of China sends the best regards to the Embassy of the Federal Republic of Germany in China.

(Sealed)
The Ministry of Foreign Affairs
The People's Republic of China

(2)   Note from the Federal Republic of Germany

Beijing
8th August, 1975

The Ministry of Foreign Affairs
The People's Republic of China
The Embassy of the Federal Republic of Germany in the People's Republic of China has the pleasure to confirm the receipt of the note from the Ministry of Foreign Affairs of the People's Republic of China, dated 8th August, 1975, the contents of which are as follows:
(contents: deleted)*
The Embassy of the Federal Republic of Germany in China has the pleasure to inform the Ministry of Foreign Affairs of the People's Republic of China that the government of the Federal Republic of Germany confirms the contents of the above mentioned note. It is also confirmed that the said note, together with this reply note, will constitute an agreement between the two governments. This agreement will be effective from today.
The Embassy of the Federal Republic of Germany in China sends its best regards to the Ministry off Foreign Affairs of the People's Republic of China.

(Stamped)
The Embassy of the Federal
Republic of Germany in China

Editor's note: **Contents deleted by the editor as they are exactly the same as the note from China.*

Exchange Notes Between China & Austria on the Mutual Benefit of Trade & Service Mark Registration

(1)   Note from China

Beijing
4th April, 1977

The Ambassador
The Embassy of Austria in
The People's Republic of China
Sir

(Signed)
Liu Zhenhua
Vice Minister
Ministry of Foreign Affairs
The People's Republic of China

(2)   Notes from Austria

Beijing
4th April, 1977

Mr. Liu Zhenhua
Vice Minister
Ministry of Foreign Affairs
The People's Republic of China
Sir,
I have the pleasure to acknowledge receipt of your letter of 4th April, 1977, the contents of which are as follows:
(Contents: deleted)*
I have the pleasure to inform you that the government of the Republic of Austria has confirmed the contents of the said notes. It is also agreed that the above mentioned note and this reply note will constitute an agreement between the governments of the two countries. This agreement will come into effect sixty days from the date of this reply letter.
I would like to send my best regards to you.

(Signed)
Ambassador
Embassy of Austria in
The People's Republic of China

*Editor's note: *The contents are deleted by the editor as they are exactly the same as the letter from China.*

Exchange Notes Between China Belgium, the Netherlands and Luxembourg on the Mutual Benefit of Trademark Registration & Protection

(1)   Note from Belgium, Holland and Luxembourg

Beijing
10th April, 1975

Mr. Li Qiang,
Minister of Foreign Trade,
The People's Repbulic of China
Sir,

We have the pleasure to inform you that, according to the Belgium, the Netherlands and Luxembourg Commodity Trademark Treaty and the appendix signed in Brussels on 19th March, 1962, the governments of Belgium, the Netherlands and Luxembourg will take concerted action and get ready to sign an agreement on trademark registration and protection on the basis of mutual benefit.

We, therefore, suggest to you that, on basis of equality nationals, companies and co-operatives of one signatory party can have commodity trademark registration and licensing rights of such trademark in the other signatory country in accordance with the laws and orders of the latter.

With regard to the Kingdom of the Netherlands this agreement is only to be implement in the Netherlands.

If your government is ready to sign, an agreement with the three governments of Belgium, the Netherlands and Luxembourg in accordance with the aforesaid conditions, we would like to suggest that this note, together with your letters sent to each one of us on the same date, will constitute an agreement between the three governments of Belgium, the Netherlands and Luxembourg and the Government of the People's Republic of China. The effective date for the commencement of this agreement will be confirmed by exchange notes.

Best regards.

(Signed)
Representative
The Government of the Kingdom of
Belgium
(Signed)
Representative
The Government of the Grand Duchy of
Luxembourg
(Signed)
Representative
The Government of the Kingdom of the
Netherlands

(2) Note from China

Beijing
10th April, 1975

The Official of Foreign Trade
The Kingdom of Belgium
Sir,
I have much pleasure in receiving the letter written together by you, on behalf of the government of Belgium and the Ambassador of the Netherlands who represents the governments of the Grand Duchy of Luxembourg and the Kingdom of the Netherlands. The contents of the letter are as follows:
(contents deleted)*
I have the pleasure to inform you that the Government of the People's Republic of China accepts the contents of the above documents. The Government of the People's Republic of China agrees that you letter together with this reply letter as well as the reply letters which I wrote today, with the same contents, to the Dutch Ambassador who represents the grand Duchy of Luxembourg and the Kingdom of Netherlands will constitute an agreement between the government of the People's Republic of China and the three governments of Belgium, the Netherlands and Luxembourg. The effective date for the commencement of this agreement will be confirmed by exchange notes.

Best regards.

(Signed)
Li Qiang
Government Representative
The People's Republic of China

(3) Note from China

Beijing
10th April, 1975

The Ambassador of the Kingdom of the Netherlands in The People's Republic of China
Sir,
I have much pleasure in receiving your letter which you wrote on behalf on the governments of the Grand Duchy of Luxembourg and the Kingdom of Netherlands. The contents of your letter are as follows:

(contents deleted)*
I have the pleasure to inform you that the Government of the People's Republic of China accepts the contents of the above documents. The Government of the People's Republic of China agrees that your letter, together with this reply letter as well as the reply letter which I wrote today, with the same contents as this reply letter, to the Foreign Trade Official of Belgium, will constitute an agreement between the Government of the People's Republic of China and the three governments of Belgium, the Netherland and Luxembourg. The effective date of this agreement will be confirmed by exchange notes.

(Signed)
Li Qiang
Government Representative
The People's Republic of China.

(4)   Note from China

Beijing
10th April, 1975

The Ambassador of the Kingdom of the Netherlands in the People's Republic of China
Sir,
I have much pleasure in receiving the letter which was jointly sent to me by you, on behalf of the Government of the Kingdom of the Netherlands, and by the Foreign Trade Official of the Kingdom of Belgium. The contents are as follows:
(contents deleted)*
I have the pleasure to inform you that the People's Republic of China accepts the contents of the above documents. The Government of the People's Republic of China agrees that your letter, together with this reply letter as well as the reply letter which I wrote today with the same contents as this reply letter (which I sent to you as the representative of the Grand Duchy of Luxembourg) and which I sent to the Foreign Trade Official of the Kingdom of Belgium will constitute an agreement between the Government of the People's Republic of China and the three governments of Belgium, the Netherlands and Luxembourg.
Best regards.

(Signed)
Government representative
The People's Republic of China

*Editor's note: *The contents are deleted by the editor as they are exactly the same as the note from the representative of the three governments.*

SECTION C: Licensing Right

Exchange Notes Between China & Thailand on Licensing Rights of Trademark Registration

(1)   Note from China

Beijing
18th January, 1977

Embassy of the Kingdom of Thailand,
The Foreign Trade Ministry of the People's Repbublic of China sends its regards to the Embassy of the Kingdom of Thailand and has the pleasure to inform the latter that both the Chinese and Thail governments have discussed the issue on preferential treatments of Trademark Registration between the two countries. The purpose of this is to strengthen the friendly relationship and promote the development of trading between our two countries. In view of this, the Foreign Trade Ministry takes the pleasure to confirm on behalf of the Government of the People's Republic of China, the preferential treatments of trademark registration, agreed by both governments as follows:
On the basis of mutual benefit and equality the corporate persons and natural persons from each of the signatory countries may apply for trademark registration and licensing rights of a registered trademark in the other signatory country in accordance with that country's regulations and rules.
The above agreement will be effective from the date when the Embassy sends its reply note.
The Foreign Trade Ministry would like to take this opportunity to send its bests regard to the Embassy of the Kingdom of Thailand.

(Stamped)
Foreign Trade Ministry
People's Republic of China

(2)   Note from Thailand

Beijing
18th January, 1977

The Foreign Trade Ministry,
The People's Republic of China.
Sir,
The Embassy of the Kingdom of Thailand would like to send its regards to the Foreign Trade Ministry of the People's Republic of China and has the pleasure to refer to the latter's note No. 1017 of Trade Promotion Law Code of 18th January 1977 (77), the contents of which are as follows. (Contents deleted *)

In view of this, the Embassy of the Kingdom of Thailand has the pleasure to imform you that the government of the Kingdom of Thailand has confirmed the contents of the above mentioned note. It is also agreed that the said note and this reply note will constitute an agreement between the governments of our two countries. The agreement shall be effective from the date when this reply note is made.

The Embassy of the Kingdom of Thailand would like to take this opportunity to express its highest respect.

(Stamped)
Embassy of The Kingdom of Thailand
in the People's Republic of China.

*Editor's note: *The contents are deleted by the editor as they are exactly the same as the note from China.*

Tobacco Monopoly Regulations of The People's Republic of China

(Promulgated by the State Council on 23rd September, 1983)

Chapter I   General Provisions

Article 1:   The present regulations to establish the State Monopoly System are formulated for the purpose of the implementation of the highly centralized and unified administration of the whole of the national tobacco industry to develop planned production, raise quality, improve supply, regulate consumption and increase financial accumulation.

Article 2:   The scope of tobacco monopoly includes:
(1)   Cigarettes, cigars, smoking tobacco, flue-cured tobacco, selected air(sun) cured tobacco;
(2)   Cigarette paper, cigarette filters;
(3)   Cigarette manufacturing equipment.

Article 3:   The establishment of the State Tobacco Monopoly Administration which exercises the overall administrative management of the tobacco monopoly system.

The establishment of the National Tobacco Corporation which pursues the unified leadership and overall management of the production, supply, sales, personnel, finances, materials, domestic and foreign trade of the tobacco industry.

The tobacco monopoly administrative authorities and business management organizations are established under provincial and county's people's governments. These establishment shall be under the joint leadership of the tobacco monopoly authority and tobacco corporation at a higher level and the local people's government, but the tobacco monopoly authority and tobacco corporation at a higher level shall be the primary leading authority.

Chapter II   Plantation and Purchase of Tobacco

Article 4:   The planned-plantation and planned-purchase of flue-cured tobacco and selected air(sun) cured tobacco shall be implemented. The State Planning Commission shall issue the plan. Without the approval of the plan-issuing authorities, no district or department is permitted to make any alteration of the plan.

Article 5:   The overall arrangement for growing area distribution of flue-cured tobacco and air(sun) cured tobacco shall be made by the tobacco corporations in accordance with the State plan. The tobacco corporations are also responsible for production and technology work such as the promotion of using good seed strains, scientific planting, priming, curing, grading and inspection of flue-cured tobacco and selected air(sun) cured toabacco.
Agriculture departments shall work in close co-ordination with regard to the tasks prescribed in the present article.

Article 6:   The unified purchase of flue-cured tobacco and selected air(sun) cured tobacco, and the redrying of tobacco are to be carried out only by the tobacco corporations. No other organization or individual is permitted to purchase or engage in this business.

Article 7:   The purchase of flue-cured tobacco and air(sun) cured tobacco shall be carried out on a contractual basis. The tobacco corporations or their authorized purchase agencies shall conclude production and purchase contracts with growers in accordance with the State plan. Growers shall make their production in accordance with the contracts signed. The tobacco corporations or their authorized purchase agencies shall organize the unified purchase in accordance with the contract provisions and the State-stipulated quality grading standards and purchase prices. Growers are not permitted to sell their products on market by themselves.
Non-planned, non-contracted and blindly developed crops of fluecured tobacco and air(sun) cured tobacco shall wholly be purchased by the tobacco corporations on floating basis.

Chapter III   Production and Sales of Cigarettes, Cigars and Smoking Tobacco

Article 8:   Planned production of cigarettes and cigars shall be implemented. The State Planning Commission shall issue mandatory plans. The people's governments and the tobacco corporations at all levels should ensure the implementation of the plans. Without the approval of the plan-issuing authorities, no alteration of the plans is permitted.

Article 9:   Cigarettes and cigars are to be produced only by factories under the tobacco corporations. No other department or individual is permitted to produce the same.
Any violation of the present article shall be subjected to the punishment of withdrawal of operational license, compulsory close-

down, cancellation of bank account and confiscation of production equipment. Cases of serious violation shall be punished by judicial authorities according to law.

Article 10: Any profit-seeking production of hand-rolled cigarettes is prohibited.Sales of hand-rolled cigarettes are prohibited.

Any violation of the present article shall be subjected to economic sanctions in addition to the confiscation of the production tools, raw materials and products. Cases of serious violation shall be punished by judicial authorities according to law.

Article 11: Production of cigarettes and cigars must be strictly in conformity with the State-stipulated standards of quality. Any product which is not in conformity with the said standards of quality, is not permitted to be delivered from the factory.

Article 12: Scientific research organizations in the tabacco industry shall be turned under the unified supervision of the National Tobacco Corporation. The overall scientific research work of the tobacco industry shall be programmed by the National Tobacco Corporation.

The National Tobacco Corporation shall organize its research and technical resources to improve the quality of tobacco and its products and to decrease the content of tar and other harmful components so as to protect consumer's health.

Article 13: The domestic market of cigarettes and cigars shall be arranged uniformly by the National Tobacco Corporation. Purchase, distribution, allocation and wholesale of cigarettes and cigars are to be operated only by the tobacco corporations and their authorized agencies. Any other department, organization or individual is not permitted to engage in such operations. Production enterprises are not permitted to sell their products by themselves.

Article 14: Any organization or individual engaged in the cigarette or cigar retail business, or in the business of producing and selling smoking-tobacco, must apply to the local tobacco monopoly authorities for the monopoly permit, and shall register with the local administration for industry and commerce applying for the operational license and subject himself to the supervision of the local tobacco monopoly authorities and the local administration for industry and commerce.

Any organization or individual without the monopoly permit and the operational license is not permitted to be engaged in cigarette and cigar retail business or in smoking-tobacco producing and selling business.

Chapter IV: Price, Trade Mark and Transportation

Article 15: The purchase price of flue-cured and selected air(sun) cured tobacco shall be formulated jointly by the State Price Bureau and the National Tobacco Coporation. The ex-works price, allocation and transfer price, wholesale price and retail price shall all be formulated by the National Tobacco Corporation.

Prices in the present article shall not be changed without the approval of the formulating authorities and shall be neither raised nor lowered in any disguised form.

Any organization or individual, not observing the State-stipulated prices, shall be subjected to punishments ranging from economic sanctions to withdrawal of the monopoly permit.

Article 16: All cigarettes and cigars must carry a registered trademark. Products without a registered trademark are forbidden to be sold on market.

Article 17: All transportation of flue-cured tobacco, selected air(sun) cured tobacco, cigarettes and cigars must have the authorization certificates issued by the tobacco corporations before transport prcedures can be implemented.

Chapter V: Production and Distribution Cigarette Paper, Cigarette Filters and Cigarette Manufacturing Equipment

Article 18: Production of cigarette paper, cigarette filters and cigarette manufacturing equipment shall be controlled by planning and at selected plants. The National Tobacco Corporation, together with the relevant supervisory authorities, shall select the specific manufacturing enterprises on the basis of competence and shall issue production permits accordingly. The enterprise supervisory authorities should organize the production according to the National Tobacco Corporation's plan.

Article 19: The National Tobacco Corporation shall conclude purchase contracts with the manufacturing enterprises to implement the unified purchase and the unified distribution of cigarette paper, cigarette filters and cigarette manufacturing equipment.
Cigarette factories are not permitted to buy these manufacturing enterprises are not permitted to sell these items by themselves.

Chapter VI: Import and Export Trade, and Foreign Economic Co-operation

Article 20: Import of technology, associated materials and cigarette manufacturing equipment; import and export of leaf tobacco, cigarettes and cigars are wholly under the unified management and administration of the National Tobacco Corporation.
Tourist agencies selling small quantity of foreign cirgarettes on consignment or commission basis, should submit their related plans to the National Tobacco Corporation for vertification and approval before proceeding.
Apart from the National Tobacco Corporation and its authorized agencies, no other organization or department is permitted to be engaged in the said import and export business.

Article 21: All activities within the tobacco industry, regarding processing using foreign materials, compensation trade, co-production and joint venture, shall be handled and organized uniformly by the National Tobacco Corporation in accordance with the State-stipulated examination procedure.

Chapter VII   Rewards and Punishments

Article 22:   The industrial and commercial administrations, tax bureaus, public security authorities and other relevant departments at all levels should work in coordination with the tobacco monopoly authorities to strengthen the management of the tobacco monopoly system. Any violation of present regulations, according to the seriousness of the cases, shall be subjected to punishments ranging from practising criticism, economic sanctions to punishment imposed by the judicial authorities according to law.

Article 23:   Any organization or individual reporting or exposing violations of the present regulations and having performed meritorious service, shall be commended or rewarded by the tobacco monopoly authorities.

Chapter VIII   Appendix

Article 24:   Detailed rules for the implementation of the present regulations shall be formulated by the State Tobacco Monopoly Administration.

Article 25:   The present regulations shall come into force on November 1, 1983. Any provisions in previous laws and regulations which contravene with present regulations, shall cease to effect. The State Tobacco Monopoly Administration shall be responsible for sorting out the said provisions according to the present promulgated regulations, and reporting them to the original issuing authorities to declare them invalid or to revise them.

Editor's Notes

Under these regulations, the State Tobacco Monopoly Administration (STMA) has been set up to administer tobacco industry in China with the following aims:
1. *to promote scheduled production*
2. *to upgrade quality of products*
3. *to improve supply*
4. *to regulate Consumption*
5. *to increase financial accumulation*

STMA is authorized by the State Council to supervise all activities related to tobacco and cigarette production; they are:
1. *production and sales of cigarettes*
2. *pricing*
3. *trademark registration*
4. *transportation*
5. *production and distribution of cigarette paper*
6. *filters and cigarette manufacturing equipment*
7. *international trade*
8. *technical cooperation with foreign countries*

III PATENT

SECTION A: Overall policy

Patent Law of the People's Republic of China

(Adopted at the Fourth Session of the Standing Committee of the Sixth National People's Congress on March 12, 1984)

I General Provisions

Article 1: This Law is enacted to protect patent rights for inventions-creations, to encourage invention-creation, to foster the spreading and application of inventions-creations, and to promote the development of science and technology, for meeting the needs of the construction of socialist modernization.

Article 2: In this Law, "inventions-creations" mean inventions, utility models and designs.

Article 3: The Patent Office of the People's Republic of China receives and examines patent applications and grants patent rights for inventions-creations that conform with the provisions of this Law.

Article 4: Where the invention-creation for which a patent is applied relates to the security or other vital interests of the state and is required to be kept secret, the application shall be treated in accordance with the relevant prescriptions of the State.

Article 5: No patent right shall be granted for any invention-creation that is contrary to the laws of the state or social morality or that is detrimental to public interest.

Article 6: For a service invention-creation made by a person in execution of the tasks of the entity to which he belongs or made by him mainly by using the material means of that entity, the right to apply for a patent belongs to the entity. For any non-service invention-creation, the right to apply for a patent belongs to the inventor or creator. After the application is approved, if it was filed by an entity under ownership by the whole people, the patent right shall be held by the entity; if it was filed by an entity under collective ownership or by an individual, the patent right shall be owned by the entity or individual.

For a service invention-creation made by any staff member or worker of a foreign enterprise, or of a Chinese-foreign joint venture enterprise located in China, the right to apply for a patent belongs to the enterprise. For any non-service invention-creation, the right to apply for a patent belongs to the inventor or creator. After the application is approved, the patent right shall be owned by the enterprise or the individual that applied for it.

The owner of the patent right and the holder of the patent right are referred to as "patentee."

Article 7: No entity or individual shall prevent the inventor or creator from filing an application for a patent for a non-service invention-creation.

Article 8: For an invention-creation made in co-operation by two or more entities, or made by an entity in execution of a commission for research or designing given to it by another entity, the right to apply for a patent belongs, unless otherwise agreed upon, to the entity which made, or to the entities which jointly made, the invention-creation. After the application is approved, the patent right shall be owned or held by the entity or entities that applied for it.

Article 9: Where two or more applicants file applications for patent for the identical invention-creation, the patent right shall be granted to the applicant whose application was filed first.

Article 10: The right to apply for a patent and the patent right may be assigned.

Any assignment, by an entity under owner-ship by the whole people, of the right to apply for a patent, or of the patent right, must be approved by the competent authority at the higher level.

Any assignment, by a Chinese entity or individual, of the right to apply for a patent, or of the patent right, to a foreigner must be approved by the competent department concerned of the State Council.

Where the right to apply for a patent or the patent right is assigned, the parties must conclude a written contract, which will come into force after it is registered with and announced by the Patent Office.

Article 11: After the grant of the patent right for an invention or utility model, except as provided for in Article 14 of this Law, no entity or individual may, without the authorization of the patentee, exploit the patent, that is make, use or sell the patented product, or use the patented process, for production or business purposes.

After the grant of the patent right for a design, no entity or individual may, without the authorization of the patentee, exploit the patent, that is, make or sell the product, incorporating the patented design, for production or business purposes.

Article 12: Any entity or individual exploiting the patent of another must, except as provided for in Article 14 of this Law, conclude with the patentee a written license contract for exploitation and pay the patentee a fee for the exploitation of the patent. The licensee has no right to authorize any entity or individual, other than that referred to in the contract for exploitation, to exploit the patent.

Article 13: After the publication of the application for a patent for invention, the applicant may require the entity or individual exploiting the invention to pay an appropriate fee.

Article 14: The competent departments concerned of the State Council and the people's governments of provinces, autonomous regions or municipalities directly under the Central Government have the power to decide, in accordance with the state plan, that any entity under the system of ownership by the whole people which is within their system or under their administration and which holds the patent right to an important invention-creation can allow other designated entities to exploit that invention-creation; and the exploiting entities shall, according to the prescriptions of the state, pay to the entity holding the patent right a fee for the exploitation. Any patent of a Chinese individual or entity under collective ownership, which is of great significance to the interests of the state or to public interest, and is in need of dissemination and application, may, after approval by the State Council at the solicitation of its competent department concerned, be treated in the same manner as those patents mentioned in the preceding paragraphs.

Article 15: The patentee has the right to affix a patent marking and to indicate the number of the patent on the patented product or on the packing of that product.

Article 16: The entity owning or holding the patent right shall award the inventor or creator of a service invention-creation a reward and, upon exploitation of the patented invention-creation, shall award the inventor or creator a reward based on the extent of spreading and application and the economic benefits yielded.

Article 17: The inventor or creator has the right to be named as such in the patent document.

Article 18: Where any foreigner, foreign enterprise or other foreign organization having no habitual residence or business office in China files an application for a patent in China, the application shall be treated under this Law in accordance with any agreement concluded between the country to which the applicant belongs and China, or in accordance with any international treaty to which both countries are party, or on the basis of the principle of reciprocity.

Article 19: Where any foreigner, foreign enterprise or other foreign organization having no habitual residence or business office in China applies for a patent, or has other patent matters to attend to, in China, he or it shall appoint a patent agency designated by the State Council of the People's Republic of China to act as his or its agent.

Where any Chinese entity or individual applies for a patent or has other patent matters to attend to in the country, it or he may appoint a patent agency to act as its or his agent.

Article 20: Where any Chinese entity or individual intends to file an application in a foreign country for a patent for invention-creation made in the country, it or he shall file first an application for patent with the Patent Office and, with the sanction of the competent department concerned of the State Council, shall appoint a patent agency designated by the State Council to act as its or his agent.

Article 21: Until the publication or announcement of the application for a patent, staff members of the Patent Office and persons involved have the duty to keep its content secret.

II Requirements for Grant of Patent Right

Article 22 : Any invention or utility model for which a patent right may be granted must possess novelty, inventiveness and practical applicability.
Novelty means that, before the date of filing, no identical invention or utility model has been publicly disclosed in publications in the country or abroad or has been publicly used or made known to the public by any other means in the country, nor has any other person filed previously with the Patent Office an application which described the identical invention or utility model and was published after the said date of filing.
Inventiveness means that, as compared with the technology existing before the date of filing, the invention has prominent substantive features and represents a notable progress and that the utility model has substantive features and represents progress.
Practical applicability means that the invention or utility model can be made or used and can produce effective results.
Article 23 : Any design for which patent right may be granted must not be identical with or similar to any design which, before the date of filing, has been publicly disclosed in publications in the country or abroad or has been publicly used in the country.
Article 24 : An invention - creation for which a patent is applied does not lose its novelty where, within six months before the date of filing, one of the following events occurred:
(1) Where it was first exhibited at an international exhibition sponsored or recognized by the Chinese Government;
(2) Where it was first made public at a prescribed academic or technological meeting;
(3) Where it was disclosed by any person without the consent of the applicant.
Article 25 : For any of the following, no patent right shall be granted:
(1) Scientific discoveries;
(2) Rules and methods for mental activities;
(3) Methods for the diagnosis or for the treatment of diseases;
(4) Food, beverages and flavourings;
(5) Pharmaceutical products and substances obtained by means of a chemical process;
(6) Animal and plant varieties;
(7) Substances obtained by means of nuclear transformation.
For processes used in producing products referred to in items (4) to (6) of the preceding paragraph, patent right may be granted in accordance with the provisions of this Law.

III Application for Patent

Article 26 : Where an application for a patent for invention or utility model is filed, a request, a description and its abstract, and claims shall be submitted. The request shall state the title of the invention or utility model, the name of the inventor or creator, the name and the address of the applicant and other related matters.

The description shall set forth the invention or utility model in a manner sufficiently clear and complete so as to enable a person skilled in the relevant field of technology to carry it out; where necessary, drawings are required. The abstract shall state briefly the main technical points of the invention or utility model.

The claims shall be supported by the description and shall state the extent of the patent protection asked for.

Article 27: On applying for a patent for exterior design, a letter of request and the drawings or photographs of the exterior design shall be submitted. Moreover, the product using the exterior design and the class to which that product belongs shall be indicated.

Article 28: The date on which the Patent Office receives the application shall be the date of filing. If the application is sent by mail, the date of mailing indicated by the postmark shall be the date of filing.

Article 29: Where any foreign applicant files an application for a patent in China for an invention or exterior design within 12 months from the date inclusive on which he first filed in a foreign country an application for a patent for the identical invention or its utility model, or within 6 months from the date inclusive on which he first filed in a foreign country an application for a patent for the identical exterior design, he may, in accordance with any agreement concluded between China and the country to which he belongs, or any international treaty to which both countries are parties, or the principle of mutual recognition of the right of priority, enjoy a right of priority, that is the date of which he first filed the application in the foreign country shall be deemed to be the date of filing the application in China. Where the applicant claims a right of priority and where one of the events listed in Article 24 of this Law occurred, the period of the right of priority shall be counted from the date on which the event occurred.

Article 30: Any applicant who claims the right of priority shall make a written declaration when the application is filed, indicating the date of filing of the earlier application in the foreign country and the country in which that application was filed, and submit, within three months, a copy of that application document, certified by the competent authority of that country; if the applicant fails to make the written declaration or to meet the time limit for submitting the document, the claim to the right of priority shall be deemed not to have been made.

Article 31: An application for a patent for invention or utility model shall be limited to one invention or utility model. Two or more inventions or utility models belonging to a single general inventive concept may be filed as one application.

An application for a patent for design shall be limited to one design incorporated in one product. Two or more designs which are incorporated in products belonging to the same class and are sold or used in sets may be filed as one application.

Article 32: An applicant may withdraw his or its application for a patent at any time before the patent right is granted.

Article 33: An applicant may amend his or its application for a patent, but may not go beyond the scope of the disclosure contained in the initial description.

IV Examination and Approval of Application for a Patent

Article 34: Where, after receiving an application for a patent for invention, the Patent Office, upon preliminary examination, finds the application to be in conformity with the requirements of this Law, it shall publish the application within 18 months from the date of filing. Upon the request of the applicant, the Patent Office may publish the application earlier.

Article 35: Upon the request of the applicant for a patent for invention, made at any time within three years from the date of filing, the Patent Office will proceed to examine the application as to its substance. If, without any justified reason, the applicant fails to meet the time limit for requesting examination as to substance, the application shall be deemed to have been withdrawn.

The Patent Office may, on its own initative, proceed to examine any application for a patent for invention as to substance when it deems it necessary.

Article 36: When the applicant for a patent for invention requests examination as to substance, he or it shall furnish pre-filing date reference materials concerning the invention.

The applicant for a patent for invention who has filed in a foreign country an application for a patent for the identical invention shall, at the time of requesting examination as to substance, furnish documents concerning any search made for the purpose of examining that application, or concerning the results of any examination made, in that country. If, without any justified reason, the said documents are not furnished, the application shall be deemed to have been withdrawn.

Article 37: Where the Patent Office, after it has made the examination as to substance of the application for a patent for invention, finds that the application is not in conformity with the provisions of this Law, it shall notify the applicant and request him or it to submit, within a specified time limit, his or its observations or to amend the application. If, without any justified reason, the time limit for making response is not met, the application shall be deemed to have been withdrawn.

Article 38: Where, after the applicant has made the observations or amendments, the Patent Office finds that the application for a patent for inventions is still not in conformity with the provisions of this Law, the application shall be rejected.

Article 39: Where it is found after examination as to substance that there is no cause for rejection of the application for a patent for invention, the Patent Office shall make a decision, announce it and notify the applicant.

Article 40: Where, after receiving the application for a patent for utility model or design, the Patent Office finds upon preliminary examination that the application is in conformity with the requirements of this Law, it shall not proceed to examine it as to substance but shall immediately made an announcement and notify the applicant.

Article 41: Within three months from the date of the announcement of the application for a patent, any person may, in accordance with the provisions of this Law, file with the Patent Office an opposition to that application. The Patent Office shall send a copy of the opposition to the applicant, to which the applicant shall respond in writing within three months from the date of its receipt; if, without any justified reason, the time limit for making the written response is not met, the application shall be deemed to have been withdrawn.

Article 42: Where, after examination, the Patent Office finds that the opposition is justified, it shall make a decision to reject the application and notify the opponent and the applicant.

Article 43: The Patent Office shall set up a Patent Re-examination Board. Where the applicant is not satisfied with the decision of the Patent Office rejecting the application, he or it may, within three months from the date of receipt of the notification, request the Patent Re-examination Board to make a re-examination. The Patent Re-examinatiion Board shall, after re-examination, make a decision and notify the applicant.

Where the applicant for a patent for invention is not satisfied with the decision of the Patent Re-examination Board rejecting the request for re-examination, he or it may, within three months from the date of receipt of the notification, institute legal proceedings in the people's court.

The decision of the Patent Re-examination Board in respect of any request by the applicant for re-examination concerning a utility model or design is final.

Article 44: Where no opposition to the application for a patent is filed or where, after its examination, the opposition is found unjustified, the Patent Office shall make a decision to grant the patent right, issue the patent certificate, and register and announce the relevant matters.

V   Duration, Cessation and Invalidation of Patent Right

Article 45: The duration of patent right for inventions shall be 15 years counted from the date of filing.

The duration of patent right for utility models or designs shall be five years counted from the date of filing. Before the expiration of the said term, the patentee may apply for a renewal for three years.

Where the patentee enjoys a right of priority, the duration of the patent right shall be counted from the date on which the application was filed in China.

Article 46: The patentee shall pay an annual fee beginning with the year in which the patent right was granted.

Article 47: In any of the following cases, the patent right shall cease before the expiration of its duration:

(1)   Where an annual fee is not paid as prescribed;

(2)   Where the patentee abandons his or its patent right by a written declaration.

Any cessation of the patent right shall be registered and announced by the Patent Office.

Article 48: Where, after the grant of the patent right, any entity or individual considers that the grant of the said patent right is not in conformity with the provisions of this Law, it or he may request the Patent Re-examination Board to declare the patent right invalid.

Article 49: The Patent Re-examination Board shall examine the request for invalidation of the patent right, make a decision and notify the person who made the request and the patentee. The decision declaring the patent right invalid shall be registered and announced by the Patent Office.

Where any party is not satisfied with the decision of the Patent Re-examination Board declaring the patent right for invention invalid or upholding the patent right for invention, such party may, within three months from receipt of the notification of the decision, institute legal proceedings in the people's court.

The decision of the Patent Re-examination Board in respect of a request to declare invalid the patent right for utility model or design is final.

Article 50 :   Any patent right which has been declared invalid shall be deemed to be non-existent from the beginning.

VI   Compulsory License for Exploitation of Patent Right

Article 51 :   The patentee himself for itself has the obligation to make the patented product, or to use the patented process, in China, or otherwise to authorize other persons to make the patented products, or to use patented process, in China.

Article 52 :   Where the patentee of an invention or utility model fails, without any justified reason, by the expiration of three years from the date of the grant of the patent right, to fulfil the obligation set forth in Article 51, the Patent Office may, upon the request of an entity which is qualified to exploit the invention or utility model, grant a compulsory license to exploit the patent.

Article 53 :   Where the invention or utility model for which the patent right was granted is technically more advanced than another invention or utility model for which a patent right has been granted earlier and the exploitation of the later invention or utility model depends on the exploitation of the earlier invention or utility model, the Patent Office may, upon the request of the later patentee, grant a compulsory license to exploit the earlier invention or utility model.

Where, according to the preceding paragraph, a compulsory license is granted, the Patent Office may, upon the request of'the earlier patentee, also grant a compulsory license to exploit the later invention or utility model.

Article 54 :   The entity or individual requesting, in accordance with the provisions of this Law, a compulsory license for exploitation shall furnish proof that it or he has not been able to conclude with the patentee a license contract for exploitation on reasonable terms.

Article 55 :   The decision made by the Patent Office granting a compulsory license for exploitation shall be registered and announced.

Article 56 :   Any entity or indivifual that is granted a compulsory license for exploitation shall not have an exclusive right to exploit and shall not have the right to authorize exploitation by any others.

Article 57 :   The entity or individual that is granted a compulsory license for exploitation shall pay to the patentee a reasonable exploitation fee, the amount of which shall be fixed by both parties in consultations. Where the parties fail to reach an agreement, the Patent Office shall adjudicate.

Article 58 :   Where the patentee is not satisfied with the decision of the Patent Office granting a compulsory license for exploitation or with the adjudication regarding the exploitation fee payable for exploitation, he or it may, within three months from the receipt of the notification, institute legal proceedings in the people's court.

VII   Protection of Patent Right

Article 59 :   The extent of protection of the patent right for invention or utility model shall be determined by the terms of the claims. The description and the appended drawings may be used to interpret the claims.
The extent of protection of the patent right for design shall be determined by the product incorporation the patented design as shown in the drawings or photographs.

Article 60 :   For any exploitation of the patent, without the authorization of the patentee, constituting an infringing act, the patentee or any interested party may request the administrative authority for patent affairs to handle the matter or may directly institute legal proceedings in the people's court. The administrative authority for patent affairs handling the matter shall have the power to order the infringer to stop the infringing act and to compensate for the damage. Any party dissatisfied may, within three months from the receipt of the notification, institute legal proceedings in the people's court. If such proceedings are not instituted within the time limit and if the order is not complied with, the administrative authority for patent affairs may approach the people's court for compulsory execution.
When any infringement dispute arises, if the patent for invention is a process for the manufacture of a product, any entity or individual manufacturing the identical product shall furnish proof of the process used in the manufacture of its or his product.

Article 61 :   Prescription for instituting legal proceedings concerning the infringement of patent right is two years counted from the date on which the patentee or any interested party obtains or should have obtained knowledge of the infringing act.

Article 62 :   None of the following shall be deemed an infringement of the patent right:
(1)   Where, after the sale of a patented product that was made by the patentee or with the authorization of the patentee, any other person uses or sells that product;
(2)   Where any person uses or sells a patented product not knowing that it was made and sold without the authorization of the patentee;
(3)   Where, before the date of filing of the application for patent, any person who has already made the same product, used the same process, or made necessary preparations for its making or using, continues to make or use it within the original scope only;
(4)   Where any foreign means of transport which temporarily passes through the territory, territorial waters or territorial airspace of China uses the patent concerned, in accordance with any agreement concluded between the country to which the foreign means of transport belongs and China, or in accordance with any international treaty to which both countries are party, or on the basis of the principle of reciprocity, for its own needs in its devices and installations;
(5)   Where any person uses the patent concerned solely for the purposes of scientific research and experimentation.

Article 63 :   Where any person passes off the patent of another person, such passing off shall be treated in accordance with Article 60 of this Law. If the circumstances are serious, any person directly responsible shall be prosecuted for his criminal liability, by applying mutatis mutandis Article 127 of the Criminal Law.

Article 64: Where any person, in violation of the provisions of Article 20 of this Law, without any authority files in a foreign country an application for a patent that divulges an important secret of the State, he shall be subject to disciplinary sanction by the entity to which he belongs or by the competent authority concerned at the higher level. If the circumstances are serious, he shall be liable under the Criminal Law.

Article 65: Where any person usurps the right of an inventor or creator to apply for a patent for a non-service invention-creation, or usurps any other right or interest of an inventor or creator prescribed by this Law, he shall be subject to disciplinary sanction by the entity to which he belongs or by the competent authority at the higher level.

Article 66: Where any staff member of the Patent Office, or any staff member concerned of the State, is in breach of his duties by pursuing personal interests or committing fraudulent acts, he shall be subject to disciplinary sanction by the Patent Office or the competent authority concerned. If the circumstances are serious, he shall be liable for criminal offence under Article 188 of the Criminal Law.

VIII Supplementary Provisions

Article 67: Any application for a patent filed with, and any other proceedings before, the Patent Office shall be subject to the payment of a fee as prescribed.

Article 68: The Implementing Regulations of this Law shall be drawn up by the Patent Office and shall enter into force after approval by the State Council.

Article 69: This Law shall enter into force on April 1, 1985.

Implementing Regulations of the Patent Law of the PRC

Approved by the State Council and promulgated by
the Patent Office of the People's Republic of China
January 19, 1985

Chapter I: General Provisions

Rule 1:   These Implementing Regulations are drawn up in compliance with the provisions of Article 68 of the Patent Law of the People's Republic of China
(hereinafter referred to as ''the Patent Laws'')

Article 2:   ''Invention'' in the Patent Law means any new technical solution relating
to product, a process or improvement thereof.
''Utility model'' in the Patent Law means any new technical solution
relating to the shape, the structure, or their combination, of a product,
which is fit for practical use.
''Design'' in the Patent Law means any new design of the shape, pattern, color, or their combination, of a product, which creates an aesthetic
feeling and is fit for industrial application.

Article 3:   Any proceedings provided for by the Patent Law and these Implementing
Regulations shall be conducted in a written form.

Article 4:   Any document submitted under the Patent Law and these Implementing
Regulations shall be in Chinese. The standard scientific and technical terms
shall be used if there is a prescribed one set forth by the State. Where
no generally accepted translation in Chinese can be found for a foreign
name or scientific or technical term, the one in the original language shall
be also indicated.
Where any certificate or certified document which is submitted in accordance with the Patent Law or these Implementing Regulations is in a
foreign language, the Patent Office may request a Chinese translation
to be also submitted within a specified time limit.

Article 5: For any document sent by mail by the Patent Office to addressee residing in any of the municipalities under the people's governments of provinces or autonomous regions, or regions of higher level, the 8th day from the date of mailing inclusive shall be presumed to be the date of receipt. Whereas for addressee residing in any other regions in China, the 16th day from the date of mailing inclusive shall be presumed to be the date of receipt.

For any document sent to the Patent Office by the applicant by mail in China, the date of mailing indicated by the postmark shall be the date of filing. If the date of mailing indicated by the postmark on the envelope is illegible, the date on which the Patent Office receives the document shall be presumed to be the date of filing, except where the date of mailing is proved by the applicant.

Article 6: The first day of any time limit prescribed in the Patent Law or these Implementing Regulations shall not be counted. Where a time limit is counted by year or by month, it shall expire on the corresponding day of the last month; if there is no corresponding day in that month, the time limit shall expire on the last day of that month.

If a time limit expires on an official holiday, the time limit shall expire on the first working day after that official holiday.

Article 7: Where the applicant, the patentee, or any interested party cannot comply with the time limit laid down by the Patent Law or these regulations on implementing or by the Patent Office because of force majeure or other justified reasons, he may within one month from the day on which the impediment is removed, state the reason and request for an extension of the time limit. However, the time limit stipulated by Article 24, Article 29, the first sentence of Article 41, Article 45 and Article 61 must be complied with.

Where before the expiration of any time limit specified by the Patent Office, an applicant with a justified reason to extend the time limit should be so request from the Patent Office by enclosing the relevant proof of the justified reason.

Article 8: Where the invention-creation for which a patent is applied for by the entity of the national defense system relates to the security of the State and is required to be kept secret, the application for patent shall be filed with the patent organization set up by the competent department of science and technology of national defense. The Patent Office shall make a decision on the basis of the observations on the examination of the application presented by the said patent organization.

Article 9: Subject to the preceding Article, the Patent Office, after receiving an application for a patent for invention-creation which is required to be examined for the purpose of security, shall send the patent for invention-creation to the competent department concerned of the State Council for examination. The said department shall, within 4 months from receipt of application, send a report on the results of the examination to the Patent Office. Where the invention-creation for which a patent is applied for is required to be kept secret, the Patent Office shall handle it as an application for confidential patent and notify the applicant accordingly.

Article 10: "Service invention-creation, made by a person in execution of the tasks of the entity of which he belongs" in Article 6 of the Patent Law refers to any invention-creation made:

(1)   in the course of performing his own duty;

(2)   in the execution of any task, other than his own duty, which was entrusted to him by the entity to which he belongs;

(3)   within one year from his resignation, retirement or change of work, where the invention-creation relates to his own duty or the other take entrusted to him by the entity to which he previously belonged.

"Material means of the entity" in Article 6 of the Patent Law refers to the entity's money, equipment, spare parts, raw materials, or technical data which are not to be disclosed to the public.

Article 11 :   "Inventor" or "creator" in the Patent Law refers to any person who has made creative contributions to the substantive features of the invention-creation. Any person who, during the course of accomplishing the invention-creation, is responsible only for organization work, or who offers facilities for making use of material means, or who takes part in other auxiliary functions, shall not be considered as inventor or creator.

Article 12 :   Two or more applicants who file, on the same day, applications for patent for the identical invention-creation, as provided for in Article 9 of the Patent Law, shall, after receiving a notification from the Patent Office, hold consultation among themselves to decide the person or persons who'shall be entitled to file the application.

Article 13 :   The patentee who has concluded any license contract for exploitation of the patent with an entity or individual shall, within three months from the entry into force of the contract, submit the contract to the Patent Office for record.

Article 14 :   "The patent agency" in Article 19, paragraph 1, and Article 20, of the Patent Law refers to the China Council for the Promotion of International Trade, the Shanghai Patent Agency, the China Patent Ltd, and other patent agencies designated by the State Council.

Article 15 :   Any applicant who appoints a patent agency for filing an application for a patent with, or for dealing with other patent matters before, the Patent Office, shall submit a power of attorney indicating the scope of the power entrusted.

Chapter II : Application for Patent

Article 16 :   Anyone who applies for a patent shall submit application documents in duplicate.

Article 17 :   "Other related matters" in Article 26, paragraph 2, of the Patent Law refer to:

(1)   the nationality of the applicant;

(2)   where the applicant is an enterprise or other organization, the name of the country in which the applicant has the principal business office;

(3)   where the applicant has appointed a patent agency, the name and address of the patent agency and the name of the patent agent;

(4)   where the applicant is an entity, the name of its representative;

(5)   where the priority of an earlier application is claimed, the relevant matters which should be indicated:

(6)   the signature or the seal of the applicant;

(7)   a list of the documents constituting the application;

(8)   a list of the documents appending the application.

Where there are two or more applicants and where they have not appointed a patent agency, they shall designate a common representative; if no common representative is designated, the applicant first named in the request shall be considered as the common representative.

Where an application for a patent for design is filed, the request shall, when necessary, also contain a brief description of the design.

Article 18: Except where the nature of an invention or utility model calls for a different manner and order of presentation, the description manual in the application for a patent for an invention or utility model shall be presented in the follwoing order:

(1)   state the title of the invention or utility model;

(2)   specify the technical field to which the invention or utility model relates;

(3)   indicate the existing technique which, as far as known to the applicant, can be regarded as useful for the understanding, searching and examination of the invention or utility model, and cite the documents reflecting such technique;

(4)   specify the task which the invention or utility model is designed to fulfil;

(5)   disclose the invention or utility model in a manner sufficiently clear and complete so as to enable a person having the ordinary skill in the relevant technical field to carry it out;

(6)   state the merits or effective results of the invention or utility model as compared with the existing technique;

(7)   brief describe the drawings, if there are any;

(8)   describe in detail the best mode contemplated by the applicant for carrying out the invention or utility model, with reference to the drawing, if any.

The description of the invention or utility model may contain chemical or mathematical formulae but no commercial advertising.

Article 19: The same sheet of drawings may contain several figures of the invention or utility model. The figures shall be numbered consecutively in Arabic numerals and arranged in numerical order.

The scale and the distinctness of the drawings shall be such that a reproduction with a linear reduction in size to two-thirds would still enable all details to be clearly distinguished.

Reference signs used in the drawings of an application shall be consistent throughout. Reference signs not appearing in the description of the invention or utility model shall not appear in the drawings.

The drawings shall not contain any other explanatory notes, except words which are indispensable.

Article 20: The claims shall define clearly and concisely the matter for which protection is sought in terms of the technical features of the invention or utility model.

If there are several claims, they shall be numbered consecutively in Arabic numerals.

The technical terminology used in the claims shall be consistent with that used in the description. The claims may contain chemical or mathematical formulae but no drawings. They shall not, except where absolutely necessary, contain such references to the description or drawing as ''as described in part . . . of the description'', or ''as illustrated in figure . . . of the drawings''.

Article 21: Claims may be independent or dependent.

An independent claim shall outline the essential technical contents of an invention or utility model and describe the indispensable technical features constituting the invention or utility model.

A dependent claim relying on the reference to one or more other claims shall refer only to the preceding claim or claims.

Article 22: Except where the nature of the invention or utility model calls for other forms of expression, an independent claim shall be presented in the following form:

(1)   a preamble portion, indicating the technical field to which the invention or utility model pertains and the technical features of the prior art which relate closely to the subject matter of the invention or utility model;

(2)   a characterizing portion, stating, in such words as ''the invention (or utility model) is characterized in that . . .'' or in similarly concise expressions, the technical features of the invention or utility model, which, in combination with the features stated in the preamble portion, it is desired to protect.

Each invention or utility model shall have only one independent claim, which shall precede all the dependent claims relating to the same invention or utility model.

Article 23: Except where the nature of the invention or utility model calls for other forms of expression, a dependent claim shall be presented in the following form:

(1)   a reference portion, indicating the serial number(s) of the claim(s) referred to. Where possible, the reference to the serial number shall be placed at the beginning of the claim(s);

(2)   a characterizing portion, which by stating the additional technical features of the invention or utility model, further defines the technical features cited in the reference portion.

Dependent claims referring to more than two other claims shall not serve as basis for any other multiple dependent claims.

Article 24: The abstract shall indicate the technical field to which the invention or utility model pertains, the technical problems to be solved, the essential technical features and the use of uses of the invention or utility model. The abstract may, where applicable, contain the chemical formula or the figure which best characterizes the invention or utility model. The whole text of the abstract shall contain preferably not more than 200 words.

Article 25: Where an application for a patent for invention concerns a micro-biological process or a product thereof and involves the use of a micro-organism which is not available to the public, the applicant shall, in addition to the other requirements provided for in the Patent Law and these Implementing Regulations:

(1) deposit a sample of the micro-organism with a depositary institution designated by the Patent Office before the date of filing, or, at the latest, on the date of filing;

(2) give in the application document relevant information of the characteristics of the micro-organism;

(3) indicate in the request the scientific name (with its Latin name) and the name of the depositary institution, the date on which the sample of the micro-organism was deposited and the file number of the deposit, and submit a receipt of deposit from that institution.

Article 26: After the publication of an application for a patent for invention relating to a micro-organism, any entity or individual which or who intends to make use of the micro-organism mentioned in the application for the purpose of experiment shall make a request to the Patent Office containing the following:

(1) the name and address of the entity or individual making the request;

(2) an undertaking by the entity or individual making the request not to make the micro-organism available to any other person;

(3) an undertaking to use the micro-organism for experimental purpose only before the grant of the patent right.

Article 27: The size of drawings or photographs of a design submitted in accordance with the provisions of Article 27 of the Patent Law shall not be smaller than 3cm x 8cm, nor larger than 19cm x 27cm.

The applicant may submit for each design one or more drawings or photographs of different angles, sides or positions so as to clearly show the object for which protection is sought. The applicant shall indicate on each drawing or photograph the angle, side or position, and mark on the top left and right of the back of drawing or photograph its consecutive number and the name of the applicant.

Article 28: Where an application for a patent for design seeking protection of colors is filed, a drawing or photograph in color, and a drawing or photograph in while and black, shall be submitted, and a statement of the colors for which protection is sought shall be made on the drawing or photograph in black and white.

Article 29: Where the Patent Office finds it necessary, it may require the applicant for a patent for design to submit a sample or model of the product incorporating the design. The volume of the sample or model submitted shall not exceed 30cm x 30cm x 30cm, and its weight shall not surpass 15 kilos. Articles easy to get rotten or broken, or articles that are dangerous may not be submitted as sample or model.

Article 30: Academic or technological meetings mentioned in item (2) of Article 24 of the Patent Law mean any academic or technological meeting organized by a competent department concerned of the State Council or by a national academic or technological association.

Article 31: Where any application for a patent falls under the provisions of item (1) or item (2) of Article 24 of the Patent Law, the applicant shall, when filing the application, make a declaration and, within a time limit of two months from the date of filing, submit a certificate issued by the entity which organized the international exhibition or academic or technological meeting, stating that the invention-creation was in fact exhibited or made public there and also the date of its exhibition or making public.

Where any application for a patent falls under the provisions of item (3) of Article 24 of the Patent Law, the Patent Office may, when necessary, require the applicant to submit the relevant proof.

Article 32: Where the applicant for a patent for invention claims priority, it or he shall, within 15 months from the date on which it or he first filed the application in a foreign country, submit the filing number accorded by that country.

Article 33: Where two or more priorities are claimed for an application for a patent, the priority period for the application shall be calculated from the earliest priority date.

Article 34: Where an application for a patent is filed by any foreigner, foreign enterprise or other foreign organization having no habitual residence or business office in China, the Patent Office may, when there is doubt, require the applicant to submit the following documents:

(1) a certificate concerning the nationality of the applicant;

(2) a certificate concerning the seat of the headquarters of a foreign enterprise or other foreign organization;

(3) a testimonial showing that the country, to which the foreigner, foreign enterprise or other foreign organization belongs, recognizes that Chinese citizens or entities are, under the same conditions applied to its nationals, entitled to patent rights and other related rights in that country.

Article 35: According to the provisions of Article 31, paragraph 1, of the Patent Law, the claims in an application for a patent for invention or utility model may be any of the following:

(1) two or more independent claims of the same category (product or process) which cannot be included in one claim;

(2) an independent claim for a product and an independent claim for a process specially adapted for the manufacture of the product;

(3) an independent claim for a product and an independent claim for a use of the product;

(4) an independent claim for a product, an independent claim for a process specially adapted for the manufacture of the product, and an independent claim for a use of the product;

(5) an independent claim for product, an independent claim for a process specially adapted for the manufacture of the product, and an independent claim for an apparatus specially designed for carrying out the process;

(6) an independent claim for a process and an independent claim for an apparatus specially designed for carrying out the process;

(7) an independent claim for a process and an independent claim for a product directly manufactured by carrying out the process.

Article 36: Where an application for a patent for design contains two or more designs in accordance with the provisions of Article 31, paragraph 2, of the Patent Law, the designs shall be numbered consecutively and the products incorporating the designs shall be indicated in the request of the application. The consecutive numbers shall be marked on the bottom left of the back of the drawings or photographs of the design.

Article 37: When withdrawing an application for a patent the application shall submit to the Patent Office a declaration stating the title of the invention-creation, the filing number and the date of filing.

Where a declaration to withdraw the application for a patent is submitted after the printing preparation has been done by the Patent Office for publication of the application documents, the application shall be published as scheduled.

Chapter III: Examination and Approval of Application for Patent

Article 38: In any of the following situations, an examiner or a member of the Patent Re-examination Board shall, on his own intiative or upon the request of the applicant or any other interested party, be excluded from exercising his function.

(1) where he is a close relative of the applicant or the patent agent;

(2) where he has an interest in the application for patent;

(3) where he has such other kinds of relations with the applicant or the patent agent that might influence the impartial examination of the application.

Where a member of the Patent Re-examination Board has taken part in the examination of the application, the provisions of the preceding paragraph shall apply.

Article 39: Upon the receipt of a request, a description (a drawing being indispensable for utility model) and one or more claims for an application for a patent for invention or utility model, or a request and one or more drawings or photographs showing the design for an application for a patent for design, the Patent Office shall accord the date of filing and a filing number, and it shall notify them to the applicant.

Article 40: If the application documents submitted do not contain a request or a description or claims, or if they are not in conformity with the provisions of Article 27 of the Patent Law, the Patent Office shall declare the application unacceptable and notify the applicant accordingly.

Article 41: Where the description of invention mentions that it contains "explanatory notes to the drawings" but the drawings are missing, the applicant shall, within the time limit specified by the Patent Office, either furnish the drawings or make a declaration for the deletion of the "explanatory notes to the drawings". If the drawings are submitted later, the date of their delivering at, or mailing to, the Patent Office shall be the date of filing of the application; if the mention of "explanatory notes of the drawings" is to be deleted, the initial date of filing shall be the date of filing of the application.

Article 42: Where an application for a patent contains two or more inventions, utility models or designs, the applicant may, at any time before the announcement of the application under Article 39 or Article 40 of the Patent Law, or after the said announcement at the time when the Patent Office considers the filing of a divisional application is justified, submit to the Patent Office a request for the division of the application and divide it on its or his own initiative into several applications.

If the Patent Office finds that the application for a patent is not in conformity with the provisions of Article 31 of the Patent Law and Rule 35 of these Implementing Regulations, it shall invite the applicant to divide the application within the specified time limit. If, without any justified reason, the applicant does not make any response within the time limit, the application shall be deemed to have been withdrawn.

Article 43: Divisional applications filed in accordance with Rule 42 of these Implementing Regulations may enjoy the date of filing of the initial application, provided that they do not go beyond the scope of disclosure contained in the initial description.

Article 44: Where, upon preliminary examination, the Patent Office finds that the application for a patent obviously falls under Article 5 or Article 25 of the Patent Law, or is obviously not in conformity with Article 18 or Article 19 of the Patent Law or Rule 2 of these Implementing Regulations, it shall invite the applicant to present its or his observation within a specified time limit. If the applicant, without any justified reason, fails to meet the time limit for presenting observations, the application shall be deemed to have been withdrawn.

Where, after the applicant has made the observations, the Patent Office still finds that the application is obviously not in conformity with the provisions of the articles and the rule cited in the preceding paragraph, the application shall be rejected.

Article 45: Where the application for patent has any of the following deficiencies, the applicant shall, within the time limit specified by the Patent Office, correct it:

(1)   the request is not presented in the prescribed form or the indications therein are not in conformity with the requirements.

(2)   the description and its drawings or the claims of the invention or utility model are not in conformity with the relevant provisions;

(3)   the application for a patent for invention or utility model does not contain an abstract;

(4)   the drawings or photographs contained in the application for a patent for design are not in conformity with the relevant provisions;

(5)   where a patent agency is appointed, no power of attorney is submitted;

(6)   any other deficiencies which call for correction.

If the application, without any justified reason, fails to meet the time limit for correcting the deficiencies, the application shall be deemed to have been withdrawn. If, after the correction, the application is still not in conformity with the relevant provisions of the Patent Law or these Implementing Regulations, it shall be rejected.

Article 46: Where the applicant requests for an earlier publication of its or his application for a patent for invention, a declaration shall be made to the Patent Office. The Patent Office shall, after preliminary examination of the application and unless it is to be rejected, publish it immediately.

Article 47: The applicant shall, when indicating in accordance with Article 27 of the Patent Law the product incorporating the design and the class to which that product belongs, refer to the classification of products for designs published by the Patent Office. Where no indication or an incorrect indication of the class to which the product incorporating the design belongs is made, the Patent Office may supply the indication or correct it.

Article 48: Any person may, from the date of publication of an application of a patent for invention till the date of the announcement of the preliminary approval after examination as to substance, submit to the Patent Office observations, with the reasons therefor, on the application which is not in conformity with the provisions of the Patent Law.

Article 49: Where the applicant for a patent for invention cannot furnish, for justified reasons, the documents of any search on the results of any examination under Article 36 of the Patent Law, he shall declare the same to the Patent Office, and submit subsequently the said documents and results to the Patent Office when they become available.

Article 50: The Patent Office shall, when proceeding on its own initiative to examine an application for a patent for invention in accordance with the provisions of Article 35, paragraph 2, of the Patent Law, notify the applicant accordingly.

Article 51: Within a period of 15 months from the date of filing or at the time when a request for examination as to substance is made, or when a response is made in regard to an opposition, the applicant for a patent for invention may amend the description and the claims of application for a patent for invention on its his own initiative.

When an amendment of the description and the claims in an application for a patent for invention or utility model is made, a replacement sheet in prescribed form shall be submitted, unless the amendment concerns only the alteration, insertion or deletion of a few words.

Article 52: The applicant for a patent for a utility model or design may, within a period from the date of filing till the date of announcement of the application for patent, or at the time when a response is made in regard to an opposition, amend its or his application on its or his own initiative. Where an amendment to an application for a patent for design is made, it shall not change the essential elements of the design.

Article 53: The situations where an application for patent shall be rejected by the Patent Office shall comprise the following:

(1) where the application does not comply with the provisions of Article 3 of the Patent Law and Rule 2 of these Implementing Regulations;

(2) where the application falls under the provisions of Article 5 or Article 25 of the Patent Law, or it does not comply with the provisions of Article 22 or Article 23 of the Patent Law;

(3) where the applicant has no right to apply for a patent according to the provisions of Article 6, Article 8 or Article 18 of the Patent Law, or cannot obtain a patent right according to the provisions of Article 9 of the Patent Law;

(4) where the application does not comply with the provisions of Article 26, paragraph 3 or paragraph 4, or Article 31 of the Patent Law;

(5) where the amendment to the application or the divisional applications go beyond the scope of disclosure contained in the initial description.

Article 54: The situations where an opposition may be filed under Article 41 of the Patent Law with regard to an application for a patent for invention or utility model, which is announced by the Patent Office, shall comprise the following:

(1)   where the invention for which a patent is applied for does not comply with the provisions of Article 3 of the Patent Law and Rule 2, paragraph 1, of these Implementing Regulations, or the utility model for which a patent is applied for does not comply with the provision of Article 3 of the Patent Law and Rule 2, paragraph 2, of these Implementing Regulations;

(2)   where the application falls under the provisions of Article 5 or Article 25 of the Patent Law, or it does not comply with the provisions of Article 22 of the Patent Law;

(3)   where the applicant has no right to apply for a patent according to Article 6, Article 8 or Article 18 of the Patent Law, or the essential elements of an application have been taken from the descriptions, drawings, models, equipment, etc., of another person, or from a process used by another person, without his consent;

(4)   where the application does not comply with the provisions of Article 26, paragraph 3 or paragraph 4 of the Patent Law;

(5)   where the amendments to the application or the divisional applications go beyond the scope of the disclosure contained in the initial description.

Article 55:   The situations where an opposition may be filed under Article 41 of the Patent Law with regard to an application for a patent for design, which is announced by the Patent Office, shall comprise the following:

(1)   where the design for which a patent is applied for does not comply with the provisions of Article 3 of the Patent Law and Rule 2, paragraph 3, of these Implementing Regulations;

(2)   where the design for which a patent is applied for falls under the provision of Article 5 of the Patent Law, or does not comply with the provision of Article 23 of the Patent Law;

(3)   where applicant has no right to apply for a patent according to Article 6, Article 8 or Article 18 of the Patent Law, or cannot obtain a patent right according to Article 9 of the Patent Law, or the essential elements of the design have been taken from the designs, drawings, photographs, articles or models of another person without his consent;

(4)   where the amendments to the application has changed the essential elements of the design.

Article 56:   Anyone who files an opposition in accordance with the provisions of Article 41 of the Patent Law shall submit the opposition, with the reasons therefore, in duplicate to the Patent Office.

Article 57:   After the receipt of the opposition, the Patent Office shall make an examination of it. Where the opposition does not conform to the prescribed requirements, the Patent Office shall notify the opponent to rectify it within the specified time limit. If the opponent fails to rectify the opposition within the specified time limit, the opposition shall be deemed not to have been filed.

Where the reasons for opposition are not stated, or the reasons for opposition does not conform to the provisions of Rule 54 or Rule 55 of these Implementing Regulations, the opposition shall be declared to be unacceptable.

Article 58 : The Patent Re-examination Board shall consist of experienced technical and legal experts designated by the Patent Office. The Director General of the Patent Office shall be the Director of the Board.

Article 59 : Where the applicant requests the Patent Reexamination Board to make a reexamination in accordance with the provisions of Article 43, paragraph 1, of the Patent Law, it or he shall file a request for re-examination and state the reasons therefore, together with the relevant supporting documents. The request and the supporting documents shall be in duplicate.

The applicant may amend its or his application for a patent at the time when it or he request reexamination, but the amendment shall be limited only to the part to which the decision of rejection of the application relates.

Article 60 : Where the request for re-examination does not comply with the pre- scribed form, the person who made the request shall rectify it within the time limit fixed by the Patent Re-examination Board. If the rectification fails to be made within the time limit, the request for re-examination shall be deemed to have been withdrawn.

Article 61 : The Patent Re-examination Board shall send the request for re-examina- tion which the Board has received to the examiner who has made the examination to make observations. The Patent Re-examination Board shall make a decision on the request and notify the applicant accordingly.

Article 62 : Where the Patent Re-examination Board finds after re-examination that the request does not comply with the provisions of the Patent Law, it shall invite the person who has made the request for re-examination to submit his observations within the specified time limit. If, without any justified reason, the time limit for making response is not met, the request for re-examination shall be deemed to have been withdrawn.

Article 63 : At any time before the Patent Re-examination Board makes its decision on the request for re-examination, the person who has made the request may withdraw his request for re-examination.

Article 64 : The Patent Office shall, after making a decision to grant the patent right, notify the applicant to pay a fee for a patent certificate within two months and claim it. Where the applicant fails to pay the fee within the time limit, it or he shall be deemed to have abandoned its or his right to obtain the patent right.

Chapter IV : Invalidation of Patent Right

Article 65 : Anyone making a request for invalidation or part invalidation of a patent right according to the provisions of Article 48 of the Patent Law shall submit the request, with the reasons therefore, to the Patent Re-examination Board. Where necessary, relevant documents shall be submitted. The request and the relevant documents shall be in duplicate.

Article 66 : Where the request for invalidation of the patent right does not comply with the prescribed form, the person who made the request shall rectify it within the time limit fixed by the Patent Re-examination Board. If the rectification fails to be made within the time limit, the request for invalidation shall be deemed to have been withdrawn.

The provisions of Rule 54 or Rule 55 of these Implementing Regulations shall be applied so far as the reason for the request for invalidation of the patent right are concerned.

Where no reasons have been stated in the request for invalidation or where the reasons stated do not comply with the provisions of Rule 54 or Rule 55 of these Implementing Regulations, the request shall be declared to be unacceptable.

Article 67: The Patent Re-examination Board shall send a copy of the request for invalidation of the patent right and a copy of the relevant documents to the patentee and invite it or him to present its or his observations within a specified time limit. Where, without any justified reasons, no response is made within the time limit, the patentee shall be deemed to have no objection to make.

Chapter V: Compulsory License for Exploitation of Patent

Article 68: Any entity requesting, in accordance with the provisions of Article 52 of the Patent Law, or any patentee requesting, under Article 53 of the Patent Law, a compulsory license for exploitation of a patent for invention or utility model, shall submit to the Patent Office a request for compulsory license, and supporting documents to show that it or he has not been able to conclude with the patentee a license contract for exploitation on resonable terms. The request and the supporting documents shall be in duplicate.

Any entity requesting, in accordance with the provisions of Article 52 of the Patent Law, a compulsory license for exploitation of a patent for invention or utility model, shall at the same time furnish documents in duplicate to show that it is in a position to exploit the patent.

The Patent Office shall, after the receipt of the request for compulsory license, invite the patentee concerned to present its or his observations within the specified time limit; where, without any justified reason, no response is made within the time limit, the patentee shall be deemed to have no objection to make.

The Patent Office shall, after having examined the request for compulsory license and the observations of the patentee, make a decision and notify the entity or patentee which made the request and the patentee concerned.

Article 69: Any entity or individual or any patentee, requesting, in accordance with the provisions of Article 57 of the Patent Law, the Patent Office to adjudicate the fees for exploitation, shall submit a request for a adjudication and furnish documents showing that the parties have not been able to conclude an agreement in respect of the amount of the fees. The Patent Office shall, after the receipt of the request, make an adjudication within three months and notify the parties accordingly.

Chapter VI: Rewards to Inventor or Creator of Service Invention-Creation

Article 70:   "Rewards" mentioned in Article 16 of the Patent Law include money prizes and remunerations which are to be awarded to inventors and creators.

Article 71:   Any entity holding a patent right shall, after the grant of the patent right, award to inventors or creators of a service invention-creation a sum of money as a prize. The sum of prize money for a patent for invention shall not be less than 200 yuan; the sum of money prize for a patent for utility model or design shall not be less than 50 yuan.

Where an invention-creation was made on the basis of an inventor's or creator's proposal adopted by the entity to which he belongs, after the grant of the patent right, the entity holding it shall award to him a money prize liberally.

Any enterprises holding the patent right may include the said money prize into its production cost; any institution holding the patent right may disburse the said money prize out of its operating expenses.

Article 72:   Any entity holding a patent right shall, after exploiting the patent for invention-creation within the duration of the patent right, draw each year from any increase in profits after taxation a percentage of $0.5\% - 20\%$ due to the exploitation of the invention or the utility model, or a percentage of $0.05\% - 0.2\%$ due to the exploitation of the design, and award it to the inventor or creator as remuneration. The entity shall, otherwise, by making reference to the said percentage, award a lump sum of money to the inventor or creator as remuneration.

Article 73:   Where any entity holding a patent right for invention-creation authorizes other entities or individuals to exploit its or his patent, it shall, after taxation, draw a percentage of $5\% - 10\%$ from the fees for exploitation it received and award it to the inventor or creator as remuneration.

Article 74:   The remuneration provided for in this chapter shall all be disbursed out of the profits derived from the making of patented products or the use of patented process and out of the fees obtained for the exploitation of the patents. The remuneration shall not be included in the normal bonus fund of the entity, nor subject to the bonus tax. But the inventor or creator shall pay tax for his income.

Article 75:   The Chinese entities under collective ownership and other enterprises may award to the inventor or creator a money prize and a remuneration by making reference to the provisions in this chapter.

Chapter VII: Administrative Authority for Patent Affairs

Article 76:   "The administrative authority for patent affairs" in Article 60 of the Patent Law and in these Implementing Regulations refers to the administrative authority for patent affairs set up by the competent departments concerned of the State Council, and the people's governments of the provinces, autonomous regions, municipalities directly under the Central Government, open cities and special economic zones.

Article 77:   Where, after the publication of an application for a patent for invention and before the grant of the patent right, any entity or individual has exploited the invention without paying appropriate fees, the patentee may, after the grant of the patent right, request the administrative authority for patent affairs to intervene in the matter, or may directly institute legal proceedings in the people's court. The administrative authority for patent affairs intervening in the matter shall have the power to decide that the entity or individual shall pay appropriate fees within the specified time limit. Where any of the parties concerned is not satisfied with the decision of the said authority, it or he may institute legal proceedings in the people's court.

The provisions of the preceding paragraph shall apply mutatis mutandis in respect of the application for a patent for utility model or design.

Article 78: Where any dispute arises between any inventor or creator, and the entity to which he belongs, as to whether an invention-creation is a service invention-creation, or whether an application for a patent is to be filed in respect of a service invention or creator may request the competent department at the higher level or the administrative authority for patent affairs of the region in which the entity is located to handle the matter.

Article 79: Where parties to any transdepartmental or transregional infringement dispute request the administrative authority for patent affairs to handle the matter, the said dispute shall be handled by the administrative authority for patent affairs of the region in which the infringement has arisen, or by the administrative authority for patent affairs of the higher competent department of the infringing entity.

Chapter VIII: Patent Register and Patent Gazette

Article 80: The Patent Office shall maintain a Patent Register in which shall be recorded the following matters relating to any patent right:
    (1)   any grant of the patent right;
    (2)   any assignment of the patent right;
    (3)   any renewals of the term of the patent right;
    (4)   any cessation and invalidation of the patent right;
    (5)   any compulsory license for exploitation of the patent;
    (6)   any changes in the name, the nationality and address of the patentee.

Article 81: The Patent Office shall publish the Patent Gaxette at regular intervals, publishing or announcing the following:
    (1)   the bibliographic data contained in the request of an application for a patent;
    (2)   the abstract of the description of an invention or utility model;
    (3)   any request for examination as to the substance of an application for a patent for invention and any decision made by the Patent Office to proceed on its own initiative to examine as to the substance of an application for a patent for invention:
    (4)   the preliminary approval after examination of an application for a patent for invention and the announcement of the application for patent for utility model or design;
    (5)   any rejection of an application for a patent;
    (6)   any decision concerning an apposition and any amendment made in an application for a patent;
    (7)   any grant of the patent right;
    (8)   any cessation of the patent right;.

(9) any invalidation of the patent right;

(10) any assignment of the patent right;

(11) any grant of compulsory license for exploitation of the patent;

(12) any renewal of the term of the patent;

(13) any withdrawal, any being deemed to have been withdrawn and any abandonment, of an application for a patent;

(14) any change in the name or address of the patentee;

(15) any notification to the applicant whose address is not known;

(16) any other related matters.

The description, its drawings and the claims of an application for a patent for invention or utility model, and drawings or photographs of an application for a patent for design shall be published in pamphlet form.

Chapter IX: Fees

Article 82: The fees which shall be paid when an application for a patent is filed with the Patent Office, or when other procedures go through the Patent Office, are as follows:

(1) application fee and application maintenance fee;

(2) examination fee, re-examination fee and opposition fee;

(3) annual fee;

(4) handling fee for transacting other patent matters: renewal fee for the patent for utility model or design, fee for a change in the bibliographic data, patent certificate fee, fee for the proof of priority, fee for a request for invalidation, fee for a request for a compulsory license, and fee for a request for adjudication on exploitation fee of a compulsory license.

The amount of fees listed above shall be prescribed by the Patent Office separately.

Article 83: Fees provided for in the Patent Law and in these Implementing Regulations may be paid to the Patent Office by way of bank or postal remittance. They may also be paid directly to the Patent Office.

Where fees are paid by way of bank or postal remittance, the applicant or the patentee shall indicate on the money order the kind of fees, the title of the invention-creation, the filing number or the patent number. In case where no such filing number or patent number has been accorded yet to the invention-creation, the applicant or the patentee or other interested parties shall indicate the date on which it or he filed the application.

Where fees are paid by way of bank or postal remittance, the date on which the transfer of such fees are ordered shall be the date of payment.

Article 84: Where the application fee is not paid at the time of filing, or if the fee paid is insufficient, the Patent Office shall notify the applicant to pay the fee or to make up the deficiency within one month from the date of filing the application. If the fee is not paid or the deficiency is not made up within the time limit, the application shall be deemed to have been withdrawn.

Article 85: Where the prescribed fees are not paid when the applicant requests examination as to substance, or re-examination, or any person files an opposition or requests an invalidation of a patent right, it or he may pay the fees within 15 days from the date on which the request is made or the opposition is filed, but the date of payment may not exceed the time limit the Patent Law prescribes for the request for examination as to substance or re-examination or for the apposition to be filed. If the payment is not made within the time limit, the request is deemed to have not been made or the opposition is deemed to have not been filed.

Article 86: Where the applicant for a patent for invention has not been granted a patent right within two years from the date of filing, it or he shall pay a fee for the maintenance of the application from the third year. The first maintenance fee shall be paid within the first month of the third year. The subsequent maintenance fees shall be paid in advance within the month before the expiration of the preceding year.

Article 87: The first annual fee shall be paid when the patent certificate is issued. Where the maintenance fee of the application for the year has already been paid at the time of the grant of a patent right, the patentee shall make up the difference on the basis of the amount of the annual fees paid in advance within the month before the expiration of the preceding year.

Article 88: Where the maintenance fee of the application or the annual fee is not paid in due time by the applicant or the patentee, or the maintenance fee or the annual fee paid is insufficient, the Patent Office shall notify the applicant or the patentee to pay the fee or to make up the deficiency within six months from the expiration of the time limit within which the maintenance fee or the annual fee was to be paid. The applicant or the patentee shall at the same time pay a surcharge which amounts to 25% that of the maintenance fee or the annual fee. Where the fees are not paid within the six months the application shall be deemed to have been withdrawn or the patent right shall be deemed lapsed from the expiration of the time limit within which the maintenance fee or the annual fee was to be paid.

Article 89: Where in accordance with the provisions of Article 45, paragraph 2, of the Patent Law, the patentee requests the renewal of the term of the patent for a utility model or design, it or he shall make the request within six months before the term expires, and at the same time pay the renewal fee. In a case where, at the expiration of the said period, the patentee fails to pay the renewal fee, the request shall be deemed to have not been made.

Article 90: Any individual who files an application for a patent or has other matters to attend to, and who has difficulties in paying the various fees prescribed by Rule 82 of these Implementing Regulations, may submit a request according to prescriptions to the Patent Office, asking for a reduction or postponement of payment.

The conditions for the reduction or postponement of the payment shall be prescribed by the Patent Office.

Chapter X: Supplementary Provisions

Article 91: Anyone may, after approval by the Patent Office, inspect or copy the files of the published or announced applications for patent, the Patent Register and any relevant supporting documents.

Article 92: Any communication with the Patent Office shall be made in the prescribed form of the Patent Office. It shall be signed or sealed by the applicant or its or his patent agent.

Article 93: Where documents or objects relating to an application for patent or patent right are submitted to the Patent Office, the number of the application or the patent and the title of the invention - creation shall be indicated. Where documents or objects are sent to the Patent Office by post, they must be registered.

Article 94: Any sheets constituting the application for patent shall be typed or printed. All the characters shall be neat and clear, and they shall be free from any alterations. Only the right side of the paper shall be used.
Drawings shall be made in black ink with the aid of drafting instruments. All lines in the drawings shall be uniformly thick and clear.

Article 95: The Patent Office shall be responsible for interpreting these Implementing Regulations.

Article 96: These Implementing Regulations shall enter into force on April 1, 1985.

SECTION B: Registration

Proclamation (No. 4) of the Patent Office of the People's Republic of China

(January 19, 1985)

Under Article 67 of the Patent Law of the People's Republic of China, any application for a patent filed with, and any other proceedings before, the Patent Office shall be subject to the payment of a fee as prescribed. The various items of patent fees to be paid are prescribed in the first paragraph of Rule 82 of the Implementing Regulations of the Patent Law of the People's Republic of China. According to the second paragraph of the same Rule, a list of the patent fees to be charged is hereby issued as follows:

Patent Fees
(unit: RMB yuan)

1.	Application fee for	
	(1) patent for invention	150
	(2) patent for utility model	100
	(3) patent for design	80
2.	Application maintenance fee for patent invention, per year	100
3.	Examination fee for application for patent for invention	400
4.	Re-examination fee for	
	(1) application for patent for invention	200
	(2) application for patent for utility model	100
	(3) application for patent for design	80
5.	Opposition fee for	
	(1) application for patent for invention	30
	(2) application for patent for utility model	20
	(3) application for patent for design	20
6.	Renewal fee for the term of patent for utility model or design	100
7.	Handling fee for making changes in the bibliographic data	10

8. Patent certificate fee for
   (1) patent for invention   100
   (2) patent for utility model   50
   (3) patent for design   50
9. Fee for the proof of priority
10. Fee for a request for invalidation of
    (1) patent for invention   300
    (2) patent for utility model   200
    (3) patent for design   150
11. Fee for a request for a compulsory license for exploitation of
    (1) patent for invention   300
    (2) patent for utility model   200
12. Fee for a request for adjudication on exploitation fee of a compulsory license   100
13. Annual fee for
    (1) patent for invention from the 1st year to the 3rd year, per year   200
        from the 4th year to the 6th year, per year   300
        from the 7th year to the 9th year, per year   600
        from the 10th year to the 12th year, per year   1200
        from the 13th year to the 15th year, per year   2400
    (2) patent for utility model
        from the 1st year to the 3rd year, per year   100
        from the 4th year to the 5th year, per year   200
        from the 6th year to the 8th year, per year   300
    (3) patent for design
        from the 1st year to the 3rd year, per year   50
        from the 4th year to the 5th year, per year   100
        from the 6th year to the 8th year, per year   200

Notes:
1. Where the applicant of the patentee is a foreigner, any of the above-listed fees shall be paid in foreign currency according to the exchange rate at the time of payment.
2. The ordinal number of years listed in Item 13 shall be counted from the filing date. The annual fee shall, beginning with the year in which the patent right was granted, be paid according to the amount prescribed for that year.

Implementing Regulations for the Reduction or Postponement of Payment for Patents by Individual Applicants

Article 1:   These implementing regulations are drawn up in compliance with Article 90 of the Patent Law of the People's Republic of China.

Article 2:   Any individual who files an application for a patent and has difficulties in paying such fees as application fee, examination fee, re-examination fee, patent renewal fee and annual fee within three years after the patent certificate is issued, may submit a request for a reduction or postponement of payment. The individual applicant or patentee is subject to paying the remaining fees in accordance with the relevant stipulations.

Article 3:   After examinations on the specific circumstances are carried out, the reduction or postponement of payment of the fees listed above will be ratified by the Patent Office. The maximum proportion for the reduction or postponement of the fees is up to 80% of the amount of the fees.

Article 4:   Any applicant or patentee who asks for a reduction or postponement of the fees is required to pay 20% of the amount of the fees and submit an application at the time of submitting other relevant applications (while the annual fee and the patent renewal fee should be paid at the stipulated date), on which wages and extra income of the applicant should be indicated at the ''cause and reason for the reduction or postponement'' column.

If an invention / creation is made by an employee of an entity within its business scope, the applicant is subject to submitting to the Patent Office, at the first time of application for a reduction or postponement of payment, a certificate issued by the entity to which he belongs proving that the invention / creation made by the applicant is beyond his scope of duty.

Article 5: Any applicant for reduction or postponement of payment or patentee whose request is in comformity with the relevant conditions should follow the implementing regulations of the Patent Law after receiving the notification issued by the Patent Office.

Article 6: All the fees postponed to be paid should be made up after the applicant or patentee has benefited financially from the invention/creation or other sources of income.

Article 7: These implementing regulations shall enter into force from April 1, 1985.

Interim Provisions Governing Patent Agent

Approved by the State Council on 4 September 1985
Promulgated by the China Patent Bureau on 12 September 1985

Article 1 :　These Regulations are formulated in order to enforce the provisions concerning agent of the ''Patent Law of the People's Republic of China''.

Article 2 :　Patent agencies shall apply for patent registration and handle other patent-relating affairs on behalf of applicants for patent registration and other clients according to Articles 19 and 20 of the ''Patent Law of the People's Republic of China''.

Article 3 :　Patent agencies referred to in these Regulations denote :
(1)　patent agencies designated by the State Council;
(2)　patent agencies established with the approval of the competent departments concerned under or the State Council and patent control organs subordinate to the people's governments of provinces, autonomous regions, municipalities directly under the central authority, open cities, and special economic zones; and
(3)　lawyers' firms qualified as patent agencies as ratified by the patent control organs of the people's governments of provinces, autonomous regions, municipalities directly under the central authority, open cities, and special economic zones.
The local patent control organs shall submit lists of patent agencies falling into the above categories 2 and 3 to the China Patent Bureau for record purposes.

Article 4 :　Patent agencies that act on behalf of their clients shall acquire from the latter a letter of authorization which perscribes the conditions of authorization and carries the seal or signature of the clients.
Patent agencies acting on behalf of their clients may charge the latter for the service according to the regulations concerned.

Article 5: Patent agencies shall employ a patent agent to handle the following affairs:
(1) rendering consultation service regarding patent;
(2) drafting documents for patent registration and handling matters related to applications for patent registration;
(3) requesting assessment and reconsideration of an application;
(4) lodging an objection against an application for patent registration and appealing for voidance of a patent registration;
(5) handling the conveyance of a patent right or franchise; and
(6) handling other affairs relating to patent.
Patent agents can be employed as patent consultants.

Article 6: A citizen who has the right to vote and to stand for election can apply for registration with the China Patent Bureau as a patent agent if he has the following qualifications:
(1) he must be a graduate majoring in science or engineering at an institute of higher learning (or have equivalent academic qualification), have proficiency in a foreign language, and have at least 3 years' experience in scientific and technological work or at least 5 years' experience in other work relating to science and technology; and
(2) he must have received training relating to the Patent Law and patent affairs and have a good knowledge of fundamental laws relating to patent agency service.
Those who are engaged in patent agency work involving foreign countries shall be familiar with preservation of industrial patents, the specific countries' and international laws and treaties concerning such; and be highly proficient in a foreign language, apart from the qualifications enumerated above.

Article 7: The China Patent Bureau and other departments and organizations such as the Ministry of Justice and the China Council for the Promotion of Foreign Trade shall form a Committee for Patent Agent Assessment to assume the following duties:
(1) assessment of the qualifications of those who apply for register as patent agents;
(2) supervising and guiding patent agency service.

Article 8: A candidate for patent agent who has passed the qualification assessment by the Committee for Patent Agent Assessment shall register as patent agent with the China Patent Bureau which grants him the professional status of patent agent by issuing him a patent agent's licence.

Article 9: A patent agent is not allowed to practice on his own but shall work with a patent agency and do the assessments by the latter.

Article 10: Patent agents who exercise their profession according to law are subject to the protection by the state law. No organization or individual shall interfere in their work.

Article 11: From the legal point of view, a patent agent's act under the authorization of a client shall be regarded as equal to an act by the client himself.

Article 12: It is obligatory for a patent agent to conceal from the public the knowledge of a patented invention to which he has access to in the practice of his profession except when the information has been disclosed.

Article 13: The Committee for Patent Agent Assessment has the right to disqualify a patent agent if he:
(1) plagiarizes the invention of this client, deliberately releases the content of his client's invention, or commits any act which severly

infringes upon the interests of his client, or;

(2) is gravely incompetent in his profession.

The Committee for Patent Agent Assessment shall notify the China Patent Bureau of its decision to disqualify a patent agent. And the China Patent Bureau shall then nullify the disqualified patent agent's registration and retrieve his patent agent's licence.

Article 14: A patent agent who commits an act described in Item 1 of Article 13 is liable to disciplinary sanction by the patent agency with which he works. Legal prosecution shall be started against such a patent agent according to law in case of gross violation.

Article 15: The right to interpret these Regulations resides in the China Patent Bureau.

Article 16: These Regulations shall go into effect on the day of promulgation.

Editor's Notes

The Patent Law of the People's Republic of China has been enforced since April 1, 1985. The legislation of this law has received popular response from all China traders. According to the Chinese Patent Office, more than one-third of the total patent applications were filed by foreigners. Due to the characteristics of patent practice, it is easily foreseen that various patent disputes will arise in the near future.

Under the present patent law and its implementing regulations, patent disputes of the following categories will be heard by the Economic Tribunals of the relevant People's Courts, they are:

1. Disputes with regard to whether a patent for invention is to be granted;
2. Disputes with regard to declaring a patent right for invalid or upholding such a right;
3. Disputes regarding a compulsory license for exploition;
4. Disputes with regard to the fee for using inventions, utility models and design during the period from publication of a patent application to the approval of a patent;
5. Disputes regarding the exploitation fee of a compulsory license;
6. Disputes regarding infringement of patent, including passing off the patent of another person but not constituting a criminal act;
7. Disputes regarding the assignment of a right to apply for a patent and a right to a patent.

For Product Safety Concerns and Information please contact our EU
representative GPSR@taylorandfrancis.com
Taylor & Francis Verlag GmbH, Kaufingerstraße 24, 80331 München, Germany

www.ingramcontent.com/pod-product-compliance
Lightning Source LLC
Chambersburg PA
CBHW070901270326
41926CB00038B/1674